Fundamentals of Real Estate APPRAISAL

9th Edition

William L. Ventolo, Jr. • Martha R. Williams, JD

Dennis S. Tosh, PhD
William B. Rayburn, PhD, MAI, CFA
Consulting Editors

Dearborn™
Real Estate Education

This publication is designed to provide accurate and authoritative information in regard to the subject matter covered. It is sold with the understanding that the publisher is not engaged in rendering legal, accounting, or other professional service. If legal advice or other expert assistance is required, the services of a competent professional person should be sought.

President: Roy Lipner
Vice-President of Product Development and Publishing: Evan M. Butterfield
Associate Publisher: Louise Benzer
Development Editor: Elizabeth Austin
Director of Production: Daniel Frey
Project Editor: Caitlin Ostrow
Typesetter: Janet Schroeder
Creative Director: Lucy Jenkins

© 2005 by Dearborn™ Real Estate Education
a division of Dearborn Financial Publishing, Inc.®

Published by Dearborn™ Real Estate Education,
a division of Dearborn Financial Publishing, Inc.®
30 South Wacker Drive
Chicago, IL 60606-7481
(312) 836-4400
http://www.dearbornRE.com

Printed in the United States of America.

05 06 07 10 9 8 7 6 5 4 3 2 1

Library of Congress Cataloging-in-Publication Data

Ventolo, William L.
   Fundamentals of real estate appraisal / William L. Ventolo, Jr. & Martha R. Williams.—
9th ed.
   p.cm.
   ISBN 1-4195-0518-1
   1. Real property—Valuation I. Williams, Martha R. II. Title.
HD1387.V45 2005
333.33'2—dc212   200502988

CONTENTS

This ninth edition of *Fundamentals of Real Estate Appraisal* covers *all* of the topics included in the prelicensing appraisal course requirements established by the Appraiser Qualification Board of The Appraisal Foundation.

As with other areas of real estate practice, the professional appraiser must keep pace with the demands of the marketplace. Technological advances have affected all facets of the real estate transaction, from first client contact to closing. Despite the availability of vast databases of market information, there is no substitute for the well-reasoned opinion of a competent appraiser. Of course, the skill and judgment required to make a reliable appraisal must begin with a thorough knowledge of appraisal principles.

Fundamentals of Real Estate Appraisal is designed to help both the student and the established professional relate appraisal theory and technique to practice. Explanations of the basic approaches to appraising are thorough, yet concise. Frequent examples, including use of forms and data grids, help bring the real world of appraising to the reader. The many exercises and achievement examinations used in the text increase its usefulness as a practical, hands-on tool by requiring reader participation.

William L. Ventolo, Jr., a former vice president of Development Systems Corporation and its subsidiary, Real Estate Education Company, received his MS in psychology from the University of Pittsburgh. Mr. Ventolo has developed and authored numerous industrial training programs and manuals, including a comprehensive dealership accounting correspondence course used by the Ford Motor Company. In addition to *Fundamentals of Real Estate Appraisal,* he has authored or coauthored many trade books and textbooks, including *The Art of Real Estate Appraisal, How to Use the Uniform Residential Appraisal Report, Mastering Real Estate Mathematics, Residential Construction, Your Home Inspection Guide,* and *Principles of Accounting.* A member of the Real Estate Educators Association, Mr. Ventolo resides in Nokomis, Florida.

Martha R. Williams, who received her JD from the University of Texas, is an author and educator and has practiced law in Texas and California. An RCE (REALTOR® Certified Executive), she has been Director of Education for the North Shore-Barrington Association of REALTORS® and the Greater Nashville Association of REALTORS®. In addition to *Fundamentals of Real Estate Appraisal,* she is author or coauthor of *The Art of Real Estate Appraisal, How to Use the Uniform Residential Appraisal Report,* the *ADA Handbook, California Real Estate Appraisal, California Real Estate Principles,* and *Agency Relationships in California Real Estate.* She is owner of the Real Estate Bookstore™, located at *www.realestatebookstore.com* and *www.r-e-b.com.* An Affiliate Member of the Appraisal Institute, President of the Association of Illinois Real Estate Educators, former officer of the Real Estate Educators Association, and member of the National Association of Real Estate Editors, Ms. Williams resides in Rochelle, Illinois.

ACKNOWLEDGMENTS

The authors wish to thank those who participated in the preparation of the ninth edition of *Fundamentals of Real Estate Appraisal*.

Illinois building codes official John E. Spurgeon, MCP, once again helped update the cost figures. Other useful reviews were provided by

James E. Jacobs, Grayson County College
Mark A. Munizzo, IFAS, The Equity Network
Lisa Musial, IFAS, Musial Appraisal Company
Terrence M. Zajac, DREI

Consulting editor Dennis S. Tosh, PhD, is a member of the finance faculty at the University of Mississippi, where he holds the J. Ed Turner Chair of Real Estate and teaches in the areas of real estate valuation and finance. He also teaches for several state and national appraisal and financial organizations. Consulting editor William B. Rayburn, PhD, MAI, CFA, is a member of the finance faculty at the University of Mississippi.

Terry V. Grissom, MBA, PhD, MAI, CRE, served as consulting editor for the fifth and sixth editions, offering the insight of his years of appraisal practice and skill as an educator.

James H. Boykin, PhD, MAI, SREA, served as consulting editor on earlier editions of this book, and his assistance was always appreciated. Reviewers of earlier editions included Richard Ransom Andrews, Carol Bohling, Robert W. Chaapel, Linda W. Chandler, Jane Chiavacci, Diana M. De Fonzo, Clay Estes, Larry E. Foote, Donald A. Gabriel, Robert C. Gorman, Ron Guiberson, George R. Harrison, Gary Hoagland, Robert Houseman, Kennard P. Howell, Alan Hummel, David J. January, Donald B. Johnson, Paul Johnson, Lowell Knapp, Frank W. Kovats, Timothy W. Lalli, Craig Larabee, Joseph H. Martin, Robert S. Martin, John F. Mikusas, Michael Milgrim, Robert L. Montney, Mark A. Munizzo, Henry E. Ormonde, Leroy Richards, Kenneth E. Ritter, Michael L. Robinson, Lawrence Sager, Richard Sorenson, Margaret E. Sprencz, Paul C. Sprencz, Bryan K. Swartwood, Jr., Ralph Tamper, Milton J. Tharp, Douglas G. Winner, and Terrence M. Zajac.

In addition to those mentioned, numerous instructors, students, and real estate professionals have offered many useful comments and suggestions over the years. We thank all who have contacted us and welcome additional comments on this edition.

Special thanks must go to Software for Real Estate Professionals, Inc., in Baton Rouge, Louisiana, for the special software included with this textbook. Derived from the company's "Appraise-It" forms processing software, the software allows the user to practice completing URAR forms.

Finally, the authors thank the staff of Dearborn Real Estate Education for their fine efforts. Elizabeth Austin, Development Editor, coordinated the manuscript revision and review with tact and patience and Daniel Frey, Director of Production, brought the manuscript through the production process. Joyce Petersen's efforts in copyediting the manuscript also are appreciated.

William L. Ventolo, Jr.
Martha R. Williams, JD, RCE

## CHAPTER 1

The Appraisal Profession

■ OVERVIEW

WEB@LINK
www.ofheo.gov

The value of real estate has risen dramatically during the past 50 years. According to the Office of Federal Housing Enterprise Oversight (OFHEO), the price of the average U.S. residence increased 12.5 percent from the first quarter of 2004 to the first quarter of 2005. Yet, the average takes into account a large variety of properties in a wide range of locations. Under such market conditions the appraisal process is even more important. Market demand still fluctuates, and not every property will increase in value, particularly over the short term. Some may actually lose value.

After many years of debate, the federal government mandated state-regulated appraiser licensing or certification for most federally related real estate transactions. The major impetus for this action came with the enactment by Congress of the Financial Institutions Reform, Recovery, and Enforcement Act of 1989 (FIRREA). Some states require licensing or certification for *all* transactions.

This chapter takes a look at the appraiser's role and discusses some of the qualifications that can help ensure a reliable, credible appraisal. The chapter also covers licensing and certification requirements and includes discussion of the Uniform Standards of Professional Appraisal Practice (USPAP) created by the Appraisal Standards Board of The Appraisal Foundation.

■ THE APPRAISER'S WORK

The professional real estate appraiser estimates the value of real property (land and/or buildings). Value may be sought for any number of reasons, such as setting a sales price or determining insurance coverage. The appraiser's client can be a buyer, a seller, a lender or other company, an attorney or estate administrator, a public agency, or a real estate broker. Although real estate brokers make many informal estimates of value, it is common practice to rely on the practiced judgment of a professional whose sole interest is in estimating the value of real property.

An appraiser's estimate of a property's value usually is in writing and may be a letter simply stating the appraiser's opinion of value. Most often, however, it is a longer document called an *appraisal report*. The proper steps must be taken to arrive at the value conclusion, regardless of the method by which it is reported. The appraiser must conduct a thorough study of the appraised property, its geographical area, historical values, and economic trends. The appraiser must be able to read a legal description and recognize the exact boundaries of the subject property. The appraiser also must have some knowledge of building construction to recognize the quality and condition of the subject property.

The appraiser must know market conditions—why some properties are more desirable than others—as well as how to analyze income and expense statements so that an evaluation of a property's potential earnings can be made.

In short, the appraiser needs some of the expertise of the surveyor, the builder, the broker, the accountant, the economist, and the mortgage lender. An appraisal takes into account the many factors that influence a property's value; therefore, an experienced appraiser can make an important contribution to any real estate transaction.

Qualifications of an Appraiser

The real estate appraiser's primary qualifications are education and experience.

Education

Colleges and private schools, as well as professional associations, offer courses in real estate appraising, but there are many other courses at both high school and college levels that give the appraiser some of the necessary educational background. The appraiser must be able to work easily with mathematical computations because he or she will be computing land and building areas and construction costs and performing all of the steps necessary to determine investment income. For this last area, a knowledge of accounting techniques is invaluable. A course in statistics also can help in studying trend indicators such as those found in census and economic reports, as well as in the overall analysis of data collected.

Geography and urban sociology also are important. Because the appraiser must be able to recognize and draw conclusions from the driving forces behind population movements and economic trends, economics and city planning courses are useful. A knowledge of building construction or engineering will help the appraiser recognize and value building components.

General real estate courses of interest to appraisers and available through colleges and private schools are geared primarily to prospective real estate salespeople and brokers, who must be licensed by their state real estate offices. Many real estate appraisers enter the field in this way—gaining the experience of handling real estate transactions and learning firsthand how the market operates.

Overlaying all of the courses and practical experience mentioned is the necessity to become technologically proficient. The modern appraisal office rennnslies heavily on electronic data gathering, recording, analysis, and reporting. The CD included with this book provides an excellent example of the tools that help make the appraiser more efficient. This topic will be discussed in greater detail later in this chapter.

Experience

In most cases, the novice appraiser will begin as a state-licensed trainee who is permitted to work only under the direct supervision of a licensed or certified appraiser. The prospective appraiser, who may perform only the range of duties authorized by the supervising appraiser's license or certification, can then develop the competence to warrant being hired for his or her appraisal skill. Government agencies and some financial institutions may have their own appraiser training programs.

Objectivity

Above all, the appraiser must remain objective in considering all of the factors relevant to the appraisal assignment. *Any* personal interest in the outcome of the appraisal must be revealed to the client, as indicated in the certification that is mandated by Standards Rule 2-3 of USPAP. As a practical matter, it is in the appraiser's best interest to avoid any assignment that could create the appearance of impropriety.

An appraiser's main credential will ultimately be the expertise that comes with performing numerous appraisals. The competent appraiser will also maintain a high level of professional practice by keeping up to date on developments within the field, reading appraisal and related publications, and attending seminars and courses.

EXERCISE 1.1

Which of the following courses would benefit a professional appraiser? Why or why not?

real estate finance
land-use planning
real estate law
real estate economics
statistics
real estate principles
urban sociology
demographics
information systems

Check your answers against those in the Answer Key at the back of the book.

Assignments Available

The service of a qualified appraiser is a recognized essential in many situations. In a real estate transaction involving either the sale or lease of real property, an appraisal may be desired to

- help set the seller's asking price;
- help a buyer determine the fairness of the asking price;
- set a value for real property when it is part of an estate;
- estimate the relative values of properties being traded;
- set value on property involved in corporate mergers, acquisitions, liquidations, or bankruptcies;
- determine the amount of a mortgage loan; or
- set rental rates.

In addition, other uses of real estate requiring appraisals include

- determining building insurance value;
- determining the effect on value of construction defects as part of a legal proceeding;
- determining property losses due to fire, storm damage, earthquake, or other disaster;
- assessing property for taxes;
- setting gift or inheritance taxes;
- estimating remodeling costs;
- valuing property as part of a marital dissolution;
- valuing property in an arbitration of a dispute;
- determining development costs;
- discovering a vacant property's most profitable use;
- ascertaining whether the present use of a property is its most profitable use; and
- establishing a value for property in a condemnation proceeding.

As time goes on, more and more of these appraisal activities have come to rely on computerized research and databases. An example is the technique called *computer assisted mass appraisal* (CAMA), useful when thousands of properties are reassessed for tax purposes. The more complex the property, however, the more the training and skill of the appraiser becomes a vital part of the valuation process.

Employment Opportunities

The types of appraisals noted above give some indication of employment opportunities available to professional real estate appraisers.

The appraiser may be self-employed, working as a sole practitioner, or perhaps using the services of a staff of other appraisers. A few appraisal companies have offices in major cities coast to coast, making use of the services of hundreds of appraisers. As with real estate sales associates employed by a brokerage, the real estate appraiser may be hired as an independent contractor, with appraisal fees divided according to the "commission split" determined in the hiring agreement.

Aside from appraisal companies, many other sources of employment are open to appraisers and, in many cases, to appraiser trainees. Appraisers' reports are used as a basis for establishing a variety of tax and condemnation values. Federal agencies, such as the Federal Housing Administration (FHA) and Department of Veterans Affairs (VA), appraise properties before insuring or guaranteeing mortgage loans. All agencies involved in such matters as road construction, urban renewal, conservation, and parkland employ appraisers.

Large industrial organizations and chain stores hire appraisers to serve their real estate departments by inspecting and judging the condition of land and buildings before entering into a purchase or lease agreement. Individuals considering the purchase or lease of real estate may hire an appraiser directly. If the appraisal will be used as part of a federally related transaction, the services of a licensed or certified appraiser probably will be required. Some states require that all appraisers be licensed or certified—even for transactions that are not federally related. Some clients also impose this requirement.

The importance of objective, accurate appraisals cannot be overstated. The wide range of activities for which the appraiser's services are required eventually touches the life of every citizen.

Appraiser Compensation

The majority of real estate appraisals are market valuations of single-family homes and are performed by self-employed appraisers. A self-employed appraiser works for a specified fee paid by the party by whom the appraiser is hired (usually a lender). In an increasingly common relationship, the appraiser may be hired (as an independent contractor or employee) by an appraisal company that contracts with a lender or other client to provide appraisal services as needed.

Appraisal fees are based on the time required to complete the appraisal process and report (the more complex the property or appraisal report required, the higher the fee will be), but they are also subject to negotiation between the appraiser and the party for whom the appraisal is prepared. Fees are thus subject to a balance between the appraiser's overhead and expenses on one hand and market competition on the other hand. Under no circumstances should the appraiser's fee be dependent on the final opinion of value, to avoid even the appearance of a conflict of interest. The appraiser's fee also cannot be based on a stipulated or subsequent event.

EXERCISE 1.2

Should an appraiser's compensation be based on the value of the property being appraised? Why or why not?

Check your answer against the one in the Answer Key at the back of the book.

■ LICENSING AND CERTIFICATION

The greatest influences on the status of the real estate appraiser came during the two decades of the 20th century in which the United States experienced its greatest economic challenges. The Great Depression of the 1930s gave birth to both the Society of Residential Appraisers as part of the United States Savings and Loan League, and the American Institute of Real Estate Appraisers under the auspices of the National Association of Real Estate Boards (now The National Association of Realtors®).

The decade of the 1980s brought many examples of economic upheaval, from the cyclic escalation and subsequent decline of real estate prices in California to the devastated marketplaces of the oil-belt states and the Northeast. These and other economic factors contributed to, and in turn were affected by, the collapse of many savings and loan institutions and led, ultimately, to the licensing of real estate appraisers.

The decade began with great promise. The *Depository Institutions Deregulation and Monetary Control Act of 1980* greatly expanded the activities of depository institutions and raised the level of federally insured accounts to $100,000. With deregulation, however, came many abuses by institutions that were ineptly and sometimes fraudulently managed. It was an era of increased competition, yet many savings and loan associations were strapped with long-term mortgage loans that yielded considerably less income than was necessary to offer the high short-term interest rates that would attract and keep depositors. To compensate, many institutions began to finance projects based on limited market analysis—projects that would have been risky ventures in the best of markets. Unfortunately, political and economic forces did not work in favor of the risk-takers. The *Tax Reform Act of 1986 (TRA '86)* eliminated the tax incentives for many investments, and the economies of the oil-belt states took a downturn. The resulting crash of real estate prices in many parts of the country proved to be the mortal blow for many overextended institutions.

Other factors contributing to the savings and loan crisis were carelessness and sometimes outright fraud in the preparation of real estate appraisals. Before the savings and loan crisis, no state required appraiser licensing or certification, and only a few states provided for voluntary certification of real estate appraisers or appraisals. At most, some states required that real estate appraisers have a real estate agent's license. This easygoing state of affairs was to be dramatically altered, however, by the federal government.

■ FIRREA

Congress took action to rescue the failed and failing savings and loans and to initiate procedures that would help prevent another such disaster by passing the *Financial Institutions Reform, Recovery, and Enforcement Act of 1989 (FIRREA)*. FIRREA established the *Office of Thrift Supervision* and the *Housing Finance Board* to supervise the savings and loans, a responsibility that had previously belonged to the Federal Home Loan Bank Board. The *Federal Savings and Loan Insurance Corporation (FSLIC)* was disbanded, and the *Federal Deposit Insurance Corporation (FDIC)* was made responsible for insuring all deposits in participating savings and loan associations as well as deposits in the participating banks it already insured.

The *Resolution Trust Corporation (RTC)* was created by FIRREA to take over, for sale or liquidation, savings and loan institutions that failed between January 1, 1989, and August 9, 1992. Its term was later extended; RTC ceased operation in 1996. The RTC was charged with acting as conservator and receiver during the *resolution* of the insolvent institutions. In addition, the RTC was given the responsibility to review and renegotiate earlier (1988) resolution agreements handled by FSLIC, although subsequent litigation has upheld some earlier agreements. RTC also took over the functions of the *Federal Asset Disposition Association (FADA)*, making RTC, during its short life, the country's largest single seller of real estate. On dissolution of RTC, its duties were taken over by FDIC.

Appraiser Licensing

One of the most important actions taken by Congress through FIRREA was the requirement that as of July 1, 1991 (later extended to January 1, 1993), all "federally related real estate appraisals" be performed *only* by appraisers *licensed* or *certified* (as required) by the state in which the real estate is located.

A certified appraiser is required for property with a transaction value of more than $1 million or complex one-unit to four-unit residential property with a transaction value greater than $250,000.

Licensed status generally is required for appraisals of one-unit to four-unit residential property, unless the size and complexity of the property indicate that a certified appraiser is necessary. Federal agency directives have indicated that appraisals of nonresidential property and complex residential property with a transaction value less than $250,000 also may be handled by licensed rather than certified appraisers.

In October 1992, Congress passed legislation that requires that any agency seeking to establish a *de minimis* value—a minimum valuation threshold below which appraiser licensing or certification is not required—determine in writing that the threshold set would not threaten the safety and soundness of lending institutions. This threshold was raised from $100,000 to $250,000, effective June 7, 1994. Currently, Fannie Mae, Freddie Mac, HUD, and the VA still require the use of state-licensed or state-certified appraisers for every appraisal, as do many lenders and other appraisal clients.

The Appraisal Foundation

WEB@LINK
www.appraisalfoundation.org

FIRREA requires that state appraiser licensing and certification qualifications and appraisal standards meet or exceed those of the Appraisal Standards Board (ASB) and the Appraiser Qualifications Board (AQB) of *The Appraisal Foundation,* a nonprofit corporation established in 1987, headquartered in Washington, D.C., and found at *www.appraisalfoundation.org.*

The **ASB** is responsible for establishing the rules for developing an appraisal and reporting its results. It has issued the *Uniform Standards of Professional Appraisal Practice (USPAP),* which have been adopted by all major appraisal groups.

The **AQB,** on the other hand, is responsible for establishing the qualifications for states to follow in the licensing, certification, and recertification of appraisers.

Appraisal organizations affiliated with The Appraisal Foundation include the American Association of Certified Appraisers, American Society of Farm Managers and Rural Appraisers, Appraisal Institute, International Association of Assessing Officers, International Right of Way Association, National Association of Independent Fee Appraisers, and National Association of Master Appraisers. Affiliate sponsors include the American Bankers Association, Farm Credit Council, Mortgage Insurance Companies of America, and National Association of REALTORS®. The Appraisal Institute of Canada is an international sponsor.

■ OTHER FEDERAL REGULATION

Ownership and use of real estate are the subject of an increasing number of federal laws and administrative regulations.

Fair Housing

The important role of all real estate professionals in providing access to housing for every resident of the United States has been recognized by Congress. The *Fair Housing Amendments Act of 1988*, effective March 12, 1989, prohibits discrimination in the selling, brokering, or appraising of residential real property because of race, color, religion, sex, handicap, familial status, or national origin. The subject of fair housing will be covered in greater detail in Chapter 6, "Data Collection."

Environmental Concerns

Regulations affecting buildings that may contain lead-based paint are only the latest evidence of heightened awareness of building construction and land development issues that affect the health and safety of occupants and others. Some of these topics will be covered in Chapter 5, "Building Construction and the Environment."

Professional Standards of Practice

The major appraisal associations have been leaders in establishing standards of appraisal practice as well as in defining ethical conduct by members of the profession. In 1985, representatives from nine appraisal groups formed an Ad Hoc Committee on Uniform Standards of Professional Appraisal Practice. The organizations included the

- American Institute of Real Estate Appraisers (since merged with the Society of Real Estate Appraisers and now known as the Appraisal Institute);
- American Society of Farm Managers and Rural Appraisers;
- Appraisal Institute of Canada;
- International Association of Assessing Officers;
- International Right of Way Association;
- National Association of Independent Fee Appraisers;
- National Society of Real Estate Appraisers; and
- Society of Real Estate Appraisers.

The standards, published in 1987 and amended several times since then, cover real estate, personal property, and business appraisals, as well as other topics. They are now the Uniform Standards of Professional Appraisal Practice (USPAP), as interpreted and amended by the Appraisal Standards Board of The Appraisal Foundation. USPAP Standards 1, 2, and 3 cover real property appraisal, real property appraisal reporting, and review appraisal. While this book is not intended to instruct students in USPAP, USPAP sections will be referred to throughout this book to help students understand how topics covered relate to current appraisal requirements.

You should keep in mind that the contents of USPAP are subject to ongoing review and modification by the Appraisal Standards Board of The Appraisal Foundation. The complete text of the Uniform Standards of Professional Appraisal Practice, proposed changes to the Standards, and information of value to both appraisers and consumers can be found at *www.appraisalfoundation.org*.

WEB LINK
www.appraisalfoundation.org

EXERCISE 1.3

1. The federal legislation that resulted in state licensing and certification of appraisers in federally related transactions was
   a. Internal Revenue Code.
   b. FIRREA.
   c. FDIC.
   d. FSLIC.

2. State appraiser licensing and certification qualifications must meet or exceed those of the
   a. Appraisal Standards Board.
   b. Appraiser Qualifications Board.

3. Appraisals in federally related transactions must meet or exceed the requirements of the
   a. Appraisal Standards Board.
   b. Appraiser Qualifications Board.

federal

4. Fannie Mae requires the use of a state-licensed or state-certified appraiser
   a. only for appraisals of property with a transaction value of more than $250,000.
   b. for all Fannie Mae-related transactions.

Check your answers against those in the Answer Key at the back of the book.

■ PROFESSIONAL SOCIETIES

As a way of establishing professional credentials and keeping up to date in the appraisal field, the appraiser may seek membership in one of the appraisal societies. Such groups usually have regular meetings, publish professional journals, hold seminars, and conduct appraisal courses. Usually they have education, experience, and examination requirements for membership.

The major appraisal and related societies follow, along with their member designations. Requirements for membership vary widely, with some being substantially more rigorous than others. Readers are urged to evaluate carefully the benefits of membership in any appraisal organization.

W E B L I N K
http://arac.lincoln-grad.org

Accredited Review Appraisers Council, San Antonio, TX
http://arac.lincoln-grad.org
Publisher of *The Review Appraiser*
Member designation: AAR (Accredited in Appraisal Review)

W E B L I N K
www.appraisers.org

American Society of Appraisers, Herndon, VA
www.appraisers.org
Publisher of *Technical Valuation,* a professional journal, and the *Appraisal and Valuation Manual*
Member designations: ASA (Senior Member), ASR (Senior Residential Member), and FASA (Fellow)

W E B L I N K
www.asfmra.org

American Society of Farm Managers and Rural Appraisers, Inc., Denver, CO
www.asfmra.org
Member designations: AFM (Accredited Farm Manager) and ARA (Accredited Rural Appraiser)

American Society of Professional Appraisers, Atlanta, GA
Member designations: CRRA (Certified Residential Real Estate Appraiser) and CCRA (Certified Commercial Real Estate Appraiser)

American Society of Real Estate Appraisers, Atlanta, GA
Member designations: RSA (Residential Senior Appraiser) and CSA (Commercial Senior Appraiser)

WEB @ LINK
www.appraisalinstitute.org

Appraisal Institute, Chicago, IL
www.appraisalinstitute.org
Publisher of *The Appraisal Journal* and *Valuation Insights and Perspectives,* as well as a number of special reports and books
Member designations: MAI (member experienced in the valuation and evaluation of commercial, industrial, residential, and other types of property, and who advises clients on real estate investment decisions), SRPA (member experienced in the valuation of commercial, industrial, residential, and other types of property), and SRA (member experienced in the analysis and valuation of residential real property)

The Appraisal Institute was created in 1990 by the merger of the American Institute of Real Estate Appraisers and the Society of Real Estate Appraisers. Appraisal Institute members who were members of one of the earlier organizations also may have one of the following designations, although these are no longer issued by the Appraisal Institute: RM (Residential Member) and SREA (Senior Real Estate Analyst).

WEB @ LINK
www.aicanada.org

Appraisal Institute of Canada, Winnipeg, Manitoba, Canada
www.aicanada.org
Publisher of *The Canadian Appraiser,* a technical journal, and *Appraisal Institute DIGEST,* a newsletter
Member designations: CRA (Canadian Residential Appraiser) and AACI (Accredited Appraiser Canadian Institute)

WEB @ LINK
www.frea.com

Foundation of Real Estate Appraisers, San Diego, CA
www.frea.com
Publisher of *Communicator* magazine

WEB @ LINK
www.iaao.org

International Association of Assessing Officers, Chicago, IL
www.iaao.org
Publisher of *The International Assessor* and the *Assessors Journal,* as well as many specialized booklets and manuals
Member designations: CPE (Certified Personalty Evaluator), AAE (Accredited Assessment Evaluator), CAE (Certified Assessment Evaluator), and RES (Residential Evaluation Specialist)

WEB @ LINK
www.irwaonline.org

International Right of Way Association, Inglewood, CA
www.irwaonline.org
Publisher of *Right of Way* magazine
Member designation: SR/WA (Senior—Right of Way Association)

WEB @ LINK
www.naifa.com

National Association of Independent Fee Appraisers, Inc., Chicago, IL
www.naifa.com
Publisher of *The Appraisal Review*
Member designations: IFA (Member), IFAS (Senior Member), and IFAC (Appraiser-Counselor)

WEB @ LINK
www.masterappraisers.com

WEB @ LINK
www.nraiappraisers.com

National Association of Master Appraisers, San Antonio, TX
www.masterappraisers.com
Publisher of *The Master Appraiser*
Member designations: MRA (Master Residential Appraiser), MFLA (Master Farm and Land Appraiser), MSA (Master Senior Appraiser), and CAO (Certified Appraisal Organization)

National Residential Appraisers Institute, Amherst, OH
www.nraiappraisers.com
Publisher of *Appraisers News Network*
Member designations: CMDA (Certified Market Data Analyst), GSA (Graduate Senior Appraiser), and SCA (Senior Certified Appraiser)

National Society of Real Estate Appraisers, Inc., Cleveland, OH
Publisher of *National Report*
Member designations: RA (Residential Appraiser), CRA (Certified Real Estate Appraiser), and MREA (Master Real Estate Appraiser)

■ THE MODERN APPRAISAL OFFICE

The typical professional appraiser of a generation ago would be flabbergasted by the inroads made by electronic media in the modern appraisal office. Even in the past ten years, the manner in which appraisal data are accumulated and analyzed and the way that the appraiser's opinion of value is transmitted to the client have undergone a transformation. With the increasing availability and range of use of small, easily programmed office computers, the appraiser must be acquainted with a variety of appraisal-based computer applications. A few of these are highlighted next, with suggestions for the equipment necessary to keep pace with the developing electronic products.

The Computer

Even the smallest real estate or appraisal office can now take advantage of the computer's storage and problem-solving capabilities. What kind of computer is best for the appraisal office? That depends on the nature of the appraisal work, the complexity of the assignments the appraiser will undertake, and the size of the appraiser's budget.

It is best to tackle the question of what computer to buy by working backward; that is, the appraiser should begin by considering the requirements of the software that will be used in everyday practice. The appraiser may have already decided to buy one of the major appraisal software packages, which could cover everything from case tracking, including data collection and report preparation, to management of the appraisal office, including billing and staffing. Most appraisal programs require a computer that is "IBM-compatible" (one that meets the operating specifications designed for IBM, Inc., products, referred to as *PCs,* or personal computers). There are far fewer applications created for the "Mac" (a computer that meets the operating specifications designed for Macintosh computers produced by Apple Computers, Inc.). There are Mac programs for all the standard forms used for residential and general appraising; however, there are more choices of software vendors for the PC. The beginning appraiser should follow the recommendations of the managing appraiser who will be reviewing his or her work to ensure compatibility.

Some state appraiser licensing offices, as well as the major appraisal associations and private education providers, offer introductory classes or seminars in computer technology and applications for the appraisal office. Because of the rapid development of more powerful computers, as well as new software to take advantage of the computer's growing data-handling capabilities, attendance at one of these classes should be useful for the experienced computer user as well as the neophyte.

In short, the computer hardware and software purchase decisions needn't be made in a vacuum. By seeking expert advice, and dealing with one of the major computer manufacturers, even the beginner can take most of the trauma out of the purchase decision. With the right information, the computer buyer should be able to invest in a system that will be adequate for three years of service. This means that the system should not only meet the appraiser's immediate needs but be expandable to cover reasonably expected additions of equipment and software.

The most important feature of the computer purchase will not be apparent until after a problem arises. Who is responsible for fixing the computer when something goes wrong, and where will the repairs be made? If the computer system is purchased with an intended period of use of three years, the most desirable warranty or service contract will be one that provides for three years of on-site maintenance, to be performed within a stated time of the request for service (48 to 72 hours, for instance). Such a warranty may require an additional fee, but will help reduce a major source of stress for the computer owner. After all, when an appraiser is relying on a functioning computer system to produce and transmit appraisals, a nonfunctioning machine means that the appraiser is virtually out of business.

What price can the appraiser expect to pay for a system capable of handling all of the operations mentioned above? That depends on many things: the system's *motherboard,* the command system, which determines how fast the system can operate; RAM, or *random access memory,* which determines how many operations the system can perform at the same time; *hard drive memory,* or data storage capacity; a *monitor* of adequate size and image definition; and the specifications of the DVD/CD drives and other peripherals. The portability of laptop and notebook computers makes them the first choice for many appraisers; functionality and storage capacity rival those of desktop machines, though at somewhat higher cost.

A basic "office suite" of software applications, including word-processing, spreadsheet, graphics, and mailing list capability, is likely to be included in the price of the basic system. The cost of appraisal-based software applications will depend on the appraiser's needs and on how much time the appraiser is willing to spend searching for the best price available. No matter what software is chosen to generate reports, it is the appraiser's responsibility to know the workings of the software well enough to ensure that no mistakes are made in the communication of the appraisal.

The Printer

Today's appraisal software not only allows a user to complete any of the numerous standard appraisal forms, it provides the form itself. The key to making a professional presentation is the quality of the printer used to print out the completed form. Best quality will be created by a laser printer capable of producing 12 or more black and white pages per minute, at a resolution of 1,200 by 1,200 dpi (dots per inch) or higher. A slower but useful second (or primary) printer would be a color ink-jet machine that can produce attractive renderings of photographs. Important considerations with any printer are the reproduction quality available, number of pages per minute the machine can produce, and cost per page, including purchase cost, expense of replacement ink or toner cartridges, and other anticipated maintenance.

The Backup System

As with any serious computer use, the appraiser should ensure that no data are lost in the event of a power failure or mechanical malfunction. The backup system properly consists of two components: (1) a battery (not just a power surge protector) to which the computer is connected to provide a secondary power supply—in essence, a cushion of time during which the computer can be shut down in the event of a power failure without loss of data—and (2) a second computer memory that can be used (and refreshed periodically) to keep a copy of everything that is stored on the computer. This can be a removable hard drive, disk, or cartridge, or an off-site source to which files can be regularly downloaded. A final word of warning: During an electrical storm, it may be prudent to shut down one's computer completely to avoid risk of data loss. There is no backup system yet invented that will survive a direct hit, or even a near-miss, from a bolt of lightning.

The Internet

Most efficient access to the resources available via the Internet requires a hard-wired system—either cable access or a dedicated T1 line. Computer modems requiring use of a telephone (dial-up) connection to a service provider are usable for limited applications. Their success depends on speed (more than 50,000 bits per second, or bps, is preferable) and availability of local access numbers. Satellite transmission is also possible, provided satellite access is available. As of this writing, wireless Internet connections have limited availability, though they will inevitably become more widely used, particularly in urban areas.

Once one is *online* (has gained access to the Internet), one can reach government, educational, and private sources of information around the globe. One can also be a recipient of communications in the form of electronic mail, or *e-mail*. One can also upload (send) and download (receive) text and graphic files. Such *electronic data interchange,* or *EDI,* allows a computer in the appraiser's office to transmit a complete appraisal report to the client almost instantaneously.

Use of the Internet by appraisers is growing exponentially every year, as more and more data sources, including multiple-listing services, provide online access to their databases. The number of government offices allowing access to public records is also growing. Information on national, regional, and local economic, employment, and other trends is readily available. There are a growing number of services specializing in data on various types of commercial and residential properties; some of these sources are listed in Chapter 6, "Data Collection." Despite numerous data sources, however, not all information available is accurate or accurately reported. USPAP requires that the appraiser verify all information used in the appraisal report.

Geographic Information Systems (GIS)

Satellite-based mapping systems have been in use for as long as satellites have orbited the earth. From their initial military and weather technology-based applications, mapping systems based on latitude and longitude are now entering the commercial marketplace. The utility of the maps, once available only from the United States Geological Survey (USGS), has been greatly expanded. Commercial services now provide (via computer disk or the Internet) reference maps that provide overlays of national, regional, and local data and are capable of incorporating the appraiser's own data. The cost of such maps will depend on the source and method of transmission.

The Camera

No modern appraisal office is complete without a digital camera that can be used to make and transmit images without the need for film or printed copy. The digital camera is a miniature version of a computer, capable of receiving images, recording them in digitized (computer-readable) format on an internal memory chip or removable memory card, and releasing them to a printer and/or another memory device, such as a computer hard drive. With a digital camera, the appraiser can import images directly to an appraisal report. If the report itself is transmitted electronically, the photos are incorporated within the report, to be viewed on the recipient's computer monitor. *Note:* Because some courts and government agencies still require printed appraisal reports with separate, professionally reproduced photos, the appraiser may need to purchase a 35-millimeter camera as well as a digital camera.

Use of Technology

In recent years, there have been many references to use of "artificial intelligence" in the appraisal process. This is a misnomer, however. The use of appropriate resources, including computers, can help an appraiser function more efficiently and more accurately, but these tools serve only as aids to the appraiser. There never will be a substitute for the skilled and informed judgment of a professional appraiser.

■ SUMMARY

The skills required of the professional appraiser touch on most areas of real estate practice. The best-qualified appraiser will have some of the abilities of the economist, city planner, surveyor, real estate developer, builder, and broker. Familiarity with appraisal-based computer applications is a necessity.

Impartiality, objectivity, knowledge of appraising fundamentals, and the quality of judgment that comes only with experience are the professional appraiser's chief credentials. The real estate appraiser's impartiality and objectivity make it unlikely that his or her prerogatives will be abused. The appraiser's knowledge and experience provide the basis for an accurate appraisal. Employment opportunities include both private and public sectors, and an appraiser may be called on for a variety of purposes.

The crisis within the savings and loan industry was the impetus for the passage by Congress of the Financial Institutions Reform, Recovery, and Enforcement Act of 1989 (FIRREA). The Resolution Trust Corporation (RTC) was charged with the sale or liquidation of failed institutions and became the largest seller of real property in the United States. Another important feature of FIRREA now in effect is the requirement that only state-licensed or state-certified appraisers be allowed to perform real property appraisals in certain federally related transactions. By helping to better define the role and responsibilities of the real estate appraiser, the new regulations will help enhance the qualifications of those who seek licensing or certification, which should, in turn, improve the level of appraisal services available.

Federal laws and regulations on such topics as fair housing and environmental issues are of increasing concern to appraisers. The professional appraisal societies provide excellent sources of appraisal information. Today's appraiser makes use of such resources to stay abreast of both legal requirements and technological innovations.

1

ACHIEVEMENT EXAMINATION

1. List at least five general course areas that would be of benefit to a real estate appraiser, in addition to real estate courses.

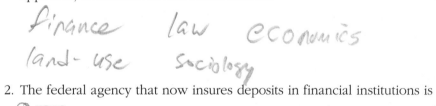

finance   law   economics
land-use   sociology

2. The federal agency that now insures deposits in financial institutions is
   a. FDIC.
   b. FSLIC.
   c. RTC.
   d. FIRREA.

3. All of the following areas of federal regulation affect appraisers *EXCEPT*
   a. appraiser licensing.
   b. fair housing.
   c. FDA.
   d. lead-based paint.

4. Appraiser qualifications that meet federal guidelines come from the
   a. Appraiser Qualification Board.
   b. Appraisal Standards Board.
   c. Resolution Trust Corporation.
   d. Appraisal Institute.

5. Every state must enact legislation to provide for appraiser licensing and certification that is consistent with criteria established by the
   a. Federal National Mortgage Association.
   b. Appraiser Qualification Board of The Appraisal Foundation.
   c. Resolution Trust Corporation.
   d. Appraisal Institute.

6. The purpose of USPAP is to

   a. delay government regulation.

   b. present information that will be meaningful to the client and will not be misleading in the marketplace.

   c. guarantee professionalism in appraisers.

   d. present information that will be useful to appraisers.

7. A certified appraiser is required for federally related transactions involving property valued at more than

   a. $250,000.

   b. $500,000.

   c. $750,000.

   d. $1 million.

Check your answers against those in the Answer Key at the back of the book.

## CHAPTER 2

Real Estate and Its Appraisal

■ OVERVIEW

Appraising has always been a unique part of the real estate industry. The appraiser's estimate of property value has a significant effect on many aspects of a real estate transaction, whether the transaction involves a sale, a transfer, a mortgage loan, or a property tax assessment or is for some other purpose. The appraiser must act as a disinterested third party; for this reason the appraiser's compensation is not based on the estimated value of the property being appraised. With no vested interest in the estimation of value, the appraiser should be able to objectively evaluate the property's relative merits, appeal, and value.

This chapter defines some of the terms that will be used throughout this book, including *appraisal, land, site, real estate, real property,* and *personal property.* A *fixture* is defined, and the legal tests for determining when an item is a fixture are provided.

You will learn how a parcel of real estate is described, how it may be owned, how its use may be restricted, and how title may be transferred.

■ BASIC CONCEPTS

put's a value on property

What Is a Real Estate Appraisal?

As defined in USPAP, an *appraisal* is the act or process of developing an opinion of value. An appraisal includes a description of the property under consideration, the appraiser's opinion of the property's condition, its utility for a given purpose, and/or its probable monetary value on the open market. The term *appraisal* is used to refer to both the *process* by which the appraiser reaches certain conclusions (USPAP Standard 1) and the written *report* in which those conclusions are communicated (USPAP Standard 2). With an objective, well-researched, and carefully documented appraisal, all parties involved, whether in a sale, lease, or other transaction, are aided in the decision-making process.

A reliable opinion of value is sought by many parties for many different reasons. The seller wants to know the value of the real estate to determine an appropriate selling price, the buyer wants to pay no more than necessary, and the broker wants to realize the maximum commission. Financial institutions, which need appraisals to assist in their underwriting decisions regardless of the loan amount, insist on an appraisal to determine the amount of money they should lend to a credit applicant. Appraisals are also used to estimate value for taxation and insurance purposes and in condemnation proceedings.

To understand how real estate is appraised, you should know how the term *real estate* is defined.

Real Estate and Real Property

Real estate is defined as the land itself and all things permanently attached to it. The definition of real estate typically includes

- land; = site
- fixtures (attachments) to land;
- anything incidental or appurtenant to land that benefits the landowner, such as an easement right to use your neighbor's driveway for access to your property; and
- anything else that is considered immovable (part of the real estate) by law, except for cultivated crops (called *emblements*) and other severable (removable) things that are sold by a contract of sale that complies with the laws regulating the sale of goods.

Land

The earth's surface, including everything under or on it, is considered *land*. The substances *under* the earth's surface may be more valuable than the surface itself. *Mineral rights* to solid substances (such as coal and iron ore), as well as those that must be removed from beneath the surface to be reduced to possession (such as oil and gas), may be transferred independently of the rest of the land. *Water rights* provide access to our increasingly important surface and underground water supplies.

When land is *improved* by the addition of streets, utilities (water, gas, electricity), sewers, and other services, it becomes a *site* and may be considered suitable for building purposes.

Within limitations, the air rights *above* the earth's surface are also considered the landowner's property. Transferable development rights of airspace have facilitated construction of highrise buildings.

Fixtures

A *fixture* is anything permanently attached to land. Fixtures include natural things that are attached by roots, such as trees and bushes, and manmade things, such as fences and buildings.

Ordinarily, improvements to real estate, including both landscaping and structures, are considered fixtures. In determining whether a specific item is a fixture, and thus part of the real estate, courts will consider the

- *method* by which the item is attached—how permanent the attachment is and the resulting economic burden of removal;
- *adaptability* of the item for the land's ordinary use;

- *relationship* of the parties;
- *intention* of the person in placing the item on the land; and
- *agreement* of the parties.

If a seller of real estate has attached something to the land, that item will be considered a fixture unless the sales contract provides otherwise or the courts determine it is not a fixture according to the criteria listed above. The appraiser must indicate whether fixtures are included in the property appraisal.

Trade Fixtures = *Personal Property*

A determination of whether an item is a fixture may also be important when property is leased. An item owned and attached to a rental space or building by a tenant and used for business purposes is called a *trade* or *chattel fixture.* Some examples of trade fixtures are gas station pumps, restaurant equipment, store shelves, and the exercise equipment in a health club.

If the tenant places an item on the land, to whom will the item belong when the lease terminates? Landlord and tenant are free to make whatever agreement they desire with regard to ownership of trade fixtures. If they have made no lease agreement or if the lease is silent on the subject of a particular fixture, state law will determine ownership of the fixture and thus whether it may be removed by the tenant.

A tenant usually may remove a trade fixture before the end of the lease term if the fixture was installed for purposes of trade, manufacture, ornament, or domestic use *and* if it can be removed without damage to the premises. Otherwise, the tenant generally is allowed to remove the fixture only if he or she believed in good faith that the fixture could be installed and subsequently removed. Of course, the tenant who is allowed to remove a trade fixture must pay for any resulting property damage. Trade fixtures that are not removed become the property of the landlord.

Bundle of Rights

The owner of real estate has the power to do certain things with it. These rights of ownership, often called the *bundle of rights,* include the rights to use, rent, sell, or give away the real estate, as well as to choose *not* to exercise any of these rights.

In some states, the rights of ownership of real estate are referred to as *real property.* In other states, the rights of ownership are included within the definition of real estate, and the terms *real estate* and *real property* are synonymous.

Traditionally, appraisers have distinguished between real estate (the land and buildings) and real property (the legal rights of ownership). In current practice, however, the terms *real estate* and *real property* are frequently used interchangeably, as is the case in this text.

The bundle of rights inherent in the ownership of real estate are what may be bought and sold in a real property transaction. In an appraisal the rights being appraised must be stated, because any limitation on the rights of ownership may affect property value. There are property rights that are reserved by law for public (government) exercise and thus limit an owner's full enjoyment of ownership rights. There also may be private restrictions on the use of real property.

Public Restrictions = *all property*

There are four public or governmental restrictions that limit the ownership of real estate. They are (1) *taxation,* (2) *eminent domain,* (3) *escheat,* and (4) *police power.* The right of *taxation* enables the government to collect taxes and to sell

T.E.E.P.

State takes it w/o heirs

the property if the taxes are not paid. In many states, growing pressure to increase the state budget or reduce a burgeoning deficit has placed additional strain on property owners. *Ad valorem* (according to value) taxation historically has taken the form of property taxes based on assessed value. *Special assessments* for particular neighborhood or regional improvements, separately itemized on property tax bills, are becoming increasingly popular. One reason for the high cost of land for new buildings in many areas is the rising level of *development fees* used to build roads, sewer systems, and other infrastructure improvements, as well as schools, parks, and other public spaces. Such costs are, of course, passed on to the homebuyer or investor. Even in areas where property tax rates are well defined, added exactions by local governing authorities, even when they don't appear on an itemized tax bill, may have a significant effect on building cost and cost of ownership.

Private property may be taken for public use, on payment of just compensation, by the right of *eminent domain*. If the owner of real property dies leaving no qualified heirs, ownership of the property may revert to the state by the right of *escheat*. The *police power* of government enables it to establish zoning ordinances, building codes, and other measures that restrict the use of real estate to protect the health, safety, morals, and general welfare of the public.

Private Restrictions

There may be private (nongovernmental) qualifications or limitations on the use of real property, most often because of *conditions, covenants, and restrictions (CC&Rs)* placed in the deed received by the property owner. CC&Rs typically benefit subdivision property owners and owners of condominium units.

The most frequently encountered private limitation on use is the *lien* created by the security instrument used to purchase the property. The instruments used to *hypothecate* (pledge) real estate as security for a debt are the *mortgage* and the *deed of trust*. The most significant difference between the two is the method by which each is enforced. A mortgage may require a court-ordered sale to be foreclosed. A deed of trust usually allows the trustee who holds title on behalf of the beneficiary (lender) to sell the property and pay off the underlying debt in the event of default by the trustor (buyer/borrower). Because of statutory protections provided to homeowners and others, the differences between the two forms of security instrument may be more theoretical than practical.

Personal Property

Any tangible items that are not permanently attached to real estate, and thus are not considered fixtures, are classified as *personal property*. Trade fixtures are included in this category because they are usually owned and installed by the tenant for the tenant's use and are to be removed by the tenant when the lease expires.

Why is it important to know the distinction between fixtures and personal property? If an item is classified as a fixture, it is part of the real estate, and its contribution to value is included in the value estimate. Items of personal property are usually not included in an appraisal.

The attachment necessary for an item to be considered a fixture would ordinarily be such that the item could be removed only by causing serious damage to either the real estate or the item itself. A window air conditioner would ordinarily be considered personal property, but if a hole were cut in a wall expressly for the installation of the air conditioner, the unit would probably be considered part of the real estate. Because the distinction between fixtures and personal property is not always obvious, appraisers should find out how these items are treated in their areas.

The parties involved in a transaction can and should agree on what items are to be considered part of the real estate. In the absence of such an agreement, however, if legal action is necessary, a court will apply the tests of a fixture listed earlier.

EXERCISE 2.1

Indicate whether each of the following is ordinarily real estate or personal property:

1. Window screens — *R E*
2. Hot tub installed in wood deck *PP RE*
3. Furnace *R E*
4. Plantation shutters *R E*
5. Central air-conditioning *R E*
6. Kitchen cabinets *R E*
7. Child's movable playhouse *P P*
8. Portable room heater *P P*
9. Rosebushes *R E*
10. The right to sell land and any building(s) attached to the land *R E*

Why is the distinction between real estate and personal property important to the appraiser?

Check your answers against those in the Answer Key at the back of the book.

LEGAL DESCRIPTIONS OF LAND

A *legal description* of land is one that describes the land in such a way that a competent surveyor could locate its boundaries using nothing more than the description.

The three basic methods used to describe land in the United States are the *lot and block system*, the *metes and bounds system*, and the *rectangular* (or *government*) *survey system*.

Lot and Block System

The *lot and block system*, also called the *lot, block, and tract system* and the *subdivision system*, is the method used to describe most residential and commercial building lots.

Individual parcels are referred to by the tract, block, and lot numbers by which they are identified in the *subdivision map* filed in the county recorder's office. The description will also name the city and county in which the tract is located and should provide the book and page number in the county recorder's office where the subdivision map appears, as well as the date the map was recorded.

Figure 2.1 shows part of a subdivision in Riverglen, California. The legal description of lot 7 is as follows: "Lot 7, Fertile Acres, Amended 35/38 (as recorded July 14, 1976, Book 186, Page 19 of maps), City of Riverglen, County of Riverside, State of California."

FIGURE 2.1
Subdivision Plat Map

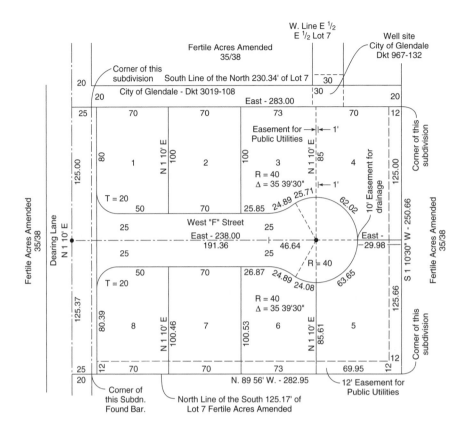

Metes and Bounds System

The *metes and bounds system* is one of the oldest known methods of surveying land in the United States and is used predominantly through the eastern states. A metes and bounds description defines the perimeter of a parcel of land by using measured distances from specified boundary markers.

A metes and bounds description starts at a *point of beginning* and follows natural or artificial boundaries, called *bounds,* for measured distances, called *metes.* Individual *monuments* or *markers* may also be referred to in the description.

Because both natural and artificial boundaries or markers may change drastically in only a few years, a metes and bounds description may be quite unreliable. Consider the following early example of such a description (illustrated in Figure 2.2), and you can imagine the difficulties of the landowner who bought the described parcel after the creek had changed its course and one of the roadways mentioned had been plowed under for farming. A tract of land located in the Village of Red Skull was described as follows:

FIGURE 2.2
Metes and Bounds Tract

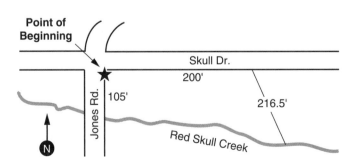

Beginning at the intersection of the East line of Jones Road and the South line of Skull Drive; thence East along the South line of Skull Drive 200 feet; thence South 15 degrees East 216.5 feet, more or less, to the center thread of Red Skull Creek; thence Northwesterly along the center line of said Creek to its intersection with the East line of Jones Road; thence North 105 feet, more or less, along the East line of Jones Road to the place of beginning.

In many areas, points of beginning have been replaced by permanent markers, and the laser transits used by modern surveyors give extremely accurate results.

Rectangular Survey System

The *rectangular survey system*, also called the *U.S. government survey system* and *section and township system*, is most useful in identifying large tracts of rural property. Land area is divided into *townships* measured and numbered starting at the intersection of a *base line* running east to west and a *principal meridian* running north to south (see Figure 2.3). Lines running east and west, parallel to the base line and spaced six miles apart, are called *township lines*. Lines that run north and south, parallel to the principal meridian, are also six miles apart and are called *range lines* (see Figure 2.4). When the horizontal township lines and the vertical range lines intersect, they form squares, called *sections*. A township is divided into 36 sections. A section of land contains 640 acres and is 1 mile square, or 5,280 feet by 5,280 feet.

Sections are numbered 1 through 36, as shown in Figure 2.5. Section 1 is always at the northeast, or upper right-hand corner of the township. The numbering proceeds right to left, left to right for the next row, right to left for the row after that, and so on. Each section in a township, in turn, can be divided into halves, quarters, and even smaller parcels based on compass point directions, as shown in the example in Figure 2.6.

FIGURE 2.3
Township Lines

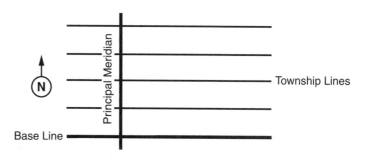

FIGURE 2.4
Range Lines

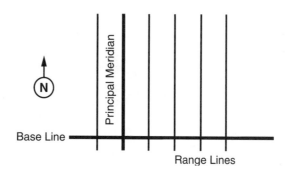

FIGURE 2.5
Sections in a Township

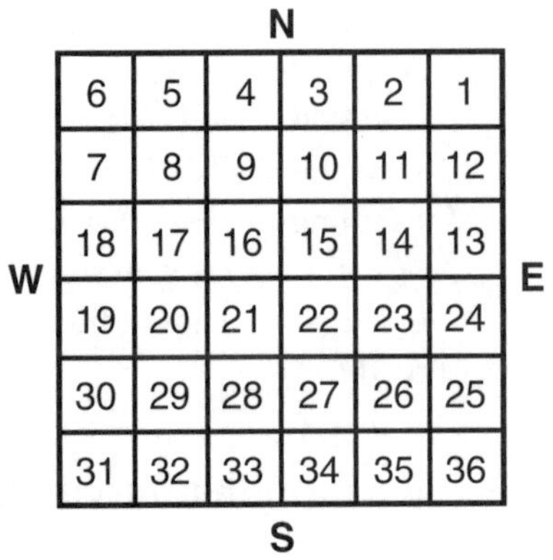

FIGURE 2.6
A Section

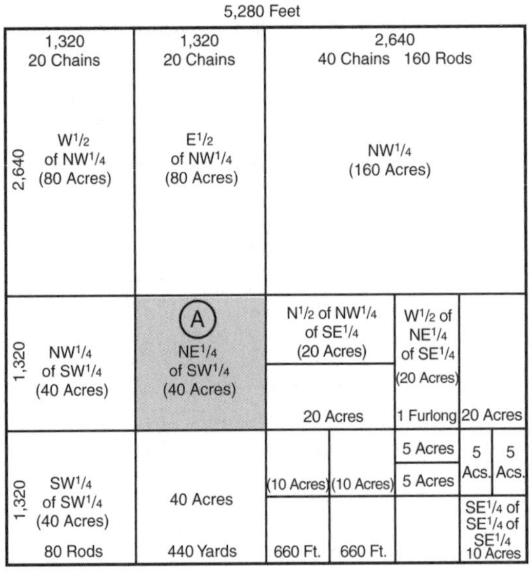

The area of a fractional part of a section is found by multiplying the fraction (or fractions) by the number of acres in a section—640. The rectangular survey system description of the 40-acre parcel labeled *A* in Figure 2.6 is "the NE¼ of the SW¼ of Section 12." If only the legal description is known, the area of the parcel can be found by multiplying: ¼ × ¼ × 640 = 40 acres.

The appraiser should be familiar with all three forms of legal descriptions and know which form or forms are accepted in the area where the appraisal is being conducted (see Figure 2.7).

EXERCISE 2.2   What is the land area covered by the parcel described as the W½ of the SW¼ of the E½ of Section 24?

Check your answer against the one in the Answer Key at the back of the book.

F I G U R E 2.7
Map of United States and Land Description Section

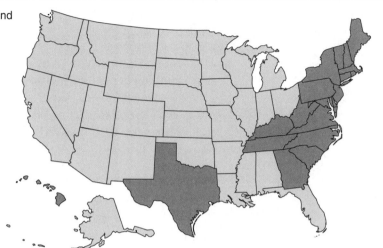

These states generally use the metes and bounds legal description:

Maine	Tennessee
Massachusetts	New Hampshire
Connecticut	Georgia
Rhode Island	North Carolina
Vermont	South Carolina
New York	Maryland
Pennsylvania	Virginia
Delaware	West Virginia
New Jersey	Texas
Kentucky	Hawaii

The remaining 30 states use the rectangular or government survey legal description.

Source: *www.outfitters.com/genealogy/land*

■ LEGAL RIGHTS AND INTERESTS

The value of real property depends on the kind of property right owned. Although the rights of ownership are spoken of as the "bundle of rights," all of the rights are not always owned by the same person or transferred together. Ownership interests in real estate are referred to as *estates in land*.

Freehold Estates

Highest form of ownership

The highest or most complete form of ownership in medieval times was the *freehold estate*. The holder of a freehold estate was not subject to the overlord but could do with the property whatever he or she chose. Freehold estates are estates of ownership. The person who owns a freehold estate can transfer the right of possession to someone else, as in a lease of the property, but the underlying right of ownership remains with the holder of the freehold estate.

Fee Simple Estate

The highest interest in real estate recognized by law is the *fee simple estate*. This generally is what we mean when we refer to property *ownership*. Fee simple ownership includes the right to use the land now and for an indefinite period of time in the future. If there are no restrictions on the ownership right, it is considered a *fee simple absolute*. Ownership that is limited in some way is a *fee simple qualified*. Any limitation on property use that could result in the loss of the ownership right is called a *fee simple defeasible*.

Examples of limitations on fee simple title are the *condition precedent* (or *fee simple determinable*), stipulating some action that must be taken before ownership will take effect, and the *condition subsequent* (or *fee simple conditional*), specifying an action or activity that, if performed, will allow the previous owner to retake possession of the property through legal action. The requirement that an heir achieve a certain age before title can be transferred is an example of a condition precedent. An example of a condition subsequent is a requirement that alcohol not be consumed on premises given to a church; if the condition is broken, the former owner can bring legal action to retake the property.

A *special limitation* is a limitation on the use of property, written so that if the stated condition is broken, title to the property automatically returns to the former owner without the need for legal action. A gift of property "so long as" it is used for a particular purpose will set up a special limitation.

Most real property appraisals are made on the basis of fee simple ownership—nothing is held back. The holder of a fee simple estate, however, may or may not own all mineral, water, and other rights associated with the land. A condition or other restriction on use of the property also may exist. The appraiser should note any such exclusions or other factors limiting the owner's use of the property as well as their effect on value.

Life Estate

A *life estate* is a present, possessory interest that lasts only as long as the life of a stated person or persons. A life estate usually is based on the life of the person who receives it, although it could be based on the life of any named person ("his mother") or persons ("her parents"). When the measuring life is that of anyone other than the holder of the life estate, it is termed a life estate *pur autre vie* (for another's life).

On the death of the person against whose life the term of possession is measured, the land becomes the property of the person named at the time the life estate was created. The ultimate recipient, called the *remainderman,* holds what is called an *estate in remainder* during the life of the holder of the life estate. Alternatively, the land could be designated to return to the person who originally gave or transferred the life estate, in which case the original owner's interest during the term of the life estate is called a *reversion.*

A life estate can be transferred by gift, sale, or lease, but its value will depend on the risk associated with its probable termination date. The interest of a remainderman or reversioner can be given away, sold, or leased, but the recipient will have no right of possession until the life estate terminates.

Nonfreehold Estates

Nonfreehold estates are those that convey only a right of use and not the underlying fee simple right of ownership.

Leasehold Estate

A nonfreehold estate is also called a *leasehold estate.* A leasehold estate is the interest of the *lessee (tenant),* who acquires a right to use property by an agreement, called a *lease,* with the fee simple owner, who is then called the *lessor (landlord).* The *leasehold* is an *estate of tenancy.* It confers a right of use for the term specified in the lease, but it does not convey ownership. A tenant has no underlying fee interest, but the tenant's leasehold estate can have value, such as when the rent paid by the tenant is less than the property's market rent—what it would command if available on the market today.

Leased Fee Estate

The *leased fee estate* is the interest retained by the landlord who conveys a leasehold estate to a tenant.

FIGURE 2.8
Easement Appurtenant

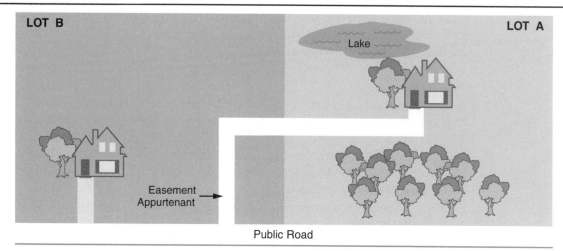

The owner of Lot A has an appurtenant easement across Lot B to gain access to his property from the paved road. In this example, Lot A is dominant and Lot B is servient.

Other Interests

Easement

An *easement* is a real property interest that conveys a limited right of use or enjoyment, such as the right to travel over a parcel of land.

Sometimes an easement benefits the owner of an adjoining parcel of land. In that case the land benefited by the easement is called the *dominant tenement*. The land over which the easement runs is called the *servient tenement*. An *easement appurtenant* is one that is said to "run with the land" because it is automatically conveyed to a new owner if title to the dominant tenement is transferred. In addition, it does not terminate if title to the servient tenement transfers (see Figures 2.8 and 2.9).

FIGURE 2.9
Easement Appurtenant and Easement in Gross

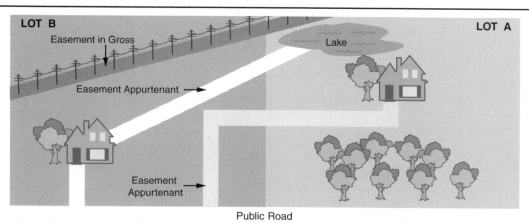

The owner of Lot B has an appurtenant easement across Lot A to gain access to the lake. For that use, Lot B is dominant and Lot A is servient. The utility company has an easement in gross across both parcels of land for its power lines. Note that Lot A also has an appurtenant easement across Lot B for its driveway. In this instance, Lot A is dominant and Lot B is servient.

An *easement in gross* belongs to an individual person or business and does not run with any parcel of land. Railroads, oil pipeline companies, and utility companies may make use of easements in gross. They do not own the underlying land but have the right to use it. Because it is considered a "personal" interest, an easement in gross usually cannot be assigned to anyone else and will terminate on the death of its owner.

License

A *license* is a temporary permission to come onto the land of another for a specific purpose. The use of land conveyed by a license is *nonexclusive* because the holder of a license has no right to keep anyone else from the property. A license can be terminated at any time without notice and is considered personal property rather than real property. An example of a license is the purchase of hunting rights on private property.

Encroachment

An *encroachment* exists when part of an improvement to land extends over the boundary line onto an adjoining parcel. Some encroachments, such as that of a fence that is a few millimeters over the border in a few places, are so slight that they are meaningless to the adjoining property owner. Occasionally, however, even a few inches of encroachment can be a grave matter, particularly when a highrise building in a congested urban area is involved. Then a few inches of encroachment may seriously impede the ability of the adjoining owner to make maximum use of that parcel. What will happen if, for instance, a 30-story building is found to encroach 10 inches onto the neighboring lot? Most likely, the owner of the neighboring lot will be entitled to compensation for the loss in value due to the inability to make full use of the property. That amount may be quite substantial if the encroachment forces the property owner to redesign a proposed structure, particularly if a conflict with the zoning or development approval process arises. An encroachment can also lead to title problems, creating an impediment to a property transfer.

■ FORMS OF PROPERTY OWNERSHIP

Title to real estate—some form of evidence of property ownership—can be held by one person, by more than one person, or in any of a variety of forms of business ownership.

Individual Ownership

Ownership by only one person is called *separate ownership* or *ownership in severalty*. The individual owner has sole control over disposition of the property and is sole recipient of any benefits that flow from it, such as rents. On the other hand, the owner in severalty also has sole liability for any debts or other obligations associated with the property, such as taxes and assessments.

In most states a married person may own real estate either as separate property or as marital property co-owned with the spouse. The distinction is critical when property is transferred. In some states, for instance, all property acquired during marriage automatically is termed *community property,* and any document attempting to convey such property must be executed (signed) by both spouses.

To avoid problems, the marital status of individuals conveying or receiving real estate always should be indicated on the deed conveying title. Common descriptive terms are *single* (never married), *unmarried* (divorced), *widow* (for surviving wife), and *widower* (for surviving husband).

Separate ownership frequently is used when a business is operated as a *sole proprietorship*. The *sole proprietor* conducts business in his or her name or under a trade name, reports business income on his or her own individual income tax return, and is solely liable for debts of the business.

Co-Ownership

When real estate is owned by two or more people, they are called *co-owners* or *concurrent owners*.

Tenancy in Common

A *tenancy in common* is created when two or more persons take title and tenancy in common is specified or when no other method of taking title is mentioned.

Tenants in common have *unity of possession*. This means that each tenant has the right to possession of the entire property and cannot be excluded by the other tenants, even if the tenants own unequal fractional interests in the property. If each of three cotenants owns one-third of a property, each still has the right to use the entire property. If there are four cotenants and one has a 40 percent interest in the property while each of the other three owns a 20 percent interest in the property, each still has the right to use the entire property. As a practical matter, cotenants who share a property will often agree on a separate portion for each to use (such as a single flat in a multiunit building), or they may agree on a separate time period during which each will have full use of the property. If the cotenants lease the property, each receives a proportionate share of the proceeds less a proportionate share of the expenses.

A tenant in common can transfer his or her interest by gift or sale or by will at death. The person to whom the property is transferred receives the same fractional interest and right of possession (see Figure 2.10). A forced sale or division of the property to dissolve the tenancy can be brought about by a lawsuit known as a *partition action*. The property will be divided into separate parcels, if possible. If the property must be sold, each of the cotenants receives a proportionate share of the proceeds less a proportionate share of expenses.

Joint Tenancy

A *joint tenancy* is a form of co-ownership that must meet certain legal requirements to be effective. There are four *unities of ownership* that are traditionally

F I G U R E 2.10
Tenancy in Common

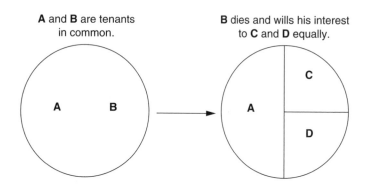

A and B are tenants in common.

B dies and wills his interest to **C** and **D** equally.

FIGURE 2.11
Joint Tenancy with Right of Survivorship

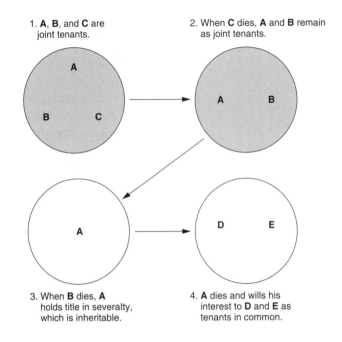

1. **A**, **B**, and **C** are joint tenants.

2. When **C** dies, **A** and **B** remain as joint tenants.

3. When **B** dies, **A** holds title in severalty, which is inheritable.

4. **A** dies and wills his interest to **D** and **E** as tenants in common.

needed to create a joint tenancy—unity of title, time, interest, and possession. *Title* must be taken by all joint tenants *at the same time,* with each receiving an equal *interest* (no unequal shares) and present right of *possession* of the property. If all four unities are present, the joint tenancy will create a *right of survivorship* (full and undivided ownership) in the last surviving joint tenant.

The most important feature of the joint tenancy is the right of survivorship, which means that a joint tenant cannot transfer title to his or her share by will. Even if the interest is specified in the will to go to someone else, the attempted transfer will be ineffectual because the right of the surviving joint tenant(s) is paramount. As each successive joint tenant dies, the surviving joint tenants acquire the deceased tenant's interest. The last survivor takes title in severalty and has all the rights of individual ownership, including the right to pass the property to his or her heirs (see Figure 2.11). In most states, the right of survivorship automatically accompanies title taken in a joint tenancy. In other states (such as North Carolina) the right of survivorship must be specifically mentioned in the instrument of conveyance (deed).

A joint tenant can transfer his or her interest in the joint tenancy while alive, but not without terminating the joint tenancy with respect to his or her interest. If there were only two joint tenants originally, the joint tenancy would be completely terminated by a transfer of one joint tenant's interest, and the two owners then would be tenants in common. If there were more than two joint tenants originally, the joint tenancy would remain in effect only for the joint tenants whose interests were not transferred. The remaining joint tenants would have a cotenancy with the new co-owner.

For example, Jeffrey, Susan, and Shirley are joint tenants with the right of survivorship in a parcel of real estate. Susan conveys her interest to Anthony. Anthony now owns a one-third interest in the parcel as a tenant in common with Jeffrey and Shirley. Jeffrey and Shirley are still joint tenants (see Figure 2.12).

FIGURE 2.12
Combination of Tenancies

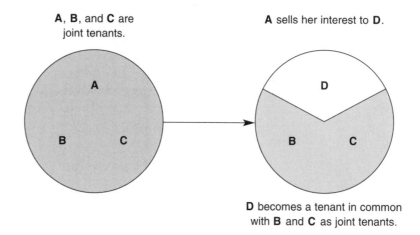

A, **B**, and **C** are
joint tenants.

A sells her interest to **D**.

D becomes a tenant in common
with **B** and **C** as joint tenants.

Marital Property

As already mentioned, married persons may have a special status as property owners. The forms of marital property ownership vary from state to state, with the two categories described next being the most common.

Community property is all property acquired by either spouse during marriage, *except* property acquired

1. by gift or inheritance,
2. with the proceeds of separate property, or
3. as income from separate property.

Property that was separate property before the marriage remains separate property afterward. The newest trend in community property states is to allow the spouses to agree in writing to change the "character" of property from separate to community or from community to separate. Community property is a holdover from Spanish law and is found in various forms in California, Arizona, Idaho, Louisiana, Nevada, New Mexico, Texas, and Washington. Because it is a form of ownership available only to married couples, community property usually is residential, although some commercial property is owned by husband and wife as community property.

Tenancy by the entirety is available in some states as a form of marital property ownership in which each spouse has an equal, undivided interest, with title passing to the survivor when one spouse dies. The right of survivorship exists only as long as the marriage, however. In the event of divorce, a tenancy by the entirety automatically becomes a tenancy in common. A tenancy by the entirety also may be terminated by agreement of the spouses or as a result of a legal proceeding brought by a joint creditor of both spouses.

Tenancy in Partnership

Two or more persons who carry on a business for profit as partners may own property for partnership purposes in a *tenancy in partnership*. All partners have the right to use the property for partnership purposes. The property can be transferred by the partnership only if the rights of all partners are transferred. Partnership property can be attached only by partnership creditors. When a partner dies, that partner's interest in partnership property goes to the surviving partners, although the heirs of the deceased are entitled to the deceased's share of business profits.

The partnership as a form of business ownership has several special features. No separate income tax is paid by the partnership. Partnership income is distributed to the partners, who are individually responsible for reporting and paying taxes on the income received. Each partner is liable for partnership debts.

A commonly used form of real estate partnership is the *joint venture,* in which the lender contributes the financing while other partners (such as the developer, landowner, construction company, or construction manager) contribute property or expertise.

Other Forms of Ownership

A *corporation* must follow the laws of the state in which it is incorporated. A *domestic corporation* is one that does business within the state where it is incorporated; a *foreign corporation* is one that does business in a state other than the state of incorporation.

Although the corporation itself is owned by *shareholders,* the corporation is recognized as a *separate legal entity.* As such, it may own, lease, and convey real estate. The day-to-day activities of the corporation are in the hands of its *officers,* who are under the overall guidance of the *board of directors.*

A benefit of incorporation is that officers, directors, and shareholders generally are not liable for corporate decisions and corporate debts. A disadvantage of incorporation is that corporate income is taxed twice—first to the corporation, then again to the shareholders when it is distributed as dividends. Income is taxed only once (when it is distributed to shareholders) if the corporation qualifies for treatment under *Subchapter S* of the Internal Revenue Code.

A *nonprofit corporation* also can own, lease, and convey real estate, but the corporation is owned by *members* rather than shareholders.

The *limited liability company (LLC)* is now recognized by most states. The exact structure and requirements of the LLC vary from state to state, but the LLC generally offers its *members* the control and income distribution benefits of the general partnership coupled with the reduced liability of the corporation.

A *trust* permits title to real estate to be held by a *trustee* for the benefit of a *beneficiary.* The property owner is the *trustor,* who establishes the trust and conveys title to the trustee, whose powers are defined in the trust document. A trust often is used as a way to convey title on behalf of minor children in the event of a parent's death.

In some states, such as Illinois, use of a *land trust* is a common way for one or more persons to hold title to avoid encumbering real estate. The trustor usually is named as the beneficiary. Because the interest of a beneficiary is considered personal property and not real estate, a judgment against the beneficiary will not create a lien against the real estate. The land trust usually lasts no longer than 20 years, although the term can be extended by agreement. If the trust term ends or the trustee is unable to locate the beneficiary, the trustee can resign and deed the property to the beneficiary or sell the property and distribute the proceeds to the beneficiary. On the beneficiary's death, title held in the land trust will pass as specified in the beneficiary's will or, if there is no will, to the beneficiary's heirs.

The *living trust* is gaining popularity as a way to hold title and avoid probate. The trustor places title to both real and personal property in the name of the trustee, but the trustor is also the beneficiary, who has the right to use the property. When the trustor/beneficiary dies, the *contingent beneficiary(ies)* named in the trust then is (are) entitled to use of the property. A living trust can be set up by a married couple as co-trustors/beneficiaries, with title going to the contingent beneficiary(ies) on the death of the second spouse.

The *real estate investment trust (REIT)* frequently has been used to secure capital for real estate purchases and pass along the benefits of depreciation and other tax deductions. Those benefits were reduced by the Tax Reform Act of 1986, however.

Special Forms of Ownership

Fee simple ownership of a parcel of real estate generally includes the land as well as all fixtures, such as buildings, attached to it. Sometimes ownership of real estate includes fewer features, and sometimes it includes more.

Condominium

A *condominium* is the absolute ownership of a unit in a multiunit building based on a legal description of the airspace the unit actually occupies, along with a specified share of the undivided interest in the *common areas* within the development. Common areas typically include the land itself, walkways, parking spaces, recreation and exercise facilities, hallways, stairs, elevators, and lobbies, as well as the foundation, exterior structure, and roof.

A condominium unit is real property that can be bought, sold, and financed just like a single-family house. The owners usually form an association to manage the commonly held real estate in accordance with detailed rules that specify the relationships among the unit owners and how the condominium operates. The expenses of management and maintenance are divided pro rata among the owners, who pay a monthly fee to the association. On occasion, unit owners may be charged a *special assessment* to pay for unusual costs that have not been adequately provided for in a reserve fund. Most states require the disclosure of condominium documents to buyers so that they can become aware of all the rules the association has adopted.

The condominium form of ownership has been used for residential apartments as well as for office and retail store space.

Cooperative

Each owner in a *stock cooperative project* is a shareholder in the corporation that holds title to real estate. Each owner receives the right to exclusive occupancy of part of the property, such as an apartment. Because the individual shares are not considered real estate, cooperative units are not financed individually, although the entire property may be financed.

Planned Unit Development

The *planned unit development (PUD)* is a type of development, as well as a zoning classification, that features individually owned parcels together with shared common areas. The planned unit development typically provides well-landscaped open areas by allowing greater density in built-up portions of the tract. PUDs have been established for residential, commercial, and industrial uses.

E X E R C I S E 2 . 3

1. What is the highest form of real property ownership?

   free simple

2. What estates in real property are owned by tenant and landlord?

   lease hold   — tenant
   lease fee — landlord

3. Mary Jones owns a house on a parcel that includes an easement over the adjoining property of Tom Yan. What is the legal term that describes the Jones property? What is the legal term that describes the Yan property?

   dominant
   serviant

4. Co-owners who have an equal right of possession coupled with a right of survivorship have what form of co-ownership?

   joint tenants

5. In what form of property ownership is an exclusive right to an identified segment of airspace conveyed along with an interest in common in the rest of the parcel?

    *Condiminium*

Check your answers against those in the Answer Key at the back of the book.

▪ TRANSFER OF TITLE

Title to real estate generally is conveyed by *deed*. The forms of deed follow.

Types of Deeds

A *deed* is a written instrument by which an owner of real estate intentionally conveys to a purchaser his or her right, title, or interest in a parcel of real estate. The owner of the real estate is referred to as the *grantor,* and the person who acquires title is called the *grantee.*

To be legally valid

- a deed must be in writing,
- there must be a description of the parties (full name and marital status),
- the grantor must be legally capable of executing the deed,
- the property must be adequately described,
- there must be a granting clause using the necessary words of conveyance (such as the word *grant*),
- the deed must be signed by the grantor(s), and
- the deed must be delivered to and accepted by the grantee.

A deed is of no effect if it is *not delivered;* that is, its delivery cannot be conditional. For instance, the grantor cannot sign the deed and give it to a third person with directions to give it to the named grantee when the grantee has performed some condition. On the other hand, the deed could be delivered and accepted with a condition placed in the deed itself so that title would be lost if the grantee failed to fulfill the condition. (The *condition precedent* and *condition subsequent* were discussed earlier in this chapter.)

Grant Deed

A *grant deed* conveys the grantor's title by use of a granting clause. The grantor makes no express warranties of title, but a grant deed carries *implied warranties* that the grantor's interest has not already been conveyed and that neither the grantor nor anyone who might claim title from the grantor has placed any encumbrance, such as a tax lien, on the property.

Quitclaim Deed

A *quitclaim deed* provides the grantee with the *least* protection of any deed. With a quitclaim deed, the grantor makes no claim to any ownership interest in the described real estate but conveys whatever interest the grantor may own, if any.

Warranty Deed

A *warranty deed* warrants expressly that the grantor has good title. With the prevalence of title insurance to protect the buyer in the event that the title turns out not to be good, this form of deed is becoming less common in most states. In some areas of the country, the grant deed has replaced the warranty deed as the most popular form of conveyance.

Bargain and Sale Deed

A *bargain and sale deed* contains no warranties against encumbrances; it only implies that the grantor holds title and possession of the property, and thus, the grantee has little legal recourse if defects later appear in the title. In some areas the bargain and sale deed is used in foreclosures and tax sales, in which case the buyer would presumably purchase title insurance for protection.

Trust Deed

The *trust deed,* or deed of trust, has already been described as a form of instrument used to hypothecate real estate as security for a debt. The trustor (owner) transfers title to the trustee (impartial third party) to hold for the benefit of the beneficiary (lender) in the event that the trustor defaults before the underlying debt is repaid.

Reconveyance Deed

When the trustor under a deed of trust has repaid the underlying debt in full, it is the duty of the beneficiary to notify the trustee so that the property can be deeded back to the trustor by means of a *reconveyance deed.*

Sheriff's Deed

A *sheriff's deed,* which contains no warranties, is given to the purchaser of property at a court-ordered sale.

Tax Deed

When property is sold by the county tax collector for nonpayment of taxes, the successful purchaser receives a *tax deed.* The quality of the title conveyed by a tax deed varies from state to state according to statutory provisions.

Recordation

A deed can be legally valid even though it is not witnessed, the signature of the grantor is not verified by anyone else, and the deed is not recorded in the county recorder's office. As a practical matter, however, acknowledgment and recording of a deed is a necessity, if only because the lender will require it.

Acknowledgment

To be recorded in the county recorder's office or other repository of title information, most states require that a deed contain an *acknowledgment* of the grantor's signature. Usually, this is accomplished by the stamp (or seal) and signature of a notary public, judge, justice of the peace, court clerk, or other person provided by law.

Recording

Recording is important because it serves as notice to the world of the transfer of title. The deed must be recorded in the appropriate office in the county where the property is located.

When properly recorded, the deed serves to place the grantee in the *chain of title* to the described property. Anyone investigating the title should be able to move *backward* through the grantee index, tracing the name of the grantor on the present deed as the grantee on the previous deed, and so on, and then *forward* through the grantor index to the present grantor. If the name of each grantor and grantee does not appear in exactly the same way on every recorded document conveyed to or from that individual, there may be a missing "link" in the chain. A fictitious name can be used to receive title, provided the same name is used to convey the property. Title cannot be conveyed to a fictitious person, although title can be conveyed to a corporation because a corporation is a recognized legal entity.

EXERCISE 2.4

1. What is the difference between a quitclaim deed and a warranty deed?

   no warranty on quit claim

2. Why is deed recordation recommended?

   notice to the world

Check your answers against those in the Answer Key at the back of the book.

■ SUMMARY

An appraisal is the act or process of developing an opinion of value. It provides a description of property as well as the appraiser's opinion of the property's condition, its utility for a given purpose, and/or its probable monetary value on the open market.

Real estate (or real property) includes land, fixtures to land, anything incidental or appurtenant to land (such as an easement right), and anything immovable by law, with certain exceptions. Land includes the earth's surface, what is under the surface (such as minerals and water), and what is above the surface. Land becomes a site suitable for building when utilities are available.

In determining whether something is a fixture to land (and thus part of the real estate), a court will look to the intention of the person who placed the item on the land, the method of attachment, the adaptability of the item for the land's ordinary use, and the agreement and relationship of the parties concerned. An appurtenance is anything used with land for its benefit.

The bundle of rights that are the rights of ownership of real property are subject to public restrictions, such as taxation, and private restrictions, typically conditions, covenants, and restrictions placed in a property owner's deed. Anything that is not real property is personal property.

The methods by which land can be described include the lot and block system (with reference to a subdivision map), the metes and bounds system (using natural or artificial boundaries), and the rectangular survey system (using townships measured along meridians and base lines).

Estates in land include the freehold estates of the fee simple estate and life estate. Nonfreehold estates include the leasehold estate owned by the lessee (tenant) and the leased fee estate owned by the lessor (landlord). Other property interests include the easement and license. An encroachment exists when part of an improvement extends onto an adjoining parcel.

Separate ownership is ownership by one person. Business ownership by one person is a sole proprietorship. Forms of co-ownership (ownership by more than one person) include tenancy in common, which has unity of possession, and joint tenancy, which has the four unities of time, title, interest, and possession. In most states, joint tenancy also carries with it the right of survivorship. A partition action can be brought by a co-owner to force a division or sale of the property. Ownership of marital property depends on the laws of the state; some states allow community property and others allow tenancy by the entirety.

A tenancy in partnership can be used by a business partnership to hold title to real estate. A corporation can hold title in its own name as a recognized legal entity. A trust permits title to be held by a trustee for the benefit of a beneficiary. Forms of trust include the land trust, living trust, and real estate investment trust.

A condominium is an ownership interest in airspace, while a cooperative is a shareholder interest in a corporation that holds title to real estate. A planned unit development includes both an individually owned parcel and a shared common area.

To be legally valid, a deed must be in writing and meet other legal requirements. Acknowledgment and recording are not necessary for validity but will serve to enter the deed in the chain of title and give notice to the world of the transfer of ownership.

ACHIEVEMENT EXAMINATION

1. The property of a person who dies leaving no heirs passes to the state by the right of

   a. acquisition.

   b. escheat.

   c. condemnation.

   d. eminent domain.

2. Condemnation of private property for public use is called the right of

   a. seizure.

   b. escheat.

   c. eminent domain.

   d. acquisition.

3. Anything that is not real property is

   a. real estate.

   b. a fixture.

   c. an appurtenance.

   d. personal property.

4. An appraisal may include a(n)

   a. property description.

   b. opinion of property condition.

   c. opinion of market value.

   d. All of the above

5. Real property includes

   a. land.

   b. fixtures and appurtenances to land.

   c. anything immovable by law, with certain exceptions.

   d. All of the above

6. The form of deed used to return title to real estate to its owner when the debt secured by a deed of trust is paid in full is the

   a. warranty deed.

   b. reconveyance deed.

   c. quitclaim deed.

   d. tax deed.

7. The form of deed that makes no warranties, express or implied, is the

   a. grant deed.

   b. reconveyance deed.

   c. quitclaim deed.

   d. tax deed.

8. Tenancy by the entirety is a form of

   a. marital property ownership.

   b. tenancy in common.

   c. business property ownership.

   d. ownership in severalty.

9. A landlord has a(n)

   a. fee simple qualified.

   b. fee simple defeasible.

   c. estate of tenancy.

   d. leased fee estate.

10. The four unities required for a joint tenancy include
   a. tenancy, location, title, and possession.
   b. time, title, interest, and possession.
   c. possession, ownership, use, and enjoyment.
   d. title, time, location, and possession.

11. An individually owned parcel includes a share of common areas in a
   a. PUD.
   b. condominium.
   c. stock cooperative.
   d. life estate.

Planned Unit Development

12. A type of real estate featuring ownership of airspace as well as an interest in common in the entire parcel is a
   a. PUD.
   b. condominium.
   c. stock cooperative.
   d. life estate.

13. If you want your children to inherit Greenacre from you, you should prefer a
   a. life estate.
   b. defeasible fee.
   c. remainder.
   d. special limitation.

14. A life estate is a(n)
   a. present, possessory interest.
   b. future interest.
   c. estate of tenancy.
   d. fee simple defeasible.

15. Property acquired by a spouse during marriage by gift or inheritance is
   a. marital property.
   b. community property.
   c. separate property.
   d. jointly owned property.

16. What are the considerations in determining whether something attached to real property is a fixture?

   P

17. A township is divided into
    a. 160 sections.
    b. 36 sections.
    c. 4 ranges.
    d. 36 meridians.

    1 mile   640 acres

18. The S½ of NW¼ of Section 16 is a parcel of
    a. 20 acres.
    b. 40 acres.
    c. 80 acres.
    d. 160 acres.

    $$640 \times \frac{1}{2} \times \frac{1}{4} =$$

19. A subdivision map is referred to in the
    a. lot and block system.
    b. lot, block, and tract system.
    c. Both a and b
    d. Neither a nor b

Check your answers against those in the Answer Key at the back of the book.

## CHAPTER 3

The Real Estate Marketplace

■ OVERVIEW

The most significant investment for most Americans is the purchase of a home. Whether a detached single-family house, a highrise condominium, a town house, a farm, a ranch, or even a houseboat, such a purchase often is well rewarded at the time of a subsequent sale, when the property's value may have increased substantially over its initial purchase price. Less frequently, particularly if a resale occurs within only a year or two, the property may not command a high enough sales price to cover both the seller's original purchase price and the expenses of sale (such as a broker's commission).

Of course, commercial property transactions are also important to the parties involved, and commercial property values can be even more volatile than those of other forms of real estate. The favorable economic indicators that encourage office and retail development may lead to overbuilt markets and empty buildings. Commercial property is typically leased, and unfavorable economic conditions can quickly lead to vacant storefronts and lowered lease rates.

In either case, a property appraisal can be valuable in making a final decision on whether to enter a transaction. An appraisal can assure either purchaser or seller that the sales price is reasonable in light of prevailing market forces.

The forces that create and affect the real estate marketplace are the subjects of this chapter. We first examine some of those forces, then define *market value*. We conclude with a discussion of some basic economic principles that contribute to real property value.

■ THE MARKET FOR REAL ESTATE

A *market* is simply a place for selling and buying. While we refer in this text to the local real estate market, in many respects there never can be a truly local real estate market. There may be locally occurring transactions (such as within a city or county), but all transactions are affected to some extent by the wider market forces within the state, region, and nation. The major forces—population level, strength of the economy, and availability of financing—can be identified separately, yet they are interconnected.

Characteristics of Real Estate Markets

Unlike the market for real estate, other goods and services are said to have *efficient* markets. The factors that compose an efficient market include

- products that are readily exchangeable for other products of the same kind;
- an ample supply of knowledgeable buyers and sellers;
- little or no government regulation influencing value;
- relatively stable prices; and
- easy product supply and transport.

A market that is at its most efficient is said to be a *perfect* market. Unfortunately, the market for real estate is far from perfect.

We can begin to define a real estate market by understanding the special factors that influence real estate as a commodity. Every parcel of real estate is considered unique and thus not interchangeable with any other parcel. Buyers and sellers of real estate frequently are unsophisticated and lack knowledge of the factors that make one parcel of real estate more valuable than another. The number of buyers and sellers frequently moves away from a state of equilibrium to create either a *seller's market* (many more buyers than sellers) or a *buyer's market* (many more sellers than buyers). Real estate is intensely regulated, with regard both to the uses to which it can be put and to the manner in which its ownership can be transferred. As a result of all these factors, as well as the fact that real estate is immovable, prices can be highly volatile.

Immobility of Real Estate

Because every parcel of real estate is unique and immobile, some of the factors that ordinarily affect supply and demand must receive somewhat different consideration.

A market is simply a forum for buying and selling, that is, a means for bringing together buyer and seller. For products other than real estate, the location of the product to be sold affects shipping costs and thus is only one of a number of determinants that affect value. The most important single factor in determining real estate value, however, is location. Land cannot be delivered to a location where it is in short supply or warehoused until it is needed. The seller of real estate can improve the property by preparing it for building or constructing or renovating improvements. The seller also can use advertising and other promotional tools to make the property's availability known to the greatest number of potential buyers. The one thing the seller of real estate cannot do is change the property's location. What the seller can do is make the property more desirable by analyzing the needs and desires of potential buyers and improving the property with those requirements in mind.

Availability of Information

Chapter 6 introduces you to some of the many sources of information available to appraisers as well as to property owners. By learning as much as possible about the economic, political, social, and environmental conditions of the area where a property is located, the appraiser can begin to assimilate the information needed to make an informed judgment, that is, one based on the appropriate indicators of market value.

Market Analysis

An analysis of the real estate marketplace must include demographic data on the area's residents. *Demography* is the scientific study of population statistics, such as births, deaths, and marriages. The overall market area can be further defined by the process called *segmentation* into specific categories of consumer preferences, including those relating to income, work, leisure activities, and other lifestyle patterns.

By knowing as much as possible about the people who make up the market area, it is possible to predict the probable demand for various types and price levels of housing as well as the commercial and industrial establishments necessary to supply the required products and services. Such *forecasts* are published regularly by various government agencies as well as research centers, industry-related companies, and trade associations.

An *absorption analysis* is a study of the number of units of residential or nonresidential property that can be sold or leased over a given period of time in a defined location. Existing space inventory must be considered in light of present demand and current or projected space surplus. In short, is there a need for new space? The overbuilding of the 1980s left many urban areas with a supply of office space that did not approach acceptable occupancy levels until the mid-1990s.

An absorption analysis usually is performed as part of a *feasibility study*, used to predict the likely success of a proposed real estate development. The feasibility study also includes a cost analysis of the proposed construction and projected return to investors.

Of course, the most complete statistics and best analyses are useless without a thoroughly up-to-date knowledge of the political climate and government forces, both local and otherwise, that may result in regulations affecting property ownership and use. A feasibility study of area growth projections for a new subdivision is incomplete if it does not take into account a proposed highway expansion through the center of the site. Without that knowledge, the use proposed by the owner or prospective purchaser might be meaningless. With that knowledge, a recommendation that the proposed use change from residential to commercial could result in a project several times as valuable.

The Cost of Credit

Few buyers of real estate could afford, or would prefer, to pay all cash for property. Interest paid on a loan used to purchase real estate is the *cost of credit* to the borrower. When the cost of credit is high, borrowers cannot qualify to buy property that would be affordable when financing is not as expensive. The cost of credit to borrowers thus has a direct impact on the price that can be paid for property.

The cost of credit depends on the availability of funds in relation to the number of potential borrowers. Credit is said to be "tight" when there is not enough financing to accommodate easily all prospective borrowers.

Sources of Capital

A *money market* fund consists of short-term financing instruments. These include U.S. Treasury bills, notes, and other government securities; municipal notes; certificates of deposit; commercial paper (corporate borrowing to finance current operations); Eurodollars (funds deposited outside the United States); and others. Because short-term loans are much in demand in the real estate industry for construction financing and other interim or "bridge" loans, rates available on the money market usually have a major impact on real estate development.

The *capital market* is the term used to describe the trading of longer-term financing instruments such as mortgages, deeds of trust, bonds, stocks, and other obligations generally maturing in more than one year. There is no one location or institution that comprises either the money market or the capital market and no sharp line of demarcation in the kinds of instruments handled by each.

Competing Investments

Investors generally fall into one of two groups, *debt investors* and *equity investors*. Debt investors are the more conservative of the two groups because they take a passive rather than an active role in management of their investments and demand a security interest in property being financed. Equity investors, who make use of what is termed *venture capital,* take a more active, though unsecured, role in the investment.

Over the years, interest in the investment potential of real estate has increased to parallel increases in real estate appreciation. In addition to financial institutions, trusts, partnerships, syndications, joint ventures, pension funds, life insurance companies, foreign investors, and other sources provided the equity capital that allowed record levels of building in the 1980s.

How Real Estate Is Financed

The lien on real estate demanded by the debt investor may take the form of either a *mortgage* or a *deed of trust,* both of which are explained below. It is important to note that even though the mortgage and deed of trust are different types of security instruments, the term *mortgage* is also used to refer to *any* instrument by which real estate is made security for a debt.

Mortgage Terms and Concepts

The security instrument is the document that *hypothecates* the real property that serves as the lender's assurance that the debt incurred will be repaid. Personal property (anything that doesn't qualify as real estate) can be *pledged* by a security instrument, rather than hypothecated. One difference between the two forms of security is that possession of personal property pledged to secure payment of a debt may be turned over to the creditor. When real estate is used as security, the debtor usually retains possession.

A *mortgage* creates a lien in favor of the *mortgagee* (lender) on the property of the *mortgagor* (property owner). The lien is enforced by the mortgagee if the mortgagor fails to meet the obligations imposed by the *promissory note* that states the terms of the loan agreement. Enforcement of a mortgage may be through a *judicial foreclosure,* which requires a court hearing, or by a sale on behalf of the mortgagee, if provided for in the mortgage instrument.

A *deed of trust,* or trust deed, is an actual transfer of title from the *trustor* (property owner) to a *trustee* (neutral third party) to be held on behalf of the lender, known as the *beneficiary.* When the debt is repaid, the beneficiary notifies the trustee, who issues a reconveyance deed that returns title to the trustor. If the trustor defaults, the trustee may sell the property to repay the underlying debt.

Mortgage Payment Plans

A mortgage debt (any debt secured by real estate, whether the security instrument used is a mortgage or deed of trust) can be repaid through a variety of payment plans.

Repayment of a mortgage debt requires payment of both *principal* (the amount borrowed) and *interest* (the charge for the borrowing). The interest rate can be *fixed* (the same for the life of the loan) or *adjustable* (varying according to an established index, such as the rate on six-month Treasury bills or the average cost of funds of FDIC-insured institutions). With either fixed-rate or adjustable-rate loans, the lender's effective yield (and the borrower's effective cost) often is increased by some form of *buydown,* an advance payment of interest called *points* or *discount points.* Each point equals 1 percent of the loan amount.

Types of Mortgages

The *fully amortized fixed-rate mortgage* requires regular payments of both principal and interest so that the loan is fully paid off at the end of the loan term. With the *adjustable-rate mortgage,* individual payments can rise or fall as the interest rate rises or falls in step with the index used.

The *graduated payment mortgage* provides lower monthly payments in the early years of the loan term, with gradual increases over five to ten years, after which payments level off for the remainder of the loan term. The *growing equity mortgage* provides a fixed interest rate but an increasing payment amount, allowing for a more rapid payoff.

The *reverse annuity mortgage,* which provides a monthly payment to a homeowner using a previously mortgage-free (or mostly mortgage-free) home as collateral with the entire loan amount plus interest due at the end of the loan term, is attracting increasing attention from older homeowners with substantial home equities. The *shared appreciation mortgage* offers a below-market interest rate and lower payments in exchange for the transfer of some equity from borrower to lender.

Elements that Create Value

For real estate or any commodity to have value, the four elements that create value must be present. These elements are demand, utility, scarcity, and transferability *(DUST).* The element of *demand* is present when someone wants the property and has the financial ability to purchase it. *Utility* means that the property can serve a useful purpose. *Scarcity* is present when the property is in short supply relative to demand. *Transferability* means that title to the property can be moved readily from one person or entity to another. When all four elements of value are present, property has a value that may be estimated by an appraiser.

When a good or service can be used to acquire another good or service, the commodities have what is termed *value in exchange.* A marketplace exists when there is no impediment to the ready exchange of goods or services. Most often, the goods or services are exchanged for their equivalent in legal tender—money. The amount of money required to bring about the exchange is the *price* of the good or service.

Many regulatory agencies and other government units, as well as individuals, incorporate in their real estate decision criteria a variety of objectives and policies that are perceived as influencing value. These criteria often define a type of value, such as one of those listed below. Nevertheless, they are typically anchored to a value-in-exchange concept, usually represented by a market value definition. The types of value defined may include

assessed value	insurable value	leased fee value
cash value	depreciated value	inheritance tax value
rental value	capitalized value	liquidation value
market value	appraised value	leasehold value
improved value	replacement value	value in use
salvage value	book value	investment value
mortgage loan value	exchange value	going-concern value

To *appraise* something means to estimate the dollar amount that represents one of its values. Appraisers for banks, savings associations, or other lenders will probably be seeking the market value of the properties they inspect for mortgage loan purposes. Depreciated cost (value) is used in one appraising approach to estimate market value; rental value may be used in another. City and county real estate taxes are based on assessed value.

Definition of Market Value

One commonly used definition of market value states that it is

 the most probable price which a property should bring in a competitive and open market under all conditions requisite to a fair sale, the buyer and seller each acting prudently and knowledgeably, and assuming the price is not affected by undue stimulus.

This definition of market value typically assumes an *arm's-length transaction* in which

- buyer and seller are typically motivated;

- both parties are well informed or well advised, and acting in what they consider their best interests;

- a reasonable time is allowed for exposure in the open market;

- payment is made in terms of cash in United States dollars or in terms of financial arrangements comparable thereto; and

- the price represents the normal consideration for the property sold unaffected by special or creative financing or sales concessions.

Sales Price

Sales price is what a property actually sells for—its transaction price. This price may differ from market value because many factors can prevent a sale from being an arm's-length transaction. The need of either of the principals (buyer or seller) to close the transaction within a short period of time will limit that party's bargaining power. On the other hand, if a seller receives an offer for less than the asking price, which is the market value of the property, but the offer is made only one week after the property is put on the market, the seller may decide that a quick sale is worth losing the higher price that might be received if the property were left on the market longer. The buyer and seller may be relatives, friends, or related companies, and one or both could voluntarily limit their bargaining power. Also, the buyer may have a pressing need to acquire the property, such as the need to add to an adjoining site.

Cost

The amount paid for a good or service is its *cost*. The cost to purchase a parcel of real estate may or may not be the same as the *price* it can command when it is sold to someone else. A developer may pay $5 million for a prime downtown lot and another $20 million to construct a highrise office building on the site. Yet if the market is flooded with similar properties and market demand thus is very low, the developer may not recoup the cost of the lot and building when the property is eventually sold.

Investment Value

Investment value is the value of a property to a particular investor, considering the investor's *cash flow* requirements. *Cash flow* is the amount of income left over after all expenses of ownership have been paid. Different investors will have different income expectations, as well as different expenses of ownership.

Before the Tax Reform Act of 1986 eliminated many of the tax advantages of real estate ownership, a property could be desirable even if it offered a *negative* cash flow (that is, it cost more to own than the income it produced) in the early period of ownership. The loss generated by the real estate could be used as a deduction to shelter other income from taxation. The amount of loss that can be carried over from real estate investments now has been greatly restricted. Determination of an individual real estate investor's after-tax position requires the services of a tax accountant or attorney.

Other Values

Value in use is property value based on a particular use, often considered as part of a broader operation or process. An example is a driving range adjacent to a golf course. The value-in-use concept offers an analytical framework to support real estate value in the context of a business's overall *going-concern value,* which also takes into account the intangible but valuable assets of an established, profitable business, such as customer good will.

The value determined by a local taxing authority as the basis for *ad valorem* property taxation is called *assessed value*. The amount for which property may be insured is its *insurable value.*

Influences on Real Estate Value

The forces of nature, as well as the human-generated effects of government, economic, and social systems, all affect the value of real estate.

Physical and Environmental

Climatic and other conditions, exacerbated by ill-planned development, can wreak havoc on both land and buildings. In California, for example, many residential and commercial buildings have been built directly over or in close proximity to known earthquake fault lines. In some tornado-prone areas of the Midwest, new subdivisions stand directly in the path of potential catastrophe. In the past two decades, multiple hurricanes, including Hugo, Andrew, and the four that occurred in 2004, inflicted heavy damage on communities in Florida and other coastal states.

The range of possible liabilities imposed on property owners for environmental reasons can be overwhelming. A special area of appraisal focusing on discovery and analysis of environmental problems has emerged.

Economic

Real estate values tend to move in cycles, mirroring the economy as a whole. With a high level of employment and regular salary increases, demand for housing and other forms of real estate will increase and prices will follow suit. When the unemployment rate rises and wage levels stagnate or decrease, the rate of mortgage loan foreclosures will increase. As more properties become available, yet fewer persons are able to afford them, market values decline. When economic conditions become more favorable, market values are stabilized and, as conditions continue to improve, may begin to rise once again.

Government and Legal

The increasing number and complexity of regulations affecting ownership and use of real estate have proven to be major influences on the cost of acquiring and owning real estate.

Although an appraiser cannot make a legal judgment, determination of the highest and best use of the property being appraised must always take into account both existing and proposed zoning.

In some states, property tax exactions require voter approval, which can be difficult to obtain. As a result, increases in development fees have been used to pass new infrastructure costs on to developers and, ultimately, property buyers.

Social

Social influences are gaining increasing recognition as harbingers of future market demand. Although the single-family detached home still is the most desired form of housing, the condominium apartment has received a measure of acceptance, particularly in urban areas. Mixed-use developments providing both residential and retail units have stimulated interest in downtown areas of both large and small cities. As more people show evidence of environmental as well as personal concerns, builders will respond to those desires, as well. The "ecologically correct" house that makes a minimal impact on the environment is only a few years down the road.

Of course, one of the most interesting phenomena of the past several decades has been the influence of the great wave of post-World War II "baby boomers" as they have grown to maturity. The economic effects of this sector of the population have been impossible to ignore. While the baby boomers were children, record levels of building were required to provide them with schools. Universities blossomed with record enrollments. When the baby boomers demanded housing, builders complied. When the baby boomers decided to have their own babies, they created a baby boomlet. As they approach retirement age, baby boomers are creating new opportunities for developers of housing designed to accommodate the needs of seniors, as well as those who require features that enhance the accessibility of the home and its fixtures.

EXERCISE 3.1   Which of the following factors are likely to prevent an arm's-length transaction?

1. Seller's immediate job transfer to another city

2. New highway construction

3. Delinquent tax sale

4. Location across the street from a grade school

5. Flooding in crawlspace not revealed by seller

6. Purchase of adjacent property for business expansion

Check your answers against those in the Answer Key at the back of the book.

■ BASIC VALUE PRINCIPLES

While many property owners could probably make a fairly accurate guess as to the current value of their property, they would still be unable to identify all or most of the factors that contribute to that value. The knowledge of precisely what those factors are, and how they influence and can be expected to influence property value, is part of what lends credence to the appraiser's estimate of market value.

The basic value principles are interrelated, and their relative importance will vary depending on particular local conditions. Supply and demand may be the paramount factor in a burgeoning oil boomtown, while in a period of economic recession competition among existing retail stores may deter development of new stores. Even climatic or geological conditions are important, as when unexpected heavy rainfall creates the threat of destructive mudslides.

It is the appraiser's task, then, to consider the subject property in light of all the factors applicable to the property's type and location, as well as the purpose of the appraisal. Principles affecting marketability (such as supply and demand) will have greater influence in the sales comparison and cost approaches, while principles affecting productivity (such as opportunity cost) will have the greatest influence in the income approach.

Anticipation

According to the principle of *anticipation,* property value may be affected by expectation of a future event. The expectations of a real estate buyer will depend to some extent on the type of property purchased. The buyer of a single-family residence usually expects to take advantage of the property's amenities as a shelter, as well as the prestige value of ownership. In the same way, some owners of commercial property enjoy the use of the facilities in conducting a business on the premises. The ability of the property to generate income is the primary expectation of most buyers of commercial and multifamily residential property. Determining the present value of the future income stream is the basis of the income approach to appraising, discussed in Chapters 11 and 12.

In addition to the benefits that flow from possession, real estate may offer a benefit that is realized only when property is sold. Real estate has historically proved to be a generally appreciating asset. As such it is usually bought with the expectation of future higher value. This *anticipation* of higher value is usually fulfilled because land offers a fixed supply to satisfy what has proved to be a continually growing demand. However, anticipation may also lower value if property rights are expected to be restricted or if the property somehow becomes less appealing to prospective buyers.

For example, a residential area scheduled to undergo condemnation for highway construction might represent anticipation in either of its forms. Owners of residential property immediately adjacent to the highway may expect property values to decline as traffic noise and pollution increase. Owners of residential property far enough away from the highway to avoid those problems may expect property values to rise as their property is made more accessible to surrounding business and shopping areas.

Land-use requirements are often anticipated by developers, who wish to be ready with the necessary residential, commercial, or industrial facilities to meet the demand they expect. The predicted need might or might not materialize, however, which is why real estate as an investment still contains an element of risk. In short, real property is very often purchased for its anticipated future benefits, whether for production of income, a tax shelter (to the extent allowed by law), or future appreciation.

Balance

Real estate is a unique, immovable product, yet it is affected by the same market forces that influence the production of other, movable items. The four factors of production are *land, labor, capital,* and *management* (also called *coordination* or *entrepreneurship*). Land will tend to be at its highest value when the four factors of production are in *balance.*

Balance also is the term used to describe a mix of land uses that maximizes land values. With the appropriate proportion of residential, commercial, and other land uses, all properties benefit by the ability of the area to attract and keep both residents and businesses.

Change

All property is influenced by the principle of *change.* No physical or economic condition remains constant. Just as real estate is subject to natural phenomena—earthquakes, tornadoes, fires, violent storms, and routine wear and tear by the elements—the real estate business (as any business) is subject to the demands of its market. It is the appraiser's job to keep aware of past and perhaps predictable effects of natural phenomena as well as the changes in the marketplace.

Competition

According to the principle of *competition,* when the supply of property in the marketplace is low relative to the demand for such property, creating excess profits for present property owners, the result is to attract more properties to the marketplace.

All types of real estate are subject to the effects of competition in some form. The value of a house will be affected by the number of other, similar houses available in the same area. If only a few properties are competing for the attention of a much larger number of buyers, those properties will command much higher prices than they would if there were many such properties for sale.

Income-producing properties are *always* susceptible to *competition.* If demand produces excess profits for a retail store, for example, similar stores will be attracted to the area. This competition tends to mean less profit for the first business. Unless total market demand increases, there probably will not be enough sales to support very many stores, and one or more will be forced out of business. Occasionally the opposite is true, and additional competitors serve as a stimulus to the area, making a center of trade for the products being sold, as in a shopping center.

Conformity, Progression, and Regression

In general, particularly in residential areas of single-family houses, buildings should follow the principle of *conformity;* that is, they should be similar in design, construction, age, condition, and market appeal to other buildings in the neighborhood.

Nonconformity may work to the advantage or disadvantage of the owner of the nonconforming property. A house that has not been well maintained but is in a neighborhood of well-kept homes will benefit from the overall good impression created by the neighborhood and its probable desirability. This is an example of the principle of *progression.* In an example of the principle of *regression,* a house that has been meticulously maintained but is in a neighborhood of homes that have not received regular repair will suffer from the generally unfavorable impression created. In the same way, an elaborate mansion on a large lot with a spacious lawn will be worth more in a neighborhood of similar homes than it would be in a neighborhood of more modest homes on smaller lots. From the appraiser's viewpoint, the major concern is whether the improvements, or components, are typical.

Contribution

In an appraisal for market value any improvement to a property, whether to vacant land or a building, is worth only what it adds to the property's market value, regardless of the improvement's construction cost. In other words, an improvement's *contribution* to the value of the entire property is counted, not its intrinsic cost. The principle of contribution is easily applied to certain housing improvements. An extensively remodeled kitchen usually will not contribute its entire cost to the value of a house. A second bathroom, however, may well increase a house's value by more than its installation cost.

The principle of conformity may overlap with the principle of contribution. For example, if a house's exterior is its major flaw and other houses nearby are well kept, the addition of new siding may be worth several times its cost because the house will then blend in with those nearby. The appraiser's opinion, therefore, should be governed by a feature's contribution to market value—not by its reported cost.

Externalities

The principle of *externalities* states that influences outside a property may have a positive or negative effect on its value. For example, the federal government's direct participation in interest rate controls, in mortgage loan guarantees, in slum clearance and rehabilitation, and so forth, has had a powerful impact on stimulating or retarding the housing supply and increasing or decreasing the level of home ownership. Values of homes and all other types of real property are directly affected by governmental action or inaction. External influences affecting value exist at regional, city, and neighborhood levels. Crime rates, population density, and income level, and even the results of student performance on standardized tests can all be found on the Internet.

Four Agents of Production

The concept of value cannot exist without a *theory of distribution* that considers the four agents of production (capital, labor, land, and management) and the return required by each in a specific enterprise. Return on capital is characterized as interest or yield. The use of labor requires compensation in the form of wages or salaries. Return on land is rent. Finally, the return to the entrepreneurial risk taker and/or coordinator of an enterprise—the management function—is profit.

Growth, Equilibrium, Decline, and Revitalization

In terms of the effects of change on real property, ordinary physical deterioration and market demand have indicated four stages through which an improved property will pass: (1) *growth,* when improvements are made and property demand expands; (2) *equilibrium* or *stability,* when the property undergoes little change; (3) *decline,* when the property requires an increasing amount of upkeep to retain its original utility while demand slackens; and (4) *revitalization* or *rehabilitation,* which may occur if demand increases, serving to stimulate property renovation.

The first three stages of a property's life cycle are also termed *development, maturity,* and *old age.* The principle of growth, equilibrium, decline, and revitalization also applies to an entire neighborhood.

Highest and Best Use

Of all the factors that influence market value, the primary consideration is the *highest and best use* of the real estate. The highest and best use of a property is its most profitable legally and physically permitted use, that is, the use that will at present provide the highest income. The highest and best use evolves from an analysis of the community, neighborhood, site, and improvements.

A highest and best use study may be made to find the most profitable use of a vacant site or to determine the validity of a proposed site utilization. If there already is a structure on the property, the highest and best use study may make one of several assumptions: the site could be considered vacant, with the cost of demolishing the existing structure taken into account when estimating profits from any other use of the site; the cost of refurbishing the existing structure could be considered in light of any increased income that might result; the structure could be considered as is, that is, with no further improvements; and the structure might be considered adaptable to new uses.

Every case must be studied on its own merits, considering zoning or other restrictive ordinances as well as current trends. For example, many gas stations have closed since the early 1970s. Before that time, most of such facilities would probably have been used again only as gas stations. With the 1980s trend toward drive-in facilities, from restaurants and dry-cleaning shops to almost every other type of retail outlet, many former gas stations were converted to other types of drive-in businesses. With the present emphasis on the environment and federal and state regulations that require the cleanup of contaminated sites, including the storage tanks and ground contamination found on property that has been used for a gasoline station, such properties are considerably less desirable.

The depth of analysis required to support the appraiser's conclusion of a property's highest and best use will depend on the nature of the report. A property's highest and best use may also be redefined at a later date, just as its appraised value may fluctuate downward or upward. The process of determining a property's highest and best use is discussed in more detail in Chapter 7, "Site Valuation."

Law of Increasing Returns and Law of Decreasing Returns

Improvements to land and structures eventually will reach a point at which they will have no positive effect on property values. As long as money spent on such improvements produces a proportionate or greater increase in income or value, the *law of increasing returns* is in effect. At the point when additional improvements bring no corresponding increase in income or value, the *law of decreasing returns* is operating.

Opportunity Cost

In the appraisal of income-producing property, *opportunity cost* is the value differential between alternative investments with differing rates of return. The appraiser considers the alternatives in selecting a rate of return for the property being appraised, which in turn will affect the final value estimate for the property.

Substitution

The value of real property is basically determined by using what is called the principle of *substitution*. The price someone is willing to pay for a property is influenced by the cost of acquiring a substitute or comparable property. If the asking price for a house is $475,000, yet a nearby, very similar property is available for only $450,000, no one is likely to offer $475,000 for the first property.

Every appraisal makes use of the principle of substitution to some extent. Its most conspicuous use is in the appraisal of single-family residences using the *sales comparison approach*. In that approach, the appraiser collects selling price information and other data on homes similar to the property being appraised (called the *subject property*) that are located in the same or a similar neighborhood and that have sold recently. The appraiser then adjusts the selling prices of those properties to account for significant differences between them and the subject property in size, style, quality of construction, and other factors likely to affect the market value of the property being appraised. For example, if the subject property has only two bathrooms and an otherwise comparable property in the same neighborhood that has sold recently has three bathrooms, the appraiser will adjust the selling price of the comparable property downward by the market value in that area of a third bathroom. Thus, if the comparable property has sold for $225,000 and the market value of a third bathroom is $7,000, the selling price of the comparable is reduced by $7,000 (to $218,000) to approximate the effect on the subject's estimated market value of the absence of a third bathroom. Other property differences may result in the selling price of a comparable property being increased to accurately reflect the estimated market value of the subject property if the subject property has a valuable feature that the comparable property lacks.

The sales comparison approach is discussed further in Chapters 6 and 10.

Supply and Demand

As with any marketable commodity, the law of *supply and demand* affects real estate. Property values will rise as demand increases and/or supply decreases. The last building lot in a desirable residential development will probably be worth much more than the first lot that was sold in the development, assuming a consistent demand.

The effect of supply and demand is most obvious on the value of older buildings in very desirable areas, usually in cities, where demographic trends (population size and distribution) may bring heavy demand for housing to neighborhoods that have already seriously deteriorated. A building in such an area, even if it required extensive remodeling to meet current building codes, might have increased in value several times because of the increased demand. Thus it should be remembered that demand relates to the supply of a particular type of property *in a given location*—not to property in general.

Surplus Productivity

The income capitalization approach to appraising, discussed in Chapters 11 and 12, makes use of the concept of the *residual value of property purchased for investment purposes*. If the expenses of ownership (capital, labor, and management) are deducted from net income, the remaining amount is termed *surplus productivity* and is considered the investor's return on the use of the land, or land rent. The expectation of profit is also expressed as the *entrepreneurial incentive* that motivates a developer to assume the risks involved with taking on a project.

Conclusion

The principles discussed are the keys to understanding *why, when*, and *how* certain factors act to influence the value of real property. If the appraiser understands these principles, he or she can form opinions based on knowledge and understanding, not guesswork.

EXERCISE 3.2   Which basic value principle(s) does each of the following case problems illustrate?

1. Carl Snyder owns a vacation home near a small town almost 300 miles from the city in which he lives and works. He doesn't use his vacation house more than three weeks every year. The last time he stayed there, he noticed that a gas station had been built a few hundred yards down the road. After talking to the owner, he discovered that a zoning change had been put into effect to allow construction of a new shopping center on land adjacent to the gas station. While Mr. Snyder's property was not rezoned, he realizes that it won't be suitable as a vacation retreat once the shopping center is built.

2. Marian Nelson customized the family room of her new home by adding a cedar-lined steam room, six-person whirlpool spa, and special ventilating system. Mrs. Nelson decided that the improvements were justified, because even though she knew she would not be living in the home for many years, she could always realize the worth of the improvements whenever she sold her home.

3. A structurally sound office building rents for $15 per square foot but lacks air-conditioning. A similar, air-conditioned building in the same neighborhood rents for $18.50 per square foot.

4. Two bookstores are located on the same city block, and both have had good business for ten years. One store is modernized with new displays, better lighting, computerized inventory control, and a coffee bar. Because the store is part of a chain, remodeling costs are absorbed without general increase in prices. The other bookstore begins losing customers.

5. A 100-unit apartment building designed for middle-income persons at least 55 years of age is in very good condition. The owners plan extensive remodeling and redecorating to be financed by raising rents as needed. The plans will probably take four years to complete. None of the apartments will be altered, but the building's exterior will be completely redone, and the lobby will be furnished with expensive carpeting, chairs, and a chandelier. The lobby remodeling is done first; the tenants seem pleased, and no major objection is made to the resultant rent increases. After the second year, however, many tenants object to the continued increases and choose not to renew their leases. The owners have difficulty finding new tenants.

6. A single-family neighborhood is located adjacent to an airport. Excessive noise caused by airplanes flying overhead and the potential danger they create have adversely affected the value of homes in the immediate area.

Check your answers against those in the Answer Key at the back of the book.

■ SUMMARY

The market for real estate is a product of statewide, regional, and national, as well as local, forces. Population level, the strength of the economy, and the availability of financing all affect the real estate market.

Markets for goods and services are called *efficient* when the products are readily exchangeable and easily transported, there is an ample supply of buyers and sellers, government regulation has little or no effect on value, and prices are stable. The market for real estate functions differently. Real estate is immobile, unique, and heavily regulated. In addition, buyers and sellers of real estate frequently lack knowledge of the factors that contribute to market value.

Market analysis begins with a study of area demographics. The market is then segmented into areas of preference, and the activities of the people that make up the segments are forecast. A feasibility study of the likely financial success of a proposed development includes an absorption analysis of the number of units.

Sources of capital for real estate development include short-term money market funds as well as longer-term capital markets. Debt investors require a security interest in the property financed, while equity investors are willing to take a riskier unsecured role.

Although we commonly refer to any financing instrument as a *mortgage*, there are differences in the creation and effect of the mortgage and deed of trust. With a mortgage, the property owner is the mortgagor and the lender is the mortgagee. With a trust deed, the property owner is the trustor, the lender is the beneficiary, and a neutral third party is the trustee, who holds title to the secured property.

Mortgage payment plans include both fixed-rate and adjustable-rate loans. Value in exchange is the ability of a good or service to command another good or service. Market value is the most probable price real estate should bring in an arm's-length transaction in which neither party is acting under duress; the property has been on the market a reasonable length of time; the property's assets and defects are known to both parties; and there are no unusual circumstances, such as favorable seller financing. Its sales price is what a property actually sells for.

The amount initially paid for a good or service is its cost to the person who owns it. Cost may or may not be the same as the item's estimated market value and its subsequent resale price. Investment value is the value to an individual investor. Value in use is based on a particular use. Assessed value is used for taxation purposes. Insurable value is the amount for which property may be insured. Going-concern value is the value of a business exclusive of the value of the real estate it occupies.

Forces affecting value include the physical and environmental, economic, governmental, legal, and social.

The basic value principles that are among the factors contributing to price increases and decreases include anticipation; balance; change; competition; conformity, progression, and regression; contribution; externalities; the four agents of production; the stages of growth, equilibrium, decline, and revitalization; highest and best use; the laws of increasing and decreasing returns; opportunity cost; the principle of substitution; the effects of supply and demand; and surplus productivity.

The four agents of production are land, labor, capital, and management. When these factors are in balance, land value should be at its highest. Opportunity cost is the difference in value created by differing rates of return. When the expenses of ownership are deducted from net income, the remainder, or surplus productivity, is attributable to land value.

ACHIEVEMENT EXAMINATION

1. The scientific study of population statistics is

   a. scientography.

   b. segmentation.

   c. demography.

   d. forecasting.

2. The amount initially paid for a good or service is its
    a. price.
    b. market value.
    c. investment value.
    (d.) cost.   *fixed*

3. Market value is based on
    a. insurable value.
    (b.) most probable price.
    c. cost.
    d. value in use.

4. Short-term financing instruments are part of the
    (a.) money market.
    b. capital market.
    c. absorption analysis.
    d. feasibility study.

5. Longer-term financing instruments are part of the
    a. money market.
    (b.) capital market.
    c. absorption analysis.
    d. feasibility study.

6. Under a deed of trust, the property owner is the
    (a.) trustor.
    b. trustee.
    c. beneficiary.
    d. reconveyancer.

7. Under a mortgage, the lender is the
    a. mortgagor.
    (b.) mortgagee.
    c. equity investor.
    d. reconveyancer.

8. Explain the difference between market value and sales price.

Identify the major value principle described in each case below.

9. A less expensive house tends to gain in value because of more expensive neighborhood houses.

Progression

10. The value of a property tends to be limited by what it costs to buy another property similar in physical characteristics, function, or income.

Substitution

11. Plans have been announced for a multimillion-dollar shopping center to be built next door to a vacant lot you own. Property values in the area of the proposed site will tend to increase as a result of this announcement.

anticipation

12. The rental value of vacant land can sometimes be greater than it would be if the land were improved with a building.

highest nearest and best use

13. In many downtown areas, parking lots make more profit than older office buildings.

highest & best use

14. An investor will probably pay more for the last 20 lots in an area where the demand for houses is great than for the first 20 lots in the same area.

supply & demand

15. The cost of installing an air-conditioning system in an apartment building is justified only if the rental increase that can be expected as a result of the installation exceeds the amount spent.

Contribution

Check your answers against those in the Answer Key at the back of the book.

## CHAPTER 4

The Appraisal Process

■ OVERVIEW

At its simplest an appraisal presents the appraiser's opinion of a property's probable monetary value on the open market. There is much more involved in even the simplest appraisal than a mere estimate of value, however.

In deriving a final opinion of value the appraiser uses several approaches to appraising—the sales comparison approach, the cost approach, and the income capitalization approach. The manner in which the appraiser applies a particular approach may be determined by the type of property being appraised and the factors of greatest importance to buyers. A single-family rental house, for instance, would not be appraised using the same method of income valuation as would an office building, even though both properties may produce income.

In this chapter you will learn the basic definition of each of the approaches to value and some of the differences in their use. You will also learn the steps involved in the appraisal process, from the appraisal assignment through the final opinion of value.

■ STEPS IN THE APPRAISAL PROCESS

An appraisal begins with a specific assignment to the appraiser, such as to estimate the market value of a single-family residence being considered for a mortgage loan. From that point, every appraisal requires the organized collection and analysis of data. Specific data about the property, general data about the surrounding area, and data applicable to the appraisal approach being used all must be researched.

The flowchart in Figure 4.1 outlines the eight steps to be followed in the appraisal process. The steps are described in the list that begins on the following page.

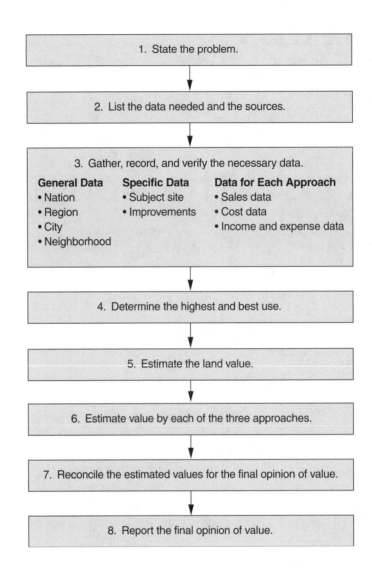

1. *State the problem.* Defining the appraisal problem includes the following:

   ■ *Identification and location of the real estate.* The property to be appraised must be identified by a complete legal description as well as a formal street address.

   ■ *Identification of the property rights to be appraised.* The typical appraisal assignment values the highest interest in real estate recognized by law—referred to as *fee simple* ownership. However, the property interest may be less than full ownership, such as a tenant's interest in a lease or the right to use an easement or right-of-way, or title may be held in partnership, by a corporation, or jointly with other individuals.

   ■ *Definition of value to be estimated.* Because the word *value* can have many interpretations, the type of value sought should always be defined so the client fully understands the basis for the reported value.

   ■ *Purpose and intended use of the appraisal.* The appraiser and client must agree on what the appraisal is to accomplish. The *purpose* of an appraisal relates to the *type of value* that is sought. The purpose of the greatest number of appraisals is to give an opinion of *market value*.

However, appraisals can be made for many other purposes—for example, to find a property's replacement cost or its insurable value.

The *intended use or function* of an appraisal is concerned with the *reason* the appraisal is being made, and the reasons may be varied. An appraisal may be made in a prospective purchase or sale, as the basis of a mortgage loan, to determine "just compensation" where property is taken under the right of eminent domain, to determine the terms of a lease, and so on.

■ *Effective date of the opinion of value.* Because real estate values are constantly changing, an opinion of value is considered valid only for the exact date specified.

■ *Any special limiting conditions.* Normally, appraisals include a statement of qualifying and limiting conditions to protect the appraiser and to inform and protect the client and other users of the appraisal.

These points will be covered in more detail later in this chapter.

Once the appraiser knows the property interest to be appraised and why the appraisal is necessary—whether for insurance purposes, to find market value, or simply to determine rental value—the approach(es) best suited to the property can be chosen. Occasionally only one approach will be appropriate, because only limited data will be available for some properties.

2. *List the data needed and the sources.* Once the appraiser knows which approach(es) will be used, the information needed can be itemized. The appraiser must be familiar enough with the sources of information to state exactly what the sources for the particular case will be.

3. *Gather, record, and verify the necessary data.* The types of data needed must be collected and recorded for future use, and the data's accuracy must be verified. This step is the most critical in the appraisal assignment, as it will form the basis for the appraiser's opinion of the property's value.

The appraiser compiles general data on the geographic and economic features of the nation, region, city, and neighborhood. Property location, as influenced by both natural and economic factors, is often of critical importance.

Regardless of the interest being appraised, specific data on the subject property (including a detailed physical description) must be obtained. Particularly when comparable properties are to be found, the physical description should include all items likely to affect market value.

Depending on the approach used, the appraiser also will gather sales data on comparable properties, cost data on construction of a like property, or income and expense data based on the property's history. All sources should be double-checked against other sources, especially when obtaining the sales price of a comparable property. In such a case, at least one of the sources should be a party to the transaction.

4. *Determine the highest and best use.* Through a highest and best use analysis the appraiser analyzes and interprets the market forces that influence the subject property to determine the property's most profitable use on which to base the final opinion of value. The appraiser may conclude that the highest and best use of the land is not its present use.

A thorough understanding of the market components that affect the value of the subject property is so important that this study is often shown in the appraisal flowchart as an additional step labeled *productivity market analysis*. Regardless of how it is categorized, the analysis requires that the appraiser take into account the physical, legal, and locational attributes present in the real estate asset—the property that is the subject of the appraisal—and consider the extent to which those attributes fulfill the requirements of the market-place. In other words, does the subject property's highest and best use satisfy the human needs that are revealed by such economic indicators as supply, demand, and absorption?

5. *Estimate the land value.* The physical features and amenities of the subject site (except for buildings) are compared with those of similar nearby sites having the same highest and best use. Adjustments are made for any significant differences, and the adjusted prices of the properties most like the subject site are used to estimate the value of the subject site.

6. *Estimate value by each of the three approaches.* Using the *sales comparison approach,* the sales prices of recently sold comparable properties are adjusted to derive an estimate of value for the property under appraisal. In the *cost approach*, the cost of property improvements, less depreciation on improvements, is added to site value. In the *income capitalization approach,* value is based on the rental income the property is capable of earning.

7. *Reconcile the estimated values for the final opinion of value.* The appraiser must correlate the information and decide what conclusions can be drawn from the volume of collected facts. The appraiser never simply averages differing value estimates. The most relevant approach, based on analysis and judgment, receives the greatest weight in determining the estimate that most accurately reflects the value sought.

8. *Report the final opinion of value.* Finally, the appraiser presents his or her conclusion of value in the reporting form requested by the client.

As you will see in Chapter 13, "Reconciliation and the Appraisal Report," the content of all appraisal reports should follow USPAP.

In Chapter 6, "Data Collection," you will learn some of the many sources of information used in a real estate appraisal.

■ BEGINNING THE APPRAISAL PROCESS

Purpose and Use of the Appraisal

The appraiser begins the *appraisal process* by stating the property being appraised and the type of value sought. *Market value* is the most frequently sought appraised value. Other types of value are highlighted in Chapter 3.

Interest(s) to Be Appraised

The form of legal interest being appraised must always be specified. Chapter 2 described the various interests in real property, including fee simple, life estate, leasehold estate, and leased fee estate. Each of these interests can be appraised. The estimated value of the interest depends on the term of the interest, any limitations on property use during that term, whether the interest is transferable, and other factors.

A fee simple absolute is the only form of ownership completely free of any other interest or estate. Even the owner of a fee simple absolute estate is subject to zoning and other governmental regulations, however. The appraisal also might be based on a partial interest, such as mineral rights.

A leasehold estate always has a definite termination date and can be valued for its remaining term.

If a residential lease does not specify a lease term, the length of time for which rent is paid is considered the lease term; for example, weekly rent implies a weekly rental term. If the time to which payment of rent applies is not specified, a month-to-month tenancy is presumed.

The value of a life estate depends on the estimated remaining life span of the person against whose life the estate is measured. If that person is elderly, the life estate obviously has less value than it would if the measuring life were that of a healthy 20-year-old who did not engage in any unusually hazardous activities.

Date of the Opinion of Value

An appraisal may be made as of any date—past, present, or future. Most often, current value is sought, and the appraiser selects the latest date possible. Most appraisers select the date of inspection of the subject property as the effective date of the appraisal. Typically, the date of the report itself would be later than the date of the appraisal. Occasionally, as in a legal proceeding, the appraiser is asked to estimate value as of a past date. Because the appraiser then has a history of market information to consider, such an appraisal may be considerably less complex than one requiring an estimate based on a future date. To estimate future value, the appraiser must extrapolate future market behavior based on current information and projected trends, an extremely difficult task. In any event, to avoid misleading the client, the appraiser should always state the assumptions under which the appraisal is made and any limitations on the use of the appraisal.

Limiting Conditions

The Federal National Mortgage Association (FNMA), now known simply as Fannie Mae, and other agencies do not expect an appraisal to be an all-encompassing process or the appraiser to spend an unlimited amount of time in preparing an appraisal report. The latest revision of the Uniform Residential Appraisal Report (URAR) form released by Fannie Mae now incorporates a *Statement of Assumptions and Limiting Conditions* to help define the appraiser's role and specify the conditions under which the appraisal is made. Fannie Mae does not allow additions or deletions to the form when it is used as part of a Fannie Mae–related appraisal. For other transactions, the appraiser may draft a customized set of limiting conditions or add to this list, as appropriate for a particular property. Figure 4.2 shows the last three pages of the six-page URAR form, which replaces all previous versions of the URAR form for Fannie Mae appraisals as of November 1, 2005. The first three pages of the form, which include property information, data analysis, and value estimate, appear throughout the remainder of this book.

You should note that the *Statement of Assumptions and Limiting Conditions* expressly limits the appraiser's responsibility for discovering and disclosing adverse conditions such as the presence of hazardous wastes and toxic substances on the property. In fact, the statement specifically provides that "the

FIGURE 4.2
Uniform Residential Appraisal Report

This report form is designed to report an appraisal of a one-unit property or a one-unit property with an accessory unit; including a unit in a planned unit development (PUD). This report form is not designed to report an appraisal of a manufactured home or a unit in a condominium or cooperative project.

This appraisal report is subject to the following scope of work, intended use, intended user, definition of market value, statement of assumptions and limiting conditions, and certifications. Modifications, additions, or deletions to the intended use, intended user, definition of market value, or assumptions and limiting conditions are not permitted. The appraiser may expand the scope of work to include any additional research or analysis necessary based on the complexity of this appraisal assignment. Modifications or deletions to the certifications are also not permitted. However, additional certifications that do not constitute material alterations to this appraisal report, such as those required by law or those related to the appraiser's continuing education or membership in an appraisal organization, are permitted.

SCOPE OF WORK: The scope of work for this appraisal is defined by the complexity of this appraisal assignment and the reporting requirements of this appraisal report form, including the following definition of market value, statement of assumptions and limiting conditions, and certifications. The appraiser must, at a minimum: (1) perform a complete visual inspection of the interior and exterior areas of the subject property, (2) inspect the neighborhood, (3) inspect each of the comparable sales from at least the street, (4) research, verify, and analyze data from reliable public and/or private sources, and (5) report his or her analysis, opinions, and conclusions in this appraisal report.

INTENDED USE: The intended use of this appraisal report is for the lender/client to evaluate the property that is the subject of this appraisal for a mortgage finance transaction.

INTENDED USER: The intended user of this appraisal report is the lender/client.

DEFINITION OF MARKET VALUE: The most probable price which a property should bring in a competitive and open market under all conditions requisite to a fair sale, the buyer and seller, each acting prudently, knowledgeably and assuming the price is not affected by undue stimulus. Implicit in this definition is the consummation of a sale as of a specified date and the passing of title from seller to buyer under conditions whereby: (1) buyer and seller are typically motivated; (2) both parties are well informed or well advised, and each acting in what he or she considers his or her own best interest; (3) a reasonable time is allowed for exposure in the open market; (4) payment is made in terms of cash in U. S. dollars or in terms of financial arrangements comparable thereto; and (5) the price represents the normal consideration for the property sold unaffected by special or creative financing or sales concessions* granted by anyone associated with the sale.

*Adjustments to the comparables must be made for special or creative financing or sales concessions. No adjustments are necessary for those costs which are normally paid by sellers as a result of tradition or law in a market area; these costs are readily identifiable since the seller pays these costs in virtually all sales transactions. Special or creative financing adjustments can be made to the comparable property by comparisons to financing terms offered by a third party institutional lender that is not already involved in the property or transaction. Any adjustment should not be calculated on a mechanical dollar for dollar cost of the financing or concession but the dollar amount of any adjustment should approximate the market's reaction to the financing or concessions based on the appraiser's judgment.

STATEMENT OF ASSUMPTIONS AND LIMITING CONDITIONS: The appraiser's certification in this report is subject to the following assumptions and limiting conditions:

1. The appraiser will not be responsible for matters of a legal nature that affect either the property being appraised or the title to it, except for information that he or she became aware of during the research involved in performing this appraisal. The appraiser assumes that the title is good and marketable and will not render any opinions about the title.

2. The appraiser has provided a sketch in this appraisal report to show the approximate dimensions of the improvements. The sketch is included only to assist the reader in visualizing the property and understanding the appraiser's determination of its size.

3. The appraiser has examined the available flood maps that are provided by the Federal Emergency Management Agency (or other data sources) and has noted in this appraisal report whether any portion of the subject site is located in an identified Special Flood Hazard Area. Because the appraiser is not a surveyor, he or she makes no guarantees, express or implied, regarding this determination.

4. The appraiser will not give testimony or appear in court because he or she made an appraisal of the property in question, unless specific arrangements to do so have been made beforehand, or as otherwise required by law.

5. The appraiser has noted in this appraisal report any adverse conditions (such as needed repairs, deterioration, the presence of hazardous wastes, toxic substances, etc.) observed during the inspection of the subject property or that he or she became aware of during the research involved in performing this appraisal. Unless otherwise stated in this appraisal report, the appraiser has no knowledge of any hidden or unapparent physical deficiencies or adverse conditions of the property (such as, but not limited to, needed repairs, deterioration, the presence of hazardous wastes, toxic substances, adverse environmental conditions, etc.) that would make the property less valuable, and has assumed that there are no such conditions and makes no guarantees or warranties, express or implied. The appraiser will not be responsible for any such conditions that do exist or for any engineering or testing that might be required to discover whether such conditions exist. Because the appraiser is not an expert in the field of environmental hazards, this appraisal report must not be considered as an environmental assessment of the property.

6. The appraiser has based his or her appraisal report and valuation conclusion for an appraisal that is subject to satisfactory completion, repairs, or alterations on the assumption that the completion, repairs, or alterations of the subject property will be performed in a professional manner.

F I G U R E 4.2
Uniform Residential Appraisal Report (continued)

APPRAISER'S CERTIFICATION: The Appraiser certifies and agrees that:

1. I have, at a minimum, developed and reported this appraisal in accordance with the scope of work requirements stated in this appraisal report.

2. I performed a complete visual inspection of the interior and exterior areas of the subject property. I reported the condition of the improvements in factual, specific terms. I identified and reported the physical deficiencies that could affect the livability, soundness, or structural integrity of the property.

3. I performed this appraisal in accordance with the requirements of the Uniform Standards of Professional Appraisal Practice that were adopted and promulgated by the Appraisal Standards Board of The Appraisal Foundation and that were in place at the time this appraisal report was prepared.

4. I developed my opinion of the market value of the real property that is the subject of this report based on the sales comparison approach to value. I have adequate comparable market data to develop a reliable sales comparison approach for this appraisal assignment. I further certify that I considered the cost and income approaches to value but did not develop them, unless otherwise indicated in this report.

5. I researched, verified, analyzed, and reported on any current agreement for sale for the subject property, any offering for sale of the subject property in the twelve months prior to the effective date of this appraisal, and the prior sales of the subject property for a minimum of three years prior to the effective date of this appraisal, unless otherwise indicated in this report.

6. I researched, verified, analyzed, and reported on the prior sales of the comparable sales for a minimum of one year prior to the date of sale of the comparable sale, unless otherwise indicated in this report.

7. I selected and used comparable sales that are locationally, physically, and functionally the most similar to the subject property.

8. I have not used comparable sales that were the result of combining a land sale with the contract purchase price of a home that has been built or will be built on the land.

9. I have reported adjustments to the comparable sales that reflect the market's reaction to the differences between the subject property and the comparable sales.

10. I verified, from a disinterested source, all information in this report that was provided by parties who have a financial interest in the sale or financing of the subject property.

11. I have knowledge and experience in appraising this type of property in this market area.

12. I am aware of, and have access to, the necessary and appropriate public and private data sources, such as multiple listing services, tax assessment records, public land records and other such data sources for the area in which the property is located.

13. I obtained the information, estimates, and opinions furnished by other parties and expressed in this appraisal report from reliable sources that I believe to be true and correct.

14. I have taken into consideration the factors that have an impact on value with respect to the subject neighborhood, subject property, and the proximity of the subject property to adverse influences in the development of my opinion of market value. I have noted in this appraisal report any adverse conditions (such as, but not limited to, needed repairs, deterioration, the presence of hazardous wastes, toxic substances, adverse environmental conditions, etc.) observed during the inspection of the subject property or that I became aware of during the research involved in performing this appraisal. I have considered these adverse conditions in my analysis of the property value, and have reported on the effect of the conditions on the value and marketability of the subject property.

15. I have not knowingly withheld any significant information from this appraisal report and, to the best of my knowledge, all statements and information in this appraisal report are true and correct.

16. I stated in this appraisal report my own personal, unbiased, and professional analysis, opinions, and conclusions, which are subject only to the assumptions and limiting conditions in this appraisal report.

17. I have no present or prospective interest in the property that is the subject of this report, and I have no present or prospective personal interest or bias with respect to the participants in the transaction. I did not base, either partially or completely, my analysis and/or opinion of market value in this appraisal report on the race, color, religion, sex, age, marital status, handicap, familial status, or national origin of either the prospective owners or occupants of the subject property or of the present owners or occupants of the properties in the vicinity of the subject property or on any other basis prohibited by law.

18. My employment and/or compensation for performing this appraisal or any future or anticipated appraisals was not conditioned on any agreement or understanding, written or otherwise, that I would report (or present analysis supporting) a predetermined specific value, a predetermined minimum value, a range or direction in value, a value that favors the cause of any party, or the attainment of a specific result or occurrence of a specific subsequent event (such as approval of a pending mortgage loan application).

19. I personally prepared all conclusions and opinions about the real estate that were set forth in this appraisal report. If I relied on significant real property appraisal assistance from any individual or individuals in the performance of this appraisal or the preparation of this appraisal report, I have named such individual(s) and disclosed the specific tasks performed in this appraisal report. I certify that any individual so named is qualified to perform the tasks. I have not authorized anyone to make a change to any item in this appraisal report; therefore, any change made to this appraisal is unauthorized and I will take no responsibility for it.

20. I identified the lender/client in this appraisal report who is the individual, organization, or agent for the organization that ordered and will receive this appraisal report.

Freddie Mac Form 70 March 2005   Page 5 of 6   Fannie Mae Form 1004 March 2005

FIGURE 4.2
Uniform Residential Appraisal Report (continued)

21. The lender/client may disclose or distribute this appraisal report to: the borrower; another lender at the request of the borrower; the mortgagee or its successors and assigns; mortgage insurers; government sponsored enterprises; other secondary market participants; data collection or reporting services; professional appraisal organizations; any department, agency, or instrumentality of the United States; and any state, the District of Columbia, or other jurisdictions; without having to obtain the appraiser's or supervisory appraiser's (if applicable) consent. Such consent must be obtained before this appraisal report may be disclosed or distributed to any other party (including, but not limited to, the public through advertising, public relations, news, sales, or other media).

22. I am aware that any disclosure or distribution of this appraisal report by me or the lender/client may be subject to certain laws and regulations. Further, I am also subject to the provisions of the Uniform Standards of Professional Appraisal Practice that pertain to disclosure or distribution by me.

23. The borrower, another lender at the request of the borrower, the mortgagee or its successors and assigns, mortgage insurers, government sponsored enterprises, and other secondary market participants may rely on this appraisal report as part of any mortgage finance transaction that involves any one or more of these parties.

24. If this appraisal report was transmitted as an "electronic record" containing my "electronic signature," as those terms are defined in applicable federal and/or state laws (excluding audio and video recordings), or a facsimile transmission of this appraisal report containing a copy or representation of my signature, the appraisal report shall be as effective, enforceable and valid as if a paper version of this appraisal report were delivered containing my original hand written signature.

25. Any intentional or negligent misrepresentation(s) contained in this appraisal report may result in civil liability and/or criminal penalties including, but not limited to, fine or imprisonment or both under the provisions of Title 18, United States Code, Section 1001, et seq., or similar state laws.

SUPERVISORY APPRAISER'S CERTIFICATION: The Supervisory Appraiser certifies and agrees that:

1. I directly supervised the appraiser for this appraisal assignment, have read the appraisal report, and agree with the appraiser's analysis, opinions, statements, conclusions, and the appraiser's certification.

2. I accept full responsibility for the contents of this appraisal report including, but not limited to, the appraiser's analysis, opinions, statements, conclusions, and the appraiser's certification.

3. The appraiser identified in this appraisal report is either a sub-contractor or an employee of the supervisory appraiser (or the appraisal firm), is qualified to perform this appraisal, and is acceptable to perform this appraisal under the applicable state law.

4. This appraisal report complies with the Uniform Standards of Professional Appraisal Practice that were adopted and promulgated by the Appraisal Standards Board of The Appraisal Foundation and that were in place at the time this appraisal report was prepared.

5. If this appraisal report was transmitted as an "electronic record" containing my "electronic signature," as those terms are defined in applicable federal and/or state laws (excluding audio and video recordings), or a facsimile transmission of this appraisal report containing a copy or representation of my signature, the appraisal report shall be as effective, enforceable and valid as if a paper version of this appraisal report were delivered containing my original hand written signature.

APPRAISER

Signature_____
Name _____
Company Name _____
Company Address_____
_____
Telephone Number _____
Email Address_____
Date of Signature and Report_____
Effective Date of Appraisal _____
State Certification #_____
or State License #_____
or Other (describe) _____ State # _____
State _____
Expiration Date of Certification or License _____

ADDRESS OF PROPERTY APPRAISED

_____
_____

APPRAISED VALUE OF SUBJECT PROPERTY $ _____

LENDER/CLIENT

Name _____
Company Name _____
Company Address_____
_____
Email Address_____

SUPERVISORY APPRAISER (ONLY IF REQUIRED)

Signature _____
Name_____
Company Name _____
Company Address_____
_____
Telephone Number _____
Email Address_____
Date of Signature _____
State Certification #_____
or State License #_____
State _____
Expiration Date of Certification or License _____

SUBJECT PROPERTY

☐ Did not inspect subject property
☐ Did inspect exterior of subject property from street
    Date of Inspection _____
☐ Did inspect interior and exterior of subject property
    Date of Inspection _____

COMPARABLE SALES

☐ Did not inspect exterior of comparable sales from street
☐ Did inspect exterior of comparable sales from street
    Date of Inspection _____

appraisal report must not be considered as an environmental assessment of the property." Nevertheless, in its guidelines for performing appraisals, Fannie Mae requires any lender who is informed by the real estate broker, property seller, purchaser, or any other party to a mortgage transaction that an environmental hazard exists on or near the property to record the information in the mortgage file, disclose it to the appraiser *and* the borrower, and comply with any other state or local disclosure laws. If the appraiser knows of any hazardous condition, it must be noted and its likely effect on the subject property's value must be commented on. The effect on value is measured by analysis of comparable market data as of the effective date of the appraisal; that is, the appraiser must use market data from properties located in the same affected area.

In short, it is in the appraiser's best interests to learn as much as possible about the types of environmental risks that are likely to be encountered, so that their presence can be considered in the valuation process. Some of these conditions are mentioned in Chapter 5, "Building Construction and the Environment." Of course, specific course work in environmental hazards is necessary for anyone who intends to act as an environmental assessor or auditor.

Above all, the appraiser must disclose the limitations and assumptions under which the appraisal is made. The Uniform Standards of Professional Appraisal Practice (USPAP) stress in Standards Rule 2-l(c) that each written or oral real property appraisal report must "clearly and accurately disclose any extraordinary assumption, hypothetical condition, or limiting condition that directly affects the appraisal and indicate its impact on value."

The certification statement required by USPAP for all written property appraisals is discussed in Chapter 13, "Reconciliation and the Appraisal Report."

FHA Appraisals

HUD (Department of Housing and Urban Development) has created some tough new standards for FHA appraisals. Appraisers who do FHA work must now complete a three-page form describing, in detail, the physical condition of a home. In the past, such responsibilities were never part of the appraiser's job description. The standards now require that appraisers pinpoint "problems with plumbing, walls, ceilings, roofs, foundations, basements, electrical systems, and heating and air-conditioning systems; soil contamination; the presence of wood-destroying insects; hazards and nuisances near homes (such as oil and gas wells); lead-based paint hazards; and other health and safety problems."

To ensure that appraisers who do FHA work will meet these government standards, the HUD program includes HUD-mandated testing. Appraisers will not be certified to do FHA appraisals until they pass the exam.

■ VALUATION APPROACHES

Each appraisal approach uses many of the principles defined in Chapter 3. In addition, each approach has its own terms and principles, some of which will be mentioned briefly in the following summaries of the three approaches. All of them will be explained fully in later chapters.

HOMES

Sales Comparison Approach

The _sales comparison_ or _market data approach_ to appraising makes the most direct use of the principle of substitution. The appraiser finds three to five (or more) properties that have sold recently and are similar to the subject property.[1] The appraiser notes any dissimilar features and makes an adjustment for each by using the following formula:

$$\text{Sale Price of Comparable Property} \pm \text{Adjustments} = \text{Indicated Value of Subject Property}$$

The appraiser adds to the sales price of a comparable property the value of a feature present in the subject property but not in the comparable. The appraiser subtracts from the sales price of the comparable property the value of a feature present in the comparable but not in the subject property. Major types of adjustments include those made for physical (on-site) features, locational (off-site) influences, conditions of sale (buyer-seller motivation and financing terms), and time from date of sale. After going through this process for each of the comparable properties, the appraiser assigns a value to the subject property that is the adjusted sales price of the comparable(s) most like the subject.

_subject has —
ADD TO comparable
subject does not have —
subtract from comparable_

EXAMPLE

House A, which sold for $355,000, is comparable to house B, the subject property, but has a garage valued at $25,000. House B has no garage. In this case, using the formula for the sales comparison approach, the market value of the subject property would be reached as shown below.

$$\$355,000 - \$25,000 = \$330,000$$

House B is valued at $330,000.

EXAMPLE

House X, the subject property, is 15 years old. A comparable property, house Y, is 15 years old and sold for $270,000 one year prior to this appraisal. Because of changes in market conditions since the sale of house Y, the appraiser has determined that 10 percent added to the sales price is an accurate reflection of the increase in property values over the year. In this case, using the formula for the sales comparison approach:

$$\$270,000 + (10\% \times \$270,000) = \text{Value of Subject Property}$$
$$\$270,000 + \$27,000 = \$297,000$$

House X is valued at $297,000.

Vacant land is valued in the same way, by finding other comparable properties and adding or subtracting, as necessary, the worth of any amenities present in either the subject or the comparable property and not in the other.

---

[1] The number of sales needed for an accurate estimate of value cannot be easily specified. Most appraisers believe that three to five comparable sales constitute a representative sample—particularly if the sales are very similar, are located close by, and have sold recently. The fewer the sales, the more carefully they should be investigated. If the quality of the data collected is questionable, a larger number of sales should be considered.

  The reason for an appraisal can also influence the number of comparable sales needed. For example, an appraisal used to establish value in a condemnation proceeding would probably require a greater number of comparable sales than one used to establish value for a mortgage loan.

Features of vacant land requiring a sales price adjustment might include installation of utilities, composition of soil, terrain, shape, zoning, and favorable location.

Cost Approach

In the *cost approach*, the appraiser estimates the value of any improvements to the land (such as structures) in terms of their reproduction or replacement cost as though *new*. The distinction between reproduction and replacement cost is discussed in Chapter 8. The appraiser then subtracts any loss in value owing to the *depreciation* of the improvements. Finally, the appraiser adds an estimate of the value of the site itself, usually found by the sales comparison approach. The formula for the cost approach is

$$\text{Reproduction or Replacement Cost of Improvements} - \text{Depreciation on Improvement(s)} + \text{Site Value} = \text{Property Value}$$

Depreciation may occur through either *deterioration* (effects of wear and tear or the elements) or *obsolescence*. Obsolescence can be *functional,* such as outmoded room layout or design, or *external,* caused by changes in factors outside the property such as zoning, the property's highest and best use, or supply and demand.

EXAMPLE

A house being appraised is similar in size, design, and quality of construction to a new house that has a construction cost of $225,000. The house being appraised has depreciated by 20 percent due to lack of maintenance and is on a lot valued separately at $40,000. Using the cost approach formula:

$225,000 – (20% × $225,000) + $40,000 = Property Value
$225,000 – $45,000 + $40,000 = $220,000

The estimated value of the property based on the cost approach is $220,000.

EXAMPLE

A warehouse that would cost $850,000 to construct today has depreciated 25 percent in its lifetime and is on land valued at $440,000. What is the property's total estimated value by the cost approach?

$850,000 – (25% × $850,000) + $440,000 = Property Value
$850,000 – $212,500 + $440,000 = $1,077,500

The estimated value of the property based on the cost approach is $1,077,500.

Income Capitalization Approach

The *income capitalization approach* is based on the net income, or investment return, that a buyer expects from the property. The price that the buyer will pay will be determined by the probable return the property will yield from the investment.

Remember that the income capitalization approach is based on *net operating income*—which is usually expressed as an annual amount. Rents are *not* net operating income. All the expenses of maintaining the building, such as upkeep and management, must be subtracted from *effective gross income* (scheduled rents plus any other income minus vacancy and collection expense factors) to realize net operating income.

If a property's net operating income for the year is known, as well as the buyer's anticipated return for the investment (stated as a capitalization rate), value can be computed by using the following formula:

$$\frac{\text{Net Operating Income}}{\text{Return (Capitalization Rate)}} = \text{Property Value}$$

or:

$$\frac{I}{R} = V$$

EXAMPLE

A buyer wants a 9 percent investment return. He is interested in a medical office building that produces a net operating income of $225,000 per year. What would the buyer be willing to pay for the building?

$$\frac{\$225,000}{9\%} = \$2,500,000$$

The property value necessary to produce the expected net operating income is $2,500,000.

The return that can be expected based on an estimated level of income and property value can be computed by using a variation of the basic income capitalization formula:

$$\frac{\text{Income}}{\text{Property Value}} = \text{Return}$$

or:

$$\frac{I}{V} = R$$

EXAMPLE

An investor estimates that a net operating income of $39,300 can be received from a building that will require an investment of $560,000. What is the investor's capitalization rate (return)?

$$\frac{\$39,300}{\$560,000} = .07017$$

The expected return, based on the income alone, is 7 percent.

A buyer who has only a certain amount to invest and wants a specific rate of return from his investment would use another variation of the formula:

$$\text{Property Value} \times \text{Return} = \text{Net Operating Income}$$

or:

$$V \times R = I$$

EXAMPLE

To receive a 12 percent return from an investment of $700,000, what would be the required net operating income of the purchased property?

$$\$700,000 \times 12\% = \$84,000$$

The net operating income would have to be $84,000.

EXERCISE 4.1

Using the formula for the approach specified, solve each of the following appraisal problems.

Sales Comparison Approach:

House X, in an Arizona community in which swimming pools are highly desired, is being appraised. It is very similar to house Y, but house Y has an in-ground swimming pool and spa valued at $27,000. House Y sold two months ago for $778,000. What is the market value of house X using the formula for the sales comparison approach?

751 K   778
                − 27

Cost Approach:

230

A retail store, built 15 years ago, has depreciated about 30 percent overall. It would cost $230,000 to build today, and similar sites are now worth $52,000. What is the market value of this store using the formula for the cost approach?

230
− 69
161 + 52 = 213 K

Income Capitalization Approach:

An apartment building provides a net annual rental income of $64,500. Investors are expecting a 12 percent return on this type of investment. What will the asking price be if it is the same as the market value found by the formula for the income capitalization approach?   645   537.5

Check your answers against those in the Answer Key at the back of the book.

■ RELATIONSHIP OF APPROACHES

The three approaches to real estate appraisal require different kinds of information, which may include data on comparable nearby property sales (sales comparison approach), building cost (cost approach), and investment return (income capitalization approach). The information available will help determine which of the appraisal methods will be given the most validity in the appraiser's opinion of the market value of the subject property.

As a general rule, the sales comparison approach is the most reliable approach with single-family residences; the cost approach is most reliable with non–income-producing property having a limited market or with special purpose properties; and the income capitalization approach is most reliable with income-producing property.

Most appraisals will require the use of more than one approach, especially when land value must be distinguished from building value. This is true when the cost approach is used to find building value. There are other instances when land value must be separated from building value, such as for tax valuation purposes. These will be discussed later in this book.

EXAMPLE

If a 45-year-old school building is to be sold, what approach would be given the most weight in determining its market value?

School buildings are not usually on the market, so there probably would be no recent comparable sales in the vicinity. If the building could be used as office or other rental space as it stood, or with a little remodeling, the income capitalization approach might be feasible. The approach given the most weight, however, would probably be the cost approach, because the high cost of constructing a similar new building would probably be the most significant selling factor.

The next step in the appraisal process is to analyze the value indications from the three approaches to arrive at the best and most supportable opinion of value. This can be either a single dollar figure or a range into which the value will most likely fall. The process the appraiser follows to do this is called *reconciliation*.

Proper analysis and reconciliation are essential to a good appraisal report. The use of accepted appraisal methods does not in itself produce a sound opinion of value. It must be combined with good judgment on the part of the appraiser, as well as experience in gathering needed information and making thorough analyses and valid interpretations of relevant data.

The reconciliation process is covered in detail in Chapter 13, "Reconciliation and the Appraisal Report."

EXERCISE 4.2

Decide which appraisal approach(es) would normally carry the most weight in valuing each of the following properties:

1. A factory   *cost income*

2. An automobile showroom and garage   *income*

3. A public building formerly used as a town hall   *cost*

4. Farmland surrounded by commercial and industrial developments
   Sales comparison

5. A one-story retail store in a busy downtown business district
   Income

6. An older, single-family residence in a neighborhood rezoned to permit highrise apartments   *Sales Comparison*

7. A medical office building in a suburban shopping center
   income

8. A single-family, owner-occupied residence
   Sales comparison

9. A place of worship

   Cost

10. A small abandoned roadside restaurant adjacent to a new apartment complex

Income

Check your answers against those in the Answer Key at the back of the book.

■ SUMMARY

The appraisal process begins with a statement of the problem, that is, the purpose of the appraisal. By gathering, recording, and verifying all of the necessary data, then analyzing and interpreting that information, the appraiser can form an opinion of value based on knowledge and understanding and not guesswork.

There are three basic approaches to determining the market value of real property. The sales comparison approach makes use of data regarding recently sold properties that are similar to the subject property. The cost approach utilizes the present construction cost of existing improvements less depreciation. The income capitalization approach makes use of the net operating income that may be expected from the property. The appraiser must use the appraisal approaches that are most reasonable in light of the type of property being appraised.

ACHIEVEMENT EXAMINATION

1. The appraisal approach that would be most useful in valuing single-family residential property is the
   a. sales comparison approach.
   b. cost approach.
   c. income capitalization approach.

2. The appraisal approach that normally would be most useful in valuing investment property is the
   a. sales comparison approach.
   b. cost approach.
   c. income capitalization approach.

3. The appraisal approach that normally would be most useful in valuing public and religious-use properties is the
   a. sales comparison approach.
   b. cost approach.
   c. income capitalization approach.

4. The reliability of an appraisal depends on the
   a. knowledge and judgment of the appraiser.
   b. accuracy of the data used.
   c. Both a and b
   d. Neither a nor b

5. Property A is a single-family residence that sold for $180,000. It is very similar to property B, which you are appraising, except that property A has a two-car garage worth $16,000. Using the formula for the sales comparison approach, calculate the market value of property B.

164 K

6. An office building has depreciated 40 percent since it was built 25 years ago. If it would cost $725,000 to build today, and if similar sites are selling for $175,000, what is the market value of the property using the formula for the cost approach?

610 K

7. You are appraising a single-story building producing net operating income of $124,000 per year. If you determine that a 9 percent return is justified on this investment, what would be your value estimate of the property using the income capitalization approach formula?

124 ÷ .09 = 1,377,777

Check your answers against those in the Answer Key at the back of the book.

## CHAPTER 5

Building Construction and the Environment

■ OVERVIEW

Real estate appraisers must know their product. In terms of residential real estate, this means knowing the construction features that determine quality, show good craftsmanship, and indicate good upkeep or show neglect, especially through visible flaws that could indicate significant structural damage. By being aware of current architectural trends and construction standards, the appraiser can gauge a property's desirability, marketability, and value. The purpose of this chapter is to explain the basic construction features of wood-frame residential houses so you can better judge and evaluate them.

Wood-frame construction, whether covered by weatherboarding or veneered with brick or stone, is the type most frequently used in single-family houses. Wood-frame houses are preferred for a number of reasons:

- They are less expensive than other types.
- They can be built rapidly.
- They are easy to insulate against heat or cold.
- Greater flexibility of design is possible, thereby enabling architects and builders to produce a variety of architectural styles.

The following building fundamentals will be considered in this chapter:

- State and municipal regulations, such as building codes
- Plans and specifications
- Architectural styles and designs
- Terms and trade vernacular used in residential construction
- The practical approach to recognizing, judging, and comparing the quality of the various house components

---

Some of the material in this chapter is adapted from *Your Home Inspection Guide* by William L. Ventolo, Jr. (Chicago: Real Estate Education Company, 1995).

This chapter also covers some of the environmental issues, such as the presence of asbestos or radon gas, that must be considered by real estate appraisers as well as brokers, developers, lenders, and others involved in real estate transactions.

PART I: PLANNING AND DESIGN

■ REGULATION OF RESIDENTIAL CONSTRUCTION

WEB LINK
www.iccsafe.org

Building codes for the construction industry were established when the Building Officials Conference of America (BOCA) combined with the National Board of Fire Insurance Underwriters to set forth rules to ensure both comfort and safety for homeowners. These standards became the forerunners of present municipal building codes. The merger of BOCA and the regional U.S. codes organizations has resulted in formation of the International Code Council, *www.iccsafe.org.*

The Federal Housing Administration (FHA) and Department of Veterans Affairs (VA) standards also have served as models for municipal building codes, which place primary importance on materials, structural strength, and safe, sanitary conditions. Such building codes set the *minimum construction standards* that must be met by builders. HUD establishes standards for manufactured homes. Such homes must meet local standards for site preparation, foundation, and utility connections, however.

■ PLANS AND SPECIFICATIONS

WEB LINK
www.aia.org

Careful plans and specifications are required to comply with building codes. These must be in sufficient detail to direct the builder in assembling the construction materials. Working drawings, called *plans* or *blueprints,* show the construction details of the building. *Specifications* are written statements that establish the quality of the materials and workmanship required.

An owner may engage an architect to design a house and prepare plans and specifications for its construction. Professional architects typically must be licensed by the state(s) in which they practice and may also join a trade association having its own membership requirements, such as the American Institute of Architects (AIA), *www.aia.org.* The architect's services may include negotiating with the builder and inspecting the progress of the construction, as well as preparing plans and specifications. Architects' fees, usually based on the hours spent on a given project, may vary from 6 percent to 15 percent of the total cost of the finished house, depending on the services rendered. The builder typically acts as *general contractor,* providing day-to-day supervision of the job site in addition to procuring building materials and hiring carpenters, plumbers, electricians, and other *subcontractors.*

Other specialists may be involved in residential construction, including the *mechanical engineer,* who provides the heating, air-conditioning, and plumbing plans and specifications; the *structural engineer,* who ensures that the foundation will support the structure and specifies the amount of steel required for reinforcing the foundation and the type and mix of concrete to be used; and the *soil engineer,* who may assist in determining the stability of the land on which the foundation is to be built. The soil engineer's investigation, coupled with the structural engineer's knowledge, will determine the details of the foundation.

Building Measurement

The size of a structure being appraised will be stated in the appraisal report and may be a critical factor in the final determination of value. The appraiser should always

■ state the basis for the measurement provided in the appraisal report;

■ verify all measurements *personally;* and

■ if a multiunit building is involved, base all measurements on the same standard for consistency.

Several commonly used standards of measurements are discussed below. The residential property standards originated with the federal agency requirements (FHA, VA, Fannie Mae, and so on).

Gross Living Area

For a single-family detached residence, size is described in terms of *gross living area (GLA),* defined as the total amount of finished habitable above-grade space, measured along the building's outside perimeter. Generally, attics, basements, and crawlspaces are not included in the measurement. Local custom may allow inclusion of other space in the calculation, if typical of the area and accepted by property buyers as equivalent to living space. For example, many areas have buildings constructed on hillsides, either *upslope* (the house is built into the hill at an elevation higher than the roadway) or *downslope* (the house is built on piers at an elevation lower than the roadway). Gross living area of such homes typically includes lower levels that are not completely above grade on all sides. The best appraisal practice is always to compare properties with others of similar construction.

For condominium apartments, size is often described in square footage of interior floor space rather than as outside wall measurement.

National Square Footage Standard

In April 1996, the Board of Standards Review of the American National Standards Institute (ANSI) adopted a voluntary national standard for measuring square footage in single-family attached and detached homes. Committee members included representatives of Fannie Mae, Freddie Mac, VA and HUD, the Appraisal Foundation, American Association of Certified Appraisers, American Institute of Architects, National Association of Home Builders, International Conference of Building Officials, National Association of REALTORS®, and numerous other organizations as well as private design building and appraising companies. The 16-page standard includes the following directives.

- Measure from the exterior face of outside walls.
- Measure to the nearest inch or tenth and report to the nearest whole square foot.
- Include only finished areas.
- Make a clear distinction between above-grade finished square footage and below-grade finished square footage and identify a level as below grade if any part of that level is below the grade line.
- Do not include openings in floors in square footage, but do include stair treads.
- Ceilings must have a height of at least seven feet except under stairs, beams, and sloping ceilings.
- Include accessory apartments and other finished areas not within the main house only if they are connected to the main house by finished hallways/stairways.
- Never consider a garage as finished space, although a garage can be calculated as unfinished square footage using ANSI guidelines.

A copy of the complete standard is available from the NAHB Research Center, Inc., (800) 638-8556 or *www.nahbrc.com.*

Gross Building Area

For multifamily residences and industrial buildings, size is described in terms of *gross building area (GBA),* defined as all enclosed floor areas (including both attics and basements), measured along the building's outside perimeter.

Gross Leasable Area

For shopping centers, size generally is described in terms of square feet of *gross leasable area (GLA),* defined as total space designed for occupancy and exclusive use of tenants (including basements), measured from outside wall surfaces to the center of shared interior walls.

The size of other multitenant commercial properties, such as office buildings, will be described as local custom dictates or, perhaps, according to the negotiating strengths of landlord and tenant. For instance, common areas (and the expense of their maintenance), including lobbies, corridors, and elevator shafts, may be apportioned among tenants on a pro rata basis—that is, in relation to the size of each tenant's exclusive-use space.

■ HOUSE STYLES

Although the details of construction are rigidly specified by building codes, house styles may vary greatly. There are no absolute standards, and real estate values rest on what potential buyers, users, and investors think is desirable as well as on what they consider to be attractive.

House styles can be grouped under two broad categories: *traditional* and *contemporary.*

Traditional Styles

Past architectural styles appeal to many prospective homeowners. Within this nostalgic design category, traditionalists have a wide range of individual styles to choose from: *Cape Cod, Victorian,* and *Georgian*—to name a few (see Figure 5.1). The handling of architectural details gives the traditional house its unique flavor. Fortunately, the detailing for many traditional houses no longer need be handcrafted because good reproductions are now mass produced. Ready-made entrance doors, mantels, moldings, and parquet floors bear a close resemblance to their handcrafted prototypes.

Contemporary Styles

Although many contemporary houses appear uncomplicated, they are often clever examples of how to make the best use of materials and space (see Figure 5.2). A distinctive contemporary look relies on the straightforward expression of the structural system itself for major design impact. One great benefit of contemporary residential architecture is its responsiveness to indoor-outdoor living. Walls of sliding glass doors, large windows, skylights, decks, terraces, and atriums all contribute to this relationship.

■ HOUSE TYPES

Today's new materials and modern techniques can make a big difference in the way houses are designed and built. The modern house, whether its style is contemporary or traditional, can exhibit the latest conveniences and building innovations.

FIGURE 5.1
Traditional House Styles

Mediterranean

Courtesy of Home Styles Publishing and Marketing

Cape Cod

Courtesy of Home Styles Publishing and Marketing

Victorian

Courtesy of Home Styles Publishing and Marketing

Farm House

Courtesy of Home Styles Publishing and Marketing

Georgian

Courtesy of Home Styles Publishing and Marketing

FIGURE 5.2
Contemporary House Style

Courtesy of Home Styles Publishing and Marketing

Large areas of double-paned glass open houses to sun, light, and view without letting in cold drafts. A good modern house has central heating, which enables homeowners to enjoy big rooms and large windows without discomfort. Air-conditioning has eliminated the need for cross-ventilation from two exposures in every room, although a house providing cross-ventilation will be attractive to the energy-conscious consumer.

The One-Story House

The one-story house, often referred to as a *ranch,* has all the habitable rooms on one level. Its great advantage is the absence of steps to climb or descend, particularly if the house is built on a concrete slab foundation or over a crawlspace, rather than a basement. Because no headroom is required above the ceiling, the roof of a one-story house is usually pitched low. The low height simplifies construction, too, but this does not necessarily mean a lower cost because foundation and roof areas are larger in proportion to total finished area than in other types of housing. The ranch is one of the easiest houses to maintain.

The One-and-a-Half-Story House

The one-and-a-half-story house, or *Cape Cod,* is actually a two-story house in which the second-floor attic space has sufficient headroom to permit up to half the area being used as livable floor area. It has two distinct advantages: economy in cost per cubic foot of habitable space and built-in expandability (see Figure 5.3).

The Two-Story House

The two-story house offers the most living space within an established perimeter; the living area is doubled on the same foundation and under the same roof. Certain economies are inherent in the two-story plan: plumbing can be aligned and winter heating is utilized to the best advantage—heat rises to the second floor after warming the ground floor. More house can be built on a smaller lot with a two-story plan. The roof is smaller, relative to the overall floor area, as is the foundation required.

The Split-Level House

The split-level has three separate levels of space. The lowest level, situated entirely or partially below the outside finished grade, usually contains the

FIGURE 5.3
Types of Houses: One-Story, One-and-a-Half-Story

ONE-STORY HOUSE

1ST FLOOR

BASEMENT

EXPANSION ATTIC

1ST FLOOR

BASEMENT

ONE-AND-A-HALF-STORY HOUSE

garage, heating and air-conditioning system, and family room. The next area—the one raised a half-flight from the lowest level—is extra space common only to a split-level house. The floor here is even with, or close to, the outside grade; it usually includes the kitchen and main living area. The sleeping level is another half-flight up, above the garage and family room.

The Split-Entry House

The split-entry design, sometimes called a *raised ranch,* is a fairly recent architectural approach to residential housing. It is basically a one-story house on an elevated foundation. The resulting greater height makes the lower level a more usable space for recreation rooms, baths, bedrooms, or other uses. In effect, the square footage of the house is doubled at a modest cost increase—merely that of finishing the rooms on the lower level (see Figure 5.4).

FIGURE 5.4
Types of Houses: Two-Story, Split-Level Styles

TWO-STORY HOUSE

2ND FLOOR
1ST FLOOR
BASEMENT

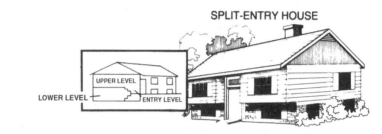

SPLIT-ENTRY HOUSE

UPPER LEVEL
LOWER LEVEL   ENTRY LEVEL

SPLIT-LEVEL HOUSE

Factory-Built Houses

Mention factory-built or manufactured housing and most people visualize "prefab" buildings and flimsy trailers. That image nags at the manufactured housing industry, which accounts for an increasing percentage of the nation's housing stock. In recent years, builders have been working hard to overcome those long-held biases against factory-built housing by turning out sturdier, better-looking products.

There are four basic types of factory-built houses, each characterized by the extent of assemblage completed in the factory and whether the house must comply with state and local building codes:

1. *Manufactured house.* This is the most complete of the factory-built houses, available usually in one or two pieces needing only to be anchored to a foundation and connected to utilities. Manufactured homes, as defined by the federal government, must meet the requirements of the Department of Housing and Urban Development. These "HUD Code" homes thus avoid

state and local building code requirements. In practice, manufactured homes often are referred to as *mobile homes* or *trailers*, even though their mobility may be limited to the journey from factory to construction site.

2. *Modular house.* This type of housing, which must meet state and local building code requirements, comes from the factory in single-room or multiple-room sections, which are then fitted together at the construction site.

3. *Panelized house.* Entire wall units, complete with electrical and plumbing installations, are constructed at the factory and transported to the site where final assembly begins. With the foundation laid, the house can be enclosed within a week. State and local building code requirements must be met.

4. *Precut house.* As the name implies, materials are delivered to the construction site already cut and ready to assemble. Each piece should fit perfectly in its place, eliminating costly time for measuring and cutting materials on site. State and local building code requirements must be met.

■ ORIENTATION: LOCATING THE HOUSE ON THE SITE

A house correctly oriented and intelligently landscaped, with windows and glass doors in the right places and adequate roof overhang, can save thousands of dollars in heating and air-conditioning bills over the years. The location of a house on its lot also contributes to full-time enjoyment and use of house and grounds. Improper positioning is probably the most common and costly mistake made in house planning today.

Topography

Topography, the "lay of the land," often dictates what style of building may be placed on the site and how the foundation of the building must be designed. A sloping site will require an engineering report to ensure a stable foundation suitable for the overall structure. A steep slope that would be considered impractical for building in some parts of the country may still be considered desirable in those parts of the country where buildable land of any kind is at a premium.

Facing to the South

Ideally, a house should be positioned on the lot so that the main living areas have the best view and also face *south*. The south side of a house receives five times as much solar heat in the winter as in summer, and the north side receives no solar heat at all during winter months.

Unless some measures of control are used, the same sunshine that helps to heat a house during the winter will make it uncomfortable during the summer. Figure 5.5 shows how this potential problem can be avoided. Because the summer sun rides high in the sky, a wide roof overhang will shade the windows by deflecting the direct heat rays. A roof overhang will not interfere with the sunshine in winter months because the winter sun travels a much lower arc and shines in at a much lower angle than the summer sun.

FIGURE 5.5
Sunlight Exposure

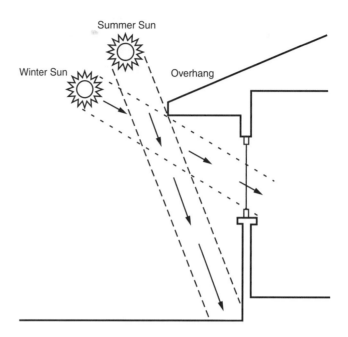

View

A decision on the location of a house can also depend on the view. If the site has an interesting long view to the east or west, it might be wise to take advantage of it, in spite of the sun factor. Even if a site does not have a good long view, a short view of a garden or patio can be just as interesting if carefully planned.

EXERCISE 5.1

1. List some economic advantages basic to the following house types:
   a. One-and-a-half-story house

   b. Two-story house

   c. Split-entry house

2. How can the orientation of a house on its lot contribute to monetary savings and the enjoyment of the house and its grounds?

Check your answers against those in the Answer Key at the back of the book.

PART II: CONSTRUCTION DETAILS

Basic knowledge of building construction will help the appraiser identify the factors that contribute to building quality and, ultimately, value.

Throughout this section of the chapter, certain terms will be followed by a bracketed number. The number refers to the corresponding term in the house diagram at the end of this chapter (see Figure 5.15), which provides an overall picture of how housing components fit together into the end product. For example, *footing* [1] means the component labeled 1 in the house diagram.

FOUNDATIONS

The foundation of the house is the substructure on which the superstructure rests. The term *foundation* includes the footings, foundation walls, columns, pilasters, slab, and all other parts that provide support for the house and transmit the load of the superstructure to the underlying earth. Foundations are constructed of cut stone, stone and brick, concrete block, or poured concrete. Poured concrete is the most common foundation material because of its strength and resistance to moisture. The two major types of foundations are *concrete slab* and *pier and beam,* shown, respectively, in Figures 5.6 and 5.7.

Concrete Slab

A *concrete slab foundation* is composed of a concrete slab supported around the perimeter and in the center by concrete beams sunk into the earth. It is made of poured concrete reinforced with steel rods. The foundation slab rests directly on the earth, with only a waterproofing membrane between the concrete and the ground. Foundations formed by a single pouring of concrete are *monolithic,* while those in which the footings and the slab are poured separately are referred to as *floating.*

Pier and Beam

In a *pier and beam foundation,* the foundation slab rests on a series of isolated columns, called *piers,* that extend above ground level. The space between the ground and the foundation is called the *crawlspace.* Each support of a pier and beam foundation consists of a *pier* [55], or column, resting on a *footing* [57], or

---

FIGURE 5.6
Concrete Slab Foundations

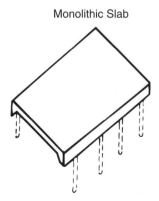

Monolithic Slab

Floating Slab

FIGURE 5.7
Pier and Beam Foundations

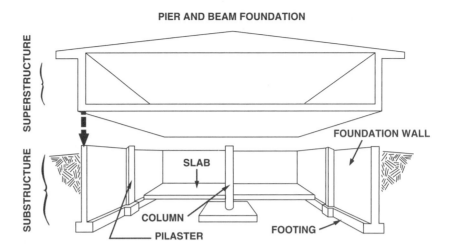

base. The pier, in turn, supports the *sill* [8], which is attached to the pier by an *anchor bolt* [7]. The *floor joists* [10] that provide the major support for the flooring are placed perpendicular to and on top of the sills.

Termite Protection

The earth is infested with termites, extremely active antlike insects that are very destructive to wood. Before the slab for the foundation is poured, the ground should be chemically treated to poison termites and thus prevent them from coming up through or around the foundation and into the wooden structure. The chemical treatment of the lumber used for sills and beams and the installation of metal *termite shields* [9] also provides protection.

Radon Gas

Radon is a colorless, odorless, tasteless radioactive gas that comes from the natural breakdown of uranium. It can be found in most rocks and soils. Outdoors, it mixes with the air and is found in low concentrations that are harmless to people. Indoors, however, it can accumulate and build up to dangerous levels. High radon levels in the home can increase risk of lung cancer (currently the only known health effect). The surgeon general has drawn attention to the danger of radon by announcing that it is second only to smoking as a cause of lung cancer.

How does radon get into a house? The amount of radon in a home depends on the home's construction and the concentration of radon in the soil underneath it. Figure 5.8 shows how radon can enter a home through dirt floors, cracks in concrete foundations, floors and walls, floor drains, tiny cracks or pores in hollow block walls, loose-fitting pipes, exhaust fans, sump pumps, and many other unsuspected places, even including the water supply.

A lot of the variation in radon levels has to do with the "airtightness" of a house: the more energy-efficient a home is, the more likely it will have higher radon levels. The average house has one complete air exchange every six to seven hours; that is, about four times a day all the air from inside the house is exchanged with outside air. The tighter the house, the more likely it is that the

FIGURE 5.8
Common Radon Entry Routes

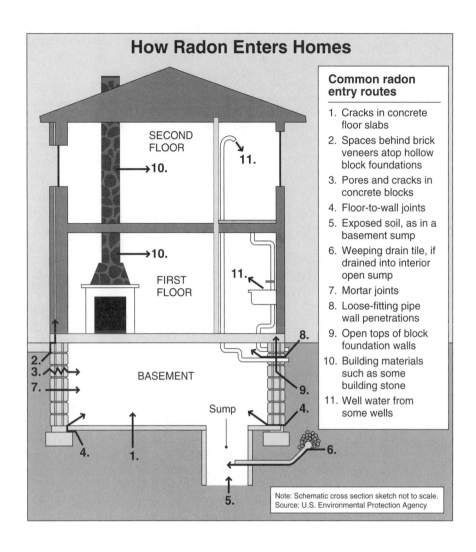

How Radon Enters Homes

SECOND FLOOR

FIRST FLOOR

BASEMENT

Sump

Common radon entry routes

1. Cracks in concrete floor slabs
2. Spaces behind brick veneers atop hollow block foundations
3. Pores and cracks in concrete blocks
4. Floor-to-wall joints
5. Exposed soil, as in a basement sump
6. Weeping drain tile, if drained into interior open sump
7. Mortar joints
8. Loose-fitting pipe wall penetrations
9. Open tops of block foundation walls
10. Building materials such as some building stone
11. Well water from some wells

Note: Schematic cross section sketch not to scale.
Source: U.S. Environmental Protection Agency

air exchange will come from beneath the house from the air over the soil, which may contain high levels of radon gas.

More information about radon, including radon-resistant construction, can be found at *www.epa.gov*.

WEB LINK
www.epa.gov

■ EXTERIOR STRUCTURAL WALLS AND FRAMING

After the foundation is in place, the exterior walls are erected. The first step in erecting exterior walls is the *framing*. The skeleton members of a building to which the interior and exterior walls are attached are called its *frame*. The walls of a frame are formed by vertical members called *studs* [15], which are spaced at even intervals and are attached to the sill. Building codes typically require that for a one-story house, the stud spacing may not exceed 24 inches on center. For a two-story house, the spacing may not exceed 16 inches. Studs rest on *plates* [12] that are secured to and rest on the *foundation wall* [4]. In constructing walls and floors, the builder will install *firestops* [43] as needed or required. These are boards or blocks nailed horizontally between studs or joists to stop drafts and retard the spread of fire. Window and door openings are framed in with wood boards. The horizontal board across the top of a window or door opening is called the *header* [26]; the horizontal board across the bottom of the opening is called the *sill*.

Figure 5.9 shows three basic types of wood frame construction: *platform*, *balloon*, and *post and beam*.

Platform Frame Construction

Today the most common type of frame construction for both one-story and two-story residential structures is *platform frame* construction. In platform construction only one floor is built at a time, and each floor serves as a platform for the next story. The wall studs are first attached to the upper and lower plates, and the entire assemblage is then raised into place and anchored to the sill.

FIGURE 5.9
Frame Construction Types

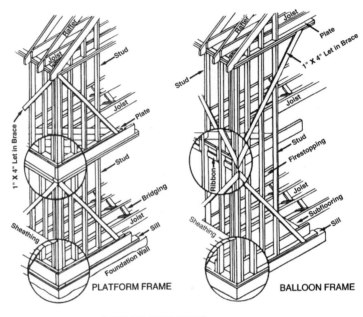

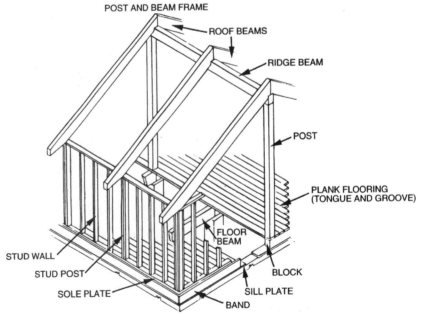

Balloon Frame Construction

The second type of framing is *balloon frame* construction, which differs from the platform method in that the studs extend continuously to the ceiling of the second floor. The second floor joists rest on *ledger boards* or *ribbon boards* set into the interior edge of the studs. The balloon method gives a smooth, unbroken wall surface on each floor level, thus alleviating the unevenness that sometimes results from settling when the platform method is used. The balloon method is usually employed when the exterior finish will be brick, stone veneer, or stucco.

Post and Beam Frame Construction

Many contemporary-style buildings utilize *post and beam frame* construction. With this method the ceiling planks are supported on beams that rest on posts placed at intervals inside the house. Because the posts provide some of the ceiling support, rooms can be built with larger spans of space between the supporting side walls. In some houses the beams are left exposed and the posts and beams are stained to serve as part of the decor.

Exterior Walls

After the skeleton of the house is constructed, the exterior wall surface must be built and the *sheathing* [19] and *siding* [20] applied. The sheathing is nailed directly to the *wall studs* [15] to form the base for the siding. Sheathing is generally insulated drywall or plywood. If the house is to have a masonry veneer, the sheathing may be gypsum board. Fabricated sheathings are available in both strip and sheet material.

After the sheathing is added, the final exterior layer, called *siding,* is applied. Siding may be asphalt, shingles, wood, aluminum, stone, brick, or other material.

Masonry Veneer versus Solid Brick

Brick *veneer* is a thin layer of brick often used as a covering on a frame house to give the appearance of a solid brick house. If the masonry is merely decorative and the walls are of wood, then the house has masonry veneer exterior finishing. On the other hand, if the brick walls provide the support for the roof structure, then the house has all masonry, or solid brick, walls. A masonry veneer house may be distinguished from a solid masonry house by the thickness of the walls; the walls of a veneered house are seldom more than eight inches thick.

Small outlets evenly spaced around the base of the masonry perimeter of a brick house are called *weep holes*. These openings provide an outlet for any moisture or condensation trapped between the brick and the sheathing of the exterior walls and are essential for proper ventilation.

Insulation

Maintaining comfortable temperatures inside the home is an important factor in construction, particularly in these days of high-cost energy. To ensure adequate protection, *insulation* [17] should be placed in the exterior walls and upper floor ceilings. *Rock wool* and *fiberglass* are commonly used insulation materials. Combinations of materials, such as fiberglass wrapped in aluminum foil or rock wool formed into batt sections that can be placed between the studs, are also available.

The effectiveness of insulation depends on its resistance to heat flow—its R-value—rather than just on its thickness. Different insulating materials have different R-values; therefore, different thicknesses are required to do the same job. The larger the R-value, the more resistance to heat flow and the better the insulation.

How much R-value is needed? The minimum property standards for federally financed construction call for R-11 or R-13 insulation within the walls and R-19 or R-22 in the attic. R-values are additive. For example, if you already have an R-13 value of insulation in a particular location and you want it to be R-35, you can use a layer of R-22 to achieve an R-35 value.

Upgraded Insulation Guidelines

The U.S. Department of Energy (DOE) has recently upgraded its insulation recommendations to homeowners, adapting its suggested minimum R-value to accommodate the country's various climates. The new R-values are now specific to ZIP code areas and take into account climate, heating and cooling needs, types of heating used, and energy prices. The DOE estimates that 50 to 70 percent of the energy used in the average American home is for heating and cooling. Yet most of the houses in the United States are not insulated to recommended levels. In an attic insulation study, for example, it was found that the average insulation level in attics is about R-20, but the DOE now recommends an average of R-40. The new guidelines cover other areas of the home as well, including ceilings, floors, exterior walls, and crawlspaces. Because insulation is relatively inexpensive, the cost/benefit ratio makes increased insulation levels worthwhile.

WEB LINK
www.energy.gov

Information about DOE programs can be found at *www.energy.gov.*

Asbestos and Urea Formaldehyde Foam Insulation

Two kinds of home insulation to be avoided are asbestos and urea formaldehyde foam insulation, or UFFI. Asbestos insulation, embedded in ceilings and walls by builders of another era, is no longer used because it is believed to cause cancer if its fibers get into the lungs. UFFI also may be a potential health hazard, and its use is banned in most parts of the United States. It often emits noxious odors and toxic fumes, causing nausea and other irritations if inhaled. If you suspect a house has either asbestos or urea formaldehyde foam insulation, bring in a qualified inspector to examine all questionable areas. More information about both of these substances can be found at *www.epa.gov.*

WEB LINK
www.epa.gov

■ ROOF FRAMING

Residential roofs are made in several styles, including gable, saltbox, hip, and flat, as shown in Figure 5.10. Roof construction includes the *rafters* [30], *sheathing* [40], and *exterior trim* or *frieze board* [42].

Exterior Trim

The overhang of a pitched roof that extends beyond the exterior walls of the house is called an *eave* [24], or *cornice,* shown in Figure 5.11. The cornice is composed of the soffit, the frieze board, the fascia board, and the extended rafters. The *frieze board* [42] is the exterior wood-trim board used to finish the exterior wall between the top of the siding or masonry and eave, or overhang,

FIGURE 5.10
Roof Designs

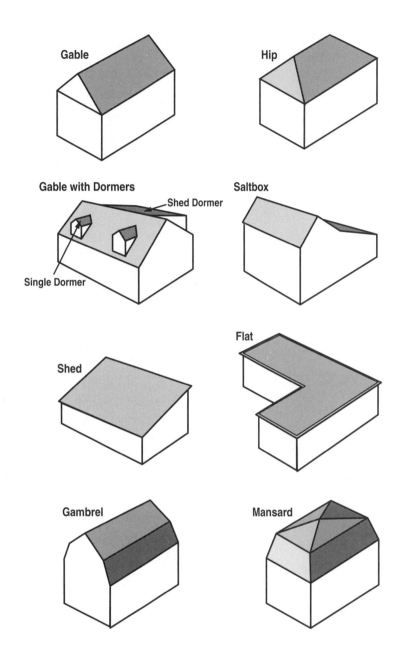

of the roof framing. The *fascia board* is an exterior wood trim used along the line of the butt end of the rafters where the roof overhangs the structural walls. The overhang of the cornice provides a decorative touch to the exterior of a house as well as some protection from sun and rain.

■ EXTERIOR WINDOWS AND DOORS

Windows and doors contribute to the overall tone of a house as well as provide a specific function. Skillfully placed doors regulate traffic patterns through the house and provide protection from intruders. Windows, in turn, admit light and a view of the exterior.

FIGURE 5.11
Eave or Cornice

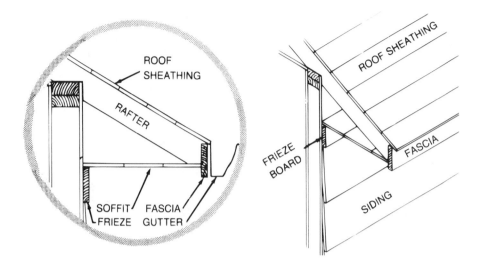

Types of Windows

Windows, shown in Figure 5.12, come in a wide variety of types and sizes, in both wood and metal (usually aluminum). Wood is preferred where temperatures fall below freezing. Although metal windows require less maintenance than wood, the frames get colder in winter and panes frost and drip from moisture condensation. Windows may be *sliding, swinging,* or *fixed.* A window might span more than one category if part of it is fixed and another part slides.

Sliding Windows

The *double-hung* window and the *single-hung window* are still the most common for new construction and for remodeling, particularly in traditional houses. The *double-hung window* has an upper and lower sash, both of which slide vertically along separate tracks. This arrangement allows cool air to come in at the bottom and warm air to go out through the top. Unfortunately, only half the window can be opened at any one time for ventilation, and it cannot be left open during a hard rain. *Single-hung* models also feature an upper and lower sash, but only the lower sash is operative. The *horizontal sliding window* moves back and forth on tracks. As with the double and single-hung types, only 50 percent of this window may be opened for fresh air. However, sliding windows usually provide more light and a better view of the outside.

Swinging Windows

Casements and jalousies are two common types of swinging windows. *Casement windows* are hinged at the side and open outward. One advantage of the casement window is that the entire window can be opened for ventilation. *Jalousie* or *louver* windows consist of a series of overlapping horizontal glass louvers that pivot together in a common frame and are opened and closed with a lever or crank. In a sunroom or sunporch, the jalousie combines protection from the weather with maximum ventilation.

Fixed Windows

A *fixed window* usually consists of a wood sash with a large single pane of insulated glass that cannot be opened for ventilation. It provides natural light and

FIGURE 5.12
Types of Windows

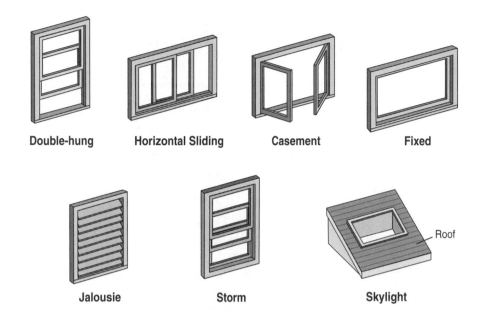

Double-hung   Horizontal Sliding   Casement   Fixed

Jalousie   Storm   Skylight

at the same time gives a clear view of the outside. Fixed windows are often used in combination with other windows.

Storm Windows

A winter necessity in most parts of the country, *storm windows* fit either on the inside or on the outside of the prime windows. Storm windows are usually made of aluminum, although older houses sometimes have wooden ones and newer houses may have the plastic type.

Storm windows can reduce summer air-conditioning bills as well as winter heating costs. Many homeowners who have air-conditioning now leave their storm windows on year-round.

The extraordinary damage created by recent hurricanes has resulted in new window glass and covering requirements in Florida and other states. The appraiser should be aware of the impact of these and other requirements on market value.

Skylights

Skylights can bring both natural illumination and the heat of the sun into rooms. A skylight lets about five times as much daylight into an area as a window of the same size. As a result, a skylight can make a small space appear brighter and larger than it actually is. A skylight is also an excellent way to bring light into a room with an obstructed or unsightly view.

Types of Doors

Exterior doors are made from wood or metal and are usually 1¾ inches thick. Interior doors usually have a thickness of 1⅜ inches.

Doors are most often classified by construction and appearance—the four most common types are *flush, panel, sliding glass,* and *storm and screen* (see Figure 5.13).

FIGURE 5.13
Types of Doors

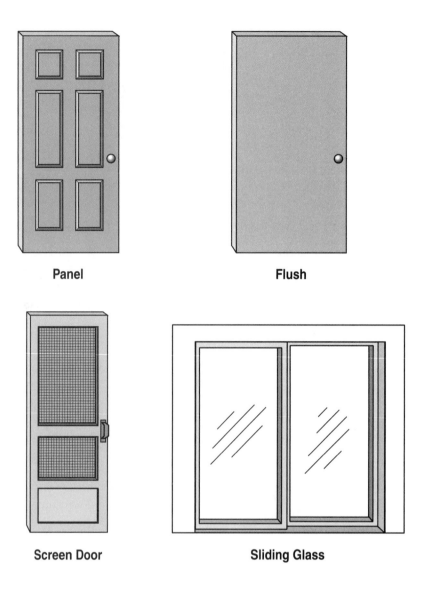

Panel

Flush

Screen Door

Sliding Glass

Flush Doors

Flush doors are most often constructed of hardwood-face panels bonded to *solid* cores or *hollow* cores of light framework. Solid cores are generally preferred for exterior doors because they provide better heat and sound insulation and are more resistant to warping. Hollow-core doors are about one-third as heavy as the solid-core type and are commonly used for interior locations, where heat and sound insulation are not critical.

Panel Doors

Available in a variety of designs, *panel* doors may be used for either interior or exterior application. They consist of *stiles* (solid *vertical* members of wood or metal) and *rails* (solid *horizontal* members of wood or metal) enclosing flat plywood or raised wood panel fillers or, in some types, a combination of wood and glass panels.

Sliding Glass Doors

Sliding glass doors have at least one fixed panel and one or more panels that slide in a frame of wood or metal. Like a window sash, the door panels are composed of stiles and rails and may hold either single or insulating glass.

Storm and Screen Doors

Storm doors are made either with fixed glass panels, to improve weather resistance, or with both screen and glass inserts, to permit ventilation and insect control. In areas with moderate year-round temperatures, *screen doors* (without glass inserts) are frequently used. Combination doors combine the functions of both storm and screen doors with interchangeable glass and screen panels. Self-storing storm doors contain the equivalent of a two-track window, accommodating two inserts in one track and another in the adjacent track. The glass and screen inserts slide up and down just as they do in a vertical storm window.

■ INTERIOR WALLS AND FINISHING

Interior walls are the partitioning dividers for individual rooms and are usually covered with *plasterboard* [46], although the older, more expensive process of covering strips of wood lath with plaster also may be used. The terms *drywall* and *wallboard* are synonymous with plasterboard. Plasterboard is finished by a process known as *taping and floating*. Taping covers the joints between the sheets of plasterboard. Floating is the smoothing out of the walls by the application of a plaster texture over the joints and rough edges where nails attach the plasterboard to the wall studs. Texturing created by a heavy layer of a plaster-like finish coat may be applied with a roller onto the plasterboard prior to painting.

The final features added to a home include *floor covering, trim, cabinet work,* and *wall finishings* of paint, wallpaper, or paneling.

Floor coverings of vinyl, asphalt tile, wood (either in strips or blocks), carpet, brick, stone, or terrazzo tile are applied over the wood or concrete subflooring.

Trim masks the joints between the walls and ceiling and gives a finished decorator touch to the room. Trim, which is usually wood, should be selected in a style that is complementary to the overall decor of the house.

Cabinet work in the home may be either custom built on-site or off-site or prefabricated in a mill. Cabinets should be well constructed to open and close properly and should correspond with the style of the house.

Wall coverings are one of the most important decorator items in the home. Paint and wallpaper should be selected for both beauty and utility. Prefinished wood fiber and plastic panels such as polyethylene-covered plywood paneling are now widely used in less formal rooms. Ceramic tiles are still used extensively as wall and floor coverings in bathrooms.

■ PLUMBING

The plumbing system in a house is actually a number of separate systems, each designed to serve a special function. The *water supply system* brings water to the house from the city main or from a well and distributes hot and cold water through two sets of pipes. The *drainage system* collects waste and used water from fixtures and carries it away to a central point for disposal outside the house. The *vent piping system* carries out of the house all sewer gases that develop in drainage lines. It also equalizes air pressure within the waste system so that waste

Lead-Based Paint

The presence of lead in paint used in housing is of major concern because of the danger of lead exposure to adults and especially children. The danger to adults includes high blood pressure, memory and concentration problems, and difficulty during pregnancy. The danger to children includes damage to the brain and nervous system, behavior and learning problems, slowed growth, and hearing loss. Deteriorating paint releases lead; renovations can release large amounts of lead into the home as well as the surrounding soil. Encapsulation using special paints that prevent lead from leaching through to the surface may be the best preventative.

As of 1978, the use of lead-based paint in housing has been prohibited by the federal government. It has been estimated that 83 percent of homes built prior to 1978 (64 million homes in all) contain lead-based paint. The Residential Lead-Based Paint Hazard Reduction Act of 1992 requires disclosure of the possible presence of lead-based paint in homes built before 1978. As of September 6, 1996, sellers and landlords owning five or more residential dwelling units must comply with disclosure requirements; the law went into effect on December 6, 1996, for sellers and landlords owning four or fewer residential dwelling units. Compliance is the responsibility of the Environmental Protection Agency (EPA). Information on legal requirements is available from the National Lead Information Center, (202) 659-1192, or

www.epa.gov/lead/nlic.htm, as well as EPA branches and state health departments.

While the law does not require that the seller or landlord conduct any testing or hazard reduction, the seller or landlord must disclose any known presence of lead and provide copies of available lead hazard evaluations and reports. The prospective buyer or renter must

- receive an EPA disclosure pamphlet (or state-approved alternative);
- have ten days in which to arrange a property inspection; and
- sign a lead warning statement and acknowledgment.

Real estate agents must inform the seller or landlord of the requirements, make sure that the buyer or renter has received the necessary documentation, and retain the signed disclosure/acknowledgment statement for three years.

It is not yet clear what the impact of the disclosure law will be on the market value of affected homes. Because all homes in a given neighborhood may contain lead-based paint, prospective homebuyers and renters may have little practical alternative. Given enough publicity, however, particularly about the potential harmful effects of lead in paint, the impact could be significant.

will flow away and not back up into fixtures. The *waste collecting* system is needed only when the main waste drain in the house is lower than sewer level under the street or when the house has more than one drainage system. The *house connection pipe system,* a single pipe, is the waste connection from the house to the city sewer line, to a septic tank, or to some other waste disposal facility.

Plumbing must be installed subject to strict inspections and in accordance with local building codes, which dictate the materials to be used and the method of installation. Sewer pipes are of cast iron, concrete, or plastic, while water pipes are of copper, plastic, or galvanized iron. Recently, wrought-drawn copper and plastic have been used more frequently because they eliminate piping joints in the foundation slab.

Plumbing Fixtures

Bathtubs, toilets, and sinks are made of cast iron or pressed steel coated with enamel. Fiberglass is a new material for these fixtures and is gaining in popularity. Plumbing fixtures have relatively long lives and often are replaced because of their obsolete style long before they have worn out.

Water Heater

Water is almost always heated by gas or electricity. Water heaters come in several capacities, ranging from 17 gallons up to 80 gallons for residential use. A 30-gallon water heater is usually the minimum size installed. After water is heated to a predetermined temperature, the heater automatically shuts off. As hot water is drained off, cold water replaces it, and the heating unit turns on automatically.

■ HEATING AND AIR-CONDITIONING

Warm-air heating systems are most prevalent in today's houses. A forced warm-air system consists of a furnace, warm-air distributing ducts, and ducts for the return of cool air. Each furnace has a capacity rated in British Thermal Units (BTUs). The number of BTUs represents the furnace's heat output from gas, oil, or electric firing. A heating and cooling engineer can determine from a building's volume, construction, insulation, and window and door sizes the furnace capacity required to provide heat for the building in the coldest possible weather.

All gas pipes for heating and cooking are made of black iron. Gas pipes are installed in the walls or overhead in the attic, where adequate ventilation is possible. They are never placed in the slab.

Almost all new homes today are centrally air-conditioned. Air-conditioning units are rated either in BTUs or in tons. Twelve thousand BTUs are the equivalent of a one-ton capacity. An engineer can determine the measurements and problems inherent in the construction and layout of the space and from this information can specify the cooling capacity required to adequately service the space or building.

Combination heating and cooling systems are common in new homes. The most prevalent is the conventional warm-air heating system with a cooling unit attached. The same ducts and blower that distribute warm air are used to distribute cool air. The cooling unit is similar to a large air conditioner.

Many heating experts believe the heat pump will eventually replace today's conventional combination heating and cooling systems. The small heat pump is a single piece of equipment that uses the same components for heating or cooling. The most commonly used system for small heat pumps takes heat out of the ground or air in winter to warm the air in the house and takes warm air out of the house in summer, replacing it with cooler air. The main drawback to the heat pump has been its initial cost. Once installed, however, it operates very economically and requires little maintenance. It works most efficiently in climates where winter weather is not severe, but new improvements make it adequate even in northern states.

Solar Heating

The increased demand for fossil fuels in recent years has forced builders to look for new sources of energy. One of the most promising sources of heat for residential buildings is *solar energy*. There are two methods for gathering solar energy: *passive* and *active*. Figure 5.5 shows the simplest form of solar heating—a *passive* system in which windows on the south side of a building take advantage of winter sunlight. A passive system can be improved inside the house by having water-filled containers that are warmed by the sun during the day and radiate warmth into the room during the night. Such a system takes up space inside the home, however, and is not compatible with most decorating schemes.

Bacteria, Fungi, and Molds

These biological agents live in air ducts, air-conditioning and heating units, and humidifiers and between wallboards and drywall. They can cause disease, allergic reactions, and respiratory illness.

The appraiser may not have the knowledge or experience needed to determine the cost of correcting environmental problems such as those discussed in this chapter. What the appraiser can do, however, is conduct a conscientious inspection of the subject property and recommend that the client bring in a qualified environmental consultant if contamination is suspected.

Even after an environmental problem has been corrected, however, the property may still suffer from what appraisers call *stigmatization*. This term refers to a continuing decline in the value of a property because of a falsely perceived environmental problem; that is, a stigmatized property may continue to lose value even though the environmental problem has been fixed or perhaps never even existed.

Stigmatization can also refer to property that has acquired an undesirable reputation because of some event that occurred on or near it, such as a violent crime or personal tragedy. A rumor suggesting that a house is haunted is another example of stigmatization.

Stigmatization issues are not about a property's physical defects but rather about opinions or perceptions, however misguided, that brand the property as undesirable. Certain issues may be the subject of state laws intended to protect property owners, in which case the appraiser could be held liable for improper disclosure. The appraiser should seek legal council when dealing with such properties.

If those considerations are unimportant and if there is adequate available sunlight, a passive solar heating system can be installed easily and at a low cost.

Most solar heating units suitable for residential use are *active* systems that operate by gathering the heat from the sun's rays with one or more *solar collectors,* as shown in Figure 5.14. Water or air is forced through a series of pipes in the solar collector to be heated by the sun's rays. The hot air or water is then stored in a heavily insulated storage tank until it is needed to heat the house. The heat production of a solar system is limited by both storage capacity and the need for good (sunny) weather, which means that most such systems must have an independent heating unit for backup. There is as yet no economical system that uses solar power to air-condition a home.

Solar heaters for swimming pools continue to provide a low-cost way of heating pool water. Solar pool heaters, in fact, constitute the largest single use for solar equipment.

■ ELECTRICAL SYSTEM

A good residential electrical system has three important characteristics. First, it must meet all National Electrical Code (NEC) safety requirements: each major appliance should have its own circuit, and lighting circuits should be isolated from electrical equipment that causes fluctuations in voltage. Second, the system must meet the home's existing needs and have the capacity to accommodate room additions and new appliances. Finally, it should be convenient; there should be enough switches, lights, and outlets located so that occupants will not have to walk in the dark or use extension cords.

Electrical service from the power company is brought into the home through the transformer and the meter into a *circuit breaker box* (or a *fuse panel* in older homes). The circuit breaker box is the distribution panel for the many electrical circuits in the house. In case of a power overload, the heat generated by the additional flow of electrical power will cause the circuit breaker to open at the breaker box, thus reducing the possibility of electrical fires. It is the responsibility of the architect or the builder to adhere to local building codes,

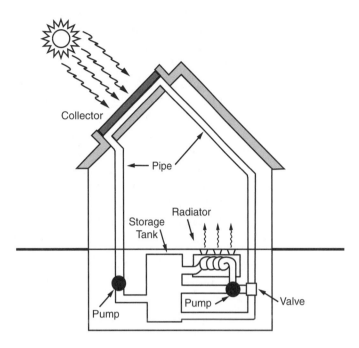

FIGURE 5.14
Active Solar Hot Water
Heating System

which regulate electrical wiring. All electrical installations are inspected by the local building authorities, which assures the homeowner of the system's compliance with the building code.

Power Requirements

Residential wiring circuits are rated by the voltage they are designed to carry. In the past, most residences were wired for only 110-volt capacity. Today, because of the many built-in appliances in use, 220-volt to 240-volt service is generally necessary. *Amperage*, the strength of a current expressed in amperes, is shown on the circuit breaker panel. The circuit breaker panel (or fuse panel) should have a capacity of at least 100 amperes. A larger service (150 to 200 or more amperes) may be needed if there is electric heat, an electric range, or if the house has more than 3,000 square feet. New wiring will be required if the existing board is only 30 to 60 amperes in capacity. If there are fewer than eight or ten circuits, it will probably be necessary to add more. Each circuit is represented by a separate circuit breaker or fuse. A house with a lot of electrical equipment may require 15 to 20 or more circuits.

Electric and Magnetic Fields

While the power of lightning is unmistakable, most people fail to realize that electricity is always around us and that the earth's magnetic field creates measurable electrical currents no matter where we are. While there is as yet no conclusive evidence of any harmful effects of *electric and magnetic fields (EMFs),* some studies have suggested a correlation between high levels of EMFs and certain types of cancers, such as leukemia. It should be noted that the EMFs linked to a slight increase in incidence of leukemia in one study were produced by continued exposure to high-voltage transmission lines, and not to the kind of fields created by ordinary home wiring and appliances. The most recent study to date indicates that there are, in fact, no measurable effects of even prolonged exposure to high-voltage transmission lines. Nevertheless, public perception of a problem (even if in error) may have an effect on the value of property located close to high-voltage transmission lines.

In the United States, high-voltage transmission lines operate at voltages between 50 and 765 kilovolts (kV), with each kV equal to 1,000 volts. Distribution lines that feed off transmission lines operate at less than 50 kV. Both types of lines carry considerably more power than the ordinary household system of 240 volts. To err on the side of safety, even with regard to ordinary household current and appliances, local utility companies are beginning to offer EMF assessments in which measurements of EMFs are made throughout the home. As a simple precaution, for instance, residents may be warned against having appliances such as a clock radio or telephone too close to the head of a bed or other location where prolonged exposure is possible.

EXERCISE 5.2

1. Where are solid-core and hollow-core doors generally used? Why?

2. Two of the separate plumbing systems in a house are the vent piping system and the water supply system. What is the purpose of each?

3. What is the major disadvantage of the heat pump?

4. List three important characteristics of a residential electrical system.

5. What is the basic difference between balloon and platform construction? Which is preferred?

Define the following features of residential construction and give the purpose of each:

6. Firestopping

7. Circuit breaker box

8. Insulation

9. Monolithic slab

10. Sill

Check your answers against those in the Answer Key at the back of the book.

Basic Terms

The following terms and concepts were introduced or discussed in this chapter. If you are not sure of the meaning or application of any of these terms, restudy that section of the chapter.

110-volt wiring	fascia board	platform frame
220-volt wiring	firestops	plasterboard
amperage	floating	post and beam frame
anchor bolt	floating slab	rafter
architectural style	floor joist	rails
asbestos	flush doors	ribbon board
balloon frame	footing	ridge
BTUs	foundation wall	R-value
building code	frame	sheathing
building plan (blueprint)	framing	siding
building specifications	frieze board	sill (beam)
casement window	insulation	sliding window
circuit breaker box	jalousie window	solar collector
collar beam	joist and rafter roof	solar heating
concrete slab foundation	lead-based paint	stiles
cornice	monolithic slab	stud
crawlspace	panel doors	taping
double-hung window	pedestal	truss roof framing
drainage system	pier	urea formaldehyde
eave	pier and beam foundation	veneer
electric and magnetic fields	piling	vent piping system
(EMFs)	plate	weep hole
exposed rafter roof framing		

■ SUMMARY

To appraise real estate successfully, an appraiser must know the fundamentals of building construction, from the design and approval process to basic construction techniques and materials. Carefully prepared plans and specifications must adhere to at least the minimum construction standards established by local building codes. Appropriate engineering is necessary to determine site and foundation requirements.

F I G U R E 5.15
Construction of a House

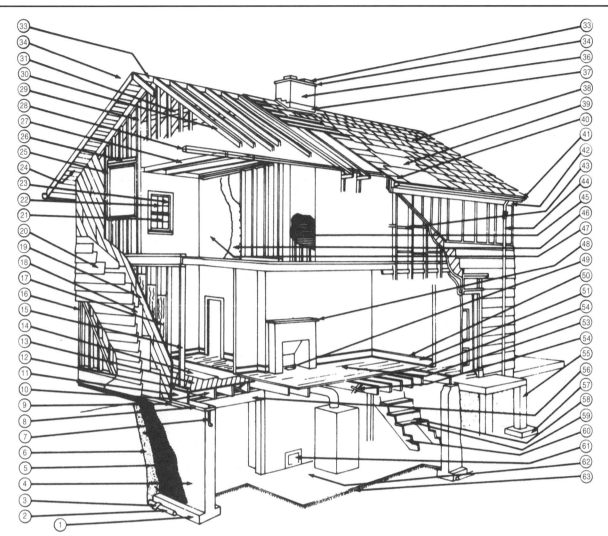

1. FOOTING
2. FOUNDATION DRAIN TILE
3. CRUSHED WASHED STONE
4. FOUNDATION WALL
5. DAMPPROOFING OR WEATHERPROOFING
6. BACKFILL
7. ANCHOR BOLT
8. SILL PLATE
9. TERMITE SHIELD
10. FLOOR JOIST
11. BAND OR BOX BEAM
12. SOLE PLATE
13. SUBFLOORING
14. BUILDING PAPER
15. WALL STUD
16. CORNER STUDS
17. INSULATION
18. HOUSE WRAP
19. WALL SHEATHING
20. SIDING
21. MULLION

22. MUNTIN
23. WINDOW SASH
24. EAVE (ROOF PROJECTION)
25. WINDOW JAMB TRIM
26. WINDOW HEADER
27. CEILING JOIST
28. TOP AND TIE PLATES
29. GABLE STUD
30. RAFTERS
31. COLLAR TIES
32. GABLE END OF ROOF
33. RIDGE BEAM
34. CHIMNEY FLUES
35. CHIMNEY CAP
36. CHIMNEY
37. CHIMNEY FLASHING
38. ROOFING SHINGLES
39. ROOFING FELT/ICE AND WATER MEMBRANE
40. ROOF SHEATHING
41. EAVE TROUGH OR GUTTER
42. FRIEZE BOARD

43. FIRESTOP
44. DOWNSPOUT
45. LATHS
46. PLASTERBOARD
47. PLASTER FINISH
48. MANTEL
49. ASH DUMP
50. BASE TOP MOULDING
51. BASEBOARD
52. SHOE MOULDING
53. FINISH MOULDING
54. CROSS BRIDGING
55. PIER
56. GIRDER
57. FOOTING
58. RISER
59. TREAD
60. STRINGER
61. CLEANOUT DOOR
62. CONCRETE BASEMENT FLOOR
63. CRUSHED WASHED STONE

A variety of house styles fall within the two broad categories of traditional and contemporary, with budget, space, and living requirements dictating size. A house should be oriented to take maximum advantage of its site, including the potential for solar heat.

The typical wood-frame house will make use of construction techniques based on a concrete slab or pier and beam foundation. A wide variety of exterior and interior wall finishes is available to suit homeowner requirements. Doors and windows also offer opportunities for individualization.

Plumbing fixtures must take into account the type of water available while suiting the needs of the residents. The choice of heating and/or cooling system is also important. The electrical system should be adequate for present as well as anticipated usage.

Environmental hazards, such as radon gas, urea formaldehyde foam insulation, lead-based paint, and mold and other biological contaminants can negatively affect the value of real estate. Appraisers are not expected to be experts in the detection of hazardous substances. If any of these conditions are suspected, a formal environmental assessment may be recommended and the appraisal made subject to the results of that determination.

5

ACHIEVEMENT EXAMINATION

1. The standard of measurement for a single-family detached residence is the

   a. gross building area.

   b. gross living area.

   c. gross leasable area.

   d. gross construction area.

For each of the following, describe the construction technique illustrated in Figure 5.15.

2. Foundation

3. Wall framing

4. Exterior walls

5. Interior walls

6. Windows

7. Floor coverings

Check your answers against those in the Answer Key at the back of the book.

CHAPTER 6

Data Collection

■ OVERVIEW

In this chapter you will review the steps in the appraisal process that require the collection of a variety of data from a variety of sources. You will examine a suggested data bank of sources, which you may supplement.

You will also learn how to use forms to help ensure the collection of adequate data regarding the subject property's neighborhood as well as the subject site and building.

In this chapter you will begin to trace the progress of a typical appraisal using the sales comparison approach by following the applicable steps outlined in the appraisal flowchart introduced in Chapter 4. A single-family residence and lot will be discussed as the sales comparison method and the general techniques used in valuing vacant sites are covered in this chapter and Chapters 7 and 10. At the end of Chapter 10, you will be given the information needed to complete your own appraisal analysis of a single-family residence using the sales comparison approach.

■ STEP 1: STATE THE PROBLEM

Prior to accepting an assignment, the appraiser must determine whether he or she has the skills necessary to perform the job competently. According to USPAP's *Competency Rule*, an appraiser who lacks the necessary knowledge or experience to perform a specific appraisal service must disclose this fact to the client before accepting the job. The appraiser may still accept the assignment, however, by indicating how he or she will gain the competence necessary to complete the assignment, which could be by associating with a qualified appraiser or retaining someone who, in fact, does possess the required knowledge or experience.

Of course, an appraiser may accept an assignment and not realize until later that the job is beyond his or her skill level or that he or she can't spend the time needed to produce competent results. At the point of such discovery, the appraiser is obligated to notify the client, and should also indicate the steps he or she will take to become competent, if the assignment is to be completed.

Once the competency issue has been settled, the first step in the appraisal process is to state the problem. The appraiser will

■ describe the subject property;

■ identify the property rights to be appraised;

■ define the value sought;

■ specify the date of valuation; and

■ determine any conditions limiting the scope of use of the appraisal.

Throughout this book, we assume that the appraiser's task is to determine the market value of the subject property.

Property Rights Conveyed

The majority of residential appraisals are of property held in fee simple ownership; that is, all of the rights of ownership are held by the current property owner. Sometimes, however, the different rights of ownership are separated and held by more than one person.

A frequent example of separation of rights of ownership with respect to residential property involves *mineral rights*. In areas that are suspected of containing oil or gas deposits, a transfer of title to real estate frequently will withhold mineral rights, title to which is retained by the transferor (the person making the transfer). The right to test for and remove the minerals may never be exercised; however, the fact that mineral rights have been separated from the other rights of ownership should be noted by the appraiser. The appraiser should also note any effect that less than fee simple ownership may be expected to have on value. If all properties in the area carry a similar reservation of mineral or other rights, there is likely to be little or no effect on market value.

A common example of a transfer of only a partial interest in commercial property is the transfer of developmental *air rights*. The fact that air rights can be transferred separately may allow a developer to accumulate the development rights of several different parcels to erect a single building that would otherwise violate zoning building height restrictions. The property from which development rights have been transferred will have its value reduced accordingly.

An *easement* creates a benefit to the dominant tenement (the land to which the easement provides ingress and egress) and a detriment to the servient tenement (the land over which the easement runs).

The full rights of ownership also include the right to dispose of the property, such as by sale, lease, or will. If the property has already been leased, however, the *leased fee* estate retained by the lessor (landlord) must be valued in light of the existing lease. The lessee—the holder of the lease—has the *leasehold* interest at the *contract* or *scheduled rent* agreed to between lessor and lessee. The leasehold interest will have value depending on the relationship of the contract rent to the prevailing *market rent* (an estimate of a property's rent potential). If market rents are higher than the rent the current lease provides, the difference between them determines the value of the leasehold interest.

In all of these examples an appraisal must take into account the exact property interest that is being valued.

EXERCISE 6.1   The exercises in this chapter and Chapter 10 give you information on the sample appraisal you will be carrying out as you study the sales comparison approach. You are to complete each exercise, referring to the explanation just covered, if necessary; then check your results against those given in the Answer Key at the back of this book. If necessary, correct your responses before proceeding to the next text discussion.

The single-family residence located at 2130 West Franklin Street, Midstate, Illinois, is to be appraised as part of a loan refinancing. State the problem, indicating the value that is being sought and the appraisal method that will be used to achieve it.

Check your answer against the one in the Answer Key at the back of the book.

■ STEP 2: LIST THE DATA NEEDED AND THE SOURCES

In the second step of the *appraisal* process the appraiser must determine the types of data needed and where they can be located. Regardless of the specific appraisal approach used, certain data must always be obtained—information about the region, city, and neighborhood, as well as facts about the property being appraised. When the sales comparison approach is used, sales data on comparable properties also must be obtained.

■ STEP 3: GATHER, RECORD, AND VERIFY THE NECESSARY DATA

The appraisal process, as discussed in Chapter 4, requires the collection or verification of data at almost every stage. Knowledge of the sources of available data and their reliability is essential if an appraisal is to be performed properly.

In step 3 of the appraisal process, as shown in the flowchart in Figure 4.1, the appraiser will need the following information:

- General data on the nation, region, city, and neighborhood
- Specific data on the subject site and improvements
- Sales data for the sales comparison approach
- Cost and accrued depreciation data for the cost approach
- Income and expense data for the income capitalization approach

Without knowledge of the sources and reliability of available data, the appraiser would be unable to perform the job properly. The type of property being appraised dictates the emphasis to be placed on the types of data collected. A factory in an industrial area, for instance, will require more services than a home in a residential area. Thus the appraiser makes an integrated analysis, moving from general data to data required for the specific appraisal approach, always keeping the subject property in mind.

■ THE DATA SOURCE LIST

Figure 6.1 lists the sources of information the appraiser may use. It also presents all of the different kinds of data needed in each step of the appraisal process and lists the sources for those items of data. Forty-five sources to which an appraiser should have access make up the Data Source List. Some of the sources already may be familiar to you; if you have ever owned real estate yourself, you will recognize even more of them. You will be referring to this source list throughout the rest of this book.

Kinds of Data Needed

Following the Data Source List are five lists that detail the types of specific information needed in each category. Each type of information called for is keyed to one or more of the 45 sources of information itemized in the source list.

EXAMPLE

In inspecting a site in a new subdivision, you notice that construction work is going on along the sides of the roadway. There are no workers present, however. How can you find out what kind of work is under way?

In the chart for specific data about the subject site, you would look up "Improvements" and find that there are four possible sources of information—numbers 1, 12, 20, and 28 in the source list. The sources are (1) personal inspection, (12) city hall or county courthouse, (20) county or city engineering commission, and (28) public utility companies. Because you have already inspected the property personally, you would contact the other sources, the most pertinent one first. In this case, the county or city engineering commission could probably tell you the reason for the construction activity. The department that issues building permits should have the information you need.

National and Regional Trends

The real estate marketplace may be defined primarily by local custom and needs, but it is strongly influenced by national and regional matters. An important area of national influence is real estate financing. The secondary market in residential mortgages and the necessity to market some commercial properties on a national basis also have given real estate financing a truly national perspective.

Demographic studies have revealed both short-term and long-term patterns in population movements across the country. Workers generally will follow employment opportunities, and in the 1970s and 1980s the oil states (Texas, Louisiana, Oklahoma, Colorado) attracted a great many former auto and steel industry personnel from states like Michigan, Ohio, and Pennsylvania. When the oil industry also proved vulnerable, some workers stayed on, but many returned to their former places of residence. The same phenomenon occurred as the new century began, when some of the high-flying high-tech companies in the San Francisco Bay Area succumbed to the effects of too much competition and vastly overoptimistic market projections. Many of the software engineers and programmers who were drawn to Silicon Valley in the 1990s returned to the stronger job markets of the East Coast (Boston) and Midwest (Chicago).

Factors other than employment also dictate population shifts. The demographics of an aging populace indicate that a certain percentage of retirees from the Midwest and Northeast continue to choose to relocate to an affordable warmer climate, such as Arizona, Nevada, or Florida, contributing to the rapid population growth in those areas.

The national economy affects the real estate marketplace most visibly during periods of recession and inflation. When demand for goods and services declines on a national basis, it may be impossible for a region or state to avoid at least some of the consequences.

F I G U R E   6.1
Data Bank

DATA SOURCE LIST

1. Personal inspection
2. Seller
3. Buyer
4. Broker
5. Salesperson
6. Register of deeds
7. Title reports
8. Transfer maps or books
9. Leases
10. Mortgages
11. Banks, savings and loans, and other lending institutions
12. City hall or county courthouse
13. Assessor's office
14. Published information on transfers, leases, or assessed valuation
15. Property managers or owners
16. Building and architectural plans
17. Accountants
18. Financial statements
19. Building architects, contractors, and engineers
20. County or city engineering commission
21. Regional or county government officials
22. Area planning commissions
23. Highway commissioner's office, road commission
24. Newspaper advertisements
25. Multiple-listing systems
26. Cost manuals (state, local, private)
27. Local material suppliers
28. Public utility companies
29. United States Bureau of the Census
30. Department of Commerce
31. Federal Housing Administration
32. Local chamber of commerce
33. Government councils
34. Local board of REALTORS®
35. National, state, or local association of home builders
36. Public transportation officials
37. Other appraisers
38. Professional journals
39. Railroad and transit authorities or companies
40. Labor organizations
41. Employment agencies
42. Plats
43. Neighbors
44. Area maps (topographic, soil)
45. Airlines and bus lines, moving companies

A. REGIONAL, CITY, NEIGHBORHOOD DATA

Types of Information	Sources	Types of Information	Sources
Topography	44	Electrical power consumption and new hookups	28
Natural resources	32, 44	Assessments	12, 13
Climate	32	Utilities or improvements available (streets, curbs, sidewalks; water; electricity; telephone; gas; sewers)	12, 28
Public transportation:		Percent built up	12, 34
Air	32, 45	Neighborhood boundaries	1, 4, 12, 42
Rail	39, 45	Predominant type of building	1, 13, 19, 22
Bus	36, 45	Typical age of buildings	1, 13, 15, 19
Subway	36, 45	Condition of buildings	1, 22, 33, 37
Route maps	1, 36	Price range of typical properties	4, 7, 15, 31, 34
Expressways	23, 44	Marketability	4, 15
Traffic patterns	12, 20, 22, 23, 36	Life cycle	4, 37
Population trends	22, 29, 32, 33	Land value trend	4, 13, 37
Family size	22	Location of facilities: churches; schools; shopping; recreational; cultural	1, 22, 44
Zoning	12, 20, 22	Avenues of approach	1, 20
Building codes	12, 19, 20	Types of services offered	28
Political organization, policies, and personnel	12, 21	Availability of personnel	22, 32
Employment level	11, 32, 33, 40	Employee amenities (shopping, eating, and banking facilities)	1
Professions, trades, or skills required	32	Marketing area	22, 32
Level of business activity and growth	11, 32	Competition	1, 32
Average family income	22, 29, 30, 32	Types of industry (light, heavy)	32
Rents and lease features	9, 15, 34	Sources of raw materials	32
Percentage of vacancies	4, 31, 34	Hazards and nuisances	1, 43
New building (amount and kind)	15, 30, 34, 35	Deed restrictions	6, 7
Building permits issued	12, 20	Changing use of area	4
Bank deposits and loans	11, 32		
Percentage of home ownership	4, 29, 34		
Tax structure and rates	12, 13		
Building permits issued	12, 20		

FIGURE 6.1
Data Bank (continued)

B. SITE DATA

Types of Information	Sources
Legal description	6
Dimensions and area	1, 6, 42
Street frontage	1, 6, 42
Location in block	6, 42
Topography	6, 44
Topsoil and drainage	19, 44
Landscaping	
Improvements:	1
Streets, curbs, sidewalks	1, 12, 20
Water; electricity; telephone; gas	28
Sewers	1, 12, 20
Tax rates and assessed valuation	12, 13
Liens and special assessments	7, 13
Zoning, codes, or regulations	12, 20, 22
Easements and encroachments	6
Status of title	7

D. SALES AND COST DATA

Types of Information	Sources
Date of sale	1 to 6, 25
Sales price	1 to 6, 25
Name of buyer and seller	1 to 6, 25
Deed book and page	6, 8, 37
Reasons for sale and purchase	2 to 5
Building reproduction cost	19, 26, 27, 40
Building replacement cost	19, 26, 27, 40
Depreciation factors:	1, 16, 19, 22, 26
Physical deterioration	
Functional obsolescence	
External obsolescence	

C. BUILDING DATA

Types of Information	Sources
Architectural style	1
Date of construction and additions	6, 13, 20
Placement of building on land	1, 20, 44
Dimensions and floor area	16, 42
Floor plan(s)	16, 20
Construction materials used (exterior and interior)	16, 19, 27
Utilities available	1, 28, 32
Interior utility and other installations:	1, 13, 16
Heating and air-conditioning	
Plumbing	
Wiring	
Special equipment, such as elevators	
Exceptions to zoning, codes, or regulations	6, 20, 22
Status of title	7
Mortgages and liens	6, 11
Condition of building	1, 13, 22

E. INCOME AND EXPENSE DATA

Types of Information	Sources
Income data (both subject and comparable properties):	
Annual income	18
Current lease terms	1, 15
Occupancy history	15, 18
Collection loss history	15, 18
Fixed expense data (both subject and comparable properties):	13, 15, 18, 38
Real estate taxes	
Insurance	
Operating expense data (both subject and comparable properties):	13, 15, 18, 38
Management	
Payroll	
Legal and accounting	
Maintenance	
Repairs	
Supplies	
Painting and decorating	
Fuel	
Electricity	
Miscellaneous	
Reserves for replacement	1, 18, 26

Surfing the Net

Of course, no source list would be current without reference to the many World Wide Web sites now available via the Internet. From its beginnings 30 years ago as a way for military information to be transmitted, then a method of communication for university researchers, the Internet has been segmented into the electronic access routes and sites that we now refer to as the World Wide Web and is accessible to virtually anyone with a computer.

It would be impossible to list even a relatively small portion of the Web sites of interest to ap-

praisers in this book. Most federal agencies, states, and many municipalities now have their own Web sites, for example, and provide a continually replenished supply of census, employment, building, and other data.

In the Web Sites section in Appendix B we have listed the names and Web addresses of those organizations we feel would be most useful to an appraiser. No doubt you will add many more Web sites to this list as you progress through the text.

Economic Base

The level of business activity in a community—particularly activity that brings income into the community from surrounding areas—defines its *economic base*. A range of businesses, from retail stores and professional offices to small-scale and large-scale manufacturing plants, can provide employment opportunities as well as the resources that allow local residents and businesses to spend their funds on local goods and services. A community's economic base also helps determine the *tax base* from which the community can draw financial support for establishment and maintenance of infrastructure (roads, bridges) and services essential to both businesses and residents.

Communities that do not have a substantial economic base in relation to their overall size are less able to provide the facilities and services that attract new residents and businesses. The "bedroom suburb" that relies on neighboring towns for products and services also must rely on the willingness and ability of residents to carry a tax load sufficient to meet local needs. The community with a reasonable amount of retail business development benefits from sales tax and other tax revenue. Furthermore, with a strong economic base, a community becomes more desirable for both businesses and residents, and that desirability is reflected in higher property values.

Examination of a community's economic base tells an appraiser something about the community's long-term economic viability and thus its likely ability to sustain real estate values.

Local Area and Neighborhood

Even communities with a population of only a few hundred residents may have well-differentiated geographic and neighborhood divisions. In this age of the tract house, neighborhoods within large communities generally are referred to by the name under which the tract was subdivided or sold. "Elm Knoll Estates" may be referred to by that name by plat map and legal description long after the knoll has been bulldozed for a playground and the last surviving elm has succumbed to disease.

Sometimes a business district defines a local area or neighborhood. Housing growth tends to radiate outward from the business hub.

Access to shopping, schools, and places of employment are all factors that make one area or neighborhood more desirable than another. The defined boundaries of a neighborhood also are important in determining whether other properties can be considered "comparable" to the property being appraised. Later in this chapter you will learn the property characteristics (building size, quality of construction, and so on) the appraiser tries to match when considering sales of recently sold properties. Location is the most important factor in comparing other properties with the subject.

Site and Improvements

Individual building lots often are more valuable when combined with other lots in a single parcel. *Assemblage* is the process of combining adjacent lots, and the increase in value that may result from ownership of the larger parcel is called *plottage.* Individual lot owners are compensated for their properties at least partly on the basis of the ultimate value of the assembled parcel. The last properties to be sold tend to command a higher price than those first sold. Nevertheless, there has been more than one example of the last holdout who wanted such an outrageous price that the offer to purchase was rescinded. More than one office or apartment project has been redesigned around a small home or business building whose owner overestimated the developer's budget and patience.

A highest and best use study should take into account the site's present zoning, physical characteristics, and existing structures. Even a relatively new building in good condition may warrant destruction if a larger building with greater profit potential can be erected on the same site.

Agricultural land entails special considerations. Soil and water testing will reveal the suitability of the land for specific crops as well as the presence of any contaminants. The necessity and availability of water for irrigation and the drainage capacity of the soil also must be taken into account. If the site contains wetlands, they may be subject to federal supervision. Other federal and state regulations may limit agricultural land use to defined purposes.

EXERCISE 6.2

Refer to the Data Bank in Figure 6.1 and list the source(s) for the following.

1. Lot size

2. New construction in the area

3. Proposed zoning changes

4. Population size

5. Nearest schools and places of worship

6. Municipal services

7. Recent zoning changes

8. Utility easements

9. Property tax assessment

Check your answers against those in the Answer Key at the back of the book.

■ DATA FORMS

The best way to make sure that no details of the property, its area, or the approaches to value are overlooked is to use a form for recording the necessary information. Such a form specifies the types of information needed and provides a place to record it. Many appraisers have developed their own forms, or make use of forms created by their clients, to provide a level of standardization and quality control for the finished appraisal report.

The rest of this chapter includes sections of the March 2005 Uniform Residential Appraisal Report (URAR) form that are used to note neighborhood data, site data, and data on the subject property's improvements. Forms for regional and city data are not given here. By using the sources listed in the Data Bank, the appraiser should be able to build an accurate profile of the region and city. Once compiled and analyzed, this information will change infrequently, but inevitably change will occur. It is the appraiser's job to keep up to date on economic indicators such as employment level, business starts (and failures), and political trends that could signal governmental policy changes affecting property values.

Neighborhood Data

Use of a form, such as the Neighborhood section of the URAR form shown in Figure 6.2, will help the appraiser gather some of the basic information needed for every appraisal report. The appraiser probably will not have to compile new neighborhood data for each appraisal, because many of the appraisals to be made will be within the same neighborhood. Some categories of neighborhood data will have to be updated at least annually, and significant change in any recorded data should be noted.

Although the Data Bank in Figure 6.1 supplies sources for much of the neighborhood information, a considerable amount of fieldwork still will be necessary. For example, when checking a neighborhood, the appraiser should note the general condition of all houses in the area. Are the homes large or small? How well are the properties landscaped? Are the lawns well kept? Do the surrounding houses conform architecturally? Answers to these questions tell much about the quality of life in the neighborhood. In most cases, visual inspection should disclose whether the neighborhood is likely to retain its character and value or to decline gradually. Not only is a thorough, firsthand knowledge of the area of tremendous value to an appraiser, it is essential for an accurate determination of the property's value.

Although most of the categories of neighborhood data are self-explanatory, some require background knowledge if the appraiser is to record them accurately. *Neighborhood boundaries,* for instance, are determined by considering the following:

■ Natural boundaries (actual physical barriers—ravines, lakes, rivers, and highways or other major traffic arteries)

■ Differences in land use (changes in zoning from residential to commercial or parkland)

■ Average value or age of homes

When recording neighborhood data, record the street name or other identifiable dividing line and note the type of area adjacent to the subject neighborhood at that boundary. A residential property adjacent to a park usually has a higher value than a similar property adjacent to a gravel pit, for instance.

FIGURE 6.2
Neighborhood Data

Note: Race and the racial composition of the neighborhood are not appraisal factors.											
Neighborhood Characteristics				**One-Unit Housing Trends**				**One-Unit Housing**		**Present Land Use %**	
Location	☐ Urban	☐ Suburban	☐ Rural	Property Values	☐ Increasing	☐ Stable	☐ Declining	PRICE AGE		One-Unit	%
Built-Up	☐ Over 75%	☐ 25–75%	☐ Under 25%	Demand/Supply	☐ Shortage	☐ In Balance	☐ Over Supply	$ (000) (yrs)		2-4 Unit	%
Growth	☐ Rapid	☐ Stable	☐ Slow	Marketing Time	☐ Under 3 mths	☐ 3–6 mths	☐ Over 6 mths	Low		Multi-Family	%
Neighborhood Boundaries								High		Commercial	%
								Pred.		Other	%
Neighborhood Description											
Market Conditions (including support for the above conclusions)											

Stage of Life Cycle

A typical neighborhood usually goes through four distinct periods in its life: *growth, equilibrium* (also called *stability*), *decline,* and *revitalization* (also called *rehabilitation*).

When an area is first developed, property values usually increase until few vacant building sites remain. At that point, the houses in the neighborhood tend to stabilize at their highest monetary value and prices rarely fluctuate downward. With increasing property deterioration, the area usually declines in both value and desirability. The process is enhanced by the availability of new housing nearby, successive ownership by lower-income residents who may not be able to afford the increasing maintenance costs of older homes, and conversion of some properties to rental units, which may not be properly maintained. As properties decrease in value, some may even be put to a different use, such as light industry, which in turn further decreases the attractiveness of the surrounding neighborhood for residential use. The neighborhood's life cycle may start over again due to *revitalization*—a period when demand increases, providing the stimulus needed for neighborhood renovation.

The classic pattern described above is the result of general economic growth coupled with increasing consumer demand and the availability of land for housing and commercial development. In recent years, this pattern has been subjected to volatile market conditions.

The 1980s began with high inflation and mortgage interest rates, placing a damper on home purchases. By the mid-1980s, however, a much lower rate of inflation, declining interest rates, and indicators of a general economic recovery helped revive the sluggish real estate housing market. The number of new building starts rose as demand increased, and the pace of development helped compensate for the slower preceding years. The Tax Reform Act of 1986 greatly limited the use of investment real estate as a tax shelter, but that limitation placed new emphasis on the necessity for prudent property analysis. A competent appraisal is an important means of helping to determine the soundness of an investment.

We are currently benefiting from several years of historically low mortgage interest rates, which helped produce record home sales in 2004. The record numbers of home sales throughout the country have been accompanied by record price appreciation as growing numbers of first-time homebuyers, move-up buyers, second-home buyers, and investors compete for the housing supply. In addition to this rising demand, housing growth may be deliberately limited in some areas for environmental or other reasons. In those areas, the period of equilibrium may be much longer than would otherwise be the case.

The appraiser must be sensitive to all of the factors that determine value, including economic, social, and governmental influences, to accurately gauge their effect on neighborhood development.

Proximity to Hazards and Nuisances

The proximity of the neighborhood, or any part of it, to hazards or nuisances has become very important. The current awareness of environmental factors and the discovery of more factors that are injurious to health or safety have made some properties undesirable. The mere potential for danger (such as that created by chemical storage facilities) may have the effect of lowering property values in nearby areas. The appraiser should be aware of these factors, as well as ones that have been alleviated (such as factory smoke pollution that may have been drastically reduced).

As a general rule, every prospective property developer in every part of the country should arrange for an independent, thorough analysis of the soil and any existing structures to determine the presence of any contaminants. Some of these, such as radon gas, are described in Chapter 5, "Building Construction and the Environment." With ongoing legal battles about who bears the responsibility for removing contaminants, the easiest way to avoid the problem is simply to avoid contaminated property. Unless a contaminant is readily apparent, an appraiser who is not specially trained to conduct an environmental assessment should not offer an opinion on the presence or absence of materials that may be deemed hazardous. Nevertheless, there may be other property detriments or nuisances, such as location in an airport flight path, that should be noted, and their impact on value considered.

Not all nuisances are readily apparent, and some are annoyances rather than hazards to health and safety. Then, too, what is acceptable to one person may be a nuisance to another. The house near the train track that most people avoid because of the noise and danger could be attractive to a train buff. The appraiser must analyze each condition to determine if it has an effect on value by researching the market.

EXERCISE 6.3

Fill out the URAR Neighborhood section that appears in Figure 6.2 with the information supplied here. All of the information pertains to the sample appraisal you will complete in this chapter and Chapter 10. When you have finished, check your completed form against the one given in the Answer Key at the back of the book. Correct all errors and fill in all missing pieces of information on your form.

The neighborhood map on the next page shows the location of 2130 West Franklin Street, Midstate, Illinois, the subject of the sample appraisal. For this appraisal you can assume that the subdivision is the neighborhood under analysis.

Midstate is a city of just over 100,000 people. The boundaries of the subdivision are Lombard Street, Cedar Street, Ellis Avenue, and Parkside Boulevard. Parkside forms a natural boundary to the south, because it separates the subdivision from parkland. Lombard divides the subdivision from expensive highrise apartments to the west, forming another boundary. Ellis to the east separates the subdivision from an area of retail stores, and Cedar Street to the north provides a boundary between the single-family residences of the subdivision and a business district and area of moderately priced apartments. Parkland is gently rolling; built-up areas are level.

This subdivision is still known locally as the "Gunderson" area, which was its name at its founding, but it has since been incorporated as a part of Midstate. In the subdivision map, fewer than 1 percent of the lots are shown as vacant, and sales of those are infrequent. The area has a few two- and three-unit buildings on Lombard Street that are about 20 years old, but the single-family homes have been built within the last 5 to 22 years, and the average age of the houses is seven years. The apartment buildings average $285,000 to $475,000 in value, make up no more than 1 percent of the entire neighborhood, and usually have one apartment that is owner-occupied.

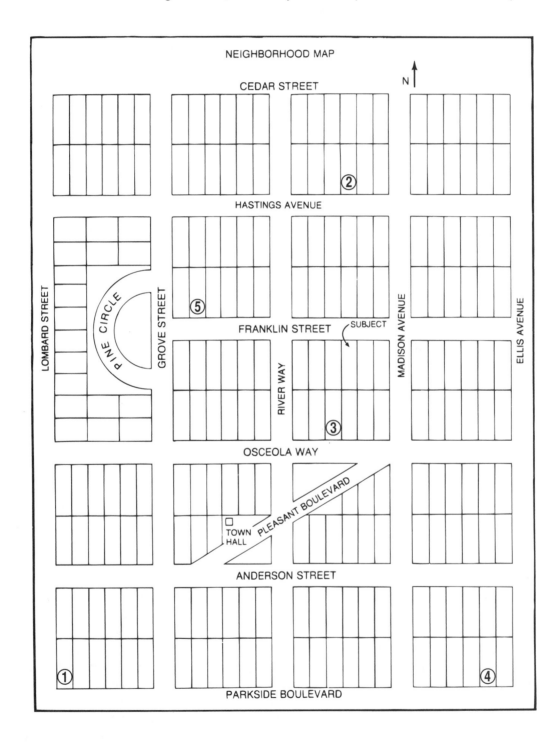

The area is considered very desirable for middle-income families (yearly income $38,000 to $45,000). About 2 percent of homes are rented. Home values are in the $160,000 to $280,000 range, with a predominant value of $240,000. Sales prices have kept up with inflation, and demand has stayed in balance with the number of homes put on the market, although average marketing time is now three months, due primarily to seasonal fluctuation. The property at 2130 West Franklin is typical of at least several dozen other properties in the area, all brick ranch houses with full basements and attached garages, on lots 50 feet by 200 feet. Other houses in the area are either split-level or two-story, the latter usually having aluminum or wood siding.

All utilities have been installed throughout the subdivision, and assessments for water and sewer lines, sidewalk installation, and asphalt street surfacing were made and paid for eight years ago when the improvements were made. The area has been incorporated, so it has city fire and police services as well as garbage collection. The property tax rate is $5 per $100 of assessed valuation, comparable to rates charged in similar nearby neighborhoods.

There is a community hospital two miles southeast at Parkside and Saginaw, and public grade schools and high schools are no more than ¾ of a mile from any home. Two private grade schools are available within a mile, and a parochial high school is within two miles.

The average size of families in this neighborhood is 3.7. Many area residents work in the nearby business district or in the commercial area, where a concentration of 40 retail stores as well as theaters and other recreational facilities offers a wide range of goods and services. Business and commercial areas are within two miles.

There is a smaller group of stores, including a supermarket and gas station, at Madison and Cedar streets and a public library branch at Cedar and Grove. Only about 1 percent of properties are devoted to commercial use.

A superhighway two miles away that bisects the central business district of Midstate connects the area to major interstate routes. There is no public transportation. The highest concentration of office and retail buildings in the business district is no more than 15 minutes by car from any house in the area, and the commercial area takes about the same time to reach. Emergency medical facilities are within a ten minute drive of any home.

There are no health hazards within the neighborhood, either from industry or natural impediments. The busiest street through the neighborhood, Madison, is still mainly residential and generally quiet. No change from current land use is predicted, and there are no nuisances, such as noise-producing factories or construction yards.

The above information should be filled in on the URAR Neighborhood Data section in Figure 6.2. When you have finished, check your form against the completed one in the Answer Key at the back of the book. Correct all errors and fill in all missing pieces of information on your form.

Site Data

The Site section of the URAR form shown in Figure 6.3 can be used to record the information needed to describe the subject site.

First, a complete and legally accurate description of the property's location must be obtained and a sketch made to show the property's approximate shape and street location. A public building or other landmark could also be shown on the sketch to help locate the site. The topography (surface features) of the site should be noted as well as the existence of any natural hazards, such as location in or near a floodplain, earthquake fault zone, or other potentially dangerous condition.

Other important features of the site are its size in square feet, location in terms of position in the block, utilities, improvements, soil composition, and

FIGURE 6.3
Site Data

Dimensions				Area		Shape		View		
Specific Zoning Classification				Zoning Description						
Zoning Compliance ☐ Legal ☐ Legal Nonconforming (Grandfathered Use) ☐ No Zoning ☐ Illegal (describe)										
Is the highest and best use of the subject property as improved (or as proposed per plans and specifications) the present use? ☐ Yes ☐ No If No, describe										
Utilities	**Public**	**Other (describe)**			**Public**	**Other (describe)**		**Off-site Improvements—Type**	**Public**	**Private**
Electricity	☐	☐		Water	☐	☐		Street	☐	☐
Gas	☐	☐		Sanitary Sewer	☐	☐		Alley	☐	☐
FEMA Special Flood Hazard Area ☐ Yes ☐ No FEMA Flood Zone					FEMA Map #			FEMA Map Date		
Are the utilities and off-site improvements typical for the market area? ☐ Yes ☐ No If No, describe										
Are there any adverse site conditions or external factors (easements, encroachments, environmental conditions, land uses, etc.)? ☐ Yes ☐ No If Yes, describe										

view. The historically higher value of a corner lot location may not hold true in residential areas having lots 50 feet or more in width. The comparative privacy of a house on a corner lot is offset if other lots offer distances of 20 feet or more between houses. Then, too, a particular corner may front on busy streets, a detriment to residential property. The opposite would be true for a commercial site, however, where a high traffic count would be desirable.

Soil composition is important because if the soil is unable to support a building, piles will have to be driven to carry the weight. A rock bed within a few feet of the surface may require blasting before a suitable foundation can be established. In either case, the cost of any extraordinary preconstruction site preparation could decrease the site's value.

Special considerations in appraisal of agricultural properties include investigation of soil and water quality as well as water supply and drainage.

Knowledge of the subject site's zoning, which will affect its future use, is necessary, as is knowledge of current zoning of surrounding areas. A site zoned for a single-family residence may be poorly used for that purpose if the neighborhood is declining and multiunit buildings are being built nearby. In such a case, the feasibility of changing the zoning to multiunit residential construction might be analyzed by making a highest and best use study.

Any part of the site that cannot be used for building purposes should be clearly designated, as should any other limitation on site use. Such limitations could raise or lower site value.

The Site Visit

Any visit to the subject property requires the permission of the property owner.

Even if the appraiser inspects only the exterior of structures or walks the property boundaries, to do so without permission can be considered trespassing.

Always contact the owner first. If the property is occupied by a tenant or anyone else other than the owner, you should make sure that your visit is anticipated, for your own pro- tection as well as out of respect for the property occupants.

Any easements or deed restrictions should be noted. An easement, for example, allows airspace or below-ground space for present or future utility installations or a right-of-way for others to travel over the property. A deed restriction, usually established by the property's subdivider, may specify the size of lots used for building, the type or style of building constructed, setbacks from property lines, or other factors designed to increase the subdivision's homogeneity and make property values more stable.

Finally, the appraiser should describe any land area(s) held in common with other property owners. A subdivision may be divided into relatively small building parcels to allow space for a greenbelt (a landscaped area available for the use of all property owners), sports facilities (such as a swimming pool, tennis court, and/or golf course), and even a clubhouse. The proximity of such features to the subject property should also be noted.

EXERCISE 6.4

The following information is applicable to the sample site at 2130 West Franklin Street. Use it to fill in the Site section of the URAR form in Figure 6.3.

The legal description of the lot is

> Lot 114 in Block 2 of Gunderson Subdivision, being part of the Northwest ¼ of the Southeast ¼ of Section 4, Township 37 North, Range 18, East of the Third Principal Meridian as recorded in the Office of the Registrar of Titles of Grove County, Illinois, on April 27, 1970.

The lot is 50 feet by 200 feet, rectangular, with 50 feet of street frontage. (The first lot dimension given is usually street frontage.) There are mercury vapor streetlights but no alley. The street is paved with asphalt, as is the driveway, which is 24 feet wide and 30 feet long. The public sidewalk and curb are concrete. The land is level, with good soil and a good view of the tree-lined street, typical of lots in the area.

Neither storm nor sanitary sewers have ever overflowed and the property is not located in a FEMA Special Flood Hazard Area. There is an easement line running across the rear ten feet of the property. The property is zoned R-1 for single-family residential use, its present use. Deed restrictions stipulate that the house must be no closer than 10 feet to side property lines, 30 feet to the street, and 50 feet from the rear property line. The current structure does not violate these restrictions. Water, gas, electric, and telephone lines have been installed. The lot is attractively landscaped, with low evergreen shrubbery across the front of the house and a view of the tree-lined parkway (the space between the sidewalk and curb). The backyard has several fruit trees. There is no evidence of any encroachment or nearby adverse land use.

When you have completed your Site Data form, check it against the one in the Answer Key at the back of the book. Correct any errors and fill in any omissions on your form.

Building Data

The Improvements section of the URAR form (Figure 6.4) is applicable to residential housing. Some of the information, such as room designations, would not be used for industrial or commercial properties. Any category that does not apply to a particular property can simply have a line drawn through it.

Exterior Features

Even before entering a single-family house, the appraiser is called on to make certain value judgments. Approaching the house from the street, the appraiser mentally records a first impression of the house, its orientation, and how it fits

FIGURE 6.4
Building Data

General Description	Foundation	Exterior Description	materials/condition	Interior	materials/condition
Units ☐ One ☐ One with Accessory Unit	☐ Concrete Slab ☐ Crawl Space	Foundation Walls		Floors	
# of Stories	☐ Full Basement ☐ Partial Basement	Exterior Walls		Walls	
Type ☐ Det. ☐ Att. ☐ S-Det./End Unit	Basement Area sq. ft.	Roof Surface		Trim/Finish	
☐ Existing ☐ Proposed ☐ Under Const.	Basement Finish %	Gutters & Downspouts		Bath Floor	
Design (Style)	☐ Outside Entry/Exit ☐ Sump Pump	Window Type		Bath Wainscot	
Year Built	Evidence of ☐ Infestation	Storm Sash/Insulated		Car Storage ☐ None	
Effective Age (Yrs)	☐ Dampness ☐ Settlement	Screens		☐ Driveway # of Cars	
Attic ☐ None	Heating ☐ FWA ☐ HWBB ☐ Radiant	Amenities	☐ Woodstove(s) #	Driveway Surface	
☐ Drop Stair ☐ Stairs	☐ Other Fuel	☐ Fireplace(s) #	☐ Fence	☐ Garage # of Cars	
☐ Floor ☐ Scuttle	Cooling ☐ Central Air Conditioning	☐ Patio/Deck	☐ Porch	☐ Carport # of Cars	
☐ Finished ☐ Heated	☐ Individual ☐ Other	☐ Pool	☐ Other	☐ Att. ☐ Det. ☐ Built-in	
Appliances ☐Refrigerator ☐Range/Oven ☐Dishwasher ☐Disposal ☐Microwave ☐Washer/Dryer ☐Other (describe)					
Finished area **above** grade contains: Rooms Bedrooms Bath(s) Square Feet of Gross Living Area Above Grade					
Additional features (special energy efficient items, etc.)					
Describe the condition of the property (including needed repairs, deterioration, renovations, remodeling, etc.).					
Are there any physical deficiencies or adverse conditions that affect the livability, soundness, or structural integrity of the property? ☐ Yes ☐ No If Yes, describe					
Does the property generally conform to the neighborhood (functional utility, style, condition, use, construction, etc.)? ☐ Yes ☐ No If No, describe					

in with the surrounding area. At the same time, the appraiser notes and records information about the landscaping. Next, the external construction materials (for the foundation, outside walls, roof, driveway, etc.) are listed and the condition of each, as well as the general external condition of the building, is rated. Finally, the appraiser measures each structure on the site, sketches its dimensions, and computes its area in square feet.

Interior Features

Once in the house, the appraiser notes and evaluates major construction details and fixtures, particularly the interior finish, the kind of floors, walls and doors, the condition and adequacy of kitchen cabinets, the type and condition of heating and air-conditioning systems, paneled rooms, fireplaces, and all other features that affect quality. The appraiser also observes the general condition of the house—for evidence of recent remodeling, the presence of cracked plaster, sagging floors, or any other signs of deterioration—and records room dimensions and total square footage. The appraiser should always inquire as to the presence of any substance requiring disclosure, such as lead-based paint.

Depreciation

Last, the appraiser notes the general condition of the building and the presence and degree of any of the three kinds of depreciation:

1. *Physical deterioration.* The effects of ordinary wear and tear and the action of the elements.

2. *Functional obsolescence.* The absence or inadequacy of features in the design, layout, or construction of the building that are currently desired by purchasers, or the presence of features that have become unfashionable or unnecessary. Fixtures such as bathtubs or vanities fall into this category. A kitchen without modern, built-in cabinets and sink would be undesirable in most areas.

3. *External obsolescence,* formerly referred to as *environmental, economic,* or *locational obsolescence.* A feature made undesirable or unnecessary because of conditions outside the property. A change of zoning from residential to commercial might make a single-family house obsolete if such usage does not fully utilize (take full monetary advantage of) the site.

The kinds of depreciation and how each affects the value of the property are explained in greater detail in the chapters on the specific appraisal approaches. When the appraiser first records building data, it is enough to make a general estimate of the degree of physical deterioration, functional obsolescence, or external obsolescence present in the property.

Multiunit Buildings

In appraising a multiunit residential building the appraiser records the building data in the same way as for a single-family house, except a multiunit building will have more information to evaluate, possibly in many categories. If apartment and room sizes are standard, this work will be greatly simplified. If there are units of many different sizes, however, each apartment must be recorded. In such a case, a floor-by-floor room breakdown would not be as useful as an apartment-by-apartment breakdown. Because most multiunit apartments are standardized, a typical floor plan that indicates the size, placement, and layout of the apartments would be the easiest and best way to show them.

There are some physical features that an appraiser may not be able to learn about a house or apartment building without actually tearing it apart. But if a checklist of items to be inspected, such as those in Figure 6.4, is prepared in advance, most of the building's deficiencies as well as its special features can be identified. If the appraiser can supply all of the required information and knows enough about construction to recognize and record any features not itemized on the list, he or she will have as thorough an analysis of the building as required for any appraisal method.

As you go through the rest of this book you will be filling out all of the forms presented in this chapter. You may review this chapter whenever necessary. If you have difficulty computing building or lot areas, refer to Chapter 15, which covers the mathematics involved in area and volume problems.

EXERCISE 6.5   The following information is applicable to the sample single-family residence at 2130 West Franklin Street. Use it to complete the Improvements section of the URAR form that appears in Figure 6.4.

The subject building is six years old, a seven-room brick ranch house with a concrete foundation. It has double-hung wood windows, wood doors, and aluminum combination storm and screen windows and doors (all only two years old). The general outside appearance and appeal of the house are good. The wood trim was recently painted, and the house probably will not be in need of tuckpointing for at least five years. The black mineral-fiber roof shingles are in good condition, as are the aluminum gutters and downspouts. The attached two-car garage is also brick, and the wood overhead door was painted at the same time as the house trim. The driveway is asphalt. The house has a full basement with a 100,000 BTU gas forced-air furnace, which is in good condition, and a central air-conditioning unit, also in good condition. There are no special energy-efficient items. The basement has concrete floor and walls, is finished with a suspended ceiling, drywall, and vinyl flooring over 50 percent of its 1,300 square feet of area and has no outside entry. There is no evidence of flooding. The wiring is 220-volt.

The house has a living room, dining room, kitchen, three bedrooms, two full bathrooms, and one half-bath. The kitchen has 12 feet of oak cabinets with built-in double basin stainless steel sink with garbage disposal, dishwasher, white range with oven and hood with exhaust fan, and white refrigerator. All appliances will be sold with the house.

The general condition of the interior living area is good. The walls and ceilings are ½-inch drywall, with ceramic tile on the lower five feet of the walls in both full bathrooms. Family room walls are wood paneled. Except for tile and wood surfaces, all of the walls are painted. Doors are wood, hollow core. Floors are hardwood, with wall-to-wall carpeting in living and dining rooms, and vinyl tile in kitchen, family room, and both bathrooms. Each full bathroom has a built-in tub and shower, lavatory with vanity, mirrored cabinet, and toilet with wall-hung tank. The half-bath has a vanity lavatory and toilet. All bathroom fixtures are white.

The house has a total of 1,300 square feet of gross living space, calculated from its exterior dimensions, and is functionally adequate. Based on its general condition, the house has an effective age of five years. There is no evidence of any adverse environmental condition on or near the property.

Check your completed Improvements section against the one in the Answer Key at the back of the book. Correct any errors and fill in any omissions.

■ DATA FOR SALES COMPARISON APPROACH

The *sales comparison approach* is the most widely used appraisal method for valuing residential property and vacant land. Using this approach, the appraiser collects sales data on comparable nearby properties that have sold recently, then makes market-derived adjustments reflecting individual differences between the subject and comparables. After necessary adjustments have been made, the appraiser selects the resultant value indication that best reflects the market value of the subject property. As a formula, the sales comparison approach is

$$\text{Sales Price of Comparable Property} \pm \text{Adjustments} = \text{Indicated Value of Subject Property}$$

The sales comparison approach relies on the principle of *substitution,* which was defined in Chapter 3. If a property identical to the one being appraised was sold recently, its sales price should be a good indicator of the price that could be commanded by the property that is the subject of the appraisal. In practice, however, the appraiser's job is not nearly as simple as that statement might suggest.

Every parcel of real estate is considered unique. Even with properties of the same design and construction built on adjacent building lots, there always will be some features that make one property different from the other. Over time, as successive owners maintain the properties in their own fashion and decorate or remodel in keeping with their tastes, the properties will become less and less similar in appearance and function. The newly built homes on unlandscaped lots that start out looking like identical twins will be quite readily distinguishable after a very short time.

The best an appraiser can do is learn as much as possible about the property being appraised so that other recently sold properties can be found that are as close as possible to the appraised property in as many features as can be identified. It is important to remember that the appraiser making an estimate of market value is making an estimate only. There is no guarantee that the estimated market value will be realized in a future sale of the appraised property. Because the sales comparison approach makes use of market data, it is also called the *market data* or *direct market comparison approach.*

The sales comparison approach can be used for many types of property, but it is particularly useful in the appraisal of a single-family residence because a home purchase generally is made by an owner/occupant who is unconcerned about the property's potential cash flow as a rental unit. Typically, what is most important to the home purchaser is the market value of the property relative to the value of other similar properties in the neighborhood, most of which also are owner-occupied.

Of course, even owner/occupants are concerned with their financial ability to carry the costs of owning a home, from mortgage and tax payments to utility bills and ordinary costs of maintenance. Owner/occupants, however, do not expect the property's potential rental value to cover all those costs. As a result, the sales price of a single-family home may be somewhat higher than its projected investment value, which is based on the cash flow the property can produce.

After all details about the subject property are known, data can be collected on sales of comparable properties. Only recent sales should be considered; they must have been arm's-length transactions, and the properties sold must be substantially similar to the subject property.

Recent Sales

To be considered in an application of the sales comparison approach, a property sale should have occurred fairly close in time to the date of appraisal. The acceptability of the sale from a time standpoint will depend on the number of sales that have taken place and the volatility of the marketplace. Within a normal market, sales no more than six months before the date of appraisal generally are acceptable. In a slow-moving market, the appraiser may have to refer to comparable sales from as long as a year earlier. In that event, the appraiser probably will need to make an adjustment to allow for the time factor. If other types of properties have increased in value over the same period, a general rise in prices may be indicated. The appraiser must determine whether the property in question is part of the general trend and, if it is, adjust the sales price of the comparable accordingly. This adjustment answers the question, "How much would this comparable property probably sell for in today's market?"

For some purposes, such as an appraisal for a federal agency, there may be a definite time limit on the sale date of comparable properties. Even if there is no time imposed by the client or agency for whom the report is being prepared, the appraiser must be alert to market trends, including both the number of overall sales and the changes in market value.

In a period of depressed prices the task of finding recent sales of comparable properties can be even more difficult for the appraiser of *commercial* property. In the best of times, in most areas commercial property sales simply are not as numerous as residential property sales, and it may be impossible for the appraiser to locate property sales that have occurred within even a year or more. The difficulty of the task is compounded if the commercial property is so unusual or has been so customized that no true comparable is available. This is one reason why the sales comparison approach may not be the best appraisal method to use for a commercial property.

The preceding discussion should make it obvious that the study of economics is a necessity for the conscientious student of appraising. The appraiser must be able to recognize economic forces in order to identify possible trends and then apply that knowledge to the facts of the appraisal. The appraiser isn't expected to second-guess the marketplace, but must be able to define its present condition and draw the appropriate conclusions.

Similar Features

In selecting comparable properties, the appraiser will be limited to sales that have occurred in the neighborhood or immediate vicinity. Because most new residential construction occurs within subdivisions developed entirely or predominantly by a single builder, finding recent sales that conform to the subject property's specifications generally presents no difficulty. The appraiser's task becomes more arduous when dealing with properties that are atypical because of either the site or the structure.

Today, when 100-lot home developments are common and some are many times that size, it may be hard to believe that such mass-produced housing is a fairly recent historical phenomenon. Through the 1930s, homes generally were designed and constructed individually for a particular client. The wider availability of financing following the New Deal reforms of the 1930s, coupled with the severe housing shortage that followed World War II, created the perfect conditions for a new type of development.

Levittown, New York, built in the late 1940s, marked the first extensive application to home-building of the economies of material purchasing and labor specialization that had been so successful in the birth of the automobile industry. By standardizing home specifications and making the most efficient use of work crews that moved from house to house on a well-coordinated schedule, William Levitt was able to offer modestly priced housing at a time when the need was great. The success of the first Levitt development did not go unnoticed, and similar subdivisions across the country soon offered a practical, affordable version of the American dream.

Many people find the uniformity of some subdivisions aesthetically unpleasing, but such uniformity is a delight for the real estate appraiser. Over the years tract builders have tried to make homes more distinctive (or "semicustomized," as they are described in advertising) by offering a range of layout and finishing material options, but most subdivision homes retain their basic similarity of form and function. Finding comparable property sales in such a neighborhood rarely is an arduous task.

The appraiser's task is more complicated when the subject property is truly distinctive, either because it has been individually designed and constructed or because the site offers special features. Then, the appraiser must accurately examine and describe the subject property to find comparables that come as close as possible to as many of the property specifications as possible. The most important features to compare will be those that have the greatest effect on value, whether positively or negatively. If the house is the design of a leading architect, and that fact is a desirable and valuable feature, the best possible comparable will be another house designed by the same architect. If the property is on a beachfront, the location may be the single most influential component of the property's value.

Site characteristics that have the greatest effect on value include location, size, view, topography, availability of utilities, and presence of mature trees and other plantings. For example, if the most outstanding feature of the property is the view, the best comparable will be a property with a similar view. If the site has a steep downhill slope, with no space flat enough for a garden or outdoor play area, the ideal comparable will be a house on a similarly restrictive lot.

If comparables that match the property's most important (valuable) feature(s) cannot be found, the value of the feature(s) must be estimated and used as an adjustment to the sales price of each of the selected comparables.

Though adjustments may be made for some differences between the subject property and the comparables, most of the following factors should be similar:

Style of house	Size of lot
Age	Size of building
Number of rooms	Terms of sale
Number of bedrooms	Type of construction
Number of bathrooms	General condition

If at all possible, the comparable properties should be from the same neighborhood as the subject property. Specific data, similar to that collected for the subject property, should be collected for completed sales of at least three comparable properties. Often, sales data on more than those three will have to be studied, because the first three properties the appraiser analyzes may not fit the general requirements listed above well enough to be used in the appraisal. What is important is that the sales chosen provide adequate support for a value conclusion. An analysis of the sales properties not used directly in the report may be helpful in establishing neighborhood values, price trends, and time adjustments.

Financing Terms

The terms of sale are of great importance, particularly if the buyer has assumed an existing loan or if the seller has helped finance the purchase. The seller may take back a note on part of the purchase price (secured by a mortgage or trust deed on the property) at an interest rate lower than the prevailing market rate. The seller may also "buy down" the buyer's high interest rate on a new loan by paying the lender part of the interest on the amount borrowed in a lump sum at the time of the sale. The argument has been made that in a buydown, the sales price has been effectively reduced by the amount the seller has paid to the lender. In any event, the sales price should be considered in light of the cost to the buyer reflected in the method used to finance the purchase. If the buyer obtained a new conventional (non–government-backed) loan and paid the remainder of the purchase price in cash, it would be sufficient to note that fact.

Ideally, because comparable properties should have comparable terms of sale, no adjustment for that factor will be necessary. However, if the appraiser has no choice but to use properties with varying financing terms, the selling prices could be adjusted to reflect those variances by using a *cash equivalency technique*. With one version of this technique, the appraiser compares the monthly payment to be made by the buyer with the required monthly payment on a new loan in the same principal amount, at the prevailing interest rate as of the sale date. The resulting percentage is applied to the amount of the purchase price represented by the principal of the low-interest loan. When this reduced amount is added to the amount paid in cash by the buyer to the seller, the result is an adjusted sales price that compensates for the effects of below-market-rate financing.

EXAMPLE

The total purchase price of a property was $200,000. The buyer made total cash payments of $50,000 and also assumed the seller's mortgage, which had a remaining principal balance of $150,000, bearing an interest rate of 7 percent, with monthly payments of $1,240.48. As of the date of sale, the mortgage had a remaining term of 20 years. Prevailing mortgages on a loan of equal amount and for a like term, as of the sale date, required a 9 percent interest rate with monthly payments of $1,349.59.

The percentage to be applied to the principal amount of the assumed loan is computed by dividing the actual required monthly payment by the payment required for a loan at the prevailing rate.

$$\frac{\$1,240.48}{\$1,349.59} = .92 \text{ or } 92\%$$

The remaining principal amount of the loan is then multiplied by that percentage to find its adjusted value.

$$\$150,000 \times .92 = \$138,000$$

The cash equivalency of the sale can be reached by adding the down payment to the adjusted value of the assumed loan.

$$\$138,000 + \$50,000 = \$188,000$$

The cash equivalency of this sale is $188,000.

If this cash equivalency technique is used to adjust the sales price of any comparable, all of the comparable properties should be so treated. Some appraisers prefer to make this adjustment for the expected holding period of the loan (typically six to eight years), rather than for the full loan term.

Note that use of a cash equivalency technique as the sole method of determining value is not permitted by such agencies as Fannie Mae. Ideally, comparable properties will have comparable terms of sale, and no adjustment for financing will be necessary. If the appraiser has no choice but to use properties with varying financing terms, their selling prices should be adjusted to reflect realistically the effect of financing in the marketplace, rather than simply being the result of a mechanical formula.

A cash equivalency technique may be useful when a buyer has assumed an existing mortgage loan or when the seller provides financing by giving the buyer a credit for some or all of the purchase price. In either situation, the appraiser will be interested in the effect on the sales price of financing that may be more or less favorable than that currently available from conventional lenders.

Seller financing may be the only alternative for a buyer who has difficulty qualifying for a loan from any other source. Another advantage of seller financing is elimination of the up-front loan fees charged by financial institutions such as banks and savings associations—termed *conventional lenders*. If the buyer doesn't have a large enough down payment for a conventional loan, a short-term second mortgage carried by the seller may enable the buyer to secure the bulk of the financing from an institution. In return for carrying all or part of the financing on the purchase, the seller may expect to receive a rate of interest that is higher than the prevailing market rate. This is most often the case when the seller's extension of credit for part of the purchase price is secured by a *second lien,* also called a *junior lien,* on the property.

The opposite situation also may occur, however. If the property has been difficult to sell because of its location or features, or if the market has few buyers for the available properties, the seller may tempt a buyer by offering financing at a rate the same as or less than the market rate. A favorable rate, combined with an easier qualifying process and no loan origination fees, can make the seller-financed home a very desirable property, even in a "buyer's market."

When would a property buyer want to assume the seller's loan? When the interest rate on the seller's loan is lower than the rate the buyer can obtain on a new loan. In addition, there may be fewer loan fees involved in a loan assumption. On the other hand, if market rates are falling, an existing loan may be a poor bargain. Then, too, an existing real estate loan can be assumed by a property buyer only if the original loan terms permit such an assumption. The promissory note that establishes the debt may have a *due-on-sale clause* that makes the entire amount still owed payable at the time of a transfer of the real estate that is used to *hypothecate* (secure) the debt.

Due-on-sale clauses, which can be enforced, currently are found in most fixed-rate mortgage loans. On the other hand, most adjustable-rate mortgages, which provide protection to the lender in the event market rates rise, specifically provide that they are assumable.

Borrowers currently benefit from historically low mortgage interest rates. With interest rates so low, the matter of loan assumability is less important; most buyers simply prefer new, low-interest loans. If mortgage interest rates rise again to the double-digit levels experienced in the early 1980s, however, loan assumability once more may become a significant selling tool.

Arm's-Length Transactions

Every comparable property must have been sold in an *arm's-length transaction,* in which neither buyer nor seller is acting under duress (greater duress, that is, than what is felt by the buyer and seller in the average transaction), the property is offered on the open market for a reasonable length of time, and both buyer and seller have a reasonable knowledge of the property, its assets, and its defects.

In most cases, the slightest indication of duress on the part of either of the principals automatically excludes a transaction from consideration. If the sale has been forced for any reason (a foreclosure, a tax sale, an estate liquidation, the need to purchase adjoining property or to sell before the owner is transferred), it is not an arm's-length transaction. If the principals are related individuals or corporations, this must be assumed to have affected the terms of the sale. Again, financing should be considered. If the down payment was extremely small, or none was required, such an exceptional situation might disqualify the sold property from consideration as a comparable, or at least require an adjustment.

Sources of Data

The preliminary search, as well as the collection of specific data, will be made from one or more of the sources listed here. All sales data, however, must be verified by one or more of the principals to the transaction. The sources are:

- *The appraiser's own records.* These offer the best sources of data. If four comparable properties are available from the appraiser's own records, only the sales prices will remain to be independently verified. (Even though the appraiser has researched the market value as thoroughly as possible, the actual selling price may not have been the same figure.)

- *Official records of deeds.* The appraiser may keep a file of transactions held within the area, but all records will be available in the county or city clerk's office. Much of the specific information needed can also be culled from these records. In localities where transfer tax stamps must be recorded on deeds, such stamps may give an indication of selling price; they are not generally reliable sources of exact selling price, however. The tax rate may be based only on the actual cash amount paid at the closing of the sale, thereby excluding assumed mortgages, for instance. Tax stamps are also usually based on rounded amounts, such as $0.50 per each $500 of financial consideration, or a fraction thereof. Merely multiplying the number of stamps by $500 in such a case could result in a final estimate that is as much as $499 more than the actual cash amount. Too many or too few stamps may also be put on the deed deliberately to mislead anyone trying to discover the property's selling price.

- *The real estate assessor's office.* If property cards can be examined, these will ordinarily reveal sales price, deed book and page, zoning, age of dwelling, lot and dwelling dimensions, and dates of additions to the house. Many assessors now make property records available electronically.

- *Records of sales* published by some local real estate boards or compiled by sales research services, often on the Internet.

- *Newspapers.* In particular, local newspapers may publish monthly or seasonal listings of sales in different neighborhoods. Any sale information taken from a newspaper should definitely be verified elsewhere, as this source is not generally reliable.

Note that, in general, information will be sought only on sales that have already closed escrow; that is, sales that have already been completed. Information on pending sales would ordinarily not be used and would be exceedingly difficult to come by in any event, given that real estate brokers, attorneys, and other agents of the principals could be in breach of their fiduciary duties if they revealed such information.

Nevertheless, in cases in which comparable property sales are rare or when a fast-moving market results in frequent price fluctuations, information on pending sales may be quite useful. For the same reasons, although asking prices of properties currently listed but not yet sold are generally not considered in a property appraisal, in some instances they may be very revealing of the current market status. If there have been relatively few sales in the area recently, for instance, and current asking prices are lower than previous sales prices, that fact should be noted by the appraiser. When combined with other factors, such as increasing length of time on the market, the appraiser may have reason to discount the value of previously recorded sales.

The appraiser should also note previous sales of the subject property that occurred within *at least* one year for one-family to four-family residential property and three years for all other property types. Close analysis of prior sales of the subject property may also indicate general market conditions.

EXERCISE 6.6

1. You need some comparables for the sample appraisal being carried out in this chapter and Chapter 10. The subject property is a house that is six years old and has three bedrooms. Name four places you would look for sales data.

2. You are appraising a subject property fitting the following description:

   Built ten years ago, has five rooms, 1 ½ baths, of average-quality construction, in a neighborhood where average annual family income is $30,000.

   There are five properties that have sold recently. These five properties are similar to the subject property except for these differences:

   Sale 1 has only one bath.
   Sale 2 is about 25 years old.
   Sale 3 needs paint.
   Sale 4 is in a slightly better neighborhood.
   Sale 5 has eight rooms and one bath.

   Which sales should be dropped from consideration as comparables, and why?

Check your answers against those in the Answer Key at the back of the book.

■ SUMMARY

The appraisal process begins with a description of the property being appraised and a statement of the type of value being sought. The ownership or other interest being appraised also must be specified. The market value of a lease depends on the length of the remaining lease term. The value of a life estate depends on the probable life expectancy of the person against whose life the estate is measured.

An appraisal can be made as of any date, but an opinion of value based on a future date requires that the appraiser make clear the assumptions on which the opinion is based.

The appraisal process involves the collection of many types of data. The appraiser must identify the kinds and sources of data necessary for an accurate property appraisal. General data on the region, city, and neighborhood, as well as specific data on the sites and buildings involved and sales, cost, and income data must be collected.

The appraiser must follow national and regional trends closely to gauge accurately their impact on market value.

Individual communities with a stable economic base are most likely to thrive in any set of circumstances. In addition to providing employment and shopping opportunities, local businesses can help bolster a community's tax base.

A parcel of real estate may be worth considerably more when it is combined with other parcels to allow construction of a much larger structure or other improvement than would otherwise be possible. The increase in value of the parcels, called *plottage,* will be enjoyed by the developer who takes the time and effort to assemble the individual lots.

The sales comparison approach, also called the *market data approach,* makes use of the principle of substitution to compare the property being appraised with comparable properties. The homebuyer who intends to occupy the home generally is less concerned than is the investor with the property's investment value based on its potential cash flow. For most homebuyers, the most important consideration is the price that other similar properties have sold for recently.

Most appraisals are based on fee simple ownership of the real estate being appraised, but some properties do not include all of the rights of ownership. Lesser interests, such as mineral or air rights, might be excluded. The property might include an extra benefit of ownership, such as an easement to travel over land owned by others. Leased fee and leasehold interests can be appraised separately.

The effect of unusual financing terms on the sales price of a comparable property must be analyzed and an adjustment made for any impact on value. Seller financing might indicate an interest rate above or below the market rate. If a loan has been assumed, the rate probably is below the current market rate.

ACHIEVEMENT EXAMINATION

1. The sales comparison approach relies on the principle of
   a. anticipation.
   b. leverage.
   c. substitution.
   d. highest and best use.

2. Another name for the sales comparison approach is the
   a. cost approach.
   b. income capitalization approach.
   c. market data approach.
   d. substitution approach.

3. The transaction price of a property is its
   a. sales price.
   b. market value.
   c. insurance value.
   d. asking price.

4. Most residential appraisals are based on

   a. the leased fee.

   b. fee simple ownership.

   c. the leasehold interest.

   d. less than fee simple ownership.

5. The appraisal process requires that the appraiser collect, record, and verify

   a. only data on the subject property's neighborhood.

   b. data on all neighborhoods in the city with which the appraiser is unfamiliar.

   c. data on an annual basis.

   d. data on the region, city, and neighborhood.

6. Ideally, the appraiser of a residential property will collect data on comparable property sales that occurred no earlier than

   a. six months prior to the date of appraisal.

   b. one year prior to the date of appraisal.

   c. 18 months prior to the date of appraisal.

   d. two years prior to the date of appraisal.

7. When choosing comparable sales for the sales comparison approach, property characteristics that should be identical or very similar to those of the subject property include

   a. size of lot and building.

   b. age of building and type of construction.

   c. number and type of rooms.

   d. All of the above

8. One method of compensating for sales that involved different terms of financing is use of the

   a. financing readjustment grid.

   b. cash equivalency technique.

   c. loan-to-value ratio.

   d. operating statement ratio.

9. To be considered comparable to the subject property, a comparable must have been sold

   a. in an arm's-length transaction.

   b. with a conventional mortgage.

   c. without any form of secondary financing.

   d. for all cash.

10. All sales data must be verified by

   a. one of the principals to the transaction.

   b. an Internet resource.

   c. the county assessor.

   d. another appraiser.

Check your answers against those in the Answer Key at the back of the book.

CHAPTER 7

Site Valuation

■ OVERVIEW

In most residential appraising, *site,* rather than *land,* is valued. As noted in Chapter 2, a site is land that is ready for its intended use and includes such improvements as grading, utilities, and access.

For most appraisals the value of the site must be determined apart from the value of any structures on it. For property tax assessment purposes, for instance, land and buildings on developed parcels are always valued separately. A portion of the assessed value will be attributed to land and a portion to buildings.

The basic principles and techniques for site inspection, analysis, and valuation are the same whether the site is vacant or improved with a house and/or other structures. Site valuation encompasses aspects of the sales comparison and income capitalization approaches to value and is an integral part of the cost approach to value.

In this chapter you will learn some of the reasons for separate valuation of a site. You will also learn some of the red flags that indicate possible environmental problems on or near the site. You will then be introduced to five methods of site valuation, with examples and exercises for four of them.

■ SEPARATE SITE VALUATIONS

As indicated above, an appraiser can estimate the value of a vacant site or of vacant land suitable for development into sites. The appraiser can also value a site separately from the improvements (structures) on it. The major reasons for separate valuations are reviewed next.

Cost Approach

Use of the cost approach to value is a primary reason for a separate site valuation, because site value must be distinguished from the cost of improvements.

$$\text{Cost of Improvements New} - \text{Depreciation on Improvements} + \text{Site Value} = \text{Property Value}$$

It is necessary to realize that although utilities can be termed *improvements* in defining a site, in the cost approach the term *improvements* usually refers to structures.

Assessments and Taxation

Assessments may require separate site valuations because they are usually based on improvements to the land itself (such as utilities) rather than on any structural changes. In the same way, most states require separate valuations of site and structures for ad valorem taxation purposes.

Because land is not considered a wasting asset, it does not depreciate. For income tax purposes, the property owner figures depreciation on structures only and thus needs to subtract the site value from the total property value.

Condemnation Appraisals

Courts and condemnors often require that the appraiser separate site and building values in eminent domain cases.

Income Capitalization

In the income capitalization approach to finding property value, one method, called the *building residual technique* (covered in detail in Chapter 12), requires that the appraiser first find land value. The appraiser then subtracts an appropriate return on this value from the net income earned by the property to produce an indication of the income available to the building.

Highest and Best Use

Every appraisal will include at least a brief statement of the property's *highest and best use*. Occasionally, an appraiser may be asked to make a highest and best use report, which is a thorough analysis of the feasibility and profitability of the entire range of uses to which the property could be put, with or without structures.

Of course, most urban and suburban land is zoned for a particular purpose. The few highly developed areas that do not have zoning (such as Houston, Texas) usually rely heavily on deed restrictions to limit density and kinds of development. Site approval and building permits also may be required. The appraiser must consider not only the most valuable present and/or prospective use of a site but also whether a zoning change or other approval necessary for a particular use is likely. Although many appraisals will be limited to present permitted land uses, occasionally the appraiser will be asked to make a broader recommendation.

The requirements of purchasers in the marketplace will define the type of property that will be most desirable. The factors that contribute to desirability are what the appraiser must consider in determining a property's probable market value. The optimum combination of factors—resulting in the optimum value—is termed the property's *highest and best use*.

Of course, a purchaser in the marketplace will have some constraints on the fulfillment of a "wish list" of real estate objectives. Those constraints—physical, legal, and financial—are discussed next.

Four Tests

In a highest and best use analysis, the appraiser must determine the use that fulfills the following four tests. The site use must be

1. physically possible,

2. legally permitted,

3. financially (or economically) feasible, and

4. maximally productive.

1. *The use must be physically possible.* A site's use may be limited by its size, shape, and topography. Does the site have sufficient access for development? Are utilities present or available? If they must be brought in, what cost is involved? Would the site be more promising as part of a larger parcel? As pointed out in Chapter 6, an individual building lot may be more valuable if it can be combined with other adjacent properties in the process called *assemblage.*

2. *The use must be legally permitted.* Some concerns that begin as geologic considerations may result in legal prohibitions, such as restrictions on building in the vicinity of an earthquake fault line. Other legal restrictions are more subjective.

In the dense thicket of local, state, and national regulations affecting real estate use, it may be difficult to believe that the concept of *zoning* is a fairly recent, 20th-century phenomenon. Zoning is an exercise of police power by a municipality or county to regulate private activity by enacting laws that benefit the health, safety, and general welfare of the public. Zoning regulations typically include

■ permitted uses,

■ minimum lot-size requirements,

■ types of structures permitted,

■ limitations on building size and height,

■ minimum setbacks from lot lines, and

■ permitted density (for example, the number of buildings per acre).

An appraisal report should always include the property's current zoning classification. Any proposed changes to the current zoning classification also should be mentioned and commented on.

Property sometimes is purchased subject to the condition that the present zoning will be changed. A request for a change of zoning may be made by appeal to the local zoning authority, usually a *zoning administrator, zoning board,* or *board of zoning adjustment.* If a property owner is unfairly burdened by a zoning restriction, a *zoning variance* may be made. The variance allows a change in the specifications ordinarily required under the zoning regulations.

A frequently encountered example of a zoning variance involves building setback requirements for residential property. If the rear of the property is a steep downslope that is unusable for all practical purposes, for example, a variance may be granted to permit the homeowner to build a deck that would ordinarily be too close to the rear property line but that allows at least some use of what would otherwise be an inaccessible area. The circumstances in each case must be considered by the local zoning board or other authority, and approval of the request should never be taken for granted.

An existing property improvement is termed a *nonconforming use* if it would not be allowed under the site's present zoning. A building that represents a nonconforming use may still be a *legal* use of the property, however, if the structure was in conformance with applicable zoning at the time it was erected. Zoning ordinances typically allow an existing structure to remain when property is rezoned for a different use, although expansion or rebuilding based on the existing use may be prohibited or limited. If that is the case, an appraisal should include an estimate of the number of years that the existing structure can be expected to remain economically viable.

A nonconforming use may represent an *underimprovement,* such as residential property in an area rezoned for commercial use, or it may represent an *overimprovement,* such as a "mom-and-pop" grocery store in an area rezoned for residential use only. Another frequent example of an overimprovement is the church in a residential area. Although the church use may be allowed under a *conditional use permit* (permission allowing a use inconsistent with zoning but necessary for the common good), use of the property for any other purpose would require separate consideration by the zoning authority.

Not all property restrictions are imposed by government. *Private restrictions* include the *conditions, covenants, and restrictions (CC&Rs)* found in the typical *declaration of restrictions* filed by a subdivision developer and incorporated by reference in the deed to each subdivision lot. Residential deed restrictions typically are enacted to ensure that property owners observe a degree of conformity in construction and upkeep of improvements and may cover such topics as architectural style, building materials and exterior colors, landscaping, and maintenance. Although deed restrictions can be enforced by any property owner who is benefited by them, they are most effective when a *homeowners' association* is formed and given the authority to act on behalf of all property owners. In many cases, the relatively minimal fee charged property owners to pay for the expenses of the homeowners' association is far outweighed by the financial benefits that flow from the improved appearance and desirability of the neighborhood.

3. *The use must be financially feasible.* A site use may be both physically possible and legally permitted, yet still be undesirable if using the site in that manner will not produce a commensurate financial return. Because market conditions affect financial feasibility, it is also possible that a use that is not financially feasible at present may become so in the future or vice versa.

For example, a site near an airport may be designated by zoning as suitable for either a hotel or a light manufacturing complex. If the area already has a relatively large number of hotels in the vicinity, resulting in a very low percentage rate of hotel-room occupancy, another hotel may not be advisable from an investment perspective. The expected rate of return per room may not justify the cost to build and maintain the facility. The same analysis would have to be made of the other allowed use; that is, would the development of the site for light manufacturing produce an adequate investment return? Often a site in what is apparently a very desirable location will remain vacant for a long time simply because the cost to develop it cannot be justified on the basis of estimated market demand for any permitted type of improvement.

4. *The use must be maximally productive.* If there is more than one legally permitted, physically possible, and financially feasible property use, which use will produce the highest financial return and thus the highest price for the property? The appraiser would analyze and compare the estimated net operating income of each present or prospective property use in light of the rate of return typically expected by investors in that type of property, to determine which use offers the highest estimated financial return and thus makes the property more valuable.

For example, assume that a vacant site in an almost completely developed suburban area that is zoned for limited commercial uses could be used for either a department store or a theater, and the terrain of the site would allow development of either. Using the income capitalization approach, the appraiser would deduct from the expected net operating income for each type of structure an amount that represents the expected rate of return for property of that type. The income remaining would then be divided by the capitalization rate assigned to the land to estimate the market value of the property for each purpose. The higher figure indicates the most productive use of the site and thus its highest and best use.

Each of these four areas of analysis is affected by the others. The amount of income that a particular use could generate is meaningless if legal approval for the use cannot be obtained. Conversely, not every legally permitted use will warrant the expenditure of funds required to bring it about. The appropriate combination of all four factors results in the single use that can be identified as the property's highest and best use.

Vacant (or as if vacant)

The traditional approach to determining highest and best use is to analyze vacant land or, if the land is improved, to study it as if it were vacant. There are several reasons why land may be studied and valued separately. First, in the cost approach and sometimes in the income capitalization approach to appraising, land value is estimated apart from the value of structures. Second, the purpose of the appraisal may be to consider the economic consequences of removing or converting an existing structure. The present structure, if any, is disregarded in the analysis of highest and best use, although the feasibility and cost of demolition and removal of an existing structure should be noted. The appraiser will then be correctly applying what has been termed the *theory of consistent use*. Both site and improvements will be valued based on the same use.

If an improved parcel is studied for its highest and best use as if vacant, that fact should be noted in the appraiser's report.

As Improved

The expense and legal approval process associated with demolition of an existing structure may make it a necessary component of the parcel. Nevertheless, there may still be some possibility of a changed use that could result in higher income potential for the property. An older building that has outlived its usefulness for one purpose may undergo a sometimes startling transformation. This is especially true during a period of intense competition that results from an overbuilt market or economic downturn (or a combination of both, as commercial property owners in many parts of the country have recently experienced). Then, a state institution that has fallen into disuse may be deemed entirely appropriate for redevelopment into condominiums, apartments, and a golf course. (For more details of the economic realities that can result in such a transaction, see "Yesterday's Grim Aslyums, Tomorrow's Grand Apartments," by Michael Corkery, *The Wall Street Journal*, July 27, 2005, page B1.)

Unlike commercial property, which may allow a variety of uses, residential property usually is zoned for exactly that, and any new structure must conform to that use. Despite the cost of demolition and removal of an existing building, however, many homes are purchased for the value of the underlying land and the prospect of tearing down the existing dwelling and erecting a new one, usually on a grand and luxurious scale. Understandably, some residents of areas where these earthbound phoenixes have arisen have taken offense at the brash and often conspicuous newcomers, and permits for conversion of such "teardown" properties have become more difficult to obtain in some communities.

Interim Use

Some properties are appraised at a time when they are not yet at their expected highest and best use. The present use in such a case is considered an *interim use*.

The classic example of an interim use is farmland in the path of development. While considering the present use an interim use and appraising it as such may appear to be a logical assumption based on the population growth trend, surrounding land uses, and present zoning, a note of caution is in order. More than one landowner has been dismayed to find that being in the path of development is no guarantee that the land will ever be allowed to develop more than grass and wildflowers. Even if present zoning allows for a range of uses, including the potential for subdivision development, a zoning ordinance can be amended by the city or county government that enacted it in the first place.

If property is "downzoned" to prohibit future development, can the property owner make a claim for compensation based on the economic loss of an expected property use? Not at the present time, unless the owner is denied *all* economically viable use of the property, as decided by the United States Supreme Court in *Lucas v. South Carolina Coastal Council,* 112 S.Ct. 2886 (1992).

EXERCISE 7.1

The major reasons for valuing sites separately from buildings have been discussed. List as many of these reasons as you can.

Check your answers against those in the Answer Key at the back of the book.

■ SITE DATA

Identification

The first step in site analysis is to identify the property. A complete and legally accurate description of the site's location must be obtained. The plot plan used to illustrate the property description should include the site's property line dimensions and show its location within a given block.

Analysis

Once the subject has been properly identified and described, it must be analyzed in detail. A report on the site's highest and best use should be an integral part of the analysis and should include the study of trends and factors influencing value, the data collection program, and the physical measurement of the site. Important features of the site are its size, location in terms of position on the block, utilities, improvements, soil composition (especially as related to grading, septic system, or bearing capacity for foundations), and whether it is located in a flood zone or an earthquake fault zone.

Knowledge of the subject site's zoning, which will affect its future use, is necessary, as is knowledge of the current zoning or imminent rezoning of surrounding properties in the area.

Finally, easements, deed restrictions, or publicly held rights-of-way should be noted. Any part of the site that cannot be used for building purposes should be clearly designated, along with other limitations on the use of the site.

■ ENVIRONMENTAL CONCERNS

With a wide range of environmental legislation now in place at both federal and state levels, identification and remediation of contaminants has become a necessary and sometimes very expensive component of property ownership. Federal regulations covering water, air, toxic substances, endangered species, wetlands, and other topics can have a profound impact on property condition as well as permitted property uses. State regulations pick up where federal regulations leave off, in many cases providing even more onerous requirements.

The first concern of the appraiser will be to identify potential or actual environmental factors that are likely to affect property value. This does not mean that every appraisal will serve as an evaluation of all environmental problems present on or affecting the subject property but, rather, that the appraiser should at least note obvious conditions and recommend further inspection. For commercial real estate, an environmental site assessment (ESA) or environmental property assessment (EPRA) is probably well-advised to protect the property owner, lender, and others involved in the transaction. Either type of inspection and analysis is beyond the scope of the average appraiser and should be undertaken only by one who is especially trained in the physical, economic, and legal ramifications of environmental conditions. What the average appraiser can do is conduct a conscientious inspection of the subject property and note suspicious conditions. These may include (and are by no means limited to) the following:

- Ponds, lakes, creeks, and other bodies of water
- Standing water or wetlands, even if seasonal
- High-power transmission lines
- Evidence of past commercial or agricultural land use
- Underground or above-ground storage tanks or drums
- Deteriorating paint
- Insulation around water pipes or ducts
- Smoke, haze, or other airborne condition
- Excessive noise
- Old building foundations or other evidence of a previous structure
- A dump site

Even a pristine site can be problematic if it is found to be the habitat for an endangered species. In short, any factor that could affect property use should be noted in the appraisal report. More information on a wide variety of topics can be found at *www.epa.gov.*

WEB LINK
www.epa.gov

Brownfields

The Environmental Protection Agency (EPA) has estimated that there are approximately 450,000 parcels of real estate in the United States that can be described as brownfields—abandoned or underutilized property that may or may not be contaminated. Pilot programs aimed at promoting a unified approach to environmental assessment, cleanup, and redevelopment have begun in 40 jurisdictions. More information about the Brownfields Action Agenda, including telephone numbers for ten regional offices can be obtained from EPA's Washington office at (202) 260-1223, or from *www.epa.gov.*

■ METHODS OF SITE VALUATION

Six methods are commonly used in appraising sites:

1. *Sales comparison method.* Sales of similar vacant sites are analyzed and compared. After adjustments are made, the appraiser arrives at an estimate of value for the subject site.

2. *Allocation method.* This method is used when the land value of an improved property must be found. The ratio of land value to building value typical of similar improved properties in the area is applied to the total value of the subject property to arrive at the land value of the subject.

3. *Abstraction method,* also called *extraction method.* When the sales price of a property is known, the cost of all improvements can be subtracted from it to find land value.

4. *Subdivision development method.* The costs of developing and subdividing a parcel of land are subtracted from the total expected sales prices of the separate sites, adjusting for the time required to sell all of the individual sites, to determine the value of the undivided raw land.

5. *Ground rent capitalization method.* When a landowner leases land to a tenant who agrees to erect a building on it, the lease is usually referred to as a *ground lease.* Ground rents can be capitalized at an appropriate rate to indicate the market value of the site. For example, assume that a site is on a long-term lease with a ground rent of $100,000 per year. If the appropriate rate for capitalization of ground rent is 10 percent, the estimated value by direct capitalization is $100,000 ÷ .10, or $1,000,000.

6. *Land residual method.*[1] The net income earned by the building is deducted from the total net income of the property; the balance is earned by the land.

The residual or leftover income is then capitalized to indicate the land value. The formula used for this method is

Property Net Income – Building Net Income = Land Net Income

Land Net Income ÷ Land Capitalization Rate = Land Value

Sales Comparison Method

There are no basic differences between the data valuation of improved properties and unimproved sites in the sales comparison method. Sales comparison analysis and valuation are discussed and illustrated in detail in Chapters 6 and 10; the basic points are simply reviewed here.

The sales comparison approach is the most reliable method of site valuation. Just as the value of a used house is estimated by the most recent sales prices of comparable houses in the neighborhood, the value of a site is judged largely by the same *comparison* method.

The appraiser's objective is to determine the probable market value of the property being appraised by interpreting the data from sales of similar properties. Because no two parcels of land are identical, there will be differences to compensate for when the appraiser compares sales properties with the subject property. Typical differences include *date of sale, location, physical characteristics, zoning and land-use restrictions, terms of financing,* and *conditions of sale.*

---

[1] Because a comprehensive treatment of the residual techniques and the capitalization process is contained in Chapter 12, "Direct and Yield Capitalization," this method of site valuation will not be covered here.

The adjustment process is an analysis designed to eliminate the effect on value of these differences. Each comparable property is likened as much as possible to the subject property. In adjusting the sales price of a comparable property, lump-sum dollar amounts or percentages are customarily used. Adjustments are always applied to the sales price of the comparable property, *not* the value of the subject property. If the comparable property is inferior in some respect to the subject property, its sales price is increased by an appropriate dollar amount or percentage. If the comparable property is superior in some category, its sales price is decreased. In the adjustment process, the appraiser then uses the modified sales prices of comparable properties in estimating the value of the subject property.

In comparing site data, whether vacant or improved, the appraiser should take care always to use the same units of measurement. For example, the sales price of a site may be expressed as a certain amount *per front foot,* based on the site's street frontage. Rural property usually is valued in *acres;* a residential subdivision lot may be valued in *square feet* or, if large enough, in acres. If lots are all very close in size or utility, value may be expressed *per lot.*

EXAMPLE	An appraisal is being made of Lot 81, Hilltop Acres Subdivision. Lot 81 is very similar to Lot 78, which sold recently for $28,000, but Lot 81 has a view of a nearby lake. By analyzing sales of other lots in Hilltop Acres, the appraiser determines that a lake view contributes $10,000 to lot value. The adjusted sales price of Lot 78 thus is $38,000, which is the indicated value of Lot 81 using this comparable in the sales comparison approach.

EXERCISE 7.2

Assume that a residential lot, 75 feet by 150 feet, sold one year ago for $20,000. In analyzing the market, you arrive at the following conclusions:

1. The subject site is 12 percent or $2,400 more valuable as a result of price increases over the year since the comparable site was sold.

2. The subject site is 10 percent or $2,000 more valuable than the comparable site with respect to location.

3. The subject site is 15 percent or $3,000 less valuable with respect to physical features.

Based on the information provided, complete the adjustment table:

	Sales Price	Date	Location	Physical Features	Net Adjustment + or −	Adjusted Price
Dollar Basis						
Percentage Basis						

Check your answers against those in the Answer Key at the back of the book.

Allocation Method

Land value may be treated as a percentage or proportion of the total value of an improved property. In many areas, land and building values have historically held a certain relationship to each other. If the approximate ratio of land value to building value is typically one to four, for instance, and a property improved

FIGURE 7.1
Abstraction Method

| $178,000 Sales Price | − $129,000 Cost of Improvements Less Depreciation | = $49,000 Land Value |

with a structure is valued at $100,000, the land value is one-fifth of that amount, or $20,000. Part of the total property value is thus *allocated* to the site and part to the improvements. Property tax assessors make such an allocation in apportioning the amount of property tax owed between land and improvements, by determining the ratio of land value to value of improvements.

Obviously, the allocation method is weak because it fails to take individual property differences into account. This method should be used only in situations where there is a lack of current sales data for vacant sites that are similar to and competitive with the subject site. It may also be useful as a gross check of an appraisal by another method.

Abstraction (Extraction) Method

A process similar to the allocation method is known as *abstraction* or *extraction*. As shown in Figure 7.1, all improvement costs (less depreciation) are deducted from the sales price, and the amount remaining is attributed to land value. In our example, the sales price of $178,000 is reduced by the $129,000 depreciated cost of improvements to determine the remaining value of $49,000 that can be considered land value.

This method, though imprecise, may be useful in appraising property when there are few sales for comparison. This is often the case with rural properties, particularly for larger parcels with improvements that represent a relatively small portion of the property's total value.

EXERCISE 7.3

In a high-income suburban residential area, the ratio of building value to land value approximates three to one. What is the land value of a typical property valued at $347,000, using the allocation method?

Check your answer against the one in the Answer Key at the back of the book.

Subdivision Development Method

The value of land with a highest and best use as a multiunit development may be found using the *subdivision development method,* also called the *land development method.* It relies on accurate forecasting of market demand, including both *forecast absorption* (the rate at which properties will sell) and *projected gross sales* (total income that the project will produce).

<table>
<tr><td>

EXAMPLE

</td><td>

A 40-acre subdivision is expected to yield 160 single-family homesites after allowances for streets, common areas, and so on. Each site should have an ultimate market value of $30,000 so that the projected sales figure for all the lots is $4,800,000 (160 × $30,000).

Based on an analysis of comparable land sales, it is concluded that lots can be sold at the rate of 60 in year 1, 70 in year 2, and 30 in year 3.

Engineers advise that the cost of installing streets, sewers, water, and other improvements will be $10,000 per lot. Other costs (sales expenses, administration, accounting, legal, taxes, overhead, etc.) are estimated at 20 percent and developer's profit at 10 percent of gross lot sales.

Problem: Assume that the highest and best use of the land is for subdivision development and that there is an active demand for homesites. What price should a developer pay for this acreage based on a sales program taking three years to complete?

</td></tr>
</table>

Solution: Total projected sales:

160 lots at $30,000 per lot		$4,800,000
Total projected development costs:		
Street grading and paving, sidewalks, curbs, gutters, sanitary and storm sewers for 160 lots at $10,000 per lot	$1,600,000	
Other costs, 20 percent of $4,800,000 (total projected sales)	960,000	
Developer's profit, 10 percent of $4,800,000 (total projected sales)	480,000	
Total development costs		3,040,000
Estimated value of raw land		$1,760,000
Raw land value per lot, $1,760,000 ÷ 160		$ 11,000

The amount that a developer should pay now in anticipation of the land's future value is computed by applying a reversion factor to its present estimated value undeveloped. The table in Figure 12.3 on page 257 lists the computed factors at specified interest rates for an investment term of 1 to 40 years. This table allows you to compute the time value of money—from some point in the future backward to the present time. In essence you are taking a sum of money to be paid later and *discounting* it, or subtracting from it the compound interest it would earn from the present time until the time when it is to be paid. By this process of discounting, you can find out what its value is today.

Note that even if the developer is also the contractor on the project, the amount of profit attributable to the development function (also referred to as *entrepreneurial profit*) usually is considered a separate item.

In this example problem, the developer's expected yield of 10 percent discounted to present worth for one year gives a reversion factor of .909; two years, a reversion factor of .826; and three years, a reversion factor of .751. The present worth of lot sales is:

In this oversimplified example, a developer would be justified in paying $1,483,790 for the raw land for subdivision purposes.

First year:	60 lots at $11,000 per lot = $660,000	
	$660,000 discounted to present worth	
	at 10% for one year (.909)	$599,940
Second year:	70 lots at $11,000 per lot = $770,000	
	$770,000 discounted to present worth	
	for two years (.826)	636,020
Third year:	30 lots at $11,000 per lot = $330,000	
	$330,000 discounted to present worth	
	for three years (.751)	247,830
	Present value of $1,760,000 discounted	
	partially 1, 2, and 3 years	$1,483,790

EXERCISE 7.4

The following building costs have been predicted for a 72-unit residential subdivision planned to utilize a 30-acre tract.

Engineering and surveying	$ 23,000
Roads	117,000
Grading and leveling all sites	46,000
Utilities	129,000
Marketing	72,000
Financing	182,000
Taxes	47,000
Administration, accounting, and other professional services	118,000
Developer's profit	200,000

Projected sales figures for the lots are

48 lots at $27,000 each, discounted to present worth at 12 percent for one year (factor: .893);
16 lots at $32,000 each, discounted to present worth at 12 percent for two years (factor: .797); and
8 lots at $36,000 each, discounted to present worth at 12 percent for three years (factor: .712).
(The higher lot prices reflect expected price increases over time.)

Estimate the market value of the raw acreage using the subdivision development method.

Determine how much a subdivider would be justified in paying for the raw land for development.

Check your answers against those in the Answer Key at the back of the book.

Ground Rent Capitalization Method

The owner of land to be developed for commercial or other purposes may choose to retain the fee simple title to the land yet lease the right to use it for building. When a landowner leases land to a tenant who agrees to erect a building on the land, the lease is usually referred to as a *ground lease*. A ground lease must be for a long enough term to make the transaction desirable to the tenant investing in the building. Such leases often run for terms of 50 years or longer, and a lease for 99 years is not uncommon.

The terms of a *ground lease,* including the *ground rent* (payment made by the tenant under a ground lease) to be paid, will vary according to the desirability of the land and the relative negotiating strengths of the parties.

The value of a ground lease usually is determined by dividing the ground rent by an appropriate *capitalization rate.* Chapter 12 of the text explains how the capitalization rate is derived. The provisions of the lease agreement must be known for a complete and accurate appraisal. The appraiser must consider the remaining length of the lease term as well as both the present rent paid and the possibility for a rent increase if the lease contains an escalation clause.

■ SUMMARY

Site value often is a separate appraisal consideration, even for property that has already been improved by the addition of structures. The site's optimum value will depend on its highest and best use, which is the use that is physically possible, legally permitted, financially feasible, and maximally productive.

A site's present legally permitted uses are determined by zoning and other regulations, as well as private restrictions such as those found in the declaration of restrictions that often accompanies subdivision parcels. A preexisting use of land that does not conform to the present zoning ordinance is termed a *nonconforming use.* A nonconforming use may ordinarily remain; however, certain restrictions are usually imposed. A *zoning variance* may be requested from the local governing body; a *conditional use permit* will allow continuation of a use that does not comply with present zoning but is of benefit to the community.

The appraiser can choose among a variety of site valuation methods, making use of sales of comparable sites (sales comparison method), income streams (land residual method), costs of development compared with projected sales income (subdivision development method), analysis of income expectation for land alone (ground rent capitalization), site-to-building value ratios (allocation method), or cost of improvements (abstraction or extraction method).

Property may be appraised for the value of its current, interim use, with the expectation that the use will change in the future. By extracting all other costs from total property value, the appraiser will arrive at the amount that is attributable solely to land value. This method primarily is useful when there are few sales of such property available for comparison. The subdivision development, or land development, method takes into account all costs, including both contractor's and developer's (entrepreneurial) profit.

A ground lease can be appraised, and its value will depend on the ground rent being paid, the length of the remaining lease term, and other specific features of the underlying lease agreement.

7

ACHIEVEMENT EXAMINATION

1. Explain how the terms *land* and *site* differ.

2. Why would an appraiser need to know site valuation

    a. in the cost approach?

    b. for tax purposes?

3. Name six site valuation techniques.

    Which method is preferred, and why?

4. Another term for developer's profit is

    a. contractor's profit.

    b. entrepreneurial profit.

    c. project profit.

    d. management profit.

5. A church in a residential area is an example of

    a. police power.

    b. forecast absorption.

    c. a nonconforming use.

    d. a private restriction.

6. Zoning is an exercise of a government's

    a. police power.

    b. power of eminent domain.

    c. right of condemnation.

    d. right of priority.

7. All improvement costs, less depreciation, are subtracted from sales price to derive land value in the process called

   a. ground rent capitalization.

   b. extraction.

   c. entrepreneurial enterprise.

   d. assemblage.

8. Private deed restrictions often are enforced through a

   a. zoning variance.

   b. zoning board.

   c. homeowners' association.

   d. housing cooperative.

Check your answers against those in the Answer Key at the back of the book.

## CHAPTER 8

The Cost Approach— Part I: Reproduction/ Replacement Cost

■ OVERVIEW

In the cost approach, the value of all property improvements (reproduction or replacement cost less depreciation) is added to site value to determine market value. In this chapter, the distinction between reproduction and replacement cost and the methods of computing building cost are explained. In Chapter 9 the different types of depreciation are analyzed.

■ COST APPROACH FORMULA

In the *cost approach*, the present cost of constructing all of the improvements on a site, less their loss in value due to accrued depreciation, is added to the value of the site as if vacant, to determine property value. The basic principle involved is that of *substitution*. The cost of a new building is substituted for that of the existing one, with some adjustment to compensate for depreciation of the existing building due to general deterioration and other factors. The appraiser will compute the cost to build a structure identical to the subject in either design and material (reproduction cost) or utility (replacement cost). The cost approach can be expressed as a formula:

$$\text{Reproduction or Replacement Cost of Improvement(s)} - \text{Accrued Depreciation} + \text{Site Value} = \text{Property Value}$$

One drawback to the cost approach is that the value of a new structure is presumed to be equal to its cost. This may not be true if the structure does not represent the highest and best use of the site. In other words, the value of an inappropriate structure, such as a large hotel on a little-traveled back road, may not equal the cost to build it.

Another drawback to the cost approach, particularly with regard to appraising single-family residences, is that builders' costs may vary greatly, depending on the number of units produced and the individual builder's profit margin. Ultimately, the appraiser may have to make market comparisons of builders' costs in the same way that selling prices are compared.

Nevertheless, the cost approach must be used when a value estimate via either the income capitalization approach or the sales comparison approach is not possible. For example, in the appraisal of special-purpose properties such as churches, schools, museums, and libraries there are no income figures available and few, if any, comparable sales.

A cost approach estimate is also needed in establishing value for insurance purposes. Insurance claims are based on the cost of restoration, or reimbursement for loss, as determined by the appraised insurance value; therefore, an insurance appraiser is mainly concerned with reproduction cost. Condemnation proceedings and real estate tax assessments are other instances in which a cost approach estimate is necessary.

The estimation of site value is a critical part of the cost approach; however, it is not developed through a costing process. Site value, as the last part of the cost approach equation, is computed by the sales comparison approach, as explained in Chapter 7. The location and amenities of the subject site (except for improvements) are compared with those of similar nearby sites. Adjustments are made for any significant differences, and the adjusted prices of the properties most like the subject site are used to estimate the value of the subject site.

Because the cost approach involves the addition of building and site values, each computed separately, it is also called the *summation* method of appraising.

REPRODUCTION COST VERSUS REPLACEMENT COST

Reproduction cost is the dollar amount required to construct an exact duplicate of improvements to the subject property at prices current as of the effective appraisal date. The *replacement cost* is the dollar amount required to construct improvements of equal utility using current construction methods and materials.

In the Cost Approach section of the URAR form, *reproduction cost* or *replacement cost* must be indicated. Determining the price of constructing an identical new property is not always feasible, however. The exacting details of workmanship present in an older home may make it impossible to duplicate today at a reasonable price. So a home with the same number, type, and size of rooms would be used to find the replacement cost, rather than the reproduction cost, of the subject property. The replacement cost of the subject's improvements is the current construction cost of improvements having the same utility, that is, those that can be used in the same way.

The construction cost, whether reproduction or replacement, will be for a *new* structure at current prices as of the effective appraisal date. The condition of the improvements at the time of the appraisal is not a factor at this point. Construction cost is a measure of the quality of a structure in terms of how expensive it would be to rebuild or replace and is not a measure of the structure's condition. An allowance for the condition of the subject property, as well as any other adverse influences, is made when accrued depreciation is subtracted in the second part of the cost approach equation.

EXERCISE 8.1

Replacement cost (rather than reproduction cost) would likely be used in valuing which of the houses shown below? Why?

Check your answers against those in the Answer Key at the back of the book.

■ DETERMINING REPRODUCTION/REPLACEMENT COST

back in time

$$250,000 \times \frac{180}{155} = \longrightarrow$$

An appraiser using the cost approach will compute the cost to duplicate property improvements, whether of the subject property itself (reproduction cost) or a functionally identical replacement (replacement cost). There are four methods for estimating the reproduction cost of a structure:

1. *Index method.* A factor representing the percentage increase of construction costs up to the date of value is applied to the original cost of the subject building.

Most common

2. *Square-foot method.* The cost per square foot of a recently built comparable structure is multiplied by the number of square feet in the subject building.

3. *Unit-in-place method.* The construction cost per unit of measure of each component part of the subject structure (including material, labor, overhead, and builder's profit) is multiplied by the number of units of that component part in the subject. Most components are measured in square feet, although certain items, such as plumbing fixtures, are estimated as complete units. The sum of the cost of the components is the cost of the new structure.

4. *Quantity survey method.* The itemized costs of erecting or installing all of the component parts of a new structure are added. Indirect costs (building permit, land survey, overhead expenses such as insurance and payroll taxes, and builder's profit) are totaled, as well as direct costs (site preparation and all phases of building construction, including fixtures).

Builder's use this

The square-foot method is the one typically used by appraisers in estimating construction costs. The quantity survey method is the one generally used by cost estimators, contractors, and builders because *all* of a structure's components are analyzed, which yields the most accurate cost estimate. This method, as well as the unit-in-place method, can be quite accurate when used by qualified cost estimators, although both are more time-consuming than the square-foot method. Because it does not take into account individual property variables, the index method generally is used only as a check of the estimate reached by one of the other methods, or when the lower level of reliability achieved is deemed acceptable.

Index Method

Although the *index method* of finding reproduction cost is rarely accurate enough to be used alone, it may serve as a useful way to verify cost figures arrived at by one of the other methods if the original construction cost of the improvements is known. Cost reporting or indexing services keep records of building cost changes over time, and sometimes from area to area. All dollar amounts are given a numerical factor relative to whatever base year is being used. By comparing the current cost index with the cost index at the time construction took place and then applying that factor to the original construction cost, an estimate of current cost can be derived. The formula used is

$$\frac{\text{Present Index}}{\text{Index at Time of Construction}} \times \text{Original Cost} = \text{Present Cost}$$

EXAMPLE

An office building constructed in 1988 for $149,000 had a cost index at that time of 177. The present cost index is 354. Using the formula:

$$\frac{354}{177} \times \$149{,}000 = \$298{,}000$$

In the example above, $298,000 is the estimated reproduction cost of the subject building. Using cost indexes successfully obviously requires that the building cost of the subject property be fairly typical; any additions or changes to the original structure would have to be taken into consideration. If a building or one of its components is fairly standard, however, the method can be useful.

The index method of finding reproduction cost is also called the *cost service index method*.

EXERCISE 8.2

The Jones residence cost $39,000 to construct in 1975. A cost index published at that time was 158.2. The current cost index from the same cost reporting service is 537.8.

What is the current indicated reproduction cost of the Jones residence by the index method?

Check your answer against the one in the Answer Key at the back of the book.

Square-Foot Method

To begin the *square-foot method* of estimating reproduction cost, the appraiser must find the dimensions of the subject structure to compute the number of square feet of ground area it covers. In collecting cost data for the square-foot method, the appraiser must find the cost of comparable new structures. The appraiser also may rely on *cost manuals* (such as those published by F.W. Dodge Corporation [*www.fwdodge.com*], Marshall and Swift Publication Company [*www.marshallswift.com*], and R. S. Means Company [*www.rsmeans.com*]) for basic construction costs. Cost manuals, which give building specifications and typical construction costs, are usually updated quarterly, sometimes even monthly. Some cost estimating services make their data available on computer software for ease and efficiency of use. Some even offer electronic linkup to their database via computer modem.

WEB LINK
www.fwdodge.com
www.marshallswift.com
www.rsmeans.com

Figure 8.1 shows a page from a typical residential construction cost manual. The overall quality of construction and type of structure are specified (in this case the structure is an economy-quality two-story house having a living area of 2,000 square feet and a perimeter of 135 linear feet). Each of the major cost components is separately itemized, including site work and provision for contractor's overhead and profit. Estimated labor time and materials and labor costs per square foot of living area are indicated. The total of all costs for this house is $62.55 per square foot. That figure would be adjusted to account for regional differences.

A sample page from a typical commercial construction cost manual is reproduced in Figure 8.2. The type of building is specified (in this case it includes both factory and office space), and its dimensions are given. Construction features are itemized, with utilities (mechanical features) listed separately. Because office and

F I G U R E 8.1
Sample Page from a Residential Construction Cost Manual

Economy 2 Story
Living Area - 2000 S.F.
Perimeter - 135 L.F.

			Labor Hours	Cost Per Square Foot Of Living Area		
				Mat.	Labor	Total
1	Site Work	Site preparation for slab; 4' deep trench excavation for foundation wall.	.034		.59	.59
2	Foundation	Continuous reinforced concrete footing, 8" deep x 18" wide; dampproofed and insulated 8" thick reinforced concrete block foundation wall, 4' deep; 4" concrete slab on 4" crushed stone base and polyethylene vapor barrier, trowel finish.	.069	2.27	3.04	5.31
3	Framing	Exterior walls - 2" x 4" wood studs, 16" O.C.; 1/2" insulation board sheathing; wood truss roof frame, 24" O.C. with 1/2" plywood sheathing, 4 in 12 pitch; 2" x 8" floor joists 16" O.C. with bridging and 5/8" plywood subfloor.	.112	4.70	5.63	10.33
4	Exterior Walls	Beveled wood siding and #15 felt building paper on insulated wood frame walls; 6" attic insulation; double hung windows; 2 flush solid core wood exterior doors with storms.	.107	7.50	4.26	11.76
5	Roofing	20 year asphalt shingles; #15 felt building paper; aluminum gutters, downspouts, drip edge and flashings.	.024	.47	.91	1.38
6	Interiors	Walls and ceilings, 1/2" taped and finished drywall, primed and painted with 2 coats; painted baseboard and trim; rubber backed carpeting 80%, asphalt tile 20%; hollow core wood interior doors.	.219	7.73	10.17	17.90
7	Specialties	Economy grade kitchen cabinets - 6 L.F. wall and base with plastic laminate counter top and kitchen sink; 30 gallon electric water heater.	.017	.83	.43	1.26
8	Mechanical	1 lavatory, white, wall hung; 1 water closet, white; 1 bathtub, enameled steel, white; gas fired warm air heat.	.061	2.12	2.17	4.29
9	Electrical	100 Amp. service; romex wiring; incandescent lighting fixtures; switches, receptacles.	.030	.58	.96	1.54
10	Overhead	Contractor's overhead and profit		3.95	4.24	8.19
		Total		30.15	32.40	62.55

FIGURE 8.2
Typical Page from a Commercial Construction Cost Manual

FACTORY AND OFFICE

One Story Brick and Concrete Block Building. Size—50' × 79'

FOUNDATION—Concrete walls, footings and piers.

WALLS—158 L/F 8" concrete block, 10' high, continuous steel sash windows, 8' high, including gutters and downspouts.

100 L/F 8" concrete block, 20' high, including 50 L/F 4" brick veneer front, 10' high, stone coping.

FLOOR—Concrete.

ROOF—Flat, tar and gravel roofing, insulated, steel decking, steel bar joists, beams and columns.

MECHANICAL FEATURES

Electric—Pipe conduit wiring, metal reflectors.

Heating—Gas unit heaters.

Plumbing—3 water closets, 3 lavatories, 1 urinal, 1 water heater.

Sprinkler—None.

OTHER FEATURES—Miscellaneous steel crane girders on building columns. One Story Brick Office Addition—22' × 50' × 10' high.

Office—Cost per Square Foot of Ground Area $70.65
Factory—Cost per Square Foot of Ground Area $40.95

factory spaces have dissimilar features (such as windows and wall height), their costs have been listed separately. Because the appraiser is interested only in the cost per square foot of a particular type and construction of building, the total cost of the example structure is not given. This example indicates a cost per square foot for office space of $70.65; factory space is $40.95 per square foot.

If the closest example in the cost manual still has significant differences from the subject building, a cost differential could be added to (or subtracted from) the cost per square foot given in the cost manual. Although cost estimates of high-ceilinged structures may utilize the *cubic-foot method* of estimating reproduction cost, a height adjustment made to the figure arrived at by the square-foot method is usually sufficient.

Both the square-foot method of estimating reproduction cost and the cubic-foot method may be referred to by the term *comparative unit method*. If that term is used, the appraiser should be sure to state the unit of measurement (square feet or cubic feet).

EXAMPLE

The following floor plan is that of a factory building with contiguous office space that approximates the example building shown in Figure 8.2. There are no significant differences between the buildings.

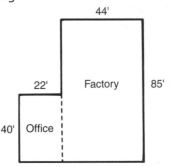

The area of the office space is 22' × 40', or 880 square feet; the area of the factory space is 44' × 85', or 3,740 square feet. Approximately 20 percent of floor area is thus office space, making this building comparable to the example, which has 22 percent office space. The reproduction cost of the office space is 880 square feet × $70.65, or $62,172. The reproduction cost of the factory space is 3,740 square feet × $40.95, or $153,153. The total estimate of the reproduction cost for the subject building is $62,172 + $153,153, or $215,325. If this building differed from the base building in the manual, then height, perimeter, or other extra adjustments to the estimate of reproduction cost would be necessary.

Regional Multipliers

Even with frequent updating, there may be a considerable time lapse between the appraisal date of a property and the publication date of a cost manual; therefore, the appraiser using the cost manual should keep informed of price increases in the area. Some cost manuals meant for national use have *regional multipliers,* so that a given example can be used for any area of the country, provided the cost estimate obtained is multiplied by the adjustment factor for that region.

Residential Appraisals

The widespread use of the appraisal report forms prepared by Freddie Mac—formerly the Federal Home Loan Mortgage Corporation—and Fannie Mae—formerly the Federal National Mortgage Association—has made the square-foot method of calculating reproduction cost a commonly used technique for residences. An example of a Freddie Mac/Fannie Mae appraisal form, the *Uniform Residential Appraisal Report (URAR),* appears at the end of Chapter 13.

With the URAR form, gross living area (derived by using the outside measurements of the house, less nonliving areas) is multiplied by cost per square foot. That figure is then added to the cost of nonliving areas and other improvements, such as garage and patio, to arrive at the total estimated cost new of all improvements.

EXAMPLE

The Smith residence is being appraised. The house has 1,800 square feet of living area, based on exterior building measurements. Current construction cost is $73 per square foot. Garage space of 550 square feet has a current construction cost of $25 per square foot. The house has a patio valued at $1,500. Other site improvements, including a driveway and landscaping, are valued at $8,500. What is the reproduction cost of the Smith property?

The improvements have a present reproduction cost new of $131,400 (1,800 × $73) plus $13,750 (550 × $25) plus $1,500 plus $8,500, for a total of $155,150.

EXERCISE 8.3

The drawing below shows the perimeter of a residence you are appraising.

A residence of similar construction, 45 feet by 50 feet and in the same area, was recently completed at a cost of $184,500. What is your cost estimate of the subject?

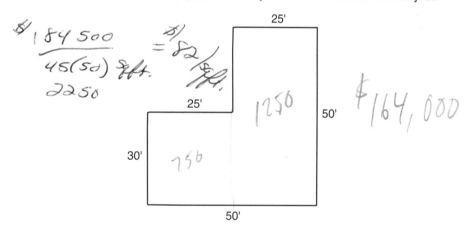

Check your answer against the one in the Answer Key at the back of the book.

Unit-in-Place Method

In the *unit-in-place method* of determining building reproduction cost, the costs of the various components of the subject structure are estimated separately, then added together to find the total cost. All of the components are itemized, each is measured where necessary, and the current construction cost per unit of measure of each component is multiplied by the number of measured units of that component in the subject building.

The unit-in-place method provides a much more detailed breakdown of the type of structure being appraised than does the square-foot method. As such, it is much more time-consuming but is likely to be more accurate than the square-foot method. As with the square-foot method, the unit-in-place method relies on cost manuals, with some allowances made (if necessary) for regional differences or recent cost increases.

A detailed breakdown of residential building costs (such as that provided in the publications of the Marshall and Swift Company) typically includes the following building components:

Foundation	Interior construction
Floor structure	Heating and cooling system
Floor covering	Electrical system
Exterior walls	Plumbing
Gable roof	Fireplace(s)
Ceiling	Appliances
Roof dormers	Stairway
Roof structure and covering	

If the costs for an industrial building were to be found in a cost manual, they might be given as shown in Figure 8.3. Cost data given at the end of Chapter 9 also show how cost figures may be broken down. *Note: Prices shown are for illustration purposes only.*

An example costing problem begins below and continues on the next four pages. The problem is based on a commercial property of standard specifications.

EXAMPLE

Using the cost data in Figure 8.3, we will compute the reproduction cost of the industrial building shown, with adjacent 50′ × 125′ parking area. The following items will be costed separately, then totaled to find the reproduction cost of the subject building: concrete foundation, roof, exterior walls, building frame, interior construction, floor, electrical, heating and A/C, plumbing, and parking area. *Later in this chapter, you will be asked to analyze and appraise a similar type of property, so study this example carefully.*

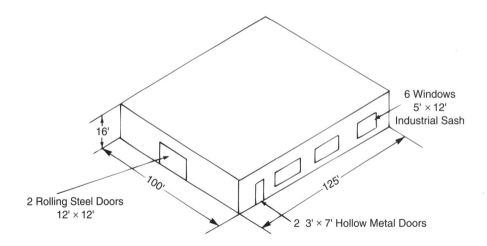

Foundation: The measured unit used for computing the construction cost of the foundation is the *linear foot,* which is a measurement of length, in this case the perimeter of the building. So

$$100' + 125' + 100' + 125' = 450'$$

FIGURE 8.3
Cost Data

Component	Cost per Measured Unit
Foundation 12″ concrete wall and footings	$30.70 per linear foot
Floor Construction 8″ reinforced concrete	$3.60 per sq. ft. of floor area
Framing 14′ steel columns, beams, and purlins	$4.50 per sq. ft. of support area
Roof Construction sheathing, 2″ polystyrene insulation, 4-ply asphalt and gravel covering	$3.70 per sq. ft.
Exterior Walls 12″ concrete block backup	$10.20 per sq. ft.
Windows industrial sash, steel, 50% vented	$14.20 per sq. ft.
Doors hollow metal, 3′ × 7′ rolling steel, chainhoist operated, 12′ × 12′	$355 per door $1,425 per door
Interior painting	$.35 per sq. ft.
Electrical wiring and fixtures	$3.10 per sq. ft. of building area
Heating and A/C	$5.30 per sq. ft. of building area
Plumbing including fixtures	$2.25 per sq. ft. of building area
Parking Area 3″ asphalt on 3″ stone base	$7.20 per sq. yd.

Because the cost is $30.70 per linear foot,

$$450 \text{ ft.} \times \$30.70 = \$13,815$$

Frame: The space occupied by the steel frame is measured in square feet of support area. The subject building has bearing walls, along with steel columns that support part of the roof area, so the portion supported by bearing walls must be subtracted from the total roof area. The roof area supported by bearing walls is considered to be halfway to the nearest frame columns. The frame columns of the subject building, as shown in the following illustration, are 25 feet apart; thus 12 ½ feet will be subtracted from each side dimension to find the roof area supported by the frame columns. In the illustration, the area supported by bearing walls is shaded, and the area supported by the steel frame is not shaded.

So

$$100' - (12 ½' + 12 ½') = 100' - 25' = 75'$$
$$125' - (12 ½' + 12 ½') = 125' - 25' = 100'$$
$$75' \times 100' = 7,500 \text{ sq. ft.}$$

The area supported by frame columns is multiplied by the cost of the steel frame, which is $4.50 per square foot.

$$7,500 \times \$4.50 = \$33,750$$

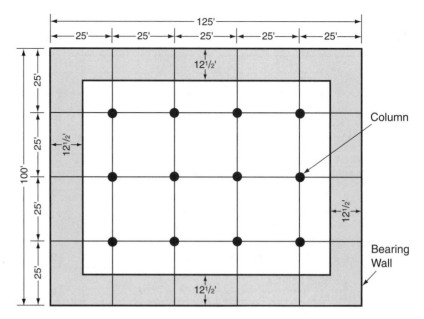

Floor: The floor is measured in square feet, so

$$100' \times 125' = 12,500 \text{ sq. ft.}$$

Because the cost is $3.60 per square foot,

$$12,500 \text{ sq. ft.} \times \$3.60 = \$45,000$$

Roof: The roof is measured in square feet, so

$$100' \times 125' = 12,500 \text{ sq. ft.}$$

Because the cost is $3.70 per square foot,

$$12,500 \text{ sq. ft.} \times \$3.70 = \$46,250$$

Exterior Walls: The walls are measured in square feet, but window and door areas must be subtracted. Per window,

$$5' \times 12' = 60 \text{ sq. ft.}$$

For six windows,

$$60 \text{ sq. ft.} \times 6 = 360 \text{ sq. ft.}$$

Per hollow metal door,

$$3' \times 7' = 21 \text{ sq. ft.}$$

For two doors,

$$21 \text{ sq. ft.} \times 2 = 42 \text{ sq. ft.}$$

Per rolling steel door,

$$12' \times 12' = 144 \text{ sq. ft.}$$

For two doors,

$$144 \text{ sq. ft.} \times 2 = 288 \text{ sq. ft.}$$

Total window and door area is

$$360 \text{ sq. ft.} + 42 \text{ sq. ft.} + 288 \text{ sq. ft.} = 690 \text{ sq. ft.}$$

Total area within the perimeters of the walls is

$$(16' \times 100' \times 2 \text{ walls}) + (16' \times 125' \times 2 \text{ walls}) = 7,200 \text{ sq. ft.}$$

Subtracting window and door areas,

$$7,200 \text{ sq. ft.} - 690 \text{ sq. ft.} = 6,510 \text{ sq. ft.}$$

Multiplying the remaining area by the cost of $10.20 per square foot,

$$6,510 \text{ sq. ft.} \times \$10.20 = \$66,402$$

Windows: Total window area, as computed above, is 360 square feet. At $14.20 per square foot,

$$360 \text{ sq. ft.} \times \$14.20 = \$5,112$$

Doors: There are two 3' × 7' hollow metal doors. At $355 per door,

$$2 \times \$355 = \$710$$

There are two 12' × 12' rolling steel doors. At $1,425 per door,

$$2 \times \$1,425 = \$2,850$$

Total cost, for all doors, is

$$\$710 + \$2,850 = \$3,560$$

Interior: Interior wall space, subtracting door and window areas, is the same as exterior wall space, or 6,510 square feet. At a cost of $.35 per square foot for painting,

$$6,510 \text{ sq. ft.} \times \$.35 = \$2,279$$

Electrical: Necessary electrical wiring and lighting fixtures for standard industrial illumination are measured per square foot of floor space. Because there are 12,500 square feet of floor space (as measured earlier), at $3.10 per square foot,

$$12,500 \text{ sq. ft.} \times \$3.10 = \$38,750$$

Heating and A/C: Measured per square foot of area served, in this case, the entire floor area. At $5.30 per square foot,

$$12,500 \text{ sq. ft.} \times \$5.30 = \$66,250$$

Plumbing: The cost of plumbing, including standard fixtures, is measured in square feet of building area. At $2.25 per square foot,

$$12,500 \text{ sq. ft.} \times \$2.25 = \$28,125$$

Parking Area:

The parking area adjacent to the building is illustrated below.

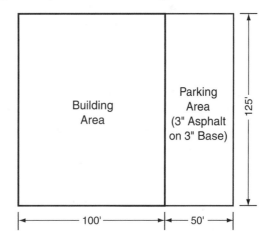

The cost of asphalt paving is measured in square yards, so

$$125' \times 50' = 6{,}250 \text{ sq. ft.}$$
$$6{,}250 \text{ sq. ft.} \div 9 = 694.4 \text{ sq. yd.}$$

At a cost of $7.20 per square yard for 3" asphalt paving on a 3" stone base,

$$694.4 \text{ sq. yd.} \times \$7.20 = \$5{,}000$$

In our sample cost analysis, no adjustments are necessary to allow for price increases since the cost data were compiled. Add all costs to arrive at the total reproduction cost of all improvements:

Foundation	$ 13,815
Frame	33,750
Floor	45,000
Roof	46,250
Exterior Walls	66,402
Windows	5,112
Doors	3,560
Interior	2,279
Electrical	38,750
Heating and A/C	66,250
Plumbing	28,125
Parking Area	5,000
	$354,293

The reproduction cost of the improvements on the subject property is $354,293. If this problem were to be carried through to find the market value estimate by the cost approach, the value of any depreciation on the improvements would have to be subtracted from the reproduction cost and the resultant figure added to the land value.

Exercise 8.4 requires that you apply what you have learned in the example problem to a similar structure. Although the measurements and construction cost information you will need are provided for you, remember that the unit-in-place method is based on accurate building specifications and measurements as well as knowledge of current construction costs.

EXERCISE 8.4

Based on the following unit-in-place costs, what is the reproduction cost estimate of a rectangular warehouse, 125' by 250'?

Foundation: concrete walls and footings at $37.30 per linear foot

Floor: reinforced concrete at $3.10 per sq. ft.

Roof: built-up tar and gravel at $2.40 per sq. ft.; roof sheathing at $.65 per sq. ft.; fiberboard insulation at $.55 per sq. ft.

Interior construction: painting and some partitions, at total cost of $4,500

Front exterior wall: common brick on concrete block, 125' long by 15' high, at $9.50 per sq. ft.; 2 windows, each 6' by 12', at $15.30 per sq. ft.; 10' by 12' drive-in door at a total cost of $1,300

Rear exterior wall: same as front wall with drive-in door, but no windows

Side exterior walls: concrete block, 250' long by 15' high, at $7.10 per sq. ft.; windows covering about 20 percent of wall area at $14.20 per sq. ft.

Steel framing: area supported by frame, 100' by 225'; with 14' eave height, at $4.50 per sq. ft.

Electrical: $3.25 per sq. ft. of floor area

Heating: $2.75 per sq. ft. of floor area

Plumbing: $1.60 per sq. ft. of floor area

Check your answer against the one in the Answer Key at the back of the book.

Quantity Survey Method

A builder or contractor estimating construction cost will need precise, up-to-date cost figures. Such an estimate usually is made by the *quantity survey method,* which necessitates a thorough itemization of all the costs expected in the construction of the building. As a result, this is the most comprehensive and accurate method of estimating reproduction cost.

Using the quantity survey method, *direct costs* (those related to materials and labor) are computed much more precisely than in the unit-in-place method. Every stage of construction is broken down into separate costs for materials and labor. The required expenditure for the electrical system, for instance, will take into account both the cost of materials at an estimated price per unit and the cost of labor for the required number of hours at the going rate per hour. Thus the appraiser must be able to estimate material unit quantities and costs as well as work times and labor rates. *Indirect costs* (those involved in necessary but not construction-related expenses, such as surveys, payroll taxes, and profit) are also added. A typical cost itemization for a 14-unit apartment building, using the quantity survey method, could include the following totals for the separate building components:

Direct Costs	
Clearing the land	$ 723
Rough and fine grading	16,753
Footings	8,760
Slabs	8,341
Entrance and stoops	4,200
Balconies	12,350
Interior stairs	575
Dampproofing	938
Rough and finished carpentry	127,390
Furring	3,480
Doors	3,560
Rough and finished hardware	11,722
Kitchen cabinets	14,250
Flooring	18,764
Refrigerators	11,920
Disposals	2,330
Gas ranges	7,386
Venetian blinds	4,800
Bathroom tile	7,297
Painting	13,750

Insulation	1,070	
Glazing	2,483	
Structural steel and lintels	4,747	
Ornamental iron	8,190	
Masonry	79,423	
Drywall	35,961	
Heating and air-conditioning	39,467	
Plumbing	44,200	
Electrical wiring	21,870	
Water mains	4,102	
Water and sewer connections	790	
Roofing and sheet metal	6,200	
Incidentals	9,340	
Cleaning, general and contract	5,900	
Landscaping	7,450	
Fence	1,800	
Temporary utilities	4,728	
Temporary roads and structures	2,857	
Streets, parking area, sidewalks, curbs, and gutters	33,689	
Sanitary and storm sewers	15,042	
Supervision and time keeping	21,785	$630,383
Indirect Costs		
Permit	$ 35	
Survey	1,980	
Layout	465	
Payroll taxes and insurance	8,570	
Builder's overhead and profit	64,000	75,050
Subtotal		$705,433
Entrepreneurial profit ($705,433 × .10)		70,543
Total Reproduction Cost New		$775,976

The last item often included in the construction cost calculation is *entrepreneurial profit* (also known as *developer's profit*), discussed briefly in Chapter 7. The management functions associated with major construction projects may be broken down into various areas of specialization. The development function may be separate from the building/contracting function; the developer may even hire a construction management firm to supervise the building contractor. As a result, the profit associated with the development function is itemized separately from the contractor's profit and other indirect costs. The developer basically is the risk taker. The amount of entrepreneurial profit ultimately received by the developer will depend on the success of the project. Of course, the element of risk also includes the possibility of loss if the project is unsuccessful.

The preceding simplified list of direct and indirect costs assumes that the builder is *not* the person developing the project, and the entry for "builder's overhead and profit" is included in indirect costs. It is more accurate (and realistic) to add the cost category for entrepreneurial profit to direct and indirect costs. In some cases, particularly when the builder/contractor works for the owner on a "build-to-suit" project, no separate entrepreneurial profit is identified. In other situations, as in this example, the contracting function is handled entirely apart from the development function and the developer has a separate profit expectation. This profit estimate should be based on market analysis. In the example, 10 percent, or $70,543, was added to reflect the market's expectation of profit.

Depending on market practice, entrepreneurial profit can be estimated as a percentage of

- direct costs,
- direct and indirect costs,
- direct and indirect costs plus land value, or
- the value of the completed project.

An appraiser using the quantity survey method obviously needs a much more comprehensive knowledge of building construction than he or she would using the square-foot or unit-in-place method. The appraiser must know every facet of building construction—almost as well as the builder does.

EXERCISE 8.5

Identify each of the following building costs as direct or indirect:

1. Payment to plumbing subcontractor

    Direct

2. Site preparation

    Direct

3. Contractor's performance bond

    Indirect

4. Barricade around construction site

    Direct

5. Builder's profit

    Indirect

6. Building permit   *Indirect*

Check your answers against those in the Answer Key at the back of the book.

■ SUMMARY

The cost approach can be a helpful tool to the appraiser in the appraisal of certain special purpose properties that are not normally bought and sold in the open market, and for all properties where there is inadequate market data. It can also be a misleading tool if solely relied on when there is adequate market data available to the appraiser.

In the cost approach, accrued depreciation is subtracted from the reproduction or replacement cost of the improvement(s), and the resulting figure is added to site value.

*must
know*

Replacement cost (current cost of a structure of comparable quality and utility) is computed when reproduction cost (current cost to construct an exact duplicate) is impractical. Reproduction or replacement cost is always based on a new structure, at current prices.

Reproduction/replacement cost can be found using the square-foot, unit-in-place, quantity survey, or index method. Each has its utility, although the quantity survey method results in the most accurate cost estimate.

ACHIEVEMENT EXAMINATION

1. The cost of improvements identical in design and material to those of the subject property is called the subject's

    a. reproduction cost.

    b. sales price.

    c. replacement cost.

    d. market value.

2. The cost of improvements identical in utility to those of the subject is called

    a. reproduction cost.

    b. sales price.

    c. replacement cost.

    d. market value.

3. In using the cost approach to appraising, the estimated construction cost of improvements usually will be based on

    a. their original cost.

    b. the cost of new improvements at current prices.

    c. book value.

    d. the national cost average of all components.

4. The index method of estimating construction cost is based on

    a. the original cost of improvements.

    b. the cost of new improvements at current prices.

    c. book value.

    d. the national cost average of all components.

5. If a commercial structure is rectangular with sides of 65 feet and 135 feet and the current local cost to build a similar structure is $45 per square foot, what is the estimated construction cost of the structure using the square-foot method?

    a. $18,000

    b. $180,000

    c. $394,875

    d. $364,500

6. A nationally based construction cost manual is acceptable for appraisal purposes if it

   a. is updated frequently.

   b. is based on median construction cost estimates.

   c. is published by a nationally recognized firm.

   d. contains regional cost multipliers.

7. In a residential appraisal utilizing the URAR form, gross living area is derived by

   a. totaling individual room areas.

   b. finding the area of the whole house based on outside measurements.

   c. finding the area of the whole house based on outside measurements, then subtracting the area of nonliving spaces.

   d. estimating all spaces based on room width, room length, and ceiling height.

8. The cost of supervising workers on a construction site is considered a(n)

   a. direct cost.

   b. overhead expense.

   c. indirect cost.

   d. incidental expense.

9. The term *entrepreneurial profit* refers to the

   a. subcontractors' profit.

   b. construction management firm's profit.

   c. developer's profit.

   d. real estate agent's profit.

10. The amount of entrepreneurial profit

    a. reflects the success of the project.

    b. is based on how project expenses are categorized.

    c. will always be the same, provided the project is completed within budget.

    d. cannot be estimated accurately.

Check your answers against those in the Answer Key at the back of the book.

CHAPTER 9

The Cost Approach— Part II: Depreciation

■ **OVERVIEW**

In the second part of the cost approach equation, depreciation is subtracted from the reproduction or replacement cost of improvements as of the date of valuation. Property value is then estimated by adding site value to the depreciated value of improvements.

This chapter explains the general types of depreciation and the methods most commonly used to estimate the amount by which a structure has depreciated. At the end of the chapter you will complete a sample appraisal of a commercial building using the cost approach.

■ **ACCRUED DEPRECIATION**

Depreciation may be defined as a loss in value from any cause. The loss in value may come from wear and tear or the presence of features that are deficient, excessive, or simply currently undesirable. There also may be external factors that cause a loss in value. *Accrued depreciation* represents the total difference between an improvement's cost new and its market value as of the date of appraisal.

Generally, there are three categories of depreciation: physical deterioration, functional obsolescence, and external obsolescence.

1. *Physical deterioration.* This is the physical wearing out of the structure, usually the most obvious form of depreciation. If a building needs painting or tuckpointing or has broken windows, cracked plaster, or water-damaged walls from a leaky roof, these are all the ordinary effects of wear and tear.

   Items exhibiting *curable physical deterioration* can be repaired or replaced economically; that is, the cost to cure the defect will result in an equal or greater increase in overall property value. The classic example is the cosmetic "fixer-upper" that is structurally sound but needs cleaning, minor repairs, and new paint to bring its appearance and appeal up to the standard of other properties in the neighborhood.

Items of physical deterioration that cannot be cured economically are placed within the category of *incurable physical deterioration*. The choice of category will not have an effect on the value estimate, provided the appraiser considers every item of depreciation only once.

2. *Functional obsolescence*. This results when layout, design, or other features are undesirable in comparison with features designed for the same functions in newer property. Functional obsolescence can be the result of a deficiency, the presence of a feature that should be replaced or modernized, or the presence of a feature that is superfluous (superadequate) for the structure's intended purpose.

   A two-story, five-bedroom house with one bathroom and only one of the bedrooms on the first floor and no bathroom on the second floor would be functionally undesirable; the same house might still be functionally undesirable if it had a second bathroom on the first floor and none on the second floor. Functional obsolescence depends on the changing requirements of homebuyers. When family rooms came into great demand, many homes were built with little or no dining room space, to allow for a family room at no major cost increase. In some areas, however, dining rooms and family rooms are both desirable, and a "formal" (separate) dining room may be a valuable feature.

   The use of replacement cost, rather than reproduction cost, eliminates the need to estimate some forms of functional obsolescence. For example, consider an older house with exceptionally high ceilings and a poor overall layout. Inherent in a replacement cost estimate would be an adjustment for the high ceilings, but not for the poor layout.

   Like physical deterioration, functional obsolescence can be either *curable* or *incurable*. If a defect is not easily remedied or economically justified, it is considered incurable. For example, a house with a poor floor plan suffers from functional obsolescence that is not easily cured. If a defect can be added, replaced, redesigned,or removed at a cost no greater than the resulting increase in property value, it is considered curable. An example might be the replacement of the original, outdated plumbing fixtures in an older house.

3. *External obsolescence* (also called *environmental, economic,* or *locational obsolescence*). This is any loss of value from causes outside the property itself and is almost always considered *incurable.* Zoning changes, proximity to nuisances, changes in land use, and market conditions can all be causes of external obsolescence. If a drive-in restaurant is constructed on a vacant lot, an adjacent residential property will probably lose value because of the increased noise and traffic.

   External obsolescence can be created by a variety of factors. It is *locational* when the property's neighborhood, community, state, or region becomes less desirable and value subsequently declines. It is *economic* when market conditions lower demand, as during a recession. It is *political* when a nearby land use is changed by the local governing body to permit a less desirable use, such as a landfill. A current example of how the national political process can affect local land values is the closure of military bases across the country. For many communities, particularly those with few other sources of employment or business revenue, the closing of a military facility will have a major impact on the local economy, including real estate values.

Care must be taken to determine whether the cause of external obsolescence has already been reflected in the appraiser's estimate of land value. While it is

The Americans with Disabilities Act

The category of functional obsolescence has been greatly expanded for commercial properties by the provisions of Title III of the Americans with Disabilities Act of 1991 (ADA). Title III requires that new places of public accommodation (as defined by the law) be built so that there are no architectural or communication barriers to prevent their accessibility to persons having a disability. Any such barriers to full accessibility that are found in existing buildings must be removed if doing so is readily achievable.

For the purposes of the law, places of public accommodation include virtually all places to which members of the public are invited, including hotels, motels, restaurants, bars, theaters, movie houses, convention centers, retail and service establishments, public transportation terminals, museums and libraries, zoos, amusement parks, schools, social service centers, and places of exercise or recreation (such as gyms and golf courses).

Examples of accommodations that may be required by the law include constructing a ramp or widening a doorway to accommodate a wheelchair, lowering counters or display shelves, providing an accessible lavatory sink and toilet, and repositioning a water fountain. The decision as to whether a particular accommodation is readily achievable is made on a case-by-case basis, but is based on the nature and cost of the action needed, the overall financial resources available, and the relationship of the site to the business or other enterprise using it, including the availability of other locations.

Unfortunately, many buildings that predate enactment of ADA require accommodations to make them fully accessible; in fact, the inspections and appraisal performed at the time of a sale or other transaction may represent the first analysis of the structure's compliance with the law. The effect on market value of necessary modifications or additions can be estimated using paired sale analysis, as described in Chapter 10.

The penalty for noncompliance with ADA can be costly. Builders are now aware of the necessity to make model homes and other marketing sites accessible, even when the homes themselves would not fall within the law's requirements. But the issue of accessibility has also been addressed by HUD. In 1997, HUD took an unprecedented action by fining a Minnesota builder for false claims that the company's townhomes and condominiums met federal requirements for accessibility by the handicapped. (Features noted by HUD that would have required little or no additional cost by the builder in order to make the units accessible included placement of wall outlets and thermostats; other features promised but not delivered included lowered thresholds and reinforcement of bathroom walls to allow future addition of grab bars.) The builder was fined $10,000, denied FHA insurance for one year, and required to make $160,000 in repairs and put funds in escrow for future repairs.

A copy of the Americans with Disabilities Act, as well as the text of the Americans with Disabilities Act Accessibility Guidelines for Buildings and Facilities (ADAAG) promulgated by the Architectural and Transportation Barriers Compliance Board, can be found in the *ADA Handbook: Employment & Construction Issues Affecting Your Business* by Martha R. Williams and Marcia L. Russell (Chicago: Real Estate Education Company, 1993). For more information on appraiser compliance with ADA, read "Appraisers and the Americans with Disabilities Act" by Richard W. Hoyt and Robert J. Aalberts in *The Appraisal Journal,* vol. LXIII, no. 3, July 1995.

Copies of the law and applicable regulations, as well as case updates and information on other news regarding ADA, are also available from the Department of Justice at its Web site *(www.ada.gov).*

---

true that land does not depreciate, the value of land can (and does) go down. Because land is always valued as if vacant, external obsolescence frequently affects highest and best use, resulting in the existing improvements being an overimprovement. In that instance, the depreciation is functional, not external.

Depreciation is the most difficult part of the cost approach equation to estimate accurately. The older the structure, the more likely it is to have deteriorated to a marked degree, often in ways not easily observable (such as corroded plumbing lines or cracked plaster hidden by wallpaper or paneling). Physical deterioration begins the moment an improvement is constructed and continues until it is no longer usable.

Depreciation (deterioration and obsolescence) may vary significantly, depending on market conditions as of the date of valuation. If demand exceeds supply, buyers may overlook many "typical" items of depreciation. For example, a single-family house located on a busy street may normally suffer from external obsolescence due to the proximity of the traffic and all of the obnoxious and noxious conditions associated with traffic. In a tight market, however, buyers may overlook, or at least not penalize as heavily, frontage on a major arterial.

A buyer's measure of depreciation may vary considerably, depending on the price range of homes in the area; for example, the lack of car storage in an older, lower-priced neighborhood may not be an item of depreciation at all. The lack of car storage in an upscale neighborhood, on the other hand, would probably be a major item of depreciation—particularly if there was no room to add car storage or if the cost to do so was high. Similarly, in lower-priced neighborhoods, buyers often are willing to do their own painting and decorating. So if a house in a lower-priced neighborhood needs painting, a buyer's measure of depreciation may be simply the cost of paint. In an upscale neighborhood, however, a house that needs painting and decorating may suffer significant deterioration because prospective buyers may take into account the cost of having professionals perform a turnkey painting and decorating job.

Every structure has an *economic life,* also called its *useful life,* during which it will be functionally useful for its original intended purpose. When a structure no longer can be used, it ceases to serve any profitable purpose. At that point, the value of the site is no higher *with* the improvement than it would be without it. In some cases, the existence of a structure may make a site *less* valuable because the cost of demolition and removal of the structure must be taken into account.

A structure's economic life may or may not coincide with its *physical life,* which is the length of time it could physically exist if allowed to remain standing. In fact, more buildings are torn down in still-usable condition than fall down from deterioration. Most buildings that are torn down are not totally derelict but have instead become uneconomic (unprofitable) in terms of the highest and best use of the site they occupy.

A structure's *effective age* reflects the quality of its construction and the degree of maintenance it has received. Any structure will suffer some physical defect eventually, whether from the elements or from the way in which it is used. Those defects will have a greater effect on improvements that were poorly constructed. If necessary maintenance and repairs are neglected, the process of deterioration is enhanced, and the physical life of the structure is shortened. On the other hand, well-constructed and well-maintained improvements benefit from a prolonged physical life.

Effective age will be greater or less than chronological age when a structure's condition differs significantly from that of similar structures in its market area that have had normal maintenance and upkeep, but no remodeling or updating of any kind. The benchmark is a typical residence that has been maintained with no significant improvements but no significant neglect.

EXAMPLE

The Smith residence was constructed 20 years ago. The Smiths have maintained their home in excellent condition, including repainting the exterior several times and re-modeling the kitchen. Similar homes in the Smiths' neighborhood are adequately maintained but not as well as the Smith home. The Smith residence thus has an effec-tive age of only 15 years.

The *remaining economic life* of a structure is the period from the date of appraisal during which it can be expected to remain useful for its original intended purpose. In determining that period, the appraiser must consider not only the present condition of the structure but also other known factors that might affect its future use or desirability, such as the use or condition of nearby property. Houses adjacent to a shopping mall may suffer from increased traffic noise, fumes, and congestion. Over time, those houses may be sold more frequently and receive less investment in upkeep and repairs than others in the same neighborhood but not as close to the shopping area.

The appraiser should always keep in mind the reaction of the market (buyers) to similar properties. The phenomenon of *gentrification* is an example of the desirability that even run-down properties may have if other factors, such as location and high demand, are strong enough.

By depreciating a structure's cost, the appraiser takes into account the probable past and future effects of its economic life, considering both its condition and outside factors.

Depreciation can be measured either directly or indirectly. The age-life method and observed condition method measure depreciation directly. The capitalized value and sales comparison methods measure depreciation indirectly.

Age-Life Method

The *age-life method* of computing depreciation (also called the *straight-line method* or *economic age-life method*) is the simplest to understand and use. It is based on the assumption that depreciation occurs at an even rate throughout the projected life of a structure. In the age-life method, accrued depreciation is estimated by comparing the effective age of the structure at the time of valuation with its total economic life. If a graph is constructed with *value* as one axis and *years of economic life* as the other axis, the line connecting the two would be a straight line. Any point on the line would indicate the structure's remaining value after the given number of years has elapsed. After 30 years, for instance, the graph shown in Figure 9.1 indicates that the structure's remaining value is $40,000; thus, the property has depreciated $40,000 ($80,000 – $40,000).

FIGURE 9.1
Age-Life Depreciation

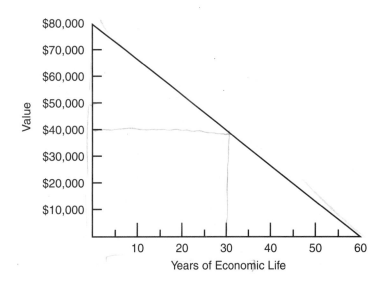

Because of differences in quality of construction and the degree of maintenance received, similar structures do not necessarily depreciate at the same rate. For this reason, appraisers normally base depreciation estimates on the *effective age* of the structure rather than the actual age.

The appraiser does not have to draw a graph to estimate depreciation by this method. A structure's loss in value can be assumed to be the ratio of its effective age to its total economic life. The formula for estimating depreciation then is

Effective Age ÷ Total Economic Life = Accrued Depreciation

A decimal figure, which may be converted to a percentage, results from this equation. This percentage is applied to the structure's reproduction or replacement cost to estimate lump-sum depreciation from all causes. The depreciation estimate is then subtracted from the cost figure to arrive at value.

EXAMPLE	The reproduction cost of a commercial building is estimated to be $800,000. The building should have an economic life of 50 years, and it is now five years old, which is also its effective age. What is its rate of depreciation, and what is its value by the cost approach (exclusive of land value)?

Using the age-life ratio, total depreciation is 10 percent (5 ÷ 50). In this example, the building is now worth $720,000:

Reproduction cost	$800,000
Less total accrued depreciation	
($800,000 × .10)	−80,000
Building value by the cost approach	$720,000

Although the age-life method is easy to apply and understand, it does have limitations:

■ It assumes that every building depreciates on a straight-line basis over the span of its economic life. This is generally not true. Depreciation varies with market conditions and the economic cycles of a neighborhood.

■ It lumps value loss from all causes into an overall estimate of depreciation.

■ It does not distinguish between curable and incurable deterioration.

■ Total economic life may be difficult to predict because it refers to a future time. Effective age is also subjective.

Variations of the Age-Life Method

In one variation of the age-life method of estimating accrued depreciation, known as the *modified effective age-life method,* the cost to cure all curable items of depreciation, both physical and functional, is estimated first. This sum is then deducted from reproduction or replacement cost new of the improvements. Finally, the age-life ratio is applied to the remaining cost to arrive at depreciation from all other causes. For example:

Replacement cost new	$500,000
Less curable items	− 50,000
Remaining cost	$450,000
Less age-life ratio	
(15 ÷ 75 = .20 × $450,000)	− 90,000
Building value	$360,000

This variation of the age-life method is most useful when the subject property has curable depreciation not typically found in sales of properties in the subject market. When the curable items of depreciation are handled separately, the appraiser may determine that utilizing a shorter effective age and/or a longer economic life expectancy in calculating the age-life ratio is appropriate.

This same kind of analysis can be applied in situations where external obsolescence is present in the subject property but not in sales of other properties in the subject market. The dollar amount of external obsolescence is estimated first and deducted from reproduction or replacement cost new; then, the age-life ratio is applied to the remaining cost to derive depreciation from all causes *except* external obsolescence. The estimated depreciation from external obsolescence is added to the estimated depreciation from the age-life method to arrive at an estimate of total depreciation.

E X E R C I S E   9 . 1

A company bought a building for $450,000 and estimated its economic life at 25 years. Compute the amount of the building's total depreciation under the age-life method after seven years.

Depriciation

$$7 \div 25 \times 450,000 = \boxed{126,000} = 324,000$$

Check your answer against the one in the Answer Key at the back of the book.

Observed Condition Method

In the *observed condition method* of computing depreciation (also known as the *breakdown method*), the appraiser estimates the loss in value for curable and incurable items of depreciation. A *curable* item is one that can be easily and economically restored or replaced, resulting in an immediate increase in appraised value. An item that would be impossible, too expensive, or not cost-effective to replace is labeled *incurable*. Following are examples in each of the three depreciation categories (physical deterioration, functional obsolescence, and external obsolescence):

1. *Physical deterioration—curable*. This category includes repairs that are economically feasible and would result in an increase in appraised value equal to or exceeding their cost. Items of routine maintenance fall into this category, as do simple improvements that can add far more than their cost to the value of the property. Fixtures and appliances should be in good working order, broken windows replaced, and landscaping tended. Exterior and interior painting often will return more than its cost by improving the overall appearance of a structure, particularly a residence.

   The loss in value due to curable physical deterioration is the cost to cure the item(s) of depreciation.

   Physical deterioration—incurable. This category includes the separate physical components of a structure, which do not deteriorate at the same rate. If roof, foundation, electrical system, and so on did deteriorate at the same rate, the economic life of a structure would simply be the economic life of its components. Unfortunately (or fortunately), the foundation of a structure typically will last far longer than its roofing material, and other items will need replacing at other times.

Generally, the individual components of a structure can be divided into *short-lived items* and *long-lived items* of incurable physical deterioration. Short-lived items are those that may be replaced or repaired once or more over the economic life of the structure. These include roof, gutters, wall coverings, cabinets, and other finishing materials. Painting and decorating could be included here or under curable physical deterioration. Loss in value due to depreciation of these items can be estimated on an individual basis or by assigning an average percentage of depreciation to the total value of all items.

Long-lived items are those that should last as long as a structure's remaining economic life. Foundation, framework, walls, ceilings, and masonry would fall within this category.

Loss in value can be based on a percentage reflecting the number of years of remaining economic life of all such items as a group, or they can be depreciated individually.

2. *Functional obsolescence—curable.* This category includes physical or design features that are inadequate or no longer considered desirable by property buyers or that are not necessary for the structure's intended use but could be added, replaced, redesigned, or removed economically (at a cost no greater than the resulting increase in value). Outmoded plumbing fixtures are usually easily replaced. Room function might be redefined at no cost if the basic room layout allowed for it, such as converting a bedroom adjacent to a kitchen to use as a family room. A closet converted to a darkroom might be easily converted back to a closet.

Loss in value from an item of curable functional obsolescence takes into account the fact that an item of remodeling or repair is more expensive when done separately than when work of the same design and specifications is performed as part of the construction of the entire structure. Thus, loss in value is the difference between the increase in total reproduction cost that would cure the item and what it would cost to cure only that item. If a kitchen suffers from lack of modern cabinets and appliances, its depreciated value is the difference between the addition to reproduction cost represented by a modernized kitchen and the cost to modernize the kitchen separately. If a modern kitchen would add $9,000 to reproduction cost and the cost as of the same date to modernize the existing kitchen by remodeling is $10,500, then $1,500 is the loss in value due to an out-of-date kitchen. Remodeling an existing structure to cure a defect is more expensive with regard to that defect than if an entirely new structure could be built without the defect.

If replacement rather than reproduction cost is used, physical or design features that exceed current requirements (a superadequacy) represent a loss in value equal to the cost to remove them; their initial construction cost and degree of physical deterioration are not considered.

Functional obsolescence—incurable. This category includes currently undesirable physical or design features that could not be easily or economically remedied. The feature might be the result of a deficiency, a lack of modernization, or a superadequacy. Many older multistory industrial structures are considered less suitable than one-story structures. Older apartments with large rooms and high ceilings might not bring as high a rent per cubic foot of space as smaller, newer apartments. The cost to correct these deficiencies is not justified. The single-family house with three or more bedrooms but only one bathroom clearly suffers from functional obsolescence that is not readily cured.

Another form of incurable functional obsolescence is the *misplaced improvement*, a structure that is inappropriate for the site on which it is located. Why would anyone put an inappropriate structure on a site? Most misplaced improvements are not planned to be that way. The reasons that an improvement is considered misplaced usually come about some time after the improvement is made. For example, a structure that is perfectly suited to its site and neighborhood may become inappropriate if the area's zoning is changed and most other properties are adapted to the new permitted use. Or a structure built in a mostly undeveloped area may eventually be surrounded by a different type of development.

EXAMPLE

The Houser family lives in a single-family residence near a downtown area. Zoning in the area, which was once solely residential, now allows limited retail and other commercial use. As a result, almost every lot on the Housers' block in this highly desirable area has been converted to a professional office or other use. The Houser residence, now located between an insurance agency and a real estate broker's office, may be considered a misplaced improvement.

The loss in value caused by incurable functional obsolescence could be estimated by comparing either the selling prices or rents of similar structures with and without the defect. Whether a misplaced improvement will result in a lowering of estimated market value will most likely depend on how adaptable the property is to any other use.

3. *External obsolescence—incurable only.* This is caused by factors not on the subject property, so this type of obsolescence cannot be considered curable. Proximity of a residence to a nuisance such as a factory would be an unchangeable factor that could not be assumed curable by the owner of the subject property. A depressed real estate market could also have a significant effect on market value. The appraiser's market analysis should be thorough enough to reveal any economic or other factors likely to affect market value.

When estimating accrued depreciation by the observed condition method, the appraiser must decide on the amount of value lost through applicable depreciation in each of the categories, as described earlier. The appraiser must be careful not to depreciate the same item more than once.

The loss in value due to external obsolescence also could be measured by comparing the selling prices or rents of similar properties, including some that are and some that are not affected by this type of depreciation. The response of buyers in the market to properties exhibiting the same type of depreciation is probably the best value indicator, but it may be difficult to isolate the loss in value due solely to that factor. For income-producing property, another way to measure loss in value due to external depreciation is by the *capitalized value method,* discussed next.

EXERCISE 9.2

Determine the depreciation category of each of the following items as specifically as you can:

1. Residential location on heavily traveled highway

E. O, incurable

2. Severe termite damage throughout a structure

P.D.   incurable

3. Need for tuckpointing (repair of mortar between bricks) on house in overall good condition

P.D.   curable

4. Office space adjacent to extremely noisy factory

E.O.

5. Newer split-level house in good condition but with potholes in asphalt driveway

P D   curable

6. Dry rot in attic beams

P D   curable

7. Major commercial airport built in 1940, with runways too short for modern jet planes

F O   curable

8. Three-bedroom house with one bathroom

F O   incurable

9. Hot water-radiator heating system

F O   curable

10. 20,000-seat sports arena with no drinking fountains

F O   incurable

Check your answers against those in the Answer Key at the back of the book.

Capitalized Value Method

The *capitalized value method* of determining depreciation is also referred to as the *rent loss method*. In this method, the appraiser determines the loss in income resulting from depreciation by comparing the income produced by similar properties, then applying a *capitalization rate* to that amount of income to determine its effect on overall property value. It is necessary to have comparable properties that possess the same defect and some that do not, to isolate the difference in rental value due solely to that cause. The following example shows how a *gross rent multiplier (GRM)* can be used to determine the loss in value attributable to an item of incurable functional obsolescence. A GRM relates the sales price of a property to its rental income. The GRM is computed by dividing the sales price of a property by its gross monthly unfurnished rent. The development, analysis, and use of multipliers is covered in Chapter 11, "The Income Capitalization Approach." More complex methods of developing a capitalization rate are discussed in Chapter 12.

EXAMPLE

The Moran residence has four bedrooms and one-and-one-half bathrooms. Comparable homes with the same number of bathrooms rent for $695 per month, while comparable homes with two full bathrooms rent for $725 per month.

The monthly difference in rent attributable to the lack of two full bathrooms is $30. That number is multiplied by a factor of 135, which is the monthly gross rent multiplier for the area. The resulting figure of $4,050 is the loss in value to the reproduction cost of the subject property that is attributable to one item of incurable functional obsolescence.

EXERCISE 9.3

A structure with an obsolete floor plan is being appraised. A comparable structure with the same floor plan rents for $980 per month. A comparable structure with a more desirable floor plan rents for $1,100 per month. If the monthly rent multiplier is 125, what is the loss in value caused by the obsolete floor plan?

Check your answer against the one in the Answer Key at the back of the book.

Market Extraction Method

The *market extraction method,* also referred to as the *market comparison* or *sales comparison* method, measures accrued depreciation directly from the subject property's market by analyzing comparable sales from which depreciation can be extracted.

Total accrued depreciation applicable to the subject can be estimated by following four steps:

1. The land value of a comparable is subtracted from its selling price to find the depreciated value of the improvements.
2. The depreciated value is subtracted from the reproduction cost of the improvements to find the dollar amount of depreciation.
3. The dollar amount of depreciation is divided by the age of the improvements to find the depreciation rate, expressed as a percent of total depreciation per year.
4. If the depreciation rate is fairly consistent for at least several comparables, the appraiser applies that percent, multiplied by the age of the subject property's improvements, to the reproduction cost of those improvements. The resulting figure is the dollar amount of depreciation for the subject property.

Property A, a lot and warehouse, sold for $350,000, has an appraised land value of $87,500, and is 16 years old. The reproduction cost of improvements is $437,500. Property B, also a lot and warehouse, sold for $400,000, has an appraised land value of $100,000, and is 12 years old. The reproduction cost of improvements is $428,600.

Property A has an improvement value of $262,500 ($350,000 – $87,500), indicating depreciation of $175,000 ($437,500 – $262,500), or 40 percent of reproduction cost ($175,000 ÷ $437,500), for a yearly depreciation rate of 2.5 percent (40% ÷ 16 years).

Property B has an improvement value of $300,000 ($400,000 – $100,000), indicating depreciation of $128,600 ($428,600 – $300,000), or 30 percent of reproduction cost ($128,600 ÷ $428,600), for a yearly depreciation rate of 2.5 percent (30% ÷ 12 years).

In the preceding example, a yearly rate of 2.5 percent could be multiplied by the age in years of the subject improvements to find the percentage of depreciation to be multiplied by the reproduction cost of the improvements.

While market extraction is a reliable method of measuring accrued depreciation, its accuracy depends on the existence of truly comparable sales of both improved properties and vacant sites. It also requires an accurate estimate of reproduction cost new of the subject improvements.

EXERCISE 9.4

A structure with an obsolete floor plan is being appraised. A comparable structure with the same floor plan recently sold for $142,000. A comparable structure with a more desirable floor plan recently sold for $156,000. What is the loss in value attributable to the floor plan?

156 – 142 ~~×14~~ =

14K

(14K)

Check your answer against the one in the Answer Key at the back of the book.

Itemizing Accrued Depreciation

To make the most accurate and thorough use of the cost approach, the appraiser must compute applicable depreciation in each category (physical deterioration, functional obsolescence, and external obsolescence), then subtract those figures from the reproduction or replacement cost of the improvement(s). The appraiser does so by listing all items within a category and determining the amount of depreciation attributable to each.

While one of the indirect methods of calculating depreciation (capitalized value or sales comparison) may be the only available method for some types of depreciation or property, in general the better approach is to estimate a percentage of depreciation for each feature. Those percentages can be computed and the resulting figures added to find the total loss in reproduction cost. Remember, a given item should not be depreciated more than once; that is, it should not appear in more than one category when values are calculated.

EXAMPLE

The following chart gives the items of curable and short-lived incurable physical deterioration found in a one-story house, as well as the reproduction cost of each item. What amount will be subtracted from the house's reproduction cost of $92,750 as curable physical deterioration, the first step in the observed condition method of determining depreciation?

Item	Reproduction Cost	Percent Depreciation	Amount of Depreciation
Exterior Painting	$1,400	60%	$840
Carpeting	2,600	20	520
Air Conditioner Compressor	1,400	70	980
Water Heater	350	100	350

Total reproduction cost of items of curable and short-lived incurable physical deterioration is $5,750 ($1,400 + $2,600 + $1,400 + $350).

Total amount of curable and short-lived incurable physical deterioration is $2,690 ($840 + $520 + $980 + $350).

Because long-lived incurable physical deterioration is usually based on general wear and tear of items not separately measured by the appraiser, the economic age-life method of computing depreciation is applied to the reproduction cost remaining *after* the full value of other items of physical deterioration has been subtracted.

EXAMPLE

In the previous example, the house is ten years old (also its effective age) and has an estimated remaining economic life of 40 years. The appraiser has determined that the amount of long-lived incurable physical deterioration is 10/50, or 20 percent of the house's remaining reproduction cost. After the full value of all items of physical deterioration is subtracted, the remaining reproduction cost is $87,000 ($92,750 – $5,750). The amount attributable to long-lived incurable physical deterioration is $17,400 (1/5 of $87,000). Total depreciation due to physical deterioration is $20,090 ($2,690 + $17,400).

The next categories, functional and external obsolescence, may be derived by one of the methods outlined in this chapter. When all categories of depreciation have been applied to the reproduction cost, the land value of the property being appraised is added to the depreciated value to determine market value by the cost approach.

EXAMPLE

There is no functional obsolescence in the house described in the preceding examples. External obsolescence due to location too close to a highway is estimated by the sales comparison method at $7,000. Land value is estimated at $44,000. Therefore:

Reproduction cost	$ 92,750
Physical deterioration	–20,090
Functional obsolescence	N/A
External obsolescence	–7,000
Depreciated building cost	$ 65,660
Site value	44,000
Property value estimate by cost approach	$109,660

EXERCISE 9.5

You are estimating the market value of a lot with a one-story industrial building that is 12 years old and has a remaining economic life of 48 years. You believe that 20 percent is an adequate depreciation deduction for everything except the following:

	Reproduction Cost	Observed Depreciation
Heating system	$12,800	60%
Plumbing	15,200	30
Electric and power	23,000	40
Floors	18,200	25
Roof	16,500	55

Additional information: The building is 125' by 160'. You estimate that it would cost $55 per square foot to reproduce the building. You estimate site value at $180,000.

What is your opinion of the property's market value?

Check your answer against the one in the Answer Key at the back of the book.

EXERCISE 9.6

The property you are asked to appraise is a ten-year-old, one-story, single-family dwellling with 1,900 sq. ft. of living area.

Given the following data, estimate reproduction cost, cost per square foot of living area, accrued depreciation, and total property value using the cost approach.

Cost data

• Direct costs (including labor, materials, equipment, and subcontractors' fees), $98,500

• Indirect costs (including profit and overhead, architect's fees, survey, legal fees, permits, licenses, insurance, taxes, financing charges, and selling expenses), $26,500

Depreciation data

Physical deterioration

• Curable physical deterioration (deferred maintenance), $5,250

• Incurable physical deterioration—short-lived items, $12,250

• Incurable physical deterioration—long-lived items:

– Observed effective age (after curing physical curable and physical incurable short-lived items and curable functional obsolescence), 5 years

– Estimated economic life expectancy, 50 years

Functional obsolescence

• Curable functional obsolescence: none

• Incurable functional obsolescence: none

External obsolescence (location too close to highway; estimated by the sales comparison method), $9,000

Site value

Estimated value of site by sales comparison approach, $40,000

Check your answers against those in the Answer Key at the back of the book.

FIGURE 9.2

Cost Approach

COST APPROACH TO VALUE (not required by Fannie Mae)		
Provide adequate information for the lender/client to replicate the below cost figures and calculations.		
Support for the opinion of site value (summary of comparable land sales or other methods for estimating site value)		

ESTIMATED ☒ REPRODUCTION OR ☐ REPLACEMENT COST NEW	OPINION OF SITE VALUE .... = $ *50,000*	
Source of cost data	Dwelling *2,000* Sq. Ft. @ $ *95* .... = $ *190,000*	
Quality rating from cost service Effective date of cost data	Sq. Ft. @ $ .... = $	
Comments on Cost Approach (gross living area calculations, depreciation, etc.)	*Extras (pool)* 20,000	
See sketch for measurement analysis. Cost estimate based on current costs of local contractors and verified by current cost manual. The depreciation estimate reflects observed effective age. Site value supported by market data on comparable sites.	Garage/Carport *625* Sq. Ft. @ $ *25* .... = $ *15,625*	
	Total Estimate of Cost-New .... = $ *225,625*	
	Less Physical	Functional	External
	Depreciation *36,000*		= $(*36,000*)
	Depreciated Cost of Improvements .... = $ *189,625*	
	"As-is" Value of Site Improvements .... = $ *8,000*	
Estimated Remaining Economic Life (HUD and VA only) Years	Indicated Value By Cost Approach .... = $ *247,625*	

Cost Approach Using the URAR Form

In the Cost Approach analysis section of the URAR form (Figure 9.2), the appraiser is required to

- estimate the value of the site;

- compute the area of the dwelling;

- estimate the reproduction cost of the dwelling at current market prices; additional lines are provided for calculating the cost of any property features not included as part of the square-foot estimate of the main living space, such as a porch, deck, or patio;

- compute the area of any garage, carport, or other structure and estimate reproduction cost at current market prices;

- estimate the amount by which the structures have depreciated;

- estimate the "as is" value of any other site improvements, such as landscaping, driveway, fences, and so on, provided they are not included in the Opinion of Site Value line;

- add site value to the depreciated cost of improvements to find the indicated value; and

- explain in the Comments section how the cost approach was applied; comment on items such as the source of cost data, types of depreciation found, and how the site value was derived.

The appraisal usually will include an addendum showing a rough sketch of the perimeter of the subject structure(s), with dimensions given in feet.

EXERCISE 9.7

Complete the blank URAR Cost Approach section provided in Figure 9.3 using the following information.

The subject property is a rectangle, 75 feet wide and 35 feet deep. There is a center front entrance but no front porch. There is a rear sliding glass door to the left of the house, opening onto a deck that is 25 feet wide by 18 feet deep. The built-in garage is 26 feet by 26 feet. The energy-efficient items on the property are the same as those enjoyed by other homes in the neighborhood—well-insulated walls, ceilings, and floors. There are no special energy-efficient fixtures.

The appraiser gathered current costs from local contractors actively engaged in building similar houses in the area. These costs were then compared to known costs published by current cost manuals. Cost estimates are based on $112 per square foot for residential construction of this quality, $20 per square foot for decking and $30 per square foot for the garage.

The subject property is 22 years old and in good overall condition. Depreciation due to physical deterioration is estimated at 20 percent and is based on the effective age of the house in relation to other houses in the area. There is no evidence of functional or external obsolescence.

Site value, including all amenities commonly found in comparable sites (such as underground utilities, storm and sanitary sewers, and concrete curbs and gutters) is estimated by analysis of comparable properties at $98,000. The value "as is" of site improvements not considered in any other category (such as the driveway and landscaping) is estimated to be $12,000.

Check your answers against those in the Answer Key at the back of the book.

FIGURE 9.3
Cost Approach

COST APPROACH TO VALUE (not required by Fannie Mae)				
Provide adequate information for the lender/client to replicate the below cost figures and calculations.				
Support for the opinion of site value (summary of comparable land sales or other methods for estimating site value)				
ESTIMATED ☐ REPRODUCTION OR ☐ REPLACEMENT COST NEW	OPINION OF SITE VALUE .... = $			
Source of cost data	Dwelling	Sq. Ft. @ $	....	=$
Quality rating from cost service Effective date of cost data		Sq. Ft. @ $	....	=$
Comments on Cost Approach (gross living area calculations, depreciation, etc.)				
	Garage/Carport	Sq. Ft. @ $	....	=$
	Total Estimate of Cost-New		....	= $
	Less Physical	Functional	External	
	Depreciation			=$( )
	Depreciated Cost of Improvements			=$
	"As-is" Value of Site Improvements			=$
Estimated Remaining Economic Life (HUD and VA only) Years	Indicated Value By Cost Approach			=$

■ SUMMARY

Accrued depreciation must be estimated, then subtracted from the reproduction or replacement cost of the improvement(s), and the resulting figure added to site value, to determine value by the cost approach.

In the appraisal of older structures in particular, the problem of measuring depreciation accurately and convincingly may be impossible. In such a case, greater emphasis should be placed on the sales comparison and/or income capitalization approaches. On the other hand, the cost approach may be the best (or only) method of evaluating special-purpose properties, such as schools.

Accrued depreciation must be estimated for each category: physical deterioration, functional obsolescence, and external obsolescence.

Depreciation may be determined using the economic age-life, observed condition, capitalized value, or market extraction method.

9

ACHIEVEMENT EXAMINATION

You now have the opportunity to apply what you have learned in Chapters 8 and 9. You will be guided through a detailed simulation of an industrial appraisal problem, in which you have to perform cost and depreciation analyses to arrive at an opinion of property value by the cost approach. You will estimate reproduction cost, depreciation, land value, and total property value.

Each computation you must record is numbered so that you can check your answer in the Answer Key at the back of the book. To make the best use of this case problem, you should check each answer as it is derived, rather than waiting until you have reached your opinion of value.

You will be using the following data in this problem:

Identification of Property:

> The subject property is located at the corner of Parker Avenue and Plymouth Road (see Exhibit A on page 187) and is improved with a one-story office and factory building, approximately 20 years old. The lot is rectangular. The building is on the west section of the lot, with parking space to the east.

Neighborhood:

> The neighborhood is located approximately four miles from the center of a small city. The immediate area is developed with various types of industrial and commercial properties, such as auto showrooms, gas stations, tool and die factories, and photographic and instrument manufacturers. The subject property is accessible to both employee automobile and truck traffic.

Public Utilities and Zoning:

> All the public utilities are installed and in service. These include gas, electricity, sewers, telephone, and water. The zoning is light industrial.

Land Value:

> On the land comparison table in Exhibit F (see page 190), there are four plots of land that are reliable indications of value for the subject property. Adjustments were made for size, location, date of sale, and desirability.

In estimating land value for this type of property, the square foot rate is the most practical measurement used in this area.

Exterior Construction:

  Foundation—12" concrete wall and footings
  Floor—6" reinforced concrete
  Exterior walls—12" common brick with block backup; jumbo face brick veneer
  Framing—steel frame with 14' eave height
  Roof—sheathing, 1⅛" fiberglass insulation, four-ply tar and gravel covering
  Windows—industrial sash, aluminum, 50 percent vented
  Doors—six 3' × 7' hollow metal; one rolling steel 12' × 12', chain hoist-operated

Interior Construction:

  Walls—painted drywall on 8' wood stud partitions in office; perimeter walls in office are painted at a cost of $.25 per square foot of wall area; 12" concrete block dividing wall (14' high) separating factory area from office area
  Floor covering—vinyl tile in office
  Ceiling—suspended mineral fiber acoustic tile
  Doors—six 3' × 7' hollow metal within office; one 3' × 7' hollow metal leading from office to factory
  Interior of factory—unfinished
  Electrical fixtures—fluorescent lights, normal lighting requirements
  Plumbing—standard fixtures
  Heating and air conditioning—both office and factory
  Miscellaneous—3" asphalt paving on 3" stone base

Physical Deterioration (Curable)—none

Physical Deterioration (Short-Lived Incurable):

  Brickwork—40%
  Roof (asphalt and gravel)—60%
  Exterior doors—75%
  Floor covering (vinyl tile) —55%
  Acoustic tile ceiling—45%
  Electric—35%
  Plumbing—30%
  Heating and air-conditioning—30%
  Asphalt paving—40%

Depreciation Deduction for Balance of Building—Physical Deterioration (Long-Lived Incurable) —25%

Functional Obsolescence (Curable)—none

Functional Obsolescence (Incurable)—5% of net value after physical deterioration

External Obsolescence—none

EXHIBIT A: PLAT PLAN AND BUILDING LAYOUT

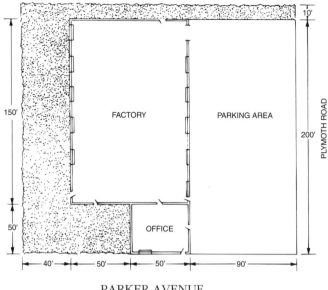

PARKER AVENUE

Compute the following:

1. total factory area   _____

2. total office area   _____

3. total building area   _____

4. building perimeter (including
   foundation wall between
   factory and office areas)   _____

5. total parking area   _____

EXHIBIT B: EXTERIOR WALL AREA

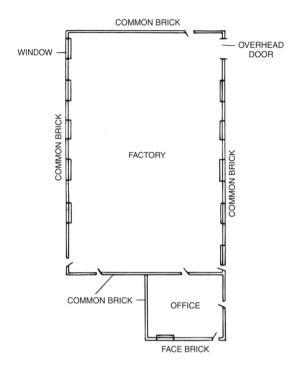

Data:

        Factory height is 14'.

        Office height is 10'.

        Overhead door is 12' × 12'.

        All other exterior doors are 3' × 7'.

        All windows are 6' × 12'.

Compute the following:

6. total area covered by common brick (including factory area above office roof and side walls) _____

7. total area covered by face brick _____

CAUTION: Door and window areas must be deducted.

EXHIBIT C: INTERIOR WALL AREA (Excluding perimeter of office)

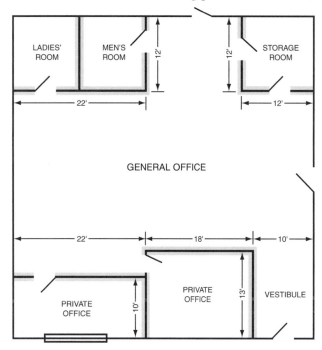

Data:

       Ceiling height is 8'.

       Doors are 3' × 7'.

       Construction is drywall on wood studs.

8. Compute the interior wall area
   for the office portion of the
   building.   _____

CAUTION: Both sides of a wall and door opening must be accounted for.

EXHIBIT D: INTERIOR WALL AREA (Perimeter of office)

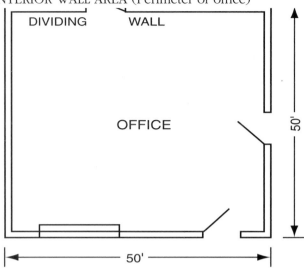

Data:

        Dividing wall height is 14'.

        Ceiling height is 8'.

        Doors are 3' × 7'.

        Window is 6' × 12'.

9. Compute the total wall area (perimeter of office only). _____

10. Compute area of concrete block dividing wall. _____

EXHIBIT E: FRAME SUPPORT

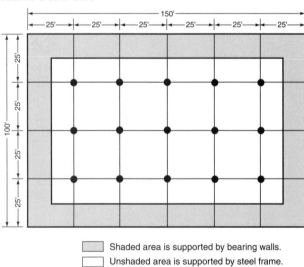

Shaded area is supported by bearing walls.
Unshaded area is supported by steel frame.

11. Compute the area supported by the steel frame. _____

EXHIBIT F: LAND COMPARISONS

Parcel	Sq. Ft. of Area	Sales Price	Sales Price per Sq. Ft.	Adjustments	Adjusted Sales Price per Sq. Ft.
A	45,000	$90,000	$2.00	+10%	$2.20
B	46,217	129,400	2.80	−20%	2.24
C	25,900	60,900	2.35	−15%	2.00
D	47,829	143,500	3.00	−25%	2.25

12. Compute the total land area of the subject property. _____

13. Compute the land value. _____

Using the cost data at the end of this chapter, compute your cost estimate for each building component listed on this and the next page. Where a cost range is given, use the highest estimate. Round off all of your answers to the nearest dollar.

14. Foundation _____

15. Exterior walls _____

16. Roof construction _____

17. Framing _____

18. Floor construction _____

19. Windows _____

20. Exterior doors _____

21. Interior construction _____

22. Electric _____

23. Plumbing _____

24. Heating and air-conditioning _____

25. Miscellaneous _____

26. Enter and total your reproduction cost figures in the list below.

REPRODUCTION COSTS

Exterior Construction:

Foundation _____

Floor construction _____

Exterior walls _____

Framing _____

Roof construction _____

Windows _____

Doors _____

Interior Construction:

Walls	_____
Floor covering	_____
Ceiling	_____
Doors	_____
Electric	_____
Plumbing	_____
Heating and air-conditioning	_____
Miscellaneous	_____
Total Reproduction Cost	_____

27. Observed depreciation:

Brickwork	_____
Roof	_____
Exterior doors	_____
Floor covering	_____
Acoustic tile ceiling	_____
Electrical	_____
Plumbing	_____
Heating	_____
Air-conditioning	_____
Asphalt paving	_____
Depreciation deduction for balance of building:	_____
Deduction for incurable functional obsolescence:	_____

28. Use the list below to determine a total property value.

COST VALUATION

Reproduction Cost	_____
Depreciation:	
Deterioration—Curable	_____
Short-Lived Incurable	_____
Long-Lived Incurable	_____
Functional Obsolescence—Curable	_____
Incurable	_____
External Obsolescence	_____
Total Accrued Depreciation	_____
Building Value Estimate	_____
Land Value Estimate	_____
Total Property Value Indicated by Cost Approach	_____

Check your solution to the case problem with the one in the Answer Key at the back of the book.

COST DATA

	Material	Specification	Cost per Unit of Measurement*
FOUNDATION	Concrete wall and footing, 4' deep, incl. excavation	8" wide 12" 16"	$20.50 per linear foot of wall 30.70 37.30
FLOOR CONSTRUCTION	Reinforced concrete, poured in place, including forms and reinforcing	4" 6" 8"	$2.50 per sq. ft. of floor 3.10 3.60
FLOOR COVERING	Nylon carpet Vinyl tile		$12.00 per sq. yd. 1.90 per sq. ft.
FRAMING	Steel frame, with steel columns, beams, and purlins	10' eave height 14' 20'	$3.70 per sq. ft. of support area 4.50 5.60

ROOF CONSTRUCTION	Wood deck
	  Sheathing
	  Fiberboard R-2.78
	  Fiberglass R-7.7
	  Polystyrene R-8
		
		½" thick
		1"
		1⅞"
		2"
			
			$ .65 per sq. ft.
			.55
			1.10
			.52

ROOF COVERING	Asphalt and gravel Polyurethane spray-on	3-ply 4-ply 1" thick 3"	$2.10 per sq. ft. 2.40 1.35 2.50
EXTERIOR WALLS	Common brick facing with block backup Jumbo face brick veneer Roman brick veneer Ribbed aluminum siding, 4" profile Steel siding, beveled, vinyl coated	8" thick 12" .040" thick 8" wide	$ 9.50 per sq. ft of wall area 10.20 3.80 7.50 2.40 per sq. ft. 1.25 per sq. ft.
DOORS	Hollow metal, 3' x 7', including frame, lockset, and hinges	exterior interior	$ 355 each 275
	Rolling steel, chain hoist operated	8' x 8' 10' x 10' 12' x 12' 20' x 16'	$ 840 each 1,175 1,425 3,200
	Pine, 3' x 7', including frame, lockset, and hinges	exterior interior	$ 290 each (incl. storm & screen) 95
	Oak, including frame, lockset, and hinges	3' x 7' x 1¾"	$ 245 each

WINDOWS	Industrial sash
	  steel, fixed
	  steel, 50% vented
	  aluminum, fixed
	  aluminum, 50% vented
			
			$11.40 per sq. ft. of window area
			14.20
			17.50
			20.10

*The figures given here are for purposes of illustration only.

COST DATA (continued)

	Material	Specification	Cost per Unit of Measurement*
INTERIOR WALLS AND PARTITIONS	Concrete block	4″ 6″ 8″ 12″	$3.20 per sq. ft. of wall area 3.70 4.05 4.40
	Drywall on wood studs, including two coats of paint		$3.15 per sq. ft. of wall area
	Drywall on metal studs, including two coats of paint		$2.70
CEILING	Mineral fiber acoustic tile, including suspension system		$1.65 per sq. ft. of ceiling area
ELECTRICAL WIRING	Fluorescent fixtures, normal lighting requirements		$3.10 per sq. ft. of building area
HEATING AND COOLING	Heating and central air-conditioning with ducts and controls		$3.70–5.75 per sq. ft. of building area
PLUMBING	Plumbing, including fixtures		$1.75–2.75 per sq. ft. of building area
MISC.	Asphalt paving on 3″ stone base	1½″ thick 3″	$4.25 per sq. yd. 7.20

*The figures given here are for purposes of illustration only.

## CHAPTER 10

The Sales Comparison Approach

■ OVERVIEW

This chapter continues the discussion of the sales comparison approach that began in Chapter 6, following the steps in the appraisal process. The exercises in this chapter carry on the sample appraisal of a single-family residence and lot. At the end of this chapter you will complete an appraisal analysis of a single-family residence using the sales comparison approach.

■ STEP 3: GATHER, RECORD, AND VERIFY THE NECESSARY DATA (CONTINUED)

Comparison Grid

The Sales Comparison Approach section of the URAR form, shown on the next page, lists the common significant property variables that warrant price adjustments. The analysis grid has space for the subject property and comparables to be described and for the sales price of each comparable to be adjusted to account for significant property differences.

The subject property and each comparable property should be identified by street address. The proximity of each comparable to the subject also should be noted, for this will be important in determining whether a value adjustment will be made for location. The sales price of each comparable, as well as the source and verification of the market data used, should be recorded. Next, the price per square foot of gross living area for the subject and comparables should be entered. The easiest way to complete the grid is to describe all the details of the subject property, then do the same for each comparable property in turn.

Although years of experience may give an appraiser some intuitive knowledge of the value of property, the figure presented in the appraisal report must be as factual as possible. It is important to remember that the adjustment value of a property feature is not simply the cost to construct or add that feature but instead what a buyer is willing to pay for it, typically a lesser amount. An opinion of market value must always consider the demands of the marketplace.

FIGURE 10.1

Sales Comparison Approach

There are	comparable properties currently offered for sale in the subject neighborhood ranging in price from $		to $	
There are	comparable sales in the subject neighborhood within the past twelve months ranging in sale price from $		to $	

FEATURE	SUBJECT	COMPARABLE SALE # 1		COMPARABLE SALE # 2		COMPARABLE SALE # 3	
Address	2130 W. Franklin	1901 Parkside Blvd.					
Proximity to Subject		Within half-mile					
Sale Price	$ N/A	$ $226,000		$		$	
Sale Price/Gross Liv. Area	$ N/A sq. ft.	$ 125.56 sq. ft.		$ sq. ft.		$ sq. ft.	
Data Source(s)		Sales agent					
Verification Source(s)		Sales agent					
VALUE ADJUSTMENTS	DESCRIPTION	DESCRIPTION	+(-) $ Adjustment	DESCRIPTION	+(-) $ Adjustment	DESCRIPTION	+(-) $ Adjustment
Sale or Financing Concessions		none					
Date of Sale/Time		6 weeks ago					
Location	quiet street	heavy traffic					
Leasehold/Fee Simple	fee simple	fee simple					
Site	50' × 200'	50' × 200'					
View	good	good					
Design (Style)	ranch/good	ranch/good					
Quality of Construction	good	good					
Actual Age	6 years	8 years					
Condition	good	good					
Above Grade	Total / Bdrms. / Baths	Total / Bdrms. / Baths		Total / Bdrms. / Baths		Total / Bdrms. / Baths	
Room Count	7 / 3 / 2.5	7 / 3 / 2					
Gross Living Area	1,825 sq. ft.	1,800 sq. ft.		sq. ft.		sq. ft.	
Basement & Finished Rooms Below Grade	full basement	full basement					
Functional Utility	adequate	adequate					
Heating/Cooling	central H/A	central H/A					
Energy Efficient Items	none	none					
Garage/Carport	2-car att.	2-car att.					
Porch/Patio/Deck	none	none					
Net Adjustment (Total)		☐ + ☐ -	$	☐ + ☐ -	$	☐ + ☐ -	$
Adjusted Sale Price of Comparables		Net Adj. % Gross Adj. %	$	Net Adj. % Gross Adj. %	$	Net Adj. % Gross Adj. %	$

(Left margin vertical text: SALES COMPARISON APPROACH)

I ☐ did ☐ did not research the sale or transfer history of the subject property and comparable sales. If not, explain

My research ☐ did ☐ did not reveal any prior sales or transfers of the subject property for the three years prior to the effective date of this appraisal.

Data source(s)

My research ☐ did ☐ did not reveal any prior sales or transfers of the comparable sales for the year prior to the date of sale of the comparable sale.

Data source(s)

Report the results of the research and analysis of the prior sale or transfer history of the subject property and comparable sales (report additional prior sales on page 3).

ITEM	SUBJECT	COMPARABLE SALE # 1	COMPARABLE SALE # 2	COMPARABLE SALE # 3
Date of Prior Sale/Transfer				
Price of Prior Sale/Transfer				
Data Source(s)				
Effective Date of Data Source(s)				

Analysis of prior sale or transfer history of the subject property and comparable sales

Summary of Sales Comparison Approach

Indicated Value by Sales Comparison Approach $

The appraiser must also avoid the temptation to make adjustments match a value that "feels" right for the subject property. The value the appraiser initially felt was the right one for the subject property may in fact be reached by further analysis. Even if this were true for every appraisal, though, it would not mean that the appraiser would have no further need to itemize specific price adjustments. The appraiser's report to the client must present the facts on which the final opinion of value was reached rather than a preconception of value. The appraiser's intuition is useful, however, if the adjusted property value is far removed from what it should be. If the value seems too high or too low, there may be adjustment factors that the appraiser has failed to consider, and more information must be gathered.

Usually there will be some dissimilarity between the subject property and a comparable. The accuracy of the market comparison approach, therefore, relies on the categories selected for adjustments and the amount of any adjustments made. The appraiser should avoid making unnecessary adjustments; that is, the appraiser should make only those adjustments considered by buyers, sellers, and tenants involved with this class of property. The categories listed on the Sales Comparison Approach grid are the most significant factors, as they have the greatest effect on value in standard residential appraisals.

Finally, the appraiser should always be careful to use properties of similar construction quality when estimating the market value of property variables. Just as the properties themselves should be similar in overall quality of construction (as mentioned below), so should individual components or details, such as a family room addition or kitchen remodeling.

Sales or Financing Concessions

As noted earlier, this is important if a sale involved nonstandard financing terms, whether in down payment, type of loan, or terms of loan.

Date of Sale/Time

An adjustment must be made if market conditions and price levels change between the date of sale of the comparable property and the date of appraisal.

Location

Because similar properties might differ in value from neighborhood to neighborhood, comparable properties should be located in the same neighborhood as the subject property, if possible. However, there may be no recourse but to find comparable properties outside the immediate area if there have been few sales, if the subject property is in a rural area, or if the subject property is atypical—such as the only three-apartment building in an area of single-family houses. In such a case, the buildings chosen as comparables should at least come from comparable neighborhoods. Even within the same neighborhood, locations can offer significant variances, such as proximity to different land uses or frontage on a heavily traveled street. A property across the street from a park would tend to be more valuable than one across the street from a railroad switchyard. As mentioned earlier, corner lots no longer automatically command higher prices for single-family residences.

Leasehold/Fee Simple

The property interests appraised should be the same for the subject property and comparables. The owner of a leasehold estate owns improvements to land, such as a building, but does not own the land itself. The owner of a fee simple estate, on the other hand, owns both the land and any improvements to it. The difference can have a significant effect on property value. The owner of a leasehold interest typically pays a ground rent, an expense that must be taken into account by a prospective property buyer. The length of the lease term also must be considered.

Site

Parcel size should be given and the site rated as good, average, fair, or poor on the basis of physical features.

View

The site should be rated as good, average, fair, or poor on the basis of view.

Design (style)

The style of a house probably should follow the rule of conformity; that is, the design should be compatible with that of others in the neighborhood.

Quality of Construction

If not the same as or equivalent to the subject property, quality of construction will be a major adjustment. Available comparables within a particular builder's subdivision typically will be of the same construction quality. Building cost estimating guides, published to assist builders (and appraisers, as you have learned in Chapter 8, "The Cost Approach—Part I: Reproduction/Replacement Cost"), can be used to rate construction quality as low, average, good, or very good to excellent.

Actual Age

Because most subdivisions are completed within a relatively short period of time, there will probably be no significant differences among comparables with respect to age. A brand-new home would likely be valued by the builder according to actual costs, overhead, and profit. In older homes of good general condition, an age difference of five years in either direction usually is not significant. Overall upkeep is of greater importance, although the age of the house may alert the appraiser to look for outmoded design or fixtures or any needed repairs.

Condition

The overall condition of each property will be noted as good, average, fair, or poor. An adjustment would be indicated if the comparable were in better or worse condition than the subject.

Above-Grade Room Count/Gross Living Area

Total number of rooms in the house, excluding bathrooms and any basement (below-grade) rooms, is listed here. The number of bedrooms and baths and the total above-grade square footage are also noted. A major adjustment would be needed if the subject property had fewer than three bedrooms and the comparables had at least three, or vice versa. Total number of full baths (lavatory, toilet, and tub or shower) and half-baths (lavatory and toilet) are tallied in this category. Modern plumbing is assumed, with an adjustment made for out-of-date fixtures.

The appraiser should confirm that the comparables were measured using a method similar to that used to measure the subject property. Total gross living area of a home generally includes only above-grade, finished living areas and not basement areas, whether completely or partially below grade, even if they are finished with the same materials and quality of construction used in the rest of the house. This is the rule applied to homes appraised for Fannie Mae using the URAR. An exception to the general rule is allowed if the below-grade living space is typical of homes in the area and is considered to add to property value; then, comparables with the same type(s) of space should be found. This is often the case in California, where hillside homes with one or more levels at least partially below grade are common.

Basement and Finished Rooms Below Grade

The appraiser should note any below-grade improvements, such as a finished basement.

Functional Utility

The building's overall compatibility with its intended use, as defined in the marketplace, should be noted. This category includes design features, such as layout and room size, that are currently desirable.

Heating/Cooling

The appraiser notes the type of heating unit and air-conditioning system, if any, of the subject and comparables.

Energy-Efficient Items

High R-factor insulation, solar heating units, or other energy conservation features should be noted.

Garage/Carport

If the subject property does not have one, any garage on a comparable property requires an adjustment. A garage on the subject property would be compared for type of construction and size.

Porch, Patio, Deck

Porch, patio, deck, fence, Florida room, pool, spa, greenhouse, or any other living or recreation area not part of the primary house area is included here. Blank lines provide additional space for entries.

An adjustment factor is indicated if either the subject property or one of the comparables has any other interior property improvement that adds to or subtracts from value. Such amenities as a fireplace, whirlpool bathtub, or luxurious finishing material (marble, granite, wood parquet, and so on) ordinarily would add to a home's value. Adjustments for these features should reflect local market expectations and buyer requirements.

■ STEP 4: DETERMINE HIGHEST AND BEST USE

The highest and best use of real estate, whether vacant or with improvements, is its most profitable legally permitted, physically possible, and financially feasible use. The highest and best use of real estate that has been improved by the erection of a structure or structures on it may take into account the existing improvements, or the land may be treated as if vacant.

Because of the wide use of zoning throughout the United States, consideration of highest and best use is generally limited to the property's present legally permitted uses. In the case of areas zoned for single-family residences, this use usually is accepted as the highest and best use. A change of zoning is occasionally possible, particularly when a subsequent nearby land use creates adverse conditions for enjoyment of residential property. As an example, property along a roadway that has become very heavily traveled by commercial vehicles as a result of nearby development may be rezoned for commercial use. Rezoning can never be assumed, however, and it usually entails a lengthy application and approval process. For the appraiser's purpose, only existing permitted land uses are considered unless otherwise specified by the client. The client may request a conditional value based on land-use changes that have a reasonable probability of occurring. If so, the appraiser must disclose the special circumstances and assumptions of the report to ensure that the report will not be misleading. The concept of highest and best use was discussed in more detail in Chapter 7, "Site Valuation."

For purposes of this chapter, the present use of all properties used in the case study and exercises will be considered their highest and best use.

■ STEP 5: ESTIMATE LAND VALUE

Because house (improvements) and lot are being valued together in the sales comparison approach, we will not make a separate estimate of land value. Land valuation techniques were discussed in Chapter 7.

■ STEP 6: ESTIMATE VALUE BY SALES COMPARISON APPROACH

Data Analysis

Because no two parcels of real estate are exactly alike, each comparable property must be analyzed and adjusted for differences between it and the subject property.

The most difficult step in using the sales comparison approach is determining the amount of each adjustment. The accuracy of an appraisal using this approach depends on the appraiser's use of reliable adjustment values. Because adjustments must reflect the activities of buyers and sellers in the market, it is the appraiser's job to research, analyze, and draw supportable conclusions from market-derived data. Unfortunately, the value of the same feature may vary for different types, sizes, and overall values of property. Until an appraiser has the background of many appraisals in a given area, more comparable properties will have to be studied than just the three to six presented in the typical appraisal report. If the appraiser completes an adjustment chart for as many as 10 to 20 or more properties, a market pattern may be more evident, and with better documentation, the value of individual differences may be estimated fairly accurately. When there have been few recent sales, the appraiser's own files can be the best source of adjustment values.

Ordinarily, an appraisal of real estate does not include any personal property on the premises. If the sales price of a comparable property includes such items, the value of the items should be noted as an adjustment factor.

Types of Adjustments
The adjustments that will be made to the sales prices of the selected comparable properties may be expressed in several ways. Most often, a *dollar adjustment* is used, to indicate

- the value of a desirable feature present in the subject property but not the comparable, resulting in a plus (+) adjustment to the sales price of the comparable; and

- the value of a desirable feature present in the comparable but not the subject property, resulting in a minus (–) adjustment to the sales price of the comparable.

The amount of the dollar adjustment is determined by using one of the methods discussed in the next section of this chapter.

Another way to adjust the sales price of a comparable is to use a *percentage adjustment,* indicating the overall effect on market value of the factor valued. This is the method often used to account for changes in market conditions as well as other changes that affect the property as a whole, such as the time from the date of sale or the property's location.

For example, market evidence may show that comparable properties located in the subject property's immediate vicinity typically have a market value that is 10 percent higher than that of properties in the vicinity of one of the comparable properties. There are many factors that could contribute to such a difference, even among properties that are in the same general neighborhood. Homes within walking distance of a school may be considered more desirable; homes near a highway with its concomitant noise and pollution may be considered less desirable. In either case, appropriate adjustment to the sales price of the comparable property would be necessary.

Another common use of a percentage adjustment is to take into account the change in market value over time. If the sale of a comparable property took place one year before the date of appraisal, and average property appreciation in the area for the same type of property has been 6 percent over the same period of time, the selling price of the comparable can be adjusted by increasing it by 6 percent.

The dollar amount of the adjustment is the appraiser's estimate of the effect on value of the identified factor. The adjustment thus is the appraiser's measurement of typical buyer reaction to the noted property difference.

Ideally, if properties could be found that were exactly alike except for one category, the adjustment value of that category would be the difference in selling prices of the two properties. Noting the individual differences of many properties at once should provide at least two such properties for every adjustment category.

Compute Adjustment Values

The *Sales Price Adjustment Chart* (or *matrix*) is a source of information for adjustment values that can be used in the sales comparison approach. The appraiser can develop such a chart and use it to substantiate dollar amounts for adjusted values.

EXAMPLE

House A is very similar to house B, except that it has a two-car attached garage, and house B does not. House A sold for $194,000; house B sold for $181,500. Because the garage is the only significant difference between the two properties, its value is the difference between the selling price of $194,000 and the selling price of $181,500. So the value of the garage is $194,000 – $181,500, or $12,500.

For the background of adjustment values, the appraiser analyzes as many properties as needed to be able to isolate each significant variable. Most neighborhoods have similar types of properties, so this is not as difficult a task as it may first appear.

This method of determining value relies on a technique called *matched pairs analysis (MPA), paired sales analysis,* or *paired data set analysis.* In matched pairs analysis, the appraiser compares the features and sales prices of comparable properties. A sufficient number of sales must be found to allow the appraiser to isolate the effect on value of the pertinent factor. Often this is not possible, and the appraiser's judgment becomes especially critical in determining the relative values to assign to multiple property variables.

The appraiser also may study the changes in sales price of the same property that has sold more than once within a defined period of time. Those prices may indicate the change in overall market conditions in that period. Of course, the appraiser must check the other factors involved in the sales to make sure that they do not involve related parties or that the presence of some other factor has not made a sale less than an arm's-length transaction. For instance, a quick resale may be necessitated by an unexpected job transfer and could have the effect of lowering the sales price. A sudden illness of the buyer and subsequent transfer of the property could also indicate a sale that does not accurately reflect market conditions. The property also could have been a "fixer-upper" with a considerably higher resale price, indicative of the extent of its rehabilitation rather than the state of the market.

There may be property differences that require no adjustment because they have no effect on the typical buyer's decision to purchase.

House A may have intricately hand-painted wainscoting in the family room; house B may have wallpaper in the family room. Yet neither property difference will require an adjustment, because the houses are perceived by buyers in the marketplace as identical to ones with plain painted walls.

Figure 10.2 is a Sales Price Adjustment Chart that has been completed for ten properties, all comparable to each other. Each relevant adjustment variable has been highlighted by a screen. *Although an appraiser ordinarily will need two or more instances of each variable as a check on the accuracy of an adjustment value, for the sake of brevity only one comparable with each variable is presented here.*

Because properties A, C, E, and J exhibit no variables, they will be used to define the standard against which the worth of each variable will be measured. Property A sold for $242,000, property C for $243,000, property E for $241,000, and property J for $242,000. Because property C shows only a slight price increase and property E only a slight price decrease, $242,000 will be used as the base house value for a typical property in the neighborhood, that is, one having the most typical property features. Each variable can now be noted and valued.

Time Adjustment

Property H is identical in features to properties A, C, E, and J, except for length of time since the date of sale. Market conditions over the past year indicate a period of general inflation. Property H was sold one year ago; properties A, C, E, and J were all sold within the past three to 11 weeks. The adjustment value to be made in the case of a year-old sale is, therefore,

$$\$242,000 - \$221,000 = \$21,000$$

The $21,000 adjustment value can be expressed as a percentage of the total cost of the property.

$$\frac{\$21,000}{\$221,000} = .09502 = 9.502\%, \text{ or simply } 9.5\%$$

In this case, the adjustment value of the variable is $21,000. If a one-year time adjustment were required for another property, the dollar value of the adjustment would be the amount derived by applying the percentage of value to that property's sales price.

Commercial Area

In this example, the $268,000 selling price of property G is considerably higher than that of properties in the residential area. On closer analysis, the appraiser discovered that property G was adjacent to the site of a new shopping mall and

FIGURE 10.2
Sales Price Adjustment Chart

Sales Price Adjustment Chart
Comparables

	A	B	C	D	E	F	G	H	I	J
SALES PRICE	$242,000	$233,000	$243,000	$247,000	$241,000	$220,000	$268,000	$221,000	$252,000	$242,000
FINANCING	75% assump.	70% assump.	75% assump.	75% assump.	70% assump.	75% assump.	70% assump.	75% assump.	70% assump.	70% assump.
DATE OF SALE	6 wks.	2 mos.	3 wks.	5 wks.	6 wks.	5 wks.	3 wks.	1 yr.	5 wks.	11 wks.
LOCATION	resid.	resid.	resid.	resid.	resid.	highway	commercial	resid.	resid.	resid.
LEASEHOLD/FEE SIMPLE	fee	fee	fee	fee	fee	fee	fee	fee	fee	fee
VIEW	good	good	good	good	good	good	good	ranch/good	good	good
SITE	50' × 200'	50' × 200'	50' × 200'	50' × 200'	50' × 200'	50' × 200'	50' × 200'	50' × 200'	50' × 200'	50' × 200'
DESIGN	ranch/good	ranch/good	ranch/good	ranch/good	ranch/good	ranch/good	ranch/good	ranch/good	ranch/good	ranch/good
CONSTRUCTION	brick	aluminum siding	brick	brick	brick	brick	brick	brick	brick	brick
AGE	8 yrs.	7 yrs.	8 yrs.	6 yrs.	6 yrs.	7 yrs.	6 yrs.	7 yrs.	6 yrs.	7 yrs.
CONDITION	good	good	good	good	good	good	good	good	good	good
NO. OF RMS./BEDRMS./BATHS	7/3/2	7/3/2	7/3/2	7/3/2½	7/3/2	7/3/2	7/3/2	7/3/2	8/4/2	7/3/2
SQ. FT. OF LIVING SPACE	1,275	1,300	1,290	1,300	1,300	1,325	1,300	1,350	1,400	1,300
OTHER SPACE (BASEMENT)	full basement	full basement	full basement	full basement	full basement	full basement	full basement	full basement	full basement	full basement
FUNCTIONAL UTILITY	adequate	adequate	adequate	adequate	adequate	adequate	adequate	adequate	adequate	adequate
HEATING/COOLING	central heat/air	central heat/air	central heat/air	central heat/air	central heat/air	central eat/air	central heat/air	central heat/air	central heat/air	central heat/air
ENERGY EFFICIENT ITEMS	none	none	none	none	none	none	none	none	none	none
GARAGE/CARPORT	2-car att.	2-car att.	2-car att.	2-car att.	2-car att.	2-car att.	2-car att.	2-car att.	2-car att.	2-car att.
OTHER EXT. IMPROVEMENTS	patio	patio	patio	patio	patio	patio	patio	patio	patio	patio
OTHER INT. IMPROVEMENTS Fireplace	one	one	one	one	one	one	one	one	one	one
TYPICAL HOUSE VALUE	$242,000	$242,000	$242,000	$242,000	$242,000	$242,000	$242,000	$242,000	$242,000	$242,000
VARIABLE FEATURE		aluminum siding		extra half bath		poor location	commercial area	year-old sale	4th bedroom	
ADJUSTMENT VALUE OF VARIABLE										

had been purchased by the mall developers for use as a parking area. Since property G represents an extraordinary situation, it should not be considered representative of the adjustment value warranted by location.

Highway Location

Property F, on a less desirable site facing a busy highway, sold for $22,000 less than the standard; therefore, this poor location indicates an adjustment of $22,000.

Commercial Area

In this example, the $268,000 selling price of property G is considerably higher than that of properties in the residential area. On closer analysis, the appraiser discovered that property G was adjacent to the site of a new shopping mall and had been purchased by the mall developers for use as a parking area. Since property G represents an extraordinary situation, it should not be considered representative of the adjustment value warranted by location.

In the next exercise, you will find the remaining adjustment values used in the sample appraisal being carried out in this chapter.

EXERCISE 10.1

Complete the adjustment valuations for construction, number of bedrooms, and number of bathrooms, as indicated by the data in the Sales Price Adjustment Chart in Figure 10.2. Record all of the adjustments computed thus far, and those you will compute yourself, in the appropriate boxes in the chart.

Time: One year ago

9.5% per year

Location: Highway

$242,000 – $220,000 = $22,000

Construction:

No. of Bedrooms:

No. of Baths:

Check your completed chart adjustments against the ones in the Answer Key at the back of the book.

Sequence of Adjustments

Some of the adjustments made to the sales prices of comparables will reflect overall property value, such as an adjustment due to sales or financing concessions. Other adjustments will be due to a specific property feature, such as the presence or absence of air-conditioning. The appraiser also may use a combination of adjustment methods, including both percentage and dollar valuations.

To reflect all adjustments accurately, the appraiser should make adjustments in sequence, with those affecting the overall property value being made first, followed by those affecting only individual property features. For example, if any adjustment is required to account for sales or financing concessions, the adjustment is made to the sales price before any other adjustment is made to determine a *normal sales price*. If an adjustment is required to account for a change in market value over time since the date of sale of the comparable, that adjustment is made next, the result being a *time-adjusted normal sales price (TANSP)*. Only after those adjustments have been made does the appraiser make a final adjustment on the basis of differences in individual property features.

The sequence of adjustments would make no difference if all of the adjustment factors were based on a dollar value rather than a percentage value. The recommended sequence of adjustments is crucial, because an adjustment in either of the first two adjustment categories—financing and time—usually is based on a percentage of total sales price. Any percentage adjustment for financing should be based on total sales price *before* any other adjustment is made. Any percentage adjustment for time should be based on the total sales price *after* any adjustment required for financing has been made. (The only other percentage adjustment that could be made before the adjustment for time would be an adjustment for seller *motivation,* as in the case of a forced sale due to employee transfer or serious illness. Seller motivation also may be referred to as *condition of sale.*)

Although no hard and fast rule can be applied to all cases, total gross adjustments, no matter how they are calculated, should probably not exceed 25 percent of a comparable's sales price.

EXERCISE 10.2

In the sample appraisal, five properties, all within one-half mile of the subject, have been selected as comparables. A description of each property and its sale is given below. In each case, property information was supplied by the sales agent. Complete the URAR Sales Comparison Approach sections of the URAR form in Figures 10.3 and 10.4 down to the Net Adj (total) line. Needed information on the subject property and comparable 1 has already been recorded. In the same way, you are to insert the necessary information for comparables 2 through 5. The ratings that the appraiser uses can be based on the definitions provided by Fannie Mae. A rating of good indicates that the subject is superior in quality in the characteristic specified to other properties in the neighborhood. A rating of average indicates that in the characteristic specified the subject is equal in quality to other properties in the neighborhood. A rating of fair indicates that in the characteristic specified the subject is inferior to what is considered acceptable in the neighborhood. A rating of poor indicates that the subject is substantially inferior to competing properties with respect to the characteristic specified. A map of the neighborhood is shown on page 117. Current market rate financing available for the purchase of homes in this price range is 8 ¼ to 8 ½ percent, with a minimum down payment of 20 percent. All of the homes are of contemporary style, with no functional obsolescence.

1. 1901 Parkside Boulevard—fee simple interest in an eight-year-old, seven-room brick ranch, in good general condition, with full basement, living room, kitchen, family room, three bedrooms, and two full baths. There are no common areas and no homeowners' association. The house, which has forced-air heating and air-con-

ditioning, has a total of 1,800 square feet of living space. Landscaping is very attractive, with several large trees, shrubs, and flower beds. The property has a view of the surrounding hills. There is a two-car attached garage. The lot is 50 feet by 200 feet. The buyer obtained an 8 ½ percent mortgage loan, making a down payment of 25 percent on the $226,000 sales price. The sale took place six weeks prior to the date of appraisal of the subject property.

2. 2135 Hastings Avenue—fee simple interest in a seven-year-old, seven-room ranch, with 1,875 square feet of space, a full basement, and forced-air heating and cooling. The house is in good condition; it is brick, with an attached two-car garage. There are three bedrooms, two full baths, living room, dining room, kitchen, and family room. The lot is 50 feet by 200 feet, with good landscaping and a view of the hills filtered through shade trees in front and back yards. There are no common areas and no homeowners' association. The buyer obtained an 8 ½ percent mortgage; the exact amount of the down payment is not known, but it was probably at least 25 or 30 percent. The purchase price was $239,000; the sale took place one year before the date of appraisal of the subject property.

3. 2129 Osceola Way—fee simple interest in a seven-room, 1,825-square-foot aluminum-sided ranch on a corner lot 50 feet by 200 feet, with attached two-car garage. The house has forced-air heating and air-conditioning. Landscaping is good and the house has a lovely view of the area. The house is eight years old and in good condition, with a living room, dining room, kitchen, family room, three bedrooms, and two full baths. There is a full basement. There are no common areas and no homeowners' association. The sales price was $238,000, and the purchase, two months before the date of this appraisal, was financed by the buyer's obtaining an 8 ¼ percent loan with a 25 percent cash down payment.

4. 2243 Parkside Boulevard—fee simple interest in an eight-room, 1,925-square-foot brick ranch on a 50-foot-by-200-foot lot, with attached two-car garage. Landscaping is good and well kept, and the six-year-old house is also in good condition. The view is of the surrounding hills. There is a living room, dining room, kitchen, family room, four bedrooms, and two full baths. There is a full basement and forced-air heating and air-conditioning. There are no common areas and no homeowners' association. The purchase price of $256,500 was financed by the buyer's paying 20 percent down and obtaining an 8 ¼ percent mortgage. The sale took place five weeks before the date of the subject appraisal.

5. 2003 Franklin Street—fee simple interest in a seven-room, 1,825-square-foot brick ranch, on a 50-foot-by-200-foot lot, with good landscaping, pretty views, and attached two-car garage. The house is seven years old, in good condition, and has a living room, dining room, kitchen, family room, three bedrooms, two full baths, and one half-bath, as well as a full basement. The house has forced-air heating and air-conditioning. There are no common areas and no homeowners' association. The sale, which took place five weeks ago, was financed by the buyer's down payment of 25 percent on an 8 ½ percent mortgage loan. The purchase price was $251,000.

Each of the comparables is functionally adequate. Record all of the data in this exercise on the Sales Comparison Approach sections of the URAR form in Figure 10.3.

At this point in many appraisals, properties considered comparables are found to be unacceptable for one or more reasons. In this group of comparables for the sample appraisal, do any of the properties seem unacceptable? If so, why?

Check your answers and your completed Sales Comparison Approach sections with those in the Answer Key at the back of the book.

F I G U R E 10.3

Comparables 1 through 3 for Exercise 10.2

There are	comparable properties currently offered for sale in the subject neighborhood ranging in price from $		to $	
There are	comparable sales in the subject neighborhood within the past twelve months ranging in sale price from $		to $	

FEATURE	SUBJECT	COMPARABLE SALE # 1		COMPARABLE SALE # 2		COMPARABLE SALE # 3	
Address	2130 W. Franklin	1901 Parkside Blvd.					
Proximity to Subject		Within half-mile					
Sale Price	$ N/A	$ $226,000		$		$	
Sale Price/Gross Liv. Area	$ N/A sq. ft.	$ 125.56 sq. ft.		$ sq. ft.		$ sq. ft.	
Data Source(s)		Sales agent					
Verification Source(s)		Sales agent					
VALUE ADJUSTMENTS	DESCRIPTION	DESCRIPTION	+(-) $ Adjustment	DESCRIPTION	+(-) $ Adjustment	DESCRIPTION	+(-) $ Adjustment
Sale or Financing Concessions		none					
Date of Sale/Time		6 weeks ago					
Location	quiet street	heavy traffic					
Leasehold/Fee Simple	fee simple	fee simple					
Site	50′ × 200′	50′ × 200′					
View	good	good					
Design (Style)	ranch/good	ranch/good					
Quality of Construction	good	good					
Actual Age	6 years	8 years					
Condition	good	good					

	Above Grade	Total	Bdrms.	Baths	Total	Bdrms.	Baths		Total	Bdrms.	Baths		Total	Bdrms.	Baths	
	Room Count	7	3	2.5	7	3	2									
	Gross Living Area	1,825 sq. ft.			1,800 sq. ft.				sq. ft.				sq. ft.			

Basement & Finished Rooms Below Grade	full basement	full basement					
Functional Utility	adequate	adequate					
Heating/Cooling	central H/A	central H/A					
Energy Efficient Items	none	none					
Garage/Carport	2-car att.	2-car att.					
Porch/Patio/Deck	none	none					
Net Adjustment (Total)		☐ + ☐ -	$	☐ + ☐ -	$	☐ + ☐ -	$
Adjusted Sale Price of Comparables		Net Adj. % Gross Adj. %	$	Net Adj. % Gross Adj. %	$	Net Adj. % Gross Adj. %	$

I ☐ did ☐ did not research the sale or transfer history of the subject property and comparable sales. If not, explain

My research ☐ did ☐ did not reveal any prior sales or transfers of the subject property for the three years prior to the effective date of this appraisal.

Data source(s)

My research ☐ did ☐ did not reveal any prior sales or transfers of the comparable sales for the year prior to the date of sale of the comparable sale.

Data source(s)

Report the results of the research and analysis of the prior sale or transfer history of the subject property and comparable sales (report additional prior sales on page 3).

ITEM	SUBJECT	COMPARABLE SALE # 1	COMPARABLE SALE # 2	COMPARABLE SALE # 3
Date of Prior Sale/Transfer				
Price of Prior Sale/Transfer				
Data Source(s)				
Effective Date of Data Source(s)				

Analysis of prior sale or transfer history of the subject property and comparable sales

Summary of Sales Comparison Approach

Indicated Value by Sales Comparison Approach $

FIGURE 10.4

Comparables 4 and 5 for Exercise 10.2

There are	comparable properties currently offered for sale in the subject neighborhood ranging in price from $		to $		
There are	comparable sales in the subject neighborhood within the past twelve months ranging in sale price from $		to $		

FEATURE	SUBJECT	COMPARABLE SALE # 4		COMPARABLE SALE # 5		COMPARABLE SALE # 6	
Address	2130 W. Franklin						
Proximity to Subject							
Sale Price	$ N/A		$		$		$
Sale Price/Gross Liv. Area	$ N/A sq. ft.	$ sq. ft.		$ sq. ft.		$ sq. ft.	
Data Source(s)							
Verification Source(s)							
VALUE ADJUSTMENTS	DESCRIPTION	DESCRIPTION	+(-) $ Adjustment	DESCRIPTION	+(-) $ Adjustment	DESCRIPTION	+(-) $ Adjustment
Sale or Financing Concessions							
Date of Sale/Time							
Location	quiet street						
Leasehold/Fee Simple	fee simple						
Site	50' × 200'						
View	good						
Design (Style)	ranch/good						
Quality of Construction	good						
Actual Age	6 years						
Condition	good						
Above Grade	Total Bdrms. Baths	Total Bdrms. Baths		Total Bdrms. Baths		Total Bdrms. Baths	
Room Count	7 3 2.5						
Gross Living Area	1,825 sq. ft.	sq. ft.		sq. ft.		sq. ft.	
Basement & Finished Rooms Below Grade	full basement						
Functional Utility	adequate						
Heating/Cooling	central H/A						
Energy Efficient Items	none						
Garage/Carport	2-car att.						
Porch/Patio/Deck	none						
Net Adjustment (Total)		☐ + ☐ -	$	☐ + ☐ -	$	☐ + ☐ -	$
Adjusted Sale Price of Comparables		Net Adj. % Gross Adj. %	$	Net Adj. % Gross Adj. %	$	Net Adj. % Gross Adj. %	$

I ☐ did ☐ did not research the sale or transfer history of the subject property and comparable sales. If not, explain

My research ☐ did ☐ did not reveal any prior sales or transfers of the subject property for the three years prior to the effective date of this appraisal.

Data source(s)

My research ☐ did ☐ did not reveal any prior sales or transfers of the comparable sales for the year prior to the date of sale of the comparable sale.

Data source(s)

Report the results of the research and analysis of the prior sale or transfer history of the subject property and comparable sales (report additional prior sales on page 3).

ITEM	SUBJECT	COMPARABLE SALE # 1	COMPARABLE SALE # 2	COMPARABLE SALE # 3
Date of Prior Sale/Transfer				
Price of Prior Sale/Transfer				
Data Source(s)				
Effective Date of Data Source(s)				

Analysis of prior sale or transfer history of the subject property and comparable sales

Summary of Sales Comparison Approach

Indicated Value by Sales Comparison Approach $

Record Information

Using the adjustment values you computed in Exercise 10.1, you are ready to complete the Sales Comparison Approach sections of the URAR form in Figures 10.5 and 10.6 for the sample appraisal being carried out in Chapter 6 and this chapter.

First, the details of the subject property are recorded as well as the selling prices of the comparables.

Then the adjustment values for the features that differ significantly from the subject property must be recorded. For example, comparable 1 is located on a major thoroughfare, while the subject property is on a quiet residential street. So the adjustment value computed earlier for location can be assigned to comparable 1 and entered in the location box for that comparable. Keep in mind that selling prices of comparable properties are adjusted to reflect the probable market value of the subject property. Because the subject property's location is generally considered a more desirable one than that of comparable 1, the adjustment value of $22,000 computed earlier must be added to the sales price of the comparable to find what the subject property would be worth. So, "+$22,000" is recorded.

An adjustment will be a plus (+) if that feature is found in the subject but not the comparable or otherwise represents a higher value for the subject property. An adjustment will be a minus (–) if that feature is present in the comparable but not the subject or otherwise represents a lower value for the subject property.

EXERCISE 10.3

Record the remaining adjustments on the Sales Comparison Approach sections of the URAR form in Figures 10.5 and 10.6. You will be recording the following adjustments, using the adjustment values you computed in the last exercise:

> Comparable 1—No. of Baths
>
> Comparable 2—No. of Baths
>
> > Date of Sale
>
> Comparable 3—Construction
>
> > No. of Baths
>
> Comparable 4—No. of Bedrooms
>
> > No. of Baths

Check your figures against those in the Answer Key at the back of the book.

Net Adjustments

Once the necessary adjustment values are recorded, they can be totaled for each comparable property. The Sales Comparison Approach section in Figure 10.7 shows the net adjustment for comparable 1. The location adjustment factor of +$22,000 is added to the adjustment factor of +$5,000 for an extra half bath, for a total adjustment of +$27,000. The + or – box must be checked as appropriate.

To find the adjusted value of comparable 1, its sales price and net adjustments are totaled. In this case $226,000 + $27,000 gives an Adjusted Sales Price of $253,000.

Fannie Mae has established guidelines for the net and gross percentage adjustments that review appraisers or loan underwriters may rely on as a general indicator of whether a property should be used as a comparable sale. Generally the total dollar amount of the net adjustments for each comparable sale should not

FIGURE 10.5

Comparables 1 through 3 for Exercise 10.3

There are ___ comparable properties currently offered for sale in the subject neighborhood ranging in price from $ ___ to $ ___ .							
There are ___ comparable sales in the subject neighborhood within the past twelve months ranging in sale price from $ ___ to $ ___ .							

FEATURE	SUBJECT	COMPARABLE SALE # 1		COMPARABLE SALE # 2		COMPARABLE SALE #3	
Address	2130 W. Franklin	1901 Parkside Blvd.		2135 Hastings Ave.		2129 Osceola Way	
Proximity to Subject		Within half-mile		Within half-mile		Within half-mile	
Sale Price	$ N/A		$ 226,000		$ 239,000		$238,000
Sale Price/Gross Liv. Area	$ N/A sq. ft.	$ 125.56 sq. ft.		$ 127.47 sq. ft.		$ 130.41 sq. ft.	
Data Source(s)		Sales agent		Sales agent		Sales agent	
Verification Source(s)		Sales agent		Sales agent		Sales agent	
VALUE ADJUSTMENTS	DESCRIPTION	DESCRIPTION	+(-) $ Adjustment	DESCRIPTION	+(-) $ Adjustment	DESCRIPTION	+(-) $ Adjustment
Sale or Financing Concessions		none		none		none	
Date of Sale/Time		6 weeks ago		1 year ago		2 months ago	
Location	quiet street	heavy traffic		quiet street		quiet street	
Leasehold/Fee Simple	fee simple	fee simple		fee simple		fee simple	
Site	50' × 200'	50' × 200'		50' × 200'		50' × 200'	
View	good	good		good		good	
Design (Style)	ranch/good	ranch/good		ranch/good		ranch/good	
Quality of Construction	good	good		good		good/alum. sd.	
Actual Age	6 years	8 years		7 years		8 years	
Condition	good	good		good		good	
Above Grade	Total / Bdrms. / Baths	Total / Bdrms. / Baths		Total / Bdrms. / Baths		Total / Bdrms. / Baths	
Room Count	7 / 3 / 2.5	7 / 3 / 2		7 / 3 / 2		7 / 3 / 2	
Gross Living Area	1,825 sq. ft.	1,800 sq. ft.		1,875 sq. ft.		1,825 sq. ft.	
Basement & Finished Rooms Below Grade	full basement	full basement		full basement		full basement	
Functional Utility	adequate	adequate		adequate		adequate	
Heating/Cooling	central H/A	central H/A		central H/A		central H/A	
Energy Efficient Items	none	none		none		none	
Garage/Carport	2-car att.	2-car att.		2-car att.		2-car att.	
Porch/Patio/Deck	none	none		none		none	
Net Adjustment (Total)		☐ + ☐ -	$	☐ + ☐ -	$	☐ + ☐ -	$
Adjusted Sale Price of Comparables		Net Adj. % Gross Adj. %	$	Net Adj. % Gross Adj. %	$	Net Adj. % Gross Adj. %	$

I ☐ did ☐ did not research the sale or transfer history of the subject property and comparable sales. If not, explain

My research ☐ did ☐ did not reveal any prior sales or transfers of the subject property for the three years prior to the effective date of this appraisal.

Data source(s)

My research ☐ did ☐ did not reveal any prior sales or transfers of the comparable sales for the year prior to the date of sale of the comparable sale.

Data source(s)

Report the results of the research and analysis of the prior sale or transfer history of the subject property and comparable sales (report additional prior sales on page 3).

ITEM	SUBJECT	COMPARABLE SALE # 1	COMPARABLE SALE # 2	COMPARABLE SALE #3
Date of Prior Sale/Transfer				
Price of Prior Sale/Transfer				
Data Source(s)				
Effective Date of Data Source(s)				

Analysis of prior sale or transfer history of the subject property and comparable sales

Summary of Sales Comparison Approach

Indicated Value by Sales Comparison Approach $

FIGURE 10.6
Comparables 4 and 5 for Exercise 10.3

There are	comparable properties currently offered for sale in the subject neighborhood ranging in price from $			to $	
There are	comparable sales in the subject neighborhood within the past twelve months ranging in sale price from $			to $	

FEATURE	SUBJECT	COMPARABLE SALE #4		COMPARABLE SALE #5		COMPARABLE SALE #6	
Address	2130 W. Franklin	2243 Parkside Blvd.		2003 Franklin Street.			
Proximity to Subject		Within half-mile		Within half-mile			
Sale Price	$ N/A	$ $256,500		$ 251,000		$	
Sale Price/Gross Liv. Area	$ N/A sq. ft.	$ 133.25 sq. ft.		$ 137.53 sq. ft.		$ sq. ft.	
Data Source(s)		Sales agent		Sales agent			
Verification Source(s)		Sales agent		Sales agent			
VALUE ADJUSTMENTS	DESCRIPTION	DESCRIPTION	+(-) $ Adjustment	DESCRIPTION	+(-) $ Adjustment	DESCRIPTION	+(-) $ Adjustment
Sale or Financing Concessions		none		none			
Date of Sale/Time		5 weeks ago		5 weeks ago			
Location	quiet street	quiet street		quiet street			
Leasehold/Fee Simple	fee simple	fee simple		fee simple			
Site	50′ × 200′	50′ × 200′		50′ × 200′			
View	good	good		good			
Design (Style)	ranch/good	ranch/good		ranch/good			
Quality of Construction	good	good		good			
Actual Age	6 years	6 years		7 years			
Condition	good	good		good			
Above Grade	Total / Bdrms. / Baths	Total / Bdrms. / Baths		Total / Bdrms. / Baths		Total / Bdrms. / Baths	
Room Count	7 / 3 / 2	8 / 4 / 2		7 / 3 / 2.5			
Gross Living Area	1,825 sq. ft.	1,925 sq. ft.		1,825 sq. ft.		sq. ft.	
Basement & Finished Rooms Below Grade	full basement	full basement		full basement			
Functional Utility	adequate	adequate		adequate			
Heating/Cooling	central H/A	central H/A		central H/A			
Energy Efficient Items	none	none		none			
Garage/Carport	2-car att.	2-car att.		2-car att.			
Porch/Patio/Deck	none	none		none			
Net Adjustment (Total)		☐ + ☐ -	$	☐ + ☐ -	$	☐ + ☐ -	$
Adjusted Sale Price of Comparables		Net Adj. % Gross Adj. %	$	Net Adj. % Gross Adj. %	$	Net Adj. % Gross Adj. %	$

I ☐ did ☐ did not research the sale or transfer history of the subject property and comparable sales. If not, explain

My research ☐ did ☐ did not reveal any prior sales or transfers of the subject property for the three years prior to the effective date of this appraisal.

Data source(s)

My research ☐ did ☐ did not reveal any prior sales or transfers of the comparable sales for the year prior to the date of sale of the comparable sale.

Data source(s)

Report the results of the research and analysis of the prior sale or transfer history of the subject property and comparable sales (report additional prior sales on page 3).

ITEM	SUBJECT	COMPARABLE SALE #1	COMPARABLE SALE #2	COMPARABLE SALE #3
Date of Prior Sale/Transfer				
Price of Prior Sale/Transfer				
Data Source(s)				
Effective Date of Data Source(s)				

Analysis of prior sale or transfer history of the subject property and comparable sales

Summary of Sales Comparison Approach

Indicated Value by Sales Comparison Approach $

exceed 15 percent of the comparable's sales price. Further, the dollar amount of the *gross* adjustment for each comparable sale should not exceed 25 percent of the comparable's sales price. The amount of the gross adjustment is determined by adding all individual adjustments without regard to the plus or minus signs.

If adjustments do not fall within Fannie Mae's net and gross percentage adjustment guidelines but the appraiser believes the comparable sales used to be the best available, as well as the best indicators of value for the subject property, an appropriate explanation must be provided.

A large total adjustment could indicate that the property sold is not a reliable comparable for the subject property.

EXERCISE 10.4

Complete the net adjustment and adjusted sales price computations for comparables 2, 3, 4, and 5 and record them on the Sales Comparison Approach sections in Figures 10.7 and 10.8.

Check your results against those in the Answer Key at the back of the book.

Value Estimate

Using the adjusted values thus compiled, the appraiser can determine the appropriate market value to assign to the subject property using the sales comparison approach.

Even when the appraiser is dealing with comparable properties that are virtually identical, the adjusted values will rarely be identical. There will usually be at least some differences in real estate transactions, however minor, that will cause selling prices to vary. A seller in one transaction may be less inclined to make a counteroffer than a seller in another transaction. Or a buyer may think that he or she has to offer a certain amount less than the asking price. After all, we are dealing with an imperfect market.

Whatever the reasons, the adjusted values of the comparable properties probably will not be identical. It is the appraiser's task to choose the adjusted value that seems to best reflect the characteristics of the subject property. In other words, which comparable is most similar to the subject property? The adjusted value of that property will most likely represent the market value of the subject property.

In step 7, the appraiser compares the value estimates reached by the cost and income approaches with that reached by the sales comparison approach. You will learn more about that process in Chapter 13, "Reconciliation and the Appraisal Report."

EXERCISE 10.5

You have already completed the Sales Comparison Approach section for this chapter's sample appraisal. Based upon what you have just read, which adjusted value indicates the appropriate opinion of market value of the subject property? Why?

Check your answers against those in the Answer Key at the back of the book.

FIGURE 10.7

Comparables 1 through 3 for Exercise 10.4

| There are | comparable properties currently offered for sale in the subject neighborhood ranging in price from $ | | | | | to $ | | . |

There are _____ comparable sales in the subject neighborhood within the past twelve months ranging in sale price from $ _____ to $ _____.

FEATURE	SUBJECT	COMPARABLE SALE # 1		COMPARABLE SALE # 2		COMPARABLE SALE # 3	
Address 2130 W.Franklin		1901 Parkside Blvd.		2135 Hastings Ave.		2129 Osceola Way	
Proximity to Subject		Within half-mile		Within half-mile		Within half-mile	
Sale Price	$ N/A		$ 226,000		$ 239,000		$ 238,000
Sale Price/Gross Liv. Area	$ N/A sq. ft.	$ 125.56 sq. ft.		$ 127.47 sq. ft.		$ 130.41 sq. ft.	
Data Source(s)		Sales agent		Sales agent		Sales agent	
Verification Source(s)		Sales agent		Sales agent		Sales agent	
VALUE ADJUSTMENTS	DESCRIPTION	DESCRIPTION	+(-) $ Adjustment	DESCRIPTION	+(-) $ Adjustment	DESCRIPTION	+(-) $ Adjustment
Sale or Financing Concessions		none		none		none	
Date of Sale/Time		6 wks ago		1 year ago	+22,700 (rounded)	2 months ago	
Location	quiet street	heavy traffic	+22,000	quiet street		quiet street	
Leasehold/Fee Simple	fee simple	fee simple		fee simple		fee simple	
Site	50' × 200'	50' × 200'		50' × 200'		50' × 200'	
View	good	good		good		good	
Design (Style)	ranch/good	ranch/good		ranch/good		ranch/good	
Quality of Construction	good	good		good		good/alum. sd	+9,000
Actual Age	6 years	8 years		7 years		8 years	
Condition	good	good		good		good	
Above Grade	Total / Bdrms. / Baths	Total / Bdrms. / Baths		Total / Bdrms. / Baths		Total / Bdrms. / Baths	
Room Count	7 / 3 / 2.5	7 / 3 / 2.5	+5,000	7 / 3 / 2	+5,000	7 / 3 / 2	+5,000
Gross Living Area	1,825 sq. ft.	1,800 sq. ft.		1,875 sq. ft.		1,825 sq. ft.	
Basement & Finished Rooms Below Grade	full basement	full basement		full basement		full basement	
Functional Utility	adequate	adequate		adequate		adequate	
Heating/Cooling	central H/A	central H/A		central H/A		central H/A	
Energy Efficient Items	none	none		none		none	
Garage/Carport	2-car att.	2-car att.		2-car att.		2-car att.	
Porch/Patio/Deck	none	none		none		none	
Net Adjustment (Total)		☒ + ☐ -	$ 27,000	☐ + ☐ -	$	☐ + ☐ -	$
Adjusted Sale Price of Comparables		Net Adj. % / Gross Adj. %	$ 253,000	Net Adj. % / Gross Adj. %	$	Net Adj. % / Gross Adj. %	$

I ☐ did ☐ did not research the sale or transfer history of the subject property and comparable sales. If not, explain

My research ☐ did ☐ did not reveal any prior sales or transfers of the subject property for the three years prior to the effective date of this appraisal.

Data source(s)

My research ☐ did ☐ did not reveal any prior sales or transfers of the comparable sales for the year prior to the date of sale of the comparable sale.

Data source(s)

Report the results of the research and analysis of the prior sale or transfer history of the subject property and comparable sales (report additional prior sales on page 3).

ITEM	SUBJECT	COMPARABLE SALE # 1	COMPARABLE SALE # 2	COMPARABLE SALE # 3
Date of Prior Sale/Transfer				
Price of Prior Sale/Transfer				
Data Source(s)				
Effective Date of Data Source(s)				

Analysis of prior sale or transfer history of the subject property and comparable sales

Summary of Sales Comparison Approach

Indicated Value by Sales Comparison Approach $

FIGURE 10.8

Comparables 4 and 5 for Exercise 10.4

| There are | comparable properties currently offered for sale in the subject neighborhood ranging in price from $ | | | | | to $ | | |

| There are | comparable sales in the subject neighborhood within the past twelve months ranging in sale price from $ | | | | | to $ | | |

FEATURE	SUBJECT	COMPARABLE SALE #4		COMPARABLE SALE #5		COMPARABLE SALE #6	
Address	2130 W.Franklin	2243 Parkside Blvd.		2003 Franklin Street			
Proximity to Subject		Within half-mile		Within half-mile			
Sale Price	$ N/A	$ 256,500		$ 251,000		$	
Sale Price/Gross Liv. Area	$ N/A sq. ft.	$ 133.25 sq. ft.		$ 137.53 sq. ft.		$ sq. ft.	
Data Source(s)		Sales agent		Sales agent			
Verification Source(s)		Sales agent		Sales agent			
VALUE ADJUSTMENTS	DESCRIPTION	DESCRIPTION	+(-) $ Adjustment	DESCRIPTION	+(-) $ Adjustment	DESCRIPTION	+(-) $ Adjustment
Sale or Financing Concessions		none		none			
Date of Sale/Time		5 wks ago		5 wks ago			
Location	quiet street	quiet street		quiet street			
Leasehold/Fee Simple	fee simple	fee simple		fee simple			
Site	50' × 200'	50' × 200'		50' × 200'			
View	good	good		good			
Design (Style)	ranch/good	ranch/good		ranch/good			
Quality of Construction	good	good		good			
Actual Age	6 years	6 years		6 years			
Condition	good	good		good			
Above Grade	Total Bdrms. Baths	Total Bdrms. Baths		Total Bdrms. Baths		Total Bdrms. Baths	
Room Count	7 3 2.5	8 4 2	–10,000	7 3 2.5			
Gross Living Area	1,825 sq. ft.	1,925 sq. ft.	+ 5,000	1,825 sq. ft.		sq. ft.	
Basement & Finished Rooms Below Grade	full basement	full basement		full basement			
Functional Utility	adequate	adequate		adequate			
Heating/Cooling	central H/A	central H/A		central H/A			
Energy Efficient Items	none	none		none			
Garage/Carport	2-car att.	2-car att.		2-car att.			
Porch/Patio/Deck	none	none		none			
Net Adjustment (Total)		☐ + ☐ -	$	☐ + ☐ -	$	☐ + ☐ -	$
Adjusted Sale Price of Comparables		Net Adj. % Gross Adj. %	$	Net Adj. % Gross Adj. %	$	Net Adj. % Gross Adj. %	$

(vertical label: SALES COMPARISON APPROACH)

I ☐ did ☐ did not research the sale or transfer history of the subject property and comparable sales. If not, explain

My research ☐ did ☐ did not reveal any prior sales or transfers of the subject property for the three years prior to the effective date of this appraisal.

Data source(s)

My research ☐ did ☐ did not reveal any prior sales or transfers of the comparable sales for the year prior to the date of sale of the comparable sale.

Data source(s)

Report the results of the research and analysis of the prior sale or transfer history of the subject property and comparable sales (report additional prior sales on page 3).

ITEM	SUBJECT	COMPARABLE SALE # 1	COMPARABLE SALE # 2	COMPARABLE SALE # 3
Date of Prior Sale/Transfer				
Price of Prior Sale/Transfer				
Data Source(s)				
Effective Date of Data Source(s)				

Analysis of prior sale or transfer history of the subject property and comparable sales

Summary of Sales Comparison Approach

Indicated Value by Sales Comparison Approach $

■ APPLICATION OF SALES COMPARISON APPROACH

The most obvious advantage of the sales comparison approach is its simplicity and rationale; by definition, it reflects the actions of market participants. In addition, it is easily understood by nonappraisers and preferred by the courts. Relying on past sales information, it gives the appearance of being the most logical and the most objective of the three approaches to forming an opinion of value. If reliable market data can be found and such information can be related to the subject property, the approach has considerable validity.

The principal limitation of the sales comparison approach is the problem of insufficient comparable sales or, even worse, a situation in which no comparable sales exist. If the subject is unique, or if there are no comparable sales available, then the approach cannot be used.

Another difficulty is the need for making accurate adjustments because two properties are seldom identical. Adjustments cannot be based on subjective (what the appraiser "feels" is right) evaluations of the differences between properties or locations. Even under the best of circumstances, differences in value due to variations among properties may be difficult to measure. Beyond this, it also may be difficult to determine whether a particular transaction was a genuine arm's-length transaction or whether peculiar circumstances affected the transaction.

Above all, the appraiser must be keenly attuned to market conditions and trends. The sales comparison approach should not become a mechanical exercise. The appraiser must always question the reliability of sales data in light of economic, political, and social market pressures.

In addition to its wide use in the appraisal of homes, the sales comparison approach is the preferred method for the appraisal of vacant land, as discussed in Chapter 7.

■ SUMMARY

The sales comparison approach relies on the collection of accurate data on both the general market and recent sales of specific properties comparable to the subject property.

The appraiser adjusts the sales price of a comparable property to reflect any differences between it and the property that is the subject of the appraisal. Either a dollar adjustment or a percentage adjustment can be made. The value of an adjustment can be computed using matched pairs analysis, also called *paired sales analysis* and *paired data set analysis*. Necessary adjustments to account for differences in financing terms or date of sale are made before other adjustments.

10

ACHIEVEMENT EXAMINATION

At the conclusion of this three-part problem, you will be asked for your opinion of the market value of a single-family residence.

1. First, determine the adjustment value for each of the significant variables by completing the Sales Price Adjustment Chart in Figure 10.9.

2. The subject property is a seven-room house with two baths and is situated on land 65 feet by 145 feet. The property is located in the central part of the neighborhood. The house is seven years old and is in good condition. Additional details on the subject property are listed in Figure 10.10. Using the adjustment values you computed in the preceding problem, complete the Sales Comparison Approach sections of the URAR form in Figures 10.10, 10.11, and 10.12.

3. In your opinion, what is the market value of the subject property?

Check your results against those in the Answer Key at the back of the book.

F I G U R E   10.9
Sales Price Adjustment Chart for Achievement Examination 10

Sales Price Adjustment Chart
Comparables

	1	2	3	4	5	6	7
SALES PRICE	$185,500	$190,000	$178,600	$186,000	$169,000	$173,500	$190,000
FINANCING	80% S/L	75% S/L	70% S/L	75% S/L	75% S/L	70% S/L	80% S/L
DATE OF SALE	2 mos. ago	3 wks. ago	1 yr. ago	2 wks. ago	1 mo. ago	8 wks. ago	3 wks. ago
LOCATION	quiet resid.	quiet resid.	quiet resid.	quiet resid.	quiet resid.	quiet resid.	quiet resid.
LEASEHOLD/FEE SIMPLE	fee	fee	fee	fee	fee	fee	fee
VIEW	good	good	good	good	good	good	good
SITE	65' × 145'	65' × 145'	65' × 145'	65' × 145'	65' × 145'	65' × 145'	65' × 145'
DESIGN	split lvl/ good	split lvl/ good	split lvl/ good	split lvl/ good	split lvl/ good	split lvl/ good	split lvl/ good
CONSTRUCTION	brick	brick	brick	brick	brick	brick	brick
AGE	7 yrs.	6½ yrs.	6 yrs.	7 ½ yrs.	7 yrs.	7 yrs.	7 yrs.
CONDITION	good	good	good	fair to good	good	good	good
NO. OF RMS./BEDRMS./BATHS	7/3/2	7/3/2	7/3/2	7/3/2	7/3/2	7/3/2	7/3/2
SQ. FT. OF LIVING SPACE	1,600	1,600	1,600	1,575	1,575	1,575	1,590
OTHER SPACE (BASEMENT)	finished half-bsmnt.	finished half-bsmnt.	finished half-bsmnt.	finished half-bsmnt.	finished half-bsmnt.	finished half-bsmnt.	finished half-bsmnt.
FUNCTIONAL UTILITY	adequate	adequate	adequate	adequate	adequate	adequate	adequate
HEATING/COOLING	central heat	central heat/air	central heat/air	central heat/air	central heat	central heat/air	central heat/air
ENERGY EFFICIENT ITEMS	none	none	none	none	none	none	none
GARAGE/CARPORT	2-car att.	2-car att.	2-car att.	2-car att.	none	none	2-car att.
OTHER EXT. IMPROVEMENTS	porch	porch	porch	porch	porch	porch	porch
OTHER INT. IMPROVEMENTS	brick fireplace	brick fireplace	brick fireplace	brick fireplace	brick fireplace	brick fireplace	brick fireplace
TYPICAL HOUSE VALUE							
VARIABLE FEATURE							
ADJUSTMENT VALUE OF VARIABLE							

FIGURE 10.10

Comparables 1 through 3 for Achievement Examination 10

FEATURE	SUBJECT	COMPARABLE SALE # 1		COMPARABLE SALE # 2		COMPARABLE SALE # 3	

There are _____ comparable properties currently offered for sale in the subject neighborhood ranging in price from $_____ to $_____

There are _____ comparable sales in the subject neighborhood within the past twelve months ranging in sale price from $_____ to $_____

FEATURE	SUBJECT	COMPARABLE SALE # 1		COMPARABLE SALE # 2		COMPARABLE SALE # 3	
Address							
Proximity to Subject							
Sale Price	$ N/A	$		$		$	
Sale Price/Gross Liv. Area	$ N/A sq. ft.	$ sq. ft.		$ sq. ft.		$ sq. ft.	
Data Source(s)							
Verification Source(s)							
VALUE ADJUSTMENTS	DESCRIPTION	DESCRIPTION	+(-) $ Adjustment	DESCRIPTION	+(-) $ Adjustment	DESCRIPTION	+(-) $ Adjustment
Sale or Financing Concessions							
Date of Sale/Time							
Location	quiet residential						
Leasehold/Fee Simple	fee simple						
Site	65' × 145'						
View	good						
Design (Style)	split-lvl/good						
Quality of Construction	good/brick						
Actual Age	7 years						
Condition	good						
Above Grade Room Count	Total 7 / Bdrms. 3 / Baths 2	Total / Bdrms. / Baths		Total / Bdrms. / Baths		Total / Bdrms. / Baths	
Gross Living Area	1,600 sq. ft.	sq. ft.		sq. ft.		sq. ft.	
Basement & Finished Rooms Below Grade	finished half basement						
Functional Utility	adequate						
Heating/Cooling	central H/A						
Energy Efficient Items	none						
Garage/Carport	none						
Porch/Patio/Deck	porch						
fireplace	brick fireplace						
Net Adjustment (Total)		☐ + ☐ -	$	☐ + ☐ -	$	☐ + ☐ -	$
Adjusted Sale Price of Comparables		Net Adj. % / Gross Adj. %	$	Net Adj. % / Gross Adj. %	$	Net Adj. % / Gross Adj. %	$

☐ I did ☐ did not research the sale or transfer history of the subject property and comparable sales. If not, explain

My research ☐ did ☐ did not reveal any prior sales or transfers of the subject property for the three years prior to the effective date of this appraisal.

Data source(s)

My research ☐ did ☐ did not reveal any prior sales or transfers of the comparable sales for the year prior to the date of sale of the comparable sale.

Data source(s)

Report the results of the research and analysis of the prior sale or transfer history of the subject property and comparable sales (report additional prior sales on page 3).

ITEM	SUBJECT	COMPARABLE SALE # 1	COMPARABLE SALE # 2	COMPARABLE SALE # 3
Date of Prior Sale/Transfer				
Price of Prior Sale/Transfer				
Data Source(s)				
Effective Date of Data Source(s)				

Analysis of prior sale or transfer history of the subject property and comparable sales

Summary of Sales Comparison Approach

Indicated Value by Sales Comparison Approach $

F I G U R E 10.11
Comparables 4 through 6 for Achievement Examination 10

| There are | comparable properties currently offered for sale in the subject neighborhood ranging in price from $ | | | to $ | | . |

| There are | comparable sales in the subject neighborhood within the past twelve months ranging in sale price from $ | | | to $ | | . |

FEATURE	SUBJECT	COMPARABLE SALE # 4		COMPARABLE SALE #5		COMPARABLE SALE #6	
Address							
Proximity to Subject							
Sale Price	$　　　　N/A		$		$		$
Sale Price/Gross Liv. Area	$　　N/A sq. ft.	$　　　sq. ft.		$　　　sq. ft.		$　　　sq. ft.	
Data Source(s)							
Verification Source(s)							
VALUE ADJUSTMENTS	DESCRIPTION	DESCRIPTION	+(-) $ Adjustment	DESCRIPTION	+(-) $ Adjustment	DESCRIPTION	+(-) $ Adjustment
Sale or Financing Concessions							
Date of Sale/Time							
Location	quiet residential						
Leasehold/Fee Simple	fee simple						
Site	65′ × 145′						
View	good						
Design (Style)	split-lvl/good						
Quality of Construction	good/brick						
Actual Age	7 years						
Condition	good						
Above Grade	Total Bdrms. Baths	Total Bdrms. Baths		Total Bdrms. Baths		Total Bdrms. Baths	
Room Count	7　3　2						
Gross Living Area	1,600 sq. ft.	sq. ft.		sq. ft.		sq. ft.	
Basement & Finished Rooms Below Grade	finished half basement						
Functional Utility	adequate						
Heating/Cooling	central H/A						
Energy Efficient Items	none						
Garage/Carport	none						
Porch/Patio/Deck	porch						
fireplace	brick fireplace						
Net Adjustment (Total)		☐ + ☐ -	$	☐ + ☐ -	$	☐ + ☐ -	$
Adjusted Sale Price of Comparables		Net Adj.　　% Gross Adj.　　%	$	Net Adj.　　% Gross Adj.　　%	$	Net Adj.　　% Gross Adj.　　%	$

I ☐ did ☐ did not research the sale or transfer history of the subject property and comparable sales. If not, explain

My research ☐ did ☐ did not reveal any prior sales or transfers of the subject property for the three years prior to the effective date of this appraisal.

Data source(s)

My research ☐ did ☐ did not reveal any prior sales or transfers of the comparable sales for the year prior to the date of sale of the comparable sale.

Data source(s)

Report the results of the research and analysis of the prior sale or transfer history of the subject property and comparable sales (report additional prior sales on page 3).

ITEM	SUBJECT	COMPARABLE SALE # 1	COMPARABLE SALE # 2	COMPARABLE SALE # 3
Date of Prior Sale/Transfer				
Price of Prior Sale/Transfer				
Data Source(s)				
Effective Date of Data Source(s)				

Analysis of prior sale or transfer history of the subject property and comparable sales

Summary of Sales Comparison Approach

Indicated Value by Sales Comparison Approach $

FIGURE 10.12

Comparable 7 for Achievement Examination 10

FEATURE	SUBJECT	COMPARABLE SALE # 7		COMPARABLE SALE #8		COMPARABLE SALE #9	
There are ___ comparable properties currently offered for sale in the subject neighborhood ranging in price from $ ___ to $ ___ .							
There are ___ comparable sales in the subject neighborhood within the past twelve months ranging in sale price from $ ___ to $ ___ .							
Address							
Proximity to Subject							
Sale Price	$ N/A		$		$		$
Sale Price/Gross Liv. Area	$ N/A sq. ft.	$ sq. ft.		$ sq. ft.		$ sq. ft.	
Data Source(s)							
Verification Source(s)							
VALUE ADJUSTMENTS	DESCRIPTION	DESCRIPTION	+(-) $ Adjustment	DESCRIPTION	+(-) $ Adjustment	DESCRIPTION	+(-) $ Adjustment
Sale or Financing Concessions							
Date of Sale/Time							
Location	quiet residential						
Leasehold/Fee Simple	fee simple						
Site	65' × 145'						
View	good						
Design (Style)	split-lvl/good						
Quality of Construction	good/brick						
Actual Age	7 years						
Condition	good						
Above Grade	Total / Bdrms. / Baths	Total / Bdrms. / Baths		Total / Bdrms. / Baths		Total / Bdrms. / Baths	
Room Count	7 / 3 / 2						
Gross Living Area	1,600 sq. ft.	sq. ft.		sq. ft.		sq. ft.	
Basement & Finished Rooms Below Grade	finished half basement						
Functional Utility	adequate						
Heating/Cooling	central H/A						
Energy Efficient Items	none						
Garage/Carport	none						
Porch/Patio/Deck	porch						
fireplace	brick fireplace						
Net Adjustment (Total)		☐ + ☐ -	$	☐ + ☐ -	$	☐ + ☐ -	$
Adjusted Sale Price of Comparables		Net Adj. % Gross Adj. %	$	Net Adj. % Gross Adj. %	$	Net Adj. % Gross Adj. %	$

I ☐ did ☐ did not research the sale or transfer history of the subject property and comparable sales. If not, explain

My research ☐ did ☐ did not reveal any prior sales or transfers of the subject property for the three years prior to the effective date of this appraisal.

Data source(s)

My research ☐ did ☐ did not reveal any prior sales or transfers of the comparable sales for the year prior to the date of sale of the comparable sale.

Data source(s)

Report the results of the research and analysis of the prior sale or transfer history of the subject property and comparable sales (report additional prior sales on page 3).

ITEM	SUBJECT	COMPARABLE SALE # 1	COMPARABLE SALE # 2	COMPARABLE SALE # 3
Date of Prior Sale/Transfer				
Price of Prior Sale/Transfer				
Data Source(s)				
Effective Date of Data Source(s)				

Analysis of prior sale or transfer history of the subject property and comparable sales

Summary of Sales Comparison Approach

Indicated Value by Sales Comparison Approach $

## CHAPTER 11

The Income Capitalization Approach

■ OVERVIEW

Under the income capitalization approach, the estimate of property value is based on the amount of income the property can be expected to produce. The process requires an accurate estimation of income and expenses and the selection of a capitalization rate and capitalization technique by which net income is processed into value.

The primary advantage of the income capitalization approach is that it approximates the thinking of the typical investor, who is interested in the dollar return on, as well as the return of, an investment in income-producing real estate.

The disadvantages of the income capitalization approach stem from the fact that in some cases, a complex set of relationships must be developed, and the complexities of income capitalization tend to confuse nonappraisers. Despite these difficulties, the income capitalization approach is an important valuation tool and must be understood by every real estate appraiser.

In this chapter, you will learn what is meant by *gross income, effective gross income,* and *net operating income.* You will also learn how to formulate and use gross rent and gross income multipliers. In Chapter 12 the capitalization rate is defined, and you will learn a direct capitalization technique by which market value may be estimated. Chapter 12 also covers the techniques of yield, or annuity, capitalization.

■ THE INCOME-BASED APPROACHES TO APPRAISAL

Income Capitalization and the Principle of Anticipation

The income capitalization approach is based on the premise that there is a relationship between the income a property can earn and the property's value. Income capitalization thus is a process of converting income into value, and the concept of anticipation is fundamental to the approach. The principle of *antic-*

ipation asserts that value is created by the expectation of benefits to be derived in the future. The price a buyer should be willing to pay for a property, therefore, would be equal to the present worth of these future benefits.

In the income capitalization approach, the appraiser reduces or *discounts* a property's anticipated future income to its present worth. This reduction recognizes the fact that an anticipated future dollar is worth less than a dollar in hand. For example, when you deposit $100 in a savings account to earn 3 percent interest compounded[1] annually, you are accepting the fact that the $103 you will receive at the end of the first year has a present value of only $100. Thus, $100 is the present value of $106 when discounted for one year at 3 percent. As you will see in Chapter 12, *yield capitalization* uses discount rates to find the present value of projected future income.

Many commercial properties are purchased to be leased to other parties. The future net income the property is capable of earning and the eventual return (residual) of the investment capital are the main benefits to the owner. For this reason the worth of the property to a prospective buyer is based largely on its earning capacity. The income capitalization approach to value translates the estimated potential income of a property into a determination of market value by the use of certain data and one of numerous income models that link different income variables to value estimates.

The usefulness of the income capitalization approach depends on the type of property under appraisal and the data available. Obviously, it is most useful for income-producing investment properties. But other properties can be appraised using an income approach technique called the *gross income/rent multiplier method,* which is similar in application to the sales comparison approach because it compares rents of similar properties with their selling prices to arrive at a determination of value for the subject property. Gross *rent* multipliers frequently are used to determine the value of single-family residences because such properties usually produce only rental income. Although these may never be rented, they usually have rental income potential, which is particularly important when an oversupply of properties, inflated prices, high mortgage interest rates, or other factors result in a weak resale market. Because industrial and commercial properties generate income from many sources other than rent, the term gross *income* multiplier is used.

■ POTENTIAL GROSS INCOME

Using the income capitalization approach, the appraiser must first estimate the property's *gross income,* which may be defined as a property's total potential income from all sources during a specified period of time, usually a year. This income typically includes rent and also any other associated non-real estate income, such as income from vending machines, laundry services, and parking.

Rent

Rent is the major source of income from most real estate. An appraiser who is gathering data for a market value appraisal using the income capitalization approach needs to know the amount of the property's *market rent,* or *economic*

---

[1] *Compound interest* means that interest is periodically added to the principal, with the result that the new balance (principal plus interest) draws interest. When the interest comes due during the compounding period (for instance, at the end of the year), the interest is calculated and accrues, or is added to the principal. See Chapter 15 for more on compound interest.

rent. Market rent is an estimate of a property's rent potential—what an investor could expect to receive in rental income if the subject space were currently available for a new tenant. In a competitive market, market rent is the standard to which the subject's rent will eventually be drawn. To find market rent, the appraiser must know what rent tenants have paid, and are currently paying, on both the subject and the comparable properties. By comparing present and past performances of the subject and similar properties, the appraiser should be able to recognize what the subject property's rent potential is and whether the property is living up to that potential.

Scheduled (Contract) Rent

Rent currently being paid by agreement between the user and the owner is called *scheduled rent* or *contract rent.* Although local custom may vary, scheduled rent is usually computed per square foot per year on income properties such as stores, offices, and warehouses. The usual practice in determining apartment rents is to compute scheduled rent per unit or room per year. Some sources of contract rent data are

- the *lessee,* the person or company renting or leasing the property;
- the *lessor,* the owner of the property;
- the property manager, who maintains the rent roll; and
- the real estate agent, if the property has been recently sold.

Historical Rent

Scheduled rent paid in past years is called *historical rent.* Historical rent information can serve as a check on the validity of current scheduled rent data. Past periodic rent increases for the subject and similar properties may indicate a trend that current scheduled rents should follow. For instance, rents in a given area may be increasing at the rate of 8 percent yearly. If the current scheduled rent of either the subject or the comparable properties is not in line with the trend, the appraiser should find the reason for the discrepancy to justify the estimate of the rental value the property could command on the current market. Recent rental trends should, of course, be emphasized in estimating the current market rental income for the appraised property.

The needed data on comparable properties for estimating market rental can be provided by owners, lessees, property management firms, and real estate brokers in the area, or perhaps previous appraisals. The following example shows how to develop and use comparable property data in determining market rental for a property to be appraised by the income capitalization approach.

EXAMPLE

The first chart on the next page shows some of the information collected on the subject and other commercial properties in the vicinity. The second chart shows how data can be converted into like units of measurement to make the comparative data more meaningful.

Properties 2 and 4 are roughly the same size as the subject; both are one-floor structures, and the rents are close. Properties 1 and 3 probably do not apply because of the big difference in size.

Property 2 rents for $2.13 per square foot, and property 4 rents for $2.05 per square foot. This suggests that the market (potential) rent of the subject property may be higher than the current scheduled rent of $1.50 per square foot.

Data for Finding Market Rent

Subject Property	Use	Hardware store
	Size	90' × 95' (one floor)
	Scheduled Rent	$12,850
Property 1	Use	Clothing store
	Size	70' × 100' (two floors)
	Scheduled Rent	$21,700
Property 2	Use	Drugstore
	Size	85' × 100' (one floor)
	Scheduled Rent	$18,105
Property 3	Use	Cleaners
	Size	105' × 120' (one floor)
	Scheduled Rent	$20,500
Property 4	Use	Grocery store
	Size	90' × 100' (one floor)
	Scheduled Rent	$18,450

	Use	Square Feet	Scheduled Rent	Rent per Square Foot per Year
Subject	Hardware	8,550	$12,850	$1.50
Property 1	Clothing	14,000	21,700	1.55
Property 2	Drugstore	8,500	18,105	2.13
Property 3	Cleaners	12,600	20,500	1.63
Property 4	Grocery store	9,000	18,450	2.05

In an actual appraisal, other factors of similarity and/or dissimilarity for selecting comparable properties must be considered. Factors to be considered include location, construction of the building, its age and condition, parking facilities, front footage, air-conditioning, and responsibilities of the tenant. If comparable properties rent for more or less than the subject, the appraiser must search for clues as to why there are rental differences. Another important factor that should be considered is the age of the leases. Although the properties may be similar, an old lease could reflect a rental level lower than prevailing rentals.

EXERCISE 11.1

You are asked to appraise a six-unit apartment building. Each apartment has one bath and five rooms: living room, dining room, kitchen, and two bedrooms. Each apartment is presently leased at $900 per apartment per year. For this problem, historical rent will be ignored. There are three other six-unit apartment buildings in the area, of similar room size and construction:

Property 1—contains two-bedroom apartments with living apartment, dining room, kitchen, and bath, renting for $1,260 per apartment per year.

Property 2—contains three-bedroom apartments with living apartment, dining room, kitchen, and bath, renting for $1,440 per apartment per year.

Property 3—contains two-bedroom apartments with living apartment, dining room, kitchen, and bath, renting for $1,176 per apartment per year.

What is the scheduled rent for the subject property?

What is the expected (market) rent for the subject property?

Check your answers against those in the Answer Key at the back of the book.

Outside Economic Factors

Various national, regional, and local factors also might have to be analyzed in deriving market rent. For example, suppose the country has been in a period of recession for the year prior to the date of an appraisal. Historical rental data may indicate a 10 percent increase per year over the preceding five years, but this rate of increase will be too high for the year immediately before the appraisal. Thus, the appraiser must keep informed of economic trends at all levels.

Assume a distribution facility that will employ hundreds of people is being built close to a town. If no new construction has begun on housing facilities, rent for dwelling space in that area most likely will increase because of the relatively low supply of, and high demand for, housing. The appraiser should be aware of this factor and take it into consideration when estimating market rent.

Using both historical and scheduled rent information for the subject and similar properties, the appraiser can derive the subject property's market rent—the amount for which the competitive rental market indicates the property should rent. This figure may be the same as, higher than, or lower than the property's present rent. The appraiser will base the potential gross income estimate on market rent added to any other income derived from the property during a one-year period.

Other Income

Not all income may be from rents. In even the smallest apartment building, the owner may have coin-operated laundry facilities for the tenants' use. Or the owner of an office or apartment building may make parking space available on the premises for the convenience of the tenants and for the income the space produces.

In making up a statement of potential gross income, market rent and other forms of income usually are itemized separately, then totaled to reflect the productivity of the property.

EXAMPLE

An appraisal for ABC Office Management, Inc., estimates the potential gross income from one of its buildings as $230,000 in scheduled rent and $9,000 from parking fees. Show the building's income in an itemized statement.

Potential Gross Income	
Scheduled rent	$230,000
Parking fees	9,000
	$239,000

The total potential gross income for the building under appraisal is $239,000.

A number of items under the potential gross income category often are reported improperly by owners or accountants not experienced in real estate. Among the more important errors are these:

- Leaving out any percentage income that may be paid if the lease is on a minimum-plus-percentage basis. This type of lease is most often found with retail stores. The lessee pays a stipulated minimum rent plus a percentage of the gross business income over a stated amount. This percentage may increase automatically as gross sales (or business) income rises. For instance, the rent may be $6,000 per year plus 8 percent of annual gross sales over $50,000 and 6 percent of gross sales over $80,000.

■ Reporting only the actual income for a year and not the total potential gross income.

■ Leaving out equivalent rents for owner-occupied areas and/or manager's quarters. These can materially affect the capitalized value of the property if the owner and/or the manager occupy substantial space.

■ Leaving out any "other" income *not* derived from rents, such as income from parking garages or lots and from the resale of electricity, heat, or air-conditioning to the tenant.

The appraiser should not accept figures and statements without verifying them by questioning either the tenants or the real estate broker or rental agent involved.

EXERCISE 11.2

You are appraising a six-unit residential property, and the only information available is the following yearly income and expense data. List the income information in statement form, then compute the estimated potential gross income.

Apartment rental income is $32,000. Outlay for janitorial service is $2,700, with another $700 for supplies. Utilities are $4,800, and maintenance and repairs amount to about $1,000. Taxes are $2,700. Income from washers and dryers is $900. Building depreciation is estimated at $2,500 per year. Rental spaces in the adjacent parking lot bring in $1,000 per year.

Check your answers against those in the Answer Key at the back of the book.

Gross Income and Gross Rent Multipliers

As mentioned earlier in this chapter, certain properties, such as single-family homes, are not purchased primarily for income. As a substitute for a more elaborate income capitalization analysis, the *gross rent multiplier (GRM)* and *gross income multiplier (GIM)* are often used in the appraisal process. Each relates the sales price of a property to its rental income.

Because they are subject to essentially the same market influences, rental prices and sales prices tend to move in the same direction and in the same proportion. If rental prices go up or down, sales prices will usually follow suit, and to the same degree. The relationship between the sales price and rental price can be expressed as a factor or ratio, which is the gross income or gross rent multiplier. The ratio is expressed as

$$\frac{\text{Sales Price}}{\text{Gross Income}} = \text{GIM} \quad \text{or} \quad \frac{\text{Sales Price}}{\text{Gross Rent}} = \text{GRM}$$

Because single-family residences usually produce only rental income, the gross rent multiplier is the method used in their appraisal. Industrial and commercial properties, which can generate income from many sources other than rent, are valued by considering their annual income from all sources.

EXAMPLE

A commercial property sold a month ago for $261,000. The annual gross income was $29,000. What is the GIM for the property?

Because the property is commercial, the annual gross income is used in the formula for finding the GIM.

$$\frac{\$261,000}{\$29,000} = 9, \text{ the GIM for this property}$$

To establish a reasonably accurate GIM, the appraiser should have recent sales and income data from at least four similar properties that have sold in the same market area and were rented at the time of sale. The resulting GIM can then be applied to the actual or projected rental of the subject property to estimate its market value. The formula would then be

$$\text{Gross Income} \times \text{GIM} = \text{Market Value}$$

EXAMPLE

Estimate of Market Value—Gross Income Multiplier Analysis

Sale No.	Market Value	Annual Gross Income	GIM
1	$100,000	$10,000	10.0
2	153,000	17,000	9.0
3	123,500	13,000	9.5
4	187,000	22,000	8.5
5	114,000	12,000	9.5
Subject	?	11,000	?

The range of GIMs applied to the subject's gross income gives

$$\$11,000 \times 8.5 = \$ 93,500$$
$$\$11,000 \times 10 = \$110,000$$

These comparisons bracket the estimate of value within reasonable limits. By using sales 1, 3, and 5 as most comparable, the appraiser concludes that the subject property's GIM should be 9.5. Therefore,

$$\$11,000 \times 9.5 = \$104,500,$$

the estimated value of the subject property.

The gross income multiplier method of estimating property value also is referred to as the *potential gross income multiplier* method. Potential gross income is income (usually annual) from all sources before any deduction for vacancy and collection losses or operating expenses. If vacancy and collection losses are deducted from gross income before the multiplier is derived, it is termed the *effective gross income multiplier.*

Because the potential gross income multiplier converts gross, rather than net, income into value, the result can be misleading. For example, consider two similar properties, each with an asking price of eight times gross income, but one property netting $10,000 per year and the other netting only $5,000 per year. (The lower net income could be caused by excessive operating expenses.) According to the GIM method, the investor ought to pay the same price for either property. This is not actually the case, however. The property with the larger net income is certainly more valuable than the other. The length of the lease term also may be a significant factor. A property nearing the end of a five-year lease term in a period of high inflation may well be generating less income than it might if the lease had been renegotiated during that period.

In other methods of direct capitalization, the multiplier concept is refined by considering not only gross income but also the lease term as well as the operating expenses incurred. It is important to use comparable properties that have similar operating expense ratios.

EXERCISE 11.3

The subject has a gross income of $18,000 per year. Information on comparable properties is listed below, with adjustment factors indicated.

Sale No.	Adjustment	Sales Price	Gross Income	GIM
1	new, long-term lease	$167,000	$18,750	
2	high operating expenses	125,000	11,500	
3	old lease	195,600	11,500	
4	low operating expense	144,000	13,400	
5	customized property	147,000	28,000	

Compute the GIM for each property. Then estimate the GIM for the subject property, taking into account the adjustment factors that indicate that a GIM should be raised or lowered to reflect special circumstances. Finally, estimate the value of the subject property.

Check your answers against those in the Answer Key at the back of the book.

■ EFFECTIVE GROSS INCOME

As discussed earlier, the appraiser's estimate of potential gross income is based on a combination of market rent plus all other income earned by the property. It is reasonable to assume, however, that some properties will not be fully rented all the time. Normally, especially during times of economic recession or overbuilt markets, many properties have vacancies. Vacancies, as well as instances of nonpayment of rent, can significantly reduce a property's income. Vacancy and collection loss allowance is usually estimated as a percentage of potential gross income.

Effective gross income is derived by totaling potential income from all sources, then subtracting vacancy and collection losses. The appropriate rate to allow for anticipated vacancy and collection losses is based on market conditions. Vacancy and collection losses rise as competition for tenants increases; they fall when the demand for desirable properties exceeds supply. In short, there is no standard rate for vacancy and collection losses that can take into account all market conditions. If comparable properties are experiencing vacancy rates of 15 percent, then that is the rate that should be assigned to the property being appraised to best reflect market conditions.

For example, assume that the potential gross income of an apartment building that derives all of its income from rent is $250,000. Historically, the subject property has had a 10 percent vacancy rate. If the rate of vacancies in the current year, based on market data analysis, does not differ from that of past years, the real or *effective gross income* of the property would be $225,000. To calculate the effective gross income for a property, the appraiser first determines the potential market rent, then adds any nonrent income. Finally, the appraiser reduces the resulting estimated potential gross income by the percentage of market rent that probably will be lost due to vacancies, collection losses, or both.

EXAMPLE

An eight-unit apartment building historically has a 4 percent vacancy rate and a 4 percent collection loss rate. A current survey of the local market also supports these vacancy estimates. The projected income for the building over the next year is $46,400 market rent, $2,000 parking income, $1,300 from vending machine income, and $800 income from laundry facilities. What is the property's effective gross income?

The effective gross income can be found most easily by first making an itemized statement of potential gross income.

Potential Gross Income	
Market rent	$46,400
Parking	2,000
Vending machines	1,300
Laundry facilities	800
	$50,500

Then vacancy and collection losses based on rental income can be computed and subtracted from potential gross income to arrive at effective gross income.

Vacancy and Collection Losses	
@ 8% of Potential Gross Income	4,040
Effective Gross Income	$46,460

The effective gross income of the subject property is $46,460.

Many factors may influence the percentage of vacancy and collection losses selected, including

- the present and past rental losses of the subject property,
- competitive conditions in the area (rental levels for the subject property and competitive buildings in the neighborhood),
- the estimate of future area population and economic trends,
- the quality of the tenants, and
- the length of the leases.

Although an allowance of 5 percent to 10 percent often is set up for vacancy and collection losses, each appraisal assignment requires that this allowance be derived from pertinent market facts.

EXERCISE 11.4

Using the income and expense information given in exercise 11.2, draw up an effective gross income statement for the subject property. The effective gross income will be based on the following vacancy and rental losses:

The apartment units are vacant for an average of one week of each year. There has also been a total rental loss of 3 percent for each of the past three years.

Check your answers against those in the Answer Key at the back of the book.

■ NET OPERATING INCOME

The value of an income-producing property is measured by the *net operating income (NOI)* it can be expected to earn during its remaining economic life or forecast income period. Net operating income is calculated by deducting the operating expenses of owning a property from its effective gross income. *Operating expenses* are the periodic expenditures needed to maintain the property and continue the production of the effective gross income. Expenses include the cost of all goods and services used or consumed in the process of obtaining and maintaining rental income. Net operating income is customarily expressed as an annual amount.

The expenses incurred depend on the property and the services provided by the owner. Apartment buildings may require a doorman, housekeeping staff for common areas, and a gardener, in addition to maintenance, insurance, property taxes, and management. Some owners of retail store properties provide the real estate and pay for the exterior maintenance of the building, insurance, and property taxes. All utilities and inside maintenance and repairs may be the responsibility of the tenant.

Classification of Operating Expenses

Operating expenses are usually grouped according to the nature of the cost incurred. Expenses may be classified as follows:

■ *Variable expenses* are the out-of-pocket costs incurred for management, wages and benefits of building employees, fuel, utility services, decorating, repairs, and other items required to operate the property. These expenses tend to vary according to the occupancy level of the property.

■ *Fixed expenses* are those costs that are more or less permanent and do not vary according to occupancy, such as real estate taxes and insurance for fire, theft, and hazards.

■ *Reserves for replacement* are allowances set up for replacement of building and equipment items that have a relatively short life expectancy. For example, reserves should be set up for heating systems, roof replacements, elevators, air conditioners, ranges, refrigerators, carpeting, and other items that routinely wear out and have to be replaced during the economic life of the building. The appraiser provides for the replacement of an item by estimating its *replacement cost* and its *remaining economic life* or *useful life*. Using a straight-line recapture method, the annual charge is found by dividing the cost of the item by the number of years of economic life. (Other methods of recapture are discussed in Chapter 12.)

Expenses for Accounting Purposes versus Expenses for Appraisal Purposes

Operating expenses for appraisal purposes do not include expenditures that are beyond the direct operation of an income-producing property. There are four types of expenses to the owner that are *not* operating expenses of real estate.

1. *Financing costs.* Property is appraised without considering available or probable financing, except under the mortgage equity capitalization method. The focus of a market value estimation is the property's productivity—its NOI.

2. *Income tax payments.* Income taxes are a powerful force and exert an influence on investment behavior, but they relate to the owner, not the property. Personal income taxes depend on the total income of a person, personal expenses, age, health, size of family, and so on, and are not treated as expenses of the property for market value appraisal purposes.

3. *Depreciation charges on buildings or other improvements.* An annual depreciation charge is an accounting method of recovering the cost of an investment over a period of time. The process of capitalization, which will be explained later, automatically provides for the recovery of the investment.

4. *Capital improvements.* Although payments may have been made for capital improvements, such as new refrigerators, ranges, or storm windows, the payments themselves are not treated as operating expenses but are taken from the replacement reserve monies.

Reconstructing the Operating Statement

Estimates of current income or expenses may be adjusted if the appraiser's study indicates that they are out of line for comparable properties or do not accurately reflect typical market conditions. The process of adjusting estimated income, eliminating inapplicable expenses, and adjusting the remaining valid expenses is called the *reconstruction* of the operating statement. It may also be described as *stabilization* of income and expenses. The objective of reconstructing the operating statement is to identify the productivity (income-producing capability) of the property. This requires consideration of expenses incurred to enable the subject property to meet the competitive standard of the market.

The operating statement can be prepared on either a *cash basis* (revenue is recorded only when received and expenses recorded only when they are actually paid) or an *accrual basis* (revenue recorded for the period is all revenue earned, whether or not it has actually been received during the period; expenses recorded for the period are all expenses incurred, whether or not they have actually been paid during the period). Individuals usually choose to keep their personal accounts on a cash basis, while businesses generally prefer accrual basis accounting and may, in fact, be required by the Internal Revenue Service to use this method. The basis of the accounting system used must be identified so that the appraiser can reconstruct the operating statement accurately.

Figure 11.1 on the next page is an operating statement for a multistory, self-service elevator apartment building. The first column of figures was prepared by the owner's accountant. The second column of figures was reconstructed by the appraiser (rounding amounts to the nearest $100). The footnotes to Figure 11.1 explain the items in the operating statement with corresponding circled numbers. (Note that the terminology used by accountants and appraisers differs somewhat. For example, the amount the appraiser categorizes as *gross income* is called *total revenue* by an accountant; the appraiser's *net income* is the accountant's *net revenue.*) All amounts on the operating statement are expressed on an annual basis.

FIGURE 11.1
Operating Statement

		Accountant's Figures	Appraiser's Adjusted Estimate
①	Gross Income (Rent)	$56,000.00	$58,700
②	Allowance for Vacancies andBad Debts	____	2,900
	Effective Gross Income	____	55,800
	Operating Expenses		
	Salaries and wages	6,000.50	6,000
	Employees' benefits	519.00	500
	Electricity	900.12	900
	Gas	3,014.60	3,000
	Water	400.10	400
	Painting and decorating	1,000.00	1,000
	Supplies	525.56	500
	Repairs	2,024.30	2,000
	Management	3,000.00	3,000
	Legal and accounting fees	800.00	800
	Miscellaneous expenses	400.00	400
	Insurance (three-year policy)	1,500.00	500
	Real estate taxes	5,100.00	5,100
	Reserves—		
③	Roof replacement	____	500
④	Plumbing and electrical	____	1,000
⑤	Payments on air conditioners	1,200.00	____
⑥	Principal on mortgage	1,500.00	____
⑦	Interest on mortgage	10,000.00	____
⑧	Depreciation—building	8,000.00	____
	Total Expenses	$45,884.38	$25,600
	Net Income	$10,115.62	$30,200

VARIABLE EXPENSES ← Salaries and wages through Miscellaneous expenses

FIXED INSURANCE ← Insurance (three-year policy), Real estate taxes

RESERVES FOR REPLACEMENT ← Reserves—Roof replacement, Plumbing and electrical

1   Income was adjusted upward to reflect the rental value of an apartment occupied by the owner.
2   Vacancy and collection losses, based on an area study, typically amount to 5 percent of gross rental income.
3   Roof replacement is expected every 20 years at a cost of $10,000, or $500 per year ($10,000 ÷ 20).
4   Plumbing and electrical replacements are based on a 20-year service life for fixtures costing $20,000, or $1,000 per year ($20,000 ÷ 20).
5   Payments for capital improvements such as air conditioners are not operating expenses.
6 & 7   Principal and mortgage interest payments are personal income deductions, not property expenses, when appraising on a "free and clear basis."
8   Depreciation is included in the accountant's figures as the owner's expense, to allow for the loss of income that will result when the property reaches the end of its useful life. (For more information on how accrued depreciation is estimated in judging the value of a property, see Chapter 9.)

EXERCISE 11.5

You are gathering data for the appraisal of a 32-unit apartment building. Using the form below, list the yearly income and expense data given in the following accountant's summary. Then compute the property's effective gross income, total expenses, and net operating income. Natural gas rates are expected to increase, perhaps by 25 percent. Because of a general increase in the tax rate, taxes should be increased by about 20 percent. Round off all figures to the nearest $100.

Property address: 759 Fourteenth Street

Rental Income	$210,000.00
Vacancy and Collection Losses	9,850.00
Salaries—Janitor	9,248.17
Employee Benefits	612.00
Management	6,000.00
Natural Gas	12,375.00
Water	3,845.67.00
Electricity	8,674.32.00
Property Taxes	6,000.00
Janitorial Supplies	673.00
Redecorating	2,000.00
Reserves for Building Replacements	2,500.00
Legal and Accounting Fees	2,400.00

Operating Statement

Potential Gross Income _____

    Allowance for Vacancy and Collection Losses _____

Effective Gross Income _____

Operating Expenses

    Variable Expenses _____

        _____

        _____

        _____

        _____

        _____

        _____

        _____

        _____

        _____

        _____

    Fixed Expenses _____

    Reserves for Replacement _____

Total Operating Expense _____

Net Operating Income _____

Check entries on your form against the tabulation in the Answer Key at the back of the book.

Applying the GRM to Residential Properties

The gross rent multiplier is a number that expresses the relationship between the sales price of a residential property and its gross monthly unfurnished rental:

$$\frac{\text{Sales Price}}{\text{Gross Rent}} = \text{GRM}$$

To establish a reasonably accurate GRM, the appraiser should have recent sales and rental data from at least three properties (a larger sample is preferred)[2] similar to the subject that have sold in the same market area and were rented at the time of sale. The appropriate GRM can then be applied to the projected rental of the subject property to estimate its market value. The formula for this step is

$$\text{Gross Rent} \times \text{GRM} = \text{Market Value}$$

The steps in applying the gross rent multiplier can be summarized:

1. Estimate the subject property's monthly market rent.
2. Calculate gross rent multipliers from recently sold comparable properties that were rented at the time of sale.
3. Based on rent multiplier analysis, derive the appropriate GRM for the subject property.
4. Estimate market value by multiplying the amount of the monthly market rent by the subject property's GRM.

Because even very similar properties rarely have the same rent or sales price, GRM analysis is likely to produce a range of multipliers. The appraiser must decide which multiplier is most appropriate for the subject property. No mathematical or mechanical formula can be substituted for careful analysis and judgment.

Following is an example of the range of data that might be collected by an appraiser trying to determine an appropriate GRM for a single-family home.

EXAMPLE

Sale No.	Sales Price	Monthly Rental	GRM (rounded)
1	$100,000	$825	121
2	110,500	875	126
3	105,500	850	124
4	112,000	890	126
5	105,250	850	124
6	104,000	845	123
Subject	?	850	?

In this example, the appraiser has estimated that the market rent for the subject property is $850. The range of GRMs derived from recent sales of comparable properties is from 121 to 126. When applied to the subject's market rent estimate, the GRMs place value between $102,850 ($850 × 121) and $107,100 ($850 × 126). These comparisons bracket the estimate of value within reasonable limits.

Because property sales 3 and 5 are most comparable to the subject property, the appraiser concludes that the subject property's GRM should be 124. The estimated value of the subject property by the gross rent multiplier method then is $850 × 124, or $105,000 (rounded).

_____

[2] To derive a more accurate GRM for appraisal purposes, the appraiser should make an effort to obtain and evaluate data on at least ten comparable rental sales—more if the subject property is located in an area in which there is a high percentage of rentals.

FIGURE 11.2
Income Approach

INCOME APPROACH TO VALUE (not required by Fannie Mae)	

Estimated Monthly Market Rent $ *850* X Gross Rent Multiplier *124*   = $ *105,400*   Indicated Value by Income Approach

Summary of Income Approach (including support for market rent and GRM) *Rental rates and sales prices of 6 properties in area were analyzed.*

Prices from $100,000 to $112,000 and rents from $825 to $890 indicate market rent of $850 and GRM of 124 for subject.

The gross rent multiplier method can be a valid indicator of market value if the subject property is located in a rental-oriented area where an abundance of viable information is available. In areas that are almost exclusively owner-occupied, rental data may be too scarce to permit the use of this method.

If the right kinds of data are available to develop valid market rent and GRM estimates, the gross rent multiplier method should be used for valuing single-family residences, if only to serve as a check against the sales comparison and cost approaches.

Income Approach Using the URAR Form

In the income approach section of the URAR form (Figure 11.2) the appraiser is required to

■ enter the subject property's monthly market rent estimate derived from the marketplace,

■ enter the GRM applicable to the subject property,

■ multiply the monthly market rent estimate by the GRM, and

■ enter the value estimate indicated by the income approach.

Operating Statement Ratios

The effect on value of varying expense levels in relation to income can be seen by studying what are termed the *operating statement ratios*. These ratios, which are derived from sales and rental data and/or the operating statements of properties similar to the subject, can be used to test the validity of the subject's estimated operating expenses.

The *operating expense ratio* is the ratio of total operating expenses to effective gross income. As a formula, the relationship can be expressed as

$$\frac{\text{Operating Expenses}}{\text{Effective Gross Income}} = \text{Operating Expense Ratio}$$

The *net income ratio* is the ratio of net operating income to effective gross income. The formula for this relationship is

$$\frac{\text{Net Operating Income}}{\text{Effective Gross Income}} = \text{Net Income Ratio}$$

The operating expense ratio and net income ratio complement each other; that is, the two ratios added together equal 1. For example, consider a building that has an effective gross income of $100,000 and total operating expenses of $25,000.

The building's operating expense ratio is $25,000 divided by $100,000, or .25. The net operating income is $100,000 less $25,000, or $75,000, making the net income ratio $75,000 divided by $100,000, or .75. The two ratios added together (.25 + .75) equal 1.

The *break-even ratio* is the ratio of the operating expenses *plus* the property's annual debt service to potential gross income. In other words, it is the ratio of funds flowing out of the property (before income taxes) to funds coming in.

The formula for the break-even ratio is

$$\frac{\text{Operating Expenses} + \text{Debt Service}}{\text{Potential Gross Income}} = \text{Break-Even Ratio}$$

The break-even ratio also can be based on effective gross income. The ratio indicates the *break-even point* at which all expenses of ownership, including financing costs, are covered by the income generated. For example, consider a building that has a potential gross income of $100,000, has operating expenses of $25,000, and requires a debt service of $55,000 at current interest rates. The property's break-even ratio is $80,000 ($25,000 + $55,000) divided by $100,000, or .80. At 80 percent occupancy (20 percent vacancy), the property will break even. Any additional reduction in the vacancy factor brought about by an increase in the occupancy rate will be profit.

Ratios vary according to the type of property being studied. For instance, a hotel usually has a break-even point that is somewhat lower than that of an office building. A 75 percent occupancy level may be considered adequate for a hotel, even though the same occupancy level (representing a vacancy factor of 25 percent) may be considered poor for an office building. By comparing the various ratios for properties comparable to the one being appraised, the appraiser can learn what kind of return is expected in the marketplace for properties producing that level of income. Ratios are particularly useful tools when they either confirm that a property's income and expenses are in line with those of other properties or indicate an abnormality that warrants further investigation.

EXERCISE 11.6

1. The ratio of total operating expenses to effective gross income is the
   a. operating expense ratio.
   b. net income ratio.
   c. effective gross income ratio.
   d. break-even ratio.

2. The ratio of net operating income to effective gross income is the
   a. operating expense ratio.
   b. net income ratio.
   c. effective gross income ratio.
   d. break-even ratio.

3. The ratio of the operating expenses plus annual debt service to potential gross income is the
   a. operating expense ratio.
   b. net income ratio.
   c. effective gross income ratio.
   d. break-even ratio.

4. A building that has an effective gross income of $50,000 and total operating expenses of $10,000 has what operating expense ratio?
   a. .10
   b. .15
   c. .20
   d. .25

5. The building described in problem 4 has what net income ratio?
   a. .80
   b. .90
   c. 1
   d. 5

Check your answers against those in the Answer Key at the back of the book.

■ SUMMARY

In the income capitalization approach, the appraiser estimates the market value of property based on its anticipated income.

Gross income includes potential property income from all sources during a specified period. Rent is the major source of income from real estate. Historical rent is scheduled, or contract, rent paid in past years. Current scheduled rent may not be the same as a property's projected market rent.

A gross income multiplier can be multiplied by the amount of gross income to derive an estimate of property value. A monthly multiplier is used for single-family residences; a yearly multiplier is used for multifamily and commercial buildings. The income multiplier method of determining value can be based on either potential gross income or effective gross income, in which case vacancy and collection losses are deducted.

By analyzing a property's operating statement, an appraiser can determine the operating expenses that are deducted from effective gross income to find net operating income. The appraiser must know whether account entries are made on a cash or an accrual basis.

The relationship of effective gross income, operating expenses, and net operating income can be expressed in several operating statement ratios that may indicate whether the property's income production is typical of the marketplace.

11

ACHIEVEMENT EXAMINATION

1. To arrive at net operating income, expenses are deducted from
   a. operating profit.
   b. gross income.
   c. effective gross income.
   d. None of these

2. In the list below, check each item that is *NOT* an expense from an appraiser's point of view.

   a. Gas and electricity

   b. Depreciation on building

   c. Water

   d. Real estate taxes

   e. Building insurance

   f. Income tax

   g. Supplies

   h. Payments on air conditioners

   i. Janitor's salary

   j. Management fees

   k. Maintenance and repairs

   l. Legal and accounting fees

   m. Principal and interest on mortgage

   n. Advertising

   o. Painting and decorating

   p. Depreciation on equipment

   q. Value of janitor's apartment (rent free)

   r. Water and sewer tax

   s. Salaries and wages of employees

   t. Reserves for replacement

   u. Payments on stoves and refrigerators

3. If a property's net income ratio is .85, what is its operating expense ratio?

   a. .15

   b. 1.50

   c. .58

   d. .015

4. Another name for contract rent is

   a. market rent

   b. scheduled rent.

   c. economic rent.

   d. surplus rent.

5. Another name for market rent is

   a. contract rent

   b. scheduled rent.

   c. economic rent.

   d. surplus rent.

6. A commercial property producing an annual gross income of $39,000 was sold two months ago for $341,250. What is the property's gross income multiplier?

 a. 7

 b. 7.75

 c. 8.5

 d. 8.75

7. A single-family residence that sold recently for $285,000 can be rented for $1,400 per month. The property's gross rent multiplier is

 a. 17

 b. 204

 c. 207

 d. 210

8. Vacancy and collection losses are deducted from gross income using a(n)

 a. potential gross income multiplier.

 b. effective gross income multiplier.

 c. gross income multiplier.

 d. gross rent multiplier.

9. In the formula for the operating expense ratio

 a. operating expenses are divided by effective gross income.

 b. effective gross income is divided by operating expenses.

 c. potential gross income is divided by effective gross income.

 d. effective gross income is divided by potential gross income.

10. In the formula for the net income ratio

 a. effective gross income is divided by potential gross income.

 b. potential gross income is divided by effective gross income.

 c. effective gross income is divided by net operating income.

 d. net operating income is divided by effective gross income.

Check your answers against those in the Answer Key at the back of the book.

## CHAPTER 12

Direct and Yield Capitalization

■ OVERVIEW

An income-based property appraisal can be made considering

- the return a property is capable of producing in a single stabilized year, using a method called *direct capitalization,* or
- the present value of the anticipated future income stream that can be expected from the property over a period of years, using a method called *yield capitalization.*

Using direct capitalization, the appraiser analyzes the market value of an income-producing property from the perspective of a new investor. The appraiser next studies the relationship between sales prices and income levels of comparable properties to derive a capitalization rate. That rate is then applied to the subject property's annual operating income, based on the income that can be expected during the first stabilized year of ownership. The resulting figure is a determination of the market value warranted by the stated level of income, assuming the same return received by comparable properties.

Using yield capitalization, the appraiser estimates the income that the property may be expected to produce in the future, then estimates the present worth of the right to receive that income. The appraiser develops a capitalization rate based on the typical investor's required return and applies that rate to the present value of the income stream to derive market value.

If there are adequate data on comparable sales with similar income expectations, direct capitalization can produce a very reliable value conclusion. If information on comparable sales is lacking, yield capitalization may provide a more reliable value estimate because an appropriate yield rate can be selected by determining what rate of return investors are requiring on investments of comparable risk.

■ DIRECT CAPITALIZATION FORMULA

The *direct capitalization formula* is

$$\frac{\text{Net Operating Income}}{\text{Capitalization Rate}} = \text{Value}$$

The four categories of data needed for an appraisal by the income approach using direct capitalization are

1. the *potential gross income* from the property, which includes the annual income from all sources;

2. the amount of the expected annual *effective gross income* from the property, estimated by subtracting anticipated vacancy and collection losses from potential gross income;

3. the *net operating income,* found by deducting normal annual operating and other expenses from the effective gross income; and

4. the *capitalization rate* for the property; that is, the rate that can be applied to the property's net annual income, the result being the appraiser's estimate of the property's value.

■ CAPITALIZATION RATE

Income-producing property is usually bought as an investment. That is, the purchaser wants the property for the return it will yield on the capital (whether owned or borrowed) used to buy it. The rate of return the investor receives is the *capitalization rate* (also called the *overall capitalization rate*), which can be expressed as a relationship between the annual net operating income a property produces and its value. Put into equation form:

$$\frac{\text{Net Operating Income}}{\text{Value}} = \text{Capitalization Rate} \quad \text{or} \quad \frac{I}{V} = R$$

EXAMPLE

An investor paid $500,000 for a building that earns a net income of $50,000 per year. What is the capitalization rate of the investment?

Using the formula $\frac{I}{V} = R$, the capitalization rate is:

$$\frac{\$50,000}{\$500,000} \text{ or } 10\%$$

The formula for the capitalization rate is useful for appraisal purposes because of its two corollaries:

$$\text{Capitalization Rate} \times \text{Value} = \text{Net Operating Income, or } R \times V = I$$

$$\frac{\text{Net Operating Income}}{\text{Capitalization Rate}} = \text{Value} \quad \text{or} \quad \frac{I}{R} = V$$

By dividing the estimated net operating income (NOI) of a property by the appropriate capitalization ("cap") rate, the property's value may be estimated.

There are several ways an appraiser can find a property's capitalization rate. The appraiser can study comparable properties that have recently sold and assume that the capitalization rate of a comparable property would be approximately the same as that of the subject. Or the appraiser can analyze the component parts of a capitalization rate and construct a rate for the subject property. Both of these methods of *direct capitalization* are discussed in this chapter.

In earlier sections we saw that the appraiser must analyze income and operating expense data to accurately estimate a property's potential gross income and compute its NOI. Using these two types of data, the appraiser compiles information from even more sources to arrive at the property's capitalization rate.

An overall *capitalization rate* may be developed by evaluating net income figures and sales prices of comparable properties.

E X A M P L E

An appraiser has determined that the annual NOI of the subject property is $130,000. By screening the market data the appraiser has compiled, a comparable property is located with an NOI of $128,000 a year that sold recently for $1,820,000. Using this comparable alone, what is the capitalization rate of the subject property?

The overall capitalization rate of the comparable property is

$$\frac{I}{V} = \frac{\$128,000}{\$1,820,000} = 7\%$$

The NOI for the subject property is $130,000, so its value is

$$\frac{I}{R} = \frac{\$130,000}{.07} = \$1,857,000$$

Of course, the appraisal would be more reliable if several comparable properties were studied to find the most appropriate capitalization rate for the subject.

By definition, comparable properties should have comparable capitalization rates. If a property the appraiser thought was comparable turns out to have a capitalization rate significantly higher or lower than that of other comparable properties, the appraiser should consider discarding that sample. Closer examination of the property or sales transaction would probably reveal extenuating circumstances (such as a transaction between related companies) that should have kept the property from consideration as a comparable.

When the income capitalization approach is used, even a slight difference in the assigned capitalization rate will have a substantial effect on the estimate of property value. If a property were assigned a capitalization rate of 9 percent and its NOI were $180,000, its value would be estimated at $180,000 ÷ .09, or $2,000,000. If the capitalization rate assigned were 8 percent, the value estimate would be $180,000 ÷ .08, or $2,250,000.

One percentage point difference in the capitalization rate would make a 12 ½ percent difference in the value estimate. By discarding extremes, the appraiser should have a narrow range of capitalization rates from which the subject property's capitalization rate can be estimated; the appraiser must use judgment in selecting a capitalization rate that is reflective of the most comparable properties.

EXERCISE 12.1

You are appraising an industrial building with an NOI of $170,000. You have previously appraised or studied the comparable properties listed below. Use all of the information you have on hand to find a suitable capitalization rate for the subject, then the subject's value. Round your answer to the nearest $100.

Property	Selling Price	Net Operating Income	Capitalization Rate
A	$1,360,000	$148,000	_____
B	940,000	110,000	_____
C	1,270,000	150,000	_____
D	1,105,000	126,000	_____
E	1,500,000	320,000	_____

Check your answers against those in the Answer Key at the back of the book.

Building a Capitalization Rate

Another way of determining a capitalization rate for the subject property is by analyzing the capitalization rate's component parts and estimating each of those components for the subject property. The two basic components of the capitalization rate are the recapture rate and the interest rate, which will be discussed next.

An investor who purchases an income-producing property expects two things:

1. Return *of* the investment. This is the right to get back the purchase price at the end of the term of ownership and is ordinarily expressed as an annual rate. Appraisers refer to this as *capital recapture.*

2. Return *on* the investment. This return is the investor's profit on the money used to purchase the property and is expressed as the *interest rate.* The interest rate is also referred to as the *discount rate, risk rate,* or *return on rate.*

Because land usually does not depreciate, its sales price at the end of the investor's period of ownership is considered adequate compensation. Buildings depreciate, however, and the investor has an asset of continually decreasing value. This anticipated future depreciation is provided for in the recapture part of the capitalization rate.

These two investment objectives can be illustrated by the following example:

EXAMPLE

The ABC Corporation owns a lot on which it builds an office building for $3 million. The building has an economic life of 20 years. The company expects to receive an annual NOI of 10 percent from the building during its economic life and also expects to have the building investment repaid over that period of time. To achieve these two objectives, the NOI of the property would have to be as follows:

$3,000,000 × .10 = $300,000 Interest (Return on investment)

$3,000,000 ÷ 20 = $150,000 Annual recapture (Return of investment)

$300,000 + $150,000 = $450,000 Annual NOI

In the above example, with an NOI of $450,000 and a value of $3 million, the building capitalization rate is $\frac{I}{V}$, or $\frac{\$450,000}{\$3,000,000}$, or 15 percent. The return *on* the investment (interest) makes up 10 percent of the capitalization rate, and the return *of* the investment (recapture) makes up 5 percent of the total capitalization rate of 15 percent.

By analyzing the factors that constitute the interest and recapture rates, the appraiser can determine a property's capitalization rate and use that and the property's net income to find its value. The recapture and interest rates are discussed next.

Selecting the Rate for Capital Recapture

Every good investment provides for a return *on* the invested capital, called the *interest* or *discount,* and a return *of* the invested capital, called *capital recapture.* In processing income produced by land only, a recapture provision is usually unnecessary. The assumption (which does not necessarily reflect the reality of the marketplace) is that land will not depreciate, and recapture can therefore be accomplished entirely through resale. A building, however, does depreciate. That is, its value decreases with the passing of time. Therefore, the appraiser must add to the interest rate a percentage that will provide for the recapture of the investment in the building.

Straight-Line Method of Recapture

The simplest, most widely used method of computing the recapture rate is the *straight-line method.* Under this method, total accrued depreciation is spread over the useful life of a building in equal annual amounts. Thus, when the building is 100 percent depreciated and presumably economically useless, all of the investment will have been returned to the investor. To find the recapture rate by the straight-line method, divide the total accrued depreciation (100 percent) by the estimated useful years of life of the building.

$$\frac{100\%}{\text{Years of Useful Life}} = \text{Annual Recapture Rate}$$

If, for example, a building has a remaining useful life of 20 years, 5 percent of the building's value should be returned annually out of NOI:

$$\frac{100\%}{20} = 5\% \text{ Recapture Rate}$$

The straight-line method of recapture requires a good deal of knowledge about the useful life of a given type of property. As a starting point, the appraiser may refer to tables, contained in various cost manuals, that deal with the useful lives of buildings by type. Then the appraiser must consider the factors unique to the subject property, such as its age, its condition, and the area in which it is located.

A building most frequently becomes useless through external or functional obsolescence, rather than through physical deterioration; that is, more buildings are torn down in still-usable condition than fall down from deterioration. For this reason, the recapture period is often referred to as *estimated remaining economic life.* An appraiser estimates the remaining economic life of a property after considering the physical, functional, and external factors involved.

Selecting the Interest Rate by the Market Extraction Method

In this method the appraiser finds the interest rate of a comparable property by subtracting the portion of the property's NOI attributable to building recapture from total NOI, then dividing the remainder by the selling price of the property.

EXAMPLE

Property X sold for $200,000. The site is valued at $50,000, and the building has a re-maining economic life of 40 years. Total NOI is $30,000.

The building value is $150,000 ($200,000 – $50,000), and the recapture rate is .025 (1/*n*, or 1 ÷ 40 years), so

$$\$150,000 \times .025 = \$3,750$$

The annual recapture of $3,750 is applied to the entire property value of $200,000 to produce an interest rate of 1.875%.

$$\$3,750 \div \$200,000 = .01875$$

The net operating income available for building recapture of $3,750 leaves $26,250 ($30,000 – $3,750) as NOI available for the property. Dividing that amount by the property's sales price:

$$\$26,250 \div \$200,000 = .13125$$

The interest rate for property X is thus 13.125 percent.

In the example above, the overall cap rate for the subject property is .13125 + .01875, or .15, which is 15 percent.

EXERCISE 12.2

Construct an interest rate for a recently sold commercial property with the following known facts: The selling price was $435,000. The site value is $125,000, and the build-ing's estimated remaining economic life is 25 years. Total net operating income is $57,000.

What is the overall cap rate for the property?

Check your answers against those in the Answer Key at the back of the book.

Band of Investment Method—Mortgage and Equity Elements

Another method commonly used to calculate an overall capitalization rate is the *band of investment method,* which considers the financial components, or "bands," of debt and equity capital required to support the investment. This method thus takes into account everyone who has a financial interest in the real estate being appraised. Not every investor will be satisfied with the same rate of return on an investment. For example, the owner may regard his or her position as riskier than that of the first or second mortgage holders. Each mortgage creates a lien on the property. If the owner defaults, the property may be sold to pay such liens, and the owner will receive only those proceeds that may remain from the sale of the property after the lienholders have been paid. Because the owner's interest is generally considered inferior to those of lienholders, the owner may require a higher total return on the investment but accept a lower cash flow return, given the value of the owner's residual interest in the property in addition to the owner's subordinated claim on the cash flow.

The band of investment method must take into account both the rate required by the lender and the rate necessary for the equity investor's desired pretax cash flow. The rate required by the lender is termed the *mortgage constant* and is annual debt service expressed as a percentage of the original principal amount. For example, a $100,000, 30-year mortgage loan at 8 percent has monthly payments of $733.78. Annual debt service is $8,805.36 ($733.78 × 12). The mortgage constant is $8,805.36 divided by $100,000, which is .088, or 8.8 percent.

The rate required by the equity investor, which is the ratio of the investor's expected pretax cash flow to the investment's value, is called the *equity capitalization rate*. The equity capitalization rate also may be referred to as the *cash on cash rate, cash flow rate,* or *equity dividend rate.*

The overall rate developed by the band of investment method thus is based on (1) the capitalization rate for debt, called the *mortgage constant,* and (2) the rate of return required (yield) on equity, called the *equity capitalization rate.* For example, assume a case in which a mortgage with a 30-year amortization period covering 80 percent of the value of the property can be obtained at 8 percent interest, and the buyer requires a return of 10 percent on the equity portion (the 20 percent of the value of the property the buyer will invest). Using the band of investment method, the overall rate could be developed as follows:

	Percent of Property's Total Value	Return Required	
Loan	.80	× .088 (mortgage constant)	= .07
Equity	.20	× .10 (equity cap rate)	= .02
Overall rate			.09 or 9%

In the example above, the overall capitalization rate of 9 percent reflects the rate of return required to attract money into the type of ownership position that results when the interests of all participants are taken into account.

Relationship of Capitalization Rate and Risk

Several generalizations can be made about the relationship between the capitalization rate and the risk of an investment.

High Risk = High Capitalization Rate
Low Risk = Low Capitalization Rate

Because high risk implies a high possibility of investment loss, a property with a high risk will have a lower selling price or value than one with a relatively low risk factor. Each of the preceding generalizations thus can be carried one step farther.

High Risk = High Capitalization Rate = Low Value
Low Risk = Low Capitalization Rate = High Value

EXERCISE 12.3

Assuming the following data, what capitalization rate would you use in appraising the subject property?

A 30-year mortgage covering 75 percent of property value can be obtained from a bank at 8 ½ percent. The mortgage constant is .092.

Equity for this type of property requires a 12 percent return.

Check your answer against the one in the Answer Key at the back of the book.

■ CAPITALIZATION TECHNIQUES USING RESIDUAL INCOME

Two techniques by which net operating income (NOI) can be capitalized into value using residual income are (1) the building residual technique and (2) the land residual technique.

In appraising, a *residual* is the income remaining after all deductions have been made. It may refer to

■ the NOI attributable to the *building* after return on land value has been deducted (building residual technique) or

■ the NOI attributable to the *land* after return on and recapture of the building value have been deducted (land residual technique).

In estimating the value of real estate, each technique will produce approximately the same answer, provided the return (interest rate) and recapture assumptions remain the same for each technique.

Building Residual Technique

To use the *building residual technique,* the appraiser must know the value of the land, which is usually found by analyzing comparable sales.

First, the appraiser deducts the amount of NOI that must be earned by the land to justify its value. The balance of the NOI must be earned by the building. This building income is then capitalized at the interest rate *plus* the rate of recapture to arrive at the building's value.

EXAMPLE

A commercial property is being appraised. The land value has been estimated at $80,000, and the typical rate of return is 12 percent, so the land itself must earn $9,600 ($80,000 × .12) if it is to justify its purchase price. The property should yield a total NOI of $37,000 yearly. The residual income to the building, therefore, is $27,400 ($37,000 – $9,600).

The capitalization rate for the building will be based on the interest rate of 12 percent (already applied to the land value) and a recapture rate of 5 percent based on an estimated remaining economic life of 20 years (100% ÷ 20 years = 5% per year). The building capitalization rate, therefore, is 17 percent (12% + 5%). The estimated building value is $27,400 ÷ .17 or $161,200 (rounded to the nearest hundred dollars).

Finally, the value of the building is added to the value of the land to arrive at the total property value, which is $241,200 ($161,200 + $80,000).

All of the information in this example problem could be itemized as follows:

Estimated Land Value		$ 80,000
NOI	$37,000	
Interest on Land Value ($80,000 × .12)	− 9,600	
Residual Income to Building	$27,400	
Capitalization Rate for Building		
Interest Rate	12%	
Recapture Rate	+5	
	17%	
Building Value ($27,400 ÷ .17)		161,200
Total Property Value		$241,200

The building residual technique is most useful when land values are stable and can be determined easily by recent sales of similar sites. This technique is also used when the construction cost of the building and the amount of accrued depreciation are difficult to measure accurately because of the building's age or unusual design.

EXERCISE 12.4

The property under appraisal is a 25-year-old apartment building producing an NOI of $50,000 a year. Compute the value of the property, assuming a remaining economic life of 40 years for the building, a 10 ½ percent interest rate, and land value estimated at $100,000.

Check your answer against the one in the Answer Key at the back of the book.

Land Residual Technique

The *land residual technique* follows the same procedure as the building residual technique—but with the building and land calculations reversed.

EXAMPLE

Assume that the NOI for a commercial property is $45,000 annually, and the value of the building has been estimated at $225,000. The appropriate interest rate for the building is 11 ⅞ percent, and the estimated recapture rate is 4 percent. What is the value of the property to the nearest $100?

Assumed Building Value		$225,000
NOI	$45,000	
Capitalization Rate for Building		
Interest Rate	11.875%	
Recapture Rate	4.0	
Total	15.875%	
Interest and Recapture on Building		
Value ($225,000 × .15875)	− 35,700	
Residual Income to Land	$ 9,300	
Land Value ($9,300 ÷ .11875)		78,300
Total Property Value		$303,300

In this example, the value of land and building together is $303,300.

The land residual technique is used (1) when the land value cannot be estimated from comparable sales or (2) when the building is new or in its early life and represents the highest and best use of the land. When a building is new, value usually is assumed to be equal to reproduction cost.

EXERCISE 12.5

A new office building valued at $3 million produces an annual NOI of $530,000. This type of property requires a 12 percent return, and the building's remaining economic life is estimated at 50 years. Estimate the total property value by the land residual technique.

Check your answer against the one in the Answer Key at the back of the book.

Valuing the Land and Building as a Whole

The land and building are valued as a single unit, rather than as separate units, when the building is very old or when it is difficult to make reliable estimates of either the land or the building value.

The appraiser analyzes sales of comparable properties and develops an NOI for each property. Then, using the formula for the capitalization rate, $\frac{I}{V} = R$, the appraiser computes a range of overall rates from which a rate appropriate to the subject property can be selected.

For example, if a comparable property producing an NOI of $12,000 sold for $100,000, then, by dividing $12,000 by $100,000, an overall rate of 12 percent is derived. This rate includes both interest and recapture. Now, if several additional properties comparable to the subject were also producing NOIs that, when divided by their selling prices, indicated a yield of approximately 12 percent, it would seem reasonable to capitalize the NOI of the subject property at the same overall rate—12 percent. Then, if the NOI of the subject were $10,000, its value by direct capitalization would be $10,000 ÷ .12, or approximately $83,000.

EXERCISE 12.6

You have been asked to appraise an income-producing property in a rural area where it is difficult to substantiate either building or land values. You have obtained the following income and selling price data on comparable properties:

	Net Operating Income	Selling Price
Property 1	$15,000	$115,400
Property 2	20,000	166,700
Property 3	12,500	100,000
Property 4	18,000	140,600
Subject	6,000	

Because all properties above are highly comparable, you feel that an average cap rate will probably be applicable to the subject. What is your estimate of value for the subject property?

Check your answer against the one in the Answer Key at the back of the book

■ YIELD CAPITALIZATION

In the process called *yield capitalization,* real estate investment return is broken down into two components: (1) an income flow for a specified number of years and (2) a capital change (a gain or loss) realized at the end of the multiyear investment period from an actual or assumed sale of the property. Yield capitalization is computed on a cash accounting basis from the investor's perspective.

Yield capitalization is an appropriate technique to use for the investor who intends to buy an income-producing property and wants to know the value of the income stream that can be expected in the future from the property. An investor planning to obtain a mortgage loan to help pay for the property will also want to know how the mortgage payments will affect the property's expected cash flow.

The tables discussed in this chapter can be used to make such calculations, but only after the appraiser has made a thorough analysis of the subject property and the degree of risk it carries as an investment. The relative permanence of the investment is considered; that is, the length of the lease term coupled with the reliability of the tenant. The capitalization method chosen by the appraiser depends on the potential stability of the income stream. Generally, the tables included here assume a relatively long-term lease and a very reliable tenant.

The discussion that follows includes the use of the *Inwood annuity table* and the reversion table, as well as the contributions of L. W. Ellwood, who explained how the various tables can be used in real estate appraisals.

■ VALUE OF ONE DOLLAR

When is a dollar worth more than a dollar? When it will be received at some time in the future. An investor who puts a dollar into an investment today wants to receive more than the dollar back when the investment matures. Sometimes a dollar is worth less than a dollar. An investor may be interested in an investment that pays back *x* number of dollars at a certain time in the future, based on an initial investment that is some amount less than *x* dollars. What is the present value of either investment? The answer to that question depends on the length of the investment term, the interest paid, and whether the interest will be compounded during the investment term.

In this computerized era, calculations that once required time-consuming application of arduous formulas or skilled consultation of lengthy charts can be accomplished by merely pushing the right buttons. The best way to use such mechanical aids, however, is with an understanding of the basis for the underlying computations.

The chart in Figure 12.1 is itself a shortcut method that shows the final figures derived from application of the formulas required to determine the value of $1 to an investor under different circumstances at an interest rate of 10 percent over an annual term from 1 to 50 years. The six functions of a dollar, as shown in columns one through six, are listed below.

1. *Future value of $1.* This column indicates the value of $1 one year from now if the dollar accumulates 10 percent interest. An investment of $1 at 10 percent interest per year will yield $1.10 at the end of one year.

2. *Future value of an annuity of $1 per year.* This column shows the total amount contributed to an *annuity* if a total of $1 is contributed every year and every year the cumulative total contributed earns 10 percent interest. At the end of year one, the total contributed is $1. At the end of year two, the

FIGURE 12.1
Six Functions of One Dollar

10.00% Annual Interest Rate

	1	2	3	4	5	6	
	Future Value of $1	Future Value Annuity of $1 per Year	Sinking Fund Factor	Present Value of $1 (Reversion)	Present Value Annuity of $1 per Year	Payment to Amortize $1	
Years							Years
1	1.100000	1.000000	1.000000	0.909091	0.909091	1.100000	1
2	1.210000	2.100000	0.476190	0.826446	1.735537	0.576190	2
3	1.331000	3.310000	0.302115	0.751315	2.486852	0.402115	3
4	1.464100	4.641000	0.215471	0.683013	3.169865	0.315471	4
5	1.610510	6.105100	0.163797	0.620921	3.790787	0.263797	5
6	1.771561	7.715610	0.129607	0.564474	4.355261	0.229607	6
7	1.948717	9.487171	0.105405	0.513158	4.868419	0.205405	7
8	2.143589	11.435888	0.087444	0.466507	5.334926	0.187444	8
9	2.357948	13.579477	0.073641	0.424098	5.759024	0.173641	9
10	2.593742	15.937425	0.062745	0.385543	6.144567	0.162745	10
11	2.853117	18.531167	0.053963	0.350494	6.495061	0.153963	11
12	3.138428	21.384284	0.046763	0.318631	6.813692	0.146763	12
13	3.452271	24.522712	0.040779	0.289664	7.103356	0.140779	13
14	3.797498	27.974983	0.035746	0.263331	7.366687	0.135746	14
15	4.177248	31.772482	0.031474	0.239392	7.606080	0.131474	15
16	4.594973	35.949730	0.027817	0.217629	7.823709	0.127817	16
17	5.054470	40.544703	0.024664	0.197845	8.021553	0.124664	17
18	5.559917	45.599173	0.021930	0.179859	8.201412	0.121930	18
19	6.115909	51.159090	0.019547	0.163508	8.364920	0.119547	19
20	6.727500	57.274999	0.017460	0.148644	8.513564	0.117460	20
21	7.400250	64.002499	0.015624	0.135131	8.648694	0.115624	21
22	8.140275	71.402749	0.014005	0.122846	8.771540	0.114005	22
23	8.954302	79.543024	0.012572	0.111678	8.883218	0.112572	23
24	9.849733	88.497327	0.011300	0.101526	8.984744	0.111300	24
25	10.834706	98.347059	0.010168	0.092296	9.077040	0.110168	25
26	11.918177	109.181765	0.009159	0.083905	9.160945	0.109159	26
27	13.109994	121.099942	0.008258	0.076278	9.237223	0.108258	27
28	14.420994	134.209936	0.007451	0.069343	9.306567	0.107451	28
29	15.863093	148.630930	0.006728	0.063039	9.369606	0.106728	29
30	17.449402	164.494023	0.006079	0.057309	9.426914	0.106079	30
31	19.194342	181.943425	0.005496	0.052099	9.479013	0.105496	31
32	21.113777	201.137767	0.004972	0.047362	9.526376	0.104972	32
33	23.225154	222.251544	0.004499	0.043057	9.569432	0.104499	33
34	25.547670	245.476699	0.004074	0.039143	9.608575	0.104074	34
35	28.102437	271.024368	0.003690	0.035584	9.644159	0.103690	35
36	30.912681	299.126805	0.003343	0.032349	9.676508	0.103343	36
37	34.003949	330.039486	0.003030	0.029408	9.705917	0.103030	37
38	37.404343	364.043434	0.002747	0.026735	9.732651	0.102747	38
39	41.144778	401.447778	0.002491	0.024304	9.756956	0.102491	39
40	45.259256	442.592556	0.002259	0.022095	9.779051	0.102259	40
41	49.785181	487.851811	0.002050	0.020086	9.799137	0.102050	41
42	54.763699	537.636992	0.001860	0.018260	9.817397	0.101860	42
43	60.240069	592.400692	0.001688	0.016600	9.833998	0.101688	43
44	66.264076	652.640761	0.001532	0.015091	9.849089	0.101532	44
45	72.890484	718.904837	0.001391	0.013719	9.862808	0.101391	45
46	80.179532	791.795321	0.001263	0.012472	9.875280	0.101263	46
47	88.197485	871.974853	0.001147	0.011338	9.886618	0.101147	47
48	97.017234	960.172338	0.001041	0.010307	9.896926	0.101041	48
49	106.718957	1057.189572	0.000946	0.009370	9.906296	0.100946	49
50	117.390853	1163.908529	0.000859	0.008519	9.914814	0.100859	50

Source: Jeffrey D. Fisher and Robert S. Martin, *Income Property Appraisal*, 2nd Edition (Chicago: Dearborn™ Real Estate Education, 2005).

total contributed is $1 for the first year, plus interest of $.10 on that dollar over the second year, plus $1 for the second year, for a total of $1 + $.10 + $1, or $2.10.

3. *Sinking fund factor.* This column shows the amount that must be invested each year of the stated term at 10 percent interest to accumulate $1. If an investor wants to accumulate $1,000,000 at the end of five years, $163,797 must be invested every year at 10 percent interest.

4. *Present value of a $1 reversion.* This column shows the amount that must be invested at 10 percent interest now in order to return $1 at the end of the stated number of years (the reversionary interest). To receive a return of $1,000,000 at the end of five years, an investment of $620,921 must be made at the beginning of the five-year term, provided interest accumulates at the rate of 10 percent per year.

5. *Present value of an annuity of $1 per year.* This column shows the present value of the right to receive an annuity of $1 per year for the stated period. An investor who wants to be paid $10,000 every year for 10 years from an annuity must contribute $61,445.67 at the start of the annuity period, provided the amount invested accumulates 10 percent interest per year.

6. *Payment to amortize $1.* This column indicates the payment amount needed to pay off a loan of $1 for the stated number of years. If $100,000 is borrowed for 15 years, the yearly payment (including both principal and interest) needed to pay the loan off in full in 15 years is $13,147.40.

When is a dollar worth more than a dollar? When it is loaned, borrowed, or spent on income-producing property. Some of the values of a dollar discussed previously will be referred to in the remaining sections of this chapter.

■ ANNUITY METHOD OF CAPITALIZATION

An *annuity* is a fixed yearly return on an investment. It may be for any number of years, if the investment is high enough to provide the return desired. The return also may be paid weekly, monthly, or quarterly, rather than yearly.

An investor who wants a return of $1,120 on a one-year investment that pays 12 percent interest has to invest $1,000. The $1,000 will be returned to the investor at the end of the year, along with interest of $120 ($1,000 × 12%), making a total of $1,120. A total return of $1,000 at 12 percent interest for one year requires an investment of $893. The investor will receive interest income of $107.16. In effect, the investor is paying $893 for the right to receive income of $107.16 and have the amount of original investment returned.

As shown above, the mathematics of computing investment amounts for one year is very simple. The total return is 100 percent of the original investment plus the interest for the time period involved (in the preceding example, 12 percent); thus, the total return is 112 percent of the original investment. Most income properties, however, are expected to yield income for more than one year. A table that may be used to find the discounted, present worth of an annuity of $1 at a stipulated interest rate for a given number of years is shown in Figure 12.2. Such an *annuity factors table* (frequently called the *Inwood table*) provides a factor to be multiplied by the desired level of yearly income (based on the interest rate and length of time of the investment) to find the present worth of the investment, that is, what the investor should pay.

FIGURE 12.2
Annuity Factors Table

					Interest Rate				
Year	10%	11%	12%	13%	14%	15%	16%	17%	18%
1	.909	.901	.893	.885	.887	.870	.862	.855	.847
2	1.736	1.713	1.690	1.668	1.647	1.626	1.605	1.585	1.566
3	2.487	2.444	2.402	2.361	2.322	2.283	2.246	2.210	2.174
4	3.170	3.102	3.037	2.974	2.914	2.855	2.798	2.743	2.690
5	3.791	3.696	3.605	3.517	3.433	3.352	3.274	3.199	3.127
6	4.355	4.231	4.111	3.998	3.889	3.784	3.685	3.589	3.498
7	4.868	4.712	4.564	4.423	4.288	4.160	4.039	3.922	3.812
8	5.335	5.146	4.968	4.799	4.639	4.487	4.344	4.207	4.078
9	5.759	5.537	5.328	5.132	4.946	4.772	4.607	4.451	4.303
10	6.145	5.889	5.650	5.426	5.216	5.019	4.833	4.659	4.494
11	6.495	6.207	5.938	5.687	5.453	5.234	5.029	4.836	4.656
12	6.814	6.492	6.194	5.918	5.660	5.421	5.197	4.988	4.793
13	7.103	6.750	6.424	6.122	5.842	5.583	5.342	5.118	4.910
14	7.367	6.982	6.628	6.302	6.002	5.724	5.468	5.229	5.008
15	7.606	7.191	6.811	6.462	6.142	5.847	5.575	5.324	5.092
16	7.824	7.379	6.974	6.604	6.265	5.954	5.668	5.405	5.162
17	8.022	7.549	7.120	6.729	6.373	6.047	5.749	5.475	5.222
18	8.201	7.702	7.250	6.840	6.467	6.128	5.818	5.534	5.273
19	8.365	7.839	7.366	6.938	6.550	6.198	5.877	5.584	5.316
20	8.514	7.963	7.469	7.025	6.623	6.259	5.929	5.628	5.353
21	8.649	8.075	7.562	7.102	6.687	6.312	5.973	5.665	5.384
22	8.772	8.176	7.645	7.170	6.743	6.359	6.011	5.696	5.410
23	8.883	8.266	7.718	7.230	6.792	6.399	6.044	5.723	5.432
24	8.985	8.348	7.784	7.283	6.835	6.434	6.073	5.746	5.451
25	9.077	8.422	7.843	7.330	6.873	6.464	6.097	5.766	5.467
26	9.161	8.488	7.896	7.372	6.906	6.491	6.118	5.783	5.480
27	9.237	8.548	7.943	7.409	6.935	6.514	6.136	5.798	5.492
28	9.307	8.602	7.984	7.441	6.961	6.534	6.152	5.810	5.502
29	9.370	8.650	8.022	7.470	6.983	6.551	6.166	5.820	5.510
30	9.427	8.694	8.055	7.496	7.003	6.566	6.177	5.829	5.517
31	9.479	8.733	8.085	7.518	7.020	6.579	6.187	5.837	5.523
32	9.526	8.769	8.112	7.538	7.035	6.591	6.196	5.844	5.528
33	9.569	8.801	8.135	7.556	7.048	6.600	6.203	5.849	5.532
34	9.609	8.829	8.157	7.572	7.060	6.609	6.210	5.854	5.536
35	9.644	8.855	8.176	7.586	7.070	6.617	6.215	5.858	5.539
36	9.677	8.879	8.192	7.598	7.079	6.623	6.220	5.862	5.541
37	9.706	8.900	8.208	7.609	7.087	6.629	6.224	5.865	5.543
38	9.733	8.919	8.221	7.618	7.094	6.634	6.228	5.867	5.545
39	9.757	8.936	8.233	7.627	7.100	6.638	6.231	5.869	5.547
40	9.779	8.951	8.244	7.634	7.105	6.642	6.233	5.871	5.548

Source: Jeffrey D. Fisher and Robert S. Martin, *Income Property Appraisal*, 2nd Edition (Chicago: Dearborn™ Real Estate Education, 2005).

The annuity table shown in Figure 12.2 may be used for investment periods from 1 to 40 years, at interest rates from 10 percent to 18 percent. Such tables are available for other investment periods and interest rates and may even reflect interest computed on a monthly, quarterly, or semiannual basis. An annuity table allows an appraiser to match the projected length of the investment with the interest rate it is expected to produce, to find the factor to be multiplied by the desired level of yearly income.

EXAMPLE

An investor wishes to receive an annual income of $6,000 for four years by making an investment earning 10 percent. What should be the amount of the original investment?

Column 1 in Figure 12.2 indicates that the annuity factor for an interest rate of 10 percent over an investment period of four years is 3.170. Multiplied by the annual income sought ($6,000 × 3.170), an initial investment figure of $19,020 is derived. In other words, a $19,020 investment for four years at 10 percent interest will yield yearly income of $6,000. At the end of the four years, the entire amount invested, plus all interest earned, will have been returned to the investor.

As stated earlier, annuity table factors may not be appropriate for every investment in real estate. The investment should be a stable one. Even though it is impossible to predict the reliability of tenants or possible changes in market usage *exactly,* the investment should have certain indicators of the stability of the income to be produced. The sound financial status of the tenant and a long-term lease should indicate a reliable income stream.

In the use of annuity tables, the number of years that the investment will be expected to yield income should be based on the remaining economic life of the property, which may coincide with the length of the lease term or projected holding period.

Building Residual Technique

Ideally, the income stream over the remaining economic life of the property will be ensured by a lease signed by a reliable client. In such a case, if land value can be estimated, the total property value can be found by using the *building residual technique.*

EXAMPLE

An appraiser is analyzing the current market value of an investment property with a land value of $100,000 (estimated by analyzing comparable sales). The retail store on the land is being leased by a major supermarket chain, which has been financially successful for 20 years and should remain so. The lease, as of the date of appraisal, will run for another 23 years. The yield rate on land and building has been calculated at 13 percent. The property provides an annual net operating income (NOI) of $36,000. What is its current market value?

The interest on the land value of $100,000 is $13,000 ($100,000 × 13%). When $13,000 is subtracted from the total annual NOI of $36,000, a *net income residual* of $23,000 ($36,000 – $13,000) may be used to derive the building value. Using the annuity table (Figure 12.2), it is determined that a 13 percent interest rate over 23 years provides a factor of 7.230. The building value is the building income multiplied by the annuity factor, or

$$\$23,000 \times 7.230 = \$166,290$$

The value of the building is $166,290. The total property value, then, is $166,290 plus the land value of $100,000, or $266,290.

The appraiser in the preceding example would record the information that follows:

Estimated Land Value		$100,000
Annual NOI before		
Recapture of Building	$36,000	
Interest on Estimated Land Value		
(@ 13% per year on $100,000)	13,000	
Annual Residual Income to Building	$23,000	
Annuity Factor (7.230, based on		
13% interest over 23 years)		
Building Value ($23,000 × 7.230)		166,290
Total Property Value		266,290
Rounded to		$266,000

EXERCISE 12.7

Use the building residual technique and the annuity table to estimate the value of a property that produces an NOI before recapture of $26,400 per year. The land is valued at $75,000, interest rate on land and building is calculated at 11 percent per year, and the current tenant has 30 years remaining on the lease.

Check your answer against the one in the Answer Key at the back of the book.

Valuing the Property as a Whole

If the property used to explain the building residual technique in the preceding example were to be treated as a whole (both land and building), the present worth of the property, with an income stream of $36,000 and an annuity factor of 7.230, would be estimated at $260,280. Or

Total Annual NOI	$36,000
Annuity Factor (23 years at 13%)	× 7.230
Present Worth of NOI	$260,280

At the end of the income stream of 23 years, however, the land will revert back to the owner. That is, although the building will have reached the end of its economic life, the land will still be valuable. The future, or reversionary, value of the land may be quite difficult to predict. The reversionary value of the land may be assumed by the appraiser to be the same as its present value, based on the appraiser's judgment of the future market value of the property.

The present worth of the whole property will be what the investor is willing to pay for the specified income stream, plus the right to the reversionary value of the land at the end of the income-producing period.

The amount that the investor should pay for the land's future value is computed by applying a reversion factor to the land's present estimated value. The *reversion table* shown in Figure 12.3 lists the computed factors at specified interest rates for an investment term of 1 to 40 years.

In the preceding example problem, an investment valued at 13 percent interest for 23 years gives a reversion factor of .060. Because the present (and assumed

FIGURE 12.3
Reversion Table

Year	10%	11%	12%	13%	14%	15%	16%	17%	18%
					Interest Rate				
1	.909	.901	.893	.885	.877	.870	.862	.855	.847
2	.826	.812	.797	.783	.769	.756	.743	.731	.718
3	.751	.731	.712	.693	.675	.658	.641	.624	.609
4	.683	.659	.636	.613	.592	.572	.552	.534	.516
5	.621	.593	.567	.543	.519	.497	.476	.456	.437
6	.564	.535	.507	.480	.456	.432	.410	.390	.370
7	.513	.482	.452	.425	.400	.376	.354	.333	.314
8	.467	.434	.404	.376	.351	.327	.305	.285	.266
9	.424	.391	.361	.333	.308	.284	.263	.243	.225
10	.386	.352	.322	.295	.270	.247	.227	.208	.191
11	.350	.317	.287	.261	.237	.215	.195	.178	.162
12	.319	.286	.257	.231	.208	.187	.168	.152	.137
13	.290	.258	.229	.204	.182	.163	.145	.130	.116
14	.263	.232	.205	.181	.160	.141	.125	.111	.099
15	.239	.209	.183	.160	.140	.123	.108	.095	.084
16	.218	.188	.163	.141	.123	.107	.093	.081	.071
17	.198	.170	.146	.125	.108	.093	.080	.069	.060
18	.180	.153	.130	.111	.095	.081	.069	.059	.051
19	.164	.138	.116	.098	.083	.070	.060	.051	.043
20	.149	.124	.104	.087	.073	.061	.051	.043	.037
21	.135	.112	.093	.077	.064	.053	.044	.037	.031
22	.123	.101	.083	.068	.056	.046	.038	.032	.026
23	.112	.091	.074	.060	.049	.040	.033	.027	.022
24	.102	.082	.066	.053	.043	.035	.028	.023	.019
25	.092	.074	.059	.047	.038	.030	.024	.020	.016
26	.084	.066	.053	.042	.033	.026	.021	.017	.014
27	.076	.060	.047	.037	.029	.023	.018	.014	.011
28	.069	.054	.042	.033	.026	.020	.016	.012	.010
29	.063	.048	.037	.029	.022	.017	.014	.011	.008
30	.057	.044	.033	.026	.020	.015	.012	.009	.007
31	.052	.039	.030	.023	.017	.013	.010	.008	.0059
32	.047	.035	.027	.020	.015	.011	.009	.007	.0050
33	.043	.032	.024	.018	.013	.010	.007	.006	.0042
34	.039	.029	.021	.016	.012	.009	.0064	.005	.0036
35	.036	.026	.019	.014	.010	.008	.0055	.004	.0030
36	.032	.023	.017	.012	.009	.007	.0048	.0035	.0026
37	.029	.021	.015	.011	.008	.006	.0041	.0030	.0022
38	.027	.019	.013	.010	.007	.005	.0036	.0026	.0019
39	.024	.017	.012	.009	.006	.0043	.0031	.0022	.0016
40	.022	.015	.011	.008	.005	.0037	.0026	.0019	.0013

future) value of the land was estimated at $100,000, the value of the reversion at the end of 23 years is $6,000 ($100,000 × .060). When the present worth of the reversion ($6,000) is added to the present worth of the net income stream ($260,280), the resulting property value is $266,280. This value is almost exactly that reached by the building residual technique. The slight discrepancy results from rounding off the annuity and reversion factors. Even this small discrepancy would be reduced if the factors were carried out to more decimal places.

EXERCISE 12.8

Using the annuity and reversion tables, estimate the value of the following property. (Record your computations below.)

The property is a two-acre site with an industrial warehouse leased to a major auto parts manufacturer at an annual rental of $30,000, which is also the NOI. The lease term will expire in 25 years, which is the estimated remaining economic life of the building. The value of the site in 25 years is expected to be $75,000 per acre. The investment should yield an income stream at 12 percent interest.

Check your answer against the one in the Answer Key at the back of the book.

■ RECAPTURE RATES

The *recapture rate* is a periodic allowance for the recovery of investment capital from the property's income stream. Annuity tables do not assume a static (unchanging from year to year) recapture rate. Slow changes in building value are assumed in the early years of the investment term, with greater changes in the last years of the investment. In the straight-line method of recapture, however, the same recapture rate is assumed for each year of the investment. The computations in Figure 12.4 show the difference in value that can result after a 25-year investment term at a 13 percent yield, using the straight-line method of recapture and the annuity table. The subject property is the one used in the preceding example.

The land value of $100,000 in both methods is the same because the sales comparison approach was used. Building value differs, however, because the annuity method allows for a slower decrease in building value over the early years of the building's life, providing a higher value in later years. The straight-line method, on the other hand, applies an equal decrease in value to be recaptured for every year of the building's economic life.

From this discussion, we can summarize the assumptions and effects of the annuity and straight-line recapture methods on income, interest, and recapture.

Under the *annuity method:*

■ The income stream does not vary but remains constant for each year of the building's economic life.

■ Interest accrues each year on the decreasing principal.

■ Recapture accounts for an increasing share of income each year.

FIGURE 12.4
Building Residual Technique (After 15 Years)

Straight-Line Method		Annuity Method	
Total Net Operating Income	$ 36,000	Total Net Operating Income	$ 36,000
Return on Land Value		Return on Land Value	
($100,000 × 13%)	13,000	($100,000 × 13%	13,000
Residual Income to Building	$ 23,000	Residual Income to Building	$ 23,000
Capitalization Rate			
Return 13%			
Recapture 4			
Total 17%			
Building Value		Building Value	
($23,000 ÷ 17%)	$135,294	($23,000 × 7.330	$168,590
Plus Land Value	100,000	Plus Land Value	100,000
Total Property Value	$235,294	Total Property Value	$268,590

Under the *straight-line method:*

■ Income decreases each year by the same amount.

■ Interest accrues each year on the decreasing property value.

■ Recapture remains constant for each year.

Figure 12.5 compares the effects of the straight-line and annuity recapture methods on income, interest, and recapture.

EXERCISE 12.9

Which of the two capitalization methods discussed in this chapter—straight-line or annuity—is appropriate in each of the following examples?

1. An office building leased by a major oil company is being appraised. The lease will run for another 22 years.

2. A building with a 20-year lease is being appraised. The lessee has hinted to the appraiser that if the building is to be sold, he will expect to renegotiate his lease with the new owner, because the rent is more than he can really afford.

Check your answers against those in the Answer Key at the back of the book.

FIGURE 12.5
Straight-Line and Annuity Methods Comparison

	Straight-Line	Annuity
Income	decreases	constant
Interest	decreases	decreases
Recapture	constant	increases

■ ELLWOOD TABLES

The late L. W. Ellwood compiled the best-known appraising tables and offered his interpretation of how they work and when they may be used. These explanations and tables are given in *Ellwood Tables for Real Estate Appraising and Financing,* Fourth Edition (©1977 by American Institute of Real Estate Appraisers).

Among the topics Ellwood covered are common formulas, their symbols, the mortgage coefficient method of finding an investment yield and capitalization rate, other equity techniques, and purchase and leaseback problems, in addition to tables for all techniques at varying interest rates.

Many of the areas explained by Ellwood, such as the Inwood annuity table and reversion table, have already been touched on in this book. For more detailed explanations of these as well as other subjects mentioned, refer to the Ellwood book and to *AIREA Financial Tables,* edited and compiled by James J. Mason (Chicago: American Institute of Real Estate Appraisers, 1981), and *Income Property Appraisal,* 2nd ed., by Jeffrey D. Fisher and Robert S. Martin (Chicago: Dearborn Real Estate Education, 2005).

■ SUMMARY

Capitalization is the relationship between income and market value. Generally speaking, income capitalization is the most important approach used in valuing income-producing property and is the one appraisers normally rely on most heavily in the final value conclusion. The reliability of this approach is, however, directly related to the quality of the data used and the proper application of income capitalization techniques.

The two ways of capitalizing income are direct capitalization and yield capitalization. Direct capitalization is the simplest mathematical process to apply, and when the rate used is supported adequately by comparable sales in the market, it is a most convincing method for estimating value.

The process of developing a capitalization rate by comparing net income figures and sales prices of comparable properties is one of the techniques of direct capitalization. A capitalization rate can also be developed by breaking down the rate's component parts and estimating each separately. The rate developed will be composed of recapture rate (return of investment) and interest rate (return on investment). The recapture rate is often derived by using the straight-line method. The interest rate is developed by using the market extraction method.

The band of investment method takes into account both the rate required by the lender (called the *mortgage constant*) and the rate necessary for the equity investor's desired pretax cash flow (called the *equity capitalization rate*). An investment with a high degree of risk will have a corresponding high capitalization rate, resulting in a low property value. A low-risk investment will have a corresponding low capitalization rate and high value.

NOI can be capitalized into value by using the building residual or land residual techniques, or by valuing the property as a whole.

Using yield capitalization, investment property value is considered the present worth of the right to receive a fixed return of both the amount invested and the interest on that amount. Yield capitalization uses discount rates to find the present value of projected future income. The discount rate used in yield capitalization should be the rate of return that typical investors in the marketplace would expect to earn on comparable properties of similar risk. An annuity table provides a factor that represents income over a stated term at a stated rate of interest. An annuity factor is applicable only if the investment is a stable one, such as a long-term lease held by a financially sound tenant.

The building residual technique can be used with an annuity table to find total present property value. Valuing land and building as a whole makes use of both annuity and reversion tables.

Building recapture can be estimated using either the straight-line method or the annuity method. The method chosen will affect income, interest, and recapture estimates.

Tables compiled by the late L. W. Ellwood are useful for a variety of investment-yield and other problems.

ACHIEVEMENT EXAMINATION

1. In income property investments

   a. low risk = low cap rate = high value.

   b. low risk = low cap rate = low value.

   c. low risk = high cap rate = low value.

   d. low risk = high cap rate = high value.

2. All other factors being equal, as the location of an income property becomes less desirable, the cap rate used will be

   a. lower.

   b. higher.

   c. less reliable.

   d. unaffected.

3. Recapture generally applies to

   a. wasting assets, such as buildings.

   b. nonwasting assets, such as land.

   c. Both a and b

   d. Neither a nor b

4. In the land residual technique, the appraiser starts with an assumption of

   a. replacement cost.

   b. building value.

   c. net capitalization.

   d. land value.

5. In the building residual technique, the appraiser starts with an assumption of

   a. replacement cost.

   b. building value.

   c. net capitalization.

   d. land value.

6. The cash on cash rate is the same as the

   a. yield capitalization rate.

   b. equity dividend rate.

   c. overall capitalization rate.

   d. break-even point.

7. Name the two component rates that are inherent in every capitalization rate.

8. Under which method are the recapture installments lowest in the earlier years?

   a. Annuity

   b. Straight-line

9. Under which method are the installments highest?

   a. Annuity

   b. Straight-line

10. Of the two recapture approaches, which would yield

    a. the highest value?

    b. the lowest value?

11. Which recapture method suggests the greatest reduction in risk?

    a. Annuity

    b. Straight-line

12. Using the following data, compute value by (a) the building residual technique and (b) the land residual technique. Round your figures to the nearest $1,000.

    Net operating income is $400,000.

    Land value is $500,000.

    Sixty-five percent of the value of the property can be borrowed at 11 percent, and equity capital for this type of investment requires a 12 percent return.

    The building's remaining economic life is 25 years.

13. In this case problem, you will estimate the market value of a property by the income capitalization approach. Round all figures to the nearest $1.

You have been asked to appraise a one-story commercial building located in a small neighborhood shopping center. The building is about 20 years old and is divided into four separate stores, all of equal size. Each store pays a yearly rental of $10,200, which is well in line with comparable properties analyzed.

The owner of the subject property lists the following items of expense for the previous year:

real estate taxes—$4,000
insurance—three-year policy—$3,000
repairs and maintenance—$2,800
mortgage payments—$8,400
legal and accounting fees—$550
miscellaneous expenses—$500

In addition to the above expense listing, you obtain the following information:

Tenants pay for their own water, heating, electricity, and garbage removal.

Repairs and general maintenance should be based on 12 percent of effective gross income.

Miscellaneous expenses should be increased to 2 percent of potential gross income.

The records of property managers indicate that vacancy and collection losses in the area run about 4 percent.

A new roof, costing $2,000 and having an average life of 20 years, was installed last year.

The gas furnace in each store can be replaced for $950 and will carry a ten-year guarantee.

Recent land sales in the area indicate that the land value of the subject property should be estimated at $55,000.

You have determined from banks in the area that 75 percent of the value of the property can be borrowed at 11 percent interest, and equity money for this type of investment requires a 13 percent return.

The building is 20 years old and appears to have depreciated about one-third.

a. On the basis of the information provided, reconstruct the operating statement.

b. Determine the appropriate capitalization rate.

c. Estimate the total property value.

14. You are appraising a commercial building earning an annual NOI before recapture of $50,000. Based on supportable information, the interest rate has been established at 15 percent. Land value has been estimated at $100,000 and the building's remaining economic life at 25 years.

    Determine the estimated value of the property in each case below.

    a. The property has year-to-year tenants of average credit risk.

    b. The property is leased for the entire 25 years to a national concern with an excellent credit rating.

Check your answers against those in the Answer Key at the back of the book.

## CHAPTER 13

Reconciliation and the Appraisal Report

■ OVERVIEW

The next step in the appraisal process is the reconciliation of the values indicated by each of the three approaches to appraising. In the *cost approach,* the cost of reproducing or replacing the structure less depreciation plus the site value was calculated. In the *income capitalization approach,* value was based on the income the property should be capable of earning. In the *sales comparison approach,* the utility of recently sold similar properties was compared with the appraised property, and the sales prices were adjusted to derive an opinion of value.

The values reached by these different techniques will almost never be the same, yet the appraiser must make a final determination of the single best supportable estimate of value. The process by which the appraiser does this is called *reconciliation.*

After the value estimates reached by the different approaches to value are reconciled, the resulting final opinion of value is presented by the appraiser to the client in as much detail as requested by the client. Although the appraiser must always fully document the research and reasoning leading to the conclusion of value, all of that background information might not be presented in the report to the client.

In this chapter you will learn what the process of reconciliation is and how it is accomplished. In addition, you will learn the types of *appraisal reports* that may be used.

■ DEFINITION OF RECONCILIATION

In theory, all of the values derived using the three major approaches should be exactly the same; that is, if the appraiser had all of the relevant data and had carried out each step in each approach without error, each value indication would be the same. In actual practice, this seldom happens. In fact, if an appraiser reaches the same value indication for all three approaches, the credibility of the appraisal report could be seriously questioned. In almost every case, the application of the three approaches naturally results in three different indications of value. In the value reconciliation process, the validity of the methods and result of each approach are weighed objectively to arrive at the single best and most supportable conclusion of value. This process is also called *correlation*.

The Process of Reconciliation

Many appraisers believe that all three approaches to value should be used in every appraisal assignment—if the appropriate kinds of data are available. Other appraisers feel that only one or two of the approaches are really necessary in typical assignments. For instance, it may be argued that the income capitalization approach does not lend itself to valuing single-family residences, because such properties are not typically bought for their income-producing capacities. The sales comparison approach would not be appropriate in valuing a special-purpose property, such as a public library or museum, because no useful comparable sale information would be available. The cost approach cannot be used to value vacant land. In reaching a decision about which approach or approaches to use, the appraiser must first understand the nature of the property and the objective of the assignment.

In reconciling, or correlating, the appraiser reviews his or her work and considers at least four factors:

1. Definition of value sought
2. Amount and reliability of the data collected in each approach
3. Inherent strengths and weaknesses of each approach
4. Relevance of each approach to the subject property and market behavior

The appraiser never averages the differing value indications. After the factors listed above are considered, the most relevant approach—cost, sales comparison, or income—receives the greatest weight in determining the amount that most accurately reflects the value sought. In addition, each of the approaches serves as a check against the others.

EXERCISE 13.1

Why is it unlikely that application of the three approaches to the same property will result in identical estimates of value?

Check your answer against the one in the Answer Key at the back of the book.

Review of the Three Approaches

To begin the reconciliation process, the appraiser verifies the steps followed in each approach. In reviewing the sales comparison approach, the appraiser should check

■ that properties selected as comparables are sufficiently similar to the subject property;

■ amount and reliability of sales data;

■ factors used in comparison;

■ logic of the adjustments made between comparable sale properties and the subject property;

■ soundness of the value estimate drawn from the adjusted sales prices of comparable properties; and

■ mathematical accuracy of the adjustment computations.

In reviewing the cost approach, the appraiser should check

■ that sites used as comparables are, in fact, similar to the subject site;

■ amount and reliability of the comparable sales data collected;

■ appropriateness of the factors used in comparison;

■ logic of the adjustments made between comparable sale sites and the subject site;

■ soundness of the value estimate drawn from the adjusted sales prices of comparable sites;

■ mathematical accuracy of the adjustment computations;

■ appropriateness of the method of estimating reproduction or replacement cost;

■ appropriateness of the unit cost factor;

■ accuracy of the reproduction or replacement cost computations;

■ market values assigned to accrued depreciation charges; and

■ for double-counting and/or omissions in making accrued depreciation charges.

In reviewing the income capitalization approach, the appraiser should check the logic and mathematical accuracy of the

■ market rents;

■ potential gross income estimate;

■ allowance for vacancy and collection losses;

■ operating expense estimate, including reserves for replacement;

■ net income estimate;

■ estimate of remaining economic life; and

■ capitalization rate and method of capitalizing.

In reviewing the gross rent multiplier method, the appraiser should check

■ that properties analyzed are comparable to the subject property and to one another in terms of locational, physical, and investment characteristics;

■ that adequate rental data are available;

■ that comparable sales were drawn from properties that were rented at the time of sale;

■ that the gross rent multiplier for the subject property was derived from current sales and current rental incomes; and

■ the mathematical accuracy of all computations.

Weighing the Choices

Once the appraiser is assured of the validity of the three value estimates, he or she must decide which is the most reliable, in terms of the value sought, for the subject property. Inherent factors may make a particular method automatically more significant for certain kinds of property (such as the income approach for investment properties). But other factors, of which the appraiser should be aware, may negate part of that significance. An economically depressed neighborhood, for instance, may make any structure virtually worthless. If the appraiser is trying to determine market value, and if the market for property in a certain neighborhood is likely to be extremely small, this fact should be reflected in the appraiser's final opinion of value.

EXAMPLE

An appraiser determining the market value of a six-unit apartment building in a neighborhood composed predominantly of two-unit to eight-unit apartment buildings arrived at the following initial estimates:

Sales Comparison Approach	$722,500
Cost Approach	758,500
Income Capitalization Approach	746,800

Based on these indications of value, the range is from $722,500 to $758,500, a difference of $36,000 between the lowest indication of value and the highest. This relatively narrow range suggests that the information gathered and analyzed is both a reasonable and a reliable representation of the market.

After value indications have been reached by each of the three approaches, the appraiser must then produce a single opinion of value based on the approach(es) supported by the most convincing factual evidence. This figure may be the same as one of the values produced by the three approaches, or it may differ from all of them, but still fall somewhere within the value range. The appraiser should have no reservations about reaching a final determination of value at either end of the range, provided his or her opinion is supported by market facts and persuasive analysis.

In reviewing the data collected for the sales comparison approach and the results drawn, the appraiser realized that this value indication should be very reliable. Other buildings in the same general condition, and with the same types of improvements, were selling for from $716,000 to $758,000. However, because all comparable sales used in the analysis required considerable adjusting, less weight was given to the sales comparison approach than would normally be expected. After allowing for specific differences, an indicated value of $722,500 was determined for the subject property by the sales comparison approach.

Next, the appraiser analyzed the information collected and the result obtained using the cost approach. The cost approach is most effective when the property is new, without functional or external obsolescence, and at its highest and best use. However, the older a property becomes, the more difficult it is to accurately estimate the proper amount of accrued depreciation. The fact that the subject building is only a few years old strengthened the $758,500 determination of value by the cost approach.

Finally, the appraiser considered the market value derived from the income capitalization approach. For several reasons, this approach seemed to have the most validity for this particular property. First, none of the apartments was owner-occupied, and the tenants were only 16 months through three-year leases. The rents charged were comparable to those for similar apartments when the leases were first signed. Since then, however, rents of other properties have risen as much as 20 percent and will probably keep rising for the next 20 months, when the leases will expire. The appraiser allowed for this in arriving at the income capitalization approach estimate. The property's current income indicated a market value of $746,800.

Even though the sales prices of comparable buildings suggested a market value of $722,500 for the subject, the building's utility as an income-producing property allows for a market value of $746,800.

Because a prudent investor for property of this type very likely will give highest consideration to an analysis of income and expenses, and because the cost approach strongly supports the income capitalization approach, the appraiser's final opinion of market value is $747,000.

The final opinion of value should be rounded to the closest practical dollar amount—in this case, the nearest thousand dollars.

EXERCISE 13.2

You are appraising a residential duplex in a well-maintained community. One unit of the property will be owner-occupied and the other unit rented, as in the past. There are many similar properties in the neighborhood, most owner-occupied with one unit used as a rental. Rents have increased slowly but consistently over the years, and there are no indications of any change in demand. No buildable lots are available in the area.

Your estimate of value by the sales comparison approach is $173,000; by the cost approach, $168,000; and by the income capitalization approach, $170,000. What will be your final opinion of market value, and why?

Check your answer against the one in the Answer Key at the back of the book.

■ RECONCILIATION IS NOT . . .

The reconciliation process can be summarized best by a discussion of what it is *not*. Value reconciliation is not the correction of errors in thinking and technique. Any corrections to be made are actually part of the review process that precedes the final opinion of value. The appraiser reconsiders the reasons for the various choices that were made throughout the appraisal framework as they affect the values reached by the three approaches.

There is no formula for reconciling the various indicated values. Rather, careful analysis and judgment, for which no mathematical or mechanical formula can be substituted, are required.

Reconciliation is also not a matter of merely averaging the three value estimates. A simple arithmetic average implies that the data and logic applied in each of the three approaches are equally reliable and should therefore be given equal weight. Certain approaches obviously are more valid and reliable with some kinds of properties than with others. But even if each value estimate were multiplied by a different factor, the appraiser would still be substituting mechanical formulas for judgment and analysis.

Finally, value reconciliation is not a narrowing of the range of value estimates. The value estimates developed from each approach are never changed—unless an error is found. Reconciliation is the final statement of reasoning and weighing of the relative importance of the facts, results, and conclusions of each of the approaches that culminates in a fully justified final opinion of market value.

TYPES OF APPRAISALS

W E B @ L I N K
www.appraisalfoundation.org

While this book is not intended to instruct students in the Uniform Standards of Professional Appraisal Practice (USPAP), it is useful to consult USPAP for general descriptions of the types of appraisals and appraisal reports currently in use. These descriptions are subject to change with future revisions of USPAP. The latest edition of USPAP can be found at *www.appraisalfoundation.org*.

At present, USPAP recognizes two types of appraisals: *limited* and *complete*. A limited appraisal is defined as "the act or process of developing an opinion of value or an opinion of value developed under and resulting from invoking the Departure Rule" (USPAP Section 1). The Departure Rule of USPAP Section 1 "permits exceptions from sections of the Uniform Standards that are classified as specific requirements rather than binding requirements."

The Departure Rule further provides that

> An appraiser may enter into an agreement to perform an assignment in which the scope of work is less than, or different from, the work that would otherwise be required by the specific requirements, provided that prior to entering into such an agreement:
>
> 1. the appraiser has determined that the appraisal process to be performed is not so limited that the results of the assignment are no longer credible;
>
> 2. the appraiser has advised the client that the assignment calls for something less than, or different from, the work required by the specific requirements and that the report will clearly identify and explain the departure(s); and
>
> 3. the client has agreed that the performance of a limited appraisal service would be appropriate, given the intended use.

A complete appraisal, on the other hand, is defined as "the act or process of developing an opinion of value or an opinion of value developed without invoking the Departure Rule" (USPAP Section 1).

TYPES OF APPRAISAL REPORTS

At present, USPAP permits three types of appraisal reports:

1. *Self-contained report.* A thorough presentation of the data, analyses, and reasoning that led to the appraiser's opinion of value.

2. *Summary report.* Although not as complete as a self-contained report, the summary report must contain sufficient information to lead the client to the appraiser's conclusion.

3. *Restricted use report.* Made for a specific client and for a stated limited purpose, the restricted use report contains virtually none of the information the appraiser used to arrive at the value conclusion.

As you can see, the key difference among the reports is the content and level of information presented. But, regardless of type, USPAP requires that each appraisal report must

- clearly and accurately set forth the appraisal in a manner that will not be misleading;

- contain sufficient information to enable the intended users of the appraisal to understand the report properly; and

- clearly and accurately disclose any extraordinary assumption, hypothetical condition, or limiting condition that directly affects the appraisal and indicate its impact on value.

It should be clear from the above that there is no substitute for a thorough understanding of USPAP requirements.

■ STYLES OF WRITTEN APPRAISAL REPORTS

Form Style Report

A *form style report* makes use of a standardized form or format to provide in a few pages a synopsis of the data supporting the conclusion of value. The type of property as well as the definition of value sought will determine the exact form used. The report is usually accompanied by location and plat maps, plot and floor plans, and photographs of the subject property and comparables.

A form report may be classified as either a summary or restricted use report, depending on the level of detail presented.

Form appraisal reports are used by agencies such as the Federal Housing Administration, Fannie Mae, banks, and insurance companies for routine property appraisals. A form is usually designed for a particular type of property being appraised for a particular purpose. The most common form report in use today for residential appraisals is the URAR. A sample appraisal showing the first two pages of the URAR form begins on page 277. Fannie Mae has also developed a form to be used in conjunction with its computerized underwriting program. This form is discussed on page 276 and is shown on page 279.

The ease of recording information makes the form report an efficient, time-saving method of presenting appraisal data. But the final opinion of value does not gain accuracy simply because it is supported by a report. The data on which the opinion is based and the experience and judgment of the appraiser are the important elements that give the appraisal validity.

Narrative Style Report

The purpose of the *narrative style report* is to give the client not only the facts about the property but also the reasoning that the appraiser used to develop the final opinion of value. The narrative style is usually classified as a self-contained report. The remainder of this chapter examines the requirements of the narrative style appraisal report.

A narrative style appraisal report ordinarily contains most or all of the sections described below.

Introduction

Title Page

An identifying label, or title page, gives the name of the appraiser and the client, the date of appraisal, and the type of property and its address.

Letter of Transmittal

Page 1 of a narrative appraisal report is the letter of transmittal, which formally presents the report to the person for whom the appraisal was made. The letter should be addressed to the client and should contain the following information: street address and a complete and accurate legal description of the subject property, property rights to be appraised, type of value sought (most often, market value), appraiser's opinion of value, effective date of the appraisal, and the appraiser's signature. Any state appraiser license or certification held should be indicated, as should any professional designations.

Table of Contents

A complete listing of the separate parts of the appraisal and all appendixes will be of great help to both the client and the appraiser and will provide an overview of the entire appraisal process.

Summary of Important Facts and Conclusions

The summary page highlights the important facts and conclusions of the report. This section should include the estimate of land value and highest and best use, the reproduction or replacement cost estimate per square foot or cubic foot, the age of the improvement(s) and its depreciated value(s), the gross rental value on a stated occupancy basis, the net income expectancy, the estimate of the value by each of the three approaches, and the final opinion of value.

Suppositions of the Appraisal

Type of Appraisal and Report Format

The report should include the type of appraisal (limited or complete) and the report format (self-contained, summary, or restricted).

Purpose of the Appraisal

The purpose of an appraisal is a statement of the appraiser's objective, which is usually to estimate market value as of a specified date. Although market value has been the main subject of this book, the content and result of the appraisal can vary greatly with its purpose. For example, in appraisals for inheritance tax, condemnation, or the sale of property, the sales comparison approach is important. For certain mortgage loan purposes, the income-producing capacity of the property would be stressed. For insurance purposes, reproduction or replacement cost data and construction features and materials would be most significant.

Definition of Value

Because the word *value* can have many interpretations, the type of value sought should always be defined in the report so the client fully understands the basis for the reported value.

Date of Value Estimate

The report must indicate the date as of which the value conclusion is applicable.

Property Rights

In most cases, the property rights to be appraised will be a fee simple interest. The appraiser, however, may be asked to estimate the value of fractional interests, or to estimate the effect on value of a change in zoning or a deed restriction, and so on. Whatever property rights are involved, they must be given in exact detail.

Statement of Assumptions and Limiting Conditions

Some general assumptions and limiting conditions typically found in an appraisal report include the following:

- It is assumed that the legal description of the property as stated in the appraisal is correct.

- The named owner of the property is assumed to be its true owner.

- Unless otherwise stated, there is no legal impediment to the marketability of the property (no "cloud on the title").

- The land has been valued at its highest and best use and the improvements at their contributory value.

- Unless otherwise stated, it is assumed that there are no hidden or unapparent property defects or adverse environmental conditions that would affect the opinion of value. No responsibility is assumed for such conditions or for any engineering or testing that might be required to discover them.

- Although information, estimates, and opinions taken from a variety of sources are considered reliable, no responsibility is taken for the accuracy of such information. *Such a statement does not relieve the appraiser of the responsibility to independently verify certain data, as discussed in this book, and to follow generally accepted appraisal methods and techniques.*

- Unless otherwise agreed, the appraiser will not be required to testify in court concerning the appraisal.

- Disclosure of the contents of the appraisal report is governed by USPAP.

Presentation of Data

National, Regional, and City Data

In a typical appraisal, most of the general data about the nation, region, and city are gathered initially from office files or previous appraisal reports. Such information should be included in the appraisal report only if it is useful in measuring the future marketability of the property—its economic life, the stability of its location, area trends, and so on. For this reason, national and regional data are generally not included in the appraisal report. Any relevant maps should be included in an appendix to help describe the region or city. When necessary, the body of the report should contain cross-references to such exhibits.

Neighborhood Data

Neighborhood data provide important background information that may influence value. Cross-references to photographs and maps can be helpful here, too. Factors such as distance to schools, public transportation, and shopping and business areas may affect property values. Such information is especially useful if the report is to be submitted to someone unfamiliar with the area. If any form of external obsolescence exists, it should be described in some detail, because it must be measured later in the appraisal report.

Financing

The report should include a brief statement about financing available in the area.

Site Data

A factual presentation of site data is needed, with cross-references to the plat map, also included in an appendix. A description of the site, including its shape, area, contour, soil, and subsoil, must be given. Census tract identification should be included when available to the appraiser.

Utilities

The important site utilities, their capacities, and how adequately they serve the present or proposed highest and best use(s) should be inventoried.

Zoning

A statement about current zoning regulations is not enough. The report should indicate whether zoning regulations are strictly enforced or a change could be easily effected. Information about the uses permitted and to what extent they conform under the present zoning also should be included. This would have an important bearing on both highest and best use and value.

Amenities

This section should contain community features, such as schools, places of worship, shopping facilities, and public services.

Description of Improvements

Among the items this section should contain are construction details and finishing, including quality, floor plan, dimensions, design and layout, age and condition, list of equipment or fixtures, and needed repairs or deferred maintenance. If physical deterioration or functional obsolescence exists, it should be described in some detail, because it will have to be valued later.

Taxes

Current assessed value, tax rate, taxes, and the likelihood of tax changes and their effects should be included.

Sales History

The price and terms of any sale of the subject property within the past three years should be included, as well as the sale of any of the comparable properties within one year before the sale date noted in the appraisal.

Data Analyses and Conclusions

Highest and Best Use Analysis

Most appraisals are based on the highest and best use to which the subject property can be put. Overimprovements or underimprovements are a part of the highest and best use concept, as is use of the site, whether proper or improper. It is not enough simply to say that the existing improvements reflect the highest and best use of the site. Some explanation or justification must be given. Remember, this is a highest and best use *analysis*—not simply an unsupported statement.

Next, each approach to value is developed separately and in enough detail for the reader to understand the basis for the appraiser's final conclusion of value.

The Cost Approach

The basic unit cost used to arrive at reproduction or replacement cost must be explained. Two buildings are seldom if ever identical, so a square-foot cost or a cubic-foot cost taken from known cost data is almost always subject to some adjustment. The measurement of depreciation resulting from physical wear and tear, layout and design, and neighborhood defects must also be explained.

The Sales Comparison Approach

In the sales comparison approach, the selling prices of properties considered comparable are used to arrive at the value of the appraised property. These comparable properties must be described in detail to illustrate the points of comparison and convince the reader that the appraiser's choices are valid comparables.

Usually it is possible to list the comparable properties on one page, bringing out both similarities and differences. A second page might show the adjustments the appraiser has developed, with a third page explaining the adjustments. Sometimes an adjustment grid showing the required adjustments is followed by a description of each comparable sale and an explanation of the adjustments made. Very large adjustments suggest that the properties are not sufficiently comparable.

The Income Capitalization Approach

In the income capitalization approach, the value of the property is based on the income it produces. Rent and expense schedules of comparable properties should be included in this section to support the appraiser's net income estimate. When available, the income history of the subject property should be listed, along with some explanation of vacancy expectations and anticipated changes in expense items.

Reconciliation and Final Conclusion of Value

Reconciliation of the value estimates derived under the sales comparison, cost, and income capitalization approaches to value is presented. The reasons for emphasizing one estimate over another should be explained clearly.

Certification of Value

The appraiser's certification is a guarantee that the appraiser or the appraiser's agent has personally inspected the property, has no present or contemplated interest in the property, and that the statements contained in the report are correct to the best of his or her knowledge.

Qualifications of Appraiser

The reader of the report will be interested in knowing the qualifications of the appraiser because experience and sound judgment are essential in the appraisal process. For this reason, a description of the appraiser's education, professional background, and appraisal experience is needed. If the appraiser is state-licensed or state-certified, this should be noted as well. It serves no purpose to include civic and social offices held or other extraneous information.

Supporting Material

Addenda

The addenda usually include tables of supporting data, maps, photographs, plat and floor plans, and résumés of leases, deeds, contracts, or other items that influenced the appraiser in reaching the final conclusion of value.

Exhibits must be neat, uncluttered, and professionally executed. An area or neighborhood plan, if included, should clearly indicate the important aspects of the area or neighborhood. When plot plans and floor plans are included in the addenda, such plans should be drawn to scale and, as in the case of other exhibits, should have a professional appearance.

EXERCISE 13.3

A suburban strip shopping center, built four years ago, is being appraised. The property is fully rented to a major supermarket chain, a variety of retail businesses, a pizzeria, and a nationally franchised ice cream parlor. The area is growing, and such businesses have flourished. As a result, there is high demand for property such as the subject, and vacant land prices in the area have increased dramatically over the past four years. Which appraisal approach(es) will probably be most important in finding the market value of the subject property, and why?

Check your answer against the one in the Answer Key at the back of the book.

■ SAMPLE APPRAISAL REPORT

A sample URAR-based appraisal report is provided in Figure 13.1. Only the sales comparison approach was used in this appraisal, so only the first two pages of the URAR form are shown.

Form 2075

Because of advanced technology and the demands of the marketplace, Fannie Mae is developing new reporting options for lenders. One such option is the *Desktop Underwriter Property Inspection Report* (Form 2075), to be used in conjunction with Fannie Mae's Desktop Underwriter computer program.

Form 2075 (Figure 13.2) is not an appraisal report. It is used in conjunction with the automated valuation model (AVM) provided by the Desktop Underwriter software.

Form 2075 allows a drive-by inspection option based on a risk assessment of the loan. The appraiser's description of the physical characteristics of the subject property is based on the drive-by inspection and what he or she believes to be reliable data sources. Such sources may include prior inspections, appraisal files, MLS data, assessment and tax records, information provided by the property owner, or other sources of information available to the appraiser.

If the property inspection reveals adverse physical deficiencies or conditions, Fannie Mae requires the lender to provide a complete interior and exterior appraisal.

Form 2075 consists of five basic sections:

1. Subject
2. Neighborhood
3. Site
4. Improvements
5. Certification and limiting conditions

FIGURE 13.1
Sample Appraisal Report

Uniform Residential Appraisal Report   File

The purpose of this summary appraisal report is to provide the lender/client with an accurate, and adequately supported, opinion of the market value of the subject property.

SUBJECT

Property Address 1101 Pleasant Drive		City Oaktown	State IL	Zip Code 60000

Borrower Arun and Richa Patel   Owner of Public Record Jay Connelly   County Crossview

Legal Description   Lot 178, Highland Park Subdivision Phase IV

Assessor's Parcel # 33-234-888-110	Tax Year N/A	R.E. Taxes $ N/A

Neighborhood Name Highland Park   Map Reference MSA 9999   Census Tract 8888

Occupant ☐ Owner ☐ Tenant ☒ Vacant   Special Assessments $ none   ☐ PUD   HOA $ ☐ per year ☐ per month

Property Rights Appraised ☒ Fee Simple ☐ Leasehold ☐ Other (describe)

Assignment Type ☒ Purchase Transaction ☐ Refinance Transaction ☐ Other (describe)

Lender/Client Oaktown National Bank   Address 324 Oaktown Boulevard, Oaktown, IL 60000

Is the subject property currently offered for sale or has it been offered for sale in the twelve months prior to the effective date of this appraisal? ☒ Yes ☐ No

Report data source(s) used, offering price(s), and date(s). Listing agent indicates property listed for sale on September 24, 20XX, at $279,900

CONTRACT

I ☒ did ☐ did not analyze the contract for sale for the subject purchase transaction. Explain the results of the analysis of the contract for sale or why the analysis was not performed.   Sales contract indicates no extraordinary financing or other terms of sale; sale is subject to completion of all stipulated construction and closing by November 30, 20XX.

Contract Price $ 279,000 Date of Contract 11-07-XX Is the property seller the owner of public record? ☒ Yes ☐ No Data Source(s)

Is there any financial assistance (loan charges, sale concessions, gift or downpayment assistance, etc.) to be paid by any party on behalf of the borrower? ☐ Yes ☒ No
If Yes, report the total dollar amount and describe the items to be paid.

NEIGHBORHOOD

Note: Race and the racial composition of the neighborhood are not appraisal factors.

Neighborhood Characteristics			One-Unit Housing Trends			One-Unit Housing		Present Land Use %	
Location ☐ Urban ☒ Suburban ☐ Rural			Property Values ☒ Increasing ☐ Stable ☐ Declining			PRICE	AGE	One-Unit	100 %
Built-Up ☒ Over 75% ☐ 25–75% ☐ Under 25%			Demand/Supply ☐ Shortage ☒ In Balance ☐ Over Supply			$ (000)	(yrs)	2-4 Unit	%
Growth ☐ Rapid ☒ Stable ☐ Slow			Marketing Time ☒ Under 3 mths ☐ 3–6 mths ☐ Over 6 mths			Low		Multi-Family	%
Neighborhood Boundaries Subject neighborhood is bordered on north by Highland Ave.,						High		Commercial	%
on east by 16th St., on south by County Rd., and on west by 20th St.						Pred.		Other	%

Neighborhood Description Subject neighborhood is 95% developed with single-family detached residences, all built within the last 10 years. Final phase of development is now underway. Amenities include concrete sidewalks and curbs and proximity one mile or less to schools, parks, and shopping.

Market Conditions (including support for the above conclusions) Business growth in Oaktown and surrounding area has resulted in steady housing demand for last 10 years. Scarcity of new homes within the city limits makes Highland Park one of the most desirable neighborhoods for both new residents and move-up buyers.

SITE

Dimensions 80' × 130' × 89' × 130'   Area 10,470 square fet   Shape Rectangular   View Residential

Specific Zoning Classification R-2   Zoning Description Residential, Single-Family

Zoning Compliance ☒ Legal ☐ Legal Nonconforming (Grandfathered Use) ☐ No Zoning ☐ Illegal (describe)

Is the highest and best use of the subject property as improved (or as proposed per plans and specifications) the present use? ☒ Yes ☐ No If No, describe

Utilities	-Public	Other (describe)		Public	Other (describe)	Off-site Improvements—Type	Public	Private
Electricity	☒	☐	Water	☒	☐	Street Blacktop	☐	☐
Gas	☒	☐	Sanitary Sewer	☒	☐	Alley	☐	☐

FEMA Special Flood Hazard Area ☒ Yes ☐ No FEMA Flood Zone   FEMA Map #   FEMA Map Date

Are the utilities and off-site improvements typical for the market area? ☒ Yes ☐ No If No, describe

Are there any adverse site conditions or external factors (easements, encroachments, environmental conditions, land uses, etc.)? ☐ Yes ☒ No If Yes, describe

IMPROVEMENTS

General Description	Foundation	Exterior Description materials/condition	Interior materials/condition
Units ☒ One ☐ One with Accessory Unit	☐ Concrete Slab ☐ Crawl Space	Foundation Walls Concrete	Floors Ceram/Wd/Good
# of Stories 2	☒ Full Basement ☐ Partial Basement	Exterior Walls Brick/Vinyl Siding	Walls Drywall/Good
Type ☐ Det. ☐ Att. ☐ S-Det/End Unit	Basement Area 1,100 sq. ft.	Roof Surface Asphalt shingle	Trim/Finish Wood/Good
☐ Existing ☐ Proposed ☒ Under Const.	Basement Finish %	Gutters & Downspouts Aluminum/Good	Bath Floor Ceram/Good
Design (Style) 2-sty/Br/Vin	☐ Outside Entry/Exit ☐ Sump Pump	Window Type Double-hung/Good	Bath Wainscot
Year Built Under const.	Evidence of ☐ Infestation	Storm Sash/Insulated Aluminum/Good	Car Storage ☐ None
Effective Age (Yrs) New const.	☐ Dampness ☐ Settlement	Screens Aluminum/Good	☐ Driveway # of Cars
Attic ☒ None	Heating ☒ FWA ☐ HWBB ☐ Radiant	Amenities ☐ Woodstove(s) #	Driveway Surface
☐ Drop Stair ☐ Stairs	☐ Other Fuel	☒ Fireplace(s) # ☐ Fence	☒ Garage # of Cars 2
☐ Floor ☐ Scuttle	Cooling ☐ Central Air Conditioning	☐ Patio/Deck ☐ Porch	☐ Carport # of Cars
☐ Finished ☐ Heated	☐ Individual ☐ Other	☐ Pool ☐ Other	☒ Att. ☐ Det. ☐ Built-in

Appliances ☒ Refrigerator ☒ Range/Oven ☒ Dishwasher ☒ Disposal ☒ Microwave ☐ Washer/Dryer ☐ Other (describe)

Finished area **above** grade contains: 7 Rooms   3 Bedrooms   2.50 Bath(s)   2,200 Square Feet of Gross Living Area Above Grade

Additional features (special energy efficient items, etc.)

Describe the condition of the property (including needed repairs, deterioration, renovations, remodeling, etc.).

Are there any physical deficiencies or adverse conditions that affect the livability, soundness, or structural integrity of the property? ☐ Yes ☐ No If Yes, describe

Does the property generally conform to the neighborhood (functional utility, style, condition, use, construction, etc.)? ☒ Yes ☐ No If No, describe

FIGURE 13.1
Sample Appraisal Report (continued)

Uniform Residential Appraisal Report
File #

There are ___ comparable properties currently offered for sale in the subject neighborhood ranging in price from $ ___ to $ ___				
There are ___ comparable sales in the subject neighborhood within the past twelve months ranging in sale price from $ ___ to $ ___				

FEATURE	SUBJECT	COMPARABLE SALE # 1	COMPARABLE SALE # 2	COMPARABLE SALE # 3
Address	1101 Pleasant Drive Oaktown	1262 Summer Terrace Oaktown	1217 Lexington Lane Oaktown	1172 Charles Street Oaktown
Proximity to Subject		.21 miles	.14 miles	.18 miles
Sale Price	$ 279,000	$ 282,500	$ 294,200	$ 272,300
Sale Price/Gross Liv. Area	$ 126.82 sq. ft.	$ 128.41 sq. ft.	$ 127.91 sq. ft.	$ 137.53 sq. ft.
Data Source(s)		Oaktown Realty	Oaktown Realty	Oaktown Realty
Verification Source(s)		Crossview County Assessor	Crossview County Assessor	Crossview County Assessor

VALUE ADJUSTMENTS	DESCRIPTION	DESCRIPTION	+(-) $ Adjustment	DESCRIPTION	+(-) $ Adjustment	DESCRIPTION	+(-) $ Adjustment
Sale or Financing Concessions		Conv Mortg No concess		Conv Mortg No concess		Conv Mortg No concess	
Date of Sale/Time		July 17, 20XX		Oct 25, 20XX		April 13, 20XX	
Location	Surbuban	Surbuban		Surbuban		Surbuban	
Leasehold/Fee Simple	Fee Simple	Fee Simple		Fee Simple		Fee Simple	
Site	80' × 130'	90' × 124'		80' × 130'		80' × 130'	
View	Residential	Residential		Residential		Residential	
Design (Style)	2-sty/Br/Vin	2-sty/Br/Vin		2-sty/Br/Vin		2-sty/Br/Vin	
Quality of Construction	Good	Good		Good		Good	
Actual Age	New const.	New const.		New const.		New const.	
Condition	Good	Good		Good		Good	
Above Grade	Total 7 Bdrms. 3 Baths 2.5	Total 7 Bdrms. 3 Baths 3	-2,500	Total 7 Bdrms. 3 Baths 2.5		Total 7 Bdrms. 3 Baths 2	+2,500
Room Count						1,980 sq. ft.	+10,000
Gross Living Area	2,200 sq. ft.	2,200 sq. ft.		2,300 sq. ft.	-3,500	990 sq. ft./	-8,000
Basement & Finished Rooms Below Grade	1,100 sq. ft./ unfinished	1,100 sq. ft./ unfinished		1,150 sq. ft./ 1,000 sf fin		1,100 sq. ft./ unfinished	
Functional Utility	Adequate	Adequate		Adequate		Adequate	
Heating/Cooling	FWA/CAC	FWA/CAC		FWA/CAC		FWA/CAC	
Energy Efficient Items							
Garage/Carport	2.0 Attached	2.0 Attached		3.0 Attached	-5,000	2.0 Attached	
Porch/Patio/Deck	Wood deck	Wood deck		Wood deck		Wood deck	
Fireplace	1/marble	1/masonry		1/marble		1/masonry	
Net Adjustment (Total)		☐ + ☒ -	$ -2,500	☐ + ☒ -	$ -16,500	☒ + ☐ -	$ 12,500
Adjusted Sale Price of Comparables		Net Adj. -0.90% Gross Adj. 0.90%	$ 280,000	Net Adj. -5.60% Gross Adj. 5.60%	$ 277,700	Net Adj. -4.60 % Gross Adj. 4.60 %	$ 284,800

I ☐ did ☐ did not research the sale or transfer history of the subject property and comparable sales. If not, explain ___ Subject property is new construction and an offer is pending. Comparable properties were sold as new construction within last year and there have been no resales since the dates of sale.

My research ☐ did ☒ did not reveal any prior sales or transfers of the subject property for the three years prior to the effective date of this appraisal.

Data source(s) ___

My research ☐ did ☒ did not reveal any prior sales or transfers of the comparable sales for the year prior to the date of sale of the comparable sale.

Data source(s) ___

Report the results of the research and analysis of the prior sale or transfer history of the subject property and comparable sales (report additional prior sales on page 3).

ITEM	SUBJECT	COMPARABLE SALE # 1	COMPARABLE SALE # 2	COMPARABLE SALE # 3
Date of Prior Sale/Transfer				
Price of Prior Sale/Transfer				
Data Source(s)				
Effective Date of Data Source(s)				

Analysis of prior sale or transfer history of the subject property and comparable sales ___

Summary of Sales Comparison Approach ___ Three similar two-story homes sold new within the last year and very close to the subject property in the same subdivision were used for comparables. The sales price of the subject falls within the value range of the comparables. The subject property was still under construction as of the date of this appraisal, and this appraisal is subject to the completion of all planned or proposed construction, as per the sales contract. The subject property is approximately 98% completed as of the date of inspection by the appraiser and is to be completed and the sale closed by November 30, 20XX.

Indicated Value by Sales Comparison Approach $ 279,000

Indicated Value by: Sales Comparison Approach $ 279,000 Cost Approach (if developed) $ ___ Income Approach (if developed) $ ___

This appraisal is made ☐ "as is", ☒ subject to completion per plans and specifications on the basis of a hypothetical condition that the improvements have been completed, ☐ subject to the following repairs or alterations on the basis of a hypothetical condition that the repairs or alterations have been completed, or ☐ subject to the following required inspection based on the extraordinary assumption that the condition or deficiency does not require alteration or repair: ___

Based on a complete visual inspection of the interior and exterior areas of the subject property, defined scope of work, statement of assumptions and limiting conditions, and appraiser's certification, my (our) opinion of the market value, as defined, of the real property that is the subject of this report is $ 279,000 , as of 11-15-20XX , which is the date of inspection and the effective date of this appraisal.

FIGURE 13.2
Form 2075

A FannieMae

Desktop Underwriter Property Inspection Report　　File No. _____

THIS PROPERTY INSPECTION REPORT IS INTENDED FOR USE BY THE LENDER/CLIENT FOR A MORTGAGE FINANCE TRANSACTION ONLY.

Property Address		City		State	Zip Code
Legal Description				County	

Assessor's Parcel No. _____　　Tax Year _____　R.E. Taxes $ _____　Special Assessments $ _____

Borrower _____　Current Owner _____　Occupant ☐ Owner ☐ Tenant ☐ Vacant

Neighborhood or Project Name _____　Project Type ☐ PUD ☐ Condominium　HOA$ ____ /Mo.

Property rights ☐ Fee Simple ☐ Leasehold　Map Reference _____　Census Tract _____

Location	☐ Urban	☐ Suburban	☐ Rural	Property values	☐ Increasing	☐ Stable	☐ Declining
Built up	☐ Over 75%	☐ 25-75%	☐ Under 25%	Demand/supply	☐ Shortage	☐ In balance	☐ Over supply
Growth rate	☐ Rapid	☐ Stable	☐ Slow	Marketing time	☐ Under 3 mos.	☐ 3-6 mos.	☐ Over 6 mos.

Single family housing		Condominium housing	
PRICE $ (000)	AGE (yrs)	PRICE (if applic.) $ (000)	AGE (yrs)
Low		Low	
High		High	
Predominant		Predominant	

Neighborhood boundaries _____

Does the site generally conform to the neighborhood in terms of size and shape? ☐ Yes ☐ No If No, describe: _____

Does the property conform to zoning regulations? ☐ Yes ☐ No If No, describe: _____

Does the present use represent the highest and best use of the property as improved? ☐ Yes ☐ No If No, describe: _____

Utilities	Public	Other		Public	Other	Off-site Improvements	Type	Public	Private
Electricity	☐		Water	☐		Street		☐	☐
Gas	☐		Sanitary sewer	☐		Alley		☐	☐

Do the utilities and off-site improvements conform to the neighborhood? ☐ Yes ☐ No If No, describe: _____

Are there any apparent adverse site conditions (easements, encroachments, special assessments, slide areas, etc.)? ☐ Yes ☐ No If Yes, describe: _____

Source(s) used for physical characteristics of property: ☐ Exterior inspection from street ☐ Previous appraisal files ☐ Assessment and tax records
☐ MLS ☐ Prior inspection ☐ Property owner ☐ Other (Describe):

No. of Stories _____　Type (Det./Att.) _____　Exterior Walls _____　Actual Age (Yrs.) _____　Manufactured Housing ☐ Yes ☐ No

Does the property generally conform to the neighborhood in terms of style, condition, and construction materials? ☐ Yes ☐ No If No, describe: _____

Are there any apparent physical deficiencies or conditions that would affect the soundness or structural integrity of the improvements or the livability of the property?
☐ Yes ☐ No If Yes, describe: _____

Are there any apparent adverse environmental conditions (hazardous wastes, toxic substances, etc.) present in the improvements, on the site, or in the immediate vicinity of the subject property? ☐ Yes ☐ No If Yes, describe: _____

APPRAISER'S CERTIFICATION: The appraiser certifies and agrees that:
1. I personally inspected from the street the subject property and neighborhood.
2. I stated in this report only my own personal unbiased, and professional analysis, opinions, and conclusions, which are subject only to the contingent and limiting conditions specified in this form.
3. I have not knowingly withheld any significant information and I believe, to the best of my knowledge, that all statements are true and correct.
4. I have no present or prospective interest in the property that is the subject of this report, and I have no present or prospective personal interest or bias with respect to the participants in the transaction.
5. I have no present or contemplated future interest in the subject property, and neither my current or future employment nor my compensation for performing this inspection is contingent on the outcome of the inspection.

SUPERVISORY APPRAISER'S CERTIFICATION: If a supervisory appraiser signed this report, he or she certifies and agrees that; I directly supervise the appraiser who prepared this report, agree with the statements and conclusions of the appraiser, agree to be bound by the appraiser's certifications numbered 4 and 5 above, and am taking full responsibility for this report.

CONTINGENT AND LIMITING CONDITIONS: The above certification is subject to the following conditions: The appraiser has noted in this report any adverse conditions (such as, but not limited to, needed repairs, the presence of hazardous substances, etc.) observed during the exterior inspection of the subject property and neighborhood. Unless otherwise stated in this report, the appraiser has no knowledge of any hidden or unapparent conditions of the property or adverse environmental conditions that would make the property more or less valuable, and has assumed that there are no such conditions and makes no guarantees or warranties, expressed or implied, regarding the condition of the property. The appraiser will not be responsible for any such conditions that do exist or for any engineering or testing that might be required to discover whether such conditions exist. Because the appraiser is not an expert in the field of environmental hazards, this report must not be considered as an environmental assessment of the property.

APPRAISER:	**SUPERVISORY APPRAISER (ONLY IF REQUIRED):**
Signature: _____	Signature: _____
Name: _____	Name: _____
Company Name: _____	Company Name: _____
Company Address: _____	Company Address: _____
Date of Report/Signature: _____	Date of Report/Signature: _____
State Certification #: _____	State Certification #: _____
or State License #: _____	or State License #: _____
State: _____	State: _____
Expiration Date of Certification or License: _____	Expiration Date of Certification or License: _____
	☐ Did ☐ Did not inspect subject property from street

10 CH.　　　　　　　　PAGE 1 OF 1　　　　　　　　Fannie Mae Form 2075　　7-97

If Form 2075 is used, the only exhibits required are a photograph that shows the front scene of the subject property and a street map that shows the location of the subject property and comparables.

If both an exterior and interior inspection of the property are required, the standard exhibits needed to support appraisal report forms such as the URAR must be included.

■ SUMMARY

In reconciling the values reached by the three appraisal approaches, the appraiser considers the value sought, the data collected and their reliability, the strengths and weaknesses of each approach, and the relevancy of each approach to the subject property.

Reconciliation is not an averaging; it is a process of reasoning and judgment by which the appraiser identifies the specific factors that result in the final opinion of value.

The appraiser's final task is to present the conclusion of value determined by reconciling the results of the appraisal approaches to the client.

USPAP recognizes two appraisal development options:

1. *Complete appraisal*—the act or process of developing an opinion of value or an opinion of value developed without invoking the Departure Rule of USPAP.

2. *Limited appraisal*—the act or process of developing an opinion of value or an opinion of value developed under and resulting from invoking the Departure Rule of USPAP.

Three appraisal reporting options are permitted:

1. *Self-contained*—provides detailed descriptions of the data, reasoning, and analyses used to arrive at the value conclusion.

2. *Summary*—presents the highlights of the information.

3. *Restricted use*—provides required information only. The client is the only intended user.

USPAP does not dictate the *style* of the appraisal report. In the form report important facts and conclusions are recorded by checking boxes and/or filling in blanks. The narrative report includes even more details of both the appraiser's research and the reasoning leading to the final conclusion of value.

ACHIEVEMENT EXAMINATION

Read the following information carefully and refer to it as often as necessary to complete the residential appraisal form on pages 286 through 288. Fill in as many items on the form as you can, then compare your own form against the one shown in the Answer Key at the back of the book. Correct any errors you made and add any information you omitted.

Legal Description:

Lot 31 in Block 4 in Hickory Gardens Unit 1, being a subdivision of part of the Southeast ¼ of Section 5, Township 30 North, Range 15, East of the Third Principal Meridian, according to the plat thereof registered in the Office of the Registrar of Titles of Dakota County, Illinois, and commonly known as: 4807 Catalpa Road, Woodview, IL 60000.

Purpose of the Appraisal:

To give an opinion of the fair market value of the subject property, held in fee simple, for possible sale purposes.

Real Estate Taxes:

The subject property is assessed for ad valorem tax purposes at $29,092. The tax rate is $7.828 per $100 of assessed value, which compares favorably with comparable suburban areas.

Neighborhood Data:

The subject property is located in a desirable neighborhood in the Central Eastern section of the Village of Woodview. The 25-year-old neighborhood is 100 percent developed with single-family residences currently ranging in value from $150,000 to $210,000. Most are valued at about $180,000, and virtually all are owner-occupied. There is no homeowners' association.

The subject's neighborhood is bounded on the East by the Village of Willow; on the South by 40th Avenue; to the West by Grand Street; and to the North by Park District land. The surrounding neighborhoods are residential communities of approximately the same age as the subject's neighborhood, with homes ranging in value from $160,000 to $250,000.

The occupants of the subject's area are mostly blue-collar workers, with median incomes ranging from $26,000 to $43,000. Employment opportunities in this area have historically been better than the national average. The neighborhood is within walking distance of public grade schools of good reputation, shopping, and transportation, and also offers several nearby parks and playgrounds. Police and fire protection have been above average. The subject's neighborhood has been well-maintained and there has been a steady demand for housing with a gradual uptrend in values during the past several years. Most houses are sold within two months of being put on the market.

Amenities:

Downtown Metroville is eight miles away, accessible by car, bus, and train; local shopping, six blocks; grade school, two blocks; high school, one mile, but accessible by bus; commuter railroad station, four blocks; expressway, two miles.

There are no detrimental influences.

Site Data:

The site is at 4807 Catalpa Road in Woodview, Dakota County, IL 60000. The site is on the north side of Catalpa between Salem and Third. The lot is a rectangle, 65' x 130' or 8,450 square feet, providing a large rear yard. There is an asphalt driveway but no alley, and there are no common areas. The street paving is also asphalt.

Sanitary and storm sewers are maintained by the city. Drainage is very good, and there is no danger of flooding. A review of the applicable flood-zone map indicates that the subject property is not located in a flood hazard area. Water is city supplied; public utility companies provide electricity and gas. There have been no major fuel supply problems in this area, and none are foreseen. Streetlights are city-maintained. Electric and telephone lines are underground.

Landscaping is typical of the neighborhood, with a sodded lawn, shrubs, and trees. The rear yard has a six-foot redwood fence.

Zoning:

The subject property is zoned "R-2, Single-Family Residence District." The subject conforms to the zoning ordinance.

Highest and Best Use:

The subject property conforms to existing zoning regulations and constitutes the highest and best use of the site.

Easements and Encroachments:

There are no easements or encroachments affecting this property, either of record or as noted by visual inspection.

Description of Improvements:

general description—a single-family residence, ranch style, containing seven rooms, three bedrooms, and two baths; contemporary open floor plan and typical room layout and dimensions

age—25 years (effective age 15 years); remaining economic life, 45 years

condition—exterior, good; interior, good

rooms—living room, dining room, family room, kitchen, three bedrooms, two baths, six closets, and two-car garage

exterior—concrete foundation, 100 percent brick veneer walls, wood-framed, double-hung windows with thermopane glass, galvanized and painted gutters, hip and gable roof with asphalt shingles, and aluminum combination storms and screens

interior (principal rooms)—vinyl tile in kitchen and bathrooms, finished oak flooring covered with wall-to-wall carpeting in other rooms; wall covering of drywall, taped and painted or papered; ceilings of drywall, taped and painted; average trim of painted pine

kitchen—modern, with maple cabinets, formica counters, vinyl flooring with carpet in dinette, double-bowl porcelain sink, hood-type exhaust fan, built-in gas oven and range, garbage disposal (new), dishwasher, and refrigerator; no pantry

bathrooms—two full baths, each with ceramic tile floor and wainscoting, built-in tub with shower, single-bowl vanity lavatory with mirrored medicine cabinet, and a two-piece built-in water closet

construction—plywood subflooring covered with oak or tile, 2" × 10" joists, steel beams and columns; galvanized pipes in good condition

basement—crawlspace

heating—very good, gas-fired, forced warm air furnace with adequate 190,000 BTU output

cooling—very good three-ton central air conditioner with adequate 190,000 BTU output

hot water heater—one-year-old, 40-gallon, gas-fired hot water heater

electrical wiring—100-amp, 220-volt system containing 12 circuit breakers

insulation—six inches above ceilings and behind drywall

garage—two-car detached, 20' × 25' with frame walls, asphalt roof, concrete floor, and wood overhead door

Miscellaneous and Extras:

The foyer of the home has a ceramic tile floor. There is wall-to-wall plush carpeting of good quality in the living room, dining room, hall, stairs, and bedrooms. The dinette and family room have wall-to-wall indoor/outdoor carpeting. The family room has a masonry fireplace. A low attic accessible by drop-stair could be used for storage, but is not floored or heated.

General Condition:

Overall, the house and garage are in good condition, with normal wear and tear. Materials and finish are somewhat better than average, but comparable to other homes in this area.

Current Market Conditions:

The current housing market is strong, reflecting a healthy local economy. Typical financing in the area is through conventional mortgages, with up to 90 percent financed at interest rates ranging from 6 percent to 8 percent, depending on the down payment. Mortgage funds are readily available.

Cost Data:

house	$95 per square foot
extra insulation	$1,200
garage	$30 per square foot
landscaping, driveway, fencing	$5,400
land value by allocation	$45,000
depreciation factors (to date)	
garage	physical 25%
	functional 0
	external 0
house	physical 25%
	functional 0
	external 0
other improvements	physical 25%

Market Data:

Adjustment value of fireplace is $5,000.

Adjustment value of finished basement is $10,000.

The subject has an assumable mortgage.

Information on comparable properties is provided in the Sales Price Adjustment Chart on page 285.

There are two comparable properties currently offered for sale in this neighborhood, priced at $178,900 and $184,500. The county tax assessor's records indicate no prior sale of any of the comparable properties within the year before each of those sales.

Income Data:

House like subject, but without fireplace, rents for $1,500.

House like subject, but without garage, rents for $1,250.

House like subject, but without garage and fireplace, rents for $1,100.

Typical Sales and Rental Statistics:

House (A) sold for $160,000 and rented for $1,200.

House (B) sold for $166,550 and rented for $1,275.

House (C) sold for $173,500 and rented for $1,300.

The square footage of the house may be computed by using the figures indicated in the diagram below.

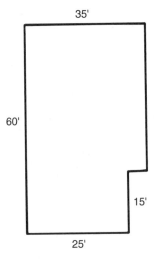

Check your completed appraisal report form against the one in the Answer Key at the back of the book.

Sales Price Adjustment Chart
Comparables

	1160 Central Park	25 Jackson	4310 W. Gladys	3840 W. Monroe	316 Iowa								
SALES PRICE	$152,000	$165,000	$177,750	$180,000	$186,240								
FINANCING	Cash	Conv.	CONV.	Conv.	Conv.								
DATE OF SALE	4 wks. ago	1 yr. ago	6 wks. ago	3 wks. ago	6 wks. ago								
LOCATION	quiet resid.	quiet resid.	quiet resid.	quiet resid.	quiet resid.								
LEASEHOLD/FEE SIMPLE	fee	fee	fee	fee	fee								
VIEW	good	good	good	good	good								
SITE	65' × 130'	65' × 130'	65' × 130'	65' × 130'	65' × 130'								
DESIGN	ranch/good	ranch/good	ranch/good	ranch/good	ranch/good								
CONSTRUCTION	good	good	good	good	good								
AGE	25 yrs.	25 yrs.	25 yrs.	25 yrs.	25 yrs.								
CONDITION	fair	good	good	good	good								
NO. OF RMS./BEDRMS./BATHS	7/3/2	7/3/2	7/3/2	7/3/2½	7/3/2								
SQ. FT. OF LIVING SPACE	1,950	2,300	1,975	1,950	1,940								
OTHER SPACE (BASEMENT)	crawlspace	crawlspace	crawlspace	crawlspace	finished basemnt.								
FUNCTIONAL UTILITY	adequate	adequate	adequate	adequate	adequate								
HEATING/COOLING	central heat/air	central heat/air	central heat/air	central heat/air	central heat/air								
ENERGY EFFICIENT ITEMS	extra insulation	extra insulation	extra insulation	extra insulation	extra insulation								
GARAGE/CARPORT	none	2-car det.	2-car det.	2-car det.	2-car det.								
OTHER EXT. IMPROVEMENTS	fence	fence	fence	fence	fence								
OTHER INT. IMPROVEMENTS	masonry fireplace	masonry fireplace	none	masonry fireplace	masonry fireplace								
TYPICAL HOUSE VALUE													
VARIABLE FEATURE													
ADJUSTMENT VALUE OF VARIABLE													

Uniform Residential Appraisal Report   File

The purpose of this summary appraisal report is to provide the lender/client with an accurate, and adequately supported, opinion of the market value of the subject property.

SUBJECT

Property Address		City	State	Zip Code
Borrower	Owner of Public Record		County	
Legal Description				
Assessor's Parcel #		Tax Year	R.E. Taxes $	
Neighborhood Name		Map Reference	Census Tract	

Occupant ☐ Owner ☐ Tenant ☐ Vacant   Special Assessments $ ☐ PUD   HOA $ ☐ per year ☐ per month
Property Rights Appraised ☐ Fee Simple ☐ Leasehold ☐ Other (describe)
Assignment Type ☐ Purchase Transaction ☐ Refinance Transaction ☐ Other (describe)
Lender/Client   Address
Is the subject property currently offered for sale or has it been offered for sale in the twelve months prior to the effective date of this appraisal? ☐ Yes ☐ No
Report data source(s) used, offering price(s), and date(s).

CONTRACT

I ☐ did ☐ did not analyze the contract for sale for the subject purchase transaction. Explain the results of the analysis of the contract for sale or why the analysis was not performed.

Contract Price $ Date of Contract   Is the property seller the owner of public record? ☐ Yes ☐ No Data Source(s)
Is there any financial assistance (loan charges, sale concessions, gift or downpayment assistance, etc.) to be paid by any party on behalf of the borrower? ☐ Yes ☐ No
If Yes, report the total dollar amount and describe the items to be paid.

NEIGHBORHOOD

Note: Race and the racial composition of the neighborhood are not appraisal factors.

Neighborhood Characteristics			One-Unit Housing Trends			One-Unit Housing		Present Land Use %	
Location ☐ Urban ☐ Suburban ☐ Rural			Property Values ☐ Increasing ☐ Stable ☐ Declining			PRICE $ (000)	AGE (yrs)	One-Unit	%
Built-Up ☐ Over 75% ☐ 25–75% ☐ Under 25%			Demand/Supply ☐ Shortage ☐ In Balance ☐ Over Supply					2-4 Unit	%
Growth ☐ Rapid ☐ Stable ☐ Slow			Marketing Time ☐ Under 3 mths ☐ 3–6 mths ☐ Over 6 mths			Low		Multi-Family	%
Neighborhood Boundaries						High		Commercial	%
						Pred.		Other	%

Neighborhood Description

Market Conditions (including support for the above conclusions)

SITE

Dimensions	Area	Shape	View

Specific Zoning Classification   Zoning Description
Zoning Compliance ☐ Legal ☐ Legal Nonconforming (Grandfathered Use) ☐ No Zoning ☐ Illegal (describe)
Is the highest and best use of the subject property as improved (or as proposed per plans and specifications) the present use? ☐ Yes ☐ No If No, describe

Utilities	Public	Other (describe)		Public	Other (describe)	Off-site Improvements—Type	Public	Private
Electricity	☐	☐	Water	☐	☐	Street	☐	☐
Gas	☐	☐	Sanitary Sewer	☐	☐	Alley	☐	☐

FEMA Special Flood Hazard Area ☐ Yes ☐ No FEMA Flood Zone   FEMA Map #   FEMA Map Date
Are the utilities and off-site improvements typical for the market area? ☐ Yes ☐ No If No, describe
Are there any adverse site conditions or external factors (easements, encroachments, environmental conditions, land uses, etc.)? ☐ Yes ☐ No If Yes, describe

IMPROVEMENTS

General Description		Foundation		Exterior Description materials/condition		Interior materials/condition	
Units ☐ One ☐ One with Accessory Unit		☐ Concrete Slab ☐ Crawl Space		Foundation Walls		Floors	
# of Stories		☐ Full Basement ☐ Partial Basement		Exterior Walls		Walls	
Type ☐ Det. ☐ Att. ☐ S-Det./End Unit		Basement Area sq. ft.		Roof Surface		Trim/Finish	
☐ Existing ☐ Proposed ☐ Under Const.		Basement Finish %		Gutters & Downspouts		Bath Floor	
Design (Style)		☐ Outside Entry/Exit ☐ Sump Pump		Window Type		Bath Wainscot	
Year Built		Evidence of ☐ Infestation		Storm Sash/Insulated		Car Storage ☐ None	
Effective Age (Yrs)		☐ Dampness ☐ Settlement		Screens		☐ Driveway # of Cars	
Attic ☐ None		Heating ☐ FWA ☐ HWBB ☐ Radiant		Amenities ☐ Woodstove(s) #		Driveway Surface	
☐ Drop Stair ☐ Stairs		☐ Other Fuel		☐ Fireplace(s) # ☐ Fence		☐ Garage # of Cars	
☐ Floor ☐ Scuttle		Cooling ☐ Central Air Conditioning		☐ Patio/Deck ☐ Porch		☐ Carport # of Cars	
☐ Finished ☐ Heated		☐ Individual ☐ Other		☐ Pool ☐ Other		☐ Att. ☐ Det. ☐ Built-in	

Appliances ☐ Refrigerator ☐ Range/Oven ☐ Dishwasher ☐ Disposal ☐ Microwave ☐ Washer/Dryer ☐ Other (describe)
Finished area **above** grade contains: Rooms   Bedrooms   Bath(s)   Square Feet of Gross Living Area Above Grade
Additional features (special energy efficient items, etc.)

Describe the condition of the property (including needed repairs, deterioration, renovations, remodeling, etc.).

Are there any physical deficiencies or adverse conditions that affect the livability, soundness, or structural integrity of the property? ☐ Yes ☐ No If Yes, describe

Does the property generally conform to the neighborhood (functional utility, style, condition, use, construction, etc.)? ☐ Yes ☐ No If No, describe

Uniform Residential Appraisal Report   File

| There are | comparable properties currently offered for sale in the subject neighborhood ranging in price from $ | | to $ | |

| There are | comparable sales in the subject neighborhood within the past twelve months ranging in sale price from $ | | to $ | |

FEATURE	SUBJECT	COMPARABLE SALE # 1		COMPARABLE SALE # 2		COMPARABLE SALE # 3	
Address							
Proximity to Subject							
Sale Price	$		$		$		$
Sale Price/Gross Liv. Area	$ sq. ft.	$ sq. ft.		$ sq. ft.		$ sq. ft.	
Data Source(s)							
Verification Source(s)							
VALUE ADJUSTMENTS	DESCRIPTION	DESCRIPTION	+(-) $ Adjustment	DESCRIPTION	+(-) $ Adjustment	DESCRIPTION	+(-) $ Adjustment
Sale or Financing Concessions							
Date of Sale/Time							
Location							
Leasehold/Fee Simple							
Site							
View							
Design (Style)							
Quality of Construction							
Actual Age							
Condition							
Above Grade	Total Bdrms. Baths	Total Bdrms. Baths		Total Bdrms. Baths		Total Bdrms. Baths	
Room Count							
Gross Living Area	sq. ft.	sq. ft.		sq. ft.		sq. ft.	
Basement & Finished Rooms Below Grade							
Functional Utility							
Heating/Cooling							
Energy Efficient Items							
Garage/Carport							
Porch/Patio/Deck							
Net Adjustment (Total)		☐ + ☐ -	$	☐ + ☐ -	$	☐ + ☐ -	$
Adjusted Sale Price of Comparables		Net Adj. % Gross Adj. %	$	Net Adj. % Gross Adj. %	$	Net Adj. % Gross Adj. %	$

☐ I did ☐ did not research the sale or transfer history of the subject property and comparable sales. If not, explain

My research ☐ did ☐ did not reveal any prior sales or transfers of the subject property for the three years prior to the effective date of this appraisal.

Data source(s)

My research ☐ did ☐ did not reveal any prior sales or transfers of the comparable sales for the year prior to the date of sale of the comparable sale.

Data source(s)

Report the results of the research and analysis of the prior sale or transfer history of the subject property and comparable sales (report additional prior sales on page 3).

ITEM	SUBJECT	COMPARABLE SALE # 1	COMPARABLE SALE # 2	COMPARABLE SALE # 3
Date of Prior Sale/Transfer				
Price of Prior Sale/Transfer				
Data Source(s)				
Effective Date of Data Source(s)				

Analysis of prior sale or transfer history of the subject property and comparable sales

Summary of Sales Comparison Approach

Indicated Value by Sales Comparison Approach $

Indicated Value by: Sales Comparison Approach $ Cost Approach (if developed) $ Income Approach (if developed) $

This appraisal is made ☐ "as is", ☐ subject to completion per plans and specifications on the basis of a hypothetical condition that the improvements have been completed, ☐ subject to the following repairs or alterations on the basis of a hypothetical condition that the repairs or alterations have been completed, or ☐ subject to the following required inspection based on the extraordinary assumption that the condition or deficiency does not require alteration or repair:

Based on a complete visual inspection of the interior and exterior areas of the subject property, defined scope of work, statement of assumptions and limiting conditions, and appraiser's certification, my (our) opinion of the market value, as defined, of the real property that is the subject of this report is $, as of   , which is the date of inspection and the effective date of this appraisal.

Uniform Residential Appraisal Report   File

(blank lined area for ADDITIONAL COMMENTS)

ADDITIONAL COMMENTS

COST APPROACH TO VALUE (not required by Fannie Mae)

Provide adequate information for the lender/client to replicate the below cost figures and calculations.

Support for the opinion of site value (summary of comparable land sales or other methods for estimating site value)

COST APPROACH

ESTIMATED ☐ REPRODUCTION OR ☐ REPLACEMENT COST NEW	OPINION OF SITE VALUE .... = $		
Source of cost data	Dwelling	Sq. Ft. @ $	.... =$
Quality rating from cost service Effective date of cost data		Sq. Ft. @ $	.... =$
Comments on Cost Approach (gross living area calculations, depreciation, etc.)			
	Garage/Carport	Sq. Ft. @ $	.... =$
	Total Estimate of Cost-New		.... = $
	Less Physical	Functional	External
	Depreciation		=$( )
	Depreciated Cost of Improvements.................................. =$		
	"As-is" Value of Site Improvements.................................. =$		
Estimated Remaining Economic Life (HUD and VA only) Years	Indicated Value By Cost Approach .... =$		

INCOME APPROACH TO VALUE (not required by Fannie Mae)

INCOME

Estimated Monthly Market Rent $ X Gross Rent Multiplier   = $ Indicated Value by Income Approach

Summary of Income Approach (including support for market rent and GRM)

PROJECT INFORMATION FOR PUDs (if applicable)

PUD INFORMATION

Is the developer/builder in control of the Homeowners' Association (HOA)? ☐ Yes ☐ No   Unit type(s) ☐ Detached ☐ Attached

Provide the following information for PUDs ONLY if the developer/builder is in control of the HOA and the subject property is an attached dwelling unit.

Legal name of project

Total number of phases   Total number of units   Total number of units sold

Total number of units rented   Total number of units for sale   Data source(s)

Was the project created by the conversion of an existing building(s) into a PUD? ☐ Yes ☐ No If Yes, date of conversion

Does the project contain any multi-dwelling units? ☐ Yes ☐ No Data source(s)

Are the units, common elements, and recreation facilities complete? ☐ Yes ☐ No If No, describe the status of completion.

Are the common elements leased to or by the Homeowners' Association? ☐ Yes ☐ No If Yes, describe the rental terms and options.

Describe common elements and recreational facilities

## CHAPTER 14

Appraising Partial Interests

■ OVERVIEW

Although we have already considered a variety of types of real estate, including single-family homes, multiunit apartment buildings, and retail and other commercial properties, there are still other forms of property interests that can be appraised. In this chapter you will learn about some of these property interests, including condominiums and time-shares. You also will learn how the interest of a lessee (tenant) can be valued.

■ TYPES OF PARTIAL INTERESTS

Thus far we have referred to real estate (land and improvements) owned outright—what is termed *fee simple* ownership. You also should be familiar with other forms of property ownership, some of which have come into use in the United States fairly recently. *Partial interests* include any interest that is less than full fee simple ownership of the entire property conveyed.

Condominiums

The *condominium* form of ownership, long popular in Europe, has been used widely in this country only since the early 1960s. The owner of a typical condominium unit owns exclusive right to the airspace that encompasses that unit, as well as an interest in the common areas. Common areas typically include the land, courtyard, walkways, parking spaces, foundation, outside walls, roof, lobby, hallways, elevators, and stairways, as well as recreational facilities such as swimming pools, golf courses, and tennis courts (see Figure 14.1). Unit owners must pay a proportional share of the maintenance and upkeep expenses of the common areas. Many residential apartments, offices, and retail stores now are held in the condominium form of legal ownership.

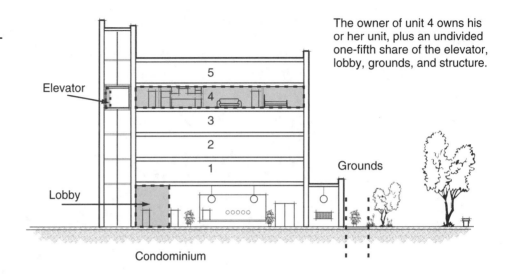

The owner of unit 4 owns his or her unit, plus an undivided one-fifth share of the elevator, lobby, grounds, and structure.

Elevator

5

4

3

2

1

Grounds

Lobby

Condominium

The residential condominium has some of the same benefits and drawbacks as rental apartment living—lack of privacy being a primary consideration. For those who cannot afford or choose not to invest in other types of property, however, the condominium is a way to own property (with all the tax and estate planning advantages that entails) yet avoid onerous yard and building maintenance.

Special appraisal considerations for condominiums include specification of both private and public areas, mention of the exact location of the subject property within the building, and consideration of the upkeep of both public areas and other units. The appraiser should note the condominium association that cares for common areas, the amount of monthly fees or other assessments charged, and any special facilities provided (such as a tennis court or swimming pool).

Appraisers generally use the sales comparison approach to value individual condominium units. In areas of high population density, well-designed and well-maintained residential condominiums have appreciated in value, though typically not as much as detached homes. In other areas a surfeit of building has resulted in more condominiums than the available demand has warranted, and prices have remained relatively flat. When a substantial number of condominium units are owned for rental investment purposes, maintenance may be more difficult, particularly if absentee landlords are slow in paying homeowner assessments.

Comparable condominium properties should be similar in building size, unit size, number of owner-occupied units, extent of common areas, and type of amenities.

Planned Unit Developments

A *planned unit development (PUD)* is a subdivision consisting of individually owned parcels or lots as well as areas owned in common.

A PUD may feature detached residences, condominiums, or town houses (houses on separately owned lots that have adjacent or party walls) and may include both residential and commercial property. Property owners pay fees and assessments to the property owners' association for upkeep of common areas.

Some PUDs comprise hundreds of separately owned lots with detached residences, one or more swimming pools, tennis courts, clubhouse, and other amenities. Of course, the more extensive the common areas, the higher will be the fees and other assessments required for proper maintenance, although spreading costs over many units can help keep expenses manageable.

The best valuation method for a PUD home or condominium unit is the sales comparison approach, ideally using similar properties in the same development.

Fannie Mae Form 1073: Individual Condominium Unit Appraisal Report

Fannie Mae Form 1073 is used to appraise a unit in a condominium project or a condominium unit in a Planned Unit Development (PUD). The revised Form 1073 is mandatory as of November 1, 2005 (Figure 14.2).

The newly revised and expanded Form 1073 now contains sections:

- describing the *scope of work* to be performed (see page four of the form),
- identifying the *intended use* of the appraiser's opinions and conclusions,
- identifying the client and other *intended users,*
- defining *market value,*
- listing the appraiser's *assumptions and limiting condition,* and
- listing the *appraiser's certifications.*

The appraiser is not permitted to make changes to this form, with the following exceptions: Fannie Mae will allow additional certifications to be added on a separate page if such certifications are required by state law, or if they cover such things as the appraiser's continuing education or membership in an appraisal organization. The appraiser may expand the scope of work to include any additional research or analysis necessary, based on the complexity of the appraisal assignment.

Time-Share Projects

The *time-share* is a relatively new and heavily promoted form of vacation property ownership, ranging from campgrounds to city apartments. A time-share purchaser receives the right to exclusive use of a portion of the property for a particular period of time each year (usually in units of one week). A time-share *estate* includes an estate (ownership) interest in the property; a time-share *use* does not.

A time-share also is best valued by the sales comparison approach. Sales prices are set by the developer based on amenities of the unit (size, special features, view) and the time of year involved. At a ski resort, for instance, a week in January is more valuable than a week in May. Holiday periods typically have the highest premium.

For some time-share projects, high initial marketing costs and limited resale potential have resulted in heavily discounted resale prices. The appraiser should examine the local market carefully, especially noting the exact ownership interest involved and the sales price and length of time on the market for resales.

FIGURE 14.2
Form 1073

Individual Condominium Unit Appraisal Report   File

The purpose of this summary appraisal report is to provide the lender/client with an accurate, and adequately supported, opinion of the market value of the subject property.

Property Address	Unit #	City	State	Zip Code

SUBJECT

Property Address _____ Unit # _____ City _____ State _____ Zip Code _____

Borrower _____ Owner of Public Record _____ County _____

Legal Description _____

Assessor's Parcel # _____ Tax Year _____ R.E. Taxes $ _____

Project Name _____ Phase # _____ Map Reference _____ Census Tract _____

Occupant ☐ Owner ☐ Tenant ☐ Vacant   Special Assessments $ _____ HOA $ _____ ☐ per year ☐ per month

Property Rights Appraised ☐ Fee Simple ☐ Leasehold ☐ Other (describe) _____

Assignment Type ☐ Purchase Transaction ☐ Refinance Transaction ☐ Other (describe) _____

Lender/Client _____ Address _____

Is the subject property currently offered for sale or has it been offered for sale in the twelve months prior to the effective date of this appraisal? ☐ Yes ☐ No

Report data source(s) used, offering price(s), and date(s).

CONTRACT

I ☐ did ☐ did not analyze the contract for sale for the subject purchase transaction. Explain the results of the analysis of the contract for sale or why the analysis was not performed.

Contract Price $ _____ Date of Contract _____ Is the property seller the owner of public record? ☐ Yes ☐ No Data Source(s) _____

Is there any financial assistance (loan charges, sale concessions, gift or downpayment assistance, etc.) to be paid by any party on behalf of the borrower? ☐ Yes ☐ No
If Yes, report the total dollar amount and describe the items to be paid.

NEIGHBORHOOD

Note: Race and the racial composition of the neighborhood are not appraisal factors.

Neighborhood Characteristics			Condominium Unit Housing Trends			Condominium Housing		Present Land Use %	
Location ☐ Urban	☐ Suburban	☐ Rural	Property Values ☐ Increasing	☐ Stable	☐ Declining	PRICE	AGE	One-Unit	%
Built-Up ☐ Over 75%	☐ 25–75%	☐ Under 25%	Demand/Supply ☐ Shortage	☐ In Balance	☐ Over Supply	$ (000)	(yrs)	2-4 Unit	%
Growth ☐ Rapid	☐ Stable	☐ Slow	Marketing Time ☐ Under 3 mths	☐ 3–6 mths	☐ Over 6 mths	Low		Multi-Family	%
Neighborhood Boundaries						High		Commercial	%
						Pred.		Other	%

Neighborhood Description _____

Market Conditions (including support for the above conclusions) _____

PROJECT SITE

Topography _____ Size _____ Density _____ View _____

Specific Zoning Classification _____ Zoning Description _____

Zoning Compliance ☐ Legal ☐ Legal Nonconforming – Do the zoning regulations permit rebuilding to current density? ☐ Yes ☐ No
☐ No Zoning ☐ Illegal (describe)

Is the highest and best use of the subject property as improved (or as proposed per plans and specifications) the present use? ☐ Yes ☐ No If No, describe

Utilities	Public	Other (describe)		Public	Other (describe)	Off-site Improvements—Type	Public	Private
Electricity	☐	☐	Water	☐	☐	Street	☐	☐
Gas	☐	☐	Sanitary Sewer	☐	☐	Alley	☐	☐

FEMA Special Flood Hazard Area ☐ Yes ☐ No FEMA Flood Zone _____ FEMA Map # _____ FEMA Map Date _____

Are the utilities and off-site improvements typical for the market area? ☐ Yes ☐ No If No, describe

Are there any adverse site conditions or external factors (easements, encroachments, environmental conditions, land uses, etc.)? ☐ Yes ☐ No If Yes, describe

PROJECT INFORMATION

Data source(s) for project information _____

Project Description ☐ Detached ☐ Row or Townhouse ☐ Garden ☐ Mid-Rise ☐ High-Rise ☐ Other (describe)

General Description	General Description	Subject Phase	If Project Completed	If Project Incomplete
# of Stories	Exterior Walls	# of Units	# of Phases	# of Planned Phases
# of Elevators	Roof Surface	# of Units Completed	# of Units	# o f Planned Units
☐ Existing ☐ Proposed	Total # Parking	# of Units For Sale	# of Units for Sale	# of Units for Sale
☐ Under Construction	Ratio (spaces/units)	# of Units Sold	# of Units Sold	# of Units Sold
Year Built	Type	# of Units Rented	# of Units Rented	# of Units Rented
Effective Age	Guest Parking	# of Owner Occupied Units	# of Owner Occupied Units	# of Owner Occupied Units

Project Primary Occupancy ☐ Principle Residence ☐ Second Home or Recreational ☐ Tenant

Is the developer/builder in control of the Homeowners' Association (HOA)? ☐ Yes ☐ No

Management Group – ☐ Homeowners' Association ☐ Developer ☐ Management Agent – Provide name of management company.

Does any single entity (the same individual, investor group, corporation, etc.) own more than 10% of the total units in the project? ☐ Yes ☐ No If Yes, describe

Was the project created by the conversion of an existing building(s) into a condominium? ☐ Yes ☐ No If Yes, describe the original use and the date of conversion.

Are the units, common elements, and recreation facilities complete (including any planned rehabilitation for a condominium conversion)? ☐ Yes ☐ No If No, describe

Is there any commercial space in the project? ☐ Yes ☐ No If Yes, describe and indicate the overall percentage of the commercial space.

F I G U R E   14.2 (continued)
Form 1073

Individual Condominium Unit Appraisal Report

File #

PROJECT INFORMATION

Describe the condition of the project and quality of construction.

Describe the common elements and recreational facilities.

Are any common elements leased to or by the Homeowners' Association? ☐ Yes ☐ No If Yes, describe the rental terms and options.

Is the project subject to ground rent? ☐ Yes ☐ No If Yes, $ _____ per year (describe terms and conditions)

Are the parking facilities adequate for the project size and type? ☐ Yes ☐ No If No, describe and comment on the effect on value and marketability.

PROJECT ANALYSIS

I ☐ did ☐ did not analyze the condominium project budget for the current year. Explain the results of the analysis of the budget (adequacy of fees, reserves, etc.), or why the analysis was not performed.

Are there any other fees (other than regular HOA charges) for the use of the project facilities? ☐ Yes ☐ No If Yes, report the charges and describe.

Compared to other competitive projects of similar quality and design, the subject unit charge appears ☐ High ☐ Average ☐ Low If High or Low, describe

Are there any special or unusual characteristics of the project (based on the condominium documents, HOA meetings, or other information) known to the appraiser?
☐ Yes ☐ No If Yes, describe and explain the effect on value and marketability.

SUBJECT UNIT DESCRIPTION

Unit Charge $ _____ per month X 12 = $ _____ per year   Annual assessment charge per year per square feet of gross living area = $ _____

Utilities included in the unit monthly assessment ☐ None ☐ Heat ☐ Air Conditioning ☐ Electricity ☐ Gas ☐ Water ☐ Sewer ☐ Cable ☐ Other (describe)

General Description	Interior materials/condition	Amenities	Appliances	Car Storage
Floor #	Floors	☐ Fireplace(s) #	☐ Refrigerator	☐ None
# of Levels	Walls	☐ Woodstove(s) #	☐ Range/Oven	☐ Garage ☐ Covered ☐ Open
Heating Type Fuel	Trim/Finish	☐ Deck/Patio	☐ Disp ☐ Microwave	# of Cars
☐ Central AC ☐ Individual AC	Bath Wainscot	☐ Porch/Balcony	☐ Dishwasher	☐ Assigned ☐ Owned
☐ Other (describe)	Doors	☐ Other	☐ Washer/Dryer	Parking Space #

Finished area **above** grade contains: Rooms   Bedrooms   Bath(s)   Square Feet of Gross Living Area Above Grade

Are the heating and cooling for the individual units separately metered? ☐ Yes ☐ No If No, describe and comment on compatibility to other projects in the market area.

Additional features (special energy efficient items, etc.)

Describe the condition of the property (including needed repairs, deterioration, renovations, remodeling, etc.).

Are there any physical deficiencies or adverse conditions that affect the livability, soundness, or structural integrity of the property? ☐ Yes ☐ No If Yes, describe

Does the property generally conform to the neighborhood (functional utility, style, condition, use, construction, etc.)? ☐ Yes ☐ No If No, describe

PRIOR SALES HISTORY

I ☐ did ☐ did not research the sale or transfer history of the subject property and comparable sales. If not, explain

My research ☐ did ☐ did not reveal any prior sales or transfers of the subject property for the three years prior to the effective date of this appraisal.
Data source(s)

My research ☐ did ☐ did not reveal any prior sales or transfers of the comparable sales for the year prior to the date of sale of the comparable sale.
Data source(s)

Report the results of the research and analysis of the prior sale or transfer history of the subject property and comparable sales (report additional prior sales on page 3).

ITEM	SUBJECT	COMPARABLE SALE # 1	COMPARABLE SALE # 2	COMPARABLE SALE # 3
Date of Prior Sale/Transfer				
Price of Prior Sale/Transfer				
Data Source(s)				
Effective Date of Data Source(s)				

Analysis of prior sale or transfer history of the subject property and comparable sales.

F I G U R E 14.2 (continued)
Form 1073

Individual Condominium Unit Appraisal Report
File #

There are ____ comparable properties currently offered for sale in the subject neighborhood ranging in price from $ ____ to $ ____ .

There are ____ comparable sales in the subject neighborhood within the past twelve months ranging in sale price from $ ____ to $ ____ .

FEATURE	SUBJECT	COMPARABLE SALE # 1		COMPARABLE SALE # 2		COMPARABLE SALE # 3	
Address and Unit #							
Project Name and Phase							
Proximity to Subject							
Sale Price	$		$		$		$
Sale Price/Gross Liv. Area	$ sq. ft.	$ sq. ft.		$ sq. ft.		$ sq. ft.	
Data Source(s)							
Verification Source(s)							
VALUE ADJUSTMENTS	DESCRIPTION	DESCRIPTION	+(-) $ Adjustment	DESCRIPTION	+(-) $ Adjustment	DESCRIPTION	+(-) $ Adjustment
Sale or Financing Concessions							
Date of Sale/Time							
Location							
Leasehold/Fee Simple							
HOA Mo. Assessment							
Common Elements and Rec. Facilities							
Floor Location							
View							
Design (Style)							
Quality of Construction							
Actual Age							
Condition							
Above Grade	Total Bdrms. Baths	Total Bdrms. Baths		Total Bdrms. Baths		Total Bdrms. Baths	
Room Count							
Gross Living Area	sq. ft.	sq. ft.		sq. ft.		sq. ft.	
Basement & Finished Rooms Below Grade							
Functional Utility							
Heating/Cooling							
Energy Efficient Items							
Garage/Carport							
Porch/Patio/Deck							
Net Adjustment (Total)		☐ + ☐ -	$	☐ + ☐ -	$	☐ + ☐ -	$
Adjusted Sale Price of Comparables		Net Adj. % Gross Adj. %	$	Net Adj. % Gross Adj. %	$	Net Adj. % Gross Adj. %	$

Summary of Sales Comparison Approach _____

Indicated Value by Sales Comparison Approach $

INCOME APPROACH TO VALUE (not required by Fannie Mae)

Estimated Monthly Market Rent $ _____ X Gross Rent Multiplier _____ = $ _____ Indicated Value by Income Approach _____

Summary of Income Approach (including support for market rent and GRM) _____

Indicated Value by: Sales Comparison Approach $ _____   Income Approach (if developed) $ _____

This appraisal is made ☐ "as is", ☐ subject to completion per plans and specifications on the basis of a hypothetical condition that the improvements have been completed, ☐ subject to the following repairs or alterations on the basis of a hypothetical condition that the repairs or alterations have been completed, or ☐ subject to the following required inspection based on the extraordinary assumption that the condition or deficiency does not require alteration or repair:

Based on a complete visual inspection of the interior and exterior areas of the subject property, defined scope of work, statement of assumptions and limiting conditions, and appraiser's certification, my (our) opinion of the market value, as defined, of the real property that is the subject of this report is $ _____ , as of _____ , which is the date of inspection and the effective date of this appraisal.

F I G U R E 14.2 (continued)
Form 1073

Individual Condominium Unit Appraisal Report   File

This report form is designed to report an appraisal of a unit in a condominium project or a condominium unit in a planned unit development (PUD). This report form is not designed to report an appraisal of a manufactured home or a unit in a cooperative project.

This appraisal report is subject to the following scope of work, intended use, intended user, definition of market value, statement of assumptions and limiting conditions, and certifications. Modifications, additions, or deletions to the intended use, intended user, definition of market value, or assumptions and limiting conditions are not permitted. The appraiser may expand the scope of work to include any additional research or analysis necessary based on the complexity of this appraisal assignment. Modifications or deletions to the certifications are also not permitted. However, additional certifications that do not constitute material alterations to this appraisal report, such as those required by law or those related to the appraiser's continuing education or membership in an appraisal organization, are permitted.

SCOPE OF WORK: The scope of work for this appraisal is defined by the complexity of this appraisal assignment and the reporting requirements of this appraisal report form, including the following definition of market value, statement of assumptions and limiting conditions, and certifications. The appraiser must, at a minimum: (1) perform a complete visual inspection of the interior and exterior areas of the subject unit, (2) inspect and analyze the condominium project, (3) inspect the neighborhood, (4) inspect each of the comparable sales from at least the street, (5) research, verify, and analyze data from reliable public and/or private sources, and (6) report his or her analysis, opinions, and conclusions in this appraisal report.

INTENDED USE: The intended use of this appraisal report is for the lender/client to evaluate the property that is the subject of this appraisal for a mortgage finance transaction.

INTENDED USER: The intended user of this appraisal report is the lender/client.

MARKET VALUE: The most probable price which a property should bring in a competitive and open market under all conditions requisite to a fair sale, the buyer and seller, each acting prudently, knowledgeably and assuming the price is not affected by undue stimulus. Implicit in this definition is the consummation of a sale as of a specified date and the passing of title from seller to buyer under conditions whereby: (1) buyer and seller are typically motivated; (2) both parties are well informed or well advised, and each acting in what he or she considers his or her own best interest; (3) a reasonable time is allowed for exposure in the open market; (4) payment is made in terms of cash in U. S. dollars or in terms of financial arrangements comparable thereto; and (5) the price represents the normal consideration for the property sold unaffected by special or creative financing or sales concessions* granted by anyone associated with the sale.

*Adjustments to the comparables must be made for special or creative financing or sales concessions. No adjustments are necessary for those costs which are normally paid by sellers as a result of tradition or law in a market area; these costs are readily identifiable since the seller pays these costs in virtually all sales transactions. Special or creative financing adjustments can be made to the comparable property by comparisons to financing terms offered by a third party institutional lender that is not already involved in the property or transaction. Any adjustment should not be calculated on a mechanical dollar for dollar cost of the financing or concession but the dollar amount of any adjustment should approximate the market's reaction to the financing or concessions based on the appraiser's judgment.

STATEMENT OF ASSUMPTIONS AND LIMITING CONDITIONS: The appraiser's certification in this report is subject to the following assumptions and limiting conditions:

1. The appraiser will not be responsible for matters of a legal nature that affect either the property being appraised or the title to it, except for information that he or she became aware of during the research involved in performing this appraisal. The appraiser assumes that the title is good and marketable and will not render any opinions about the title.

2. The appraiser has provided a sketch in this appraisal report to show the approximate dimensions of the improvements. The sketch is included only to assist the reader in visualizing the property and understanding the appraiser's determination of its size.

3. The appraiser has examined the available flood maps that are provided by the Federal Emergency Management Agency (or other data sources) and has noted in this appraisal report whether any portion of the subject site is located in an identified Special Flood Hazard Area. Because the appraiser is not a surveyor, he or she makes no guarantees, express or implied, regarding this determination.

4. The appraiser will not give testimony or appear in court because he or she made an appraisal of the property in question, unless specific arrangements to do so have been made beforehand, or as otherwise required by law.

5. The appraiser has noted in this appraisal report any adverse conditions (such as needed repairs, deterioration, the presence of hazardous wastes, toxic substances, etc.) observed during the inspection of the subject property or that he or she became aware of during the research involved in performing this appraisal. Unless otherwise stated in this appraisal report, the appraiser has no knowledge of any hidden or unapparent physical deficiencies or adverse conditions of the property (such as, but not limited to, needed repairs, deterioration, the presence of hazardous wastes, toxic substances, adverse environmental conditions, etc.) that would make the property less valuable, and has assumed that there are no such conditions and makes no guarantees or warranties, express or implied. The appraiser will not be responsible for any such conditions that do exist or for any engineering or testing that might be required to discover whether such conditions exist. Because the appraiser is not an expert in the field of environmental hazards, this appraisal report must not be considered as an environmental assessment of the property.

6. The appraiser has based his or her appraisal report and valuation conclusion for an appraisal that is subject to satisfactory completion, repairs, or alterations on the assumption that the completion, repairs, or alterations of the subject property will be performed in a professional manner.

FIGURE 14.2 (continued)
Form 1073

Individual Condominium Unit Appraisal Report   File

APPRAISER'S CERTIFICATION: The Appraiser certifies and agrees that:

1. I have, at a minimum, developed and reported this appraisal in accordance with the scope of work requirements stated in this appraisal report.

2. I performed a complete visual inspection of the interior and exterior areas of the subject property. I reported the condition of the improvements in factual, specific terms. I identified and reported the physical deficiencies that could affect the livability, soundness, or structural integrity of the property.

3. I performed this appraisal in accordance with the requirements of the Uniform Standards of Professional Appraisal Practice that were adopted and promulgated by the Appraisal Standards Board of The Appraisal Foundation and that were in place at the time this appraisal report was prepared.

4. I developed my opinion of the market value of the real property that is the subject of this report based on the sales comparison approach to value. I have adequate comparable market data to develop a reliable sales comparison approach for this appraisal assignment. I further certify that I considered the cost and income approaches to value but did not develop them, unless otherwise indicated in this report.

5. I researched, verified, analyzed, and reported on any current agreement for sale for the subject property, any offering for sale of the subject property in the twelve months prior to the effective date of this appraisal, and the prior sales of the subject property for a minimum of three years prior to the effective date of this appraisal, unless otherwise indicated in this report.

6. I researched, verified, analyzed, and reported on the prior sales of the comparable sales for a minimum of one year prior to the date of sale of the comparable sale, unless otherwise indicated in this report.

7. I selected and used comparable sales that are locationally, physically, and functionally the most similar to the subject property.

8. I have not used comparable sales that were the result of combining a land sale with the contract purchase price of a home that has been built or will be built on the land.

9. I have reported adjustments to the comparable sales that reflect the market's reaction to the differences between the subject property and the comparable sales.

10. I verified, from a disinterested source, all information in this report that was provided by parties who have a financial interest in the sale or financing of the subject property.

11. I have knowledge and experience in appraising this type of property in this market area.

12. I am aware of, and have access to, the necessary and appropriate public and private data sources, such as multiple listing services, tax assessment records, public land records and other such data sources for the area in which the property is located.

13. I obtained the information, estimates, and opinions furnished by other parties and expressed in this appraisal report from reliable sources that I believe to be true and correct.

14. I have taken into consideration the factors that have an impact on value with respect to the subject neighborhood, subject property, and the proximity of the subject property to adverse influences in the development of my opinion of market value. I have noted in this appraisal report any adverse conditions (such as, but not limited to, needed repairs, deterioration, the presence of hazardous wastes, toxic substances, adverse environmental conditions, etc.) observed during the inspection of the subject property or that I became aware of during the research involved in performing this appraisal. I have considered these adverse conditions in my analysis of the property value, and have reported on the effect of the conditions on the value and marketability of the subject property.

15. I have not knowingly withheld any significant information from this appraisal report and, to the best of my knowledge, all statements and information in this appraisal report are true and correct.

16. I stated in this appraisal report my own personal, unbiased, and professional analysis, opinions, and conclusions, which are subject only to the assumptions and limiting conditions in this appraisal report.

17. I have no present or prospective interest in the property that is the subject of this report, and I have no present or prospective personal interest or bias with respect to the participants in the transaction. I did not base, either partially or completely, my analysis and/or opinion of market value in this appraisal report on the race, color, religion, sex, age, marital status, handicap, familial status, or national origin of either the prospective owners or occupants of the subject property or of the present owners or occupants of the properties in the vicinity of the subject property or on any other basis prohibited by law.

18. My employment and/or compensation for performing this appraisal or any future or anticipated appraisals was not conditioned on any agreement or understanding, written or otherwise, that I would report (or present analysis supporting) a predetermined specific value, a predetermined minimum value, a range or direction in value, a value that favors the cause of any party, or the attainment of a specific result or occurrence of a specific subsequent event (such as approval of a pending mortgage loan application).

19. I personally prepared all conclusions and opinions about the real estate that were set forth in this appraisal report. If I relied on significant real property appraisal assistance from any individual or individuals in the performance of this appraisal or the preparation of this appraisal report, I have named such individual(s) and disclosed the specific tasks performed in this appraisal report. I certify that any individual so named is qualified to perform the tasks. I have not authorized anyone to make a change to any item in this appraisal report; therefore, any change made to this appraisal is unauthorized and I will take no responsibility for it.

20. I identified the lender/client in this appraisal report who is the individual, organization, or agent for the organization that ordered and will receive this appraisal report.

Freddie Mac Form 465   March 2005   Page 5 of 6   Fannie Mae Form 1073   March 2005

F I G U R E   14.2 (continued)
Form 1073

Individual Condominium Unit Appraisal Report   File

21. The lender/client may disclose or distribute this appraisal report to: the borrower; another lender at the request of the borrower; the mortgagee or its successors and assigns; mortgage insurers; government sponsored enterprises; other secondary market participants; data collection or reporting services; professional appraisal organizations; any department, agency, or instrumentality of the United States; and any state, the District of Columbia, or other jurisdictions; without having to obtain the appraiser's or supervisory appraiser's (if applicable) consent. Such consent must be obtained before this appraisal report may be disclosed or distributed to any other party (including, but not limited to, the public through advertising, public relations, news, sales, or other media).

22. I am aware that any disclosure or distribution of this appraisal report by me or the lender/client may be subject to certain laws and regulations. Further, I am also subject to the provisions of the Uniform Standards of Professional Appraisal Practice that pertain to disclosure or distribution by me.

23. The borrower, another lender at the request of the borrower, the mortgagee or its successors and assigns, mortgage insurers, government sponsored enterprises, and other secondary market participants may rely on this appraisal report as part of any mortgage finance transaction that involves any one or more of these parties.

24. If this appraisal report was transmitted as an "electronic record" containing my "electronic signature," as those terms are defined in applicable federal and/or state laws (excluding audio and video recordings), or a facsimile transmission of this appraisal report containing a copy or representation of my signature, the appraisal report shall be as effective, enforceable and valid as if a paper version of this appraisal report were delivered containing my original hand written signature.

25. Any intentional or negligent misrepresentation(s) contained in this appraisal report may result in civil liability and/or criminal penalties including, but not limited to, fine or imprisonment or both under the provisions of Title 18, United States Code, Section 1001, et seq., or similar state laws.

SUPERVISORY APPRAISER'S CERTIFICATION: The Supervisory Appraiser certifies and agrees that:

1. I directly supervised the appraiser for this appraisal assignment, have read the appraisal report, and agree with the appraiser's analysis, opinions, statements, conclusions, and the appraiser's certification.

2. I accept full responsibility for the contents of this appraisal report including, but not limited to, the appraiser's analysis, opinions, statements, conclusions, and the appraiser's certification.

3. The appraiser identified in this appraisal report is either a sub-contractor or an employee of the supervisory appraiser (or the appraisal firm), is qualified to perform this appraisal, and is acceptable to perform this appraisal under the applicable state law.

4. This appraisal report complies with the Uniform Standards of Professional Appraisal Practice that were adopted and promulgated by the Appraisal Standards Board of The Appraisal Foundation and that were in place at the time this appraisal report was prepared.

5. If this appraisal report was transmitted as an "electronic record" containing my "electronic signature," as those terms are defined in applicable federal and/or state laws (excluding audio and video recordings), or a facsimile transmission of this appraisal report containing a copy or representation of my signature, the appraisal report shall be as effective, enforceable and valid as if a paper version of this appraisal report were delivered containing my original hand written signature.

APPRAISER

Signature _____
Name _____
Company Name _____
Company Address _____

_____
Telephone Number_____
Email Address _____
Date of Signature and Report _____
Effective Date of Appraisal _____
State Certification # _____
or State License #_____
or Other _____ State # _____
State _____
Expiration Date of Certification or License _____

ADDRESS OF PROPERTY APPRAISED

_____
_____

APPRAISED VALUE OF SUBJECT PROPERTY $_____
LENDER/CLIENT
Name _____
Company Name _____
Company Address _____
Email Address _____

SUPERVISORY APPRAISER (ONLY IF REQUIRED)

Signature _____
Name _____
Company Name _____
Company Address _____

_____
Telephone Number _____
Email Address _____
Date of Signature _____
State Certification # _____
or State License # _____
State _____
Expiration Date of Certification or License _____

SUBJECT PROPERTY
☐ Did not inspect subject property
☐ Did inspect exterior of subject property from street
　　Date of Inspection _____
☐ Did inspect interior and exterior of subject property
　　Date of Inspection _____

COMPARABLE SALES
☐ Did not inspect exterior of comparable sales from street
☐ Did inspect exterior of comparable sales from street
　　Date of Inspection _____

Freddie Mac Form 465   March 2005   Page 6 of 6   Fannie Mae Form 1073   March 2005

Manufactured Homes

Factory-built homes now account for almost one-third of all new single-family home purchases in the United States. The federal government refers to a home constructed in a factory, including both completely enclosed homes and those that consist of components to be assembled on site, as a *manufactured home*. Such homes must meet the National Manufactured Home Construction and Safety Standards covering design, construction, durability, fire resistance, and energy efficiency.

Well-maintained manufactured home subdivisions, offering generous lot space with lawn areas, well-paved streets, swimming pools, and other facilities, can be inviting places to live and may increase in value. Manufactured homes offer housing that usually is much more affordable than alternatives. Unfortunately, strict zoning has limited their availability in most urban areas.

Special considerations for manufactured homes appraised by the sales comparison approach include the age and size of the home, its location, and, if applicable, space rental cost, lease term, subdivision amenities, and upkeep of the subdivision grounds and other units.

Some forms of manufactured housing, such as those using panelized construction, may be required to conform to local building codes and thus are considered equivalent to homes constructed entirely on site.

Other Forms of Ownership

Other partial interests include the *life estate, easement, cooperative,* and various forms of *co-ownership. Tenants in common* share an *undivided interest* in the property that is the subject of the cotenancy. This means that each tenant has the right to use the entire property, regardless of the fractional interest owned. The value of a tenant in common's interest is based on that fraction.

Joint tenants, who share the unities of title, time, interest, and possession, cannot have unequal interests. A joint tenancy also includes the right of survivorship, which means that a joint tenant cannot convey the property interest without destroying the joint tenancy. The joint tenancy has value while the tenant lives because the tenant is entitled to full use of the property, but the ultimate value of a joint tenant's interest depends on the actuarial likelihood that the joint tenant will be the last survivor.

If all cotenants are willing to join in a conveyance of co-ownership property, the property's value should be the same as it would be under individual ownership of the fee simple title. An individual tenant's interest, valued separately, will depend on the type of property and the terms of the cotenancy. The appraiser must consider the likely desirability of the property to a potential buyer. If use of the property is easily divisible, such as a three-unit building owned by three tenants in common under an agreement giving each the right to occupy a separate unit, the valuation process will be less complicated.

EXERCISE 14.1   What special considerations would be taken into account when appraising the following property interests?

1. Condominium

2. PUD

3. Time-share

4. Manufactured home

Check your answers against those in the Answer Key at the back of the book.

■ APPRAISING LEASE INTERESTS

In previous chapters we referred to the owner of a leased property as the *lessor* or *landlord* and to the person who leases the property as the *lessee* or *tenant.* When the scheduled rent the lessee pays is the same as the market rent, or economic potential of the property, both parties receive full value for their lease and investment dollar. If the scheduled rent (contract rent) is lower or higher than market rent, however, one party gains and the other loses the amount of the difference. How the lessor's and lessee's interests are defined and evaluated is discussed next.

Definition of Terms

Leased Fee

An owner who leases property for a given period of time creates a *leased fee,* which represents the lessor's interest and rights in the real estate. In return for the lease that permits the tenant to occupy and use the property, the lessor receives a stipulated fee or rental and retains the right to repossess the property at the termination of the lease. The value of the rental payments plus the remaining property value at the end of the lease period, known as the *reversion,* make up the lessor's interest in the property. This leased fee interest may be sold or mortgaged, subject to the rights of the tenant.

Leasehold Estate

A second interest created by a lease belongs to the tenant. It is referred to as the *leasehold estate,* or the lessee's interest and rights in the real estate. Because the lessee is obligated under the terms of the lease to pay rent, the lessee's interest in the property can have value only if the agreed-on scheduled rent is less than the prevailing market rental, or economic rent. If the agreed-on scheduled rent is higher than the prevailing market rent, the difference is termed *excess rent* and the tenant has a negative leasehold interest.

A lessee may make substantial improvements to a parcel under the terms of a ground lease. A *ground lease* is defined as a lease of land only, on which the tenant usually owns a building or is required to build as specified in the lease.

An important benefit of the lessee's leasehold estate is the right to mortgage leasehold improvements by using them as security for the repayment of a debt. The lessee's interest in the improvements usually is *subordinated* (made secondary) to the interest of the *mortgagee* (the holder of the mortgage).

Sandwich Lease

When a tenant has a leasehold estate of value, the tenant may sublet that interest. By doing so, the tenant creates what is known as a *sandwich lease,* and the value of the property is then divided among three interests: the lessor's, the original or prime lessee's, and the sublessee's. The interest of the sublessee under a sandwich lease is called a *subleasehold.*

Creation of Lease Interests

The statute of frauds in most states requires that a lease that will terminate more than one year from the date of agreement must be in writing to be enforceable in a court of law. Oral agreements for leases of one year or less are usually enforceable; however, it is good business practice to put all lease agreements in writing.

A lease agreement may cover one or more of the following topics:

Gross Lease

In a *gross lease* the tenant usually pays a fixed rental over the period of the lease, and the landlord pays all expenses of ownership, such as taxes, assessments, and insurance.

Net Lease

Under a *net lease,* in addition to the rent, the tenant pays part or all of the property charges, such as taxes, assessments, insurance, and maintenance.

Triple Net Lease

In a *triple net lease,* also known as a *net, net, net lease* or *absolute net lease,* the tenant pays *all* operating and other expenses *plus* a fixed rent. These expenses include taxes, assessments, insurance, utilities, and maintenance.

Percentage Lease

In a *percentage lease,* the tenant usually pays a minimum guaranteed base rent plus a percentage of *gross income* earned by the business. The amount paid over the base is called *overage rent.* The percentage paid may change (usually, it decreases) as gross income increases. For example, the rent may be $1,000 per month plus 3 percent of gross income over $6,000 per month and 1 percent of gross income over $10,000 per month.

Either a gross lease or a net lease may be a percentage lease.

Excess Rent and Deficit Rent

Excess rent is the amount by which scheduled rent exceeds market rent at the time of the appraisal. Excess rent is created by a lease that is favorable to the *lessor* and is likely the result of a strong rental market. *Deficit rent*, on the other hand, is the amount by which market rent exceeds scheduled rent at the time of the appraisal. Deficit rent is created by a lease favorable to the *tenant* and is usually the result of a weak rental market. Because excess rent and deficit rent result from a lease contract rather than the income potential of the property, their effect is often considered a non-realty element of value.

Escalator Clause

An *escalator clause* provides for periodic increases in rents based on any increase in one of a number of indexes, such as the *consumer price index (CPI)* or the *wholesale price index (WPI).*

Renewal Options

The lease may provide that the lessee has the right at the end of the lease term to renew the lease for the same term or some other stated period. A *renewal option* usually includes a rent increase at a stated percentage or based on an index or other formula. The existence of a renewal option at a rate favorable to the lessee will make the lessee's interest that much more valuable and the lessor's interest that much less valuable. Because the right to exercise a renewal option is entirely at the discretion of the lessee, it usually is considered a benefit to the lessee rather than the lessor.

Tenant Improvements

Most leased office and other commercial buildings are built, finished, or remodeled according to the requirements of a particular tenant. Frequently, original construction does not include interior partitioning, which is completed only after a lease is entered into so that the space can be finished to suit the tenant's needs. Either the lessor or the lessee may be obligated to pay for such *tenant improvements,* as the lease provides. If the lessor pays, the rent will be higher than it would be otherwise; if improvements are made by the tenant, the rent may be lower than otherwise.

Other Lease Provisions

A lease may contain a *tax-stop clause* that allows the landlord to charge the tenant for any increase in taxes over a specified level. An *expense-stop clause* works in the same way to pass increases in building maintenance expenses on to tenants on a pro rata basis. A *purchase option,* or *right of first refusal,* may accompany a lease of real property. The purchase price may be provided in the lease agreement or it may be based on a stated formula.

EXERCISE 14.2

1. Scheduled rent that is higher than market rent creates
   a. overage rent.
   b. gross rent.
   c. excess rent.
   d. escalator rent.

2. The amount paid over minimum base rent in a percentage lease is
   a. overage rent.
   b. gross rent.
   c. excess rent.
   d. escalator rent.

3. The lease under which the tenant pays a fixed rental and the landlord pays all expenses of ownership is the
   a. gross lease.
   b. triple net lease.
   c. net lease.
   d. percentage lease.

4. An index will be referred to in a(n)
   a. gross lease.
   b. triple net lease.
   c. escalator clause.
   d. expense-stop clause.

5. The interest of a sublessee is a
   a. leasehold.
   b. leased fee.
   c. subleasehold.
   d. sandwich lease.

6. Increases in maintenance costs are passed on to tenants under a(n)
   a. tax-stop clause.
   b. expense-stop clause.
   c. gross lease.
   d. escalator clause.

Check your answers against those in the Answer Key at the back of the book.

■ LEASED FEE AND LEASEHOLD VALUATIONS

Because changing conditions affect the value of real estate, leases made prior to the current period may be for amounts above or below the current market figures. If market rent exceeds scheduled rent, the property owner is, in effect, transferring part of the property interest to the tenant, thus creating a positive leasehold interest. On the other hand, if scheduled rent exceeds market rent, a negative leasehold interest (referred to as a *lease premium*) exists, and the unfavorable lease, in a sense, is a liability of the lessee. If the difference between scheduled rent and market rent becomes too heavily weighted in the owner's favor, the tenant may try to renegotiate the terms of the lease or perhaps may even default. If scheduled rent and market rent are the same, the tenant's interest in the property is of zero value.

The principle involved in the valuation of lease interests is similar to that of capitalized income valuation under the annuity or Inwood method. The value of the lessor's and the lessee's interests is found by capitalizing the present value of the income each receives and adding the reversionary value of the land, or land and building, at the expiration of the lease term. Ordinarily, the lessor receives the reversionary value of the property. But some leases provide for payments to the lessee by the lessor for any improvements made by the lessee that will ultimately revert to the lessor.

In valuing lease interests, the appraiser must first carefully study the detailed provisions of the lease to determine the rights and obligations of the owner and tenant. Then, the valuation of leased fee and leasehold interests is basically a matter of dividing the value of the property into separate values attributable to each of the various interests. As a general rule, the total of the various interests in the property will approximate the value of the property under free and clear ownership, but may be somewhat more or less.

The examples in this chapter give leased property situations and suggested methods of appraisal. The examples shown are typical of situations involving relatively long-term leases and assume no remaining building value at the end of the lease term. Other leases require different assumptions. Note, too, that capitalization rates must always have adequate market support. The first example illustrates the valuation of an investment property free and clear of any lease interests.

EXAMPLE

A property earning a net operating income of $48,000 per year is rented on an annual basis to one tenant. The remaining economic life of the building is 25 years, and the current market value of the land is estimated at $100,000. The rate of interest for similar investments is 14 percent. Based on these facts, and using the *building residual technique,* the value of the property is obtained.

Estimated Land Value		$100,000
Net Operating Income	$48,000	
Land Income ($100,000 × 14%)	14,000	
Residual Income to Building	$34,000	
Capitalization Rate for		
Building:	14%	
Interest Rate	4	
Recapture Rate	18%	
Building Value ($34,000 ÷ 18%)		188,889
Total Property Value		$288,900 (rounded)

The following series of examples, all based on the same hypothetical property but with varying conditions as to term of lease and amount of rent under the lease, illustrate the valuation of leased fee and leasehold interests.

EXAMPLE

Assume that the property described in the previous example is now leased to a nationally known company on a 25-year lease at the same net annual rent of $48,000, equal to market rent. The building is considered of no value at the end of the lease term. Because of the increased security, and therefore the decreased risk, in having the property leased for a long period of time by a national company, the interest rate (sometimes called *risk rate*) has been lowered from 14 percent to 12 percent. The interest rate applicable to reversion is assumed to be 14 percent.

Based on these facts, and using the Inwood method of capitalization, the value of the leased fee is derived as follows:

Net Operating Income	$ 48,000
[1]Annuity Factor (25 yrs. @ 12%)	7.843
Present Worth of Net Income	$376,500 (rounded)
[2] Present Worth of Reversion	
(25 yrs. @ 14%)	
($100,000 × .038 reversion factor)	3,800
Total Property Value	$380,300

In the preceding example, the lower risk rate of 12 percent results in an increase in the value of the investment (from $288,900 to $380,300).

EXAMPLE

The property is leased to a nationally known company on a 25-year lease, but the net operating income is only $40,000, $8,000 below the market rent. The appraiser in this instance must estimate the value of the two affected interests—leased fee and leasehold. Because of the greatly reduced risk brought on by the long lease to a national company at a scheduled rent well below the market rent, the interest rate has been lowered to 11 percent. The interest rate applicable to reversion is unchanged at the 14 percent rate assumed earlier.

The leased fee interest can be computed as follows:

Net Operating Income	$ 40,000
Annuity Factor (25 yrs. @ 11%)	8.422
Present Worth of Net Income	$336,900 (rounded)
Present Worth of Reversion	
(25 yrs. @ 14%)	
($100,000 × .038 reversion factor)	3,800
Value of the Leased Fee Interest	$340,700

The leasehold interest can be computed as follows:

Market Rent	$ 48,000
Scheduled Rent	40,000
Excess Rent	$ 8,000
Present Worth of Excess Rent	
Discounted @ 15%	6,464
Value of Leasehold Interest	$ 51,700 (rounded)
Total Value of Leased Fee and Leasehold	
Interests ($340,700 + $51,700)	$392,400

---

[1] See Figure 12.2 (Annuity Factors Table).
[2] See Figure 12.3 (Reversion Table).

In the preceding example, it is obvious that the lessee has an interest in the property that can be measured annually in terms of the difference between the rental value of the property today and the actual rent paid to the landlord. This would also be the value of the lessee's interest if a sandwich lease were to be created, with (under these facts) the sublessee's scheduled rent equal to the market rent. To measure the lessee's leasehold interest, the excess rent must be capitalized over the term of the lease. Because the excess rent arises out of a leasehold interest, it is subject to the covenants and conditions of the lease and is less secure; therefore, the interest rate used (15 percent) is higher than the 14 percent rate used to value the property under free and clear ownership.

E X A M P L E

The scheduled rent is $52,000 per year, or $4,000 higher than the current market rent. A higher interest rate (15 percent) will be applied to the excess rent portion of the total income because it may not continue for the length of the lease.

The leased fee interest can be computed as follows:

Present Value of Market Rent (from page 303)	$376,500
Value of Reversion	3,800
	$380,300
Excess Rent Discounted @ 15% ($4,000 x 6.464 annuity factor)	25,900 (rounded)
Value of Leased Fee Interest	$406,200

When scheduled rent is higher than market rent, as in the last example, the value of the lessor's interest increases. This happens even though the excess rent is capitalized at a higher rate because the tenant may default if he or she is paying more rent than may ordinarily be expected.

E X E R C I S E   1 4 . 3

1. Explain how a leasehold estate is created.

2. Using the figures given in the example above, what is the value of the leased fee interest if scheduled rent is $54,000? If scheduled rent is $50,000?

Check your answers against those in the Answer Key at the back of the book.

■ SUMMARY

A property interest to be appraised is not always an undivided fee simple interest. A condominium is the undivided ownership of the airspace that a unit actually occupies, plus an undivided interest in the ownership of the common elements, which are owned jointly with the other condominium unit owners. A planned unit development (PUD) includes individual ownership of a detached home and lot, town home and lot, or condominium, along with shared ownership of common areas. A time-share divides ownership into increments of time. Manufactured homes require special consideration of their location.

Property under co-ownership may be difficult to sell, and its value will be affected commensurately if all owners do not take part in the transaction.

Excess rent is any amount by which scheduled rent is greater than market rent. Deficit rent is the amount by which market rent exceeds scheduled rent. A lessee may mortgage property improvements. A subleasehold is the interest of a sublessee.

A lease may be described by the manner in which rent is determined, as in a gross lease, net lease, triple net lease (net, net, net lease), or percentage lease. Overage rent is any amount paid over the base minimum under a percentage lease. With an escalator clause, lease payments can increase on the basis of an index (for example, the consumer price index)

The lessee may have the right to renew the lease under the same or revised terms. The lease also may provide the lessee a purchase option or right of first refusal. Tenant improvements are made to suit the tenant and may be paid for by either landlord or tenant. Tax-stop and expense-stop clauses work to pass on to the lessee any increase in tax or expense payments that would otherwise be the obligation of the landlord.

Because the annuity method of capitalization is based on the premise that income will remain scheduled and predictable throughout the term of a long lease, it is almost always used in valuing leased fee and leasehold interests.

A leasehold interest can have value only if the scheduled rent under the lease is less than the market rent value of the property free of lease. In a sense, a leasehold interest has many of the characteristics of first mortgage equity. If there is a sublessee who also has an interest (which may occur when scheduled rent is less than market rent), the middleman (the prime lessee) is referred to as a *sandwich lessee*. The sublessee's interest will have risk characteristics similar to a second mortgage. Thus, the capitalization of either the prime lessee's interest or the sublessee's interest normally will warrant a higher capitalization rate than that of the lessor's interest.

The sum of the values of the various lease interests tends to equal the value of the property under free and clear ownership. However, if the scheduled rent paid by a reliable lessee exceeds the market rent, the sum of the values of the various interests could exceed the value of the real estate free and clear.

14

ACHIEVEMENT EXAMINATION

An industrial property with a 30-year lease to a highly rated tenant calls for an annual rental of $36,000. Data on comparative properties indicate that the market rent of the subject property is $45,000 per year.

The lessor is virtually assured of receiving the rent, as long as it remains below market rent. In the opinion of the appraiser, an appropriate rate of interest for a low-risk investment of this type is 11 percent. The lessee, on the other hand, has an interest that is subject to variation in value. If market conditions change and the per year rental value is no longer a favorable one, the value of the leasehold estate will be reduced considerably or even eliminated. To reflect the lessee's risk, the appraiser estimates the leasehold rate at 14 percent. The annuity factor for 30 years at 14 percent is 7.003.

If land value at the expiration of the lease is determined to be $150,000 and the building is assumed to be worthless at the time, what is the value of the leased fee interest?

What is the value of the leasehold interest?

Check your answers against those in the Answer Key at the back of the book.

## CHAPTER 15

Appraisal Math and Statistics

■ OVERVIEW

Math is used every day in the real estate business. Sometimes it may involve a simple measurement of land area. At other times it may involve a complex investment analysis that requires the use of sophisticated computers programmed with compound interest schedules and multiple regression tables.

This chapter provides a review of the mathematics involved in computing land area and building area and volume. Other mathematical computations with which the appraiser should be familiar, such as compound interest, are also discussed. The chapter ends with a brief introduction to statistics. Statistical analysis has particular application to the work of the appraiser because appraisers are continually drawing inferences about populations or markets from samples.

Because readers will have varying degrees of knowledge and experience in math computations, the Achievement Examination at the end of this chapter may be taken to review such computations. It will serve as an indication of whether all of the material in this chapter should be studied.

■ CALCULATORS

Calculators are a great aid in the real estate business, and you should know how to use one. State licensing exams generally will allow you to use a silent, handheld calculator, as long as it does not have a printout tape. A common four-function calculator (+, −, ×, ÷, plus % and √ keys) is sufficient for most problems you will encounter on the job or on exams. Most models have the ability to store and recall numbers in a built-in memory, which reduces the need to write down answers to be used in subsequent calculations.

Some of the material in this chapter is adapted from *Mastering Real Estate Mathematics*, 6th edition, by Ventolo, Tamper, and Allaway (Chicago: Real Estate Education Company, 1995).

If you plan to buy a new calculator, however, a good-quality *financial calculator* might be a better choice. This type of calculator will have a memory and also be capable of performing all the mathematical and financial operations you probably will need. A financial calculator will include these additional function keys:

n	the number of interest compounding periods
i	the amount of interest per compounding period
PMT	the payment
PV	the present value
FV	the future value

These five keys on the financial calculator can handle almost every conceivable problem dealing with finance. Although proficiency with the calculator does not guarantee success on exams or on the job, there is little doubt that it does provide a critical edge.

■ PERCENTS

Percent (%) means per hundred or per hundred parts. For example, 50 percent means 50 parts out of a total of 100 parts (100 parts equal 1 whole), and 100 percent means all 100 of the 100 total parts, or 1 whole unit.

Converting Percents to Decimals

To change a percent to a decimal, move the decimal point *two places to the left* and drop the percent sign (%). All numbers have a decimal point, although it is usually not shown when only zeros follow it.

EXAMPLE

99 is really 99.0

 6 is really 6.0

$1 is the same as $1.00

So, percents can be readily converted to decimals.

EXAMPLE

99%	=	99.0%	=	.990	=	.99
6%	=	6.0%	=	.060	=	.06
70%	=	70.0%	=	.700	=	.70

Note: Adding zeros to the *right* of a decimal point after the last figure does not change the value of the number.

Converting Decimals to Percents

This process is the reverse of the one you just completed. Move the decimal point *two places to the right* and add the % sign.

EXAMPLE

.10 = 10%
1.00 = 100%
.98 = 98%
.987 = 98.7%

Percentage Problems

Percentage problems usually involve three elements: *percent* (rate), *total,* and *part.*

EXAMPLE

percent		total		part
10%	of	100	is	10

Look at the example that follows. A problem involving percentages is really a multiplication problem. To solve this problem, you first convert the percentage to a decimal, then multiply.

EXAMPLE

What is 20% of 150?

150 × 20% = ?
20% = .20
150 × .20 = 30

Answer: 20% of 150 is 30.

A generalized formula for solving percent problems is

$$\text{Total} \times \text{Percent} = \text{Part}$$

To solve a percent problem, you must know the value of two of the elements of this formula. The value that you must find is called the *unknown* (most often shown in the formula as x).

EXAMPLE

If 25 percent of the houses in your area are less than 10 years old and there are 600 houses, how many houses are less than 10 years old?

Total	×	Percent	=	Part
600	×	25%	=	x
600	×	.25	=	150

Two additional formulas can be derived from the basic formula, *percent × total = part.* The diagram below will help you remember them.

$$\frac{\text{PART}}{\text{TOTAL} \quad \times \quad \text{PERCENT}}$$

Because *part* is over *percent* in the diagram, you make a fraction of these two elements when looking for a *total.*

$$\textbf{Total} = \frac{\text{Part}}{\text{Percent}}$$

Because *part* is over *total,* you make a fraction of these two elements when looking for a *percent.*

$$\textbf{Percent} = \frac{\text{Part}}{\text{Total}}$$

Because *percent* and *total* are both in the lower part of the diagram, multiply these two to get the *part*.

$$\text{Total} \times \text{Percent} = \textbf{Part}$$

E X A M P L E

If 25 percent of the houses in your area are less than 10 years old and this amounts to 150 houses, how many houses are there in your area?

Solution: State the formula.

$$\text{Total} = \frac{\text{Part}}{\text{Percent}}$$

Substitute values.

$$\text{Total} = \frac{150}{.25}$$

Solve the problem.
Total = 600

E X A M P L E

There are 600 houses in your area, and 150 of them are less than 10 years old. What percentage of the houses are less than 10 years old?

Solution: $\text{Percent} = \dfrac{\text{Part}}{\text{Total}}$

$$\text{Percent} = \frac{150}{600}$$

Percent = .25 or 25%

Problem-Solving Strategy

Let's take a look at how to solve *word* problems. Here's the five-step strategy you should use.

1. Read the problem carefully.
2. Analyze the problem, pick out the important factors, and put those factors into a simplified question, disregarding unimportant factors.
3. Choose the proper formula for the problem.
4. Substitute the figures for the elements of the formula.
5. Solve the problem.

If you use this strategy throughout this chapter and wherever it applies in this text, you'll have an easier time with word problems.

E X A M P L E

Consider an example that applies the five-step strategy to a typical real estate problem.

1. Read the following problem carefully.

   A house sold for $140,600, which was 95 percent of the original list price. At what price was the house originally listed?

2. Analyze the problem, pick out the important factors, and put those factors into a question.

$140,600 is 95 percent of what?

3. Choose the proper formula for the problem.

$$\text{Total} = \frac{\text{Part}}{\text{Percent}}$$

4. Substitute the figures for the elements of the formula.

$$\text{Total} = \frac{\$140{,}600}{.95}$$

5. Solve the problem.

$$\text{Total} = \$148{,}000$$

Let's try another problem, one that you've dealt with in earlier chapters on income capitalization.

Assume a property earns a net operating income of $26,250 per year. What percentage of net operating income (rate) is this, if the property is valued at $210,000? You can solve this problem using the capitalization formulas you worked with earlier.

$$\frac{\text{Income}}{\text{Rate} \mid \text{Value}} \qquad \frac{\text{Part}}{\text{Total} \mid \text{Percent}}$$

Both formulas above are really the same. Think of *total* as *value, part* as *income,* and *percent* as *rate.*

Solution: Restate the problem:

What percent of $210,000 is $26,250?

What formula will you use?

$$Rate = \frac{Income}{Value} \qquad \text{or} \qquad R = \frac{I}{V}$$

Solve the problem:

$$\$26{,}250 \div \$210{,}000 = .125 \text{ or } 12.5\%$$

As you have seen, in working with problems involving percents, there are several ways of stating the same relationship.

For example, you can say that

$$P = B \times R$$

where

P is the percentage of the whole.

B is the base, or whole.

R is the rate.

Or

$$I = RV$$

where

I is the amount of income.

R is the rate.

V is the value or whole.

Or

Part = Whole × Rate

Or

Part = Total × Percent

To find out how many square feet are in 20 percent of an acre, you must first know how many square feet there are in an acre. This number is 43,560. The problem can be solved by using any one of the formulas above.

E X A M P L E

Part	=	Whole	×	Rate
Part	=	43,560 sq. ft.	×	20%
Part	=	43,560 sq. ft.	×	.20
Part	=	8,712 sq. ft.		

E X E R C I S E 15.1

1. If houses in your area have increased in value 8 percent during the past year and the average price of houses sold last year was $95,000, what is the average price of houses sold today?

$102,600

2. Mr. Jonas purchased a house for $125,000 and sold it for $140,000. What percent profit did he make on his investment?

140−125 ÷ 125 = 12%

125 = 12%

Check your answers against the ones in the Answer Key at the back of the book.

■ INTEREST

Interest is the cost of using someone else's money. A person who borrows money is required to repay the loan *plus* a charge for interest. This charge will depend on the amount borrowed (principal), the length of time the money is used (time), and the percent of interest agreed on (rate). Repayment, then, involves the return of the principal plus a return on the principal, called *interest*.

There are two types of interest, *simple interest* and *compound interest*.

Simple Interest

Simple interest is interest earned on only the original principal, not on the accrued interest. Interest is always payable for a particular period, whether daily, monthly, annually, or based on some other schedule. With simple interest, the amount earned at the end of each period is withdrawn or placed in a separate account.

The formula for computing simple interest is

$$\text{Principal} \times \text{Rate} \times \text{Time} = \text{Interest}$$

For example, the interest owed on a loan of $1,000 for 180 days at a rate of 10 percent per year is $1,000 × .10 × (180/360), which can be simplified to $1,000 × .10 × ½, which equals $50.

The formula for computing simple interest is used to determine the amount of up-front *points* (also called *discount points*) that a lender may require as part of the fee for a mortgage loan.

For example, a loan in the amount of $160,000 may require payment of two points at the time of closing. In that case, the borrower must be prepared to pay $160,000 × 2 percent, which is $160,000 × .02, or $3,200, to the lender as a condition of receiving the loan.

In computing a loan's annual percentage rate (APR) for federal mortgage loan disclosure purposes, one point (1%) paid at the time of origination is considered roughly equal to a one-eighth increase in the rate charged over the life of the loan. This means that if a loan of $160,000 at an interest rate of 8 percent requires a payment of two points up front, the annual percentage rate—the actual interest rate paid—is closer to 8 ¼ percent. This figure is computed by adding 8% + (2 × ⅛%), which is 8% + ⅜%, which can be simplified to 8 ¼%.

Compound Interest

The term *compound interest* means that the interest is periodically added to the principal, and, in effect, the new balance (principal plus interest) draws interest. The annual interest rate may be calculated at different intervals, such as annually, semiannually, quarterly, monthly, or daily. When the interest comes due during the compounding period (for instance, at the end of the month), the interest is calculated and accrues, or is added to the principal.

The annuity and other capitalization techniques covered in Chapter 12 make use of tables of factors derived from formulas that represent the change in return over time at various interest rates. Annuity and reversion factors can be used to determine the amount that must be invested at the required interest rate to yield the desired return. The annuity factors shown in Figure 12.2 represent the *present value of $1 per period*. The reversion factors shown in Figure 12.3 represent the *present value of $1*.

The factors shown in Figure 15.1 represent the *future value of $1*.

The formula for computing future investment value when interest is compounded is

$$\text{Principal} \times (1 + \text{interest rate})^n = \text{Future Value}$$

or

$$P\,(1 + i)^n = S$$

In the formula, *i* stands for the interest rate, *n* stands for the number of compounding periods (such as daily or monthly), and *S* stands for the sum of principal and all accumulated interest. The interest rate calculation $(1 + i)^n$ does not

FIGURE 15.1
10% Compound Interest (Future Value of $1)

	Conversion Period				
Year	Daily	Monthly	Quarterly	Semiannual	Annual
1	1.105 171	1.104 713	1.103 813	1.102 500	1.100 000
2	1.221 403	1.220 391	1.218 403	1.215 506	1.210 000
3	1.349 859	1.348 182	1.344 889	1.340 096	1.331 000
4	1.491 825	1.489 354	1.484 506	1.477 455	1.464 100
5	1.648 721	1.645 309	1.638 616	1.628 895	1.610 510
6	1.822 119	1.817 594	1.808 726	1.795 856	1.771 561
7	2.013 753	2.007 920	1.996 495	1.979 932	1.948 717
8	2.225 541	2.218 176	2.203 757	2.182 875	2.143 589
9	2.459 603	2.450 448	2.432 535	2.406 619	2.357 948
10	2.718 282	2.707 041	2.685 064	2.653 298	2.593 742

have to be computed separately for every problem. Instead, it can be found in a table of compound interest factors, such as the one shown in Figure 15.1, which indicates the factor to be applied to find the future value of $1 at the interest rate and for the period specified.

For example, the factor for computing the future value of $1 at the end of 10 years at 10 percent interest, compounded *daily,* is 2.718282. Using the preceding formula, the future value of an investment of $1,000 at 10 percent interest compounded daily will be $1,000 × 2.718282, or $2,718.28. An initial investment of $1,000 at 10 percent interest compounded *annually* for 10 years would require a factor of 2.593742, for a total future value of $2,593.74. The more frequent the compounding (in these examples, daily rather than annually), the greater the ultimate return.

Another factor table useful to the investor indicates the individual payment amounts needed to amortize a loan at the required interest rate over the desired period. Figure 15.2 shows the monthly payment required to amortize a loan of $1 at the interest rates indicated. The monthly payment needed to amortize a loan of $100,000 at 10 percent interest over 20 years can be found by applying the factor of .0097 to the loan amount:

$$\$100,000 \times .0097 = \$970 \text{ monthly installment}$$

Values in monthly installment tables are frequently expressed in terms of the required payment per $1,000 of loan value. The factor for a loan of $1,000 at 9 percent interest for a term of one year is 8.75. (The decimal point in each factor shown in Figure 15.2 would be moved two places to the right to show the factor for a loan of $1,000.)

EXERCISE 15.2

A house you like can be bought with a $90,000 loan and $18,000 cash. The interest rate is 9 percent and the lender requires a loan fee of 1 ½ points. What amount of interest must be paid to obtain the loan, and what will the monthly payment be if the loan term is 30 years? (Use the appropriate table in this chapter).

1.5 % of loan

90 K loan
18 K cash   .0081 × 90K = $ 729

Check your answer against the one in the Answer Key at the back of the book.

.015 × 90K   1350

FIGURE 15.2
Monthly Installment Required to Amortize $1

			Interest Rate			
Term of Years	9%	9 ½%	10%	10 ½%	11%	11 ½%
1	.0875	.0877	.0880	.0882	.0884	.0887
2	.0457	.0460	.0462	.0464	.0467	.0469
3	.0318	.0321	.0323	.0326	.0328	.0330
4	.0249	.0252	.0254	.0257	.0259	.0261
5	.0208	.0211	.0213	.0215	.0218	.0220
6	.0181	.0183	.0186	.0188	.0191	.0193
7	.0161	.0164	.0167	.0169	.0172	.0174
8	.0147	.0150	.0152	.0155	.0158	.0160
9	.0136	.0139	.0141	.0144	.0147	.0150
10	.0127	.0130	.0133	.0135	.0138	.0141
15	.0102	.0105	.0108	.0111	.0114	.0117
20	.0090	.0094	.0097	.0100	.0104	.0107
25	.0084	.0088	.0091	.0095	.0099	.0102
30	.0081	.0085	.0088	.0092	.0096	.0100
35	.0079	.0083	.0086	.0090	.0094	.0098
40	.0078	.0082	.0085	.0089	.0093	.0097

■ AREA AND VOLUME

Many mathematical computations occur throughout the appraisal of any structure, from the simplest one-room warehouse to the most complex apartment or office building. The appraiser must find the square footage of the appraised site, the number of square feet of usable structure space, and the total square feet of the ground area the structure covers. In addition, one of the methods used in the cost approach to appraisal requires the measurement of cubic feet of space occupied by the structure.

The appraiser should know how to compute the area (and volume, where applicable) of any shape. Property boundaries, particularly those measured by the method known as *metes and bounds* (also called *courses and distances*), often are not regularly shaped, and structures usually are not.

Area of Squares and Rectangles

To review some basics about shapes and measurements:

The space inside a two-dimensional shape is called its *area*.

A *right angle* is the angle formed by one-fourth of a circle. Because a full circle is 360 degrees and one-fourth of 360 degrees is 90 degrees, a right angle is a 90-degree angle.

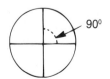

A *rectangle* is a closed figure with four sides that are at right angles to each other.

A *square* is a rectangle with four sides of equal length. A square with sides each one inch long is a *square inch*. A square with sides each one foot long is a *square foot*.

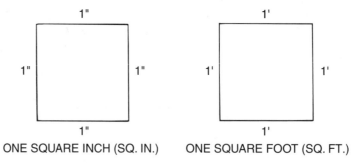

ONE SQUARE INCH (SQ. IN.)   ONE SQUARE FOOT (SQ. FT.)

Note:

The symbol for *inch* is ".

The symbol for *foot* is '.

The abbreviations are *in.* and *ft.*

The following formula may be used to compute the area of any rectangle:

$$\text{Area} = \text{Length} \times \text{Width}$$

$$A = L \times W$$

The area of the following rectangle, using the formula, is 5" × 6", or 30 square inches.

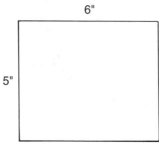

The term *30 inches* refers to a straight line 30 inches long. The term *30 square inches* refers to the area of a specific figure. When inches are multiplied by inches, the answer is in square inches. Likewise, when feet are multiplied by feet, the answer is in square feet.

Square feet are sometimes expressed by using the *exponent* [2]; for example, 10 ft.[2] is read 10 feet squared and means 10' × 10', or 100 square feet.

An exponent indicates how many times the number, or unit of measurement, is multiplied by itself. This is called the *power* of the number or unit of measure. The exponent is indicated at the upper right of the original number or unit of measurement (for example, 10^3 would equal $10 \times 10 \times 10$; 10^4, $10 \times 10 \times 10 \times 10$).

The area of the rectangle at the left, below, is 4' × 6', or 24 square feet. The area of the square at the right, below, is 5 yards × 5 yards, or 25 square yards.

E X A M P L E

Mr. Blair has leased a vacant lot that measures 60 feet by 160 feet. How much rent will he pay per year, if the lot rents for $.35 per square foot per year?

To solve this problem, the area of the lot must be computed first.

$$A = L \times W = 160' \times 60' = 9,600 \text{ sq. ft.}$$

The number of square feet is then multiplied by the price per square foot to get the total rent.

$$9,600 \times \$.35 = \$3,360$$

Front Foot Versus Area

In certain situations, a tract of land may be priced at $X per *front foot*. Typically, this occurs where the land faces something desirable, such as a main street, a river, or a lake, thus making the frontage the major element of value.

For example, consider the following tract of land facing (fronting on) a lake.

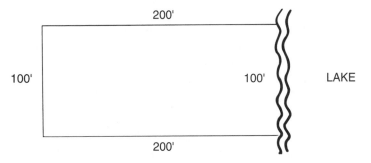

The area of the lot is 20,000 square feet (100' × 200'). If this lot sells for $100,000, its price could be shown as $5 per square foot ($100,000 ÷ 20,000 square feet) or $1,000 per front foot ($100,000 ÷ 100 front feet).

Conversions—Using Like Measures for Area

When area is computed, all dimensions used must be given in the *same kind of unit*. When a formula is used to find an area, units of the same kind must be used for each element of the formula, with the answer as square units of that kind. So inches must be multiplied by inches to arrive at square inches, feet must be multiplied by feet to arrive at square feet, and yards must be multiplied by yards to arrive at square yards.

If the two dimensions to be multiplied are in different units of measure, one of the units of measure must be converted to the other. The following chart shows how to convert one unit of measure to another.

12 inches = 1 foot	
36 inches = 1 yard	
3 feet = 1 yard	
To convert feet to inches, *multiply the number of feet by 12.*	(*ft.* × 12 = in.)
To convert inches to feet, *divide the number of inches by 12.*	(*in.* ÷ 12 = ft.)
To convert yards to feet, *multiply the number of yards by 3.*	(*yd.* × 3 = ft.)
To convert *feet* to *yards,* *divide the number of feet by 3.*	(*ft.* ÷ 3 = yd.)
To convert *yards* to *inches,* *multiply the number of yards by 36.*	(*yd.* × 36 = in.)
To convert *inches* to *yards,* *divide the number of inches by 36.*	(*in.* ÷ 36 = yd.)

EXERCISE 15.3

Solve the following problems:

1. 12″ × 3′= _____3_____ square feet or ____432____ square inches

2. 15″ × 1.5′ = __1.875__ square feet or ____270____ square inches

3. 72″ × 7′ = ____42____ square feet or __6048__ square inches

4. What is the area of the square below in square inches?

1'

144

5. 1,512 square inches = __10.5__ square feet.

144 sq inch per foot

6. Mr. Johnson's house is on a lot that is 75 feet by 125 feet. What is the area of his lot?

9375

Check your answers against those in the Answer Key at the back of the book.

To convert square inches, square feet, and square yards, use the following chart

To convert square feet to square inches, *multiply the number of square feet by 144.*	*(sq. ft. × 144 = sq. in.)*
To convert square inches to square feet, *divide the number of square inches by 144.*	*(sq. in. ÷ 144 = sq. ft.)*
To convert square yards to square feet, *multiply the number of square yards by 9.*	*(sq. yd. × 9 = sq. ft.)*
To convert square feet to square yards, *divide the number of square feet by 9.*	*(sq. ft. ÷ 9 = sq. yd.)*
To convert square yards to square inches, *multiply the number of square yards by 1,296.*	*(sq. yd. × 1,296 = sq. in.)*
To convert square inches to square yards, *divide the number of square inches by 1,296.*	*(sq. in. ÷ 1,296 = sq. yd.)*

Area of Triangles

A triangle *is a closed figure with three straight sides and three angles. Tri* means *three.*

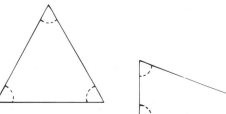

The 4-square-inch figure at the left, next page, has been cut in half by a straight line drawn between its opposite corners to make two equal triangles.

When one of the triangles is placed on a square-inch grid, it is seen to contain ½ sq. in. + ½ sq. in. + 1 sq. in., or 2 sq. in.

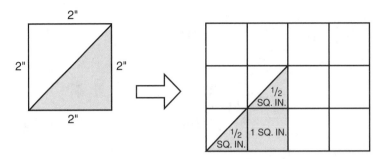

The area of the triangle below is 4.5 sq. ft.

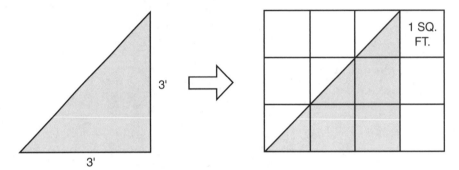

The square-unit grid is too cumbersome for computing large areas. It is more convenient to use the formula for finding the area of a triangle.

> Area of triangle A = ½ (Base × Height)
>
> ½ (BH)

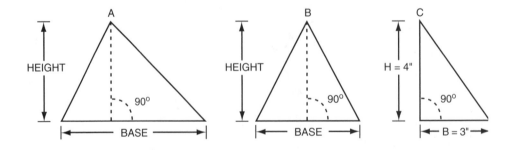

The *base* is the side on which the triangle sits. The *height* is the straight line distance from the tip of the uppermost angle to the base. The height line must form a 90-degree angle to the base. The area of triangle C above is:

$$A = ½(BH) = ½(3" × 4") = ½(12 \text{ sq. in.}) = 6 \text{ sq. in.}$$

EXERCISE 15.4

The diagram below shows a lakefront lot. Compute its area.

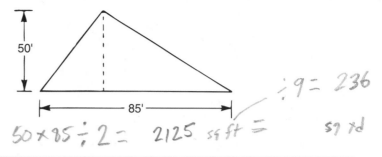

$$50 \times 85 \div 2 = 2125 \text{ sq ft} = \qquad \div 9 = 236 \quad sq\,yd$$

Check your answer against the one in the Answer Key at the back of the book.

Area of Irregular Closed Figures

Here is a drawing of two neighboring lots.

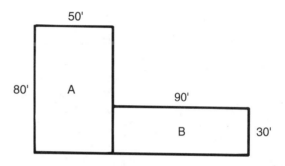

To find the total area of both lots:

lot A = 50' × 80' = 4,000 sq. ft.

lot B = 90' × 30' = 2,700 sq. ft.

both lots = 4,000 sq. ft. + 2,700 sq. ft. = 6,700 sq. ft.

Two rectangles can be made by drawing one straight line inside Figure 1 below. There are two possible positions for the added line, as shown in Figures 2 and 3.

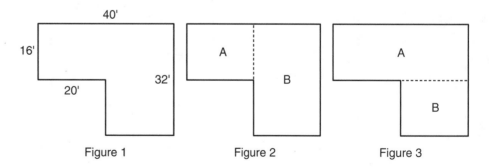

Figure 1   Figure 2   Figure 3

Using the measurements given in Figure 1, the total area of the figure may be computed in one of two ways:

area of A = 20' × 16' = 320 sq. ft.

area of B = 32' × (40' − 20') = 32' × 20' = 640 sq. ft.

total area = 320 sq. ft. + 640 sq. ft. = 960 sq. ft.

or:

area of A = 40' × 16' = 640 sq. ft.

area of B = (40' − 20') × (32' − 16') = 20' × 16' = 320 sq. ft.

total area = 640 sq. ft. + 320 sq. ft. = 960 sq. ft.

The area of an irregular figure can be found by dividing it into regular figures, computing the area of each, and adding all of the areas together to obtain the total area.

EXERCISE 15.5

1. This figure has been divided into rectangles, as shown by the broken lines. Compute the area of the figure.

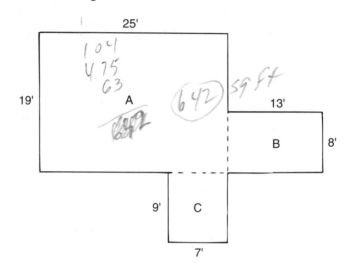

2. Make a rectangle and a triangle by drawing a single line through the figure below, then compute the area of the figure.

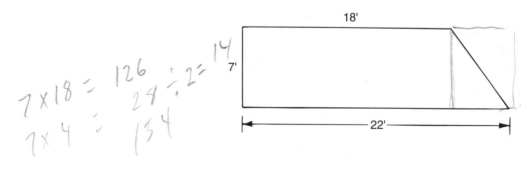

3. Compute the area of each section of the figure below. Then, compute the total area.

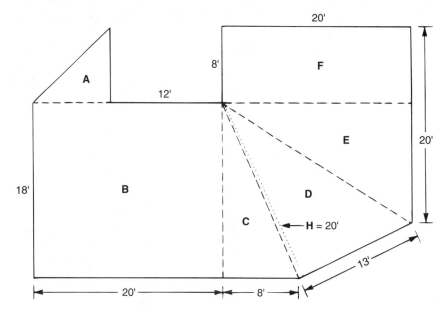

Check your answers against those in the Answer Key at the back of the book.

Living Area Calculations

Real estate appraisers frequently must compute the amount of living area in a house.

The living area of a house is the area enclosed by the outside dimensions of the heated and air-conditioned portions of the house. This excludes open porches, garages, and such.

When measuring a house in preparation for calculating the living area, these steps should be followed:

1. Draw a sketch of the foundation.

2. Measure *all* outside walls.

3. If the house has an attached garage, treat the inside garage walls that are common to the house as outside walls of the house.

4. Measure the garage.

5. Convert inches to tenths of a foot (so that the same units of measurement are used in the calculations).

6. Before leaving the house, check to see that net dimensions of opposite sides are equal. If not, remeasure.

7. Section off your sketch into rectangles.

8. Calculate the area of each rectangle.

9. Add up the areas, being careful to *subtract* the area of the garage, *if necessary*.

10. Before leaving the house, *always* recheck the dimensions.

EXERCISE 15.6 What is the living area of the house shown in the sketch below? Follow the steps above and remember to compute each area separately.

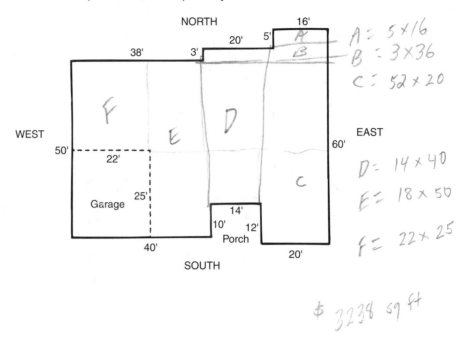

A = 5×16
B = 3×36
C = 52×20

D = 14×40
E = 18×50
F = 22×25

$ 3238 sq ft

Check your answer against the one in the Answer Key at the back of the book.

Volume

When a shape has more than one side and encloses a space, the shape has *volume,* defined as the space that a three-dimensional object occupies.

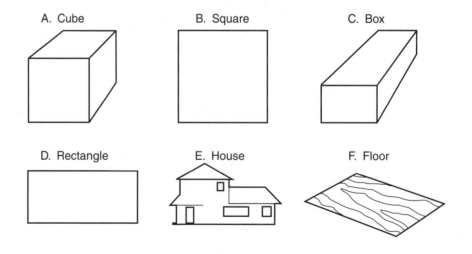

Of the above shapes, A, C, and E have volume; B, D, and F have area only.

Flat shapes—squares, rectangles, triangles, and so on—do not have *volume*. Flat shapes have two dimensions (length and width *or* height), and shapes with volume have three dimensions (length, width, *and* height).

Technically speaking, each shape with three dimensions can also be measured in terms of its surface area. For example, a bedroom has volume because it has three dimensions—length, width, and height; however, *one wall* can be measured as *surface area,* or area = length × width.

Cubic Units

A *cube* is made up of six squares. Look at the six sides of the following cube.

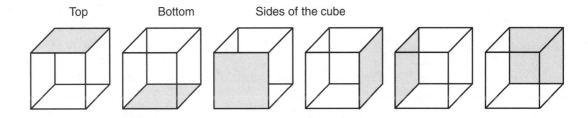

Volume is measured in *cubic* units. Each side of the cube below measures one inch, so the figure is *one cubic inch,* or *1 cu. in.*

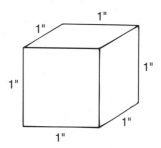

There are four cubic feet in the figure below. The exponent³ may also be used to express cubic feet; that is, 1 ft.³ is one cubic foot.

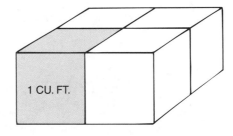

Using the formula for computing volume,

Volume of box A = *L* × *W* × *H* = 6"× 3" × 9" = 162 cu. in.

Volume of box B = *L* × *W* × *H* = 9' × 6' × 3' = 162 cu. ft.

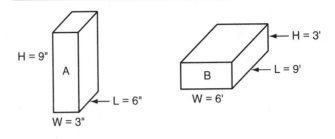

$$V \text{ (volume)} = L \text{ (length)} \times W \text{ (width)} \times H \text{ (height)}$$

E X A M P L E

A building's construction cost was $450,000. The building is 60 feet long, 45 feet wide, and 40 feet high, including the basement. What was the cost of this building per cubic foot?

$$V = L \times W \times H = 60' \times 45' \times 40' = 108{,}000 \text{ cu. ft.}$$

$$\text{Cost per cubic foot} = \frac{\text{Total cost}}{\text{Volume}} = \frac{\$450{,}000}{108{,}000 \text{ cu. ft.}} = \$4.166$$

The cost per cubic foot of this building is $4.17 (rounded).

Conversions—Using Like Measures for Volume

To convert cubic inches, cubic feet, and cubic yards, use the chart below.

To convert cubic feet to cubic inches, *multiply the number of cubic feet by 1,728.*	*(cu. ft. × 1,728 = cu. in.)*
To convert cubic inches to cubic feet, *divide the number of cubic inches by 1,728.*	*(cu. in. ÷ 1,728 = cu. ft.)*
To convert cubic yards to cubic feet, *multiply the number of cubic yards by 27.*	*(cu. yd. × 27 = cu. ft.)*
To convert cubic feet to cubic yards, *divide the number of cubic feet by 27.*	*(cu. ft. ÷ 27 = cu. yd.)*
To convert cubic yards to cubic inches, *multiply the number of cubic yards by 46,656.*	*(cu. yd. × 46,656 = cu. in.)*
To convert cubic inches to cubic yards, *divide the number of cubic inches by 46,656.*	*(cu. in. ÷ 46,656 = cu. yd.)*

E X A M P L E

How many cubic yards of space are there in a flat-roofed house that is 30 feet long, 18 feet wide, and 10 feet high?

$$V = L \times W \times H = 30' \times 18' \times 10' = 5{,}400 \text{ cu. ft.}$$
$$\text{cu. yd.} = \text{cu. ft.} \div 27 = 5{,}400 \text{ cu. ft.} \div 27 = 200 \text{ cu. yd.}$$

Volume of Triangular Prisms

To compute the volume of a three-dimensional triangular figure, called a *prism* (e.g., an A-frame house), use the following formula:

$$\text{Volume} = \frac{1}{2}\,(B \times H \times W)$$

To compute the volume of the following house, first divide the house into two shapes, S and T.

Find the volume of S.

$$V = \frac{1}{2}\,(B \times H \times W) = \frac{1}{2} \times (22' \times 8' \times 35') =$$
$$\frac{1}{2}\,(6,160 \text{ cu. ft.}) = 3,080 \text{ cu. ft.}$$

Find the volume of T.

$$V = 22' \times 35' \times 10' = 7,700 \text{ cu. ft.}$$

Total volumes S and T.

$$3,080 \text{ cu. ft.} + 7,700 \text{ cu ft.} = 10,780 \text{ cu. ft.}$$

EXERCISE 15.7

Complete the following problems.

1. 8' × 7' = _____ sq. ft. = _____ sq. in. = _____ sq. yd.

   9' × 3' × 2' = _____ cu. ft. = _____ cu. in. = _____ cu. yd.

2. Find the total ground area covered by a building with the perimeter measurements shown below.

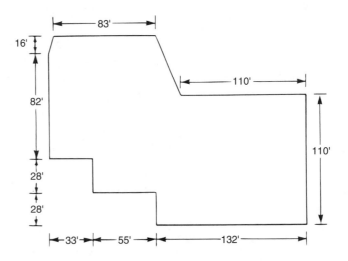

3. The building on the next page has a construction cost of $45 per cubic yard. What is the total cost of this building?

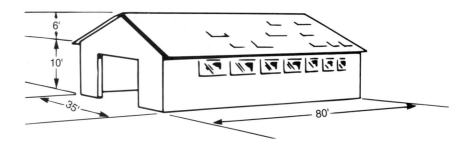

Check your answers against those in the Answer Key at the back of the book.

■ STATISTICS

Statistics is the science of collecting, classifying, and interpreting information based on the number of things. Economists often make use of statistics to support theories and conclusions. Appraisers, too, can use statistics to support the assumptions that allow an estimate of value. Some of the commonly used statistical terms are defined in the following paragraphs.

Population and Sample

In the language of statistics, a *variate* is a single item in a group. One single-family home is a variate. All variates in a group make up a *population*. For example, in Pittsburgh, Pennsylvania, the population of single-family homes consists of all the single-family homes in that city.

Appraisers are rarely, if ever, able to deal with the total population. It may be too expensive or too time-consuming to gather the details on all the population. The appraiser must, therefore, rely on a *sample* of the population. A sample is defined as some of the population or some of the variates in that population.

A single number or attribute, called a *parameter,* can be used to describe an entire group or population of variates. For example, all the house sales in a community in a given year can be described by the total dollar amount of all the sales. The total, or sum, of all variates is called an *aggregate*.

Organization of Numerical Data

To facilitate interpretation and analysis, statistical data must be arranged or grouped in an orderly way. There are two principal methods of arranging numerical data. In one method each of the various values or variates is presented in order of size. This arrangement is called an *array*.

In the second method of arranging numerical data, called a *frequency distribution,* the values are grouped to show the frequency with which each size or class occurs.

The dollar amounts $100,000, $102,000, $150,000, $175,000, $150,000, $165,000, $150,000, $100,000, and $150,000, which represent home sales in a neighborhood,

FIGURE 15.3 An Array	House Sales
	$175,000
	165,000
	150,000
	150,000
	150,000
	150,000
	102,000
	100,000
	100,000
Number of sales	9

have less meaning when presented in this unorganized manner than when presented in an array (Figure 15.3) or in a frequency distribution (Figure 15.4).

Measures of Central Tendency

In analyzing data the first task is to describe the information in precise terms of measurement. Basic concepts of measurement used in statistics include *measures of central tendency.* A measure of central tendency describes the typical variate in a population. For example, the *typical sales price* for a single-family home and the *typical rent* for a square foot of office space are measures of central tendency.

Three common statistical measures are the *mean,* the *median,* and the *mode.* All three measure central tendency and are used to identify the typical variate in a population or sample.

Mean
The *mean* is the average; that is, the sum of the variates divided by the number of variates. For example, in Figure 15.3, the mean price of the houses sold is $1,242,000 divided by 9, or $138,000.

Median
The *median* is found by dividing the number of variates into two equal groups. If the number of variates is odd, the median is the single variate at the middle. If the number of variates is even, the median is the arithmetic mean of the two variates closest to the middle from each end. In Figure 15.3, the median home price is $150,000.

Mode
The *mode* is the most frequently occurring variate. In Figure 15.4, the mode is $150,000.

Selecting a Measure of Central Tendency
Before an appraiser selects one measure of central tendency, he or she should consider the following:

■ The arithmetic mean is the most familiar measure of central tendency and can be conveyed to a client quickly and easily.

FIGURE 15.4
Frequency Distribution

Sales	Frequency
$175,000	1
165,000	1
150,000	4
102,000	1
100,000	2
Number of sales	9

- The arithmetic mean is affected by extreme values and might not represent any of the variates in a population. For example, the arithmetic mean of 5, 10, 15, 20, and 500 is 110.

- The median is not affected by extreme variates as is the arithmetic mean. For example, the median in the above item is 15. So, in samples of population where the variances are great, the median is a much better indicator than the average, or mean.

- The mode might represent an actual situation. For example, the population of apartments per building might have an arithmetic mean of 11.25, a median of 12.5, and a mode of 12. It is more realistic to discuss 12 units per building as opposed to 11.25 or 12.5. The mode, therefore, is most useful when a number of units have the same value.

Measures of Dispersion

Obtaining representative values other than measures of central tendency is often desirable. *Measures of dispersion* may be computed to measure the spread of the data; that is, to determine whether variates are grouped closely about the mean or median or are widely scattered or dispersed. Three common measures of dispersion are the *range*, the *average deviation,* and the *standard deviation*.

Range

The *range* is a measure of the difference between the highest and lowest variates. The range of prices in Figure 15.3 is $175,000 minus $100,000, or $75,000.

Average Deviation

The *deviation* is the measure of how widely the individual variates in a population vary. The *average deviation* measures how far the average variate differs from the mean. The formula for the average deviation finds the mean of the sum of the absolute differences (plus and minus signs are ignored) of each of the variates from the mean of the variates. The average deviation is also called the average *absolute* deviation because absolute differences are used, making all the values positive.

In Figure 15.5, the average deviation is 5.78 (52 ÷ 9). This means that, on the average, the test scores deviated from the mean by 5.78 points.

Standard Deviation

The *standard deviation* measures the differences between individual variates and the entire population by taking the square root of the sum of the squared differences between each variate and the mean of all the variates in the population, divided by the number of variates in the population. In Figure 15.5, the

FIGURE 15.5
Average Deviation and Standard Deviation

Scores on Real Estate Test	Deviations from Mean	Squares of Deviation
94	12	144
91	9	81
85	3	9
84	2	4
82	0	0
78	− 4	16
77	− 5	25
75	− 7	49
72	−10	100
Total 738	52	428

Mean = 82 (738 ÷ 9)

Median = 82

Mode   In the illustrated population of test scores there is no mode.

Range = 22

Average Deviation = 5.78 (52 ÷ 9)

Standard Deviation = 6.90 ($\sqrt{}$ of 428 ÷ 9)

standard deviation is 6.90 (428 ÷ 9 = 47.56; the square root of 47.56 is 6.896, rounded to 6.90).

Note: The formula for computing the standard deviation in this example holds true only when the entire population is considered. If a sample of a population is used, as is typically the case in real estate appraising, the sum of the squared differences from the mean is divided by the number of variates in the sample minus one. One is subtracted from the number of variates in a sample to adjust for the one degree of freedom that is lost when the mean is computed.

Regression Analysis—An Old Technique with a New Use

In the past few years, advances in personal computer technology have brought about a profound revolution in the way appraisals are performed. The availability of ever cheaper and more powerful personal computers has elevated an old theoretical valuation technique to the cutting edge of appraisal technology—one that is within the means of even the smallest appraisal office. This technique is called *multiple linear regression analysis.*

Regression analysis makes use of basic principles of statistics, some of which are discussed in this chapter, to analyze comparable sales and determine line-item adjustments. A single regression analysis can consist of millions of individual calculations. Until a few years ago, the rigorous computations required to make use of this technique made it impractical for most fee appraising. Such calculations were simply not feasible, given the limited capability of even the state-of-the-art personal computers of ten years ago. With today's equipment and software, however, they are a relatively trivial matter. Software with built-in regression analysis can enter recommended adjustment values automatically as the appraiser completes the URAR form. The result is not only to make the appraisal process more efficient but also to give the appraiser's value conclusions a high degree of accuracy, even in difficult rural markets where good comparable sales data can be hard to find.

With the aid of regression analysis, appraisers can make subtle predictions about the market that would be impossible otherwise. Perhaps more important is the level of accuracy possible because the technique provides detailed statistical justification for the values derived.

A thorough treatment of the use of regression analysis in appraising is beyond the scope of this text, but books, courses, and other materials explaining how to use this technique are available.

■ SUMMARY

Many mathematical concepts are involved in the study of appraisal, ranging from simple arithmetic to sophisticated statistical techniques.

The use of tables can help the investor or appraiser determine what is necessary to achieve a stated financial goal.

Knowing the terminology of statistics can help the appraiser understand the significance of the data collected and how they affect property value. Proponents of the statistical approach claim that it offers an objective method of analysis, and that any appraiser can master the technique by taking a course in elementary statistics.

ACHIEVEMENT EXAMINATION

1. A property has an assessed value of $45,000. If the assessment is 36 percent of market value, what is the market value?

   45K ÷ .36 = 125 K
   50K ÷ .06 = 8⃠3⃠3⃠3⃠3⃠3⃠8⃠ 833,333

2. A property valued at $200,000 produces a net operating income of $24,000 per year. What percentage of value (rate) does this property earn?

   24K ÷ 200K = 12 %

3. Find the total area of the figure below.

450

A   375.0

B   3575
        550

C

$ 4,500
 ÷ 9 =
     800

5q yd = 9

100 - 65 = 35 - 15 = 20

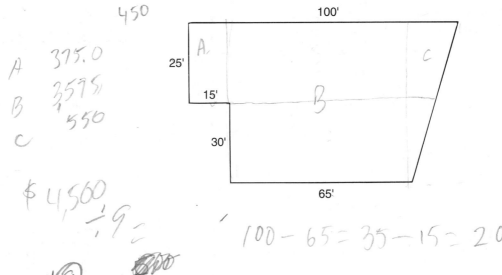

4. The house below would cost $2.75 per cubic foot to build. What would be the total cost, at that price?

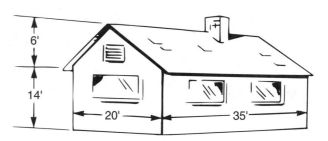

5. What is the total area of the figure below in square feet?

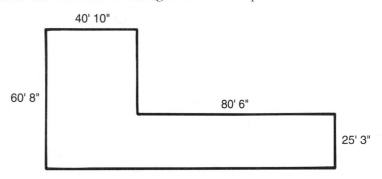

6. What is the living area of the house shown in the sketch below?

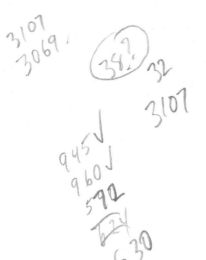

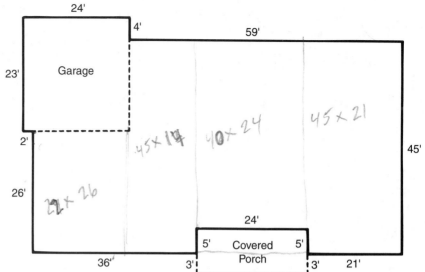

7. The average of all variates is the
   a. mean.
   c. median.
   b. mode.
   d. range.

8. The center of all variates is the
   a. mean.
   c. median.
   b. mode.
   d. range.

9. The difference between the highest and lowest variates is the
   a. mean.
   c. median.
   b. mode.
   d. range.

10. The mean of five house sales prices of $100,000, $75,000, $175,000, $200,000, and $150,000 is
    a. $140,000.
    c. $700,000.
    b. $150,000.
    d. $175,000.

11. The median of the house sales prices in question 10 is
    a. $140,000.
    c. $700,000.
    b. $150,000.
    d. $175,000.

12. The aggregate of the house sales prices in question 10 is
    a. $140,000.
    c. $700,000.
    b. $150,000.
    d. $175,000

13. Using Figure 15.1, calculate the value in five years of an investment of $7,500 at 10 percent interest compounded daily.
    a. $20,387
    c. $12,340
    b. $12,365
    d. $12,290

14. To determine the value in eight years of an investment of $10,000 at 10 percent interest compounded annually, the applicable factor is
    a. 2.143589.
    b. 2.357948.
    c. 1.948717.
    d. 2.182875.

15. Using Figure 15.2, calculate the monthly payment required to amortize a loan of $270,000 at 9½ percent interest for a term of 40 years.
    a. $221.40
    b. $2,241
    c. $2,403
    d. $2,214

16. The factor used to find the monthly payment required to amortize a loan of $147,000 at 11 percent interest over 30 years is
    a. .0092.
    b. .0096.
    c. .0100.
    d. .0097.

Check your answers against those in the Answer Key at the back of the book.

State Real Estate Appraiser Licensing/ Certification Boards

Alabama Real Estate Appraiser Board
> P. O. Box 304355
> Montgomery, AL 36130-4355
> *www.reab.state.al.us/*

Alaska Board of Certified Real Estate Appraisers
> P. O. Box 110806
> Juneau, AK 99811-0806
> *www.dced.state.ak.us/occ/papr.htm*

Arizona Board of Appraisal
> 1400 West Washington, Ste. 360
> Phoenix, AZ 85007
> *www.appraisal.state.az.us/*

Arkansas Appraiser Licensing and Certification Board
> 2725 Cantrell Rd., Ste. 202
> Little Rock, AR 72202
> *www.state.ar.us/alcb/*

California Office of Real Estate Appraisers
> 1102 Q St., Ste. 4100
> Sacramento, CA 95814
> *www.orea.ca.gov/*

State of Colorado Board of Real Estate Appraisers
> 1900 Grant St., Ste. 600
> Denver, CO 80203
> *www.dora.state.co.us/real-estate/appraisr/appraisr.htm*

Connecticut Real Estate Appraisal Commission
   State Office Building, Room G-8A
   165 Capitol Ave.
   Hartford, CT 06106
   www.ct.gov/dcp/cwp/view.asp?a=1624&Q=276078&PM=1

Delaware Council on Real Estate Appraisers
   861 Silver Lake Blvd.
   Dover, DE 19904
   www.dpr.delaware.gov/boards/realestateappraisers/vto.shtml

District of Columbia DCRA/OPLA
   941 North Capitol St. NE, Room 7200
   Washington, DC 20002
   www.dcra.dc.gov

Florida Department of Business and Professional Regulation
   1940 North Monroe St.
   Tallahassee, FL 32399-0750
   www.state.fl.us/dbpr/re/index.shtml

Georgia Real Estate Appraisers Board
   International Tower
   229 Peachtree St. NE, Ste. 1000
   Atlanta, GA 30303-1605
   www.grec.state.ga.us/

Hawaii Real Estate Appraiser Program
   P. O. Box 3469
   Honolulu, HI 96801
   www.hawaii.gov/dcca/areas/pvl/programs/realestateappraiser/

Idaho Real Estate Appraiser Board
   Owyhee Plaza
   1109 Main St., Ste. 220
   Boise, ID 83702-5642
   https://www.ibol.idaho.gov/rea.htm

Illinois Real Estate Appraisal Division
   500 East Monroe St., Ste. 500
   Springfield, IL 62701-1509
   www.obre.state.il.us/realest/APPRAISAL.HTM

Indiana Professional Licensing Agency
   Attn: Real Estate Appraiser Licensure and Certification Board
   302 West Washington St.
   Indianapolis, IN 46204
   www.in.gov/pla/bandc/appraiser/

Iowa Real Estate Appraiser Examining Board
1920 S.E. Hulsizer Rd.
Ankeny, IA 50021-3941
www.state.ia.us/government/com/prof/realappr/realappr.htm

Kansas Real Estate Appraisal Board
1100 SW Wannamaker Rd., Ste. 104
Topeka, KS 66604
www.accesskansas.org/kreab

Kentucky Real Estate Appraisers Board
2480 Fortune Dr., Ste. 120
Lexington, KY 40509
www.kreab.ky.gov/

Louisiana Real Estate Appraisers Board
5222 Summa Court
Baton Rouge, LA 70809
www.lreasbc.state.la.us/

Maine Board of Real Estate Appraisers
#35 State House Station
Augusta, ME 04333-0035
www.state.me.us/pfr/olr/categories/cat37.htm

Maryland Commission of Real Estate Appraisers and Home Inspectors
500 North Calvert St.
Baltimore, MD 21202-3651
www.dllr.state.md.us/license/occprof/reappr.html

Commonwealth of Massachusetts
Board of Registration of Real Estate Appraisers
239 Causeway St., Ste. 500
Boston, MA 02114-2130
www.mass.gov/dpl/boards/ra/index.htm

Michigan State Board of Real Estate Appraisers
P. O. Box 30018
Lansing, MI 48909
www.michigan.gov/appraisers

Minnesota Department of Commerce
85-7th Place East, Ste. 60
St. Paul, MN 55101
www.state.mn.us/cgi-bin/portal/mn/jsp/home.do?agency=Commerce

Mississippi Real Estate Commission
P. O. Box 12685
Jackson, MS 39236-2685
www.mrec.state.ms.us/

Missouri Real Estate Appraisers Commission
P. O. Box 1335
Jefferson City, MO 65102-1335
www.pr.mo.gov/appraisers.asp/

Montana Board of Real Estate Appraisers
301 S. Park Ave., Ste. 400
P. O. Box 200513
Helena, MT 59620-0513
www.discoveringmontana.com/dli/bsd/
license/bsd_boards/rea_board/board_page.asp

Nebraska Real Estate Appraiser Board
P. O. Box 94963
Lincoln, NE 68509-4963
www.appraiser.ne.gov

Nevada Real Estate Division
788 Fairview Dr., Ste. 200
Carson City, NV 89701-5453
www.red.state.nv.us/

New Hampshire Real Estate Appraiser Board
State House Annex, Room 426
25 Capitol St.
Concord, NH 03301-6312
www.nh.gov/nhreab/

New Jersey Real Estate Appraiser Board
P. O. Box 45032
Newark, NJ 07101
www.state.nj.us/lps/ca/nonmedical/reappraisers.htm

New Mexico Real Estate Appraisers Board
2550 Cerrillos Rd.
Santa Fe, NM 87505
www.rld.state.nm.us/b&c/reappraisers/index.htm

New York Department of State
Division of Licensing Services
84 Holland Ave.
Albany, NY 12208-3490
www.dos.state.ny.us/lcns/appraise.htm

North Carolina Appraisal Board
P. O. Box 20500
Raleigh, NC 27619-0500
www.ncappraisalboard.org/

North Dakota Real Estate Appraiser
Qualifications and Ethics Board
P. O. Box 1336
Bismarck, ND 58502-1336
www.ext.nodak.edu/extpubs/agecon/market/ec752-4w.htm

Ohio Department of Commerce
Division of Real Estate & Professional Licensing
615 West Superior Ave., 12th Floor
Cleveland, OH 44113-1801
www.com.state.oh.us/real/appmain.htm

Oklahoma Insurance Department
Real Estate Appraiser Board Division
2401 NW 23rd St., Ste. 28
Oklahoma City, OK 73107
www.oid.state.ok.us/agentbrokers/realestate.html

Oregon Appraiser Certification and Licensure Board
1860 Hawthorne Ave. NE, Ste. 200
Salem, OR 97303
www.oregonaclb.org

Pennsylvania State Board of Certified Real Estate Appraisers
P. O. Box 2649
Harrisburg, PA 17105-2649
www.dos.state.pa.us/bpoa/cwp/view.asp?a=1104&q=432589

Division of Commercial Licensing & Regulation
Real Estate Appraisers Section
233 Richmond St.
Providence, RI 02903
www.dbr.state.ri.us/real_estate.html

South Carolina Real Estate Appraisers Board
P. O. Box 11847
Columbia, SC 29211-1847
www.llr.state.sc.us/POL/RealEstateAppraisers/
www.llr.state.sc.us/pol.asp

South Dakota Department of Revenue and Regulation
Appraiser Certification Program
445 East Capitol Ave.
Pierre, SD 57501-3185
www.state.sd.us/appraisers

Tennessee Real Estate Appraiser Commission
500 James Robertson Parkway, Ste. 620
Nashville, TN 37243-1166
www.state.tn.us/commerce/boards/treac

Texas Appraiser Licensing and Certification Board
P. O. Box 12188
Austin, TX 78711-2188
www.talcb.state.tx.us

Utah Division of Real Estate
P. O. Box 146711
Salt Lake City, UT 84114-6711
www.commerce.utah.gov/dre/applicensing.html

Vermont Board of Real Estate Appraisers
81 River St.
Montpelier, VT 05609-1106
http://vtprofessionals.org/opr1/appraisers/

Virginia Department of Professional and Occupational Regulation
Board for Real Estate Appraisers
3600 West Broad St., 5th Floor
Richmond, VA 23230-4817
www.dba.state.va.us/licenses/resources.asp?SECTION_ID=61

Washington Department of Licensing
Real Estate Appraisers Licensing Program
P. O. Box 9015
Olympia, WA 98507-9015
www.dol.wa.gov/app/appfront.htm

West Virginia Real Estate Appraiser
Licensing and Certification Board
2110 Kanawha Blvd. East, Ste. 101
Charleston, WV 25311
www.wvs.state.wv.us/appraise/

Wisconsin Department of Regulation and Licensing
Real Estate Appraisers Board
P. O. Box 8935
Madison, WI 53708-8935
http://drl.wi.gov/index.htm

Wyoming Certified Real Estate Appraiser Board
2020 Carey Ave., Ste. 100
Cheyenne, WY 82002-0180
http://realestate.state.wy.us/

Web Sites

Accredited Review Appraisers Council
http://arac.lincoln-grad.org

American Institute of Architects
www.aia.org

American Real Estate Society
www.aresnet.org

American Society of Appraisers
www.appraisers.org

American Society of Farm Managers and Rural Appraisers, Inc.
www.asfmra.org

American Society of Home Inspectors
www.ashi.org

Americans with Disabilities Act
www.ada.gov

Appraisal Foundation
www.appraisalfoundation.org

Appraisal Institute
www.appraisalinstitute.org

Appraisal Institute of Canada
www.aicanada.org

Appraisal Qualifications Board
www.appraisalfoundation.org/aqb.htm

Appraisal Standards Board
www.appraisalfoundation.org/asb.htm

Association of Appraiser Regulatory Officials
www.aaro.net

Building Owners and Managers Association International
www.boma.org

Bureau of Labor Statistics
stats.bls.gov

Bureau of Land Management
www.glorecords.blm.gov

Bureau of Transportation Statistics
www.bts.gov

Census Bureau
www.census.gov

A Citizen's Guide to Radon, Revised 2004 (EPA)
www.epa.gov/radon/pubs/citguide.html

Commercial Investment Real Estate Institute
www.ccim.com

Department of Energy
www.energy.gov

Department of Housing and Urban Development
www.hud.gov

Department of Housing and Urban Development: RESPA
www.hud.gov/offices/hsg/sfh/res/respamor.cfm

Department of Veteran Affairs
www.va.gov

Environmental Protection Agency
www.epa.gov

Fannie Mae
www.fanniemae.com
www.efanniemae.com

Fannie Mae Foundation
www.fanniemaefoundation.org

Federal Agricultural Mortgage Corporation (Farmer Mac)
www.farmermac.com

Federal Deposit Insurance Corporation
www.fdic.gov

Federal Emergency Management Agency
www.fema.com

Federal Housing Administration
www.hud.gov/offices/hsg/fhahistory.cfm

Federal Reserve Board
www.federalreserve.gov

Freddie Mac
www.freddiemac.com

Fedworld Information Network
www.fedworld.gov

Foundation of Real Estate Appraisers
www.frea.com

F.W. Dodge Corporation
www.fwdodge.com

Ginnie Mae
www.ginniemae.gov

Inman News Service
www.inman.com

The Inside Story: A Guide to Indoor Air Quality (EPA)
www.epa.gov/iaq/pubs/insidest.html

Internal Revenue Service Publications
www.irs.gov/formspubs/index.html

International Association of Assessing Officers
www.iaao.org

International Code Council
www.iccsafe.org

International Real Estate Directory
www.ired.com

International Right of Way Association
www.irwaonline.org

Manufactured Housing Institute
www.mgfhome.org

Municipal Code Corporation
www.municode.com

Marshall & Swift Publication Company
www.marshallswift.com

National Association of Home Builders
www.nahb.org

National Association of Home Builders Research Center, Inc.
www.nahbrc.com

National Association of Independent Fee Appraisers
www.naifa.com

National Association of Master Appraisers
www.masterappraisers.com

National Association of Real Estate Brokers
www.nareb.com

National Association of REALTORS®
www.realtor.com
www.realtor.org

National Lead Information Center
www.epa.gov/lead/nlic.htm

National Residential Appraisers Institute
www.nraiappraisers.com

National Safety Council's Environmental Health Center
www.nsc.org/ehc/lead.htm

Office of Federal Housing Enterprise Oversight
www.ofheo.gov

Real Estate Educators Association
www.reea.org

Realty Times
www.realtytimes.com

R. S. Means Company
www.rsmeans.com

State Appraisal Requirements

State	Prelicense Requirements	CE Requirements	Prelicense Distance	CE Distance
Alabama	75–180 hrs	28 hrs every 2 yrs	Yes	Yes
Alaska	75–180 hrs	28 hrs every 2 yrs	No	Yes
Arkansas	90–180 hrs	28 hrs every 2 yrs	No	Yes, for 7 hrs
Arizona	90–180 hrs	28 hrs every 4 yrs	No	No
California	90–180 hrs	56 hrs every 4 yrs	Yes*	Yes*
Colorado	75–180 hrs	42 hrs every 3 yrs	Yes	Yes
Connecticut	75–180 hrs	28 hrs every 2 yrs	Yes	Yes
Delaware	75–180 hrs	28 hrs every 2 yrs	Yes	Yes
District of Columbia	90–180 hrs	28 hrs, 7 must be USPAP	Yes	Yes
Florida	75–180 hrs	30 hrs per renewal period	No	Yes
Georgia	75–180 hrs	14 hrs every yr	Yes	Yes
Hawaii	90–180 hrs	20 hrs every 2 yrs	No	Yes
Idaho	75–180 hrs	15 hrs every yr	No	No
Illinois	75–180 hrs	28 hrs every 2 yrs	Yes	Yes
Indiana	90–180 hrs	28 hrs every 2 yrs	No	No
Iowa	120–180 hrs	28 hrs every 2 yrs	Yes	Yes
Kansas	90–180 hrs	42 hrs every 3 yrs	Yes*	Yes*
Kentucky	75–180 hrs	14 credits for each yr	No	Yes*
Louisiana	75–180 hrs	30 hrs every 2 yrs	Yes	Yes
Maine	75–180 hrs	28 hrs every 2 yrs	No	Yes
Maryland	75–180 hrs	42 hrs every 3 yrs	No	No
Massachusetts	45–180 hrs	45 hrs every 3 yrs	No	Yes
Michigan	75–180 hrs	28 or 14 hrs every 2 yrs	No	Yes
Minnesota	90–180 hrs	30 hrs every 2 yrs	No	No
Mississippi	75–180 hrs	20 hrs every 2 yrs	Yes	Yes
Missouri	90–180 hrs	28 hrs every 2 yrs	No	Yes
Montana	90–180 hrs	31 hrs every 2 yrs	No	Yes
Nebraska	90–180 hrs	28 hrs every 2 yrs	No	Yes
Nevada	75–180 hrs	30 hrs every 2 yrs	Yes	Yes*
New Hampshire	75–180 hrs	14 hrs/yr for 3 yrs	No	Yes

State	Prelicense Requirements	CE Requirements	Prelicense Distance	CE Distance
New Jersey	75–180 hrs	7 hrs USPAP every 2, yrs 28 hrs every 2 yrs	Yes	Yes
New Mexico	75–180 hrs	42 hrs every 3 yrs	No	Yes, for 14 hrs
New York	90–180 hrs	28 hrs every 2 yrs	No	Yes
North Carolina	90–180 hrs	28 hrs every 2 yrs	No	Yes, up to 7 hrs
North Dakota	15–180 hrs	42 hrs every 3 yrs	Yes, up to 40 hrs	N/A
Ohio	90–180 hrs (voluntary)	13 hrs every yr	No	No
Oklahoma	75–180 hrs	42 hrs every 3 yrs	No	Yes, for 21 hrs
Oregon	75–180 hrs	28 hrs every 2 yrs	Yes	Yes
Pennsylvania	120–180 hrs	28 hrs every 2 yrs	No	No
Rhode Island	75–180 hrs	28 hrs every 2 yrs	No	Yes
South Carolina	75–180 hrs	28 hrs every 2 yrs	No	No
South Dakota	75–180 hrs	28 hrs every 2 yrs	Yes	Yes
Tennessee	90–180 hrs	28 hrs every 2 yrs	No	Yes, for 7 hrs
Texas	90–180 hrs	28 hrs every 2 yrs	Yes	Yes
Utah	90–180 hrs	28 hrs every 2 yrs	Yes	Yes
Vermont	90–180 hrs	28 hrs every 2 yrs	Yes	Yes, for 14 hrs
Virginia	75–180 hrs	28 hrs every 2 yrs	Yes	Yes
Washington	90–180 hrs	14 hrs every yr	Yes	Yes, for 14 hrs
West Virginia	90–180 hrs	14 hrs every yr	No	No
Wisconsin	90–180 hrs	28 hrs every 2 yrs	Yes	Yes
Wyoming	90–180 hrs	45 hrs every 3 yrs	Yes	Yes

* With restrictions. Check your state board for details.

Note: **These requirements were last updated in 2005, and your state's requirements may have changed. Please contact your state appraisal board for the most up-to-date information.**

Uniform Standards of Professional Appraisal Practice

Uniform Standards of Professional Appraisal, 2005
USPAP is subject to ongoing critique and to additions and corrections. This appendix includes the 2005 version of USPAP; for the most recent version, please visit The Appraisal Foundation Web site at *www.appraisalfoundation.org.*

The Uniform Standards of Professional Appraisal Practice (USPAP) are copy-written and promulgated by the Appraisal Foundation. The standards include the following sections:

Introduction
    Preamble
    Ethics Provision
    Competency Provision
    Jurisdictional Exception
    Supplemental Standards
    Definitions
Standard 1
    Real Property Appraisal
Standard 2
    Real Property Appraisal, Reporting
Standard 3
    Real Property Appraisal and Reporting
Standard 4
    Real Estate/Real Property Consulting
Standard 5
    Real Estate/Real Property Consulting, Reporting
Standard 6
    Mass Appraisal and Reporting
Standard 7
    Personal Property Appraisal
Standard 8
    Personal Property Appraisal, Reporting
Standard 9
    Business Appraisal
Standard 10
    Business Appraisal, Reporting
Statements on Appraisal Standards

The introduction and standards 1 through 3 of USPAP appear in this appendix, reprinted with the permission of The Appraisal Foundation.

UNIFORM STANDARDS OF
PROFESSIONAL APPRAISAL PRACTICE
as promulgated by the
Appraisal Standards Board of
The Appraisal Foundation

PREAMBLE

The purpose of the *Uniform Standards of Professional Appraisal Practice* (USPAP) is to promote and maintain a high level of public trust in appraisal practice by establishing requirements for appraisers. It is essential that appraisers develop and communicate their analyses, opinions, and conclusions to intended users of their services in a manner that is meaningful and not misleading.

The Appraisal Standards Board promulgates USPAP for both appraisers and users of appraisal services. The appraiser's responsibility is to protect the overall public trust and it is the importance of the role of the appraiser that places ethical obligations on those who serve in this capacity. USPAP reflects the current standards of the appraisal profession.

USPAP does not establish who or which assignments must comply. Neither The Appraisal Foundation nor its Appraisal Standards Board is a government entity with the power to make, judge, or enforce law. Compliance with USPAP is required when either the service or the appraiser is obligated to comply by law or regulation, or by agreement with the client or intended users. When not obligated, individuals may still choose to comply.

USPAP addresses the ethical and performance obligations of appraisers through DEFINITIONS, Rules, Standards, Standard Rules, and Statements.

ETHICS RULE

To promote and preserve the public trust inherent in professional appraisal practice, an appraiser must observe the highest standards of professional ethics. This ETHICS RULE is divided into four sections: Conduct, Management, Confidentiality, and Record Keeping. The first three sections apply to all appraisal practice, and all four sections apply to appraisal practice performed under Standards 1 through 10.

> Comment: This Rule specifies the personal obligations and responsibilities of the individual appraiser. However, it should also be noted that groups and organizations engaged in appraisal practice share the same ethical obligations.

Compliance with USPAP is required when either the service or the appraiser is obligated by law or regulation, or by agreement with the client or intended users, to comply. In addition to these requirements, an individual should comply any time that individual represents that he or she is performing the service as an appraiser.

An appraiser must not misrepresent his or her role when providing valuation services that are outside of appraisal practice.

> Comment: Honesty, impartiality, and professional competency are required of all appraisers under these *Uniform Standards of Professional Appraisal Practice* (USPAP). To document recognition and acceptance of his or her USPAP-related responsibilities in communicating an appraisal, appraisal review, or appraisal consulting assignment completed under USPAP, an appraiser is required to certify compliance with USPAP. (See Standards Rules 2-3, 3-3, 5-3, 6-8, 8-3, and 10-3.)

Conduct (ETHICS RULE)

An appraiser must perform assignments ethically and competently, in accordance with USPAP and any supplemental standards agreed to by the appraiser in accepting the assignment. An appraiser must not engage in criminal conduct. An appraiser must perform assignments with impartiality, objectivity, and independence, and without accommodation of personal interests.

In appraisal practice, an appraiser must not perform as an advocate for any party or issue.

> Comment: An appraiser may be an advocate only in support of his or her assignment results. Advocacy in any other form in appraisal practice is a violation of the ETHICS RULE.

An appraiser must not accept an assignment that includes the reporting of predetermined opinions and conclusions.

An appraiser must not communicate assignment results in a misleading or fraudulent manner. An appraiser must not use or communicate a misleading or fraudulent report or knowingly permit an employee or other person to communicate a misleading or fraudulent report.

An appraiser must not use or rely on unsupported conclusions relating to characteristics such as race, color, religion, national origin, gender, marital status, familial status, age, receipt of public assistance income, handicap, or an unsupported conclusion that homogeneity of such characteristics is necessary to maximize value.

> Comment: An individual appraiser employed by a group or organization that conducts itself in a manner that does not conform to these Standards should take steps that are appropriate under the circumstances to ensure compliance with the Standards.

Management (ETHICS RULE)

The payment of undisclosed fees, commissions, or things of value in connection with the procurement of an assignment is unethical.

> Comment: Disclosure of fees, commissions, or things of value connected to the procurement of an assignment must appear in the certification and in any transmittal letter in which conclusions are stated. In groups or organizations engaged in appraisal practice, intra-company payments to employees for business development are not considered to be unethical. Competency, rather than financial incentives, should be the primary basis for awarding an assignment.

It is unethical for an appraiser to accept an assignment, or to have a compensation arrangement for an assignment, that is contingent on any of the following:

1. **the reporting of a predetermined result (e.g., opinion of value);**
2. **a direction in assignment results that favors the cause of the client;**
3. **the amount of a value opinion;**
4. **the attainment of a stipulated result; or**
5. **the occurrence of a subsequent event directly related to the appraiser's opinions and specific to the assignment's purpose.**

Advertising for or soliciting assignments in a manner that is false, misleading, or exaggerated is unethical.

> Comment: In groups or organizations engaged in appraisal practice, decisions concerning finder or referral fees, contingent compensation, and advertising may not be the responsibility of an individual appraiser, but for a particular assignment, it is the responsibility of the individual appraiser to ascertain that there has been no breach of ethics, that the assignment is prepared in accordance with these Standards, and that the report can be properly certified when required by Standards Rules 2-3, 3-3, 5-3, 6-8, 8-3, or 10-3.

Confidentiality (ETHICS RULE)

An appraiser must protect the confidential nature of the appraiser-client relationship.

An appraiser must act in good faith with regard to the legitimate interests of the client in the use of confidential information and in the communication of assignment results.

An appraiser must be aware of, and comply with, all confidentiality and privacy laws and regulations applicable in an assignment*.

An appraiser must not disclose confidential information or assignment results prepared for a client to anyone other than the client and persons specifically authorized by the client; state enforcement agencies and such third parties as may be authorized by due process of law; and a duly authorized professional peer review committee except when such disclosure to a committee would violate applicable law or regulation. It is unethical for a member of a duly authorized professional peer review committee to disclose confidential information presented to the committee.

> Comment: When all confidential elements of confidential information are removed through redaction or the process of aggregation, client authorization is not required for the disclosure of the remaining information, as modified.

*NOTICE: Pursuant to the passage of the Gramm-Leach-Bliley Act in 1999, numerous agencies have adopted new privacy regulations. Such regulations are focused on the protection of information provided by consumers to those involved in financial activities "found to be closely related to banking or usual in connection with the transaction of banking". These activities have been deemed to include "appraising real or personal property." (Quotations are from the Federal Trade Commission, Privacy of Consumer Financial Information; Final Rule, 16 CFR Part 313)

Record Keeping (ETHICS RULE)
An appraiser must prepare a workfile for each appraisal, appraisal review, or appraisal consulting assignment. The workfile must include:

- **the name of the client and the identity, by name or type, of any other intended users;**
- **true copies of any written reports, documented on any type of media;**
- **summaries of any oral reports or testimony, or a transcript of testimony, including the appraiser's signed and dated certification; and**
- **all other data, information, and documentation necessary to support the appraiser's opinions and conclusions and to show compliance with this Rule and all other applicable Standards, or references to the location(s) of such other documentation.**

An appraiser must retain the workfile for a period of at least five (5) years after preparation or at least two (2) years after final disposition of any judicial proceeding in which the appraiser provided testimony related to the assignment, whichever period expires last.

An appraiser must have custody of his or her workfile, or make appropriate workfile retention, access, and retrieval arrangements with the party having custody of the workfile.

> Comment: A workfile preserves evidence of the appraiser's consideration of all applicable data and statements required by USPAP and other information as may be required to support the appraiser's opinions, conclusions, and recommendations. For example, the content of a workfile for a Complete Appraisal must reflect consideration of all USPAP requirements applicable to the specific Complete Appraisal assignment. However, the content of a workfile for a Limited Appraisal need only reflect consideration of the USPAP requirements from which there have been no departure and that are required by the specific Limited Appraisal assignment.
>
> A photocopy or an electronic copy of the entire actual written appraisal, appraisal review, or appraisal consulting report sent or delivered to a client satisfies the requirement of a true copy. As an example, a photocopy or electronic copy of the Self-Contained Appraisal Report, Summary Appraisal Report, or Restricted Use Appraisal Report actually issued by an appraiser for a real property appraisal assignment satisfies the true copy requirement for that assignment.

Care should be exercised in the selection of the form, style, and type of medium for written records, which may be handwritten and informal, to ensure that they are retrievable by the appraiser throughout the prescribed record retention period.

A workfile must be in existence prior to and contemporaneous with the issuance of a written or oral report. A written summary of an oral report must be added to the workfile within a reasonable time after the issuance of the oral report.

A workfile must be made available by the appraiser when required by state enforcement agencies or due process of law. In addition, a workfile in support of a Restricted Use Appraisal Report must be sufficient for the appraiser to produce a Summary Appraisal Report (for assignments under STANDARDS 2 and 8) or an Appraisal Report (for assignments under STANDARD 10), and must be available for inspection by the client in accordance with the Comment to Standards Rules 2-2(c)(ix), 8-2(c)(ix), and 10-2(b)(ix).

COMPETENCY RULE

Prior to accepting an assignment or entering into an agreement to perform any assignment, an appraiser must properly identify the problem to be addressed and have the knowledge and experience to complete the assignment competently; or alternatively, must:

1. **disclose the lack of knowledge and/or experience to the client before accepting the assignment;**
2. **take all steps necessary or appropriate to complete the assignment competently; and**
3. **describe the lack of knowledge and/or experience and the steps taken to complete the assignment competently in the report.**

   Comment: Competency applies to factors such as, but not limited to, an appraiser's familiarity with a specific type of property, a market, a geographic area, or an analytical method. If such a factor is necessary for an appraiser to develop credible assignment results, the appraiser is responsible for having the competency to address that factor or for following the steps outlined above to satisfy this COMPETENCY RULE.

   The background and experience of appraisers varies widely, and a lack of knowledge or experience can lead to inaccurate or inappropriate appraisal practice. The COMPETENCY RULE requires an appraiser to have both the knowledge and the experience required to perform a specific appraisal service competently.

   If an appraiser is offered the opportunity to perform an appraisal service but lacks the necessary knowledge or experience to complete it competently, the appraiser must disclose his or her lack of knowledge or experience to the client before accepting the assignment and then take the necessary or appropriate steps to complete the appraisal service competently. This may be accomplished in various ways, including, but not limited to, personal study by the appraiser, association with an appraiser reasonably believed to have the necessary knowledge or experience, or retention of others who possess the required knowledge or experience.

   In an assignment where geographic competency is necessary, an appraiser preparing an appraisal in an unfamiliar location must spend sufficient time to understand the nuances of the local market and the supply and demand factors relating to the specific property type and the location involved. Such understanding will not be imparted solely from a consideration of specific data such as demographics, costs, sales, and rentals. The necessary understanding of local market conditions provides the bridge between a sale and a comparable sale or a rental and a comparable rental. If an appraiser is not in a position to spend the necessary amount of time in a market area to obtain this understanding, affiliation with a qualified local appraiser may be the appropriate response to ensure development of credible assignment results.

   Although this Rule requires an appraiser to identify the problem and disclose any deficiency in competence prior to accepting an assignment, facts or conditions uncovered during the course of an assignment could cause an appraiser to discover that he or she lacks the required knowledge or experience to complete the assignment competently. At the point of such discovery, the appraiser is obligated to notify the client and comply with items 2 and 3 of this Rule.

DEPARTURE RULE

This Rule permits exceptions from sections of the Uniform Standards that are classified as specific requirements rather than binding requirements. The burden of proof is on the appraiser to decide before accepting an assignment and invoking this Rule that the scope of work applied will result in opinions or conclusions that are credible. The burden of disclosure is also on the appraiser to report any departures from specific requirements.

An appraiser may enter into an agreement to perform an assignment in which the scope of work is less than, or different from, the work that would otherwise be required by the specific requirements, provided that prior to entering into such an agreement:

1. **the appraiser has determined that the appraisal process to be performed is not so limited that the results of the assignment are no longer credible;**
2. **the appraiser has advised the client that the assignment calls for something less than, or different from, the work required by the specific requirements and that the report will clearly identify and explain the departure(s); and**
3. **the client has agreed that the performance of a limited appraisal service would be appropriate, given the intended use.**
   <u>Comment</u>: Not all specific requirements are *applicable* to every assignment. When a specific requirement is *not applicable* to a given assignment, the specific requirement is irrelevant and therefore no departure is needed.

A specific requirement is *applicable* when:

- it addresses factors or conditions that are present in the given assignment, or
- it addresses analysis that is typical practice in such an assignment.

A specific requirement is *not applicable* when:

- it addresses factors or conditions that are not present in the given assignment,
- it addresses analysis that is not typical practice in such an assignment, or
- it addresses analysis that would not provide meaningful results in the given assignment.

Of those specific requirements that are *applicable* to a given assignment, some may be *necessary* in order to result in opinions or conclusions that are credible. When a specific requirement is *necessary* to a given assignment, departure is not permitted.

Departure is permitted from those specific requirements that are *applicable* to a given assignment but *not necessary* in order to result in opinions or conclusions that are credible.

A specific requirement is considered to be both *applicable* and *necessary* when:

- it addresses factors or conditions that are present in the given assignment, or
- it addresses analysis that is typical practice in such an assignment, and
- lack of consideration for those factors, conditions, or analyses would significantly affect the credibility of the results.

Typical practice for a given assignment is measured by:
- the expectations of the participants in the market for appraisal services, and
- what an appraiser's peers' actions would be in performing the same or a similar assignment.

If an appraiser enters into an agreement to perform an appraisal service that calls for something less than, or different from, the work that would otherwise be required by the specific requirements, Standards Rules 2-2(a)(xi), 2-2(b)(xi), 2-2(c)(xi), 6-7(p), 8-2(a)(xi), 8-2(b)(xi), 8-2(c)(xi), 10-2(a)(x), and 10-2(b)(x) require that the report clearly identify and explain departure(s) from the specific requirements.

Departure from the following development and reporting Rules is not permitted: Standards Rules 1-1, 1-2, 1-5, 1-6, 2-1, 2-2, 2-3, 3-1, 3-2, 3-3, 4-1, 4-2, 5-1, 5-2, 5-3, 6-1, 6-3, 6-6, 6-7, 6-8, 7-1, 7-2, 7-5, 7-6, 8-1, 8 2, 8 3, 9-1, 9-2, 9-3, 9-5, 10-1, 10-2, and 10-3. This restriction on departure is reiterated throughout the document with the reminder: "This Standards Rule contains binding requirements from which departure is not permitted."

The DEPARTURE RULE does not apply to the DEFINITIONS, PREAMBLE, ETHICS RULE, COMPETENCY RULE, JURISDICTIONAL EXCEPTION RULE or SUPPLEMENTAL STANDARDS RULE.

JURISDICTIONAL EXCEPTION RULE

If any part of these Standards is contrary to the law or public policy of any jurisdiction, only that part shall be void and of no force or effect in that jurisdiction.

Comment: The purpose of the JURISDICTIONAL EXCEPTION RULE is strictly limited to providing a saving or severability clause intended to preserve the balance of USPAP if one or more of its parts are determined to be contrary to law or public policy of a jurisdiction. By logical extension, there can be no violation of USPAP by an appraiser disregarding, with proper disclosure, only the part or parts of USPAP that are void and of no force and effect in a particular assignment by operation of legal authority. It is misleading for an appraiser to disregard a part or parts of USPAP as void and of no force and effect in a particular assignment without identifying in the appraiser's report the part or parts disregarded and the legal authority justifying this action.

As used in the JURISDICTIONAL EXCEPTION RULE, law means a body of rules with binding legal force established by controlling governmental authority. This broad meaning includes, without limitation, the federal and state constitutions; legislative and court-made law; and administrative rules, regulations, and ordinances. Public policy refers to more or less well-defined moral and ethical standards of conduct, currently and generally accepted by the community as a whole, and recognized by the courts with the aid of statutes, judicial precedents, and other similar available evidence. Jurisdiction refers to the legal authority to legislate, apply, or interpret law in any form at the federal, state, and local levels of government.

SUPPLEMENTAL STANDARDS RULE

These Uniform Standards provide the common basis for all appraisal practice. Supplemental standards applicable to assignments prepared for specific purposes or property types may be issued (i.e., published) by government agencies, government sponsored enterprises, or other entities that establish public policy. An appraiser and client must ascertain whether any such published supplemental standards in addition to these Uniform Standards apply to the assignment being considered.

Comment: The purpose of the SUPPLEMENTAL STANDARDS RULE is to provide a reasonable means to augment USPAP with requirements that add to the requirements set forth by USPAP.

Supplemental standards cannot diminish the purpose, intent, or content of the requirements of USPAP.

Upon agreeing to perform an assignment that includes acceptable supplemental standards, an appraiser is obligated to competently satisfy those supplemental standards, as well as applicable USPAP requirements.

An appraiser who represents that an assignment is or will be completed in compliance with agreed-upon supplemental standards and who then knowingly fails to comply with those supplemental standards violates the ETHICS RULE, or who then inadvertently fails to comply with those supplemental standards violates the COMPETENCY RULE. (See the ETHICS RULE and the COMPETENCY RULE.)

DEFINITIONS

For the purpose of these Standards, the following definitions apply:

ADVOCACY: representing the cause or interest of another, even if that cause or interest does not necessarily coincide with one's own beliefs, opinions, conclusions, or recommendations.

APPRAISAL: (noun) the act or process of developing an opinion of value; an opinion of value. (adjective) of or pertaining to appraising and related functions such as appraisal practice or appraisal services.

> **Complete Appraisal**: the act or process of developing an opinion of value or an opinion of value developed without invoking the DEPARTURE RULE.

> **Limited Appraisal**: the act or process of developing an opinion of value or an opinion of value developed under and resulting from invoking the DEPARTURE RULE.

> Comment: An appraisal must be numerically expressed as a specific amount, as a range of numbers, or as a relationship (e.g., not more than, not less than) to a previous value opinion or numerical benchmark (e.g., assessed value, collateral value).

APPRAISAL CONSULTING: the act or process of developing an analysis, recommendation, or opinion to solve a problem, where an opinion of value is a component of the analysis leading to the assignment results.

> Comment: An appraisal consulting assignment involves an opinion of value but does not have an appraisal or an appraisal review as its primary purpose.

APPRAISAL PRACTICE: valuation services performed by an individual acting as an appraiser, including but not limited to appraisal, appraisal review, or appraisal consulting.

> Comment: *Appraisal practice* is provided only by appraisers, while *valuation services* are provided by a variety of professionals and others. The terms *appraisal, appraisal review,* and *appraisal consulting* are intentionally generic and are not mutually exclusive. For example, an opinion of value may be required as part of an appraisal review and is required as a component of the analysis in an appraisal consulting assignment. The use of other nomenclature for an appraisal, appraisal review, or appraisal consulting assignment (e.g., analysis, counseling, evaluation, study, submission, or valuation) does not exempt an appraiser from adherence to the *Uniform Standards of Professional Appraisal Practice.*

APPRAISAL REVIEW: the act or process of developing and communicating an opinion about the quality of another appraiser's work that was performed as part of an appraisal, appraisal review, or appraisal consulting assignment.

> Comment: The subject of an appraisal review assignment may be all or part of a report, workfile, or a combination of these.

APPRAISER: one who is expected to perform valuation services competently and in a manner that is independent, impartial, and objective.

> Comment: Such expectation occurs when individuals, either by choice or by requirement placed upon them or upon the service they provide by law, regulation, or agreement with the client or intended users, represent that they comply. (See PREAMBLE.)

APPRAISER'S PEERS: other appraisers who have expertise and competency in the same or a similar type of assignment.

ASSIGNMENT: a valuation service provided as a consequence of an agreement between an appraiser and a client.

ASSIGNMENT RESULTS: an appraiser's opinions and conclusions developed specific to an assignment.

> Comment: Assignment results include an appraiser's:
> - opinions or conclusions developed in an appraisal assignment, such as value;
> - opinions of adequacy, relevancy, or reasonableness developed in an appraisal review assignment; or
> - opinions, conclusions, or recommendations developed in an appraisal consulting assignment.

ASSUMPTION: that which is taken to be true.

BIAS: a preference or inclination that precludes an appraiser's impartiality, independence, or objectivity in an assignment.

BINDING REQUIREMENTS: all or part of a Standards Rule of USPAP from which departure is not permitted. (See DEPARTURE RULE.)

BUSINESS ENTERPRISE: an entity pursuing an economic activity.

BUSINESS EQUITY: the interests, benefits, and rights inherent in the ownership of a business enterprise or a part thereof in any form (including, but not necessarily limited to, capital stock, partnership interests, cooperatives, sole proprietorships, options, and warrants).

CLIENT: the party or parties who engage an appraiser (by employment or contract) in a specific assignment.

> Comment: The client identified by the appraiser in an appraisal, appraisal review, or appraisal consulting assignment (or in the assignment workfile) is the party or parties with whom the appraiser has an appraiser-client relationship in the related assignment, and may be an individual, group, or entity.

CONFIDENTIAL INFORMATION: information that is either:
- identified by the client as confidential when providing it to an appraiser and that is not available from any other source; or
- classified as confidential or private by applicable law or regulation*.

*NOTICE: For example, pursuant to the passage of the Gramm-Leach-Bliley Act in November 1999, some public agencies have adopted privacy regulations that affect appraisers. As a result, the Federal Trade Commission issued a rule focused on the protection of "non-public personal information" provided by consumers to those involved in financial activities "found to be closely related to banking or usual in connection with the transaction of banking." These activities have been deemed to include "appraising real or personal property." (Quotations are from the Federal Trade Commission, Privacy of Consumer Financial Information; Final Rule, 16 CFR Part 313.)

COST: the amount required to create, produce, or obtain a property.

> Comment: *Cost* is either a fact or an estimate of fact.

EXTRAORDINARY ASSUMPTION: an assumption, directly related to a specific assignment, which, if found to be false, could alter the appraiser's opinions or conclusions.

> Comment: Extraordinary assumptions presume as fact otherwise uncertain information about physical, legal, or economic characteristics of the subject property; or about conditions external to the property, such as market conditions or trends; or about the integrity of data used in an analysis.

FEASIBILITY ANALYSIS: a study of the cost-benefit relationship of an economic endeavor.

HYPOTHETICAL CONDITION: that which is contrary to what exists but is supposed for the purpose of analysis.

> Comment: Hypothetical conditions assume conditions contrary to known facts about physical, legal, or economic characteristics of the subject property; or about conditions external to the property, such as market conditions or trends; or about the integrity of data used in an analysis.

INTANGIBLE PROPERTY (INTANGIBLE ASSETS): nonphysical assets, including but not limited to franchises, trademarks, patents, copyrights, goodwill, equities, securities, and contracts as distinguished from physical assets such as facilities and equipment.

INTENDED USE: the use or uses of an appraiser's reported appraisal, appraisal review, or appraisal consulting assignment opinions and conclusions, as identified by the appraiser based on communication with the client at the time of the assignment.

INTENDED USER: the client and any other party as identified, by name or type, as users of the appraisal, appraisal review, or appraisal consulting report by the appraiser on the basis of communication with the client at the time of the assignment.

JURISDICTIONAL EXCEPTION: an assignment condition that voids the force of a part or parts of USPAP, when compliance with part or parts of USPAP is contrary to law or public policy applicable to the assignment.

MARKET VALUE: a type of value, stated as an opinion, that presumes the transfer of a property (i.e., a right of ownership or a bundle of such rights), as of a certain date, under specific conditions set forth in the definition of the term identified by the appraiser as applicable in an appraisal.

> Comment: Forming an opinion of market value is the purpose of many real property appraisal assignments, particularly when the client's intended use includes more than one intended user. The conditions included in market value definitions establish market perspectives for development of the opinion. These conditions may vary from definition to definition but generally fall into three categories:
>
> 1. the relationship, knowledge, and motivation of the parties (i.e., seller and buyer);
> 2. the terms of sale (e.g., cash, cash equivalent, or other terms); and
> 3. the conditions of sale (e.g., exposure in a competitive market for a reasonable time prior to sale).
>
> *Appraisers are cautioned to identify the exact definition of market value, and its authority, applicable in each appraisal completed for the purpose of market value.*

MASS APPRAISAL: the process of valuing a universe of properties as of a given date using standard methodology, employing common data, and allowing for statistical testing.

MASS APPRAISAL MODEL: a mathematical expression of how supply and demand factors interact in a market.

PERSONAL PROPERTY: identifiable tangible objects that are considered by the general public as being "personal" - for example, furnishings, artwork, antiques, gems and jewelry, collectibles, machinery and equipment; all tangible property that is not classified as real estate.

PRICE: the amount asked, offered, or paid for a property.

> Comment: Once stated, *price* is a fact, whether it is publicly disclosed or retained in private. Because of the financial capabilities, motivations, or special interests of a given buyer or seller, the price paid for a property may or may not have any relation to the value that might be ascribed to that property by others.

REAL ESTATE: an identified parcel or tract of land, including improvements, if any.

REAL PROPERTY: the interests, benefits, and rights inherent in the ownership of real estate.

> Comment: In some jurisdictions, the terms *real estate* and *real property* have the same legal meaning. The separate definitions recognize the traditional distinction between the two concepts in appraisal theory.

REPORT: any communication, written or oral, of an appraisal, appraisal review, or appraisal consulting service that is transmitted to the client upon completion of an assignment.

> Comment: Most reports are written and most clients mandate written reports. Oral report requirements (see the Record Keeping section of the ETHICS RULE) are included to cover court testimony and other oral communications of an appraisal, appraisal review, or appraisal consulting service.

SCOPE OF WORK: the amount and type of information researched and the analysis applied in an assignment. Scope of work includes, but is not limited to, the following:

- the degree to which the property is inspected or identified;
- the extent of research into physical or economic factors that could affect the property;
- the extent of data research; and
- the type and extent of analysis applied to arrive at opinions or conclusions.

SIGNATURE: personalized evidence indicating authentication of the work performed by the appraiser and the acceptance of the responsibility for content, analyses, and the conclusions in the report.

> Comment: A signature can be represented by a handwritten mark, a digitized image controlled by a personalized identification number, or other media, where the appraiser has sole personalized control of affixing the signature.

SPECIFIC REQUIREMENTS: all or part of a Standards Rule of USPAP from which departure is permitted under certain limited conditions. (See DEPARTURE RULE.)

SUPPLEMENTAL STANDARDS: requirements issued by government agencies, government sponsored enterprises, or other entities that establish public policy which add to the purpose, intent and content of the requirements in USPAP, that have a material effect on the development and reporting of assignment results.

> Comment: Supplemental standards are published in regulations, rules, policies, and other similar documents, and have the same applicability to all properties or assignments in a particular category or class regardless of the contracting entity.

> Contractual agreements that are unique to the contracting entity and which apply specifically to a particular property or assignment are not supplemental standards.

VALUE: the monetary relationship between properties and those who buy, sell, or use those properties.

> Comment: *Value* expresses an economic concept. As such, it is never a fact but always an opinion of the worth of a property at a given time in accordance with a specific definition of value. In appraisal practice, value must always be qualified - for example, market value, liquidation value, or investment value.

VALUATION SERVICES: services pertaining to aspects of property value.

> Comment: Valuation services pertain to all aspects of property value and include services performed both by appraisers and by others.

WORKFILE: documentation necessary to support an appraiser's analyses, opinions, and conclusions.

STANDARD 1: REAL PROPERTY APPRAISAL, DEVELOPMENT

In developing a real property appraisal, an appraiser must identify the problem to be solved and the scope of work necessary to solve the problem, and correctly complete research and analysis necessary to produce a credible appraisal.

<u>Comment</u>: STANDARD 1 is directed toward the substantive aspects of developing a competent appraisal of real property. The requirements set forth in STANDARD 1 follow the appraisal development process in the order of topics addressed and can be used by appraisers and the users of appraisal services as a convenient checklist.

<u>Standards Rule 1-1 (This Standards Rule contains binding requirements from which departure is not permitted.)</u>

In developing a real property appraisal, an appraiser must:

(a) **be aware of, understand, and correctly employ those recognized methods and techniques that are necessary to produce a credible appraisal;**

<u>Comment</u>: This Rule recognizes that the principle of change continues to affect the manner in which appraisers perform appraisal services. Changes and developments in the real estate field have a substantial impact on the appraisal profession. Important changes in the cost and manner of constructing and marketing commercial, industrial, and residential real estate as well as changes in the legal framework in which real property rights and interests are created, conveyed, and mortgaged have resulted in corresponding changes in appraisal theory and practice. Social change has also had an effect on appraisal theory and practice. To keep abreast of these changes and developments, the appraisal profession is constantly reviewing and revising appraisal methods and techniques and devising new methods and techniques to meet new circumstances. For this reason, it is not sufficient for appraisers to simply maintain the skills and the knowledge they possess when they become appraisers. Each appraiser must continuously improve his or her skills to remain proficient in real property appraisal.

(b) **not commit a substantial error of omission or commission that significantly affects an appraisal; and**

<u>Comment</u>: In performing appraisal services, an appraiser must be certain that the gathering of factual information is conducted in a manner that is sufficiently diligent, given the scope of work as identified according to Standards Rule 1-2(f), to ensure that the data that would have a material or significant effect on the resulting opinions or conclusions are identified and, where necessary, analyzed. Further, an appraiser must use sufficient care in analyzing such data to avoid errors that would significantly affect his or her opinions and conclusions.

(c) **not render appraisal services in a careless or negligent manner, such as by making a series of errors that, although individually might not significantly affect the results of an appraisal, in the aggregate affects the credibility of those results.**

<u>Comment</u>: Perfection is impossible to attain, and competence does not require perfection. However, an appraiser must not render appraisal services in a careless or negligent manner. This Standards Rule requires an appraiser to use due diligence and due care.

Standards Rule 1-2 (This Standards Rule contains binding requirements from which departure is not permitted.)

In developing a real property appraisal, an appraiser must:

(a) identify the client and other intended users;

(b) identify the intended use of the appraisers opinions and conclusions;

Comment: Identification of the intended use is necessary for the appraiser and the client to decide:

- the appropriate scope of work to be completed, and
- the level of information to be provided in communicating the appraisal.

An appraiser must not allow a clients objectives or intended use to cause an analysis to be biased.

(c) identify the type and definition of value and, if the value opinion to be developed is market value, ascertain whether the value is to be the most probable price:

(i) in terms of cash; or

(ii) in terms of financial arrangements equivalent to cash; or

(iii) in other precisely defined terms; and

(iv) if the opinion of value is to be based on non-market financing or financing with unusual conditions or incentives, the terms of such financing must be clearly identified and the appraisers opinion of their contributions to or negative influence on value must be developed by analysis of relevant market data;

Comment: When developing an opinion of market value, the appraiser must also develop an opinion of reasonable exposure time linked to the value opinion.

(d) identify the effective date of the appraisers opinions and conclusions

(e) identify the characteristics of the property that are relevant to the type and definition of value and intended use of the appraisal, including:

(i) its location and physical, legal, and economic attributes;

(ii) the real property interest to be valued;

(iii) any personal property, trade fixtures, or intangible items that are not real property but are included in the appraisal;

(iv) any known easements, restrictions, encumbrances, leases, reservations, covenants, contracts, declarations, special assessments, ordinances, or other items of a similar nature; and

(v) whether the subject property is a fractional interest, physical segment, or partial holding;

Comment on (i)(v): If the necessary subject property information is not available because of assignment conditions that limit research opportunity (such as conditions that preclude an onsite inspection or the gathering of information from reliable third-party sources), an appraiser must:

- obtain the necessary information before proceeding, or
- where possible, in compliance with Standards Rule 1-2(g), use an extraordinary assumption about such information.

An appraiser may use any combination of a property inspection and documents, such as a physical legal description, address, map reference, copy of a survey or map, property sketch, or photographs, to identify the relevant characteristics of the subject property. Identification of the real property interest appraised can be based on a review of copies or summaries of title descriptions or other documents that set forth any known encumbrances. The information used by an appraiser to identify the property characteristics must be from sources the appraiser reasonably believes are reliable.

An appraiser is not required to value the whole when the subject of the appraisal is a fractional interest, a physical segment, or a partial holding.

(f)   **identify the scope of work necessary to complete the assignment;**

Comment: The scope of work is acceptable when it is consistent with:

- the expectations of participants in the market for the same or similar appraisal services; and
- what the appraisers peers actions would be in performing the same or a similar assignment in compliance with USPAP.

An appraiser must have sound reasons in support of the scope of work decision and must be prepared to support the decision to exclude any information or procedure that would appear to be relevant to the client, an intended user, or the appraiser's peers in the same or a similar assignment.

An appraiser must not allow assignment conditions or other factors to limit the extent of research or analysis to such a degree that the resulting opinions and conclusions developed in an assignment are not credible in the context of the intended use of the appraisal.

(g)   **identify any extraordinary assumptions necessary in the assignment; and**

Comment: An extraordinary assumption may be used in an assignment only if:

- it is required to properly develop credible opinions and conclusions;
- the appraiser has a reasonable basis for the extraordinary assumption;
- use of the extraordinary assumption results in a credible analysis; and
- the appraiser complies with the disclosure requirements set forth in USPAP for extraordinary assumptions.

(h)   **identify any hypothetical conditions necessary in the assignment.**

Comment: A hypothetical condition may be used in an assignment only if:

- use of the hypothetical condition is clearly required for legal purposes, for purposes of reasonable analysis, or for purposes of comparison;
- use of the hypothetical condition results in a credible analysis; and
- the appraiser complies with the disclosure requirements set forth in USPAP for hypothetical conditions.

Standards Rule 1-3 (This Standards Rule contains specific requirements from which departure is permitted. See the DEPARTURE RULE.)

When the value opinion to be developed is market value, and given the scope of work identified in accordance with Standards Rule 1-2(f), an appraiser must:

(a) identify and analyze the effect on use and value of existing land use regulations, reasonably probable modifications of such land use regulations, economic supply and demand, the physical adaptability of the real estate, and market area trends; and

Comment: An appraiser must avoid making an unsupported assumption or premise about market area trends, effective age, and remaining life.

(b) develop an opinion of the highest and best use of the real estate.

Comment: An appraiser must analyze the relevant legal, physical, and economic factors to the extent necessary to support the appraisers highest and best use conclusion(s).

Standards Rule 1-4 (This Standards Rule contains specific requirements from which departure is permitted. See the DEPARTURE RULE.)

In developing a real property appraisal, an appraiser must collect, verify, and analyze all information applicable to the appraisal problem, given the scope of work identified in accordance with Standards Rule 1-2(f).

(a) When a sales comparison approach is applicable, an appraiser must analyze such comparable sales data as are available to indicate a value conclusion.

(b) When a cost approach is applicable, an appraiser must:

(i) develop an opinion of site value by an appropriate appraisal method or technique;

(ii) analyze such comparable cost data as are available to estimate the cost new of the improvements (if any); and

(iii) analyze such comparable data as are available to estimate the difference between the cost new and the present worth of the improvements (accrued depreciation).

(c) When an income approach is applicable, an appraiser must:

(i) analyze such comparable rental data as are available and/or the potential earnings capacity of the property to estimate the gross income potential of the property;

(ii) analyze such comparable operating expense data as are available to estimate the operating expenses of the property;

(iii) analyze such comparable data as are available to estimate rates of capitalization and/or rates of discount; and

(iv) base projections of future rent and/or income potential and expenses on reasonably clear and appropriate evidence.

> Comment: In developing income and expense statements and cash flow projections, an appraiser must weigh historical information and trends, current supply and demand factors affecting such trends, and anticipated events such as competition from developments under construction.

(d) **When developing an opinion of the value of a leased fee estate or a leasehold estate, an appraiser must analyze the effect on value, if any, of the terms and conditions of the lease(s).**

(e) **An appraiser must analyze the effect on value, if any, of the assemblage of the various estates or component parts of a property and refrain from valuing the whole solely by adding together the individual values of the various estates or component parts.**

> Comment: Although the value of the whole may be equal to the sum of the separate estates or parts, it also may be greater than or less than the sum of such estates or parts. Therefore, the value of the whole must be tested by reference to appropriate data and supported by an appropriate analysis of such data.

> A similar procedure must be followed when the value of the whole has been established and the appraiser seeks to value a part. The value of any such part must be tested by reference to appropriate data and supported by an appropriate analysis of such data.

(f) **An appraiser must analyze the effect on value, if any, of anticipated public or private improvements, located on or off the site, to the extent that market actions reflect such anticipated improvements as of the effective appraisal date.**

(g) **An appraiser must analyze the effect on value of any personal property, trade fixtures, or intangible items that are not real property but are included in the appraisal.**

> Comment: Competency in personal property appraisal (see STANDARD 7) or business appraisal (see STANDARD 9) may be required when it is necessary to allocate the overall value to the property components. A separate appraisal, developed in compliance with the Standard pertinent to the type of property involved, is required when the value of a non-realty item or combination of such items is significant to the overall value.

(h) **When appraising proposed improvements, an appraiser must examine and have available for future examination:**

(i) **plans, specifications, or other documentation sufficient to identify the scope and character of the proposed improvements;**

(ii) **evidence indicating the probable time of completion of the proposed improvements; and**

(iii) **reasonably clear and appropriate evidence supporting development costs, anticipated earnings, occupancy projections, and the anticipated competition at the time of completion.**

> Comment: Development of a value opinion for a subject property with proposed improvements as of a current date involves the use of the hypothetical condition that the described improvements have been completed as of the date of value when, in fact, they have not.

> The evidence required to be examined and maintained may include such items as contractors estimates relating to cost and the time required to complete construction, market and feasibility studies, operating cost data, and the history of recently completed similar developments. The appraisal may require a complete feasibility analysis.

Standards Rule 1-5 (This Standards Rule contains binding requirements from which departure is not permitted.)

In developing a real property appraisal, when the value opinion to be developed is market value, an appraiser must, if such information is available to the appraiser in the normal course of business:

(a)   analyze all agreements of sale, options, or listings of the subject property current as of the effective date of the appraisal; and

(b)   analyze all sales of the subject property that occurred within the three (3) years prior to the effective date of the appraisal.

    Comment: See the Comments to Standards Rules 2-2(a)(ix), 2-2(b)(ix), and 2-2(c)(ix) for corresponding reporting requirements relating to the availability and relevance of information.

Standards Rule 1-6 (This Standards Rule contains binding requirements from which departure is not permitted.)

In developing a real property appraisal, an appraiser must:

(a)   reconcile the quality and quantity of data available and analyzed within the approaches used; and

(b)   reconcile the applicability or suitability of the approaches used to arrive at the value conclusion(s).

    Comment: See the Comments to Standards Rules 2-2(a)(ix), 2-2(b)(ix), and 2-2(c)(ix) for corresponding reporting requirements.

STANDARD 2: REAL PROPERTY APPRAISAL, REPORTING

In reporting the results of a real property appraisal, an appraiser must communicate each analysis, opinion, and conclusion in a manner that is not misleading.

Comment: STANDARD 2 addresses the content and level of information required in a report that communicates the results of a real property appraisal.

STANDARD 2 does not dictate the form, format, or style of real property appraisal reports. The form, format, and style of a report are functions of the needs of users and appraisers. The substantive content of a report determines its compliance.

Standards Rule 2-1 (This Standards Rule contains binding requirements from which departure is not permitted.)

Each written or oral real property appraisal report must:

(a)   clearly and accurately set forth the appraisal in a manner that will not be misleading;

(b)   contain sufficient information to enable the intended users of the appraisal to understand the report properly; and

(c)   clearly and accurately disclose all assumptions, extraordinary assumptions, hypothetical conditions, and limiting conditions used in the assignment.

Comment: Examples of extraordinary assumptions or hypothetical conditions might include items such as the execution of a pending lease agreement, atypical financing, a known but not yet quantified environmental issue, or completion of onsite or offsite improvements.

Standards Rule 2-2 (This Standards Rule contains binding requirements from which departure is not permitted.)

Each written real property appraisal report must be prepared under one of the following three options and prominently state which option is used: Self-Contained Appraisal Report, Summary Appraisal Report, or Restricted Use Appraisal Report.

Comment: When the intended users include parties other than the client, either a Self-Contained Appraisal Report or a Summary Appraisal Report must be provided. When the intended users do not include parties other than the client, a Restricted Use Appraisal Report may be provided.

The essential difference among these three options is in the content and level of information provided.

An appraiser must use care when characterizing the type of report and level of information communicated upon completion of an assignment. An appraiser may use any other label in addition to, but not in place of, the label set forth in this Standard for the type of report provided.

The report content and level of information requirements set forth in this Standard are minimums for each type of report. An appraiser must supplement a report form, when necessary, to ensure that any intended user of the appraisal is not misled and that the report complies with the applicable content requirements set forth in this Standards Rule.

A party receiving a copy of a Self-Contained Appraisal Report, Summary Appraisal Report, or Restricted Use Appraisal Report in order to satisfy disclosure requirements does not become an intended user of the appraisal unless the appraiser identifies such party as an intended user as part of the assignment.

(a)   The content of a Self-Contained Appraisal Report must be consistent with the intended use of the appraisal and, at minimum:

(i)   state the identity of the client and any intended users, by name or type;

Comment: An appraiser must use care when identifying the client to ensure a clear understanding and to avoid violations of the Confidentiality section of the ETHICS RULE. In those rare instances when the client wishes to remain anonymous, an appraiser must still document the identity of the client in the workfile but may omit the client's identity in the report.

Intended users of the report might include parties such as lenders, employees of government agencies, partners of a client, and a client's attorney and accountant.

(ii)   **state the intended use of the appraisal;**

(iii)   **describe information sufficient to identify the real estate involved in the appraisal, including the physical and economic property characteristics relevant to the assignment;**

Comment: The real estate involved in the appraisal can be specified, for example, by a legal description, address, map reference, copy of a survey or map, property sketch and/or photographs or the like. The information can include a property sketch and photographs in addition to written comments about the legal, physical, and economic attributes of the real estate relevant to the purpose and intended use of the appraisal.

(iv)   state the real property interest appraised;

Comment: The statement of the real property rights being appraised must be substantiated, as needed, by copies or summaries of title descriptions or other documents that set forth any known encumbrances.

(v)   **state the type and definition of value and cite the source of the definition;**

Comment: Stating the definition of value also requires any comments needed to clearly indicate to intended users how the definition is being applied.

When reporting an opinion of market value, state whether the opinion of value is:

- in terms of cash or of financing terms equivalent to cash, or
- based on non-market financing or financing with unusual conditions or incentives.

When an opinion of market value is not in terms of cash or based on financing terms equivalent to cash, summarize the terms of such financing and explain their contributions to or negative influence on value.

(vi)   **state the effective date of the appraisal and the date of the report;**

Comment: The effective date of the appraisal establishes the context for the value opinion, while the date of the report indicates whether the perspective of the appraiser on the market or property use conditions as of the effective date of the appraisal was prospective, current, or retrospective.

Reiteration of the date of the report and the effective date of the appraisal at various stages of the report in tandem is important for the clear understanding of the reader whenever market or property use conditions on the date of the report are different from such conditions on the effective date of the appraisal.

(vii)   **describe sufficient information to disclose to the client and any other intended users of the appraisal the scope of work used to develop the appraisal;**

Comment: This requirement is to ensure that the client and intended users whose expected reliance on an appraisal may be affected by the extent of the appraiser's investigation are properly informed and are not misled as to the scope of work. The appraiser has the burden of proof to support the scope of work decision and the level of information included in a report.

When any portion of the work involves significant real property appraisal assistance, the appraiser must describe the extent of that assistance. The signing appraiser must also state the name(s) of those providing the significant real property appraisal assistance in the certification, in accordance with SR 2-3.

(viii)   **clearly and conspicuously:**

- **state all extraordinary assumptions and hypothetical conditions; and**
- **state that their use might have affected the assignment results;**

(ix)   **describe the information analyzed, the appraisal procedures followed, and the reasoning that supports the analyses, opinions, and conclusions;**

Comment: The appraiser must be certain the information provided is sufficient for the client and intended users to adequately understand the rationale for the opinion and conclusions.

When reporting an opinion of market value, a summary of the results of analyzing the subject sales, options, and listings in accordance with Standards Rules 1-5 is required. If such information is unobtainable, a statement on the efforts undertaken by the appraiser to obtain the information is required. If such information is irrelevant, a statement acknowledging the existence of the information and citing its lack of relevance is required.

(x)   **state the use of the real estate existing as of the date of value and the use of the real estate reflected in the appraisal; and, when reporting an opinion of market value, describe the support and rationale for the appraisers opinion of the highest and best use of the real estate;**

Comment: The report must contain the appraiser's opinion as to the highest and best use of the real estate, unless an opinion as to highest and best use is unnecessary, such as in insurance valuation or "value in use" appraisals. When reporting an opinion of market value, the appraisers support and rationale for the opinion of highest and best use is required. The appraisers reasoning in support of the opinion must be provided in the depth and detail required by its significance to the appraisal.

(xi)   **state and explain any permitted departures from specific requirements of STANDARD 1 and the reason for excluding any of the usual valuation approaches; and**

Comment: A Self-Contained Appraisal Report must include sufficient information to indicate that the appraiser complied with the requirements of STANDARD 1, including any permitted departures from the specific requirements. The amount of detail required will vary with the significance of the information to the appraisal.

When the DEPARTURE RULE is invoked, the assignment is deemed to be a Limited Appraisal. Use of the term "Limited Appraisal" makes clear that the assignment involved something less than or different from the work that could have and would have been completed if departure had not been invoked. The report of a Limited Appraisal must contain a prominent section that clearly identifies the extent of the appraisal process performed and the departures taken.

The reliability of the results of a Complete Appraisal or a Limited Appraisal developed under STANDARD 1 is not affected by the type of report prepared under STANDARD 2. The extent of the appraisal process performed under STANDARD 1 is the basis for the reliability of the value conclusion.

(xii)   **include a signed certification in accordance with Standards Rule 2-3.**

(b)   **The content of a Summary Appraisal Report must be consistent with the intended use of the appraisal and, at a minimum:**

Comment: The essential difference between the Self-Contained Appraisal Report and the Summary Appraisal Report is the level of detail of presentation.

     (i)   **state the identity of the client and any intended users, by name or type;**

         Comment: An appraiser must use care when identifying the client to ensure a clear understanding and to avoid violations of the Confidentiality section of the ETHICS RULE. In those rare instances when the client wishes to remain anonymous, an appraiser must still document the identity of the client in the workfile but may omit the client's identity in the report.

         Intended users of the report might include parties such as lenders, employees of government agencies, partners of a client, and a client's attorney and accountant.

     (ii)   **state the intended use of the appraisal;**

     (iii)   **summarize information sufficient to identify the real estate involved in the appraisal, including the physical and economic property characteristics relevant to the assignment;**

         Comment: The real estate involved in the appraisal can be specified, for example, by a legal description, address, map reference, copy of a survey or map, property sketch, and/or photographs or the like. The summarized information can include a property sketch and photographs in addition to written comments about the legal, physical, and economic attributes of the real estate relevant to the type and definition of value and intended use of the appraisal.

     (iv)   **state the real property interest appraised;**

         Comment: The statement of the real property rights being appraised must be substantiated, as needed, by copies or summaries of title descriptions or other documents that set forth any known encumbrances.

     (v)   **state the type and definition of value and cite the source of the definition;**

         Comment: Stating the definition of value also requires any comments needed to clearly indicate to the intended users how the definition is being applied.

         When reporting an opinion of market value, state whether the opinion of value is:

         ▪   in terms of cash or of financing terms equivalent to cash, or
         ▪   based on non-market financing or financing with unusual conditions or incentives.

         When an opinion of market value is not in terms of cash or based on financing terms equivalent to cash, summarize the terms of such financing and explain their contributions to or negative influence on value.

(vi)   **state the effective date of the appraisal and the date of the report;**

Comment: The effective date of the appraisal establishes the context for the value opinion, while the date of the report indicates whether the perspective of the appraiser on the market or property use conditions as of the effective date of the appraisal was prospective, current, or retrospective.

Reiteration of the date of the report and the effective date of the appraisal at various stages of the report in tandem is important for the clear understanding of the reader whenever market or property use conditions on the date of the report are different from such conditions on the effective date of the appraisal.

(vii)   **summarize sufficient information to disclose to the client and any intended users of the appraisal the scope of work used to develop the appraisal;**

Comment: This requirement is to ensure that the client and intended users whose expected reliance on an appraisal may be affected by the extent of the appraiser's investigation are properly informed and are not misled as to the scope of work. The appraiser has the burden of proof to support the scope of work decision and the level of information included in a report.

When any portion of the work involves significant real property appraisal assistance, the appraiser must summarize the extent of that assistance. The signing appraiser must also state the name(s) of those providing the significant real property appraisal assistance in the certification, in accordance with SR 2-3.

(viii)   **clearly and conspicuously:**

- **state all extraordinary assumptions and hypothetical conditions; and**
- **state that their use might have affected the assignment results;**

(ix)   **summarize the information analyzed, the appraisal procedures followed, and the reasoning that supports the analyses, opinions, and conclusions;**

Comment: The appraiser must be certain that the information provided is sufficient for the client and intended users to adequately understand the rationale for the opinions and conclusions, including reconciliation of the data and approaches, in accordance with Standards Rule 1-6.

When reporting an opinion of market value, a summary of the results of analyzing the subject sales, options, and listings in accordance with Standards Rule 1-5 is required. If such information is unobtainable, a statement on the efforts undertaken by the appraiser to obtain the information is required. If such information is irrelevant, a statement acknowledging the existence of the information and citing its lack of relevance is required.

(x)   **state the use of the real estate existing as of the date of value and the use of the real estate reflected in the appraisal; and, reporting an opinion of market value, summarize the support and rationale for the appraisers opinion of the highest and best use of the real estate;**

Comment: The report must contain the appraiser's opinion as to the highest and best use of the real estate, unless an opinion as to highest and best use is unnecessary such as in insurance valuation or "value in use" appraisals. When reporting an opinion of market value, a summary of the appraisers support and rationale for the opinion of highest and best use is required. The appraisers reasoning in support of the opinion must be provided in the depth and detail required by its significance to the appraisal.

(xi)   **state and explain any permitted departures from specific requirements of STANDARD 1 and the reason for excluding any of the usual valuation approaches; and**

Comment: A Summary Appraisal Report must include sufficient information to indicate that the appraiser complied with the requirements of STANDARD 1, including any permitted departures from the specific requirements. The amount of detail required will vary with the significance of the information to the appraisal.

When the DEPARTURE RULE is invoked, the assignment is deemed to be a Limited Appraisal. Use of the term "Limited Appraisal" makes clear that the assignment involved something less than or different from the work that could have and would have been completed if departure had not been invoked. The report of a Limited Appraisal must contain a prominent section that clearly identifies the extent of the appraisal process performed and the departures taken.

The reliability of the results of a Complete Appraisal or a Limited Appraisal developed under STANDARD 1 is not affected by the type of report prepared under STANDARD 2. The extent of the appraisal process performed under STANDARD 1 is the basis for the reliability of the value conclusion.

(xii)   **include a signed certification in accordance with Standards Rule 2-3.**

The content of a Restricted Use Appraisal Report must be consistent with the intended use of the appraisal and, at a minimum:

(i)   **state the identity of the client, by name or type;**

Comment: An appraiser must use care when identifying the client to ensure a clear understanding and to avoid violations of the Confidentiality section of the ETHICS RULE. In those rare instances when the client wishes to remain anonymous, an appraiser must still document the identity of the client in the workfile but may omit the client's identity in the report.

(ii)   **state the intended use of the appraisal;**

Comment: The intended use of the appraisal must be consistent with the limitation on use of the Restricted Use Appraisal Report option in this Standards Rule (i.e., client use only).

(iii)   **state information sufficient to identify the real estate involved in the appraisal;**

Comment: The real estate involved in the appraisal can be specified, for example, by a legal description, address, map reference, copy of a survey or map, property sketch, and/or photographs or the like.

(iv)   **state the real property interest appraised;**

(v)   **state the type of value, and cite the source of its definition;**

(vi)   **state the effective date of the appraisal and the date of the report;**

Comment: The effective date of the appraisal establishes the context for the value opinion, while the date of the report indicates whether the perspective of the appraiser on the market or property use conditions as of the effective date of the appraisal was prospective, current, or retrospective.

(vii)   **state the extent of the process of collecting, confirming, and reporting data or refer to an assignment agreement retained in the appraisers workfile that describes the scope of work to be performed;**

Comment: When any portion of the work involves significant real property appraisal assistance, the appraiser must state the extent of that assistance. The signing appraiser must also state the name(s) of those providing the significant real property appraisal assistance in the certification, in accordance with SR 2-3.

(viii)   **clearly and conspicuously:**

- **state extraordinary assumptions and hypothetical conditions; and**
- **state that their use might have affected the assignment results;**

(ix)   **state the appraisal procedures followed, state the value opinion(s) and conclusion(s) reached, and reference the workfile;**

Comment: An appraiser must maintain a specific, coherent workfile in support of a Restricted Use Appraisal Report. The contents of the workfile must be sufficient for the appraiser to produce a Summary Appraisal Report. The file must be available for inspection by the client (or the clients representatives, such as those engaged to complete an appraisal review), state enforcement agencies, such third parties as may be authorized by due process of law, and a duly authorized professional peer review committee except when such disclosure to a committee would violate applicable law or regulation.

When reporting an opinion of market value, information analyzed in compliance with Standards Rule 1-5 is significant information that must be disclosed in a Restricted Use Appraisal Report. If such information is unobtainable, a statement on the efforts undertaken by the appraiser to obtain the information is required. If such information is irrelevant, a statement acknowledging the existence of the information and citing its lack of relevance is required.

(x)   **state the use of the real estate existing as of the date of value and the use of the real estate reflected in the appraisal; and, when reporting an opinion of market value, state the appraisers opinion of the highest and best use of the real estate;**

Comment: The report must contain a statement of the property uses both as is and as reflected in the appraisal and include the appraisers opinion as to the highest and best use of the real estate, unless an opinion as to highest and best use is unnecessary such as in insurance valuation or "value in use" appraisals. If an opinion of highest and best use is required, the appraisers reasoning in support of the opinion must be stated in the depth and detail required by its significance to the appraisal or documented in the workfile and referenced in the report.

(xi)   **state and explain any permitted departures from applicable specific requirements of STANDARD 1; state the exclusion of any of the usual valuation approaches; and state a prominent use restriction that limits use of the report to the client and warns that the appraisers opinions and conclusions set forth in the report cannot be understood properly without additional information in the appraisers workfile; and**

Comment: When the DEPARTURE RULE is invoked, the assignment is deemed to be a Limited Appraisal. Use of the term "Limited Appraisal" makes it clear that the assignment involved something less than or different from the work that could have and would have been completed if departure had not been invoked. The report of a Limited Appraisal must contain a prominent section that clearly identifies the extent of the appraisal process performed and the departures taken.

The Restricted Use Appraisal Report is for client use only. Before entering into an agreement, the appraiser should establish with the client the situations where this type of report is to be used and should ensure that the client understands the restricted utility of the Restricted Use Appraisal Report.

(xii)   **include a signed certification in accordance with Standards Rule 2-3.**

Standards Rule 2-3 (This Standards Rule contains binding requirements from which departure is not permitted.)

Each written real property appraisal report must contain a signed certification that is similar in content to the following form:

I certify that, to the best of my knowledge and belief:

—   the statements of fact contained in this report are true and correct.

—   the reported analyses, opinions, and conclusions are limited only by the reported assumptions and limiting conditions and are my personal, impartial, and unbiased professional analyses, opinions, and conclusions.

—   I have no (or the specified) present or prospective interest in the property that is the subject of this report and no (or the specified) personal interest with respect to the parties involved.

—   I have no bias with respect to the property that is the subject of this report or to the parties involved with this assignment.

—   my engagement in this assignment was not contingent upon developing or reporting predetermined results.

—   my compensation for completing this assignment is not contingent upon the development or reporting of a predetermined value or direction in value that favors the cause of the client, the amount of the value opinion, the attainment of a stipulated result, or the occurrence of a subsequent event directly related to the intended use of this appraisal.

—   my analyses, opinions, and conclusions were developed, and this report has been prepared, in conformity with the *Uniform Standards of Professional Appraisal Practice.*

—   I have (or have not) made a personal inspection of the property that is the subject of this report. (If more than one person signs this certification, the certification must clearly specify which individuals did and which individuals did not make a personal inspection of the appraised property.)

—   no one provided significant real property appraisal assistance to the person signing this certification. (If there are exceptions, the name of each individual providing significant real property appraisal assistance must be stated.)

Comment: A signed certification is an integral part of the appraisal report. An appraiser who signs any part of the appraisal report, including a letter of transmittal, must also sign this certification.

In an assignment that includes only assignment results developed by the real property appraiser(s), any appraiser(s) who signs a certification accepts full responsibility for all elements of the certification, for the assignment results, and for the contents of the appraisal report. In an assignment that includes personal property, business or intangible asset assignment results not developed by the real property appraiser(s), any real property appraiser(s) who signs a certification accepts full responsibility for the real property elements of the certification, for the real property assignment results, and for the real property contents of the appraisal report.

When a signing appraiser(s) has relied on work done by others who do not sign the certification, the signing appraiser is responsible for the decision to rely on their work. The signing appraiser(s) is required to have a reasonable basis for believing that those individuals performing the work are competent and that their work is credible.

The names of individuals providing significant real property appraisal assistance who do not sign a certification must be stated in the certification. It is not required that the description of their assistance be contained in the certification, but disclosure of their assistance is required in accordance with SR 2-2(a), (b), or (c)(vii), as applicable.

Standards Rule 2-4 (This Standards Rule contains specific requirements from which departure is permitted. See DEPARTURE RULE.)

An oral real property appraisal report must, at a minimum, address the substantive matters set forth in Standards Rule 2-2(b).

Comment: Testimony of an appraiser concerning his or her analyses, opinions, and conclusions is an oral report in which the appraiser must comply with the requirements of this Standards Rule.

See the Record Keeping section of the ETHICS RULE for corresponding requirements.

STANDARD 3:
APPRAISAL REVIEW, DEVELOPMENT AND REPORTING

In performing an appraisal review assignment, an appraiser acting as a reviewer must develop and report a credible opinion as to the quality of another appraiser's work and must clearly disclose the scope of work performed.

Comment: Appraisal review is the act or process of developing and communicating an opinion about the quality of all or part of the work of another appraiser that was performed as part of an appraisal, appraisal review, or appraisal consulting assignment. The reviewer's opinion about quality must encompass the completeness, adequacy, relevance, appropriateness, and reasonableness of the work under review, developed in the context of the requirements applicable to that work.

The COMPETENCY RULE applies to the reviewer, who must correctly employ those recognized methods and techniques necessary to develop credible appraisal review opinions and also avoid material errors of commission or omission. A misleading or fraudulent appraisal review report violates the ETHICS RULE.

Appraisal review requires the reviewer to prepare a separate report setting forth the scope of work and the results of the appraisal review.

Appraisal review is distinctly different from the cosigning activity addressed in Standards Rules 2-3, 5-3, 6-8, 8-3, and 10-3. To avoid confusion between these activities, a reviewer performing an appraisal review must not sign the work under review unless he or she intends to accept the responsibility of a cosigner of that work.

Standards Rule 3-1(This Standards Rule contains binding requirements from which departure is not permitted.)

In developing an appraisal review, the reviewer must:

(a) **identify the reviewer's client and intended users, the intended use of the reviewer's opinions and conclusions, and the purpose of the assignment;**

Comment: The intended use is in the context of the client's use of the reviewer's opinions and conclusions; examples include, without limitation, quality control, audit, qualification, or confirmation. The purpose of the assignment relates to the reviewer's objective; examples include, without limitation, to evaluate compliance with relevant USPAP requirements, with a client's requirements, or with applicable regulations.

A reviewer must ascertain whether the purpose of the assignment includes the development of his or her own opinion of value about the subject property of the work under review.

If the purpose of the assignment includes the reviewer developing his or her own opinion of value about the subject property of the work under review, that opinion is an appraisal whether it:

- concurs with the opinion of value in the work under review, as of the date of value in that work or a different date of value; or

- differs from the opinion of value in the work under review, as of the date of value in that work or a different date of value

(b) identify the:

(i) **subject of the appraisal review assignment,**

(ii) **effective date of the review,**

(iii) **property and ownership interest appraised (if any) in the work under review,**

(iv) **date of the work under review and the effective date of the opinion or conclusion in the work under review, and**

(v) **appraiser(s) who completed the work under review, unless the identity was withheld.**
Comment: The subject of an appraisal review assignment may be all or part of a report, a workfile, or a combination of these, and may be related to an appraisal, appraisal review, or appraisal consulting assignment.

(c) **identify the scope of work to be performed:**

Comment: A reviewer must take appropriate steps to identify the precise extent of the review process to be completed in an assignment. The reviewer must have sound reasons in support of the scope of work decision, and the resulting opinions and conclusions developed in the assignment must be credible and consistent with the intended use of the review.

In making the scope of work decision, the reviewer must identify any extraordinary assumptions necessary in the assignment. An extraordinary assumption may be used in an appraisal review assignment only if:

- it is required to properly develop credible opinions and conclusions;

- the reviewer has a reasonable basis for the extraordinary assumption;

- use of the extraordinary assumption results in a credible analysis; and

- the reviewer complies with the disclosure requirements set forth in SR 3-2(d) for extraordinary assumptions.

The appraisal review must be conducted in the context of market conditions as of the effective date of the opinion in the work being reviewed. Information available to the reviewer that could not have been available to the appraiser as of or subsequent to the date of the work being reviewed must not be used by a reviewer in the development of an opinion as to the quality of the work under review.

When the scope of work of the assignment includes a requirement for the reviewer to develop his or her own opinion of value, the following apply:

The reviewer's scope of work in developing his or her own opinion of value may be different from that of the work under review.

The effective date of the reviewer's opinion of value may be the same or different from the date of the work under review.

The reviewer is not required to replicate the steps completed by the original appraiser. Those items in the work under review that the reviewer concludes are credible and in compliance with the applicable development Standard (STANDARD 1, 3, 4, 6, 7, or 9) can be extended to the reviewer's value opinion development process on the basis of an extraordinary assumption by the reviewer. Those items not deemed to be credible or in compliance must be replaced with information or analysis by the reviewer, developed in conformance with STANDARD 1, 3, 4, 6, 7, or 9, as applicable, to produce a credible value opinion.

The reviewer may use additional information available to him or her that was not available to the original appraiser in the development of his or her value opinion; however, the reviewer must not use such information as the basis to discredit the original appraiser's opinion of value.

(d)   develop an opinion as to the completeness of the material under review, given the scope of work applicable in the assignment;

Comment: The reviewer is required to develop an opinion as to the completeness of the work under review within the context of the requirements applicable to that work.

(e)   **develop an opinion as to the apparent adequacy and relevance of the data and the propriety of any adjustments to the data, given the scope of work applicable in the assignment;**

Comment: When reviewing a mass appraisal report and considering the propriety of any adjustment to value for isolated differences in data, the reviewer must develop an opinion as to the use of the coefficients from decomposition of a statistical model.

(f) develop an opinion as to the appropriateness of the appraisal methods and techniques used, given the scope of work applicable in the assignment, and develop the reasons for any disagreement; and

(g) develop an opinion as to whether the analyses, opinions, and conclusions are appropriate and reasonable, given the scope of work applicable in the assignment, and develop the reasons for any disagreement.

Comment: When reviewing a mass appraisal report, the reviewer must develop an opinion as to the standards of accuracy and adequacy of the mass appraisal testing performed and develop the reasons for any disagreement.

Standards Rule 3-2 (This Standards Rule contains binding requirements from which departure is not permitted.)

In reporting the results of an appraisal review, the reviewer must:

(a) state the identity of the client, by name or type, and intended users; the intended use of the assignment results; and the purpose of the assignment;

(b) state the information that must be identified in accordance with Standards Rule 3-1(b);

Comment: If the identity of the appraiser(s) in the work under review was withheld, state that fact in the review report.

(c) state the nature, extent, and detail of the review process undertaken (i.e., the scope of work) identified in accordance with Standards Rule 3-1(c) ;

Comment: When any portion of the work involves significant appraisal, appraisal review, or appraisal consulting assistance, the reviewer must state the extent of that assistance. The signing reviewer must also state the name(s) of those providing the significant assistance in the certification, in accordance with SR 3-3.

(d) state the opinions, reasons, and conclusions required in Standards Rule 3-1(d-g), given the scope of work identified in compliance with Standards Rule 3-1(c);

Comment: When the scope of an appraisal review assignment includes the reviewer expressing his or her own opinion of value, the reviewer must:

1. state which information, analyses, opinions, and conclusions in the material under review that the reviewer accepted as credible and used in developing the reviewer's opinion of value;

2. summarize any additional information relied on and the reasoning and basis for the reviewer's opinion of value; and

3. state all assumptions and limiting conditions; and

4. clearly and conspicuously:

    • state all extraordinary assumptions and hypothetical conditions connected with the reviewer's opinion of value; and
    • state that their use might have affected the assignment results.

The reviewer may include his or her own value opinion within the appraisal review report itself without preparing a separate appraisal report. However, data and analyses provided by the reviewer to support a different value conclusion must match, at a minimum, the reporting requirements for a Summary Appraisal Report for a real property appraisal (SR 2-2(b)) and a personal property appraisal (SR 8-2(b)), an appraisal consulting report for real property appraisal consulting (SR 5-2), a mass appraisal report for mass appraisal (SR 6-7), and an appraisal report for business appraisal (SR 10-2(a)).

(e)   **include all known pertinent information; and**

> Comment: The reviewer must be certain that the information provided is sufficient for the client and intended users to adequately understand the rationale for the reviewer's opinion and conclusions.

(f)   **include a signed certification in accordance with Standards Rule 3-3.**

Standards Rule 3-3 (This Standards Rule contains binding requirements from which departure is not permitted.)

Each written appraisal review report must contain a signed certification that is similar in content to the following form:

I certify that, to the best of my knowledge and belief:

— **the facts and data reported by the reviewer and used in the review process are true and correct.**

— **the analyses, opinions, and conclusions in this review report are limited only by the assumptions and limiting conditions stated in this review report and are my personal, impartial, and unbiased professional analyses, opinions, and conclusions.**

— **I have no (or the specified) present or prospective interest in the property that is the subject of work under review and no (or the specified) personal interest with respect to the parties involved.**

— **I have no bias with respect to the property that is the subject of the work under review or to the parties involved with this assignment.**

— **my engagement in this assignment was not contingent upon developing or reporting predetermined results.**

— **my compensation is not contingent on an action or event resulting from the analyses, opinions, or conclusions in this review or from its use.**

— **my analyses, opinions, and conclusions were developed and this review report was prepared in conformity with the *Uniform Standards of Professional Appraisal Practice*.**

— **I have (or have not) made a personal inspection of the subject property of the work under review. (If more than one person signs this certification, the certification must clearly specify which individuals did and which individuals did not make a personal inspection of the subject property of the work under review.)**

— **no one provided significant appraisal, appraisal review, or appraisal consulting assistance to the person signing this certification. (If there are exceptions, the name of each individual(s) providing appraisal, appraisal review, or appraisal consulting assistance must be stated.)**

Comment: A signed certification is an integral part of the appraisal review report. A reviewer who signs any part of the appraisal review report, including a letter of transmittal, must also sign this certification.

Any reviewer(s) who signs a certification accepts full responsibility for all elements of the certification, for the assignment results, and for the contents of the appraisal review report.

When a signing reviewer(s) has relied on work done by others who do not sign the certification, the signing reviewer is responsible for the decision to rely on their work. The signing reviewer(s) is required to have a reasonable basis for believing that those individuals performing the work are competent and that their work is credible.

The names of individuals providing significant appraisal, appraisal review, or appraisal consulting assistance who do not sign a certification must be stated in the certification. It is not required that the description of their assistance be contained in the certification, but disclosure of their assistance is required in accordance with SR 3-2(c).

For reviews of business or intangible asset appraisal reports, the inspection portion of the above certification is not applicable.

Standards Rule 3-4 (This Standards Rule contains specific requirements from which departure is permitted. See DEPARTURE RULE.)

An oral appraisal review report must address the substantive matters set forth in Standards Rule 3-2.

Comment: Testimony of a reviewer concerning his or her appraisal review opinions and conclusions is an oral report in which the reviewer must comply with the requirements of this Standards Rule.

See the Record Keeping section of the ETHICS RULE for corresponding requirements.

abatement   Stopping or reducing of amount or value, as when assessments for ad valorem taxation are abated after the initial assessment has been made.

absentee landlord   An owner of an interest in income-producing property who does not reside on the premises and who may rely on a property manager to oversee the investment.

absolute fee simple title   A title that is unqualified. Fee simple is the best title that can be obtained. (See also *fee simple*.)

absorption analysis   A study of the number of units of residential or nonresidential property that can be sold or leased over a given period of time in a defined location. (See also *feasibility study*.)

abstraction   Method of finding land value in which all improvement costs (less depreciation) are deducted from sales price. Also called *extraction*.

access   A way to enter and leave a tract of land, sometimes by easement over land owned by another. (See also *egress* and *ingress*.)

accessibility   The relative ease of entrance to a property by various means, a factor that contributes to the probable most profitable use of a site.

accessory buildings   Structures on a property, such as sheds and garages, that are secondary to the main building.

accretion   Land buildup resulting from the deposit by natural action of sand or soil washed up from a river, lake, or sea.

accrual basis   In accounting, a system of allocating revenue and expense items on the basis of when the revenue is earned or the expense incurred, not on the basis of when the cash is received or paid out.

accrued depreciation   (1) For accounting purposes, total depreciation taken on an asset from the time of its acquisition. (2) For appraisal purposes, the difference between reproduction or replacement cost and the appraised value as of the date of appraisal.

accrued expenses   Expenses incurred that are not yet payable. In a closing statement, the accrued expenses of the seller typically are credited to the purchaser (taxes, wages, interest, etc.).

acquisition appraisal   A market value appraisal of property condemned or otherwise acquired for public use, to establish the compensation to be paid to the owner.

acre   A measure of land, 208.71 by 208.71 feet in area, being 43,560 square feet, 160 square rods, or 4,840 square yards.

actual age   The number of years elapsed since the original structure was built. Sometimes referred to as *historical* or *chronological age*.

adjustable-rate mortgage (ARM)   A financing technique in which the lender can raise or lower the interest rate according to a set index, such as the rate on six-month Treasury bills or the average cost of funds of FDIC-insured institutions. (See also *amortized mortgage*.)

adjustment   Decrease or increase in the sales price of a comparable property to account for a feature that the property has or does not have in comparison with the subject property.

ad valorem   According to value (Latin); generally used to refer to real estate taxes that are based on assessed property value.

adverse land use   A land use that has a detrimental effect on the market value of nearby properties.

aesthetic value   Relating to beauty, rather than to functional considerations.

age-life method of depreciation   A method of computing accrued depreciation in which the cost of a building is depreciated at a fixed annual percentage rate; also called the *straight-line method*.

aggregate   In statistics, the sum of all individuals, called *variates*.

air rights   The right to use the open space above the physical surface of the land, generally allowing the surface to be used for some other purpose.

allocation method   The allocation of the appraised total value of the property between land and building. The allocation may be accomplished either on a ratio basis or by subtracting a figure representing building value from the total appraised value of the property.

allowance for vacancy and collection losses   The percentage of potential gross income that will be lost due to vacant units, collection losses, or both.

amenities The qualities and state of being pleasant and agreeable; in appraising, those qualities that are attached to a property and from which the owner derives benefits other than monetary; satisfaction of possession and use arising from architectural excellence, scenic beauty, and social environment.

amortized mortgage A mortgage loan in which the principal and interest are payable in periodic installments during the term of the loan so that at the completion of all payments there is a zero balance.

annuity A fixed, regular return on an investment.

annuity method A method of capitalization that treats income from real property as a fixed, regular return on an investment. For the annuity method to be applied, the lessee must be reliable and the lease must be long term.

anticipation, principle of The principle that the purchase price of property is affected by the expectation of its future appeal and value.

appraisal An estimate of quantity, quality, or value; the process through which conclusions of property value are obtained; also refers to the report setting forth the process of estimating value. (See also *appraisal process*.)

Appraisal Foundation, The Nonprofit corporation established in 1987 and headquartered in Washington, D.C., sponsored by major appraisal and appraisal-related professional and trade groups.

appraisal methods The approaches used in the appraisal of real property. (See *cost approach, income capitalization approach, sales comparison approach*.)

appraisal process A systematic analysis of the factors that bear on the value of real estate; an orderly program by which the problem is defined; the work necessary to solve the problem is planned; the data involved are acquired, classified, analyzed, and interpreted into an estimate of value; and the final opinion of value is presented in the form requested by the client.

appraisal report An appraiser's written opinion to a client of the value sought for the subject property as of the date of appraisal, giving all details of the appraisal process.

Appraisal Standards Board Created by The Appraisal Foundation and responsible for establishing minimum standards of appraisal competence.

appraised value An estimate by an appraiser of the amount of a particular value, such as assessed value, insurable value, or market value, based on the particular assignment.

appraiser One who estimates value.

Appraiser Qualification Board Created by The Appraisal Foundation and responsible for establishing minimum requirements for licensed and certified appraisers and licensing and certifying examinations.

appreciation Permanent or temporary increase in monetary value over time due to economic or related causes.

approaches to value Any of the following three methods used to estimate the value of real estate: cost approach, income capitalization approach, and sales comparison approach.

appurtenance Anything used with land for its benefit, either affixed to land or used with it, that will pass with the conveyance of the land.

arm's-length transaction A transaction in which both buyer and seller act willingly and under no pressure, with knowledge of the present conditions and future potential of the property, and in which the property has been offered on the open market for a reasonable length of time and there are no unusual circumstances.

array An arrangement of statistical data according to numerical size.

assemblage The combining of two or more adjoining lots into one larger tract to increase their total value.

assessed value The value placed on land and buildings by a government unit (assessor) for use in levying annual real estate taxes.

assessment The imposition of a tax, charge, or levy, usually according to established rates. (See also *special assessment*.)

assessor One who determines property values for the purpose of ad valorem taxation.

asset Property that is owned and has value, such as cash or real or personal property.

average deviation In statistics, the measure of how far the average individual, or variate, differs from the mean of all variates.

balance The appraisal principle that states that the greatest value of a property will occur when the type and size of the improvements are proportional to each other as well as to the land.

band of investment A method of developing a discount rate based on (1) the rate of mortgage interest available, (2) the rate of return required on equity, and (3) the debt and equity share in the property. A variation of this method is used to compute an overall capitalization rate.

bargain and sale deed A deed that contains no warranties against liens or other encumbrances but implies that the grantor has the right to convey title.

base line A reference survey line of the government or rectangular survey, being an imaginary line extending east and west and crossing a principal meridian at a definite point.

base rent The minimum rent payable under a percentage lease.

bench mark A permanent reference mark (PRM) used by surveyors in measuring differences in elevation.

benchmark The standard or base from which specific estimates are made.

beneficiary The person who is to receive the benefits from a trust fund.

book value The value of a property as an asset on the books of account; usually, reproduction or replacement cost, plus additions to capital and less reserves for depreciation.

breakdown method (See *observed condition depreciation*.)

break-even point That point at which total income equals total expenses.

break-even ratio The ratio of operating expenses *plus* the property's annual debt service to potential gross income.

building capitalization rate The sum of the discount and capital recapture rates for a building.

building codes Rules of local, municipal, or state governments specifying minimum building and construction standards for the protection of public safety and health.

building residual technique A method of capitalization using net income remaining to building after interest on land value has been deducted.

bundle of rights A term often applied to the rights of ownership of real estate, including the rights of using, renting, selling, or giving away the real estate or *not* taking any of these actions.

CAMA. Computer Assisted Mass Appraisal Use of computerized databases and techniques in valuing commercial and residential properties for tax assessment purposes.

capital Money and/or property comprising the wealth owned or used by a person or business enterprise to acquire other money or goods.

capitalization The process employed in estimating the value of a property by the use of an appropriate capitalization rate and the annual net operating income expected to be produced by the property. The formula is expressed as

$$\frac{\text{Income}}{\text{Rate}} = \text{Value}$$

capitalization rate The percentage rate applied to the income a property is expected to produce to derive an estimate of the property's value; includes both an acceptable rate of return on the amount invested (yield) and return of the actual amount invested (recapture).

capital recapture The return of an investment; the right of the investor to get back the amount invested at the end of the term of ownership or over the productive life of the improvements.

capitalized value method of depreciation A method of computing depreciation by determining loss in rental value attributable to a depreciated item and applying a gross rent multiplier to that figure.

cash basis A system of recognizing revenue and expense items only at the time cash is received or paid out.

cash equivalency technique Method of adjusting a sales price downward to reflect the increase in value due to assumption or procurement by buyer of a loan at an interest rate lower than the prevailing market rate.

cash flow The net spendable income from an investment, determined by deducting all operating and fixed expenses from gross income. If expenses exceed income, a *negative* cash flow is the result.

cash flow rate (See *equity capitalization rate*.)

cash on cash rate (See *equity capitalization rate*.)

chain A surveyor's unit of measurement equal to four rods or 66 feet, consisting of 100 links of 7.92 inches each; ten square chains of land are equal to one acre.

change, principle of The principle that no physical or economic condition ever remains constant.

chattels Tangible personal property items.

client One who hires another person as a representative or agent for a fee.

closing statement The computation of financial adjustments required to close a real estate transaction, computed as of the day of closing the sale; used to determine the net amount of money the buyer must pay to the seller to complete the transaction, as well as amounts to be paid to other parties, such as the broker or escrow holder. (See also *settlement*.)

code of ethics Rules of ethical conduct, such as those that govern the actions of members of a professional group.

community property A form of property ownership in which husband and wife have an equal interest in property acquired by either spouse during the time of their marriage. Community property does not include property that each spouse owned prior to marriage or property received by gift or inheritance or as the proceeds of separate property.

comparables Properties that are substantially equivalent to the subject property.

comparative unit method (See *square-foot method*.)

comparison method (See *sales comparison approach*.)

competition, principle of The principle that a successful business attracts other such businesses, which may dilute profits.

complete appraisal The act or process of estimating value or an estimate of value, performed without invoking the Departure Rule of the Uniform Standards of Professional Appraisal Practice.

compound interest Interest paid on both the original investment and accrued interest.

condemnation Taking private property for public use through court action, under the right of eminent domain, with compensation to the owner.

conditional use permit Approval of a property use inconsistent with present zoning because it is in the public interest. For example, a church or hospital may be allowed in a residential district.

conditions, covenants, and restrictions (CC&Rs)
Private limitations on property use placed in the deed received by a property owner, typically by reference to a Declaration of Restrictions.

condominium   The absolute ownership of an apartment or a commercial unit, generally in a multiunit building, by a legal description of the airspace that the unit actually occupies, plus an undivided interest in the ownership of the common elements, which are owned jointly with the other condominium unit owners.

> **common elements**   All portions of the land, property, and space that make up a condominium property that include land, all improvements and structures, and all easements, rights, and appurtenances and exclude all space composing individual units. Each unit owner owns a definite percentage of undivided interest in the common elements.

> **parcel**   The entire tract of real estate included in a condominium development; also referred to as a *development parcel.*

> **unit**   One ownership space in a condominium building or a part of a property intended for independent use and having lawful access to a public way. Ownership of one unit also includes a definite undivided interest in the common elements.

conformity, principle of   The principle that buildings should be similar in design, construction, and age to other buildings in the neighborhood to enhance appeal and value.

contiguous   Adjacent; in actual contact; touching.

contract   An agreement entered into by two or more legally competent parties who, for a consideration, undertake to do or to refrain from doing some legal act or acts.

contract rent   (See *scheduled rent.*)

contribution, principle of   The principle that any improvement to a property, whether to vacant land or a building, is worth only what it adds to the property's market value, regardless of the improvement's actual cost.

conventional loan   A mortgage loan, made with real estate as security, that is neither insured by the FHA nor guaranteed by the VA.

conveyance   A written instrument, such as a deed or lease, by which title or an interest in real estate is transferred.

cooperative   A multiunit residential building with title in a trust or corporation that is owned by and operated for the benefit of persons living within it, who are the beneficial owners of the trust or the stockholders of the corporation, each possessing a proprietary lease granting occupancy of a specific unit in the building.

corporation   An association of shareholders, created under law, having a legal identity separate from the individuals who own it.

correction lines   A system of compensating for inaccuracies in the rectangular survey system due to the curvature of the earth. Every fourth township line (24-mile intervals) is used as a correction line on which the intervals between the north and south range lines are remeasured and corrected to a full six miles.

correlation   (See *reconciliation.*)

cost   The amount paid for a good or service.

cost approach   The process of estimating the value of a property by adding the appraiser's estimate of the reproduction or replacement cost of property improvements, less depreciation, to the estimated land value.

cost index   Figure representing construction cost at a particular time in relation to construction cost at an earlier time, prepared by a cost reporting or indexing service.

cost service index method   (See *index method.*)

covenant   An agreement written into deeds and other instruments promising performance or nonperformance of certain acts or stipulating certain uses or nonuses of property.

cubic-foot method   A method of estimating reproduction cost by multiplying the number of cubic feet of space a building encloses by the construction cost per cubic foot.

curable depreciation   A depreciated item that can be restored or replaced economically. (See also *functional obsolescence—curable* and *physical deterioration—curable.*)

data   Information pertinent to a specific appraisal assignment. Data may be *general* (relating to the economic background, the region, the city, and the neighborhood) or *specific* (relating to the subject property and comparable properties in the market).

datum   A horizontal plane from which heights and depths are measured.

debt investors   Investors who take a relatively conservative approach, typically taking a passive role in investment management while demanding a security interest in property financed.

declaration of restrictions   Document filed by a subdivision developer and referenced in individual deeds to subdivision lots that lists all restrictions that apply to subdivision properties. (See also *deed restrictions.*)

decreasing returns, laws of   The situation in which property improvements no longer bring a corresponding increase in property income or value.

deed   A written instrument that conveys title to or an interest in real estate when properly executed and delivered.

deed of trust   (See *trust deed.*)

deed restrictions   Provisions in a deed limiting the future uses of the property. Deed restrictions may take many forms: they may limit the density of buildings, dictate the types of structures that can be erected, and prevent buildings from being used for specific purposes or used at all. Deed restrictions may impose a myriad of limitations and conditions affecting the property rights appraised.

default   Failure to perform a duty or meet a contractual obligation.

demised premises   Property conveyed for a certain number of years, most often by a lease.

demography   The statistical study of human populations, especially in reference to size, density, and distribution. Demographic information is of particular importance to people involved in market analyses and highest and best use analyses in determining potential land uses of sites.

depreciated cost   For appraisal purposes the reproduction or replacement cost of a building, less accrued depreciation to the time of appraisal.

depreciation   For appraisal purposes, loss in value due to any cause, including physical deterioration, functional obsolescence, and external obsolescence. (See also *obsolescence.*)

depth factor
An adjustment factor applied to the value per front foot of lots that vary from the standard depth.

development   (See *neighborhood life cycle.*)

direct capitalization   Selection of a capitalization rate from a range of overall rates computed by analyzing sales of comparable properties and applying the following formula to each:

$$\frac{Income}{Value} = Rate, \quad \frac{I}{V} = R$$

direct costs   Costs of erecting a new building involved with either site preparation or building construction, including fixtures.

direct market comparison approach   (See *sales comparison approach.*)

discount rate   (See *interest rate.*)

disintegration   (See *neighborhood life cycle.*)

easement   A right to use the land of another for a specific purpose, such as a right-of-way or for utilities; a nonpossessory interest in land. An *easement appurtenant* passes with the land when conveyed.

economic base   The level of business activity in a community—particularly activity that brings income into the community from surrounding areas.

economic life   The period of time during which a structure may reasonably be expected to perform the function for which it was designed or intended.

economic obsolescence   (See *external obsolescence.*)

economic rent   (See *market rent.*)

EDI. Electronic Data Interchange   Transmission of information, including completed appraisal forms or other documents, via modem from one computer to another.

effective age   The age of a building based on the actual wear and tear and maintenance, or lack of it, that the building has received.

effective demand   The desire to buy coupled with the ability to pay.

effective gross income   Estimated potential gross income of a rental property from all sources, less anticipated vacancy and collection losses.

egress   A way to leave a tract of land; the opposite of ingress. (See also *access.*)

eminent domain   The right of a federal, state, or local government or public corporation, utility, or service corporation to acquire private property for public use through a court action called *condemnation,* in which the court determines whether the use is a necessary one and what the compensation to the owner should be.

encroachment   A building, wall, or fence that extends beyond the land of the owner and illegally intrudes on land of an adjoining owner or a street or an alley.

encumbrance   Any lien (such as a mortgage, tax lien, or judgment lien), easement, restriction on the use of land, outstanding dower right, or other interest that may diminish the value of property to its owner.

entrepreneurial profit   The amount of profit attributable to the development function.

environmental obsolescence   (See *external obsolescence.*)

equalization   The raising or lowering of assessed values for tax purposes in a particular county or taxing district to make them equal to assessments in other counties or districts.

equilibrium   (See *neighborhood life cycle.*)

equity   The interest or value that an owner has in real estate over and above any mortgage or other lien or charge against it.

equity capitalization rate   A rate that reflects the relationship between a single year's before-tax cash flow and the equity investment in the property. The before-tax cash flow is the net operating income less the annual debt service payment, and the equity is the property value less any outstanding loan balance. The equity capitalization rate, when divided into the before-tax cash flow, gives an indication of the value of the equity. Also called *cash on cash rate, cash flow rate,* or *equity dividend rate.*

equity dividend rate   (See *equity capitalization rate.*)

equity investors   Investors making use of what is termed *venture capital* to take an unsecured and thus relatively risky part in an investment.

escalator clause   A clause in a contract, lease, or mortgage providing for increases in wages, rent, or interest, based on fluctuations in certain economic indexes, costs, or taxes.

escheat   The reversion of property of a decedent who died intestate (without a will) and without heirs to the state or county as provided by state law.

escrow   The closing of a transaction through a disinterested third person called an *escrow agent* or *escrow holder,* who holds funds and/or documents for delivery on the performance of certain conditions.

estate   The degree, quantity, nature, and extent of ownership interest that a person has in real property.

estate in land   The degree, quantity, nature, and extent of interest a person has in real estate.

estate in remainder   The remnant of an estate that has been conveyed to take effect and be enjoyed after the termination of a prior estate; for instance, when an owner conveys a life estate to one party and the remainder to another. (For a case in which the owner retains the residual estate, see *estate in reversion.*)

estate in reversion   An estate that comes back to the original holder, as when an owner conveys a life estate to someone else, with the estate to return to the original owner on termination of the life estate.

excess income   (See *excess rent.*)

excess rent   The amount by which scheduled rent exceeds market rent.

expense   The cost of goods and services required to produce income.

expense-stop clause   Lease provision to pass increases in building maintenance expenses on to tenants on a pro rata basis.

external obsolescence   Loss of value from forces outside the building or property, such as changes in optimum land use, legislative enactments that restrict or impair property rights, and changes in supply-demand relationships.

externalities   The principle that outside influences may have a positive or negative effect on property value.

feasibility study   An analysis of a proposed subject or property with emphasis on the attainable income, probable expenses, and most advantageous use and design. The purpose of such a study is to ascertain the probable success or failure of the project under consideration.

Federal Reserve Bank System   Central bank of the United States established to regulate the flow of money and the cost of borrowing.

fee simple   The greatest possible estate or right of ownership of real property, continuing without time limitation. Sometimes called *fee* or *fee simple absolute.*

fee simple defeasible   Any limitation on property use that could result in loss of the right of ownership.

fee simple qualified   Ownership of property that is limited in some way.

FHA   The Federal Housing Administration. Insures loans made by approved lenders in accordance with its regulations.

final opinion of value   The appraiser's opinion of the defined value of the subject property, arrived at by reconciling (correlating) the estimates of values derived from the sales comparison, cost, and income approaches.

Financial Institutions Reform, Recovery, and Enforcement Act of 1989 (FIRREA)   Federal legislation that mandates state licensing or certification for appraisers performing appraisals in certain federally related transactions.

first mortgage   A mortgage that has priority as a lien over all other mortgages.

fixed expenses   Those costs that are more or less permanent and do not vary in relation to the property's occupancy or income, such as real estate taxes and insurance for fire, theft, and hazards.

fixed-rate mortgage   (See *amortized mortgage.*)

fixture   Anything affixed to land, including personal property attached permanently to a building or to land so that it becomes part of the real estate.

foreclosure   A court action initiated by a mortgagee or lienor for the purpose of having the court order that the debtor's real estate be sold to pay the mortgage or other lien (mechanic's lien or judgment).

form appraisal report   Any of the relatively brief standard forms prepared by agencies such as the Federal Home Loan Mortgage Corporation and Federal National Mortgage Association and others for routine property appraisals.

freehold   An estate in land in which ownership is for an indeterminate length of time.

frequency distribution   The arrangement of data into groups according to the frequency with which they appear in the data set.

front foot   A standard of measurement, being a strip of land one foot wide fronting on the street or waterfront and extending the depth of the lot. Value may be quoted per front foot.

functional obsolescence   Defects in a building or structure that detract from its value or marketability, usually the result of layout, design, or other features that are less desirable than features designed for the same functions in newer property.

functional obsolescence—curable   Physical or design features that are no longer considered desirable by property buyers but could be replaced or redesigned at relatively low cost.

functional obsolescence—incurable   Currently undesirable physical or design features that are not easily remedied or economically justified.

GIS. Geographic Information Systems   Various types of software that make use of a computerized database to produce maps based on satellite imaging–derived reference points on the earth's surface.

going concern value   The value existing in an established business property compared with the value of selling the real estate and other assets of a concern whose business is not yet established. The term takes into account the goodwill and earning capacity of a business.

grant deed   A type of deed in which the grantor warrants that he or she has not previously conveyed the estate being granted to another, has not encumbered the property except as noted in the deed, and will convey to the grantee any title to the property the grantor may later acquire.

grantee   A person who receives a conveyance of real property from a grantor.

grantor   The person transferring title to or an interest in real property to a grantee.

gross building area   All enclosed floor areas, as measured along a building's outside perimeter.

gross income   (See *potential gross income.*)

gross income multiplier   A figure used as a multiplier of the gross income of a property to produce an estimate of the property's value.

gross leasable area   Total space designed for occupancy and exclusive use of tenants, measured from outside wall surfaces to the center of shared interior walls.

gross lease   A lease of property under the terms of which the lessee pays a fixed rent and the lessor pays all property charges regularly incurred through ownership (repairs, taxes, insurance, and operating expenses).

gross living area   Total finished, habitable, above-grade space, measured along the building's outside perimeter.

gross market income   (See *potential gross income.*)

gross rent multiplier   (See *gross income multiplier.*)

ground lease   A lease of *land only* on which the lessee usually owns the building or is required to build as specified by the lease. Such leases are usually long-term net leases; the lessee's rights and obligations continue until the lease expires or is terminated for default.

ground rent   Rent paid for the right to use and occupy land according to the terms of a ground lease.

growing equity mortgage (GEM)   A type of loan that rapidly increases the equity in a property by increasing the monthly payments a certain percentage each year and applying those increases to the principal.

highest and best use   The legally and physically possible use of land that is likely to produce the highest land (or property) value. It considers the balance between site and improvements as well as the intensity and length of uses.

historical cost   Actual cost of a property at the time it was constructed.

historical rent   Scheduled (or contract) rent paid in past years.

holdover tenancy   A tenancy in which the lessee retains possession of the leased premises after the lease has expired and the landlord, by continuing to accept rent from the tenant, thereby agrees to the tenant's continued occupancy.

homeowners' association   Organization of property owners in a residential condominium or subdivision development, usually authorized by a declaration of restrictions to establish property design and maintenance criteria, collect assessments, and manage common areas.

Hoskold sinking fund table   A table that supplies a factor by which a property's annual net income may be multiplied to find the present worth of the property over a given period at a given rate of interest.

HUD   Department of Housing and Urban Development.

improved land   Real property made suitable for building by the addition of utilities and publicly owned structures, such as a curb, sidewalk, street-lighting system, and/or sewer.

improvements   Structures of whatever nature, usually privately rather than publicly owned, erected on a site to enable its utilization, e.g., buildings, fences, driveways, and retaining walls.

income capitalization approach   The process of estimating the value of an income-producing property by capitalization of the annual net operating income expected to be produced by the property during its remaining economic life.

increasing returns, law of   The situation in which property improvements increase property income or value.

incurable depreciation   A depreciated item that would be impossible or too expensive to restore or replace.

independent contractor   A person who contracts to do work for another by using his or her own methods and without being under the control of the other person regarding how the work should be done. Unlike an employee, an independent contractor pays all of his or her expenses, personally pays income and Social Security taxes, and receives no employee benefits. Many real estate salespeople are independent contractors.

index method   An appraisal technique used to estimate reproduction or replacement cost. The appraiser multiplies the original cost of construction by a price index for the geographic area to allow for price changes.

indirect costs   Costs of erecting a new building not involved with either site preparation or building construction; for example, building permit, land survey, overhead expenses such as insurance and payroll taxes, and builder's profit.

industrial district or park   A controlled development zoned for industrial use and designed to accommodate specific types of industry, providing public utilities, streets, railroad sidings, and water and sewage facilities.

ingress   The way to enter a tract of land. Often used interchangeably with *access*. (See also *access*.)

installment contract   A contract for the sale of real estate by which the purchase price is paid in installments over an extended period of time by the purchaser, who is in possession, with the title retained by the seller until a certain number of payments are made. The purchaser's payments may be forfeited on default.

insurable value   The highest reasonable value that can be placed on property for insurance purposes.

interest   A percentage of the principal amount of a loan charged by a lender for its use, usually expressed as an annual rate.

interest rate   Return on an investment; an interest rate is composed of four component rates—*safe rate, risk rate, nonliquidity rate,* and *management rate.*

management rate   Compensation to the owner for the work involved in managing an investment and reinvesting the funds received from the property.

nonliquidity rate   A penalty charged for the time needed to convert real estate into cash.

risk rate   An addition to the safe rate to compensate for the hazards that accompany investments in real estate.

safe rate   The interest rate paid by investments of maximum security, highest liquidity, and minimum risk.

interim use   A temporary property use awaiting transition to its highest and best use.

intestate   Dying without a will or without having made a valid will. Title to property owned by someone who dies intestate will pass to his or her heirs as provided in the law of descent of the state in which the property is located.

investment value   The worth of investment property to a specific investor.

Inwood annuity table   A table that supplies a factor to be multiplied by the desired yearly income (based on the interest rate and length of time of the investment) to find the present worth of the investment.

joint tenancy   Ownership of real estate between two or more parties who have been named in one conveyance as joint tenants. On the death of a joint tenant, the decedent's interest passes to the surviving joint tenant(s) by the right of survivorship.

joint venture   The joining of two or more people to conduct a specific business enterprise. A joint venture is similar to a partnership in that it must be created by agreement between the parties to share in the losses and profits of the venture. It is unlike a partnership in that the venture is for one specific project only, rather than for a continuing business relationship.

land   The earth's surface in its natural condition, extending down to the center of the globe, its surface and all things affixed to it, and the air space above the surface.

land capitalization rate   The rate of return, including interest, on land only.

land development method   (See *subdivision development method*.)

landlocked parcel   A parcel of land without any access to a public road or way.

landlord   One who owns property and leases it to a tenant.

land residual technique   A method of capitalization using the net income remaining to the land after return on and recapture of the building value have been deducted.

land trust   A trust originated by the owner of real property in which real estate is the only asset. Because the interest of a beneficiary is considered personal property and not real estate, a judgment against the beneficiary will not create a lien against the real estate. Thus land trusts are popular when there are multiple owners who seek protection against the effects of divorce, judgments, or bankruptcies of each other.

latent defect   Physical deficiencies or construction defects not readily ascertainable from a reasonable inspection of the property, such as a defective septic tank or underground sewage system, or improper plumbing or electrical wiring.

lease   A written or oral contract for the possession and use of real property for a stipulated period of time, in consideration for the payment of rent. Leases for more than one year generally must be in writing.

leased fee   The lessor's interest and rights in the real estate being leased.

leasehold estate   The lessee's right to possess and use real estate during the term of a lease. This is generally considered a personal property interest.

legal description   A statement identifying land by a system prescribed by law. (See also *lot and block system, metes and bounds description,* and *rectangular survey system*.)

lessee   The person to whom property is leased by another; also called a *tenant*.

lessee's interest   An interest having value only if the agreed-on rent is less than the market rent.

lessor   The person who leases property to another; also called a *landlord*.

lessor's interest   The value of lease rental payments plus the remaining property value at the end of the lease period.

letter of transmittal   First page of a narrative appraisal report, in which the report is formally presented to the person for whom the appraisal was made.

levy   To impose or assess a tax on a person or property; the amount of taxes to be imposed in a given district.

license   (1) The revocable permission for a temporary use of land—a personal right that cannot be sold. (2) Formal permission from a constituted authority (such as a state agency) to engage in a certain activity or business (such as real estate appraisal).

lien   A right given by law to certain creditors to have their debts paid out of the property of a defaulting debtor, usually by means of a court sale.

life estate   An interest in real or personal property that is limited in duration to the lifetime of its owner or some other designated person or persons.

limited appraisal   The act or process of estimating value, or an estimate of value, performed under and resulting from invoking the Departure Provision of the Uniform Standards of Professional Appraisal Practice.

living trust   An arrangement in which a property owner (trustor) transfers assets to a trustee, who assumes specified duties in managing the asset. After the payment of operating expenses and trustee's fees, the income generated by the trust property is paid to or used for the benefit of the designated beneficiary. The living trust is gaining popularity as a way to hold title and avoid probate of trust assets.

lot and block system   Method of legal description of an individual parcel of land by reference to tract, block, and lot numbers and other information by which the parcel is identified in a recorded subdivision map. Also called *lot, block, and tract system* and *subdivision system.*

maintenance expenses   Costs incurred for day-to-day upkeep, such as management, wages and benefits of building employees, fuel, utility services, decorating, and repairs.

manufactured home   A structure transportable in one or more sections, designed and equipped to contain not more than two dwelling units to be used with or without a foundation system; does not include a recreational vehicle.

marital property   (See *community property* and *tenancy by the entirety.*)

markers   (See *monuments.*)

market   A place or condition suitable for selling and buying.

market comparison approach   (See *sales comparison approach.*)

market comparison method of depreciation   (See *sales comparison method of depreciation.*)

market data approach   (See *sales comparison approach.*)

market extraction method of depreciation   (See *sales comparison method of depreciation.*)

market price   (See *sales price.*)

market rent   The amount for which the competitive rental market indicates property should rent. An estimate of a property's rent potential.

market value   The most probable price real estate should bring in a sale occurring under normal market conditions.

mean   The average of all items included within a group, calculated by dividing the sum of the individual items, or variates, by the number of variates.

mechanic's lien   A lien created by statute that exists in favor of contractors, laborers, or materialmen who have performed work or furnished materials in the erection or repair of a building.

meridian   (See *principal meridian.*)

metes and bounds description   A method of legal description specifying the perimeter of a parcel of land by use of measured distances from a point of beginning along specified boundaries, or bounds, using monuments, or markers, as points of reference.

mile   A measurement of distance, being 1,760 yards or 5,280 feet.

monuments   Natural or artificial objects used to define the perimeter of a parcel of land using the metes and bounds method of legal description.

mortgage   A conditional transfer or pledge of real property as security for the payment of a debt; also, the document used to create a mortgage lien.

mortgage constant   The first-year debt payment divided by the beginning loan balance.

mortgagee   The lender in a loan transaction secured by a mortgage.

mortgagor   An owner of real estate who borrows money and uses his or her property as security for the loan.

narrative appraisal report   A detailed written presentation of the facts and reasoning behind an appraiser's opinion of value.

neighborhood   A residential or commercial area with similar types of properties, buildings of similar value or age, predominant land-use activities, and natural or fabricated geographic boundaries, such as highways or rivers.

neighborhood life cycle   The period during which most of the properties in a neighborhood undergo the stages of development, equilibrium, decline, and revitalization.

> **decline**   Properties require an increasing amount of upkeep to retain their original utility and become less desirable.
>
> **development (growth)**   Improvements are made, and properties experience a rising demand.
>
> **equilibrium**   Properties undergo little change; also called *stability.*
>
> **revitalization**   Property renovations occur in response to demand; also called *rehabilitation.*

net income ratio   The ratio of net operating income to effective gross income.

net lease   A lease requiring the tenant to pay rent and part or all of the costs of maintenance including taxes, insurance, repairs, and other expenses of ownership. Sometimes known as an *absolute net lease, triple net lease,* or *net, net, net lease.*

net operating income (NOI)   Income remaining after operating expenses are deducted from effective gross income.

nonconforming use   A once lawful property use that is permitted to continue after a zoning ordinance prohibiting it has been established for the area; a use that differs sharply from the prevailing uses in a neighborhood.

observed condition depreciation   A method of computing depreciation in which the appraiser estimates the loss in value for all items of depreciation. (See also *incurable depreciation* and *curable depreciation.*)

obsolescence   Lessening of value from out-of-date features as a result of current changes in property design, construction, or use; an element of depreciation. (See also *external obsolescence* and *functional obsolescence.*)

occupancy   Possession and use of property as owner or tenant.

occupancy rate   The percentage of total rental units occupied and producing income.

operating expense ratio   The ratio of total operating expenses to effective gross income.

operating expenses   The cost of all goods and services used or consumed in the process of obtaining and maintaining income. (See also *fixed expenses, maintenance expenses,* and *reserves for replacement.*)

operating statement   The written record of a business's gross income, expenses, and resultant net income.

operating statement ratio   Relationship of a property's expenses to income, found by dividing total operating expenses by effective gross income.

opportunity cost   The value differential between alternative investments with differing rates of return.

option   A right given for a valuable consideration to purchase or lease property at a future date, for a specified price and terms. The right may or may not be exercised at the option holder's (optionee's) discretion.

orientation   Positioning a structure on its lot with regard to exposure to the sun, prevailing winds, privacy, and protection from noise.

overage rent   Rent paid over a base amount in a percentage lease.

overall capitalization rate   A rate of investment return derived by comparing the net income and sales prices of comparable properties.

overall rate   The direct ratio between a property's annual net income and its sales price.

overimprovement   An improvement to property that is more than warranted by the property's highest and best use and thus not likely to contribute its cost to the total market value of the property.

ownership in severalty   Individual ownership of real estate, not to be confused with the use of the word *several* to mean "more than one"; also called *tenancy in severalty, sole tenancy,* or *separate ownership.*

paired sales analysis   A method of estimating the amount of adjustment for the presence or absence of any feature by pairing the sales prices of otherwise identical properties with and without the feature in question. A sufficient number of sales must be found to allow the appraiser to isolate the effect on value of the pertinent factor (also called *paired data set analysis* and *matched pairs analysis*).

parameter   A single number or attribute of the individual things, persons, or other entities in a population.

partial interest   Any property interest that is less than full fee simple ownership of the entire property.

partnership   An association of two or more individuals who carry on a continuing business for profit as co-owners. Under the law a partnership is regarded as a group of individuals rather than as a single entity.

percentage lease   A lease commonly used for commercial property that provides for a rental based on the tenant's gross sales at the premises. It generally stipulates a base monthly rental, plus a percentage of any gross sales exceeding a certain amount.

personal property   Items that are tangible and movable and do not fit the definition of realty; chattels.

physical deterioration—curable   Loss of value due to neglected repairs or maintenance that are economically feasible and, if performed, would result in an increase in appraised value equal to or exceeding their cost.

physical deterioration—incurable   Loss of value due to neglected repairs or maintenance of short-lived or long-lived building components that would not contribute comparable value to a building if performed.

physical life   The length of time a structure can be considered habitable, without regard to its economic use.

planned unit development (PUD)   A subdivision consisting of individually owned residential and/or commercial parcels or lots as well as areas owned in common.

plat   A map representing a parcel of land subdivided into lots, showing streets and other details or a single site.

plottage value   The subsequent increase in the unit value of a group of adjacent properties when they are combined into one property in a process called *assemblage.*

point of beginning   Place at which a legal description of land using the metes and bounds method starts.

police power   The right of the government to impose laws, statutes, and ordinances to protect the public health, safety, and welfare. Includes zoning ordinances and building codes.

possession   The right of the owner to occupy property. When property is occupied by a tenant, the owner has constructive possession by right of title.

potential gross income   A property's total potential income from all sources during a specified period of time.

prepaid items of expense   Expense items, such as insurance premiums and tax reserves, that have been paid in advance of the time that the expense is incurred. Prepaid expenses typically are prorated and credited to the seller in the preparation of a closing statement.

price   The amount of money set or paid as the consideration in the sale of an item at a particular time.

principal   (1) A sum lent or employed as a fund or investment—as distinguished from its income or profits; (2) the original amount (as of a loan) of the total due and payable at a certain date; or (3) a party to a transaction—as distinguished from an agent.

principal meridian   One of 35 north and south survey lines established and defined as part of the U.S. government or rectangular survey system.

profit-and-loss statement   (See *operating statement*.)

prorations   The adjustment of taxes, interest, insurance, and/or other costs on a pro rata basis as of the closing of a sale. (See also *closing statement*.)

purchase money mortgage   A note secured by a mortgage or trust deed given by the buyer, as mortgagor, to the seller, as mortgagee, as part of the purchase price of real estate.

quantity survey method   A method for finding the reproduction cost of a building in which the costs of erecting or installing all of the component parts of a new building, including both direct and indirect costs, are added.

quitclaim deed   A conveyance by which the grantor transfers whatever interest he or she has in the land, without warranties or obligations.

range   A measure of the difference between the highest and lowest items in a data set.

real estate   Land; a portion of the earth's surface extending downward to the center of the earth and upward into space including fixtures permanently attached thereto by nature or by man, anything incidental or appurtenant to land, and anything immovable by law; freehold estate in land.

real estate broker   Any person, partnership, association, or corporation that, for compensation or valuable consideration, sells or offers for sale, buys or offers to buy, or negotiates the purchase, sale, or exchange of real estate; or that leases or offers to lease, or rents or offers for rent any

real estate or the improvement thereon for others. Such a broker must secure a state license. For a license to be issued to a firm, it is usually required that all active partners or officers be licensed real estate brokers.

real estate investment trust (REIT)   Trust ownership of real estate by a group of individuals who purchase certificates of ownership in the trust, which in turn invests the money in real property and distributes the profits to the investors free of corporate income tax.

real estate salesperson   Any person who, for compensation or valuable consideration, is employed either directly or indirectly by a real estate broker to sell or offer to sell; or to buy or offer to buy; or to negotiate the purchase, sale, or exchange of real estate; or to lease, rent, or offer for rent any real estate; or to negotiate leases thereof or improvements thereon. Such a salesperson must secure a state license.

real property   The rights of ownership of real estate, often called the *bundle of rights;* for all practical purposes, synonymous with real estate.

recapture rate   The percentage of a property's original cost that is returned to the owner as income during the remaining economic life of the investment.

reconciliation   The step in the appraisal process in which the appraiser reconciles the estimates of value received from the sales comparison, cost, and income capitalization approaches to arrive at a final opinion of market value for the subject property.

reconstruction of the operating statement   The process of eliminating the inapplicable expense items for appraisal purposes and adjusting the remaining valid expenses, if necessary.

reconveyance deed   A deed used by a trustee under a deed of trust to return title to the trustor.

rectangular survey system   A system established in 1785 by the federal government, which provides for the surveying and describing of land by reference to principal meridians and base lines; also called *U.S. government survey system* and *section and township system*.

regional multipliers   Adjustment factors by which standard cost figures can be multiplied to allow for regional price differences.

remainder   The remnant of an estate that has been conveyed to take effect and be enjoyed after the termination of a prior estate; for instance, when an owner conveys a life estate to one party and the remainder to another. (For the case in which the owner retains the residual estate, see *reversion*.)

remainderman   The party designated to receive a remainder estate. There are two types: *vested* remainderman (one who is known and named) and *contingent* remainderman (one whose identity is not certain or who is to be selected).

remaining economic life The number of years of useful life left to a building from the date of appraisal.

renewal option Lease provision that allows the lessee to renew the lease for the same term or some other stated period, usually with a rent increase at a stated percentage or based on an index or other formula.

rent Payment under a lease or other arrangement for use of a property.

rent loss method of depreciation (See *capitalized value method of depreciation.*)

replacement cost The current construction cost of a building having exactly the same utility as the subject property.

reproduction cost The current construction cost of an exact duplicate of the subject building.

reserves for replacement Allowances set up for replacement of building and equipment items that have a relatively short life expectancy.

residual In appraising, the value remaining after all deductions have been made.

resolution trust corporation (RTC) Federal agency created by the Financial Institutions Reform, Recovery, and Enforcement Act of 1989 to oversee management and liquidation of assets of failed savings and loan associations.

reverse annuity mortgage (RAM) An instrument designed to aid elderly homeowners by providing them a monthly income over a period of years in exchange for equity they have acquired in their homes. RAM borrowers typically may obtain up to 80 percent of the appraised value of free-and-clear property.

reversion The remnant of an estate that the grantor (as opposed to a third party) holds after he or she has granted a limited estate such as a leasehold or life estate to another person and that will return or revert back to the grantor. (See also *remainder.*)

right-of-way The right that one has to travel over the land of another; an easement.

riparian rights Rights of an owner of land that borders on or includes a stream, river, lake, or sea. These rights include definition of (and limitations on) access to and use of the water, ownership of streambed, navigable water, and uninterrupted flow and drainage. (See also *accretion.*)

risk rate (See *interest rate.*)

rod A measure of length, 16 ½ feet.

safe rate (See *interest rate.*)

sales comparison approach The process of estimating the value of property through examination and comparison of actual sales of comparable properties; also called the *direct market comparison* or *market data approach.*

sales comparison method of depreciation Way of estimating loss in value through depreciation by using sales prices of comparable properties to derive the value of a depreciated item. Also called the *market data method* and the *market extraction method.*

salesperson (See *real estate salesperson.*)

sales price The actual price that a buyer pays for a property.

sandwich lease The ownership interest of a sublessee.

scheduled rent Rent paid by agreement between lessor and lessee; also called *contract rent.*

second mortgage A mortgage loan secured by real estate that has previously been made security for an existing mortgage loan. Also called a *junior mortgage* or *junior lien.*

selling price The actual price that a buyer pays for a property.

settlement The process of closing a real estate transaction by adjusting and prorating the required credits and charges.

shared appreciation mortgage (SAM) A loan designed for borrowers whose current income is too low to qualify for another type of mortgage. The SAM loan makes the lender and the borrower partners by permitting the lender to share in property appreciation. In return, the borrower receives a lower interest rate.

sheriff's deed Deed given by a court to effect the sale of property to satisfy a judgment.

sinking fund method Use of a factor by which a property's annual net income may be multiplied to find the present worth of the property over a given period at a given rate of interest.

site Land suitable for building purposes, usually improved by the addition of utilities or other services.

special assessment A charge against real estate made by a unit of government to cover the proportional cost of an improvement, such as a street or sewer.

special-purpose property Property that has unique usage requirements, such as a church or a museum, making it difficult to convert to other uses.

square-foot method A method for finding the reproduction cost of a building in which the cost per square foot of a recently built comparable structure is multiplied by the number of square feet in the subject property.

standard deviation A measure of the difference between individual entities, called *variates,* and an entire population, in which the square root of the sum of the squared differences between each variate and the mean of all the variates in the population is divided by the number of variates in the population.

statistics The science of collecting, classifying, and interpreting information based on the number of things.

straight-line method of depreciation (See *age-life method of depreciation.*)

straight-line recapture A method of capital recapture in which total accrued depreciation is spread over the useful life of a building in equal amounts.

subdivision A tract of land divided by the owner into blocks, building lots, and streets by a recorded subdivision plat. Compliance with local regulations is required.

subdivision development method A method of valuing land to be used for subdivision development. It relies on accurate forecasting of market demand, including both forecast absorption (the rate at which properties will sell) and projected gross sales (total income that the project will produce); also called the *land development method.*

subleasehold The interest of a sublessee under a sandwich lease.

subletting The leasing of premises by a lessee to a third party for a part of the lessee's remaining term.

substitution, principle of The basic appraisal premise that the market value of real estate is influenced by the cost of acquiring a substitute or comparable property.

summation method Another name for the cost approach to appraising.

supply and demand, principle of A principle that the value of a commodity will rise as demand increases and/or supply decreases.

survey The process of measuring land to determine its size, location, and physical description; also, the map or plat showing the results of a survey.

tax deed The instrument used to convey legal title to property sold by a governmental unit for nonpayment of taxes.

tax-stop clause A clause in a lease providing that the lessee will pay any increase in taxes over a base or an initial year's taxes.

tenancy by the entirety The joint ownership, recognized in some states, of property acquired by husband and wife during marriage. On the death of one spouse the survivor becomes the owner of the property.

tenancy in common A form of co-ownership by which each owner holds an undivided interest in real property as if he or she were sole owner. Each individual owner has the right to partition. Unlike joint tenants, tenants in common have the right of inheritance.

tenancy in severalty (See *ownership in severalty.*)

tenant One who has possession of real estate; an occupant, not necessarily a renter; the lessee under a lease. The estate or interest held is called a *tenancy.*

time-share Estate or use interest in real property for a designated time period each year.

title The evidence of a person's right to the ownership and possession of land.

topography Surface features of land; elevation, ridges, slope, contour.

trade fixtures Articles of personal property installed by a commercial tenant under the terms of a lease. Trade fixtures are removable by the tenant before the lease expires and are not true fixtures.

triple net lease (See *net lease.*)

trust A fiduciary arrangement whereby property is conveyed to a person or an institution, called a *trustee,* to be held and administered on behalf of another person or entity, called a *beneficiary.* The one who conveys the trust is called the *trustor.*

trust deed An instrument used to create a mortgage lien by which the borrower conveys title to a trustee, who holds it as security for the benefit of the note holder (the lender); also called a *deed of trust.*

trustee The holder of bare legal title in a deed of trust loan transaction.

trustor The borrower in a deed of trust loan transaction.

underimprovement An improvement that is less than a property's highest and best use.

Uniform Standards of Professional Appraisal Practice (USPAP) Minimal criteria for appraisal competency promulgated by The Appraisal Foundation at the direction of Congress, to be applied to appraisals that require the services of a state-licensed or certified appraiser.

unit-in-place method A method for finding the reproduction cost of a building in which the construction cost per square foot of each component part of the subject building (including material, labor, overhead, and builder's profit) is multiplied by the number of square feet of the component part in the subject building.

useful life (See *economic life.*)

use value The value of a property designed to fit the specific requirements of the owner but that would have little or no use to another owner. Also referred to as *value-in-use.*

usury Charging interest in excess of the maximum legal rate.

vacancy and collection losses (See *allowance for vacancy and collection losses.*)

valuation principles Factors that affect market value, such as the principles of substitution, highest and best use, supply and demand, conformity, contribution, increasing and decreasing returns, competition, change, stage of life cycle, anticipation, externalities, balance, surplus productivity, opportunity cost, and agents of production.

value The power of a good or service to command other goods or services in exchange; the present worth of future rights to income and benefits arising from ownership.

value in exchange   The value of goods and services in exchange for other goods and services, or money, in the marketplace; an economic concept of market value.

VA mortgage   A mortgage loan on approved property made to a qualified veteran by an authorized lender and guaranteed by the Department of Veterans Affairs to limit possible loss by the lender.

variance   (See *zoning variance.*)

variate   In statistics, an individual thing, person, or other entity.

vendee   Buyer.

vendor   Seller.

warranty deed   A deed in which the grantor fully warrants good clear title to the property.

yield   Income produced by an investment. Usually used to refer to equity investments.

yield capitalization   Method used to estimate value from annual net operating income by applying a capitalization rate derived by analyzing each of the rate's component parts to provide both return on and return of the investment.

zoning   Municipal or county regulation of land use within designated districts or *zones*. Zoning is an application of a state's *police power* to regulate private activity by enacting laws that benefit the public health, safety, and general welfare. Zoning may affect use of the land, lot sizes, type of structure permitted, building heights, setbacks, and density.

zoning ordinance   Regulation of the character and use of property by a municipality or other government entity through the exercise of its police power.

zoning variance   An exemption from a zoning ordinance or regulation permitting a structure or use that would not otherwise be allowed.

ANSWER KEY

■ CHAPTER 1

Exercise 1.1

All of the courses listed would benefit a professional appraiser because they touch on topics that must be understood in order to prepare a well-reasoned appraisal report.

Exercise 1.2

An appraiser's compensation should not depend on the estimate of value obtained, to avoid even the appearance of impropriety. The appraiser's compensation may, however, reflect the complexity of the work required in dealing with the subject property.

Exercise 1.3

1. b
2. b
3. a
4. b

Achievement Examination 1

1. Numerous courses, such as economics, geography, sociology, city planning, accounting, statistics
2. a
3. c
4. a
5. b
6. b
7. d

■ CHAPTER 2

Exercise 2.1

Real estate or real property: 1, 2, 3, 4, 5, 6, 9, 10
Personal property: 7, 8
If an item were personal property, it could not be considered in estimating the value of real property. On the other hand, if the item were real estate, then its contribution to the value of the real property would have to be estimated.

Exercise 2.2

40 acres

Exercise 2.3

1. Fee simple absolute, or fee simple
2. Tenant owns a leasehold estate; landlord owns a leased fee estate.
3. Mary Jones's land is the dominant tenement. Tom Yan's land is the servient tenement.
4. Joint tenancy
5. Condominium

Exercise 2.4

1. The grantor of a quitclaim deed makes no warranty that he or she actually owns any interest to convey in the described property; any interest that is owned, however, will be conveyed by the deed.
2. Recording a deed serves notice to the world of the title transfer if the deed is recorded in the county where the property is located.

Achievement Examination 2

1. b
2. c
3. d
4. d
5. d
6. b
7. c
8. a
9. d
10. b
11. a
12. b
13. c
14. a
15. c

16. Whether something attached to real property is a fixture may be determined by considering the intention of the person who placed the item on the land, the method of attachment, the adaptability of the thing for the land's ordinary use, the agreement of the parties, and the relationship of the parties.

17. b

18. c

19. c

■ CHAPTER 3

Exercise 3.1

Likely to prevent an arm's-length transaction: 1, 3, 5, 6

Exercise 3.2

1. Highest and best use, change, conformity

2. Contribution, laws of increasing and decreasing returns

3. Contribution, laws of increasing and decreasing returns, competition

4. Competition, contribution

5. Laws of increasing and decreasing returns, contribution

6. Externalities

Achievement Examination 3

1. c

2. d

3. b

4. a

5. b

6. a

7. b

8. Market value is an estimate of the worth of a property. Sales price is the actual selling price of a property.

9. Progression

10. Substitution

11. Anticipation

12. Highest and best use

13. Highest and best use

14. Supply and demand

15. Contribution

■ CHAPTER 4

Exercise 4.1

Sales comparison approach: $778,000 − $27,000 = $751,000 (Value of house X)
Cost approach: $230,000 − (30% × $230,000) + $52,000 = Property value
$230,000 − $69,000 + $52,000 = $213,000
Income capitalization approach: $64,500 ÷ 12% = $537,500

Exercise 4.2

1. Cost

2. Income capitalization

3. Cost

4. Sales comparison

5. Income capitalization

6. Sales comparison

7. Income capitalization

8. Sales comparison

9. Cost

10. Income capitalization

Achievement Examination 4

1. a   3. b

2. c   4. c

5. Value of property B: $180,000 − $16,000 = $164,000

6. $725,000 − (40% × $725,000) + $175,000 = Property value
$725,000 − 290,000 + $175,000 = $610,000

7. $124,000 ÷ 9% = $1,377,800 (rounded to nearest hundred dollars)

■ CHAPTER 5

Exercise 5.1

1. a. One-and-a-half-story house: there is economy in cost per cubic foot of habitable space and built-in expandability.

   b. Two-story house: plumbing can be lined up; winter heating is used to the best advantage (heat rises); more house can be built on a smaller piece of property.

   c. Split-entry house: the square footage of the house is doubled at a modest cost increase by finishing the rooms on the lower level.

2. If a house is oriented with the main living areas facing south, it can result in savings in heating and air-conditioning costs. Orientation also contributes to the enjoyment of a house if it takes advantage of a natural view and the maximum amount of land is allocated for private use.

Exercise 5.2

1. Solid cores are generally preferred for exterior doors because they provide better heat and sound insulation and are more resistant to warping. Hollow-core doors are about a third as heavy as the solid-core type and are commonly used for interior locations where heat and sound insulation are not as critical.

2. The *water supply system* brings water to the house from a well or city main and distributes hot and cold water through two sets of pipes. The *vent piping system* carries out of the house all sewer gases from drainage lines.

3. The main drawback to the heat pump is its initial cost. Once installed, however, the heat pump operates very economically and requires little maintenance.

4. 1. *Safety*—The system must meet all NEC requirements.
   2. *Capacity*—The system must meet the home's existing needs and have the capacity to accommodate room additions and new appliances.
   3. *Convenience*—There should be enough switches, lights, and outlets, and they should be located so that occupants will not have to walk in the dark or use extension cords.

5. *Balloon* construction differs from the *platform* method in that the studs are continuous, extending to the ceiling of the second floor, rather than shorter lengths, extending the length of one floor at a time. The platform method is usually preferred.

6. *Firestopping:* Boards or blocks nailed between studs or joists to stop drafts and retard the spread of fire.

7. *Circuit breaker box:* The distribution panel for the many electrical circuits in the house. If a circuit is overloaded, the heat generated by the additional flow of electrical power will cause the circuit breaker to open at the breaker box. By removing the overload and allowing the breaker to cool, the switch in the circuit breaker box may be turned to "on" and electrical service restored.

8. *Insulation:* Batts or loose fill placed in outside walls or ceilings to prevent loss of heat from structure in winter and transfer of heat into structure in summer.

9. *Monolithic slab:* Concrete slab forming foundation area of structure. Monolithic concrete is poured in a continuous process so there are no separations due to different setting times.

10. *Sills:* The horizontal members of the foundation that are secured to the piers by the anchor bolts to prevent the house from sliding from its foundation.

Achievement Examination 5

1. b
2. monolithic concrete slab
3. balloon frame
4. wood sheathing covered with building paper, and siding (probably wood)
5. plaster over wallboard
6. could be either single or double hung
7. finished wood on first floor; unfinished concrete in basement

■ CHAPTER 6

Exercise 6.1

The property being appraised is the single-family residence located at 2130 West Franklin Street, Lakeside, Illinois. Fee simple property rights are to be appraised. The purpose of the appraisal is to estimate market value, which is the most probable price the property should bring in a sale occurring under normal market conditions. The date of valuation is the date of the report.

As a general rule, the sales comparison approach is most useful in valuing properties of this type.

Exercise 6.2

1. (1) Personal inspection

   (6) Register of deeds

   (42) Plats

2. (19) Building architects, contractors, and engineers

   (12) City hall or county courthouse

   (20) County or city engineering commission

3. (12) City hall or county courthouse

   (20) County or city engineering commission

   (22) Area planning commissions

4. (22) Area planning commissions

   (29) United States Bureau of the Census

   (32) Local chamber of commerce

   (33) Government councils

5. (1) Personal inspection

   (22) Area planning commissions

   (44) Area maps

6. (1) Personal inspection

   (12) City hall or county courthouse

   (22) Area planning commissions

   (32) Local chamber of commerce

   (44) Area maps

   (28) Public utility companies

7. (12) City hall or county courthouse

   (20) County or city engineering commission

   (22) Area planning commissions

8. (6) Register of deeds

   (7) Title reports

9. (7) Title reports

   (12) City hall or county courthouse

   (13) Assessor's office

Exercise 6.3

Note: Race and the racial composition of the neighborhood are not appraisal factors.

Neighborhood Characteristics			One-Unit Housing Trends				One-Unit Housing		Present Land Use %	
Location ☒ Urban	☐ Suburban	☐ Rural	Property Values ☒ Increasing	☐ Stable	☐ Declining		PRICE	AGE	One-Unit	95%
Built-Up ☒ Over 75%	☐ 25–75%	☐ Under 25%	Demand/Supply ☐ Shortage	☒ In Balance	☐ Over Supply		$ (000)	(yrs)	2-4 Unit	1%
Growth ☐ Rapid	☐ Stable	☒ Slow	Marketing Time ☐ Under 3 mths	☒ 3–6 mths	☐ Over 6 mths		160 Low	5	Multi-Family	%

Neighborhood Boundaries *Cedar, Parkside, Ellis, and Lombard define this* — 280 High 22 Commercial 1%
predominantly residential neighborhood known as the Gunderson area. — 240 Pred. 7 Other *Vac* 1%

Neighborhood Description *Fifteen-minute commute time to downtown Midstate and convenient schools, shopping and health care facilities continue to make the Gunderson area very desirable and demand for homes has been consistent.*

Market Conditions (including support for the above conclusions) *Although sales prices have kept pace with inflation, a seasonal slowdown has resulted in an average marketing time of three months. This remains a healthy market, however, with no indication of a downturn.*

Exercise 6.4

Dimensions *50' × 200'*   Area *10,000 sq. ft.*   Shape *Rectangular*   View *Residential*

Specific Zoning Classification *R-2*   Zoning Description *Residential, Single-Family*

Zoning Compliance ☒ Legal   ☐ Legal Nonconforming (Grandfathered Use)   ☐ No Zoning   ☐ Illegal (describe)

Is the highest and best use of the subject property as improved (or as proposed per plans and specifications) the present use? ☒ Yes   ☐ No If No, describe

Utilities	Public	Other (describe)		Public	Other (describe)	Off-site Improvements—Type	Public	Private
Electricity	☒	☐	Water	☒	☐	Street *Asphalt*	☒	☐
Gas	☒	☐	Sanitary Sewer	☒	☐	Alley	☐	☐

FEMA Special Flood Hazard Area ☐ Yes ☒ No FEMA Flood Zone   FEMA Map #   FEMA Map Date

Are the utilities and off-site improvements typical for the market area? ☒ Yes ☐ No If No, describe

Are there any adverse site conditions or external factors (easements, encroachments, environmental conditions, land uses, etc.)? ☒ Yes ☐ No If Yes, describe

Apparent utility easement across rear ten feet of site.

Exercise 6.5

General Description		Foundation		Exterior Description materials/condition	Interior materials/condition
Units ☒ One ☐ One with Accessory Unit		☐ Concrete Slab ☐ Crawl Space		Foundation Walls *Concrete/good*	Floors *Wd/tile/carpet/Gd*
# of Stories *1*		☒ Full Basement ☐ Partial Basement		Exterior Walls *Brick/good*	Walls *Drywall/Good*
Type ☒ Det. ☐ Att. ☐ S-Det./End Unit		Basement Area *1,300* sq. ft.		Roof Surface *Mineral-fiber shingles/Gd*	Trim/Finish
☒ Existing ☐ Proposed ☐ Under Const.		Basement Finish *50* %		Gutters & Downspouts *Aluminum/Gd*	Bath Floor *Vinyl tile/Good*
Design (Style) *Ranch/brick*		☐ Outside Entry/Exit ☐ Sump Pump		Window Type *Wood double-hung/Gd*	Bath Wainscot *Ceramic/Gd*
Year Built *6 yrs. ago*		Evidence of ☐ Infestation		Storm Sash/Insulated *Aluminum/Gd*	Car Storage ☐ None
Effective Age (Yrs) *5*		☐ Dampness ☐ Settlement		Screens *Aluminum/Good*	☒ Driveway # of Cars
Attic	☒ None	Heating ☒ FWA ☐ HWBB ☐ Radiant		Amenities ☐ Woodstove(s) #	Driveway Surface *Asphalt*
☐ Drop Stair	☐ Stairs	☐ Other Fuel *Gas*		☐ Fireplace(s) # ☐ Fence	☒ Garage # of Cars *2*
☐ Floor	☐ Scuttle	Cooling ☒ Central Air Conditioning		☐ Patio/Deck ☐ Porch	☐ Carport # of Cars
☐ Finished	☐ Heated	☐ Individual ☐ Other		☐ Pool ☐ Other	☒ Att. ☐ Det. ☐ Built-in

Appliances ☒Refrigerator ☒Range/Oven ☒Dishwasher ☒Disposal ☐Microwave ☐Washer/Dryer ☒Other (describe) *Range Fan/Hood*

Finished area **above** grade contains: *6* Rooms   *3* Bedrooms   *1.50* Bath(s)   *1,300* Square Feet of Gross Living Area Above Grade

Additional features (special energy efficient items, etc.)

Describe the condition of the property (including needed repairs, deterioration, renovations, remodeling, etc.). *Overall good exterior and interior condition of improvements noted with no indication of functional inadequacies.*

Are there any physical deficiencies or adverse conditions that affect the livability, soundness, or structural integrity of the property? ☐ Yes ☐ No If Yes, describe

Does the property generally conform to the neighborhood (functional utility, style, condition, use, construction, etc.)? ☒ Yes ☐ No If No, describe

Exercise 6.6

1. records on previous appraisals; county clerk's office; principals involved; brokers or salespeople

2. Sale 2 should be dropped from consideration because of its age. Sale 5 should be dropped because it has three more rooms than the subject; if the only difference was its having only one bathroom, it could still be considered as a comparable.

Achievement Examination 6

1. c
2. c
3. a
4. b
5. d
6. a
7. d
8. b
9. a
10. a

■ CHAPTER 7

Exercise 7.1

1. to value vacant sites
2. to apply the cost approach to value
3. to levy special assessments for public improvements
4. for taxation purposes
5. to estimate building depreciation
6. to apply the building residual technique
7. may be required in condemnation appraising
8. to determine if the site is realizing its highest and best use

Exercise 7.2

	Sales Price	Time	Location	Physcial Features	Net Adj. + or –	Adjusted Price
Dollar basis	$20,000	+ $2,400	$2,000	– $3,000	+ $1,400	$21,400
Percentage basis	$20,000	+ 12%	+ 10%	– 15%	+ 7%	$21,400

Exercise 7.3

Land value is $347,000 ÷ 4, or $86,750.

Exercise 7.4

Total projected sales:

48 lots at $27,000 per lot	$1,296,000	
16 lots at $32,000 per lot	512,000	
8 lots at $36,000 per lot	288,000	
72		$2,096,000

Total projected development costs — 934,000
Estimated value of raw land — $1,162,000
Raw land value per lot: $1,162,000 ÷ 72 — $16,139

Present worth of lot sales:

First year: 48 lots at $16,139 per lot = $774,672

$774,672 discounted to present worth at
12 percent for one year (.893) $ 691,782

Second year: 16 lots at $16,139 per lot = $258,224

$258,224 discounted to present worth
at 12 percent for two years (.797)   205,805

Third year: 8 lots at $16,139 per lot = $129,112

$129,112 discounted to present worth
at 12 percent for three years (.712)   91,928

Amount subdivider should pay for raw land $ 989,515

Achievement Examination 7

1. The earth's surface, and everything under it or on it, is considered *land.* When the land is improved by the addition of utilities (water, gas, electricity) or other services (such as sewers), it becomes a *site* and may be considered suitable for building purposes.

2. a. In applying the cost approach, site value must be distinguished from the cost of improvements, as indicated by the following formula:

$$\text{Cost of Improvements New} - \text{Depreciation on Improvements} + \text{Site Value} = \text{Estimated Property Value}$$

   b. In computing depreciation for tax purposes, site value must be subtracted from total property value, because land is not depreciable.

3. Sales comparison method; allocation method; abstraction method; subdivision development method; ground rent capitalization; land residual method.

   The sales comparison approach is preferred whenever sales of similar vacant sites are available. The underlying presumption is that recent sales of comparable sites competitive with the subject site are the most reliable guide to the probable current market behavior and reactions of informed buyers.

4. b
5. c
6. a
7. b
8. c

■ CHAPTER 8

Exercise 8.1

The house shown in the bottom photograph:
It is an old house that cannot be economically produced today.

Exercise 8.2

537.8 ÷ 158.2 × $39,000 = $132,580

Exercise 8.3

Area of comparable building: 45' × 50' = 2,250 sq. ft.
$184,500 ÷ 2,250 = $82 (cost per square foot)

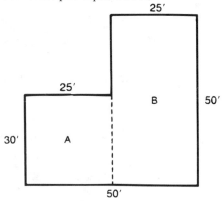

A = 30' × 25'	750 sq. ft.
B = 25' × 50'	1,250 sq. ft.
Total area	2,000 sq. ft.

Cost estimate: 2,000 sq. ft. × $82 = $164,000

Exercise 8.4

Unit-in-place costs:

Foundation		
Perimeter, 750 ft. @ $37.30		$ 27,975
Floor		
31,250 sq. ft. @ $3.10		96,875
Roof		
31,250 sq. ft. @ $3.60 ($2.40 + $.65 + $.55)		112,500
Interior construction		
Painting and partitions		4,500
Front exterior wall		
125' × 15' = 1,875 sq. ft.		
– 144 sq. ft. for windows		
– 120 sq. ft. for door =		
1,611 sq. ft. @ $9.50	$ 15,305	
Windows 144 sq. ft. @ $15.30	2,203	
Door	1,300	18,808

Rear exterior wall

1,875 sq. ft. – 120 sq. ft. = 1,755 sq. ft. @ $9.50	$ 16,673	
Door	1,300	17,973

Side exterior walls

500' × 15' = 7,500 sq. ft. – 20% for windows = 6,000 sq. ft. @ $7.10	$ 42,600	
Windows 1,500 sq. ft. @ $14.20	21,300	63,900

Steel framing
Area supported by frame

100' × 225' = 22,500 sq. ft. @ $4.50	101,250

Electric

31,250 sq. ft. @ $3.25	101,563

Heating

31,250 sq. ft. @ $2.75	85,938

Plumbing

31,250 sq. ft. @ $1.60	50,000
Total Reproduction Cost	$ 681,282

$681,282 ÷ 31,250 sq. ft. = about $21.80 per sq. ft.

Exercise 8.5

1. direct
2. direct
3. indirect
4. direct
5. indirect
6. indirect

Achievement Examination 8

1. a
2. b
3. b
4. a
5. c
6. d
7. c
8. a
9. c
10. a

■ **CHAPTER 9**

Exercise 9.1

Age-life method:

    Total depreciation = 28% (7 ÷ 25)

    Dollar amount of accrued depreciation = $126,000 ($450,000 × .28)

Exercise 9.2

1. External obsolescence—incurable
2. Physical deterioration—long-lived incurable
3. Physical deterioration—short-lived incurable
4. External obsolescence—incurable
5. Physical deterioration—curable
6. Physical deterioration—short-lived incurable
7. Functional obsolescence—incurable
8. Functional obsolescence—incurable
9. Functional obsolescence—incurable
10. Functional obsolescence—curable

Exercise 9.3

$1,100 − $980 = $120 loss in rent

$120 × 125 monthly rent multiplier = $15,000 loss in property value

Exercise 9.4

$156,000 − $142,000 = $14,000 loss in property value

Exercise 9.5

	Reproduction Cost	Observed Depreciation	Amount of Depreciation
heating system	$12,800	60%	$ 7,680
plumbing	15,200	30	4,560
electric and power	23,000	40	9,200
floors	18,200	45	8,190
roof	16,500	55	9,075
Total	$85,700		$ 38,705

Reproduction cost: 125' × 160' = 20,000 sq. ft.

                  20,000 × $55 = $1,100,000

Depreciation itemized above		− 85,700
Balance of building depreciation	$1,014,300 × .20	202,860
Total depreciation		$241,565

Applying the formula for the cost approach:

      $1,100,000 − $241,565 + $180,000 = $1,038,435 property value

Exercise 9.6

Estimated reproduction cost new of improvements

Direct costs	$98,500	
Indirect costs	26,500	
Total reproduction cost		$125,000

Cost per square foot of living area

($125,000 ÷ 1,900 sq. ft.), $65.79

Estimated accrued depreciation
Physical deterioration

Curable	$ 5,250	
Incurable—short-lived	12,250	– 17,500
Reproduction cost of long-lived items		$107,500
Incurable—long-lived:		
5 (effective age) ÷ 50 (economic life)		× .10
Incurable—long-lived		$ 10,750
Total physical deterioration		

($5,250 + $12,250 + $10,750) = $28,250

Summation and value indication by the cost approach to value

Estimated reproduction cost new of improvements		$125,000
Estimated accrued depreciation		
Physical deterioration	$28,250	
Functional obsolescence	0	
External obsolescence	9,000	
Total estimated accrued depreciation		– 37,250
Estimated reproduction cost less accrued depreciation		$ 87,750
Estimated site value		+40,000
Indicated value by the cost approach		$127,750

Exercise 9.7

COST APPROACH TO VALUE (not required by Fannie Mae)				
Provide adequate information for the lender/client to replicate the below cost figures and calculations.				
Support for the opinion of site value (summary of comparable land sales or other methods for estimating site value)				
ESTIMATED ☒ REPRODUCTION OR ☐ REPLACEMENT COST NEW	OPINION OF SITE VALUE		=$ *98,000*	
Source of cost data	Dwelling *2,625* Sq. Ft. @ $ *112*		=$*294,000*	
Quality rating from cost service Effective date of cost data	*Deck 450* Sq. Ft. @ $ *20*		=$ *9,000*	
Comments on Cost Approach (gross living area calculations, depreciation, etc.)				
Cost estimate supported by current costs of local	Garage/Carport *676* Sq. Ft. @ $ *30*		=$ *20,280*	
contractors verified by current cost manual.	Total Estimate of Cost-New		= $*323,280*	
Depreciation based on observed physical deterioration	Less Physical	Functional	External	
and age of property. Site value suggested by market	Depreciation *65,000*			=$(*65,000*)
data on comparable sites.	Depreciated Cost of Improvements			=$*258,280*
	"As-is" Value of Site Improvements			=$ *12,000*
Estimated Remaining Economic Life (HUD and VA only) Years	Indicated Value By Cost Approach			=$*368,280*

Achievement Examination 9

1. Total factory area: 100' × 150' = 15,000 sq. ft.

2. Total office area: 50' × 50' = 2,500 sq. ft.

3. Total building area: 15,000 sq. ft. + 2,500 sq. ft. = 17,500 sq. ft.

4. Building perimeter:

   100' + 150' + 50' + 50' + 50' + 50' + 200' = 650 linear ft.

5. Total parking area: 90' × 200' = 18,000 sq. ft. = 2,000 sq. yd.

6. Area covered by common brick:

100' + 150' + 50' + 150' = 450' × 14'	6,300 sq. ft.	
Plus area above office roof 50' × 4'	200	
Plus area along office walls		
50' + 50' = 100' × 10'	1,000	7,500 sq. ft.
Less— Door area 12' × 12'	144 sq. ft.	
5 (3' × 7')	105	
Window area 10 (6' × 12')	720	− 969
Total area covered by common brick		6,531 sq. ft.

7. Area covered by face brick:

50' × 10'		500 sq. ft.
Less— Door area 3' × 7'	21 sq. ft.	
Window area 6' × 12'	72	− 93
Total area covered by face brick		407 sq. ft.

8. Interior wall area for office:

Private office 32' × 2 sides = 64' × 8'	512 sq. ft.	
Private office 34' × 2 sides = 68' × 8'	544	
Storage room 24' × 2 sides = 48' × 8'	384	
Washrooms 46' × 2 sides = 92' × 8'	736	2,176 sq. ft.
Less door area 6 (3' × 7') × 2 sides		− 252
Total interior wall area for office		1,924 sq. ft.

9. Perimeter of office:

50' + 50' + 50' + 50' = 200' × 8'		1,600 sq. ft.
Less— Door area 3(3' × 7')	63 sq. ft.	
Window area 6' × 12'	72	− 135
Total perimeter of office		1,465 sq. ft

10.
50' × 14'	700 sq. ft.
Less one door 3' × 7'	− 21
Total	679 sq. ft.

11. Steel frame: 75' × 125' = 9,375 sq. ft.

12. Total land area: 210' × 230' = 48,300 sq. ft.

13. Land value:

    Of the four sales listed, the price of only the smallest parcel, C, appears to be out of line. The remaining sales are priced from $2.20 to $2.25 per square foot, a narrow range.

    Because no additional information is given, and parcel D is closest to the subject lot in size, $2.25 per square foot seems appropriate in estimating the land value.

    Land value = 48,300 sq. ft. × $2.25 = $108,675

14. Foundation: 650 linear feet, 12" concrete @ $30.70 = $19,955

15. Exterior walls:

Common brick, 12" block, 6,531 sq. ft. @ $10.2	$66,616
Jumbo face brick veneer 407 sq. ft. @ $3.80	1,547
Total for exterior walls	$68,163

16. Roof construction:

sheathing	$ .65
1⅞" fiberglass insulation	1.10
4-ply tar and gravel covering	2.40
Total	$4.15

    17,500 sq. ft. of building area @ $4.15 = $72,625

17. Framing: 9,375 sq. ft. @ $4.50 = $42,188

18. Floor construction:

    17,500 sq. ft. 6" reinforced concrete @ $3.10 = $54,250

19. Windows: 11 (6' × 12') = 792 sq. ft. @ $20.10 = $15,919

20. Exterior doors:

6 (3' × 7') metal @ $355	$2,130
12' × 12' rolling steel @ $1,425	1,425
Total for exterior doors	$3,555

21. Interior construction:

Wall area for office (drywall on wood studs), 1,924 sq. ft. @ $3.15	$6,061
Concrete block dividing wall 679 sq. ft. @ $4.40	2,988
Perimeter of office 1,465 sq. ft. @ $.25 (painting)	366
Total for walls	$9,415

    Doors: 7 (3'× 7') @ $275 = $1,925

    Floor covering: 2,500 sq. ft. vinyl tile in office @ $1.90 = $4,750

    Ceiling (office): 2,500 sq. ft. mineral fiber acoustic tile @ $1.65 = $4,125

22. Electric: 17,500 sq. ft. @ $3.10 = $54,250

23. Plumbing: 17,500 sq. ft. @ $2.75 = $48,125

24. Heating and air-conditioning: 17,500 sq. ft. @ $5.75 = $100,625

25. Miscellaneous:

    Parking area: 2,000 sq. yd. @ $7.20 = $14,400

26. Reproduction Costs:

Exterior construction

Foundation	$ 19,955
Floor construction	54,250
Exterior walls	68,163
Framing	42,188
Roof construction	72,625
Windows	15,919
Exterior doors	3,555

Interior construction

Walls	9,415
Floor covering	4,750
Ceiling	4,125
Interior doors	1,925
Electrical	54,250
Plumbing	48,125
Heating and air-conditioning	100,625

Miscellaneous

Parking	14,400
Total reproduction cost	$514,270

27. Depreciation

Observed depreciation, deterioration—short-lived incurable

brickwork $68,163 × 40%	$ 27,265
roof (asphalt and gravel) $42,000 × 60%	25,200
exterior doors $3,555 × 75%	2,666
floor (vinyl tile) $4,750 × 55%	2,613
acoustic tile ceiling $4,125 × 45%	1,856
electrical $54,250 × 35%	18,988
plumbing $48,125 × 30%	14,438
heating and air-conditioning $100,625 × 30%	30,188
asphalt paving $14,400 × 40%	5,760
Deterioration—short-lived incurable	$128,974

Total reproduction cost	$514,270	
Full cost of short-lived incurable items	−339,993	
Balance of building	$174,277	
Deterioration—long-lived incurable	× .25	43,569
Total physical deterioration		$172,543

Incurable functional obsolescence

Net value after physical deterioration: $514,270 − 172,543 = $341,727

Incurable functional obsolescence: $341,727 × 5% = $17,086

28. Cost valuation

Reproduction cost		$514,270
Depreciation:		
Deterioration—curable	0	
—short-lived incurable	$128,974	
—long-lived incurable	43,569	
Functional obsolescence		
—curable	0	
—incurable	17,086	
External obsolescence	0	
Total accrued depreciation		−189,629
Building value estimate		324,641
Land value estimate		108,675
Total property value indicated by cost approach		$433,316

■ CHAPTER 10

Exercise 10.1 (See form on page 412.)

Construction: Aluminum siding, rather than brick

$242,000 − $233,000 = $9,000

No. of Bedrooms: 4 (1 extra)

$252,000 − $242,000 = $10,000

No. of Baths: extra ½ bath

$247,000 − $242,000 = $5,000

Exercise 10.2 (See forms on pages 413 and 414.)

No. All properties are similar to the subject and should be considered in this appraisal.

Exercise 10.3 (See forms on pages 415 and 416.)

Exercise 10.4 (See forms on pages 417 and 418.)

Exercise 10.5

Because the value range (excluding comparable 2) is close and comparable 5 required no adjustment, it is reasonable to estimate that the subject property has a market value of $251,000.

Achievement Examination 10 (See pages 419–422.)

3. $173,500 is the indicated market value of the subject property by the sales comparison approach.

E X E R C I S E   10.1
Sales Price Adjustment Chart

Sales Price Adjustment Chart
Comparables

	A	B	C	D	E	F	G	H	I	J
SALES PRICE	$242,000	$233,000	$243,000	$247,000	$241,000	$220,000	$268,000	$221,000	$252,000	$242,000
FINANCING	80% conv.	90% conv.	80% conv.	95% conv.	90% conv.	95% conv.	90% conv.	80% conv.	90% conv.	80% conv.
DATE OF SALE	6 wks.	2 mos.	3 wks.	5 wks.	6 wks.	5 wks.	3 wks.	1 yr.	5 wks.	11 wks.
LOCATION	resid.	resid.	resid.	resid.	resid.	highway	commercial	resid.	resid.	resid.
LEASEHOLD/FEE SIMPLE	fee	fee	fee	fee	fee	fee	fee	fee	fee	fee
VIEW	good	good	good	good	good	good	good	good	good	good
SITE	50' × 200'	50' × 200'	50' × 200'	50' × 200'	50' × 200'	50' × 200'	50' × 200'	50' × 200'	50' × 200'	50' × 200'
DESIGN	ranch/good	ranch/good	ranch/good	ranch/good	ranch/good	ranch/good	ranch/good	ranch/good	ranch/good	ranch/good
CONSTRUCTION	brick	aluminum siding	brick	brick	brick	brick	brick	brick	brick	brick
AGE	8 yrs.	7 yrs.	8 yrs.	6 yrs.	6 yrs.	7 yrs.	6 yrs.	7 yrs.	6 yrs.	7 yrs.
CONDITION	good	good	good	good	good	good	good	good	good	good
NO. OF RMS./BEDRMS./BATHS	7/3/2	7/3/2	7/3/2	7/3/2½	7/3/2	7/3/2	7/3/2	7/3/2	8/4/2	7/3/2
SQ. FT. OF LIVING SPACE	1,475	1,500	1,490	1,500	1,500	1,525	1,500	1,550	1,600	1,500
OTHER SPACE (BASEMENT)	full basement	full basement	full basement	full basement	full basement	full basement	full basement	full basement	full basement	full basement
FUNCTIONAL UTILITY	adequate	adequate	adequate	adequate	adequate	adequate	adequate	adequate	adequate	adequate
HEATING/COOLING	central heat/air	central heat/air	central heat/air	central heat/air	central heat/air	central heat/air	central heat/air	central heat/air	central heat/air	central heat/air
ENERGY EFFICIENT ITEMS	none	none	none	none	none	none	none	none	none	none
GARAGE/CARPORT	2-car att.	2-car att.	2-car att.	2-car att.	2-car att.	2-car att.	2-car att.	2-car att.	2-car att.	2-car att.
OTHER EXT. IMPROVEMENTS	patio	patio	patio	patio	patio	patio	patio	patio	patio	patio
OTHER INT. IMPROVEMENTS Fireplace	one	one	one	one	one	one	one	one	one	one
TYPICAL HOUSE VALUE	$242,000	242,000	242,000	242,000	242,000	242,000	242,000	242,000	242,000	242,000
VARIABLE FEATURE		aluminum siding		extra half bath		poor location	commercial area	year-old sale	4th bedroom	
ADJUSTMENT VALUE OF VARIABLE		$9,000		$5,000		$22,000	$26,000	$21,000	$10,000	

EXERCISE 10.2
Sales Comparison Approach

Uniform Residential Appraisal Report   File

There are	comparable properties currently offered for sale in the subject neighborhood ranging in price from $		to $	.
There are	comparable sales in the subject neighborhood within the past twelve months ranging in sale price from $		to $	.

FEATURE	SUBJECT	COMPARABLE SALE # 1		COMPARABLE SALE # 2		COMPARABLE SALE # 3	
Address 2130 W. Franklin		1901 Parkside Blvd.		2135 Hastings Ave.		2129 Osceola Way	
Proximity to Subject		Within half-mile		Within half-mile		Within half-mile	
Sale Price	$ N/A	$ 226,000		$ 239,000		$ 238,000	
Sale Price/Gross Liv. Area	$ N/A sq. ft.	$ 125.56 sq. ft.		$ 127.47 sq. ft.		$ 130.41 sq. ft.	
Data Source(s)		Sales agent		Sales agent		Sales agent	
Verification Source(s)		Sales agent		Sales agent		Sales agent	
VALUE ADJUSTMENTS	DESCRIPTION	DESCRIPTION	+(-) $ Adjustment	DESCRIPTION	+(-) $ Adjustment	DESCRIPTION	+(-) $ Adjustment
Sale or Financing Concessions		None		None		None	
Date of Sale/Time		6 weeks ago		1 year ago		2 months ago	
Location	quiet street	heavy traffic		quiet street		quiet street	
Leasehold/Fee Simple	fee Simple	fee Simple		fee Simple		fee Simple	
Site	50¢ ´200¢	50¢ ´200¢		50' ×200'		50' ×200'	
View	good	good		good		good	
Design (Style)	ranch/good	ranch/good		ranch/good		ranch/good	
Quality of Construction	good	good		good		gd/alum.sid.	
Actual Age	6 years	8 years		7 years		8 years	
Condition	good	good		good		good	
Above Grade	Total	Bdrms.	Baths	Total	Bdrms.	Baths	
Room Count	7 3 2.5	7 3 2		7 3 2		7 3 2.5	
Gross Living Area	1,825 sq. ft.	1,800 sq. ft.		1,875 sq. ft.		1,825 sq. ft.	
Basement & Finished Rooms Below Grade	full basement	full basement		full basement		full basement	
Functional Utility	adequate	adequate		adequate		adequate	
Heating/Cooling	central H/A	central H/A		central H/A		central H/A	
Energy Efficient Items	none	none		none		none	
Garage/Carport	2-car att.	2-car att.		2-car att.		2-car att.	
Porch/Patio/Deck	none	none		none		none	
Net Adjustment (Total)		☐ + ☐ -	$	☐ + ☐ -	$	☐ + ☐ -	$
Adjusted Sale Price of Comparables		Net Adj. %		Net Adj. %		Net Adj. %	
		Gross Adj. %	$	Gross Adj. %	$	Gross Adj. %	$

I ☐ did ☐ did not research the sale or transfer history of the subject property and comparable sales. If not, explain

My research ☐ did ☐ did not reveal any prior sales or transfers of the subject property for the three years prior to the effective date of this appraisal.

Data source(s)

My research ☐ did ☐ did not reveal any prior sales or transfers of the comparable sales for the year prior to the date of sale of the comparable sale.

Data source(s)

Report the results of the research and analysis of the prior sale or transfer history of the subject property and comparable sales (report additional prior sales on page 3).

ITEM	SUBJECT	COMPARABLE SALE # 1	COMPARABLE SALE # 2	COMPARABLE SALE # 3
Date of Prior Sale/Transfer				
Price of Prior Sale/Transfer				
Data Source(s)				
Effective Date of Data Source(s)				

Analysis of prior sale or transfer history of the subject property and comparable sales

Summary of Sales Comparison Approach

EXERCISE 10.2 (continued)
Sales Comparison Approach

Uniform Residential Appraisal Report   File

| There are | comparable properties currently offered for sale in the subject neighborhood ranging in price from $ | | | | to $ | | . |
| There are | comparable sales in the subject neighborhood within the past twelve months ranging in sale price from $ | | | | to $ | | . |

FEATURE	SUBJECT	COMPARABLE SALE # 4		COMPARABLE SALE #5		COMPARABLE SALE # 3	
Address 2130 W. Franklin		2243 Parkside Blvd.		2003 Franklin St.			
Proximity to Subject		Within half-mile		Within half-mile			
Sale Price	$ N/A		$ 256,500	$ 251,000		$	
Sale Price/Gross Liv. Area	$ N/A sq. ft.	$133.25 sq. ft.		$137.53 sq. ft.		$ sq. ft.	
Data Source(s)		Sales agent		Sales agent			
Verification Source(s)		Sales agent		Sales agent			
VALUE ADJUSTMENTS	DESCRIPTION	DESCRIPTION	+(-) $ Adjustment	DESCRIPTION	+(-) $ Adjustment	DESCRIPTION	+(-) $ Adjustment
Sale or Financing Concessions		none		none			
Date of Sale/Time		5 weeks ago		5 weeks ago			
Location	quiet street	quiet street		quiet street			
Leasehold/Fee Simple	fee Simple	fee Simple		fee Simple			
Site	50¢ × 200¢	50¢ × 200¢		50' × 200'			
View	good	good		good			
Design (Style)	ranch/good	ranch/good		ranch/good			
Quality of Construction	good	good		good			
Actual Age	6 years	6 years		7 years			
Condition	good	good		good			
Above Grade	Total Bdrms. Baths	Total Bdrms. Baths		Total Bdrms. Baths		Total Bdrms. Baths	
Room Count	7 3 2.5	8 4 2		7 3 2.5			
Gross Living Area	1,825 sq. ft.	1,925 sq. ft.		1,825 sq. ft.		sq. ft.	
Basement & Finished Rooms Below Grade	full basement	full basement		full basement			
Functional Utility	adequate	adequate		adequate			
Heating/Cooling	central H/A	central H/A		central H/A			
Energy Efficient Items	none	none		none			
Garage/Carport	2-car att.	2-car att.		2-car att.			
Porch/Patio/Deck	none	none		none			
Net Adjustment (Total)		☐ + ☐ -	$	☐ + ☐ -	$	☐ + ☐ -	$
Adjusted Sale Price of Comparables		Net Adj. %		Net Adj. %		Net Adj. %	
		Gross Adj. %	$	Gross Adj. %	$	Gross Adj. %	$

I ☐ did ☐ did not research the sale or transfer history of the subject property and comparable sales. If not, explain

My research ☐ did ☐ did not reveal any prior sales or transfers of the subject property for the three years prior to the effective date of this appraisal.

Data source(s)

My research ☐ did ☐ did not reveal any prior sales or transfers of the comparable sales for the year prior to the date of sale of the comparable sale.

Data source(s)

Report the results of the research and analysis of the prior sale or transfer history of the subject property and comparable sales (report additional prior sales on page 3).

ITEM	SUBJECT	COMPARABLE SALE # 1	COMPARABLE SALE # 2	COMPARABLE SALE # 3
Date of Prior Sale/Transfer				
Price of Prior Sale/Transfer				
Data Source(s)				
Effective Date of Data Source(s)				

Analysis of prior sale or transfer history of the subject property and comparable sales

Summary of Sales Comparison Approach

Indicated Value by Sales Comparison Approach $

EXERCISE 10.3
Sales Comparison Approach

Uniform Residential Appraisal Report   File

There are	comparable properties currently offered for sale in the subject neighborhood ranging in price from $					to $	
There are	comparable sales in the subject neighborhood within the past twelve months ranging in sale price from $					to $	

FEATURE	SUBJECT	COMPARABLE SALE # 1	+(-) $ Adjustment	COMPARABLE SALE # 2	+(-) $ Adjustment	COMPARABLE SALE # 3	+(-) $ Adjustment
Address	2130 W.Franklin	1901 Parkside Blvd.		2135 Hastings Ave.		2129 Osceola Way	
Proximity to Subject		Within half-mile		Within half-mile		Within half-mile	
Sale Price	$ N/A	$ 226,000		$ 239,000		$ 238,000	
Sale Price/Gross Liv. Area	$ N/A sq. ft.	$ 125.56 sq. ft.		$ 127.47 sq. ft.		$ 130.41 sq. ft.	
Data Source(s)		Sales agent		Sales agent		Sales agent	
Verification Source(s)		Sales agent		Sales agent		Sales agent	
VALUE ADJUSTMENTS	DESCRIPTION	DESCRIPTION	+(-) $ Adjustment	DESCRIPTION	+(-) $ Adjustment	DESCRIPTION	+(-) $ Adjustment
Sale or Financing Concessions		none		none		none	
Date of Sale/Time		6 wks ago		1 year ago	+22,700	2 months ago	
Location	quiet street	heavy traffic	+22,000	quiet street	(rounded)	quiet street	
Leasehold/Fee Simple	fee simple	fee simple		fee simple		fee simple	
Site	50' × 200'	50' × 200'		50' × 200'		50' × 200'	
View	good	good		good		good	
Design (Style)	ranch/good	ranch/good		ranch/good		ranch/good	
Quality of Construction	good	good		good		good/alum. sd	+9,000
Actual Age	6 years	8 years		7 years		8 years	
Condition	good	good		good		good	
Above Grade	Total / Bdrms. / Baths	Total / Bdrms. / Baths		Total / Bdrms. / Baths		Total / Bdrms. / Baths	
Room Count	7 / 3 / 2.5	7 / 3 / 2	+5,000	7 / 3 / 2	+5,000	7 / 3 / 2	+5,000
Gross Living Area	1,825 sq. ft.	1,800 sq. ft.		1,875 sq. ft.		1,825 sq. ft.	
Basement & Finished Rooms Below Grade	full basement	full basement		full basement		full basement	
Functional Utility	adequate	adequate		adequate		adequate	
Heating/Cooling	central H/A	central H/A		central H/A		central H/A	
Energy Efficient Items	none	none		none		none	
Garage/Carport	2-car att.	2-car att.		2-car att.		2-car att.	
Porch/Patio/Deck	none	none		none		none	
Net Adjustment (Total)		☐ + ☐ -	$	☐ + ☐ -	$	☐ + ☐ -	$
Adjusted Sale Price of Comparables		Net Adj. %		Net Adj. %		Net Adj. %	
		Gross Adj. %	$	Gross Adj. %	$	Gross Adj. %	$

I ☐ did ☐ did not research the sale or transfer history of the subject property and comparable sales. If not, explain

My research ☐ did ☐ did not reveal any prior sales or transfers of the subject property for the three years prior to the effective date of this appraisal.

Data source(s)

My research ☐ did ☐ did not reveal any prior sales or transfers of the comparable sales for the year prior to the date of sale of the comparable sale.

Data source(s)

Report the results of the research and analysis of the prior sale or transfer history of the subject property and comparable sales (report additional prior sales on page 3).

ITEM	SUBJECT	COMPARABLE SALE # 1	COMPARABLE SALE # 2	COMPARABLE SALE # 3
Date of Prior Sale/Transfer				
Price of Prior Sale/Transfer				
Data Source(s)				
Effective Date of Data Source(s)				

Analysis of prior sale or transfer history of the subject property and comparable sales

Summary of Sales Comparison Approach

Indicated Value by Sales Comparison Approach $

EXERCISE 10.3 (continued)
Sales Comparison Approach

Uniform Residential Appraisal Report
File #

There are	comparable properties currently offered for sale in the subject neighborhood ranging in price from $					to $	
There are	comparable sales in the subject neighborhood within the past twelve months ranging in sale price from $					to $	

FEATURE	SUBJECT	COMPARABLE SALE #4		COMPARABLE SALE #5		COMPARABLE SALE #6	
Address	2130 W. Franklin	2243 Parkside Blvd.		2003 Franklin Street.			
Proximity to Subject		Within half-mile		Within half-mile			
Sale Price	$ N/A	$ $256,500		$ 251,000		$	
Sale Price/Gross Liv. Area	$ N/A sq. ft.	$ 133.25 sq. ft.		$ 137.53 sq. ft.		$ sq. ft.	
Data Source(s)		Sales agent		Sales agent			
Verification Source(s)		Sales agent		Sales agent			
VALUE ADJUSTMENTS	DESCRIPTION	DESCRIPTION	+(-) $ Adjustment	DESCRIPTION	+(-) $ Adjustment	DESCRIPTION	+(-) $ Adjustment
Sale or Financing Concessions		none		none			
Date of Sale/Time		5 weeks ago		5 weeks ago			
Location	quiet street	quiet street		quiet street			
Leasehold/Fee Simple	fee simple	fee simple		fee simple			
Site	50' × 200'	50' × 200'		50' × 200'			
View	good	good		good			
Design (Style)	ranch/good	ranch/good		ranch/good			
Quality of Construction	good	good		good			
Actual Age	6 years	6 years		7 years			
Condition	good	good		good			
Above Grade	Total Bdrms. Baths	Total Bdrms. Baths		Total Bdrms. Baths		Total Bdrms. Baths	
Room Count	7 3 2.5	8 4 2	-10,000	7 3 2.5			
Gross Living Area	1,825 sq. ft.	1,925 sq. ft.	+5,000	1,825 sq. ft.		sq. ft.	
Basement & Finished Rooms Below Grade	full basement	full basement		full basement			
Functional Utility	adequate	adequate		adequate			
Heating/Cooling	central H/A	central H/A		central H/A			
Energy Efficient Items	none	none		none			
Garage/Carport	2-car att.	2-car att.		2-car att.			
Porch/Patio/Deck	none	none		none			
Net Adjustment (Total)		☐ + ☐ -	$	☐ + ☐ -	$	☐ + ☐ -	$
Adjusted Sale Price of Comparables		Net Adj. % Gross Adj. %	$	Net Adj. % Gross Adj. %	$	Net Adj. % Gross Adj. %	$

☐ I did ☐ did not research the sale or transfer history of the subject property and comparable sales. If not, explain

My research ☐ did ☐ did not reveal any prior sales or transfers of the subject property for the three years prior to the effective date of this appraisal.

Data source(s)

My research ☐ did ☐ did not reveal any prior sales or transfers of the comparable sales for the year prior to the date of sale of the comparable sale.

Data source(s)

Report the results of the research and analysis of the prior sale or transfer history of the subject property and comparable sales (report additional prior sales on page 3).

ITEM	SUBJECT	COMPARABLE SALE # 1	COMPARABLE SALE # 2	COMPARABLE SALE # 3
Date of Prior Sale/Transfer				
Price of Prior Sale/Transfer				
Data Source(s)				
Effective Date of Data Source(s)				

Analysis of prior sale or transfer history of the subject property and comparable sales

Summary of Sales Comparison Approach

Indicated Value by Sales Comparison Approach $

EXERCISE 10.4
Sales Comparison Approach

Uniform Residential Appraisal Report   File

There are ___ comparable properties currently offered for sale in the subject neighborhood ranging in price from $ ___ to $ ___							
There are ___ comparable sales in the subject neighborhood within the past twelve months ranging in sale price from $ ___ to $ ___							

FEATURE	SUBJECT	COMPARABLE SALE # 1		COMPARABLE SALE # 2		COMPARABLE SALE # 3	
Address	2130 W.Franklin	1901 Parkside Blvd.		2135 Hastings Ave.		2129 Osceola Way	
Proximity to Subject		Within half-mile		Within half-mile		Within half-mile	
Sale Price	$ N/A	$ 226,000		$ 239,000		$ 238,000	
Sale Price/Gross Liv. Area	$ N/A sq. ft.	$ 125.56 sq. ft.		$ 127.47 sq. ft.		$ 130.41 sq. ft.	
Data Source(s)		Sales agent		Sales agent		Sales agent	
Verification Source(s)		Sales agent		Sales agent		Sales agent	
VALUE ADJUSTMENTS	DESCRIPTION	DESCRIPTION	+(-) $ Adjustment	DESCRIPTION	+(-) $ Adjustment	DESCRIPTION	+(-) $ Adjustment
Sale or Financing Concessions		none		none		none	
Date of Sale/Time		6 wks ago		1 year ago	+22,700 (rounded)	2 months ago	
Location	quiet street	heavy traffic	+22,000	quiet street		quiet street	
Leasehold/Fee Simple	fee simple	fee simple		fee simple		fee simple	
Site	50′ × 200′	50′ × 200′		50′ × 200′		50′ × 200′	
View	good	good		good		good	
Design (Style)	ranch/good	ranch/good		ranch/good		ranch/good	
Quality of Construction	good	good		good		good/alum. sd.	+9,000
Actual Age	6 years	8 years		7 years		8 years	
Condition	good	good		good		good	
Above Grade	Total 7 / Bdrms. 3 / Baths 2.5	Total 7 / Bdrms. 3 / Baths 2	+5,000	Total 7 / Bdrms. 3 / Baths 2	+5,000	Total 7 / Bdrms. 3 / Baths 2	+5,000
Room Count							
Gross Living Area	1,825 sq. ft.	1,800 sq. ft.		1,875 sq. ft.		1,825 sq. ft.	
Basement & Finished Rooms Below Grade	full basement	full basement		full basement		full basement	
Functional Utility	adequate	adequate		adequate		adequate	
Heating/Cooling	central H/A	central H/A		central H/A		central H/A	
Energy Efficient Items	none	none		none		none	
Garage/Carport	2-car att.	2-car att.		2-car att.		2-car att.	
Porch/Patio/Deck	none	none		none		none	
Net Adjustment (Total)		☒ + ☐ -	$ 27,000	☒ + ☐ -	$ 27,700	☒ + ☐ -	$ 14,000
Adjusted Sale Price of Comparables		Net Adj. ___% Gross Adj. ___%	$ 253,000	Net Adj. ___% Gross Adj. ___%	$ 266,700	Net Adj. ___% Gross Adj. ___%	$ 252,000

I ☐ did ☐ did not research the sale or transfer history of the subject property and comparable sales. If not, explain

My research ☐ did ☐ did not reveal any prior sales or transfers of the subject property for the three years prior to the effective date of this appraisal.

Data source(s)

My research ☐ did ☐ did not reveal any prior sales or transfers of the comparable sales for the year prior to the date of sale of the comparable sale.

Data source(s)

Report the results of the research and analysis of the prior sale or transfer history of the subject property and comparable sales (report additional prior sales on page 3).

ITEM	SUBJECT	COMPARABLE SALE # 1	COMPARABLE SALE # 2	COMPARABLE SALE # 3
Date of Prior Sale/Transfer				
Price of Prior Sale/Transfer				
Data Source(s)				
Effective Date of Data Source(s)				

Analysis of prior sale or transfer history of the subject property and comparable sales

Summary of Sales Comparison Approach

Indicated Value by Sales Comparison Approach $ ___

E X E R C I S E 10.4 (continued)
Sales Comparison Approach

Uniform Residential Appraisal Report

File #

There are	comparable properties currently offered for sale in the subject neighborhood ranging in price from $				to $	
There are	comparable sales in the subject neighborhood within the past twelve months ranging in sale price from $				to $	

FEATURE	SUBJECT	COMPARABLE SALE #4		COMPARABLE SALE #5		COMPARABLE SALE #6	
Address	2130 W. Franklin	2243 Parkside Blvd.		2003 Franklin Street.			
Proximity to Subject		Within half-mile		Within half-mile			
Sale Price	$ N/A		$ $256,500		$ 251,000		$
Sale Price/Gross Liv. Area	$ N/A sq. ft.	$ 133.25 sq. ft.		$ 137.53 sq. ft.		$ sq. ft.	
Data Source(s)		Sales agent		Sales agent			
Verification Source(s)		Sales agent		Sales agent			
VALUE ADJUSTMENTS	DESCRIPTION	DESCRIPTION	+(-) $ Adjustment	DESCRIPTION	+(-) $ Adjustment	DESCRIPTION	+(-) $ Adjustment
Sale or Financing Concessions		none		none			
Date of Sale/Time		5 weeks ago		5 weeks ago			
Location	quiet street	quiet street		quiet street			
Leasehold/Fee Simple	fee simple	fee simple		fee simple			
Site	50′ × 200′	50′ × 200′		50′ × 200′			
View	good	good		good			
Design (Style)	ranch/good	ranch/good		ranch/good			
Quality of Construction	good	good		good			
Actual Age	6 years	6 years		7 years			
Condition	good	good		good			
Above Grade	Total | Bdrms. | Baths	Total | (Bdrms) | (Baths)		Total | Bdrms. | Baths		Total | Bdrms. | Baths	
Room Count	7 | 3 | 2.5	8 | 4 | 2	−10,000	7 | 3 | 2.5		| |	
Gross Living Area	1,825 sq. ft.	1,925 sq. ft.	+5,000	1,825 sq. ft.		sq. ft.	
Basement & Finished Rooms Below Grade	full basement	full basement		full basement			
Functional Utility	adequate	adequate		adequate			
Heating/Cooling	central H/A	central H/A		central H/A			
Energy Efficient Items	none	none		none			
Garage/Carport	2-car att.	2-car att.		2-car att.			
Porch/Patio/Deck	none	none		none			
Net Adjustment (Total)		☐ + ☒ −	$ 5,000	☐ + ☐ −	$ -0-	☐ + ☐ −	$
Adjusted Sale Price of Comparables		Net Adj. % Gross Adj. %	$ *251,000*	Net Adj. % Gross Adj. %	$ *251,000*	Net Adj. % Gross Adj. %	$

I ☐ did ☐ did not research the sale or transfer history of the subject property and comparable sales. If not, explain

My research ☐ did ☐ did not reveal any prior sales or transfers of the subject property for the three years prior to the effective date of this appraisal.

Data source(s)

My research ☐ did ☐ did not reveal any prior sales or transfers of the comparable sales for the year prior to the date of sale of the comparable sale.

Data source(s)

Report the results of the research and analysis of the prior sale or transfer history of the subject property and comparable sales (report additional prior sales on page 3).

ITEM	SUBJECT	COMPARABLE SALE # 1	COMPARABLE SALE # 2	COMPARABLE SALE # 3
Date of Prior Sale/Transfer				
Price of Prior Sale/Transfer				
Data Source(s)				
Effective Date of Data Source(s)				

Analysis of prior sale or transfer history of the subject property and comparable sales

Summary of Sales Comparison Approach

Indicated Value by Sales Comparison Approach $

ACHIEVEMENT EXAMINATION 10
Sales Price Adjustment Chart

Sales Price Adjustment Chart

	Comparables						
	1	2	3	4	5	6	7
SALES PRICE	$185,500	$190,000	$178,600	$186,000	$169,000	$173,500	$190,000
FINANCING	80% S/L	75% S/L	70% S/L	75% S/L	75% S/L	70% S/L	80% S/L
DATE OF SALE	2 mos. ago	3 wks. ago	1 yr. ago	2 wks.ago	1 mo. ago	5 wks. ago	3 wks. ago
LOCATION	quiet resid.	quiet resid.	quiet resid.	quiet resid.	quiet resid.	quiet resid.	quiet resid.
LEASEHOLD/FEE SIMPLE	fee	fee	fee	fee	fee	fee	fee
SITE	65' × 145'	65' × 145'	65' × 145'	65' × 145'	65' × 145'	65' × 145'	65' × 145'
VIEW	good	good	good	good	good	good	good
DESIGN	split lvl./ good	split lvl./ good	split lvl./ good	split lvl./ good	split lvl./ good	split lvl./ good	split lvl./ good
CONSTRUCTION	brick	brick	brick	brick	brick	brick	brick
AGE	7 yrs.	6½ yrs.	6 yrs.	7½ yrs.	7 yrs.	7 yrs.	7 yrs.
CONDITION	good	good	good	fair to good	good	good	good
NO. OF RMS./BEDRMS./BATHS	7/3/2	7/3/2	7/3/2	7/3/2	7/3/2	7/3/2	7/3/2
SQ. FT. OF LIVING SPACE	1,600	1,600	1,600	1,575	1,575	1,575	1,590
OTHER SPACE (BASEMENT)	finished half-bsmnt.	finished half-bsmnt.	finished half-bsmnt.	finished half-bsmnt.	finished half-bsmnt.	finished half-bsmnt.	finished half-bsmnt.
FUNCTIONAL UTILITY	adequate	adequate	adequate	adequate	adequate	adequate	adequate
HEATING/COOLING	central heat	central heat/air	central heat/air	central heat/air	central heat	central heat/air	central heat/air
ENERGY EFFICIENT ITEMS	none	none	none	none	none	none	none
GARAGE/CARPORT	2-car att.	2-car att.	2-car att.	2-car att.	none	none	2-car att.
OTHER EXT. IMPROVEMENTS	porch	porch	porch	porch	porch	porch	porch
OTHER INT. IMPROVEMENTS	brick fireplace	brick fireplace	brick fireplace	brick fireplace	brick fireplace	brick fireplace	brick fireplace
TYPICAL HOUSE VALUE	$190,000	$190,000	$190,000	$190,000	$190,000	$190,000	$190,000
VARIABLE FEATURE	No Central Air	-	Yr.-Old Sale	Condition	No Central Air No Garage	No Garage	-
ADJUSTMENT VALUE OF VARIABLE	$4,500	-	$11,400	$4,000	$21,000	$16,500	-

ACHIEVEMENT EXAMINATION 10
Sales Comparison Approach

Uniform Residential Appraisal Report   File

There are		comparable properties currently offered for sale in the subject neighborhood ranging in price from $			to $		
There are		comparable sales in the subject neighborhood within the past twelve months ranging in sale price from $			to $		

FEATURE	SUBJECT	COMPARABLE SALE # 1		COMPARABLE SALE # 2		COMPARABLE SALE # 3	
Address							
Proximity to Subject							
Sale Price	$ N/A	$ 185,500		$ 190,000		$ 178,600	
Sale Price/Gross Liv. Area	$ N/A sq. ft.	$ 115.94 sq. ft.		$ 118.75 sq. ft.		$ 111.63 sq. ft.	
Data Source(s)							
Verification Source(s)							
VALUE ADJUSTMENTS	DESCRIPTION	DESCRIPTION	+(-) $ Adjustment	DESCRIPTION	+(-) $ Adjustment	DESCRIPTION	+(-) $ Adjustment
Sale or Financing Concessions		none		none		none	
Date of Sale/Time		2 months ago		3 weeks ago		1 year ago	+11,400
Location	quiet residential	quiet res.		quiet res.		quiet res.	
Leasehold/Fee Simple	fee simple	fee simple		fee simple		fee simple	
Site	65' × 145'	65' × 145'		65' × 145'		65' × 145'	
View	good	good		good		good	
Design (Style)	split-lvl/good	split-lvl/good		split-lvl/good		split-lvl/good	
Quality of Construction	good/brick	good/brick		good/brick		good/brick	
Actual Age	7 years	7 years		6½ years		6 years	
Condition	good	good		good		good	
Above Grade	Total	Bdrms.	Baths	Total	Bdrms.	Baths	Total	Bdrms.	Baths	Total	Bdrms.	Baths
Room Count	7	3	2	7	3	2		7	3	2		7	3	2	
Gross Living Area	1,600 sq. ft.	1,600 sq. ft.		1,600 sq. ft.		1,600 sq. ft.	
Basement & Finished Rooms Below Grade	finished half basement	finished half basement		finished half basement		finished half basement	
Functional Utility	adequate	adequate		adequate		adequate	
Heating/Cooling	central H/A	central H/A	+4,500	central H/A		central H/A	
Energy Efficient Items	none	none		none		none	
Garage/Carport	none	2-car att.	-16,500	2-car att.	-16,500	2-car att.	-16,500
Porch/Patio/Deck	porch	porch		porch		porch	
fireplace	brick fireplace	brick fireplace		brick fireplace		brick fireplace	
Net Adjustment (Total)		☐ + ☒ -	$ 12,000	☐ + ☒ -	$ 16,500	☐ + ☒ -	$ 5,100
Adjusted Sale Price of Comparables		Net Adj. % Gross Adj. %	$ 173,500	Net Adj. % Gross Adj. %	$ 173,500	Net Adj. % Gross Adj. %	$ 173,500

I ☐ did ☐ did not research the sale or transfer history of the subject property and comparable sales. If not, explain

My research ☐ did ☐ did not reveal any prior sales or transfers of the subject property for the three years prior to the effective date of this appraisal.

Data source(s)

My research ☐ did ☐ did not reveal any prior sales or transfers of the comparable sales for the year prior to the date of sale of the comparable sale.

Data source(s)

Report the results of the research and analysis of the prior sale or transfer history of the subject property and comparable sales (report additional prior sales on page 3).

ITEM	SUBJECT	COMPARABLE SALE # 1	COMPARABLE SALE # 2	COMPARABLE SALE # 3
Date of Prior Sale/Transfer				
Price of Prior Sale/Transfer				
Data Source(s)				
Effective Date of Data Source(s)				

Analysis of prior sale or transfer history of the subject property and comparable sales

Summary of Sales Comparison Approach

ACHIEVEMENT EXAMINATION 10 (continued)

Sales Comparison Approach

Uniform Residential Appraisal Report   File

| There are | comparable properties currently offered for sale in the subject neighborhood ranging in price from $ | | | to $ | | | . |
| There are | comparable sales in the subject neighborhood within the past twelve months ranging in sale price from $ | | | to $ | | | . |

FEATURE	SUBJECT	COMPARABLE SALE # 4		COMPARABLE SALE # 5		COMPARABLE SALE # 6	
Address							
Proximity to Subject				✕			
Sale Price	$ N/A	$ 186,000		$ 169,000		$ 173,500	
Sale Price/Gross Liv. Area	$ N/A sq. ft.	$ 118.10 sq. ft.		$ 107.30 sq. ft.		$ 110.16 sq. ft.	
Data Source(s)							
Verification Source(s)							
VALUE ADJUSTMENTS	DESCRIPTION	DESCRIPTION	+(-) $ Adjustment	DESCRIPTION	+(-) $ Adjustment	DESCRIPTION	+(-) $ Adjustment
Sale or Financing Concessions		none		none		none	
Date of Sale/Time		2 weeks ago		1 month ago		5 weeks ago	
Location	quiet residential	quiet res.		quiet res.		quiet res.	
Leasehold/Fee Simple	fee simple	fee simple		fee simple		fee simple	
Site	65' × 145'	65' × 145'		65' × 145'		65' × 145'	
View	good	good		good		good	
Design (Style)	split-lvl/good	split-lvl/good		split-lvl/good		split-lvl/good	
Quality of Construction	good/brick	good/brick		good/brick		good/brick	
Actual Age	7 years	7½ years		7 years		7 years	
Condition	good	fair to good	+4,000	good		good	
Above Grade	Total Bdrms. Baths	Total Bdrms. Baths		Total Bdrms. Baths		Total Bdrms. Baths	
Room Count	7 3 2	7 3 2		7 3 2		7 3 2	
Gross Living Area	1,600 sq. ft.	1,575 sq. ft.		1,575 sq. ft.		1,575 sq. ft.	
Basement & Finished Rooms Below Grade	finished half basement	finished half basement		finished half basement		finished half basement	
Functional Utility	adequate	adequate		adequate		adequate	
Heating/Cooling	central H/A	central H/A		central H	+4,500	central H/A	
Energy Efficient Items	none	none		none		none	
Garage/Carport	none	2-car att.	-16,500	none		none	
Porch/Patio/Deck	porch	porch		porch		porch	
fireplace	brick fireplace	brick fireplace		brick fireplace		brick fireplace	
Net Adjustment (Total)		☐ + ☒ - $ 12,500		☒ + ☐ - $ 4,500		☐ + ☐ - $ -0-	
Adjusted Sale Price of Comparables		Net Adj. % Gross Adj. % $ 173,500		Net Adj. % Gross Adj. % $ 173,500		Net Adj. % Gross Adj. % $ 173,500	

I ☐ did ☐ did not research the sale or transfer history of the subject property and comparable sales. If not, explain

My research ☐ did ☐ did not reveal any prior sales or transfers of the subject property for the three years prior to the effective date of this appraisal.

Data source(s)

My research ☐ did ☐ did not reveal any prior sales or transfers of the comparable sales for the year prior to the date of sale of the comparable sale.

Data source(s)

Report the results of the research and analysis of the prior sale or transfer history of the subject property and comparable sales (report additional prior sales on page 3).

ITEM	SUBJECT	COMPARABLE SALE # 1	COMPARABLE SALE # 2	COMPARABLE SALE # 3
Date of Prior Sale/Transfer				
Price of Prior Sale/Transfer				
Data Source(s)				
Effective Date of Data Source(s)				

Analysis of prior sale or transfer history of the subject property and comparable sales

Summary of Sales Comparison Approach

ACHIEVEMENT EXAMINATION 10 (continued)
Sales Comparison Approach

Uniform Residential Appraisal Report   File

There are	comparable properties currently offered for sale in the subject neighborhood ranging in price from $		to $		.
There are	comparable sales in the subject neighborhood within the past twelve months ranging in sale price from $		to $		

FEATURE	SUBJECT	COMPARABLE SALE # 7		COMPARABLE SALE # 8		COMPARABLE SALE # 9	
Address							
Proximity to Subject							
Sale Price	$ N/A	$ *$190,000*		$		$	
Sale Price/Gross Liv. Area	$ N/A sq. ft.	$ *119.50* sq. ft.		$ sq. ft.		$ sq. ft.	
Data Source(s)							
Verification Source(s)							
VALUE ADJUSTMENTS	DESCRIPTION	DESCRIPTION	+(-) $ Adjustment	DESCRIPTION	+(-) $ Adjustment	DESCRIPTION	+(-) $ Adjustment
Sale or Financing Concessions		*none*					
Date of Sale/Time		*3 weeks ago*					
Location	quiet residential	*quiet res.*					
Leasehold/Fee Simple	fee simple	*fee simple*					
Site	65' × 145'	*65' × 145'*					
View	good	*good*					
Design (Style)	split-lvl/good	*split-lvl/good*					
Quality of Construction	good/brick	*good/brick*					
Actual Age	7 years	*7 years*					
Condition	good	*good*					
Above Grade	Total Bdrms. Baths	Total Bdrms. Baths		Total Bdrms. Baths		Total Bdrms. Baths	
Room Count	7 3 2	7 3 2					
Gross Living Area	1,600 sq. ft.	*1,590* sq. ft.		sq. ft.		sq. ft.	
Basement & Finished Rooms Below Grade	finished–16,500 half basement	*finished half basement*					
Functional Utility	adequate	*adequate*					
Heating/Cooling	central H/A	*central H/A*					
Energy Efficient Items	none	*none*					
Garage/Carport	none	*2-car att.*	−16,500				
Porch/Patio/Deck	porch	*porch*					
fireplace	brick fireplace	*brick fireplace*					
Net Adjustment (Total)		☐ + ☒ -	$ 16,500	☐ + ☐ -	$	☐ + ☐ -	$
Adjusted Sale Price of Comparables		Net Adj. % Gross Adj. %	$ 173,500	Net Adj. % Gross Adj. %	$	Net Adj. % Gross Adj. %	$

I ☐ did ☐ did not research the sale or transfer history of the subject property and comparable sales. If not, explain

My research ☐ did ☐ did not reveal any prior sales or transfers of the subject property for the three years prior to the effective date of this appraisal.
Data source(s)

My research ☐ did ☐ did not reveal any prior sales or transfers of the comparable sales for the year prior to the date of sale of the comparable sale.
Data source(s)

Report the results of the research and analysis of the prior sale or transfer history of the subject property and comparable sales (report additional prior sales on page 3).

ITEM	SUBJECT	COMPARABLE SALE # 1	COMPARABLE SALE # 2	COMPARABLE SALE # 3
Date of Prior Sale/Transfer				
Price of Prior Sale/Transfer				
Data Source(s)				
Effective Date of Data Source(s)				

Analysis of prior sale or transfer history of the subject property and comparable sales

Summary of Sales Comparison Approach

Indicated Value by Sales Comparison Approach $

■ **CHAPTER 11**

Exercise 11.1

Scheduled rent:

$900 per room per year or $900 × 5 rooms = $4,500 per year per unit

$4,500 per year per unit × 6 units = $27,000 per year

Market rent:

Because property 2 is an apartment building that contains apartments with three bedrooms, it has been dropped as a comparable sale.

Property 1: $1,260 × 5 rooms = $6,300 per year per unit

$6,300 per year per unit × 6 units = $37,800 per year

Property 3: $1,176 × 5 rooms = $5,880 per year per unit

$5,880 per year per unit × 6 units = $35,280 per year

If the comparable properties reflect typical rents in the area, then rental income ranges from $35,280 per year to $37,800 per year, or from $1,176 per room per year to $1,260 per room per year. The subject property should be expected to rent for about $1,220 per room per year, or $36,600 annually.

Exercise 11.2

Apartment rental income	$32,000
Income from washers and dryers	900
Rent on parking space	1,000
Potential gross income	$33,900

Exercise 11.3

Sale No.	Adjustment	GIM
1	+	8.9
2	–	10.9
3	–	17.0
4	+	10.7
5	–	5.3

Sales 3 and 5 appear out of line. The range for the subject, then, is between 8.9 and 10.9, and weighted toward the high side by the indicated adjustments.

Our estimate:

GIM = 10.8

Value of subject property = $18,000 × 10.8 = $194,400

Exercise 11.4

Apartment rental income	$32,000
Income from washers and dryers	900
Rent on parking space	1,000
Potential gross income	$33,900

Six units provide 312 possible weeks of rent
(6 × 52 = 312).
Six weeks of vacancy means a 2% vacancy loss
(6 × 312 = .019).
Vacancy and collection losses

(2% + 3% = 5%) × $33,900	1,695
Effective gross income	$32,205

Exercise 11.5

Potential gross income		$210,000
Allowance for vacancy and collection losses		− 9,900
Effective gross income		$200,100
Variable expenses:		
Salaries—janitor	$ 9,200	
Employee benefits	600	
Management	6,000	
Natural gas (+25%)	15,500	
Water	3,800	
Electricity	8,700	
Janitorial supplies	700	
Redecorating	2,000	
Legal and accounting fees	2,400	
Fixed expenses:		
Taxes (+20%)	7,200	
Reserves for replacement	2,500	
Total operating expenses		58,600
Net operating income		$141,500

Exercise 11.6

1. a
2. b
3. d
4. c
5. a

Achievement Examination 11

1. c
2. b, f, h, m, p, u
3. a
4. b
5. c
6. d

7. b

8. b

9. a

10. d

CHAPTER 12

Exercise 12.1

Property	Capitalization rate (rounded)
A	10.9
B	11.7
C	11.8
D	11.4
E	21.3

The capitalization rate of property E appears out of line with the rest of the comparables and should be discarded.

Based on the four remaining comparables, the value of the subject property is in a range from about $144,100 ($17,000 ÷ .118) to about $156,000 ($17,000 ÷ .109).

Exercise 12.2

Sales price	$435,000
Site value	−125,000
Building value	$310,000
Recapture rate = 100% ÷ 25 years =	× .04
NOI available for building recapture	$ 12,400

Interest rate (building) = $12,400 ÷ $435,000 property value = .0285 = 2.85%

Total NOI	$ 57,000
NOI for building recapture	− 12,400
NOI available for site	$ 44,600

Interest rate = $44,600 ÷ $435,000 = .1025 = 10 ¼%

Overall cap rate = 10.25% + 2.85% = 13.10%

Exercise 12.3

Loan (.75 × .092)	.069
Equity (.25 × .12)	.030
Overall rate	.099 or 9.9%

Exercise 12.4

Estimated land value		$100,000
Net operating income	$50,000	
Interest on land value ($100,000 × 10 ½%)	−10,500	
Residual income to building	$39,500	
Cap rate for building		
Interest rate	10.5%	
Recapture rate (100% ÷ 40)	2.5	
Building value (rounded) $39,500 ÷ .13	13.0%	303,800
Total property value		$403,800

Exercise 12.5

Estimated building value		$3,000,000
Net operating income	$530,000	
Cap rate for building		
Interest rate:	12%	
Recapture rate (100% ÷ 50)	2	
Total	14%	
Discount and recapture on building		
value ($3,000,000 × .14)	−420,000	
Residual income to land	$110,000	
Land value $110,000 ÷ .1095 (rounded)		917,000
Total property value		$3,917,000

Exercise 12.6

Average cap rate = .1257

Subject: $\dfrac{I}{R} = V$ $16,000 ÷ .1257 = $127,300 (rounded)

Exercise 12.7

Estimated land value		$ 75,000
Total net operating income	$26,400	
Interest on land value ($75,000 × 11%)	8,250	
Residual income to building	$18,150	
Building value (using annuity factor of 8.694 × $18,150)		157,796
Total property value		$232,796

Exercise 12.8

Total operating net income	$ 30,000
Annuity factor (25 years at 12%)	× 7.843
Present worth of net operating income	$235,290
Reversion factor (25 years at 12% = .059)	
Present worth of reversion ($150,000 × .059)	8,850
Total value of property	$244,140

Exercise 12.9

1. Annuity
2. Straight-line

Achievement Examination 12

1. a
2. b
3. a
4. b
5. d
6. b
7. Interest rate

   Recapture rate
8. a
9. b
10. Highest—annuity; lowest—straight-line
11. a
12. Interest rate: 65% × 11%   =   7.15%

                     35% × 12%   =   4.20%

                          Total   =   11.35%

    Recapture rate: 100% ÷ 25 yrs. = 4%

    a. Building residual technique:

Estimated land value		$ 500,000
Net operating income	$400,000	
Interest on land value		
($500,000 × .1135)	– 56,750	
Residual income to building	$343,250	
Cap rate for building		
Interest rate 11.35%		
Recapture rate 4.00		
15.35%		
Building value (rounded)		
($343,250 ÷ .1535)		2,236,000
Total property value		$2,736,000

b. Land residual technique:

Estimated building value		$2,236,000
Net operating income	$400,000	
Cap rate for building		
Interest rate 11.35%		
Recapture rate <u>4.00</u>		
15.35%		
Interest and recapture on building value		
($2,236,000 × .1535)	<u>−343,226</u>	
Residual income to land	$ 56,774	
Land value (rounded) $56,774 ÷ .1135		<u>500,000</u>
Total property value		$2,736,000

13. a. Reconstruction of operating statement:

Potential gross income		
(4 stores × $10,200 per yr.)		$40,800
Allowance for vacancy and collection losses (4%)		<u>− 1,632</u>
Effective gross income		$39,168
Variable expenses:		
Repairs and maintenance		
(12% of effective gross income)	$4,700	
Legal and accounting fees	550	
Miscellaneous expense	816	
Fixed expenses:		
Insurance ($3,000 ÷ 3 yrs.)	1,000	
Real estate taxes	4,000	
Reserves for replacement:		
Roof ($2,000 ÷ 20 yrs.)	100	
Furnaces ($950 × 4 ÷ 10 yrs.)	<u>380</u>	
Total operating expenses		<u>11,546</u>
Net operating income		$27,622

b. Capitalization rate estimate:

Interest rate		
First mortgage (75% × 11%)	8.25%	
Equity (25% × 13%	<u>3.25</u>	
Total interest rate	11.5%	
Recapture rate (100% ÷ 40 yrs. remaining economic life)		<u>2.5</u>
Total capitalization rate		14.0%

c. Estimate of total property value:

Building residual technique

Estimated land value	$ 55,000

Net operating income	$27,622
Interest on land value ($55,000 × 11.5%)	6,325
Residual income to building	$21,297

Cap rate for building

Interest rate	11.5%
Recapture rate	2.5
	14.0%

Building value rounded ($21,297 ÷ .14)	152,121
Total property value	$207,121

14. The value indications are different in cases "a" and "b" because of different assumptions in types of income streams and methods of recapturing capital.

a. Building residual—straight-line method

Estimated land value		$100,000
Net operating income	$ 50,000	
Return on land value ($100,000 × .15)	− 15,000	
Residual income to building	$ 35,000	

Cap rate for building

Interest rate	15%
Recapture rate	+4
	19%

Building value ($35,000 ÷ .19) (rounded)		184,211
Total value of property		$284,211

b. Property residual—annuity method

Total net operating income	$ 50,000
Annuity factor (25 years at 15%)	× 6.464
Present worth of net operating income	$323,200
Present worth of reversion—$100,000 × .030	
(25 years at 15%)	3,000
Total value of property	$326,200

or

Building residual—annuity method

Estimated land value		$100,000
Residual income to building	$35,000	
Annuity factor (25 years @ 15%)	× 6.464	
Value of building		226,240
Total value of property		$326,240

■ CHAPTER 13

Exercise 13.1

All three approaches involve many variables that will affect the estimate of value. In the cost approach, the many factors contributing to construction cost and property depreciation must be recognized and evaluated. The sales comparison approach is successful only when recent sales of comparable properties are available. Even single-family residences may have many individual differences, entailing price adjustments that in turn rely on accurate estimations of the value of property features. The income capitalization approach relies on accurate income analysis and may involve complex computations.

Exercise 13.2

The cost approach valuation is somewhat lower than the others, but because no new construction is possible in the area, reliance on this estimate would be unrealistic. The other estimates are roughly comparable. The income approach valuation reflects the fact that rents in the area have been fairly stable, and there are no economic indicators of a significant change in either direction. Because most such properties are owner-occupied, a positive factor as indicated by the upkeep of the area, the market value estimate is probably more accurate than that reached solely by the income capitalization approach. The final opinion of market value, as the most probable price the property can command, thus should be $173,000.

Exercise 13.3

The income capitalization and cost approaches will be most important in valuing the subject property. The cost approach will set the upper limit of value, as there is land available for similar construction. The income capitalization approach is important because of the property's income-producing abilities and potential. The value reached by the income capitalization approach will be influenced by the existence of major tenants, who may be financially sound but who also may benefit from long-term contracts that may not reflect the recent dramatic increases in property values in the area.

Achievement Examination 13

See the completed first three pages of the URAR form that appear on pages 431–433.

ACHIEVEMENT EXAMINATION 13
Uniform Residential Appraisal Report

Uniform Residential Appraisal Report   File

The purpose of this summary appraisal report is to provide the lender/client with an accurate, and adequately supported, opinion of the market value of the subject property.

SUBJECT

Property Address 4807 Catalpa Road	City Woodview State IL Zip Code 60000
Borrower Owner of Public Record	County Dakota

Legal Description attached to this report
Assessor's Parcel #   Tax Year   R.E. Taxes $ 2,278
Neighborhood Name   Map Reference   Census Tract
Occupant ☒ Owner ☐ Tenant ☐ Vacant Special Assessments $ ☐ PUD HOA $ ☐ per year ☐ per month
Property Rights Appraised ☒ Fee Simple ☐ Leasehold ☐ Other (describe)
Assignment Type ☐ Purchase Transaction ☐ Refinance Transaction ☐ Other (describe)
Lender/Client   Address
Is the subject property currently offered for sale or has it been offered for sale in the twelve months prior to the effective date of this appraisal? ☒ Yes ☐ No
Report data source(s) used, offering price(s), and date(s).

CONTRACT

I ☐ did ☐ did not analyze the contract for sale for the subject purchase transaction. Explain the results of the analysis of the contract for sale or why the analysis was not performed.

Contract Price $ Date of Contract Is the property seller the owner of public record? ☐ Yes ☐ No Data Source(s)
Is there any financial assistance (loan charges, sale concessions, gift or downpayment assistance, etc.) to be paid by any party on behalf of the borrower? ☐ Yes ☐ No
If Yes, report the total dollar amount and describe the items to be paid.

NEIGHBORHOOD

Note: Race and the racial composition of the neighborhood are not appraisal factors.

Neighborhood Characteristics	One-Unit Housing Trends	One-Unit Housing	Present Land Use %
Location ☐ Urban ☒ Suburban ☐ Rural	Property Values ☒ Increasing ☐ Stable ☐ Declining	PRICE AGE	One-Unit 100 %
Built-Up ☒ Over 75% ☐ 25–75% ☐ Under 25%	Demand/Supply ☐ Shortage ☒ In Balance ☐ Over Supply	$ (000) (yrs)	2-4 Unit %
Growth ☐ Rapid ☒ Stable ☐ Slow	Marketing Time ☒ Under 3 mths ☐ 3–6 mths ☐ Over 6 mths	Low	Multi-Family %
Neighborhood Boundaries Boundaries are shown on attached map		High	Commercial %
		Pred.	Other %

Neighborhood Description Subject property is located in a desirable subdivision in the Central Eastern section of the Village of Woodview. Schools, shopping, and other necessary facilities and services are within a reasonable distance.

Market Conditions (including support for the above conclusions) Steady demand for housing with a gradual uptrend in values reflects a relatively healthy local economy. Conventional financing readily available with interest rates at 6% to 8%. The desirability of this neighborhood is reflected by the fact that most homes are sold within 2 months of being put on the market.

SITE

Dimensions 65' × 130' Area 8,450 squre feet Shape rectangular View tree-lined st/typical
Specific Zoning Classification R-2 Zoning Description Single-family residence
Zoning Compliance ☒ Legal ☐ Legal Nonconforming (Grandfathered Use) ☐ No Zoning ☐ Illegal (describe)
Is the highest and best use of the subject property as improved (or as proposed per plans and specifications) the present use? ☒ Yes ☐ No If No, describe

Utilities	Public	Other (describe)		Public	Other (describe)	Off-site Improvements—Type	Public	Private
Electricity	☒	☐	Water	☒	☐	Street	☒	☐
Gas	☒	☐	Sanitary Sewer	☒	☐	Alley	☐	☐

FEMA Special Flood Hazard Area ☐ Yes ☒ No FEMA Flood Zone FEMA Map # FEMA Map Date
Are the utilities and off-site improvements typical for the market area? ☒ Yes ☐ No If No, describe
Are there any adverse site conditions or external factors (easements, encroachments, environmental conditions, land uses, etc.)? ☐ Yes ☒ No If Yes, describe
Underground electric and telephone lines; no easements or encroachments

IMPROVEMENTS

General Description	Foundation	Exterior Description materials/condition	Interior materials/condition
Units ☒ One ☐ One with Accessory Unit	☐ Concrete Slab ☒ Crawl Space	Foundation Walls Concrete/gd	Floors Vinyl/cpt/oak/gd
# of Stories 1	☐ Full Basement ☐ Partial Basement	Exterior Walls Brick veneer/gd	Walls Drywall/paint/gd
Type ☒ Det. ☐ Att. ☐ S-Det./End Unit	Basement Area sq. ft.	Roof Surface Asphlt.shingle/gd	Trim/Finish Wood/Avg
☒ Existing ☐ Proposed ☐ Under Const.	Basement Finish %	Gutters & Downspouts Galv./paint/gd	Bath Floor Ceram/gd
Design (Style) Ranch	☐ Outside Entry/Exit ☐ Sump Pump	Window Type Wood double-hung/gd	Bath Wainscot Ceram/gd
Year Built 25 years ago	Evidence of ☐ Infestation	Storm Sash/Insulated Comb.alum/gd	Car Storage ☐ None
Effective Age (Yrs) 15	☐ Dampness ☐ Settlement	Screens Comb.alum/gd	☒ Driveway # of Cars 2
Attic ☐ None	Heating ☒ FWA ☐ HWBB ☐ Radiant	Amenities ☐ Woodstove(s) #	Driveway Surface Asphalt
☒ Drop Stair ☐ Stairs	☐ Other Fuel	☐ Fireplace(s) # ☐ Fence	☒ Garage # of Cars
☐ Floor ☐ Scuttle	Cooling ☒ Central Air Conditioning	☐ Patio/Deck ☐ Porch	☐ Carport # of Cars
☐ Finished ☐ Heated	☐ Individual ☐ Other	☐ Pool ☐ Other	☐ Att. ☒ Det. ☐ Built-in

Appliances ☒ Refrigerator ☒ Range/Oven ☒ Dishwasher ☒ Disposal ☐ Microwave ☐ Washer/Dryer ☒ Other (describe) Oven fan/hood
Finished area above grade contains: 7 Rooms 3 Bedrooms 2.00 Bath(s) 1,950 Square Feet of Gross Living Area Above Grade
Additional features (special energy efficient items, etc.) 6" insulation above ceiling and behind drywall; 6' redwood fence around rear yard.
Describe the condition of the property (including needed repairs, deterioration, renovations, remodeling, etc.). Overall, house and garage are in good shape with normal wear and tear indicating 25% depreciation. There is no evidence of functional or external obsolescence.

Are there any physical deficiencies or adverse conditions that affect the livability, soundness, or structural integrity of the property? ☐ Yes ☒ No If Yes, describe
No detrimental influences.

Does the property generally conform to the neighborhood (functional utility, style, condition, use, construction, etc.)? ☒ Yes ☐ No If No, describe

Freddie Mac Form 70 March 2005   Page 1 of 6   Fannie Mae Form 1004 March 2005

ACHIEVEMENT EXAMINATION 13 (continued)
Uniform Residential Appraisal Report

Uniform Residential Appraisal Report   File

There are	2	comparable properties currently offered for sale in the subject neighborhood ranging in price from $ 178,90.00		to $ 184,500.00	
There are	5	comparable sales in the subject neighborhood within the past twelve months ranging in sale price from $ 152,000.00		to $ 186.240.00	

FEATURE	SUBJECT	COMPARABLE SALE # 1		COMPARABLE SALE # 2		COMPARABLE SALE # 3	
Address	4807 Catalpa Road	4310 W. Gladys		3840 W. Monroe		316 Iowa	
Proximity to Subject							
Sale Price	$		$ 177,750		$ 180,000		$ 186,240
Sale Price/Gross Liv. Area	$ sq. ft.	$ 90.00 sq. ft.		$ 92.31 sq. ft.		$ 96.00 sq. ft.	
Data Source(s)							
Verification Source(s)							
VALUE ADJUSTMENTS	DESCRIPTION	DESCRIPTION	+(-) $ Adjustment	DESCRIPTION	+(-) $ Adjustment	DESCRIPTION	+(-) $ Adjustment
Sale or Financing Concessions		conventional		conventional		conventional	
Date of Sale/Time		6 wks. ago		3 wks. ago		6 wks. ago	
Location	Suburban	quiet res.		quiet res.		quiet res.	
Leasehold/Fee Simple	fee simple	fee simple		fee simple		fee simple	
Site	8,450 sq. ft.	65′ × 130′		65′ × 130′		65′ × 130′	
View	good/street	good/street		good/street		good/street	
Design (Style)	ranch	ranch		ranch		ranch	
Quality of Construction	good	good		good		good	
Actual Age	25 yrs.	25 yrs.		25 yrs.		25 yrs.	
Condition	good	good		good		good	
Above Grade	Total Bdrms. Baths	Total Bdrms. Baths		Total Bdrms. Baths		Total Bdrms. Baths	
Room Count	7 3 2	7 3 2		7 3 2		7 3 2	
Gross Living Area	1,950 sq. ft.	1,975 sq. ft.		1,950 sq. ft.		1,940 sq. ft.	
Basement & Finished Rooms Below Grade	crawlspace	crawlspace		crawlspace		finished basement	−10,000
Functional Utility	adequate	adequate		adequate		adequate	
Heating/Cooling	central h/a	central h/a		central h/a		central h/a	
Energy Efficient Items	extra insulation	equal		equal		equal	
Garage/Carport	2-car detached	2-car detached		2-car detached		2-car detached	
Porch/Patio/Deck							
Fireplace	masonry	none	+5,000	masonry		masonry	
Fence	fence	fence		fence		fence	
Net Adjustment (Total)		☒+ ☐-	$ 5,000	☐+ ☐-	$	☐+ ☒-	$ −10,000
Adjusted Sale Price of Comparables		Net Adj. 2.80 % Gross Adj. 2.80 %	$ 182,750	Net Adj. % Gross Adj. %	$ 180,000	Net Adj. −5.40 % Gross Adj. 5.40 %	$ 176,240

I ☒ did ☐ did not research the sale or transfer history of the subject property and comparable sales. If not, explain

My research ☐ did ☒ did not reveal any prior sales or transfers of the subject property for the three years prior to the effective date of this appraisal.
Data source(s)   County tax assessor
My research ☐ did ☒ did not reveal any prior sales or transfers of the comparable sales for the year prior to the date of sale of the comparable sale.
Data source(s)   County tax assessor
Report the results of the research and analysis of the prior sale or transfer history of the subject property and comparable sales (report additional prior sales on page 3).

ITEM	SUBJECT	COMPARABLE SALE # 1	COMPARABLE SALE # 2	COMPARABLE SALE # 3
Date of Prior Sale/Transfer				
Price of Prior Sale/Transfer				
Data Source(s)				
Effective Date of Data Source(s)				

Analysis of prior sale or transfer history of the subject property and comparable sales

Summary of Sales Comparison Approach

Indicated Value by Sales Comparison Approach $ 180,000

Indicated Value by: Sales Comparison Approach $ 180,000   Cost Approach (if developed) $ Income Approach (if developed) $ 169,000

This appraisal is made ☒ "as is", ☐ subject to completion per plans and specifications on the basis of a hypothetical condition that the improvements have been completed, ☐ subject to the following repairs or alterations on the basis of a hypothetical condition that the repairs or alterations have been completed, or ☐ subject to the following required inspection based on the extraordinary assumption that the condition or deficiency does not require alteration or repair:

Based on a complete visual inspection of the interior and exterior areas of the subject property, defined scope of work, statement of assumptions and limiting conditions, and appraiser's certification, my (our) opinion of the market value, as defined, of the real property that is the subject of this report is
$, as of   , which is the date of inspection and the effective date of this appraisal.

Uniform Residential Appraisal Report   File

ADDITIONAL COMMENTS

COST APPROACH TO VALUE (not required by Fannie Mae)

Provide adequate information for the lender/client to replicate the below cost figures and calculations.

Support for the opinion of site value (summary of comparable land sales or other methods for estimating site value)

COST APPROACH					
ESTIMATED ☒ REPRODUCTION OR ☐ REPLACEMENT COST NEW	OPINION OF SITE VALUE			= $	45,000
Source of cost data	Dwelling	1,950 Sq. Ft. @ $	90	= $	175,500
Quality rating from cost service Effective date of cost data		Sq. Ft. @ $		= $	
Comments on Cost Approach (gross living area calculations, depreciation, etc.)			Extra insulation		1,200
Depreciation based on normal wear and tear for well-maintained	Garage/Carport	500 Sq. Ft. @ $	30	= $	15,000
property with effective age of 15 years.	Total Estimate of Cost-New			= $	191,700
	Less Physical	Functional	External		
	Depreciation 47,925			= $(	47,925)
	Depreciated Cost of Improvements			= $	143,775
	"As-is" Value of Site Improvements			= $	8,400
Estimated Remaining Economic Life (HUD and VA only) Years	Indicated Value By Cost Approach			= $	197,175

INCOME APPROACH TO VALUE (not required by Fannie Mae)

INCOME	
Estimated Monthly Market Rent $ 1,300 X Gross Rent Multiplier 130 = $ 169,000 Indicated Value by Income Approach	
Summary of Income Approach (including support for market rent and GRM) Comparable home sales prices/monthly rental income:	
$160,000/$1,200; $166,500/$1,275; $173,500/$1,300.	

PROJECT INFORMATION FOR PUDs (if applicable)

PUD INFORMATION

Is the developer/builder in control of the Homeowners' Association (HOA)? ☐ Yes ☐ No   Unit type(s) ☐ Detached ☐ Attached

Provide the following information for PUDs ONLY if the developer/builder is in control of the HOA and the subject property is an attached dwelling unit.

Legal name of project

Total number of phases   Total number of units   Total number of units sold

Total number of units rented   Total number of units for sale   Data source(s)

Was the project created by the conversion of an existing building(s) into a PUD? ☐ Yes ☐ No   If Yes, date of conversion

Does the project contain any multi-dwelling units? ☐ Yes ☐ No   Data source(s)

Are the units, common elements, and recreation facilities complete? ☐ Yes ☐ No   If No, describe the status of completion.

Are the common elements leased to or by the Homeowners' Association? ☐ Yes ☐ No   If Yes, describe the rental terms and options.

Describe common elements and recreational facilities

■ CHAPTER 14

Exercise 14.1

1. condominium building size, unit size, number of owner-occupied units, common areas, amenities, monthly fees, or other assessments

2. PUD size of development, common areas, amenities, fees, or assessments, use of comparable properties in the same development

3. time-share ownership interest, amenities, time of year, resale market

4. manufactured home age and size of home, lot size, lawn areas, streets, park amenities, upkeep, space rental cost, and lease term

Exercise 14.2

1. c

2. a

3. a

4. c

5. c

6. b

Exercise 14.3

1. A leasehold estate is created (may be valued) when scheduled rent under the lease is less than the fair market rental, or economic rent.

2. $419,100

   $393,200

Achievement Examination 14

Leased fee interest:

Net operating income	$ 36,000
Annuity factor (30 years @ 11%)	× 8.694
Present worth of net income	$312,984
Present worth of reversion	
($150,000 × .044 reversion factor)	6,600
Value of the leased fee interest	$319,584

Leasehold interest:

Market rent	$ 45,000
Scheduled rent	36,000
Excess rent	$ 9,000
Present worth of excess rent discounted at 14%	× 7.003
Value of leasehold interest	$ 63,027

Total value of leased fee and leasehold interests =

$319,584 + $63,027 = $382,611 rounded to $382,600.

■ **CHAPTER 15**

Exercise 15.1

1. $95,000 × .08 = $7,600

$95,000 + 7,600 = $102,600 *or*

$95,000 × 1.08 = $102,600

2. $140,000 − $125,000 = $15,000

$15,000 ÷ $125,000 = .12 = 12%

Exercise 15.2

$90,000 × .015 = $1,350 interest

$90,000 × .0081 = $729 per month

Exercise 15.3

1. 3 square feet or 432 square inches

2. 1.875 square feet or 270 square inches

3. 42 square feet or 6,048 square inches

4. 144 square inches

5. 10.5 square feet

6. 75 feet × 125 feet = 9,375 square feet

Exercise 15.4

$A = ½ (BH) = ½ (50' × 85') = ½ (4,250$ sq. ft.$) = 2,125$ sq. ft.

Exercise 15.5

1. Area of A = 25' × 19' = 475 sq. ft.

Area of B = 13' × 8' = 104 sq. ft.

Area of C = 9' × 7' = 63 sq. ft.

Total area = 642 sq. ft.

2. Area of rectangle:

$A = L × W = 18' × 7' = 126$ sq. ft.

Area of triangle:

$A = ½ (BH) = ½ (22' − 18') × 7' = ½ (4' × 7') = ½ (28$ sq. ft.$) = 14$ sq. ft.

Total area = 126 sq. ft. + 14 sq. ft. = 140 sq. ft.

3. Area of A = $½ (20'− 12') × 8' = 32$ sq. ft.

Area of B = 18' × 20' = 360 sq. ft.

Area of C = $½ (8' × 18') = 72$ sq. ft.

Area of D = $½ (13' × 20') = 130$ sq. ft.

Area of E = $½ ×20' − 8') × 20' = 120$ sq. ft.

Area of F = 8' × 20' = 160 sq. ft.

Total area = (32 + 360 + 72 + 130 + 120 + 160) sq. ft. = 874 sq. ft.

Exercise 15.6

AREA

A	= 5' × 16'	=	80 sq. ft.
B	= 3' × (20' + 16') = 3' × 36'	=	108
C	= 12' × 20'	=	240
D	= 10' × (40' − 22') = 10' × 18'	=	180
E	= (50' − 25') × 22' = 25' × 22'	=	550
F	= (50' − 10') × (74' − 22') = 40' × 52'	=	2,080
	TOTAL	=	3,238 sq. ft.

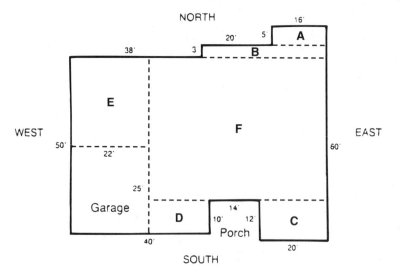

Exercise 15.7

1. 8' × 7' = 56 sq. ft. = 8,064 sq. in. = 6 sq. yd. (rounded)

   9' × 3' × 2'= 54 cu. ft. = 93,312 cu. in. = 2 cu. yd.

2. A. B = (33' + 55') − 83' = 5'   ½ (5' × 16') = 40 sq. ft.

   B. 83' × 16' = 1,328 sq. ft.

   C. B = 132' − 110' = 22'   H = (16' + 82' + 28' + 28') − 110' = 44'

   ½ (22' × 44') = 484 sq. ft.

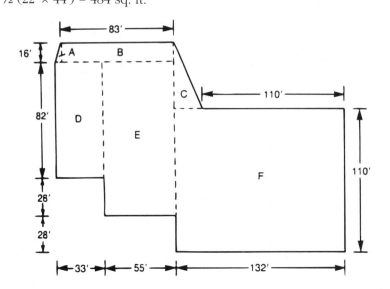

D. 82' × 33' = 2,706 sq. ft.

E. 55' × (82' + 28') = 55' × 110' = 6,050 sq. ft.

F. 132' × 110' = 14,520 sq. ft.

Total area = 40 sq. ft. + 1,328 sq. ft. + 484 sq. ft. + 2,706 sq. ft. +
     6,050 sq. ft. + 14,520 sq. ft. = 25,128 sq. ft.

3. 80' × 35' × 10' = 28,000 cu. ft. ÷ 27 = 1,037.037 cu. yd.

½ (80' × 35' × 6') = 8,400 cu. ft. ÷ 27 = 311.111 cu. yd.

1,037.037 cu. yd. + 311.111 cu. yd. = 1,348.148 cu. yd.

1,348.148 cu. yd. × $45 = $60,666.66

Achievement Examination 15

1. $45,000 ÷ .36 = $125,000

2. $24,000 ÷ $200,000 = .12 = 12%

3.

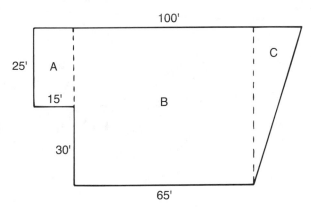

A = 25' × 15' = 375 sq. ft.

B = 65' × (30' + 25') = 65' × 55'= 3,575 sq.ft.

C = ½ (*BH*)   B = 100' − (15' + 65') = 20'

H = 30' + 25' = 55' ½ × (20' × 55') = 550 sq. ft.

Total area = 375 sq. ft. + 3,575 sq. ft. + 550 sq. ft. = 4,500 sq. ft.

4. 35' × 20' × 14' = 9,800 cu. ft.

½ (35' × 20' × 6') = 2,100 cu. ft.

9,800 cu. ft. + 2,100 cu. ft. = 11,900 cu. ft.

11,900 × $2.75 = $32,725

5. 40.83' × 60.67' = 2,477 sq. ft. (rounded)

80.5' × 25.25' = 2,033 sq. ft. (rounded)

Total area = 4,510 sq. ft. (rounded)

6.

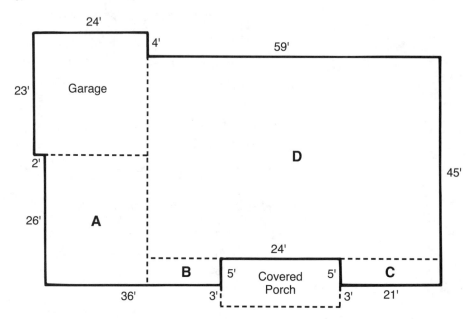

AREA

A = 26' × (24' − 2') = 26' × 22'   572 sq. ft.

B = 36' − (24' − 2') = 36' − 22' = 14' × 5'   70

C = 21' × 5'   105

D = 59' × (45' − 5') = 59' × 40'   2,360

             TOTAL   3,107 sq. ft.

7. a

8. c

9. d

10. a

11. b

12. c

13. b

14. a

15. d

16. b

INDEX

A

AACI (accredited appraiser Canadian Institute), 10
AAE (accredited assessment evaluator), 10
Aalberts, Robert J., 171
AAR (accredited in appraisal review), 9
Above-grade room count, 198–99
Absorption analysis, 43
Abstraction site valuation, 140, 142
Accessibility, 171
Accredited Review Appraisers Council, 9
Accrual basis, 231
Accrued depreciation, 169, 185
    itemizing, 180–82
Acknowledgment, 36
Acre valuation, 140
Active solar energy, 97, 98
Actual age, 198
ADA. *See* Americans with Disabilities Act
ADA Handbook: Employment & Construction Issues Affecting Your Business, 171
Addenda, 275–76
Adjustable-rate mortgage, 45
Adjustment
    net, 209, 212
    sequence, 205–6
    types of, 200–201
Ad valorem taxes, 20, 47
AFM (accredited farm manager), 9
Age-life depreciation method, 173–75
Aggregate, 328
Agricultural land, 112
AIA. *See* American Institute of Architects
Air conditioner, 97
Air rights, 18, 106
AIREA Financial Tables, 260
Allocation site valuation, 140, 141–42
Amenities, 274
American Association of Certified Appraisers, 7, 77
American Bankers Association, 7
American Institute of Architects (AIA), 76, 77
American Institute of Real Estate Appraisers, 5, 8, 10, 260
American National Standards Institute (ANSI), 77

American Society of Appraisers, 9
American Society of Farm Managers and Rural Appraisers, 7, 8, 9
American Society of Professional Appraisers, 9
American Society of Real Estate Appraisers, 9
Americans with Disabilities Act (ADA), 171
Americans with Disabilities Act Accessibility Guidelines, 171
Amortizing one dollar, 314–15
Amperage, 99
Anchor bolt, 86
Annual percentage rate (APR), 313
Annuity capitalization method, 253, 258, 259, 302, 305
Annuity factors table, 253, 254, 255
ANSI. *See* American National Standards Institute
Anticipation, 49–50, 221–22
Apple Computers, 11
Appraisal, 17–18, 36
    beginning process of, 62–67
    fees, 5
    intended use, function of, 61, 272
    steps in, 59–62
    suppositions for, 272–73
    types of, 270, 272
Appraisal and Valuation Manual, 9
Appraisal Foundation, 1, 7, 77
Appraisal Institute, 7, 8, 10
Appraisal Institute of Canada, 7, 8, 10
Appraisal Institute DIGEST, 10
Appraisal Journal, The, 10, 171
Appraisal report, 2, 265
    format, 272
    sample, 276–80
    styles of, 271–76
    types of, 270–71, 280
Appraisal Review, The, 10
Appraisal Standards Board, 1, 7, 8
Appraisal and Valuation Manual, 9
Appraise, 46
Appraiser
    assignments, 3–4
    certifications, 291
    compensation, 5
    employment opportunities for, 4–5

qualifications of, 2–3, 275
    records, 128
    work of, 1–2
Appraiser Qualifications Board (AQB), 7
"Appraisers and the Americans with Disabilities Act," 171
Appraisers News Network, 11
APR. *See* Annual percentage rate
AQB. *See* Appraiser Qualifications Board
ARA (accredited rural appraiser), 9
Area, 315–24
    conversions, 318–19
Arm's-length transaction, 46, 127
Array, 328
As if vacant, 137
As improved, 137
ASA (senior member), 9
Asbestos, 90
ASR (senior residential member), 9
Assemblage, 112
Assessments, 134
Assessor's office, 128
Assessors Journal, 10
Assumptions, 273, 291
Automated valuation model (AVM), 276
Average deviation, 330, 331
AVM. *See* Automated valuation model

B

Baby boomers, 48
Backup system, 13
Bacteria, 98
Balance, 50
Balloon construction, 88, 89
Band of investment method, 246–47
Bargain and sale deed, 35
Base line, 23
Basement, 199
Beneficiary, 32, 44
Blueprints, 76–78
Board of directors, 32
Board of zoning adjustment, 135
BOCA. *See* Building Officials Conference of America
Bounds, 22
Breakdown depreciation, 175–78
Break-even point, 236
Break-even ratio, 236

How To Install Your URAR Software

The software package with this edition of *Fundamental of Real Estate Appraisal* allows you to practice completing standard Uniform Residential Appraisal Report forms. This install CD includes everything you need to easily review and print out three different sets of sample data. Then, using the information found in any one of the three data sets, you can fill in an electronic version of a URAR form. When you are done, you can file your work or print it out and compare it to the corresponding suggested solutions also found in the install. There is also an internal "Help" feature available if you run into difficulty. To access the software, follow the step-by-step instructions.

Note: This software is designed to run on an Windows PC or compatible computer. Although it might be possible to run this software on a Mac using Virtual PC, this implementation is not provided by this installation and would entail the abilities of your Mac to run PC software. Mac support for PC implementation would therefore have to be provided by your Mac retailer rather than by SFREP.

Installation:

1. Put in your CD.
2. It should automatically start.
   a. If it does not start automatically, then the auto run is probably disabled on your computer.
   b. In that case, leave the CD in your computer.
   c. Click on *Start-My Computer*
   d. Double click on the *CD drive.*
   e. Double click on *AI* and then double click on *Install.*
3. Do not change any options during installation.
4. Follow the installation prompts by clicking *Setup, OK, OK.*

Registration:

1. *Your Name Here* will appear on all appraiser fields until you configure the software for your personal use. To do this, please follow these steps:
2. Click *Start-Programs-Appraise It-Registration* (or click *Start-Run* and type *c:\tra\register.exe*).
3. Click *Ok.*
4. **Do not change the company information!** It should read:

Fundamentals of Real Estate Appraisal
Call Software for Real Estate Professionals
for more information.
828-587-3737

5. Leave approval code as is: 1H-USVJ-TSUL4IVFJ
6. **Do not change the above information!** Instead, click *Define Users.*
7. Click *Edit.* Replace *your name here* with your personal name.
8. Then click *OK, OK, OK* until all the dialog boxes are closed.

By installing this software, you accept and agree to the bound by the following licensing agreement: 1) Use of this software is limited to the purchaser of this text. 2) You may not duplicate the software. 3) You may not modify, alter, adapt, merge, decompile or reverse engineer the software. 4) You may not remove or obscure any copyright notices. 5) Use of this software is limited to educational purposes only; commercial use is not permitted.